THE NATIONAL RESEARCH AND EDUCATION NETWORK (NREN):

RESEARCH AND POLICY PERSPECTIVES

INFORMATION MANAGEMENT, POLICY, AND SERVICES
Charles R. McClure and Peter Hernon, Editors

THE NATIONAL RESEARCH AND EDUCATION NETWORK (NREN):

RESEARCH AND POLICY PERSPECTIVES

BY:

CHARLES R. McCLURE
ANN P. BISHOP
PHILIP DOTY
HOWARD ROSENBAUM

SYRACUSE UNIVERSITY
SCHOOL OF INFORMATION STUDIES
SYRACUSE, NEW YORK 13244

ABLEX PUBLISHING CORPORATION
NORWOOD, NEW JERSEY

Printed in the United States of America

Library of Congress Cataloging-in-Publication Data

McClure, Charles R.
    The National Research and Education Network (NREN) : research and
policy perspectives / by Charles R. McClure ... [et al.].
        p.   cm.
    Includes bibliographical references and index.
    ISBN 0-89391-813-X
    1. Communication in science--United States. 2. Research--United
States. 3. Information networks--United States.   I. Title.
Q179.94.M33 1991
001.2'0285'46--dc20   91-14028
                                                                   CIP

Ablex Publishing Corporation
355 Chestnut St.
Norwood, NJ 07648

TABLE OF CONTENTS

TABLE OF CONTENTS (continued)

LIST OF FIGURES AND TABLES

FIGURES

TABLES

PREFACE

Development of the proposed National Research and Education Network (NREN) may be the single most important factor affecting the ability of the United States to manage information resources effectively in the 1990s. The potential impacts of the NREN on the nation's research and educational infrastructure are still being identified and assessed. While some of the benefits of national networking are difficult to predict, it is clear that the design and implementation of some type of national, coordinated, high-speed network is essential if the United States is to maintain a leadership role in high-performance computing and electronic networking and increase its overall national productivity and competitiveness.

This book, The National Research and Education Network (NREN): Research and Policy Perspectives, provides an overview and status report on the progress made in developing such a network as of early 1991. Further, it reports on a number of investigations that provide a research and policy perspective on the NREN and computer-mediated communication (CMC). Equally important, the book brings together a number of key source documents that have directed the development of the NREN. Thus, it is intended to serve as a handbook on NREN development, a sourcebook of important NREN policy statements, and a report on research conducted at Syracuse University on topics related to electronic networks.

Developments with the NREN have occurred so rapidly that it is increasingly difficult to identify all relevant literature and policy instruments. The review of these sources in the main body of the book and the material included in the appendices are intended to provide a unified source of information about the NREN, its development, and key issues yet to be resolved. Another purpose of this book is to offer some assessments of previously untested claims and assumptions about the NREN. Such assessments are part of a small, but growing, effort to determine the significance of national research networks to scholarly communication and research and to consider policy strategies to promote the most effective and beneficial utilization of these networks.

As 1991 unfolds and new initiatives and issues related to the design and development of the NREN are debated, we believe it is essential that policy makers consider the research, policy, and user perspectives discussed in this book. Considering these perspectives, especially the user perspective, may be the difference between designing an NREN that is only a technical success, as opposed to a network that increases the overall effectiveness and efficiency with which researchers, educators, and others gain access to and use information resources to enhance the overall competitiveness of the United States. Clearly, this country requires the latter. Further, no matter what the fate of the proposed NREN, national research and education networking is here to stay; thus, the relevance of the issues and perspectives discussed in this book do not depend upon the outcome of any single Federal initiative.

Portions of this book are based on contract reports completed originally for the U.S. Congress, Office of Technology Assessment (OTA). Chapters 6, 8, and 9 contain some material that appeared in the report Electronic Networks, The Research Process, and Scholarly Communication (Contract No. L3-2225) by Charles R. McClure, Ann Bishop, and Philip Doty. Chapters 7 and 8 contain some material that appeared in the report Scientific Norms and Electronic Research Networks (Contract No. N3-2550.0) by Philip Doty, Ann Bishop, and Charles R. McClure. Chapter 5 is an edited version of the report How Electronic Networks are Changing Science: Implications for a National Research and Education Network (Contract No. L3-5395-0) by Susan Koch.

The authors acknowledge the support from OTA in conducting the original studies. Moreover, we recognize the support and assistance of Frederick W. Weingarten who served as OTA project director for the Syracuse University study team during the completion of these contract reports. The authors also wish to acknowledge the assistance provided by Dean Donald A. Marchand at the School of Information Studies and Vice President Benjamin R. Ware at Syracuse University in support of these studies. The book could not have been completed without the expert assistance and production work provided by Ms. Beth Mahoney and the editorial and research assistance of Linda Schamber and Susan E. Holm, also at the School of Information Studies.

Charles R. McClure
Ann P. Bishop
Philip Doty
Howard Rosenbaum
February 20, 1991

INTRODUCTION

CHAPTER 1

During the 1980s, the Federal government initiated a number of important programs related to national networking. Congress also proposed the development of a national high-speed, high-capacity telecommunications network, dubbed the National Research and Education Network (NREN). The NREN aims to achieve national goals by improving the nation's electronic communication infrastructure and encouraging the development of more electronic information services and resources. The present book stems from the authors' desire to chronicle the rise of the proposed NREN and to explore issues related to its use by the research community.

Indeed, the development of the NREN may be the single most important information policy and management issue to confront the United States in the 1990s. A national electronic network has the potential to affect large segments of society. National and international "connectivity" to a range of information services and resources can have a pervasive and significant impact on the manner in which a society operates. To a large degree, however, we are unable to predict what the impacts from national networking might be and how they might affect established societal institutions. This situation is due, in part, to the limited amount of formal investigation that has occurred on topics related to national telecommunications systems and to network uses and policies.

National telecommunications networks for information sharing among scientists and engineers have been in existence for several decades. Today, the number of new technologies and uses seems to be skyrocketing. National research networking began in 1969, when the Defense Advanced Research Projects Research Agency (DARPA) of the Department of Defense funded the development of the first successful prototype packet-switching telecommunications network for its researchers and engineers, known as ARPANET. Since then, applications for electronic communication and computing have grown steadily among research, education, and library communities. In 1984, NSF began establishing national supercomputer centers and designing a high-speed telecommunications backbone, known as NSFNET, to provide access to the centers for scientists and engineers in a variety of disciplines. NSFNET is part of the Internet, an extensive system of local, regional, national, and international networks that connects an estimated one million users. BITNET, a cooperative network founded in 1981, is widely used by members of noncommercial research and education institutions.

BITNET, along with the Computer & Science Network (CSNet), became the Corporation for Research and Education Networking (CREN) in 1989. It currently connects more than 1200 sites around the world.

The number of available network resources and services increased greatly in the 1980s, along with people's familiarity with the technology. Networking is gradually becoming a more familiar tool in the classroom, laboratory, office, and library. Current network services that foster informal and formal communication include:

- Electronic mail for exchanging messages
- File transfer for transmitting papers and data
- Online bulletin boards for posting queries and participating in discussions
- Online newsletters and journals for sharing news and research results.

These services make it easier to collaborate with geographically dispersed colleagues, tap the expertise of a wide range of contacts, and provide instruction to remote learners.

Networks also currently provide online access to a variety of remote information resources and other research and education tools, such as:

- Library catalogs and databases
- Commercial, governmental, and not-for-profit information services
- Supercomputers
- Specialized software
- Specialized research instruments (e.g., telescopes), applications (e.g., medical imaging), and databases (e.g., satellite data).

Electronic services and resources facilitate both traditional and innovative research and education activities. Networks offer individuals at small or geographically remote institutions a lifeline to their colleagues and an opportunity to perform cutting-edge research.

This chapter provides an introduction to basic concepts and developments in national networking and briefly describes the policy origins of the NREN. It also argues for the need to consider social and behavioral factors in the design, implementation, management, and evaluation of information technologies such as electronic networks. The chapter concludes with a description of the purposes and organization of this book.

THE DEVELOPMENT OF THE NREN

The cost of telecommunications is decreasing, while the connectivity, speed, and power of electronic networks and related computing resources are increasing. Today's patchwork system of electronic networks is being used by more and more people. Within this context, the Federal government has made a formal commitment to harnessing and directing the development of high-performance computing and networking resources. One major focus of the national commitment is the proposed NREN. Such a network is envisioned as an electronic superhighway system that would allow researchers, business people, educators, and students around the country to communicate with each other and to access a broad range of research tools and information resources.

National Networking Policy Initiatives

In October 1988, Senator Albert Gore of Tennessee introduced S. 2918, the National High-Performance Computer Technology Act of 1988 (Congress, Senate, 1988a). The Act defined the government's role in high-performance computing and proposed the creation of a high-capacity, fiber optic network to link and broaden access to supercomputer centers throughout the United States. Congressman Doug Walgren introduced a companion bill, H.R. 3131, in the House of Representatives (Congress, House, 1989b). These bills were not passed, however, nor were similar bills introduced in 1989 and 1990. New versions were introduced in 1991. Executive branch interest and intentions regarding national networks were crystallized in two reports produced by the Office of Science and Technology Policy (1987 and 1989a). The legislative and executive branch policy initiatives complement each other and support many of the same basic objectives. Some of the fundamental provisions of these initiatives include:

- Establishing a Federal High Performance Computing Program in which science agencies and national libraries will fund and conduct research and develop technologies and resources appropriate for the NREN
- Mandating the creation of the NREN -- to link over 1,000 Federal and industrial laboratories, educational institutions, libraries, and other facilities -- over the next five years

- Promoting the development of a number of electronic information resources and services on the NREN, such as directories of users and databases; electronic journals and books; access to computerized research facilities, tools, and databases; access to commercial information resources and services; and user support and training
- Funding the development of supercomputers and advanced software to help resolve certain "grand challenges" in science and engineering.

Problems remain, however, in deciding which provisions deserve priority and which Federal agencies are to play a lead role in developing and coordinating high-performance computing initiatives. Some of the major constituencies concerned with national networking initiatives are:

- The research and education communities
- Librarians and other information providers
- Information technology manufacturers and other members of the information industry
- Federal and other policy makers
- Policy analysts and scholars.

All of these groups have their own views on strategies for NREN implementation.

The main goals of Federal initiatives are to help the U.S. maintain its lead in high-performance computing and to improve national productivity. The government sees continued research and development in high-performance computing and networking as critical to the country's competitiveness, security, scientific and technological advancement and, ultimately, the general welfare of its citizens. Although the emphasis of these initiatives, to date, is on advanced research computing applications, they also have the potential to create widespread changes in computing and communications for a much broader base of users, such as those in the education and library communities. Much as the interstate highway system was an investment in the nation's transportation infrastructure, the NREN is seen by some of its promoters as an investment in the nation's information infrastructure, and they expect the national information highway system to bring similar, widespread benefits.

Addressing the need to develop support mechanisms and services for the information infrastructure, Robert Kahn, President of the Corporation for National Research Initiatives, warned that the informa-

tion highway is "more than just laying down concrete. We need the connecting roads, the highway services, and the transportation functions" (Congress, Senate, 1988b, p. 38). One difficulty, however, lies in the expectation of easily quantifiable and immediate short-term payoffs from infrastructure investments. As noted by William Wulf of the National Science Foundation, investment in a national research network, like any investment in any kind of infrastructure, cannot be measured easily or effectively, despite its having a major impact on scientific productivity (Congress, Senate, 1988b, p. 90). Wulf's observation is echoed by Leonard Kleinrock of the National Research Council and the University of California: "There is no reliable measure that you can apply to predict profits from investment in infrastructure" (Congress, Senate, 1988b, p. 29). While some of the positive results of an NREN would be evident fairly quickly, a broad range of effects would be fully felt only in the long term, measurable in decades. Wenk (1986, p. 129) plainly identified the "unspoken demand of sponsors (public or private) for quick results" as one of the major problems faced by researchers in all fields today.

Need for a User Perspective

The Federal government, as well as a number of for-profit and not-for-profit organizations, is moving ahead with plans that can bring the NREN into being by the middle of the 1990s. There is overwhelming support among many stakeholder groups for a national, high-speed electronic network that will link scientists and researchers in the Federal government, the academic research community, and the private sector. Much of the current debate about the potential impact of networks on R&D productivity is based on untested assumptions, such as:

- Most researchers possess the skills, training, resources, and physical ability to take full advantage of research networks.
- All researchers will eventually be enthusiastic, sophisticated, and habitual users of networks.
- High-performance computing and advanced telecommunications networks will virtually eliminate the strictures of time and space, thereby fostering easy and productive long-distance collaborations.
- The next generation of users will acquire their skills as a matter of course during their education.

- The NREN will make scientific communication more widespread and efficient.
- The NREN will increase scientific productivity, and scientists will want to integrate it into their research activities.
- Networks will help achieve the wider and more democratic distribution of research resources.
- The use of networks is "contagious," and the existence of the NREN will fuel demand, access, and use.

These assumptions underlie most claims of increased research productivity and enhanced international competitiveness. They may be accurate representations of the potential role that the NREN will play in scientists' and engineers' daily research and communication activities, but as yet little formal investigation of these assumptions has been done.

This book emphasizes the need to bring a user perspective to the design, implementation, and management of electronic network systems and services. A user perspective asks:

- How can the use of electronic networks facilitate the tasks and goals of particular communities of users?
- What problems do particular groups of users face in attempting to exploit networks for the accomplishment of those tasks and goals?
- What design, management, and policy strategies can alleviate those problems and maximize network use and effectiveness?

These questions can be addressed by utilizing a range of qualitative and quantitative empirical techniques from the fields of information science, management, communications, sociology, and psychology.

A user perspective assumes that information technologies should not be designed and implemented according to technical criteria alone, but should take into account the particular communication behavior, information use patterns, and work environments of potential users. Adopting this perspective will help network designers, managers, and users:

- Avoid conflicts
- Understand and estimate the impact and benefits of network use
- Choose appropriate network designs, features, and services

- Devise appropriate strategies for marketing network services and promoting network use
- Develop effective policies for network management and use
- Develop appropriate mechanisms for user training and support
- Evaluate the effects of network implementation.

The authors believe that maintaining a user perspective will result in the development of a new model for understanding communication and work in the electronic age and will encourage successful network designs and policies.

Those responsible for designing and implementing national research networks must attempt to identify and address a number of social and behavioral issues related to the integration of communication and analytic tools into the working lives of network users. User-based policies will incorporate an understanding of, for example, the culture of the communities and subcommunities involved; the relationship between community norms and the use of electronic networks; effects of networks on collaboration and scholarly communication; definitions of eligible users and acceptable uses; relationships among users in academia, government, and the private sector; and the training and support of onsite and remote users of networked facitities.

PURPOSES AND ORGANIZATION OF THIS BOOK

While this book does try to bridge the gap between national network policy development and user-based research, it is not a comprehensive treatment of all the issues and topics related to national networking initiatives. It concentrates on issues related specifically to research, as opposed to education, applications. It does not consider international issues related to electronic networks, nor does it discuss technical, legal, or finanacial aspects of network development. Rather, this book adopts a user perspective toward the evolving electronic networking environment and brings together background information, research, and selected original policy documents in one sourcebook (see the Appendices).

This book is primarily concerned with research on and issues surrounding the development and implementation of the NREN. Thus, it includes little discussion of U.S. information policy per se. For background information on Federal information policy, legislation dealing with information technology, and policy related to scientific and technical information (STI) see McClure, Hernon, and Relyea (1989); McClure and Hernon (1989); and Office of Technology Assessment (1988).

Purposes of the Book

A major aim of this book is to provide information and background material related to the NREN, current as of February 1991. Developments with the NREN have occurred so rapidly that it is increasingly difficult to identify relevant literature and policy instruments. The review of these sources in the main body of the book and the material included in the appendices are intended to provide a unified source of information about the NREN, its development, and key issues yet to be resolved. Another purpose of this book is to offer some assessments of previously untested claims and assumptions about the NREN. Such assessments are part of a small, but growing, effort to determine the significance of national research networks to scholarly communication and research and to consider policy strategies to promote the most effective and beneficial utilization of these networks.

There is a broad range of work that needs to be done to plan for, implement, and manage the proposed NREN. This book is a first step in that direction and aims to:

- Identify and analyze current trends and policy issues in electronic networking as they relate to the research process and scholarly communication
- Provide an overview of key literature and policy instruments related to the NREN
- Report the findings of a study that examined the role of social and behavioral factors in electronic network use
- Explore the role and importance of scientific norms for the design and implementation of the NREN
- Offer recommendations to increase the effectiveness of the proposed NREN
- Bring together a selection of key source documents, reports, and policy instruments as a reference aid.

This discussion aims to contribute to the overall effectiveness and usefulness of the evolving NREN and of other electronic networks.

Organization of the Book

The book represents the compilation of a number of research efforts conducted by the authors. Although the chapters are organized and presented in a particular order, each can stand alone. This section offers a short summary of subsequent chapters so readers can identify chapters of interest.

Chapter 2, "Development of the National Research and Education Network," reviews key documents and policy issues related to the creation of the NREN. After a brief discussion of the development of high-speed national electronic networks, it reviews recent government documents, Congressional hearings, pending legislation, and articles in the popular and professional press that have focused on the design, development, implementation, and use of the NREN.

Chapter 3, "NREN Benefits, Problems, and Policy Issues: Views from the Literature," reviews proposed benefits that have been associated with the development of the NREN, identifies and analyzes possible problems related to the NREN, and provides an overview of key policy implications and issues identified from the literature.

Chapter 4, "Research on Computer-Mediated Communication and its Significance for the NREN," discusses current research on CMC and electronic networks. The purposes of this chapter are two-fold. First, it seeks to present a selective review of some current research into CMC in a variety of settings and from the perspectives of several social science disciplines. Second, it attempts to describe the research context, based on a combination of methodological techniques, within which the research reported in Chapters 6 and 7 took place.

Chapter 5, "Electronic Networks and Science," written by Susan Koch of Indiana University, discusses how electronic networks may affect the way in which science is conducted. It focuses on the impacts of electronic networks on the scientific enterprise and the effects of the use of electronic networks on the individual researcher, on the organization within which the individual conducts scientific activity, and on science as a whole. The chapter identifies key factors to be considered in designing, managing, and operating electronic networks for scientists and engineers.

Chapter 6, "Impact of Networks on Research: Results from an Empirical Study," describes an empirical study of the impacts of high-speed electronic networks on scientific communication and the research process. Using multiple data collection and analysis strategies, this exploratory study describes the ways in which users' current networking experiences have affected the research process and patterns of scientific communication, and analyzes current trends and policy issues in networking as they relate to scientific research and communication.

Chapter 7, "Scientific Norms and the Use of Electronic Research Networks," discusses the relationships among scientific norms, researchers' network behavior and attitudes, and the development of the NREN. Typically, these norms are not adequately considered in the design of electronic networks, leading to unforeseen problems in the routine operation of these networks, user frustration, and a general underutilization of network resources.

Chapter 8, "User Perspectives on Electronic Networks," reports the views and comments of network users who participated in the study described in Chapter 6. It offers insights on national network development from those who belong to one of its chief user groups. The chapter concludes with a discussion of possible strategies to incorporate the views of users into the design of the proposed NREN.

Chapter 9, "Issues, Recommendations, and Prospects," offers a review of the key social and behavioral issues that are likely to affect the design of the NREN and offers recommendations to allow policy makers and other interested stakeholders to resolve these issues. It also contains a status report on developments and activities related to the NREN as of early 1991.

A number of key reports, pieces of proposed legislation, a glossary, a substantial bibliography, and other source material are also included at the end of the book. These appendices and other sources provide a context for current policy decisions and debates; they represent current Federal and other policy views and recommendations for developing and implementing the NREN.

Network policy makers, scientists and engineers, scholars and educators, as well as network managers and administrators, and readers interested in scientific communication and the sociology of science, are among those who should find this book useful. It serves as a sourcebook on NREN and provides a bridge between national network policy development and research based on the needs and problems of network users. Readers can turn to the book for an overview of the historical and policy development of the proposed NREN through early 1991, a review

important literature on computer-mediated communication, a discussion of important issues related to national networking initiatives, and a description of the results of selected investigations of network use in the research community.

Development of the National Research and Education Network

Chapter 2

Some people envision a time in the near future when there will be fundamental changes in the ways in which scientific research and communication, information seeking and delivery, and other scholarly activities are done. Scholars, scientists, and researchers in the United States will be able to use a high-speed, wide-band, electronic network stretching from coast to coast to communicate with each other as easily as if they were using the telephone. They will be able to access remote databases, use specialized instruments, and work on supercomputers, all without leaving their offices. Large-scale collaborative research among geographically dispersed researchers will become the rule, not the exception.

This change is expected by many to be a consequence of the implementation of the proposed National Research and Education Network (NREN) and its integration into the daily routines of scientific research and other scholarly activities. However, closer examination of writings concerned with the development of the NREN reveals that this vision, while seductive, should not be taken as a forecast of an inevitable future. There are many significant and difficult questions that must be explored before the NREN can be brought into existence.

This chapter contains a selective review of key writings related to the design and implementation of the NREN, and it is divided into two sections:

- An overview of the proposed NREN, including its recent history, development, and goals
- A discussion of recent government reports, Congressional legislation and hearings, and articles that have appeared in the popular and professional press discussing the design, development, implementation, and use of the NREN.

Four key themes that emerge from this review of the literature are:

- There is overwhelming support for the construction and implementation of the NREN for use by the Federal government, academia, the library community, and the private sector.
- A consensus seems to be emerging that an important goal of the NREN should be to provide access to high-performance computing and other network resources to many different kinds of users.
- Many commentators, both inside and outside the Federal government, believe that the establishment of the NREN is essential to American efforts to

maintain a competitive edge in certain sectors of the global economy.

- Commentators and policy makers have not yet reached a consensus on many of the important issues involved in the design, development, and implementation of the proposed NREN.

The review of this literature indicates that there is a pressing need for empirically based information about the ways in which existing electronic networks are currently used by scientists, engineers, and educators and the ways in which they foresee using an expanded and enhanced national research network. This kind of information is critical for policy makers and network managers, who must decide how the NREN is to be developed, implemented, funded, and operated on a day-to-day basis.

BACKGROUND, DESCRIPTION, AND GOALS OF THE PROPOSED NREN

Science and advanced information networking technologies have become increasingly intertwined during the last two decades. Scientists and engineers are beginning to demand rapid and reliable access to remote supercomputing resources and databases and to other researchers with whom they wish to collaborate. This is especially true of scientists and engineers engaged in a set of complex and fundamental questions called "Grand Challenges" by the National Research Council (NRC) (1988a, p. 33). These researchers are also becoming dissatisfied with the abilities of existing networks to meet their research and communication needs.

According to a recent report by the Congressional Office of Technology Assessment (OTA), (Office of Technology Assessment, 1989c, p. 28):

> There is substantial agreement in the scientific and higher education community about the pressing national need for a broad bandwidth state of the art research network . . . . Increasing demand on network capacity has quickly saturated each network upgrade. In addition, the fast growing demand on network capacity is overburdening the current informal administrative arrangements for running the Internet.

For the full text of this report, <u>High Performance Computing & Networking for Science: Background Paper</u>, see Appendix K.

There is also a developing consensus within the Federal government that information networking technology has become an integral component in science and technology. A national research network, operating as the backbone of a national information infrastructure, is seen by many to be a powerful tool which will enable the United States to strengthen its position in the global economy. This trend has been recognized by Congress and has spurred recent legislation intended to describe the initial stages of proposed development, clarify the Federal agency and departmental roles and responsibilities in the planning and development process, and determine funding levels of the NREN.

In order to help increase U. S. competitiveness in the computer industry and the rest of the manufacturing sector, Senator Albert Gore and others recently introduced S. 272, the <u>High-Performance Computing Act of 1991</u>, which stated that (Congress, Senate, 1991b, p. 2, 3):

> It is the purpose of Congress in this Act to help ensure the continued leadership of the United States in high-performance computing and its applications. This requires that the United States Government - (1) expand Federal support for research, development, and application of high-performance computing in order to - (A) establish a high-capacity national research and education network.

In the House, Congressman Brown and others introduced H.R. 656, the <u>High-Performance Computing Act of 1991</u>, which contained almost exactly the same language as the Senate legislation (Congress, House, 1991, p. 2). This legislation is an indication of the growing belief within the Federal government that Congress and the Administration should take a proactive role in the development of the NREN and the national information infrastructure needed to support it. For the full text of S. 272, see Appendix E.

History of National Networking

The Internet, a network of computer networks, was initially developed by the Defense Advanced Research Projects Agency (DARPA) (Gould, 1990a, p. 4). The original purpose of the Internet was to allow geographically dispersed researchers to share scientific data and computing resources by providing them with access to otherwise incompatible networks (Britten, 1990, p. 104). Beginning with ARPANET in 1969, DARPA has played a major role in creating and funding a series of networks that have become interconnected and share a common communications protocol, called TCP/IP (Terminal Control Protocol/ Internet Protocol) (LaQuey, 1989, p. 33). This protocol is a set of rules which allows messages to be sent quickly and easily among different types of computers and from one network to another.

The success of TCP/IP and other advances in networking technology led to such heavy network use that, by 1983, there were approximately 60 networks connected to ARPANET. By this time, according to Lynch and Preston, "the concept of the Internet with multiple wide-area networks connecting myriad institutional LANs (local area networks) was institutionalized" (1990, p. 279). In 1983, recognizing that a significant portion of the total network traffic was produced by academic researchers, the Department of Defense sought to relinquish its management of the Internet. Its first move was to channel the traffic associated with military research and development programs onto MILNET, a separate network with restricted access. ARPANET was left to handle the traffic of the research and education community (Gould, 1990c, p.4). ARPANET and MILNET formed major parts of the backbone of the Internet, which was the name given to the loosely organized networks which had become linked to ARPANET by 1983. For the full text of Gould'd report, <u>The Federal Research Internet and the National Research and Education Network: Prospects for the 1990s</u>, see Appendix M.

The National Science Foundation (NSF) took over the coordination of the Internet in 1985 and began to fund the development of the National Science Foundation Network (NSFNET), a national, high-speed telecommunications backbone that originally connected six supercomputing centers set up under the agency's auspices (Wintsch, 1989, p. 34). This backbone has been expanded to include 13 nodes, each of which is the hub of a regional network, composed in turn of interlinked campus networks. By 1988,

NSFNET was in place, "thus effectively superseding the older ARPANET backbone," which was phased out the following year (Lynch and Preston, 1990, p. 279). Regional and academic networks quickly began to connect to the NSFNET backbone; starting with about 60 networks on ARPANET in 1983, the Internet now contains around 700 networks, with some 60,000 host computers and an estimated one million users.

Most of these networks allow remote log in, file transfer, electronic mail, and other services. Currently, there are more than 1,000 colleges and universities which can communicate with each other across the Internet. Other Federal agencies and departments such as the Department of Energy (DoE) and the National Space and Aeronautics Administration (NASA) also manage their own Internet networks. Thus, the Internet has become a network which (Gould, 1990c, p. 1):

> Supports a vast, multidisciplinary community of researchers within government, universities, and industry, including physicists, electrical engineers, mathematicians, medical researchers, chemists, astronomers, computer scientists, and social scientists. It allows users of any one of the thousands of computers it connects to have access to distant resources such as supercomputers and scientific databases.

The growth of the Internet has not occurred according to any unified logic or plan. At the Federal level, for example, management of the Internet has been the responsibility of the Federal Research Internet Coordinating Committee (FRICC), which is attached to the Office of Science and Technology Policy (OSTP) in the Executive Office of the President. Below the Federal level, however, the management structure of the Internet can best be described as decentralized, with decision and policy-making authority located at the host site and individual networks. In other words, the Internet actually "consists of autonomous entities that are interconnected" (LaQuey, 1989, p. 34).

As a result, the Internet does not provide its users with directions or easy ways to access all of its member networks and resources. There are a number of problems that contribute to the lack of connectivity. They are (Gould, 1990a, p. 7):

- The extent to which networks are fragmented

- The technical limitations on the types of hardware and software that can be used on the Internet
- The weakness of gateways between networks
- The lack of training and support for users and the absence of documentation about the member networks and their procedures.

Different member networks offer different services and often have different policies governing access and use. Wintsch summarizes this situation (1989, p. 34):

> Neither fast enough for computer scientists nor smooth enough for scholars with limited knowledge of computers, the present Internet is at best a rough prototype of what FCCSET [Federal Coordinating Council for Science, Engineering, and Technology] has in mind for the turn of the century, and is a far cry from fulfilling the promise scientists . . . believe networking holds. Using it at all has been likened to an excursion into Babel.

As a consequence, what a user can do on the Internet depends on the particular member network to which he or she belongs and the extent to which the user is knowledgeable about the complexities of network communication protocols and procedures. Some scientists and researchers are so discouraged by the daunting problem of managing communication on the Internet that they do not even want to send electronic mail (Wintsch, 1989, p. 34).

Description of the NREN

The Federal government, academia, and the private sector have turned their attention to resolving problems associated with network use, envisioning a "user friendly, unified high-speed research network with nationwide coverage" (Gould, 1990b, p. 5; for the full text of this report, Building the National Research and Education Network, see Appendix N). Early discussions about this network revolved around the creation of a "national research network" (NRN), but, by early 1989, proponents of the network began to include "education" in its name (Kahin, 1990, p. 1). The plan, as of 1991, is to transform part of the Internet into the NREN, and, until recently, the Federal Research Internet Coordinating Committee (FRICC) has had the lead role in the process. FRICC's three-stage plan to create the NREN entails (Office of Technology Assessment, 1989c, p. 34):

- Stage 1: upgrade and interconnect existing agency networks into a jointly funded and managed T1 (1.5 Mb/s) National Networking Testbed.
- Stage 2: integrate national networks into a T3 (45 Mb/s) backbone by 1993.
- Stage 3: push a technological leap to a multigigabit NREN starting in the mid-1990s.

A North American T1 line has a speed of 1.544 megabits per second, and is considered to be a high-speed line; a T3 line has a speed of 45 megabits per second, which represents an increase in transmission speed by a factor of 30 (Quarterman, 1990, p. 134). By the end of the third stage, the NREN will have achieved speeds of multigigabits, or several thousand million bits per second (Wintsch, 1989, p. 34). It will also integrate "four levels of increasingly complex and flexible capability" (Office of Technology Assessment, 1989c, p. 23): physical wire/fiber optic common carrier highways; user-defined, packet-switched networks; basic network operations and services; and research, education, database, and information services accessible to network users. Stage 1 is well underway, and work has begun on Stage 2. Stage 3 "might coincide with a transition from Government sponsorship to commercial network service paid for by users" (Gould, 1990d, p. 8; for the full text of this report, High Performance Computing: An Overview, see Appendix L).

Currently, there is both an existing, or interim, NREN and a proposed NREN. The interim NREN is developing within the structure and operations of the Internet, and, at this point, it is difficult to separate what belongs to the interim NREN and what belongs to the Internet. The networks that are currently part of the interim NREN tend to operate independently, although they "must often abide by guidelines set by the regional network(s) they connect to and by the NSFNET" (Gould, 1990b, p. 3). Some of these networks are nonprofit, some are funded by joint ventures among academic, governmental, and private sector partners, and some "have no organizational or legal status, existing only as projects or accounts within a member institution." At the beginning of 1991, the interim NREN's approximately one million users had links to Federal networks and to industrial and research networks in Canada, Europe, Central and South America, and the Pacific Rim.

The proposed NREN is being developed out of public policy debates over and legislation concerning national high-speed networking efforts. The vision of the proposed NREN is of a high-speed transcontinental network of networks which will allow the rapid and transparent transmission of billions of bits of information per second among users in the Federal government, the educational community, and the private sector. According to Huray and Nelson (1990, p. 23), "when network legislation passes, the NSFNET will be declared to be NREN-1."

The proposed NREN is expected to have a three-tiered structure derived from the structure of the Internet. The first tier will be NSFNET, serving as the national backbone, which will be managed by Advanced Network and Services, Inc. (ANS). ANS is a nonprofit organization created by Merit, Inc. (current managers of the Internet), IBM, and MCI Communications Corporation (ANS, 1990, p. 1), whose stated purpose is to complement and support the development of the NREN as proposed by Congress (*Link Letter*, 1990a, p. 1). In December 1990, NSF announced that "operational deployment of NSFNET's new T3 backbone reached the halfway point" with high-speed connections in place at end nodes in Ann Arbor, Michigan; Urbana-Champaign, Illinois; San Diego, California; and Palo Alto, California (*Link Letter*, 1990b, p. 1). In early 1991, work is expected to be completed linking the remaining end nodes at Pittsburgh, Pennsylvania; Cambridge, Massachusetts; Ithaca, New York; and Argonne, Illinois. When this work has been completed, NSFNET will be the foundation of "the world's fastest openly available network for research and education" (*Link Letter*, 1990b, p. 9).

The second tier will be made up of regional networks. Currently, these range from networks within a state that are multicounty or less in scope, such as the Bay Area Regional Research Network (BARRNET), to serving an entire state, such as the New York State Education and Research Network (NYSERNET), to networks that cover several states, such as the Southeastern Universities Research Association Network (SURANET).

The third tier will be made up of smaller networks that operate within educational, Federal, and private sector sites. Because the NREN is being developed within the Internet, it is not entirely clear where the former will begin and the latter will end; at this point, they can perhaps best be described as existing alongside each other.

Current development of the NREN is not proceeding according to any uniform plan. Work on the NSFNET backbone is the most organized segment of the process, but thus far there is little coordination of efforts on the second and third tiers. There is legisla-

tion in Congress which, if enacted, will provide a more coherent plan for the implementation of a high-performance computing program, of which the development of the NREN is a significant part. If, for example, S. 272 is passed, a total of $195,000,000 will be appropriated for the development and support of the NREN between 1992 and 1996 (Congress, Senate, 1991b; for the full text of S. 272, see Appendix E). Appropriating funding is an important step in the development and implementation of the NREN, but the efficient allocation of these funds will depend on policy makers' grasp of the issues involved in the debate over the purposes and goals of this network. What are the goals that have thus far been set for the NREN?

Goals of the NREN

A number of goals have been proposed for the NREN. One fundamental goal is to establish an "[a]round-the-clock, high quality" network that will be the backbone of an advanced, permanent information infrastructure (Office of Technology Assessment, 1989c, p. 21). Based on a goal of open access, the network is expected to provide wide-spread connectivity linking scientists, researchers, educators, and library and information professionals in the Federal government, academia, and the private sector. As a consequence, the NREN will be able to achieve broad national goals, such as enhancing national competitiveness, productivity, and technology transfer. By enabling users to communicate with each other rapidly, across organizational and disciplinary boundaries, the NREN is expected to greatly reduce the time that is needed for innovations to flow from the laboratory to the marketplace.

Another goal is to extend access to supercomputing and other network resources and services to more users. According to Gould, "an extensive array of information resources will likely become stitched together by the NREN to form a more cohesive electronic information infrastructure," allowing users to search very large databases, use electronic bulletin boards, participate in ongoing computer conferences, explore software libraries, and share time on expensive, geographically distant, and previously inaccessible equipment (1990b, p. 7). Such universal access is expected to enable scientists to use distributed computing from remote locations in their research (Wintsch, 1989, p. 32).

The NREN is expected to greatly increase the abilities of scientists and researchers to engage in large-scale collaboration. Lederberg and Uncapher argue that the NREN is needed to support a "National Collaboratory," a combination of technology, tools, and infrastructure whose goal is to build "no less than a distributed intelligence, fully and seamlessly networked, with fully supported computational assistance designed to accelerate the pace and quality of discourse, and a broadening of the awareness of discovery" (1989, p. 3). The intent of a Collaboratory is allow geographically dispersed scientists to work with each other as if they were in the same laboratory.

A technical goal, as noted earlier, is to make the NREN transparent to users. Achieving such a level of transparency will require a very high degree of standardization and a friendly user interface throughout the network. It will also require that network planners and designers to take into account the education and training of users, who must be able to understand and perform the procedures necessary to maximize their use of the NREN.

The NREN is also expected to serve as a testbed for research and experimentation on data communications technology. According to OTA, prior experiences with networking have demonstrated that "generic technologies developed for the Internet . . . transfer readily into general data-networking applications" (1989c, p. 25). In this way, the NREN could have an impact on the rate of technology transfer in high-performance computing and communication between the research and manufacturing sectors.

In summary, major goals commonly proposed for the NREN in government reports include:

- Providing an advanced information infrastructure linking the Federal government, academia, and the private sector
- Enhancing the economic competitiveness of the United States by facilitating communication among scientists, engineers, and educators, improving scientific and research productivity, and speeding up the rate of technology transfer between the research and manufacturing sectors
- Extending the full range of network resources and services, including supercomputing resources, to all users
- Enabling scientists and researchers in different disciplines to engage in large-scale remote collaboration

- Supporting the development of a National Collaboratory
- Making the research and educational networking transparent to users by standardizing network protocols and procedures
- Serving as a testbed for research and development on high-speed networks and high-performance computing.

A concise description of NREN goals was provided by OTA, which stated that the proposed network (1989c, p. 26):

> Would link universities, national laboratories, non-profit institutions and government research organizations, private companies doing government-supported research and education, and facilities such as supercomputers, experimental instruments, databases, and research libraries. Network research, as a joint endeavor with industry, would create and transfer technology for eventual commercial exploitation, and serve the data networking needs of research and higher education into the next century.

The NREN has the potential to be one of the most significant technological developments in information networking and data communications of the century. Many of its supporters believe that the NREN may alter the way in which science is conducted in this country, and implications of NREN development have been widely discussed in the literature. As will be made clear in Chapters 6 and 7, however, such a belief may be rooted in a set of overly optimistic assumptions about the ways in which scientists and researchers perceive and use networks.

SUPPORT FOR THE PROPOSED NREN

This section examines key writings supporting the establishment of the NREN. It first describes reports produced by Federal agencies and private sector advisors to the Federal government, legislation introduced in Congress related to the NREN, and the testimony of witnesses before Congressional committees. It then describes articles that have appeared in the popular and professional press. Finally, it reports on the response of the library community to the NREN. Generally, all of these sources reflect enthusiastic support for establishing such a national research and education network.

Support for the NREN within the Government

Reports to the government

The concept of a national high-speed data and communication network has captured the imagination of many in academia, the Federal government, and the private sector. Figure 2-1 summarizes the key governmental reports discussed in this section.

The 1987 OSTP report, <u>A Research and Development Strategy for High Performance Computing</u>, was one of the earliest and most influential statements of the need for Federal involvement in high-performance computing. Written by FCCSET under a 1986 Congressional mandate, the report proposed a broad national agenda for advanced information technologies in several areas. The Federal government, according to FCCSET, should develop a long-range strategy to support basic research on high-performance computers and software technology and algorithms, and should provide long-term support for the training of computer scientists, researchers in computational science, and in computer technologies. The report also explicitly recognized the critical importance of networking technologies as important means to "develop large scale distributed approaches to the collaborative solution of computational problems in science, engineering, and other applications areas" (Office of Science and Technology Policy, 1987, p. 18).

Although brief, this report indicated high-level Executive branch interest in the idea of networking, recommending that the Federal government establish partnerships with industry and academia to "coordinate research and development for a research network to provide a distributed computing capability" that links these three sectors (Office of Science and Technology Policy, 1987, p. 21). FCCSET regarded this matter as one of some urgency, noting that in Europe and Japan research and development in high-speed networking technologies was being "aggressively" pursued by government-industry coalitions (p. 18). This R&D activity, the report suggested, would soon pose a serious challenge to the United States' continued leadership in high-performance computing, networking technologies, and software development.

The high-performance computing strategy proposed by FCCSET was a national policy statement intended to focus the efforts of the Federal govern-

ment, the educational community, and the private sector on a common set of problems. Noting that "Federally-funded computing research . . . continues to be the major source of innovation for computing technology and a primary catalyst for industrial development," the report called for the implementation of the various components as rapidly as possible (Office of Science and Technology Policy, 1987, p. 4).

In the following year, there were reports from private sector advisors to the Federal government that echoed the concerns expressed by FCCSET. With a mandate from the National Research Council (NRC), the Computer Science and Technology Board and the Commission on Physical Sciences, Mathematics, and Resources published a report, <u>The National Challenge in Computer Science and Technology</u> (National Research Council, 1988a), which explicitly linked a national computer network with "maximizing the benefits in productivity and competitiveness" that are created by the United States computer industry (p. 5). Realizing that the design and implementation of a national research network would be a multifaceted problem, the authors recommended that funding be made available in four different areas (p. 33):

- The identification and investigation of "Grand Challenges" in computer science
- The development of strategies to recruit and train the next generation of researchers
- The introduction of advanced computing equipment into the research environment
- Increases in the number of basic research projects.

With these recommendations, the NRC took the position that there must be considerable research and development on the information and scientific infrastructure within which a national computer network, such as the NREN, would function.

Also in 1988, the National Research Network Review Committee, the Computer Science and Technology Board, and the Commission on Physical Sciences, Mathematics, and Resources, under the auspices of the NRC, released <u>Toward A National Research Network</u> (National Research Council, 1988b). This report dealt primarily with the evaluation of FCCSET's 1987 network proposal. After a cogent discussion of several of the major concerns, observations, implementation strategies, and issues surrounding the establishment of a national computer network, the NRC concluded that "there is a clear and urgent need for a national research network. This nation

Figure 2-1. Key Reports on the NREN

A Research and Development Strategy for High Performance Computing. (1987). Office of Science and Technology Policy.

This report proposed a broad national agenda for advanced information technologies. It recognized the critical importance of networking technologies as important "means to develop large scale distributed approaches to the collaborative solution of computational problems in science, engineering, and other applications areas" (p. 18). It also recommended that the Federal government establish partnerships with industry and academia to "coordinate research and development for a research network to provide a distributed computing capability that links" (p. 21) these three sectors.

The National Challenge in Computer Science and Technology. (1988). National Research Council.

This report explicitly links a national computer network with "maximizing the benefits in productivity and competitiveness" which are created by the United States computer industry (p. 5). The authors of the report envisioned "a nationwide computer communications capability that would enable any computer in the United States to communicate with any other computer easily, reliably and over a broad range of speeds" (p. 14).

The report recommends that funding be made available in four different areas (p. 33): the identification and investigation of "grand challenges" in computer science; the development of strategies to recruit and train the next generation of researchers; the introduction of advanced computing equipment into the research environment; increases in the number of basic research projects.

Toward A National Research Network. (1988). National Research Council.

This report primarily deals with the evaluation of a network proposal, developed by the Federal Coordinating Council for Science, Engineering, and Technology (FCCSET), calling for the creation of a "high-performance, national computer network for researchers" (p. vii). After a cogent discussion of several of the major concerns, observations, implementation strategies, and issues surrounding the establishment of a national research network, the NRC concludes that "there is a clear and urgent need for a national research network" (p. 39).

Information Technology and the Conduct of Research: The User's View. (1989). Panel on Information Technology and the Conduct of Research.

This report recommended that research institutions and the Federal Government should collaborate on a national high-speed computer network for use by all qualified researchers. It suggests that OSTP and the Federal agencies responsible for supporting and conducting research and development should "plan and fund a nationwide infrastructure for computer based research communication" (p. 52). The report is important because it emphasized the importance of involving the users of such a network in the planning and implementation stages.

High Performance Computing and Networking: Background Paper. (1989). Office of Technology Assessment.

This report argues that there have been shifts in the thinking of policy makers giving higher priority to "the development of a very high capacity national scientific network," or "internet," which would be a fundamental component in a national data communications infrastructure (p. 17). It also outlines a coherent plan for the establishment of this network and of the components of the infrastructure which must be concurrently developed.

The Federal High Performance Computing Program. (1989). Office of Science and Technology Policy.

This report describes in greater detail various components of the strategy outlined in OSTP's 1987 report.

stands to gain considerably from the many direct and indirect benefits that would accrue from an NREN" (p. 39). This call was echoed on the floors of the Senate and the House, where legislators had been grappling with the issue of a national research network for several years prior to the NRC report.

The Office of Science and Technology Policy (1989) released a subsequent report, The Federal High Performance Computing Program, in which FCCSET described the various components of the strategy laid out in its 1987 report in greater detail. It proposed a five-year R&D policy that sought to integrate the efforts of the Federal government, the academic community, and the private sector in the development of high-performance computing hardware and software, a national network, an infrastructure to support the network, and educational programs to train the next generation of scientists and researchers. The goals of the program are to maintain the United States' economic competitiveness and leadership position in high-performance computing, encourage innovation in this area by stimulating the diffusion and assimilation of new technologies, and increase productivity. In relation to the strategy for networking, FCCSET argued that (Office of Science and Technology Policy, 1989, p. 31):

> Today's Internet is far from uniform in the type and quality of service provided, and it does not yet reach the entire research community. Even so, expanding the Internet and enhancing its performance as far as technology allows will still fall far short of what can and should be accomplished. The goal of this component . . . is to create a new NREN which operates at rates of gigabits per second nationwide. This tremendous challenge is within the grasp of the United States in the next ten years.

For the full text of this report, see Appendix I.

Responding to this sense of urgency, numerous calls came forth for the establishment of a national electronic highway which could connect researchers in Federal laboratories, academia, and the private sector. The National Academy of Sciences sponsored a study of the use of information technology and networks by researchers in various disciplines (Panel on Information Technology and the Conduct of Research, 1989). The study concluded that OSTP and the Federal agencies responsible for supporting and conducting

research and development should "plan and fund a nationwide infrastructure for computer based research communication" (1989, p. 52). For the Executive Summary of this report, see Appendix J.

In its 1989 draft report, High Performance Computing and Networking, OTA maintained that there have been recent shifts in the thinking of policy makers, who are currently giving higher priority to "the development of a very high capacity national scientific network," which would become a fundamental component in a national data communications and information infrastructure (1989b, p. 17). Also in 1989, OTA published High Performance Computing and Networking for Science: Background Paper, a report which argued that (1989c, p. 21):

> Policy action is needed, if Congress wishes to see the evolution of a full-scale national research and education network. The existing 'internet' of scientific networks is a fledgling. . . . Academics, policy makers, and researchers around the world agree on the pressing need to transform it into a permanent infrastructure.

Congress has been cognizant of the need to consider the extent to which there should be Federal involvement in the creation, implementation, and operation of a national computer network and has been grappling with the policy implications of the establishment of a national network for at least the last ten years.

Recent Legislation and the NREN

In this section, several pieces of legislation are examined. Each was written with the intention of enacting components of the Federal government's high-performance computing program. With the exception of the National Science Foundation Authorization Act for Fiscal Year 1987 (P. L. 99-383), none had been passed into law by Congress at the time this chapter was written. The bills to be reviewed are:

- S. 1067, National High Performance Computing Act of 1989 (Called the *original version*)
- S. 1067, National High Performance Computing Act of 1990 (As reported out of the Commerce Committee, called the *second version*)
- S. 1067, National High Performance Computing Act of 1990 (Passed by the Senate, called the *third version*)

- S. 272, <u>National High Performance Computing Act of 1991</u>
- H. R. 3131, <u>National High Performance Computing Technology Act of 1989</u>
- H. R. 4329, <u>American Technology Preeminence Act of 1990</u>
- S. 1976, <u>Department of Energy High-Performance Computing Act of 1989</u> (Called the *original version*)
- S. 1976, <u>Department of Energy High-Performance Computing Act of 1990</u> (Called the *second version*)
- S. 343, <u>Department of Energy High-Performance Computing Act of 1991</u>.

Although work is proceeding on a national network through Executive branch and private sector efforts, it is clear that legislation made at the Federal level will also have major impacts on the proposed NREN.

The purpose of this section is to trace the development of the proposed NREN through the legislative debate on the ways in which the Federal government should best carry out the strategies of the High-Performance Computing (HPC) program outlined by Executive branch agencies. This is important because the debate reveals many of the critical policy issues whose resolution will determine the structure of the NREN, the process of its implementation, management, and evolution, and the ways in which it will eventually be used. In the discussion below, only the portions of the legislation dealing with the NREN are considered. Specific language in these bills will be referred to by both Section and page number.

Senator Albert Gore of Tennessee has been a key player in the proposal of the NREN. In 1986, Senator Gore sponsored S. 2594, the <u>Supercomputer Network Study Act,</u> which was integrated into the <u>National Science Foundation Authorization Act for Fiscal Year 1987</u> (P. L. 99-383). The law directed NSF to investigate the potential of fiber optics for networks intended to link NSF supercomputers located around the country. It also directed OSTP to study "critical problems and current and future options regarding communication networks" which would link research computers, including supercomputers, at academic and Federal research facilities. This mandate was the impetus for OSTP's initial 1987 study of high-performance computing.

S. 1067

In October 1988, Senator Gore introduced S. 2918, the <u>National High Performance Computing Technology Act of 1988</u> (Congress, Senate, 1988a). This bill contained two important titles, Title II, National Computer Research Network, and Title III, National Information Infrastructure (Henderson, 1990b). In May 1989, Senators Gore and Jeffords introduced S. 1067, the <u>National High Performance Computing Technology Act of 1989</u> (Congress, Senate, 1989b), legislation similar to S. 2918. S. 1067 was referred to the Committee on Commerce, Science, and Transportation. A companion bill, H.R. 3131, which had the same title and was identical in structure to the Senate bill, was introduced in the House of Representatives by Congressman Walgren and others in August 1989 (Congress, House, 1989b). For the full text of the original version of S. 1067, see Appendix B.

Neither bill passed in its respective chamber, and the Senate version was carried over into the 101st Congress' second session as S. 1067, the <u>High Performance Computing Act of 1990</u> (Congress, Senate, 1990a). This second version of the bill contained a number of changes and a favorable recommendation by the Committee on Commerce, Science, and Transportation. For the full text of this version of S. 1067, see Appendix C. A third version of S. 1067 was passed by the Senate in October 1990, again with changes, but it made no further progress by the end of the session (Congress, Senate, 1990b). For the full text of this version of S. 1067, see Appendix D. The bill has been reintroduced into the first session of the 102nd Congress as S. 272, the <u>High-Performance Computing Act of 1991</u> (Congress, Senate, 1991; see Appendix E). This new version of the bill also contains some significant changes.

The original version of S. 1067 was an attempt to write legislation that would define Federal involvement in high-performance computing (HPC). Based on OSTP's plan for an HPC program, this bill also sought to assign responsibilities within the Federal government and authorize funding for the components of the plan. Developed in consultation with industry and certain Federal agencies, the bill had six titles, the first three of which directly involved the NREN. In relation to the NREN, a major goal of S. 1067 was to outline a leading role for the Federal government in the creation of a high-speed, high-capacity network that would operate over a fiber optic backbone, linking some 1,300 sites in government, industry, and academia by 1996 (Congress, Senate, 1989b, p. 2).

Title I of S. 1067 amended the <u>National Science and Technology Policy, Organization, and Priorities Act of 1976</u> by clarifying the role of the Federal government in the national HPC program; this appeared as a new section, Title VI. FCCSET was charged with developing and implementing a five-year plan that would set overall goals and priorities for the program and determine the roles, responsibilities, and budgets of Federal agencies and departments involved in the program. FCCSET was also responsible for overseeing interagency coordination and that "agencies work together to connect their computer networks and . . . improve, share, and distribute computer software they have developed" (Congress, Senate, 1989b, p. 3). In this title, NSF was made the lead agency in the creation of the NREN when it was given the tasks of "providing for the establishment, by 1996, of a 3 gigabit-per-second national computer network" and of developing and supporting an information infrastructure for the network (p. 9).

Title II again designated NSF as the lead agency in the Federal effort to create the NREN, and included DoD, DoE, the Department of Commerce (DoC), and NASA as the main supporting agencies. As described in Section 201(a)(1-5), the NREN would (Congress, Senate, 1989b, p. 13):

- Link government, industry, and the higher education community
- Be developed in close cooperation with the computer and telecommunications industry
- Be designed and developed with the advice of potential users in government, industry, and higher education
- Have accounting mechanisms that allow users or groups of users to be charged for their usage of the network, where appropriate
- Be phased out when commercial networks can meet the networking needs of American researchers.

While somewhat vague, these characteristics described a national network that would be the product of a massive cooperative venture involving many of the major sectors of American society.

Section 202 of this title also described other agency and department responsibilities. FCCSET was required to create a National Network Advisory Committee with representatives from the scientific research community, academia, and the private sector. This group would bring together network users and experts to provide technical and policy information to FCCSET and the agencies that would construct and operate the network. R&D on advanced network technology was assigned to DoD, which, through

DARPA, would work on the hardware and software needed to run the NREN. The National Institute of Standards and Technology (NIST), in cooperation with the National Security Agency (NSA), was responsible for deriving a set of standards for interoperability, common user interfaces, and network security procedures. The National Telecommunications and Information Administration (NTIA) was to examine the positive and negative effects of current Federal telecommunications laws on the participation of the private sector in the data transmission field. This bill appropriated $400 million between FY1990 and FY1994 to NSF for the "research, development, and implementation" of the NREN (p. 15).

Title III designated NSF as the lead agency in the establishment of a "national science and technology infrastructure of data bases and knowledge banks accessible through" the NREN (Congress, Senate, 1989b, p. 16). As described in Section 301, the five major components of this infrastructure would be:

- A directory of network users
- Provision for access to unclassified Federal scientific databases, including weather data, census data, economic data, and remote sensing satellite data
- Rapid prototyping of computer chips and other devices using centralized facilities connected to the network
- Databases and knowledge banks for use by artificial intelligence programs
- Provision for international collaboration among researchers.

NSF was empowered to work closely with DoC, the National Oceanic and Atmospheric Administration (NOAA), NIST, the Bureau of the Census, DoD, NSA, and other appropriate agencies. Interestingly, there was no section in this title authorizing appropriations for the development of the information infrastructure.

The second version of S. 1067, retitled the National High Performance Computing Act of 1990, was favorably reported by the Senate Committee on Commerce, Science, and Transportation and had a structure similar to that of the original version of the bill, although there were significant changes in language. The changes in this version of the bill reflected a subtle shift in the Federal Government's approach to implementing the HPC program as the Committee attempted to widen the base of government and private sector support for and involvement in the program. This version of the bill was written to provide a balanced and comprehensive plan for the implementation of OSTP's HPC program. Because the different components of the program were designed to be interdependent, the bill created a plan where "progress in high-performance computing . . . [would be] hindered if the pace of development in any one area . . . [were] not as fast as in other areas" (Congress, Senate, 1990a, p. 4). For the full text of the Senate Committee on Commerce, Science, and Transportation's report, High-Performance Computing Act of 1990, see Appendix F (Congress, Senate, 1990c).

In Title I, Section 602(a)(2)(B), FCCSET's involvement in the determination of Federal funding to carry out the components of the plan was made more specific by requiring that it "describe the levels of Federal funding for each agency" (Congress, Senate, 1990a, p. 26). The list of agencies expected to participate in the plan was extended to include NTIA, the Department of Education (DoEd), the Library of Congress (LC), the National Library of Medicine, and the National Agricultural Library. FCCSET was also explicitly directed to work with industry, the National Research Council, and academic, State, and other groups (p. 28).

A clause from the original version was deleted which had required FCCSET to consult with actual and potential users of HPC research through an advisory board that would be staffed by members of the educational community and the private sector (Congress, Senate, 1989b, p. 7). In Section 602(c) of the second version, OSTP is directed to set up a High-Performance Computing Advisory Panel which would provide FCCSET with independent assessments of the program's progress, potential problems and possible revisions to the plan, and the ability of the program to contribute to continued U. S. leadership in HPC (Congress, Senate, 1990a, p. 28).

Section 102 of the second version was a new amendment to the National Science and Technology Policy, Organization, and Priorities Act of 1976 (P. L. 94-282), which described the functions of FCCSET necessary for it to play a leading role in the effort to formulate policies dealing with scientific and technical activities that spanned agency and departmental boundaries. The Council was empowered to coordinate cooperative ventures within the Federal government and domestic and international ventures among governmental, academic, and industrial research communities. FCCSET was also given the power to

delegate tasks to employees of Federal agencies involved in the program (Congress, Senate, 1990a, p. 37).

Instead of merely "providing for the establishment" of the NREN (Congress, Senate, 1989b, p. 8), NSF was, in Section 602(d)(1)(A) of the second version, given the "primary responsibility" for establishing what was now described as a "multi-gigabit" network (Congress, Senate, 1990a, p. 28). In addition, NSF was instructed to "maintain, expand, and upgrade its existing computer networks" until such time as the NREN would be operational (p. 28). While previously required to develop an "information infrastructure," this term was deleted from the second version, and NSF was instead directed to make information services and databases available over computer networks (p. 29).

There were also changes in agency and departmental responsibilities and tasks. NIST still had the task of defining standards, but was instructed to cooperate with industry and to use an open standards-setting process. Instead of having to develop new standards to protect network security and privacy, NIST was now able to adopt existing standards, if they were deemed appropriate. The general responsibilities of DoD did not change, but the Office of Naval Research was deleted from the list of DoD agencies explicitly involved in the program.

A more subtle change occurred in the section describing the role of DoE in the program. Originally, DoE was to make "unclassified computer technology research readily available to American industry" (Congress, Senate, 1989b, p. 10). In the second version, "unclassified computer research" was to be made "available to North American companies" (Congress, Senate, 1990a, p. 32). By deleting reference to "technology," research on such HPC components as software, protocols, and algorithms was included, as long as it was unclassified. Adding "North American" was an attempt to encourage joint ventures in HPC between American and Canadian companies.

There was more of an academic, library, and information professional presence in this version. In Section 602(d)(1)(G), DoEd, which did not appear in the original version, was given the task of establishing library connections to the NREN in order to facilitate the dissemination of library and information services over the network. In Section 602(d)(1)(H), the Library of Congress (LC) and the other national libraries were to "compile, develop, and maintain electronic data bases . . . [and] provide for dissemination of, access to, and use" of these and other resources over the NREN (Congress, Senate, 1990a, pp. 32, 33).

In Title II, the NREN was again described as a multigigabit network. The five characteristics listed in Section 201(a)(1-5) of the original version (Congress, Senate, 1989b, p. 13) had been expanded to eight. In Section 201(1-8) of the second version, the new characteristics were (Congress, Senate, 1990b, pp. 38, 39):

- Provide computer users with access to supercomputers, computer databases, and other research facilities (section 2)
- Provide users of libraries and other educational institutions with access to the Network and information resources (section 3)
- Be established in a manner which fosters and maintains competition and private sector investment in high-speed data networking within the telecommunications industry (section 6).

There were also deletions and additions to other characteristics. In Section 201(1), which described the range of institutions to be connected to the NREN, the word "higher" was removed from "higher education," indicating that secondary and elementary schools would eventually be linked to the NREN. Section 201(4), which described the cooperative role of the private sector in the program, noted that the NREN was to be developed in close association with the information industry, which was added to the computer and telecommunications industries as partners in the program. In Section 201(7), the NREN was expected to have accounting mechanisms, but now these were to be applied only where "technically feasible." These mechanisms were to be used to charge users "where appropriate" for their "usage of the network and copyrighted materials available over the Network" (p. 39). This change represented both a more tentative approach to the problem of user fees and a recognition of the importance of protecting copyrighted materials in electronic form.

In Section 202(1)(A), FCCSET was directed to establish a Federal Networking Advisory Committee which would be staffed by representatives "from the interests involved in existing Federal research networks" and the NREN (Congress, Senate, 1990a, p. 39). In addition to the name change, this group was no longer expected to provide FCCSET with policy advice, and its membership no longer had to be drawn from "all the interests" involved in the program (Congress, Senate, 1989b, p. 13). The list of

constituencies from which the membership was to be drawn was deleted from the second version of the bill. There was also a new stipulation included in Section 202(1)(B) that the report that FCCSET would have to submit to Congress would have to contain a "plan for the eventual commercialization" of the NREN (p. 40).

There were two changes in agency responsibilities. Instead of having to cooperate with NSA and other agencies in the development of standards, NIST was only to consult with them, although consultation was to explicitly involve NSF and the private sector. NTIA was still expected to investigate the effects of telecommunications laws on the private sector, but the scope of the study was extended to include current state laws. A new requirement was that NTIA had to provide the Administration with a report on this investigation within one year of the bill becoming law (Congress, Senate, 1990a, p. 41).

The National Science Foundation, instead of having to coordinate the development of an infrastructure, was instead to "promote development" of the information services of Section 301 of Title III. The National Technical Information Service (NTIS), DoE, the National Institutes of Health (NIH), LC, the U.S. Geological Survey, and the Department of Agriculture were added to the list of agencies from which NSF would seek assistance. There was also a clarification of the way in which other relevant agencies could be brought into this effort; in this version, the Director of OSTP was explicitly given the authority to identify such agencies.

Also in this section, the list of information services was expanded from five to eight; the new services were (Congress, Senate, 1990a, p. 42):

- Directories of databases available over the network (section 2)
- Digital libraries to video programming, books, and journals stored in electronic form and other computer data (section 4)
- Orientation and training of users of databases and networks (section 5)
- Commercial information services to researchers using the network (section 6).

There were also changes made in the remaining services on this list. Instead of simply providing access to unclassified Federal scientific databases, Section 301(3) required NSF to promote the development of means of identifying and cataloging this information. Instead of having to provide for international collaboration among researchers, Section 301(8) required NSF to promote the use of "technology to support computer-based collaboration that allows researchers around the Nation to share information and instrumentation" (p. 42). This version of the bill appropriated $195 million to NSF for the R&D and development of the NREN between FY1991 and 1995. It also appropriated $338 million to NASA, an undetermined amount of which was to be earmarked for the NREN.

The third version of S. 1067 was similar in structure to the version that was reported to the Senate by the Committee on Commerce, Science, and Transportation, but it also contained significant changes and some reorganization of sections. Title I in this version changed the title of the bill to The High-Performance Computing Act of 1990, and in Section 101, the amended Title added to the National Science and Technology Policy, Organization, and Priorities Act of 1976 was renumbered as Title VII. This title began with Section 701, in which FCCSET was required to manage the interagency coordination of the HPC program. In Section 701(a)(3), which listed the agencies and departments involved in the plan, NSA and LC were deleted and the Department of Agriculture was added to the list. However, the involvement of LC was preserved in Section 710(a)(4), which stated that "the plan shall take into consideration the present and planned activities" of LC (Congress, Senate, 1990b, p. 8).

Section 602(d)(2)(A-F) of the second version, which detailed agency and departmental collaboration in the program, was moved to Section 701((a)(5)(A-H) with the following additions (Congress, Senate, 1990b, p. 9):

* Accelerate the development of high-performance computer systems, subsystems, and associated software (F)
* Provide the technical support and research and development of high-performance computer software and hardware needed to address Grand Challenges (G)
* Identify agency rules, regulations, policies, and practices which can be changed to significantly improve utilization of Federal high-performance computing and network facilities, and make recommendations to such agencies for appropriate changes (H).

The stipulation to promote software interoperability was deleted, but software "portability" was added as a goal to Section 701(a)(5)(B). In addition to cooperating with industry in the development of software, agencies were encouraged to exchange software, where appropriate. A new clause, Section 701(a)(6), required FCCSET to include in the plan security policies for the network. The agencies and departments participating in the program would then be expected to develop and implement security plans to "protect Federal research computer networks and information resources accessible" through the networks in accordance with these network-wide policies (p. 9).

Section 701(b) of Title VII, which further explicated the role of FCCSET, maintained the Council's role as the lead group in the formulation of the plan, and added an explicit responsibility to handle interagency coordination of the program. However, it also seemed to restrict the powers of FCCSET, because it deleted the Council's responsibility for implementation of the plan from Section 701(b)(1) (Congress, Senate, 1990b, p. 9). Further restriction of FCCSET's role occurred in the next sentence, where, instead of being able to coordinate the HPC R&D activities of participating agencies and departments, it was now only able to "recommend ways to coordinate" these activities (p. 10). The formation of the High-Performance Computing Advisory Panel, which was introduced in the second version (Congress, Senate, 1990a, p. 28), created the specific task of the Director of OSTP. The members who would serve on this panel were to be "prominent representatives from industry and academia, who are specially qualified to provide . . . advice and information" about HPC. Section 106, which further discussed the functions of FCCSET, was incorporated without change from Section 102 in the second version of the bill.

In Section 102 of the third version of the bill, which paralleled Title II, Section 201 of the second version, the phrase "in cooperation with" was deleted from the sentence which, in the second version, clearly indicated that NSF was the lead agency in the establishment of the NREN. All of the agencies listed were given an equivalent role in this part of the program. In Section 102(b)(1), computer users were to be afforded "appropriate access" to network resources; this addition seemed to reflect a step back from the assumption of a network based on open access (Congress, Senate, 1990b, p. 15). There was no indication of how appropriateness of access requests would be determined, or who would make such judgments.

There were also two additions to the characteristics of the NREN; it was expected to (p. 14):

- Be established in a manner which promotes research and development leading to deployment of commercial data communications and telecommunications standards (4)
- Be phased into commercial operation as commercial networks can meet the networking needs of American researchers and educators (6).

These characteristics indicated a change in the way in which the future of the NREN had been portrayed. Instead of being phased out at some point, these sentences suggested that, at some as yet undetermined time, the NREN would be taken over by the private sector. The academic community was also added to the population of users whose networking needs were to be met by commercial networks in the private sector.

Section 202(1), which in the second version had required FCCSET to establish a Federal Networking Advisory Committee, was deleted from the third version. However, Section 102(f) required FCCSET to create an "entity or entities" to manage the development, implementation, and operation of the NREN. This unnamed group was to set "goals, strategy, and priorities" for the NREN, clarify the involvements of Federal agencies and departments, and develop a method to coordinate their activities. Once the NREN was operational, this group was to "oversee . . . [its] operation and evolution," handle the interagency network linkages, and "develop conditions for access to the network" (Congress, Senate, 1990b, pp. 13, 14). The lines of authority between this group and FCCSET were not made clear in this section, and it seemed that their responsibilities in relation to the development of the NREN overlapped to some extent.

There were several changes in the responsibilities of participating agencies and departments. In Section 102(d), DoD, which had the lead role in R&D of hardware and software needed for the NREN in the second version, was directed to support such R&D (Congress, Senate, 1990b, p. 14). NIST's basic task did not change, but in Section 102(g)(2), it no longer had to consult with NSF, NSA, other agencies, or with industry. In addition, the stipulation that an open standards setting process be used was deleted (p. 16).

Section 103(a) described the role of NSF in the HPC program. While carrying over several of the tasks from Section 602(d)(1)(A) of the second version

(Congress, Senate, 1990a, p. 29), the first two sentences were deleted, removing a general description of NSF's responsibilities in relation to the types of research it was mandated to fund. However, an explicit requirement was added directing NSF to make funds available to researchers wanting access to supercomputers. Also, the sentence from the second version which gave NSF primary responsibility for the establishment of the NREN was deleted. Title III, Section 301, which in the second version detailed the role of NSF in providing information services (p. 41) was incorporated into Section 103(b)(1) of the third version. NSF was directed to promote the development of these services, and the involvement of other agencies and departments was no longer mandatory. The list of services also underwent changes in the third version, with three deletions from the list of eight, and changes to three of the remaining five. The directory of databases, digital libraries, and the rapid prototyping of integrated circuits and other devices were omitted. What remained were (Congress, Senate, 1990b, p. 18):

- The provision of directories of users and services
- Databases of unclassified Federal scientific data
- Training users of databases and networks
- Access to commercial information services to researchers using the Network
- Technology to support computer-based collaboration that allows researchers around the Nation to share information and instrumentation.

The inclusion of a directory of services was an addition to the list, as was the stipulation that NSF only find ways to provide access to commercial information services, instead of providing the services themselves. The requirement to identify, catalog, and provide for access to the Federal scientific databases was also deleted.

Title II of the third version of S. 1067 incorporated substantial portions of S. 1976, the Department of Energy High Performance Computing Act of 1990, which will be examined below. This was the result of a compromise struck by the Senate Committee on Commerce and the Committee on Energy and Natural Resources. This Title greatly expanded the proposed role of DoE in the development, implementation, and operation of the NREN. Section 202(a) required the Secretary of Energy to establish a HPC program that would have the same priorities and goals as the program developed by FCCSET (Congress, Senate, 1990b, p. 25). In Section 203(a)(1, 2), DoE was directed to "provide for a high-performance computer network . . . to link the government, research, industry, and educational constituencies of the Department" (p. 26). DoE was given authority to either create new networks or to use existing ones, including the NREN. As will be seen in the discussion of S. 1976 below, this stipulation removes DoE as the lead agency in the creation of the NREN. The bill appropriated to NSF $95 million dollars for R&D and support of the NREN between FY1991 and 1993.

Although S. 1067 did unanimously pass the Senate in October 1990, no further action was taken on the bill because of what occurred in the House. According to Ebbinghouse (1990, p. 3):

> It was a long hard fight for the bipartisan bill. Among the biggest problems the bill faced in the House was the two billion dollar price tag, especially since there was no indication of where the money would come from . . . these were tough times for a 'massive spending bill.' So when the House passed a watered down version of the bill, and attached it to a larger package, the Senate killed it, and with it what was left of S. 1067.

Further commentary on the demise of S. 1067 was provided by Paul Peters, Director of the Coalition for Networked Information (CNI), who stated that the version of the bill that was passed by the Senate (the third version) was not acceptable to CNI, EDUCOM, the educational community, and other library and information professional constituencies. He argued that the bill had been compromised in order to gain the support of the Senate Energy Committee and, as a consequence, several important elements of the bill had been deleted. The NSF was no longer the lead agency in the effort to establish the NREN, and there was no longer a "strong commitment to a uniform network architecture and the standards that enable the implementation of such an architecture" (1990, p. 1). In addition, much of the language that had provided for education and service elements was deleted.

S. 1976

In November 1989, Senators Johnston, Gore, and McClure introduced S. 1976, the Department of Energy High-Performance Computing Act of 1989 (Congress, Senate, 1989a). The bill renewed the call for Federal involvement in the development of a national high-performance computing program to support the development of a high-speed, national research and education network. Section 2(a)(10) gave a leading role in the creation and management of a national HPC program to DoE, and directed DoE to use the framework set out in the 1989 OSTP report The Federal High Performance Computing Program (pp. 3, 4). Section 3(b)(2)(A) ordered DoE to establish a high-capacity national research and education computer network, effectively replacing NSF with DoE as the lead agency in the HPC program (p. 6). For the full text of the original version of S. 1976, see Appendix G.

The scope of the mandate given to DoE by this bill was broad. Section 3(b)(1), (2)(A-F) stipulated that within one year of the bill's becoming law, DoE would be responsible for developing a five-year plan which would (Congress, Senate, 1989a, pp. 5-8):

- Summarize ongoing HPC programs at DoE
- Detail DoE's contribution to the program resulting in the establishment of the NREN
- Make clear DoE's involvement in the development of databases, services, and research facilities which will be available on the NREN
- Set funding levels for the various components of the program
- Determine the roles its laboratories will play in the program.

This list does not exhaust the responsibilities that were detailed in this section, but it does include those that would directly affect the design and construction of the NREN.

Section 4(a) contained similar language to Section 102(a) of the third version of S. 1067 (Congress, Senate, 1990b, p. 13), except that it listed the Secretary of DoE first. It required that the NREN be constructed by 1996, and Section 4(b)(1-7) listed the major characteristics of the network. The NREN had to (Congress, Senate, 1989a, pp. 7-8):

- Link government, industry, and the higher education community
- Provide computer users at more than 1,000 universities, Federal laboratories, and industrial laboratories with access to supercomputers, computer databases, and other research facilities
- Be developed in close cooperation with the computer and telecommunications industries

- Be designed and developed with the advice of potential users in government, industry, and the higher education community
- Be established in a manner which fosters and maintains competition in high-speed data networking within the telecommunications industry
- Have accounting mechanisms which allow users or groups of users to be charged for their usage of the network, where appropriate
- Be phased out when commercial networks can meet the networking needs of American researchers.

The bill appropriated $100 million for DoE to develop the NREN between FY1991 and FY1995 (p. 9). After S. 1976 was read twice, it was sent to the Committee on Energy and Natural Resources.

The second version of S. 1976 was favorably reported by the Committee on Energy and Natural Resources in July 1990, with an amendment (Congress, Senate, 1990e, p. 1). Section 3(a) and (a)(1) stated that one purpose of the bill was to direct the Secretary of Energy to establish an HPC program that would include the NREN. Section 5 detailed DoE's role in the HPC program and grounded DoE's authority in the Federal Non-Nuclear Research and Development Act of 1974. For the full report by the Senate Committee on Energy and Natural Resources, including the text of this version of S. 1976, see Appendix H.

Section 6(a) made DoE the lead department in the creation of the NREN, which was to (Congress, Senate, 1990e, p. 2):

- Have a multigigabit-per-second data transmission capacity
- Enable government, industry, educational institutions, and others to link together, as may be appropriate
- Be developed with the advice of potential users
- Have mechanisms that allow users to be charged appropriately for the use of the NREN
- Be subject to such terms, conditions, charges, and limitations as the Secretary deems reasonable
- Be operational by no later than 1996
- Be eliminated or sold to the private sector, in accordance with applicable law, when the networking needs provided by the NREN can be satisfied by other means.

The NREN that would be built by DoE would differ from the one envisioned in S. 1067. It would be open to users outside of government, academia, and private industry. Advice would be sought from a wider group of potential users, not just high-profile and prominent network experts. The management of the NREN would be firmly centered in DoE, subject to the directives of the Secretary of Energy. Finally, the future of the network was left open; it could be sold or simply eliminated.

Section 7(a) took another step toward locating control of the HPC program within DoE by calling for the creation of a Federal Interagency High-Performance Computing Task Force. This task force was to be chaired by the Secretary of Energy, and its members would include the Secretary of Commerce, the Secretary of Defense, the Administrator of NASA, the Director of NSF, and others as deemed appropriate by the Chair (Congress, Senate, 1990e, p. 3). Section 7(b) stated that the purposes of this group were to develop and coordinate a government-wide strategy for the efficient use of Federal computing resources by agencies. The description of the elements of the computing strategy which followed in Section 7(e)(1-9) was similar to the tasks that were assigned to FCCSET in the first two versions of S. 1067, in Section 602(a)(2) (Congress, Senate, 1990a, p. 26), and to an unnamed group in the third version, in Section 102(f)(2) (Congress, Senate, 1990b, p. 15).

The Task Force, however, was assigned additional responsibilities. It had to examine agency rules, regulations, policies, and practices to determine which ones inhibited the use of HPC and make recommendations for changes. It was to be responsible for the dissemination of information concerning the availability of HPC facilities and networking services and the ways these resources could be accessed to users in the government, academia, and the private sector. Finally, in Section 7(e)(7), the Task Force would be given the authority to "determine who outside the Federal government should have access to" high-performance computing and the NREN, "if anyone, and the appropriate terms and conditions for such access" (Congress, Senate, 1990e, p. 4). The Act appropriated $675 million to DoE to carry out the provisions of the bill, but there was no indication of the amount to be earmarked for the development and implementation of the NREN.

H. R. 4329

In August 1989, Representative Doug Walgren of Pennsylvania introduced H.R. 3131, the National High Performance Computer Technology Act of 1989, the companion bill to the original version of S. 1067 (Congress, House, 1989b). Major portions of H.R. 3131 were incorporated into H.R. 4329, the American Technology Preeminence Act, introduced by Representative Roe and others on March 21, 1990 (Congress, House, 1990a). The bill received a favorable report with an amendment from the Committee on Science, Space, and Technology in May 1990. Title IV, Section 403 dealt with the national HPC program, and amended the National Science and Technology Policy, Organization, and Priorities Act of 1976 by adding Title VII, the National High Performance Computer Technology Program. This section updated and integrated key elements of Titles I and II of H.R. 3131 and incorporated some critical language from S. 1976. It stated that the 1989 OSTP report "provides a framework for a multiagency computer technology program" to be followed closely by FCCSET, which was designated as the lead agency in the formulation of this program (p. 33).

In this title, FCCSET was still responsible for developing a national HPC Plan, but in Section 703(a)(1), its mandate to implement the plan was dropped. FCCSET was directed in Section 703(b)(3) to establish an "advisory board which shall include representatives from universities and industry who are involved in research and development activities in high performance computing" (Congress, House, 1990a, p. 37). Board members were given the charge of acting as independent observers and evaluators of the plan, particularly in terms of its "balance among components" and its "effectiveness . . . in maintaining American leadership in computing and networking."

In addition, Section 703(a)(4)(B), which described the functions that the NREN was expected to fulfill, contained some significant alterations, as compared to previous legislation (Congress, House, 1990a, pp. 35-36). It specified neither NREN's speed nor the number of institutions it would connect. It included a sentence taken from Section 4(b)(6) of the original version of S. 1976, which required that the network be "established in a manner which fosters and maintains competition . . . within the telecommunications industry" that had not appeared in H.R. 3131 or the original version of S. 1067.

DoE had been designated the lead agency in S. 1976, but was not mentioned in H.R. 4329. The amended Title VII followed H.R. 3131 and the early versions of S. 1067 rather closely. The presence of the library and information professions was also missing from this bill. Finally, this legislation did not contain any appropriations for the development and implementation of the HPC program.

S. 272

In January 1991, Senator Gore introduced S. 272, the High-Performance Computing Act of 1991. The bill was very similar in structure to the third version of S. 1067 passed by the Senate in 1990, but there were several important changes. In Section 5, which contained the amended Title VII, the central role of FCCSET in developing and coordinating the HPC program was reasserted. In Section 701(a)(2)(c), FCCSET was authorized to describe funding levels for agencies, departments, and specific HPC activities, including the establishment of the NREN (Congress, Senate, 1991b, p. 6).

Most importantly, in Section 6(f)(1) (p. 14), FCCSET was given the task of overseeing the network. This task previously was the responsibility of an unnamed "entity or entities" to be appointed by FCCSET in the third version of S. 1067 (Congress, Senate, 1990b, p. 15). The functions of FCCSET described in Section 106 of the third version of S. 1067 were deleted, as was Title II, the section describing the Department of Energy HPC program (Congress, Senate, 1990b, pp. 21-30). The bill appropriated $195 million to NSF for NREN research and development.

When introducing S. 272, Senator Gore commented that (1991, p. S1999):

> Perhaps the most important contribution this bill will make to our economic security is the National Research and Education Network, the cornerstone of the program funded by this bill. By 1996, this fiber-optic computer network would connect more than 1 million people at more than 1,000 colleges in all 50 states . . . . This network will speed research and accelerate technology transfer, so that the discoveries made in our university laboratories can be quickly and effectively turned into profits for American companies.

He went on to discuss the effects that the NREN and its supporting technologies would have on education in libraries and in American homes. Gore's optimism has, in large part, been echoed in Congress at the many hearings that have been held on the NREN over the last several years.

S. 343

In February 1991, Senator Johnston and others introduced S. 343, the Department of Energy High-Performance Computing Act of 1991 (Congress, Senate, 1991a). This bill was similar to S. 1976, although there were some changes. In a strong challenge to the tone of S. 272, Section 2(c)-(e) stated that DoE was the Federal agency with the "greatest degree of expertise and knowledge in the research, development and use of high-performance computers, associated software and networks" and was therefore "particularly well-equipped. . .to design, implement and manage a multi-gigabit per-second nationwide computer network" (p. 2). Section 5 maintained DoE's key role in the establishment of an HPC program, giving it many of the responsibilities assigned to FCCSET and NSF in S. 272. For the full text of S. 343, see Appendix O.

However, the network described in Section 6(a)(1)-(4) is not the NREN. Called the "Federal High-Performance Computer Network," it was intended to link agencies and departments within the Federal government, although the Secretary of Energy was authorized to allow people to be connected as deemed appropriate. As in S. 1976, DoE can build this network or can make use of other governmental networks provided, in an addition to Section 6(a)(4), "that the Federal department or agency concurs in such use" (p. 5). In S. 1976, the NREN was mentioned by name in this context, in this version, it was not. In what may be an indication that this network was intended to compete with the NREN, Section 6(4)(b) orders DoE to use their network for research and education, making it available to "undergraduate and graduate students, post-doctoral fellows, and faculty" in computational science and related fields in American higher education (p. 5).

Despite the apparent dispute over the nature of the Federal Government's commitment to a national computer network, there is an underlying support of the concept of such a network, whether the NREN is managed and operated by NSF and FCCSET, or the Federal High-Performance Computer Network is run by DoE. This support cuts across political and public and private sector boundaries; this is evident in the Congressional hearings that have been held over the past decade.

Congressional Hearings

During a series of hearings in 1988 and 1989, the call for a national research and education network has come under critical but largely positive scrutiny from industry, academia, and the Federal government. For a summary of key Congressional hearings on the NREN, see Figure 2-2.

The Senate Subcommittee on Science, Technology, and Space held a hearing in August 1988 on Computer Networks and High Performance Computing (Congress, Senate, 1988b), the purposes of which were, according to Senator Gore (p. 2):

> To look at what researchers need, ways to pay for an improved National Research Network, whether or not government agencies are working together well to develop the network that all can use, and where . . . [the U.S. is] in relation to other nations' networks.

All the witnesses at this hearing voiced strong support for the establishment of the NREN.

Dr. Paul Huray, chairman of the FCCSET Committee on Computer Research and Applications, described a three-level network structure for the NREN with a national backbone and smaller networks at regional and institutional levels. Huray described how FRICC had been working to achieve this vision of the NREN by integrating existing governmental networks, beginning with the linking of the National Science Foundation's NSFNET with DARPA's ARPANET, DoE's MFNET, and NASA's NASNET.

Leonard Kleinrock, chairman of the NRC's National Research Network Review Committee, stated that his committee "strongly endorsed" the creation of the NREN (Congress, Senate, 1988b, p. 18), as did Robert E. Kahn, President of the Corporation for National Research Initiatives (p. 20). In his testimony, Kenneth M. King, President of EDUCOM, discussed the role of BITNET as a low-speed national network linking research institutions and universities and allowing electronic mail and small file transfer (p. 68). He expressed his organization's support for the NREN by drawing the analogy that, "like the national highway system, a high-speed network is an essential

Figure 2.2. Key Congressional Hearings on the NREN, 1988-1990

House:

The U.S. Supercomputing Industry . . . Hearings. (June 20, 1989). House Subcommittee on Science, Research, and Technology.

Witnesses at this hearing discussed the current status of the U. S. supercomputing industry and indicated that, while it is still leading the world, the industry must continue to innovate if it is to maintain its position in the face of foreign competition. The NREN, in the eyes of many, is expected to be an important tool in the process of research and development.

High Performance Computing . . . Hearings. (October 3, 1989). House Subcommittee on Science, Research, and Technology.

Testimony was given by representatives of industry, the Federal Government, and higher education that a high-speed computer network was essential to continued efforts to maintain the competitive presence of the U. S. in high-performance computing.

Hearings on H. R. 3131: National High-Performance Computing Technology Act. (March 14, 1990). House Subcommittee on Science, Research, and Technology.

The testimony was largely favorable, with support coming from witnesses representing the Executive branch, government agencies, the private sector, and higher education. Some important statements were made by the representatives from the Federal government; for example, Dr. Fred Weingarten of OTA argued that the "key policy question regarding information technology and science is how the government's role should be defined," not whether or not the government should become involved in promoting change in information technology research (p. 3). Dr. D. Allen Bromley, of OSTP, provided the Bush administration's views on H. R. 3131.

Senate:

Computer Networks and High Performance Computing. (August 11, 1988). Senate Subcommittee on Science, Technology, and Space.

The purposes of this hearing were to look at what researchers need, ways to pay for an improved National Research Network, whether or not government agencies are working together well to develop the network that all can use, and where . . . [the U.S. is] in relation to other nations' networks (p. 2). Testimony was given concerning the possibilities of linking existing networks into a "national backbone" to form the NREN.

S. 1067 - Supercomputing and Information Superhighways. (June 21, 1989). Senate Subcommittee on Science, Technology, and Space.

In his opening remarks, Senator Gore stated that the NREN "is the most important, most cost effective investment that the Federal government can make in American science and technology . . . this is an investment the Federal government must make" (p. 2). Many witnesses agreed, arguing that it will be a "vital component" of the technological infrastructure needed to ensure that the United States will maintain its position as a world leader in high-performance computing (p. 7). Dr. William Wulf of NSF described the extent to which the NSF has implemented a "new 1.5 megabit/second NSFNET backbone" which as the "core of a rapidly developing 'internet'" links some 250 research institutions and allows researchers to use "over 100,000 computers" (p. 3).

Figure 2.2. Key Congressional Hearings on the NREN, 1988-1990 (continued)

<u>S. 1067 - Visualization, Artificial Intelligence, and Advanced Computing Software</u>. (July 26, 1989). Senate Subcommittee on Science, Technology, and Space

During this hearing, witnesses from industry and academia expressed their support for the NREN. For example, Dr. Karl-Heinz Winkler, Deputy Director for Science, Technology, and Education at the National Center for Supercomputer Applications at the University of Illinois, asserted that the "establishment of a high performance national digital computational infrastructure will be the key for the future economic development of the United States" (p. 3).

<u>Computer Technology and the New Age of Information</u>. (September 15, 1989). Senate Subcommittee on Science, Space, and Technology

Support for the NREN was presented by witnesses from research institutions, industry, and libraries. Referring to the extensive holdings of the Library of Congress, James Billington, the Librarian of Congress, stated that "the proposed high speed, high capacity National Research and Education Network could greatly facilitate . . . [a] broadening access to all our resources" (p. 4). In his remarks, John Seely Brown, the Vice President of Advanced Research at XEROX Palo Alto Research Center, concluded with the statement that "the aim of this testimony has been to throw enthusiastic support behind the concept and the potential" of the NREN (p. 10).

component of the national research infrastructure because it provides access to expensive shared resources" (p. 74).

In June 1989, the Senate Subcommittee on Science, Technology, and Space held a hearing on S. 1067 (Congress, Senate, 1989d). In his opening remarks, Senator Gore stated that the NREN "is the most important, most cost effective investment that the Federal government can make in American science and technology . . . [and] an investment the Federal government must make" (p. 2). Sheryl Handler, president of Thinking Machines Corporation, agreed with Gore's statement and recommended that government move quickly to establish the 2 gigabit NREN because it would become a "vital component" of the technological infrastructure needed for the United States to maintain its position as a world leader in high-performance computing (p. 7).

In his testimony, William Wulf, the Assistant Director for Computer and Information Science and Engineering of NSF, described the extent to which NSF had implemented a "new 1.5 megabit/second NSFNET backbone" which as the "core of a rapidly developing 'internet'" linked some 250 research institutions and allows researchers to use "over 100,000 computers" (Congress, Senate, 1989d, p. 3). If the requisite funding were to be made available, Wulf expected that NSF could begin implementation of

phase two of the OSTP strategy, a 45-megabit-per-second-network, in 1990, two years ahead of the schedule outlined by OSTP in 1987.

While obviously in favor of the continued development of the NREN, Wulf concluded his testimony by opposing the original version of S. 1067 because of several technical details in the bill which, in his opinion, would attempt to implement OSTP goals through legislation, instead of administrative action. He mentioned four specific objections to the proposed legislation (Congress, Senate, 1990d, p.10):

- The provision to authorize appropriations for OSTP, which it would then allocate to other agencies, would be at variance with OSTP's charter.
- The authorizations would be incremental to an existing research effort which was not clarified in the legislation and could not be uniquely related to existing budgetary categories.
- FCCSET would be granted operational and policy-making responsibilities which would be in distinct contrast to its current advisory role defined by the 1976 OSTP charter.
- If NSF were to receive additional, unrequested funding, it could have an adverse impact on existing programs and priorities.

Wulf argued that S. 1067 would restrict responsiveness to future requirements for high-performance computing and would "hamper the effectiveness of the interagency process as requirements and technologies change" (p. 10).

Hearings on S. 1067 by the Senate Subcommittee on Science, Technology, and Space continued in July 1989 (Congress, Senate, 1989d). Witnesses from industry and academia again expressed their support for the NREN. Karl-Heinz Winkler, Deputy Director for Science, Technology, and Education at the National Center for Supercomputer Applications at the University of Illinois, asserted that the establishment of a high-performance digital computational infrastructure would be critical for the future economic development of the United States (p. 3).

Further support was presented by witnesses from research institutions, industry, and libraries during Computer Technology and the New Age of Information, a hearing held in September 1989 by the same Senate subcommittee (Congress, Senate, 1989c). Referring to the extensive holdings of LC, James Billington, the Librarian of Congress, stated that "the proposed high speed, high capacity National Research and Education Network could greatly facilitate broadening access to all our resources" (p. 4). In his remarks, John Seely Brown, the Vice President of Advanced Research at XEROX Palo Alto Research Center, concluded with the statement that "the aim of this testimony has been to throw enthusiastic support behind the concept and the potential" of the NREN (p. 10).

On March 14 and 15, 1990, the House Subcommittee on Science, Research, and Technology held two days of hearings on H.R. 3131 (Congress, House, 1990d). The testimony was largely favorable, with support coming from witnesses representing the Executive branch, government agencies, the private sector, and higher education. Some important statements were made by the representatives from the Federal government. After a discussion of the benefits expected to accompany the NREN, Fred Weingarten of OTA argued that the "key policy question regarding information technology and science is how the government's role should be defined," not whether or not the government should become involved in promoting change in information technology research (p. 3). He stated that legislation such as H.R. 3131 was necessary to provide for coordination among Federal programs and agencies developing a "nationwide, even global infrastructure" to support high-perfor-

mance computing (p. 6). Weingarten asserted that broader NREN policy objectives should be legislated and concluded that legislation was needed to ensure that the NREN, when implemented, would fully serve the educational goals that have been set for it by Congress.

D. Allen Bromley, the Director of OSTP, provided the Bush administration's views on H.R. 3131. Based on an assumption of the continuation of the increasing rate of change in computer and information technology, Bromley argued that flexibility had to be the most important characteristic of any legislation intended to direct the Federal government's involvement in research and development in this area (Congress, House, 1990d, pp. 4-5):

> Any plan which 'locks in' programs within specific agencies could prevent flexibility in out-years. Likewise, specifying budgets for individual agencies five years in advance may lead to misallocated resources as circumstances and opportunities change, as they surely will. For this reason, I cannot approve of any legislation - however well intentioned - that might constrain even one current reexamination of the Federal High Performance Computing Program.

He suggested that successful legislation would have the capacity to allow agencies to annually evaluate their involvement in an HPC program in light of the changing environment in information networking.

Bromley indicated that administration support for the high-performance computing initiative remained strong. This could be seen, he argued, in the budgetary process, where the initiative had consistently been given a high priority, and in the high-level policy meeting called by OSTP in January 1990, which involved a gathering of representatives from those agencies whose work supported the initiative. Bromley noted that his office had also begun to "restructure and revitalize FCCSET and all of the FCCSET committees" in an effort to improve their effectiveness in achieving the goals set out in the 1989 OSTP report on the High Performance Computing Program (Congress, House, 1990d, p. 3).

Wulf, speaking in his capacity as the chairperson of the FCCSET Subcommittee on Networking, discussed recent developments which had affected the development of the NREN. He reported that the Federal Networking Council (FNC) had begun to meet and stated that "for the first time, we have a body to coordinate the complex operational and evolutionary development of the present internet" (p. 7). Wulf saw this as a major development, because, in his opinion, the FNC represented the beginnings of a governance mechanism for the NREN. The FNC was expected to draw upon several different constituencies as it began to carry out its mandate, including (Congress, House, 1990d, p. 7):

> The broader community of users and providers of networks and network services — representatives of academia, public and private research institutions, and the computer and telecommunications industries.

He described FCCSET as conducting research on technology required for the NREN in the form of five high-speed testbed networks, each of which "involves university-industry cooperation on a subset of the total problem . . . in the context of some real application domain" (p. 8). Wulf argued that this cooperation was important because it provided a platform for technology transfer and a setting within which new ideas and products could be tested.

It is clear that there is considerable support for the NREN within certain groups in the Federal government. In reports, hearings, and in proposed legislation, many different stakeholders have argued that the NREN be established as quickly as possible. There are five major themes running through this material on high-speed and high-performance electronic networking:

- The development and implementation of the NREN will assist the United States in maintaining its competitive edge in science, engineering, and HPC.
- The NREN will become the technical backbone of an advanced, integrated electronic information infrastructure.
- The Federal government will take a leading role in the establishment of the NREN.
- A coalition among the Federal government, academia, and industry will be necessary to ensure that the needs of the users are considered during the design and construction of an NREN.
- The NREN will be used to facilitate remote collaborative research because it will provide large-scale distributed computing at high speeds and with wide bandwidth.

Many of these themes have also been discussed elsewhere, such as in the popular media and in publications designed for particular professional audiences.

Support for the NREN in the Popular and Professional Press

Prefiguring the involvement of the Federal government in national networking efforts, Newell and Sproull (1982) argued that computer networks were becoming an increasingly important component of scientific activity. They foresaw that scientists would change their styles of work because network technologies would offer them tools which would enable them to conduct research more efficiently and productively. Denning (1985), writing in American Scientist, briefly sketched the history and evolution of computer networks and predicted that they would become a more pervasive medium of information transfer among scientists.

Recently, government involvement in national networking has received mass media attention. Articles by Markoff in the New York Times have described the growing support for the NREN among scientists, researchers, and politicians and have explained some of the basic characteristics and benefits of high-speed information networking to a lay audience. He has discussed the legislation proposed by Senator Gore (1988a), how the advent of extensive computer networking would change scientific communication and styles of working (1989c), the advantages that would accrue from the increased use of networking by scientists (1989b), and the ability of parallel processing to improve the analysis of large data sets (1989a). He has also written about the Corporation for National Research Initiatives (CNRI), noting that Robert Kahn, its founder (1990b, p. 6):

> [H]as successfully orchestrated a remarkable coalition that brings together major corporate competitors, government agencies and educational institutions. All have agreed to take part in the research necessary to create a fully integrated, high speed national network of computers, possibly early next century, that will unleash a tremendous burst of scientific, educational and economic activity.

The work being done at CNRI is part of the basic research necessary to develop the technological structure for the network; Markoff described this research as the "basic 'plumbing' . . . plotting the details of how it would work - and, not incidentally, how it would be paid for" (1990, p. 6).

In a recent issue of <u>Computerworld</u>, Horwitt discussed the basic structure of NREN, the policy issues surrounding its funding and construction, and some of the benefits that are expected from its implementation. She emphasized the enthusiasm that is present in the research and academic communities and singled out the "commercial vendor community, which has already shown a strong interest in the NREN project" (1989, p. 104). LaQuey, in an article discussing several of the major computer networks which currently serve the academic community, commented that the NREN (1989, p. 65):

> Would unify government sponsorship and management of what are now separately sponsored (but well-interconnected) internets owned by the National Science Foundation, NASA, the Department of Defense, and the Department of Energy. The basis for the new network would be the NSFnet and the successor to ARPANET - the Defense Research Internet.

In <u>Government Computer News</u>, Olsen (1989) indicated that if current traffic patterns did not change, the National Science Foundations' NSFNET would be saturated by 1991.

Writing in <u>IEEE Spectrum</u>, C. Gordon Bell, Vice President for R&D at Ardent Computer Corporation, argued that existing networks are too fragmented and are unable to meet the current needs of researchers in academia, industry, and the Federal government. In his opinion, "the most viable solution is a national research network organized and maintained by the Federal government" (1988, p. 54). Bell, who chaired the FCCSET Subcommittee on Computer Networking, Infrastructure, and Digital Communication, described the three-staged approach originally proposed for the NREN in the 1987 OSTP report and adopted by FRICC in 1989.

In 1988, <u>EDUCOM Bulletin</u> devoted its Summer/Fall issue to the NREN. Titled <u>Public and Private Initiatives to Create a National Education and Research Network</u>, this issue presented a number of papers delivered by representatives of academia and the private sector at National Net '88, an annual conference sponsored by EDUCOM (1988). The major

themes appearing in this issue included the management and financing of the NREN, questions of access and types of use, and the problem of the transition from existing networks to the NREN. According to Kenneth King, the purpose of the conference was to "begin the process of forging an alliance among government, industry, and higher education to create a national instruction and research network" (p. 2).

Press treatment of the idea of the NREN has been very positive. Many of the articles dealing with the NREN have stressed the need for a high-speed electronic network. Two main themes are that high-speed, high-performance networks will significantly change the ways in which scientists and researchers do their work and that if network traffic continues to increase at current rates, existing networks will be saturated before the turn of the century. It then becomes clear that there is considerable interest in the NREN among the research and academic communities and in the private sector and that the Federal government will have to resolve major policy issues concerning the NREN, including issues of management, financing, and access. The material reviewed in this chapter also offers detailed discussions of specific benefits and problems associated with such a major undertaking. Some of these will be discussed in Chapter 3.

<u>Reactions to the NREN in the Library Community</u>

Although the NREN has received attention in the popular and professional press since the mid-1980s, the library community did not take much interest in issues related to the proposed network until late 1988. At a December 1988 meeting of the LC Network Advisory Committee (NAC) and EDUCOM, the two groups agreed to "work together in a coalition whose purpose is to achieve . . . [a] common vision . . . [of] interconnected networks," of which the NREN was to be the exemplar (Henderson, 1990a, p. 1). Although the American Library Association (ALA) was represented on the NAC, the NREN did not become a formal Committee agenda item for ALA until their 1989 Midwinter meeting; since that time it has been on the agenda at all subsequent meetings. By June 1989, ALA had established regular coverage of NREN legislation and hearings in their newsletters and on the ALANET electronic mail system.

At a meeting of the Federal Library and Information Center Committee (FLICC) which was held in December 1989, a spokesperson for ALA's Washington D.C. office, Carol Henderson, discussed the original versions of S. 1067, H.R. 3131, and several key reports dealing with the NREN. She suggested that an important role for the library community would be in support of the development of a "bibliographic infrastructure," particularly in terms of the creation of directories and indexes to electronic information. Henderson emphasized that (Federal Library and Information Center Committee, 1990b, p. 3):

> There have been continuing discussions between the library networking community and EDUCOM on plans for this network, particularly on standards compatibility . . . . The university computing and library networking community have been discussing these issues as well as the variety of linkages and contributions the library community could make to this whole effort.

At this same meeting, James Benn, a research associate at the U.S. National Commission on Libraries and Information Science (NCLIS), took a somewhat critical look at the proposed NREN. He "criticized the vagueness of the legislation, saying that the terms 'education' and 'network' would be difficult to define in practice" (p. 4). He also questioned whether the legislation included the library community in the phrase "American researcher," stating that "the only mention of libraries is in the formation of the National Network Advisory Agency, and this is in an advisory capacity" (p. 4).

At Congressional hearings on Computer Technology and the New Age of Information (Congress, Senate, 1989c) held in September 1989, representatives from several national libraries gave testimony in favor of the NREN. James Billington, the Librarian of Congress, along with Henriette Avram, Assistant Librarian for Processing Services at LC, and Daniel Masys, Director of the Lister Hill National Center for Biomedical Communications, National Library of Medicine, argued that a national high-speed computer network could, in time, be the underpinning of a "library without walls" and that the increased access to library resources would greatly expand both the role and the usefulness of libraries linked to the network.

Further support for the NREN was provided by Paul Gherman, the Director of Libraries at Virginia Polytechnic Institute and State University, who spoke before the House Subcommittee on Science, Research, and Technology's hearings on H.R. 3131 (Congress,

House, 1990d). He ended his testimony by stating that (American Library Association, 1990b, p. 4):

> The original vision for the NREN was to make supercomputing more broadly available to scientists and researchers. It was a very worthwhile initiative. However, I believe the vision the library community has presented to you here today sees in the NREN the possibility of transforming the very basis of scholarly communication in our nation. This vision offers a new efficiency, quality, and speed by which information can be accessed.

Testimony at this hearing was one of the first and most important steps in providing Congress with a library perspective on the proposed NREN.

On January 10, 1990, a resolution supporting the NREN was adopted by the ALA Council. Originating in the ALA's Library and Information Technology Association (LITA), this resolution directs the ALA to "work to improve legislative and other proposals to increase opportunities for multitype library participation and leadership in, and contributions to" the NREN (American Library Association, 1990). A similar, but more specific resolution was adopted by the Special Libraries Association (SLA) on June 9, 1990. The wording of this resolution differed from the ALA's resolution by explicitly supporting the second version of S. 1067 and H.R. 3131. It emphasized that the basis of the SLA's support lay in the legislation's stipulations for "specific roles for libraries . . . in the proposed National Research and Education Network" (Special Libraries Association, 1990).

Lobbying by library groups led to a series of proposed amendments to the third version of S. 1067 that were presented to Senate staff in February 1990. These amendments were incorporated into the networking technology bill passed by the Senate in 1990 (Congress, Senate, 1989b). This effort included representatives from ALA, the Association of Research Libraries (ARL), the Chief Officers of State Library Agencies, SLA, and the U.S. National Commission on Libraries and Information Science. Commenting on this lobbying effort, Henderson stated that (1990a, p. 3):

> The amendments and supporting rationale, designed to strengthen library linkages to the NREN, were discussed with staff of the Senate Science, Technology, and Space Sub-

committee on February 1. Most of these suggestions were incorporated into the revised bill subsequently approved by the parent Commerce, Science, and Transportation Committee. The amendments were also discussed with House subcommittee staff.

ALA has also responded to the Commerce Department's NTIA, which, in January 1990, had asked for public comments on a range of policy issues related to the domestic telecommunications infrastructure. In their response, submitted in April 1990, ALA "recommended support of NREN development with public access through the nation's libraries" (p. 4).

In March 1990, at the National Net '90 Conference, ARL, CAUSE (the Association for the Management of Information Technology in Higher Education) and EDUCOM announced the formation of the Coalition for Networked Information (CNI). This organization is mandated to promote the provision of information resources and services on existing networks and on proposed interconnected networks and to address the related public policy issues which are expected to accompany the development and implementation of the NREN. According to DeCandido and Rogers (1990, p. 14):

> Nearly 60 institutions and organizations have already committed to joining the Coalition for Networked Information, and sponsorship is being provided by Apple Computer, Digital Equipment Corporation, IBM, and Xerox. Basic issues that the coalition needs to address include intellectual property rights, standards, licensing, cost recovery fees, and economic models for the project.

The vision which underlies the work of the CNI is that of the "virtual library," a collection of information resources located at geographically dispersed sites that will be widely available to researchers and scholars through computers and interconnected networks. The NREN is seen as "an essential step toward this compelling future" (Association of Research Libraries, CAUSE, and EDUCOM, 1989, p. 1).

During the annual ALA conference in June 1990, LITA sponsored a program entitled "The Promise of the Proposed National Research and Education Network (NREN) for Improved Information Access" which had 1,000 attendees. The purpose of this program was to (Parkhurst, 1990b, p. 1):

Bring information about the NREN before a broad library audience, to promote understanding of the complex issues involved, to monitor legislation, and to participate in the formal and informal coalitions that have developed and will be developed to promote the NREN.

At this meeting, an information packet containing papers and bibliographies on the NREN was distributed as an initial step in raising the awareness of the library community about the proposed network, the legislation which defines it, and the policy issues involved in the debate.

One position paper by Brownrigg, recently commissioned by LITA, focused on NREN issues of concern to the library community. Based on an assumption of a "convergence of libraries and networking," Brownrigg's argument was that "there is good reason that libraries should connect to the NREN" because many of the information services and communication functions expected to be part of the routine operation of the NREN are library services and functions (Brownrigg, 1990, p. 56). He described a form of the "virtual library" where a "consortium of public libraries would use the NREN to connect their online catalogs," creating a (p. 62):

> "Universal borrowing card" so that library users in America's mobile society could move from public library to public library and use each as if it were the same library. Collections so united would be richer and more accessible than that of the Library of Congress.

Brownrigg also identified a range of policy issues that the library community should consider as it becomes more involved in the debate over the NREN. Briefly, these included (pp. 58-60):

- Funding and cost recovery, because new federal dollars likely will be required to sustain a national network that will meet the needs of American education and research; the inclusion of library and information services into the debate may be crucial in gaining taxpayer support.
- The governance and management of the NREN; what should be the role of libraries?
- Privacy, because for the library profession, one issue will be how to achieve a balance between open access and privacy/security.

- The use of network resources, because the challenge for traditional librarians is to readjust further the professional focus from communication primarily by print to communication by electronics.
- The movement toward a network-wide set of standards.
- The definition of fair use, because there is a fundamental problem for libraries in using the NREN as the carrier for electronic library services without a resolution of the issue of commercial traffic.

Brownrigg concluded with a set of 10 principles which, in his opinion, should be used to frame the policy debate over the form and operation of the NREN. These principles included such concepts as an extension of the First Amendment to electronic communication over the NREN, the establishment of the NREN as a free market, and universal interconnectivity.

In a recent issue of Academic Computing, Larsen discussed the possibilities of developing what he called the "Colibratory," a distributed electronic library (1990, p. 22). Commenting that two important trends in academic and scientific work are connectivity and the shared access to geographically remote, networked resources, Larsen argued that "scholars are increasingly expecting to be able to meet more of their basic information access needs through the network connections to their personal workstations." He also focused attention on the needs of users of the distributed electronic library (p. 24):

> Network development has largely focused on building the underlying communications infrastructure, with rather little regard being given to an information architecture serving the user of the network. As the network expands in coverage, capability, and capacity, increasing attention must be given to the services offered to network users. Network users must be able to find the resources they seek on the network easily. This means that more resources must be available on the network, and that an organized, intuitive means of finding them must be available.

Larsen based his concept of the Colibratory on Kenneth King's (1988) vision of a networked scholarly community which would provide global access to all

significant information resources and the ability to easily maneuver through the network to access whatever resources are needed.

Larsen proposed that the NREN be used as a testbed to design and implement a distributed electronic information system. He suggested that the "online Internet Resource Guide" which contains downloadable pages of Postscript text maintained on an NSF Network Service Center (NNSC) computer be made "accessible and searchable online, like a library catalog" (1990, p. 35). Development of the Colibratory will require the coordinated efforts of network designers, information providers, and network users. This collaboration, he concluded, must begin early in the development of the NREN and must receive as much attention as the technical development of the network.

A similar theme was expressed by Cline who discussed the role of information resources in the NREN. She argued that the NREN's "real value will result from the information resources and services made available to a broad user community" (1990, p. 30). There would be online directories listing the holdings of the virtual library that would be easily navigated by users at remote locations. According to Cline, "the 'virtual library' will be a key part of the new academic and research infrastructure and will advance the academic mission - the creation and use of knowledge" (p. 33).

There is support growing in the library community for the NREN, due, in part, to the increased efforts of organizations such as LITA to disseminate information about the proposed network. The formation of interest and lobbying groups is beginning, and groups such as CNI are becoming important players in the debate over the NREN. There is also specific interest in such information infrastructure-related tasks as the development of directories and indexes for electronic or digital information, and there is a renewed interest in the library literature in the concept of the virtual library, or library without walls, which is expected to be made possible by the NREN. It is likely that the library community's interest in the NREN will continue to grow and become better focused on specific issues as people become more aware of these issues. As interest increases, there will be a need for the library community to put forward specific proposals for how and why libraries might participate in the NREN.

Conclusion

It is clear that there is considerable support within the Federal government, in academia, and in the private sector for the creation of a national high-speed electronic network. An examination of the popular and professional press also reveals a keen interest in the idea of the NREN. There is a growing awareness and involvement within the library community that has led to successful lobbying efforts and increased attention to such issues as equity of access, definitions of acceptable use, and the meaning of the word "education" in the title of the proposed network. With such a range of communities now aware of and interested in the NREN, there has also been a wide-ranging discussion of national networking benefits and problems and of related policy issues that must be resolved before the development and implementation of the network can begin. The presentation and analysis of these perceived benefits, problems, and policy issues are the focus of Chapter 3.

NREN BENEFITS, PROBLEMS, AND POLICY ISSUES: VIEWS FROM THE LITERATURE

CHAPTER 3

As seen in the previous chapter, many people contend that the NREN could greatly improve scientific research and communication, increase scientific productivity, and enhance the competitiveness of the United States in the global economy. There could also be little or no change in the ways in which scientific research is conducted and in the existing patterns of network use. It is possible that the NREN could represent a massive Federal, academic, and private sector investment that produces little return. Indeed, many of the proposed benefits of NREN rest largely on untested assumptions about network use.

In this chapter, the benefits, problems, and policy issues emerging from the public debate over the NREN are examined. The chapter is divided into three sections:

- A review of major benefits expected to emerge from the development of an NREN
- An identification and analysis of possible problems related to the NREN
- An overview of key policy implications and issues identified from the literature discussed in the previous sections.

Three main themes emerge from this analysis of the policy-oriented debate over the NREN:

- Much discussion has occurred about the benefits associated with the NREN, but there has been much less discussion of potential problems.
- Many of the viewpoints are based on untested assumptions about the impacts of electronic networks on scientific research, communication, and productivity.
- There is a plethora of policy issues associated with the NREN that must be resolved if the network is to be integrated successfully into the nation's scientific information infrastructure.

One major conclusion of this chapter is that there is a need for empirical research which investigates the impacts of high-speed electronic networks on scientific productivity from a user's perspective. Such research is needed so that policy makers and other stakeholders in the development and implementation of the NREN can make decisions on the basis of current and valid information.

BENEFITS EXPECTED TO EMERGE FROM THE NREN

Much of the commentary that has appeared in the literature not only stresses the importance of establishing the NREN, it also describes a wide range of benefits that are expected to emerge from the integration of such a network into the routines of R&D work and into the work of educators, information professionals, and librarians. Figure 3-1 summarizes the major benefits which many commentators have linked to the NREN; some of these are discussed below.

Enhancing U. S. Competitiveness

Considerable agreement exists that a national network will enhance the competitiveness of the United States in the global economy by ensuring continued U. S. leadership in the fields of science and technology. The NREN is expected to provide a testbed that would help maintain the leadership position of the U.S. in high-performance computing and networking. Further, the NREN is expected to provide widespread access to research resources, thus supporting advances in many areas of science and technology that would improve national economic competitiveness (Gould, 1990d, p. 2). The relationship between the NREN and American economic competitiveness has been discussed in numerous Federal government reports (Office of Technology Assessment, 1989a, 1989c; Gould, 1990a, p. 1; National Research Council, 1988a), Congressional hearings (Congress, House, 1989a; Congress, House, 1990c; Congress, Senate, 1989c; Congress, Senate, 1989d; Congress, Senate, 1989e), and in the press (Bell, 1988; Hancock, 1988, p. 5; McAdams, Vietorisz, Dougan and Lombardi, 1988; Roberts, 1990, p. 11).

The potential contribution of the NREN to American competitiveness was described by the National Research Council (1988b, p. 1, 4):

> Data obtained by this committee regarding current and anticipated research activities demonstrate that an NREN could dramatically improve the productivity and quality of the U. S. research community. Through these direct benefits, plus commercial spinoffs from associated computer and network research, an NREN could greatly promote U. S. competitiveness in a multiplicity of disciplines.

But we must not hesitate, for our foreign competitors are busy at work with their own national research networks (e.g., the RACE program in Europe and the national network projects in Canada, Japan, and in newly industrializing countries such as Singapore. . .). If we are successful in the NREN development, our competitive advantage will continue to grow.

The importance of the NREN, following this line of argument, lies in its ability to give the United States a competitive edge in the global economy. An initial benefit is that the use of the NREN by scientists and researchers would allow American companies to maintain their domination of the global high-performance computing market, staving off the challenge of the Japanese into the next century (Gould, 1990d, p. 10). As new technologies begin to enter other sectors of the American economy, the abilities of these sectors to compete will also be enhanced.

Equal Access to Supercomputers

A second benefit of a national research network is that it will "provide supercomputing power to anyone with access to the network" (Gore, 1989, p. 7). The idea of equal access to supercomputers is attractive to many commentators because it is expected to extend the power of networks to greater numbers of researchers, especially at smaller institutions (National Research Council, 1988b, p. 10; Huray, in Congress, Senate, 1988a, p. 16; Auguston, in Congress, House, 1989a, p. 1; King, in Congress, Senate, 1988b, p. 64; Wulf, in Congress, Senate, 1988b, p. 90), reducing their isolation from the greater scientific community (King, in Congress, Senate, 1988b, p. 3). According to Handler, "This country must be the first to have every scientist, business person and student using supercomputers" (Congress, Senate, 1989d, p. 8). This would produce what David Clark of MIT has called "a leveling of the playing field" (in Wintsch, 1989, p. 32). In addition, according to the 1987 Office of Science and Technology Policy report, "a well-coordinated national network . . . could reduce the number of sites needed for the physical presence of supercomputers" (1987, p. 19).

Figure 3-1. Benefits Associated with the NREN

Enhancing U. S. Competitiveness

- The NREN will enhance the competitiveness of the United States in the global economy by ensuring continued U. S. leadership in the fields of science and technology, particularly in the global high-performance computing market
- The NREN can dramatically improve the productivity and quality of the U. S. research community

Access to Supercomputers

- The NREN will provide supercomputing power to anyone with access to the network
- The NREN will extend the power of the network to greater numbers of researchers, especially at smaller institutions, reducing their isolation from the larger scientific community
- The NREN could reduce the number of sites needed for the the physical presence of supercomputers
- Increased access to supercomputers would lead to many subsequent benefits, such as truly distributed computing, where a given job is executed on several different machines as appropriate, the analysis of very large data sets, increased access to large, remote databases, and the creation of national knowledge bank or digital library
- More open access to supercomputing resources through the NREN will also allow the private sector to begin experimenting with the high-performance computing abilities of supercomputers and, as a consequence, may spur purchases of these machines by industry.

Removing Constraints from the Research Process

- The NREN would remove constraints of time, costs, and distance from the research and development process, increasing the efficiency of scientific communication and encouraging a wider range of users to become involved in networking.

Increasing Collaboration among Researchers

- The potential for collaboration among researchers will increase, once any computer can easily and reliably communicate with any other computer over a broad range of data rates
- This will lead to the sharing of software and databases, and the natural association of geographically distributed but functionally complementary individuals
- By facilitating the computations and scientific communication, the NREN will help immensely in enhancing limited scientific research manpower
- The NREN will support the development and operation of a national collaboratory

Increasing the Rate of Knowledge and Technology Transfer

- By improving the speed with which research can be conducted and information can be exchanged, the pace of innovations will increase, as will the rates at which knowledge and technology transfer take place
- As scientific productivity increases, there will be commercial spinoffs which will flow to industry, as well as cooperative programs for research and development among academic researchers, Federal researchers, and industry.

Additional Benefits of Access to Supercomputers

Many agree that the increased access to supercomputers would lead to many subsequent benefits such as the advent of truly distributed computing (National Research Council, 1988b, p. 16), the analysis of very large data sets (Panel on Information Technology and the Conduct of Research, 1989, p. 1), increased access to large, remote databases (King, in Congress, Senate, 1988a, p. 3; Handler, in Congress, Senate, 1989d, p. 3), and the creation of "national knowledge bank" (Kahn, in Congress, Senate, 1988a, p. 40) or "digital library" (New York State Library and the Nelson A. Rockefeller Institute of Government, 1989, p. 6; Gore, in Congress, Senate, 1989c, p. 3; Wulf, in Congress, Senate, 1989d, p. 2; Kahn, 1988, p. 21).

These network resources and services would also allow scientists, engineers, and other researchers to undertake what the Federal government calls the "Grand Challenges" of science, "fundamental problem[s] in science and engineering, with broad economic and scientific impact, whose solution[s] will require the application of high-performance computing resources" (Congress, Senate, 1990c, p. 24). Examples of Grand Challenges include the human genome project, computer modeling of global weather patterns for predictive purposes, and semiconductor design. According to OSTP, progress on these problems is often severely limited by current processing and memory capacities (1989, p. 8). In addition, current networks have neither broad enough bandwidth nor sufficient speed for scientists and engineers to work on these problems at locations removed from supercomputer sites. The NREN is expected to remedy these technical difficulties, allowing scientists, engineers, and researchers to more quickly and easily access supercomputing resources from remote locations.

There may also be economic benefits to the widening of access to supercomputing resources available over the NREN. More open access to supercomputers will also allow the academic community and the private sector to begin experimenting with the high-performance computing (HPC) abilities of supercomputers and, as a consequence, may spur purchases of these machines by these sectors.

Removing Constraints from the Research Process

Another benefit is that the NREN would remove constraints of time, costs, and distance from the R&D process (Panel on Information Technology and the Conduct of Research, 1989, p. 12). Wintsch reported that "the resulting increases in the efficiency of scientific communication will encourage a wider range of users to become involved in networking and will also lead to a series of related benefits" (1989, p. 32). For example, Federal laboratories and research laboratories in the private sector could increase the rate at which technology transfer occurs because of their increased abilities to gain access to remote instrumentation, databases, and to the results of other scientists' and engineers' research. Preprints of current work in electronic form which are sent out over networks and the emergence of online refereed electronic journals indicate that the NREN has a vast potential to alter the process of scientific communication. In addition, the NREN will allow scientists, engineers, and other researchers to transfer larger amounts of information across greater distances faster than ever before. Access to information and data held in nodes on the network can reduce costs to individual organizations by eliminating unnecessary duplication of effort in knowledge creation.

Increasing Collaboration Among Researchers

The potential for collaboration among researchers will increase (Gould, 1989, p. 1; National Research Council, 1988b, p. 5; Winkler, in Congress, Senate, 1989e, p. 8; Nagel, in Congress, Senate, 1989e, p. 10; Walgren, 1988, p. 9; Bloch, 1988, p. 11; Huray, in Congress, Senate, 1988b, p. 11, 16) once any computer can easily and reliably communicate with any other computer. As the phenomenon of large-scale collaborative science increases, it will, according to Bromley, lead to "the sharing of software and databases, and the natural association of geographically distributed but functionally complementary individuals" (Congress, House, 1989b, p. 9).

Robert Dickinson, Deputy Head of the Interdisciplinary Climate Systems Section at the National Center for Atmospheric Research, agreed with Bromley, stating that "by facilitating computations and scientific communication [networks] help immensely in enhancing our limited research manpower" (Congress, Senate, 1988b, p. 51). John Seely Brown argued that a well-designed NREN will permit the "leveraging of the nation's knowledge base" because it will "empower . . . collaboration" (Congress, Senate, 1989b, p. 2). Bloch envisioned such collaboration as occurring in a "workplace without walls," the culmination of which will be a new form of production that he called "telemanufacturing" (1988, p. 11).

A workshop held at the Rockefeller University in March 1989 examined and enthusiastically supported the concept of a "National Collaboratory," which, according to Lederberg and Uncapher, is "a resource that would use networking and computer technology to support remote interaction" among scientists (1989, p. i). Science is essentially a social activity, and the Collaboratory could be an integral element of the research process because it "will provide seamless access to colleagues, instruments, data, information, and knowledge" (1989, p. 6) and, as argued by Lederberg and Uncapher, a high-speed national network would be the foundation for Collaboratory activities (1989, p. 1).

Increasing the Rate of Knowledge and Technology Transfer

By improving the speed with which research can be conducted and information can be exchanged, the pace of innovation will increase, as will the rates at which knowledge and technology transfer take place (Rollwagen, in Congress, Senate, 1989d, p. 7; Wulf, in Congress, House, 1989a, p. 2; Lucky, in Congress, Senate, 1989d, p. 1; Dickinson, in Congress, Senate, 1989c, p. 51; Bloch, 1988, p. 11). As scientific productivity increases, there will be what Kleinrock called commercial spinoffs (Congress, Senate, 1988b, p. 21), which will flow to industry as well as cooperative programs for research and development among academic researchers, Federal researchers, and industry (Kutler, in Congress, Senate, 1988b, p. 56). The NREN is expected to facilitate large-scale joint ventures among the Federal government, academia, and the private sector.

Benefits to the Private Sector

In the long run, the private sector is expected to realize and take advantage of the enormous profit potential of the NREN. In early congressional hearings, representatives from the private sector emphasized benefits resulting from the NREN's ability to transfer research results to the private sector more quickly. The current Senate version of the high-performance computing bill, S. 272 (see Appendix E) explicitly mentioned several important private sector benefits that will occur as a consequence of Federal involvement in the development of the NREN. In

Section 6(6)(c), the bill stated that the NREN will be (Congress, Senate, 1991, p. 9):

- Developed in close cooperation with the computer, telecommunications, and information industries
- Established in a manner which fosters and maintains competition and private sector investment in high-speed data networking within the telecommunications industry
- Established in a manner which promotes research and development leading to deployment of commercial data communications and telecommunications standard
- Phased into commercial operation as commercial networks can meet the networking needs of American researchers and educators.

This legislation clearly considers Federal involvement in the development of the NREN as short term, and indicates that the private sector will assume the management and operation of the network when such time arrives as commercial network service providers can compete at a national level. The Federal government is also attempting to involve the private sector in the planning, design, and implementation of the NREN, seeking out industry input into these processes.

Testimony by Wulf summed up the benefits of networking (Congress, Senate, 1989c, p. 2):

> It is clear that networks increase the productivity of researchers, by allowing them to collaborate with a larger set of colleagues, by giving them access to data collected at remote sites, and by giving them access to unique resources. Networks can also effectively increase the pool of researchers, for example, by making it possible for the faculty of four-year and minority institutions to become full participants in research projects based elsewhere.
>
> More important than either of the above, however, is that networks allow research to be undertaken that simply couldn't be done otherwise.

There is considerable speculation about the benefits that are expected to accrue from the development and use of the NREN (see Figure 3-1). These benefits, however, are largely based on untested assumptions and optimistic expectations. One of the main themes of this book is that there is a need for rigorous, empirical research to test these assumptions, leading to clearly defined policies intended to maximize the benefits of the NREN. The results of such a study are reported in Chapters 6 and 7.

PROBLEMS ASSOCIATED WITH THE NREN

There has also been some discussion of problems associated with the proposed NREN. These problems can be divided into two broad categories. First, there are those which are based on perceptions of current networking difficulties. These are important because they represent issues which must be resolved either technically or through policy decisions if the NREN is to be successfully implemented and used. Second, there is a category of problems which are based on speculation about networking difficulties that will arise as more scientists and researchers and other users begin to use the NREN more extensively. There has been less discussion of these problems, perhaps reflecting the difficulty of analyzing a network which is slowly coming into existence and has not yet taken a clearly recognizable form. Figure 3-2 summarizes both categories of networking problems discussed below.

Problems with Existing Networks

Fragmentation

One major problem with existing networks is fragmentation (Gould, 1989, p. 2; Huray, in Congress, Senate, 1988b, p. 10; National Research Council, 1988b, p. 1). According to the National Research Council "computer networks of today . . . are islands unto themselves" (1988a, p. 15). There are more than 100 large networks in the United States, and there is, at best, only limited coordination among them (Gore, in Congress, Senate, 1988b, p. 2). The lack of connectivity mitigates against collaborative research (Bloch, 1988, p. 12) and the rapid exchange of information, so that scientific productivity is "severely hampered by . . . [the] inability to effectively link . . . to supercomputers, to the large scientific databases, and to . . . colleagues" (Kleinrock, in Congress, Senate, 1988b, p. 20). The inability to establish communication networks linking researchers is not the only consequence of a lack of interconnection among networks.

Fragmentation also means that there is unequal access to computing resources for users, further increasing the gap between the high-profile scientific elite and the rest of the research community (National Research Council, 1988b, p. 1; Panel on Information Technology and the Conduct of Research, 1987, p. 16). Fragmentation also means that networking applications and networked resources are more difficult to identify and use.

The lack of connectivity among networks persists, in part, because of several factors:

- There is little standardization among the communication protocols that govern the transmission of data and messages (Quarterman, 1990, p. 215).
- There is a distinct lack of standards for inter-network operations (Ricart, 1989, p. 28; National Research Council, 1988a, p. 15; Panel on Information Technology and the Conduct of Research 1989, p. 20).
- There are inconsistencies among the policies which determine standards of acceptable usage on many networks (Fuchs, 1988, p. 47).

In general, there has been little incentive for existing networks to develop a set of technical and use-oriented standards. The debates surrounding the NREN, however, have increased many network users' and managers' awareness of the importance of connectivity.

Limited Capacity of Existing Networks

Another concern is "the low quality of many research networks" (National Research Council, 1988a, p. 19). According to Senator Gore, existing networks "are more like left turn lanes at rush hour today - low capacity, overloaded, and unable to keep up with demand" (1989, p. 31). This problem may be attributed to several factors. Many existing networks are, for the most part:

- Technically incompatible, with different protocols and addressing conventions
- Heterogeneous (Gould, 1989b, p. 1; McAdams, in Congress, Senate, 1988b, p. 106), with different management policies and different purposes
- Managed in a style best described as "anarchic" (Panel on Information Technology and the Conduct of Research, 1989, p. 22).

Figure 3-2. Problems Associated with Networking

Problems with Existing Networks

Fragmentation

- There are over 100 large networks in the United States and there is, at best, only limited coordination among them
- Fragentation means that there is unequal access to computing resources, further increasing the gap between the high-profile scientific elite and the rest of the research community
- There is little standardization among networks' communications protocols, there is a lack of standards for inter network operations, and there are inconsistencies among networks' policies which determine standards of acceptable usage

Limited Capacity of Existing Networks

- Many networks are low capacity, overloaded, and unable to keep up with demand
- Many networks are managed in a style best described as "anarchic"
- The performance of underlying network technology has not kept pace with the increased demands of users

Lack of User Friendliness

- Many users in the scientific and research community are dissatisfied with the amount of effort they must expend to acquire networking knowledge and skills
- Instruction, documentation, and troubleshooting support are in many cases scarce
- Users find that inconsistent format and retrieval process make the process of gaining access to data stored in different networks too difficult

Problems Which May Accompany the NREN

Social Impacts of the NREN on Science

- The roles of the Federal government as a major funder of both the NREN and scientific research may lead to a conflict of interest where funding goes to proposals featuring heavy NREN use
- Access and use of the NREN among the scientific elite may buttress a self-reinforcing elite structure in science
- It is also possible that increased access to the NREN could create a level playing field in American science

Increasing the Burden on Scientists

- Scientists may have to devote considerable time to documenting their use of the NREN
- Charge- and performance-based elements may have to be factored into proposals, increasing the complexity of the grant-writing process
- Increased collaboration may involve scientists in extended negotiations as they work out the intricacies of NREN use

Figure 3-2. Problems Associated with Networking (continued)

Access

- There is a conflict between the assumption of the need for open access to the NREN and the assumption that restricted access is necessary to protect certain users and their organizations
- There is no clear formulation of what will constitute a "qualified user"

Threats to Security and Privacy

- There may be threats to network and information security and to the privacy of users
- There may be a need for different levels of access and protection for different services and resources

Technological Problems

- Cost-effective technologies for high-speed high-bandwidth networking have not yet been successfully demonstrated on a large scale

According to Hancock, there is evidence of "redundancy, incompatibility and inadequacy" in many networks (1988, p. 7).

The Office of Science and Technology Policy characterized the problem of low quality by asserting that national networks (1987, p. 18):

> Have low capacity, are overloaded, and fail to interoperate successfully. These [networks] . . . have been expanded to increase the numbers of users and connections but the performance of the underlying network technology has not kept pace with the increased demands. Therefore, the networks which, in the 1970s had significant impact in enabling collaboration, are now barriers. Capacity . . . is orders of magnitude less than the rates required.

As a consequence, some members of the research community are frustrated by the mismatch between the high-performance processing equipment that they wish to use and the low-performance computer networks over which their data must travel (National Research Council, 1988b, p. 1).

Lack of User Friendliness

Another problem is that many existing networks are not "user friendly" (Kleinrock, in Congress, Senate, 1988b, p. 21). Many users in the scientific and research community are dissatisfied with the amount of effort that they must expend to acquire and update networking knowledge and skills. Networks currently require that users acquire specialized knowledge and skills. Since "instruction, documentation, and troubleshooting support . . . are in many cases scarce," successful network users are typically those "who have developed a degree of expertise in computer networking technology" through the course of their own work (Gould, 1989, p. 2).

Several factors contribute to this lack of user friendliness:

- There are few easily available directories of users, facilities, and network addresses (Panel on Information Technology and the Conduct of Research, 1989, p. 12; Bromley, in Congress, House, 1989b, p. 8; Huray, in Congress, Senate, 1988b, p. 10).
- It is often difficult for researchers to gain access to data stored by other researchers or in even the best commercially maintained databases because of inconsistent formats and retrieval procedures (Gould, 1990a, p. 15).

- Users often have difficulties understanding and using network addressing conventions for different networks.
- Users become frustrated with the inability of existing networks to transfer visual information and large data files successfully (Gould, 1990a, p. 15).
- Many networks offer unreliable service.

In spite of the attention paid to users' problems, these writings display a surprising lack of concern with the need for user support, education, and training. There seems to be an implicit assumption that the next generation of researchers will acquire networking skills much in the way that they learn how to drive a car. Until networks become easier to use, many scientists and researchers may be reluctant to expend the time and effort needed to learn how to overcome these obstacles.

Problems Which May Accompany the NREN

Social Impacts of the NREN on Science

If the NREN is successful and becomes an integral part of the research process, it may have a significant impact on the ways in which science is conducted. Because of the extent of government involvement in the funding, planning, implementation, and operation of the NREN, there may be conflicts over the Federal government's roles as a funder, user, and participant in research (Office of Technology Assessment, 1989c, p. 3). Because of the vested interest that the Federal government would have in the success of the NREN, there could be a possibility that funding decisions would be swayed by the degree to which use of the NREN is featured in funding proposals submitted by researchers.

In a discussion of the effects of information technology on organizations, Attewell and Rule (1988, p. 566) argue that those technologies which:

Alter the quality and availability of information are likely to shift balances of power between various groups of organizational actors . . . . The rerouting of information may also create new dependencies between parts of organizations and dissolve old ones, paving the way for structural changes.

The impacts of information technology on organizations might be extended to the institution of science, suggesting at least three scenarios:

- There could be no changes in the ways in which science is conducted.
- A buttressing of the existing self-reinforcing elite structure of science may occur, where the NREN would be implemented and most heavily used by the most prestigious institutions and researchers first, thus further increasing their prestige and control over resources. This situation could have a detrimental effect on other institutions and users and vitiate the leveling of the research and networking playing field, one of the primary goals of the NREN.
- A level playing field, brought about by open access to the NREN, could democratize access to important research and networking resources.

Which outcome would be most likely to occur is not at all clear, nor is it clear that policy makers, network designers, administrators, and user communities have considered these possibilities. Attempts to discern which scenario could result from the implementation and use of the NREN are made more difficult by the fact that there are many other cultural and organizational factors which will affect the way in which the NREN evolves and is implemented.

Increasing the Burden on Scientists

If the NREN becomes an essential tool in scientific research, one problem that scientists may have to face is the increased administrative burden that will accompany network use. There will be a need for record keeping to account for tasks performed, resources accessed, services used, and time spent on the NREN. Such information will be essential if user charges must be assessed and if network managers wish to evaluate the performance of the NREN. These charge- and performance-based elements may have to be factored into research and funding proposals, making the grant-writing process more complex. This accounting use will seriously degrade network capacity and performance, based on the experiences of telephone, online, and other service providers.

The NREN is also expected to enable scientists and researchers to engage in more extensive collaboration. The "Collaboratory" obligates network users engaged in collaborative research to establish and maintain relationships among themselves and their institutions. Scientists may have to negotiate the allocation of computing and other resources and develop policies on a case-by-case basis to deal with the sharing of the data and information collected during the research process. Research is needed to determine the amount of time that scientists currently must commit to record keeping and other activities that support network use for research and scientific communication.

In addition to the extra administrative burden imposed by increased networking, it is also possible that scientists may find themselves overloaded with more information from their network collaborations and involvements than they can reasonably handle. Information overload is a source of difficulty for researchers now. In an increasingly electronic environment, the issue will only intensify, especially because the role of information intermediaries for quality control and filtering is as yet undefined for networked environments.

Access

The NREN will allow users to establish communication networks that cut across disciplinary, organizational, and political boundaries. According to Roberts (1989, p. 11), "by its nature and charter, the NREN will span the boundaries of the public and private sectors of the economy." To maximize the potential for increases in productivity, the population of users should be as large as possible. The possibility of open access to the NREN, however, highlights the conflict between the assumption that the network should be available to all qualified users, however defined, and the assumption that certain groups have the right to exercise control over access to certain types of information products and services. The former is a norm fundamental to the world view of many scientists and essential to the formation of an informed electorate, and the latter is a norm associated with national security concerns for the Federal government and control of proprietary information for the private sector and some academics. To further complicate matters, there is no clear definition of the knowledge, skills, and job or personal characteristics that will define a "qualified user." The term remains problematic.

Threats to Security and Privacy

Two related problems which may occur if the NREN is open to a broad spectrum of users are threats to network and information security and to the privacy of users. Users will want to have easy access to the variety of services and resources on the network, but will also want to operate with the knowledge that there is a minimal threat to the integrity of these services and resources.

Potential security issues include (Office of Technology Assessment, 1989c, p. 6):

- Developing, as necessary, different levels of access and protection for different services and resources on the NREN; some may need to be as open and public as possible, while others will need a very high level of protection
- Preventing unauthorized access to network services and resources and to users' private files and machines
- Protecting the network from worms, viruses, and related threats
- Intellectual property protection, because electronic formats, coupled with a communications network, erode the ability to control copying and dissemination.

The security problem is a critical one for network managers and policy makers because "the security of the entire system depends on the security of its weakest link, so some minimum degree of security will have to be maintained throughout the system" (Koch, 1989, p. 23). The problem of network security will increase in difficulty and complexity as more nodes are connected to the NREN. When access is available on university campuses, industrial laboratories, and throughout the Federal government, and when collaboration and the free flow of information are encouraged, there will be a pressing need for adequate security procedures. If network security cannot be adequately maintained, the resulting problems may restrict the free flow of information over the NREN and discourage users from fully exploiting network capabilities.

Technological Problems

Unless a number of critical technological problems are resolved, the promise of the NREN may be difficult to achieve. According to Wintsch, the resolution of these problems (1989, p. 32):

Must quickly lead to cost-effective technologies. Needed in particular are technologies for exploiting enough of the bandwidth in optical fibers to support heavy and variable flows of information. High speed communications also depend on ultrafast switches . . . and on algorithms that are capable of managing traffic moving at the rates optical fibers promise.

She argued that while the basic research in these areas is being conducted in laboratories around the country, only the beginnings of solutions have emerged. The NREN, if it is to be established as currently envisioned, will have to make use of optical technology, new network and processing architectures, and as-of-yet undeveloped software. There are hints that the challenges can be met, "but the ideal components have yet to emerge" (p. 37). Further, there are fundamental disagreements about what the ideal components of the NREN might be.

The material reviewed for this chapter identified five major categories of problems associated with the NREN:

- The possibility of negative impacts on the social structure of science
- The increased administrative burden as use of the NREN increases
- The tension between norms of open access and the desire to control certain types of network services and resources
- The need to protect networks from unauthorized access and users from invasion of privacy
- The challenges inherent in developing the hardware and software that will support the high-speed, broad bandwidth requirements of the NREN.

Due to the complexity of these problems and the number of stakeholders affected, these problems will have to be resolved at the highest organizational and policy levels (see Figure 3-2).

POLICY ISSUES INVOLVED IN THE DEBATE OVER THE NREN

Many of the benefits that are expected to accompany the integration of the NREN into science will not emerge as users begin to explore the network. Nor will the problems fade away as existing networks are integrated into the NREN. There is a need for careful consideration of network policy to ensure that the NREN can achieve its goals, produce the expected benefits, and resolve some fundamental problems. Because there are great uncertainties in the networking, political, and telecommunications environments, "there is no straightforward or well-accepted model for the 'best' way to design, manage, and upgrade the future national research network" (Office of Technology Assessment, 1989c, p. 29).

According to Roberts (1989, p. 11):

In some ways the widespread support and enthusiasm for the NREN is a double-edged sword, because it creates a lightening rod for this large constellation of issues, many of which are beyond the ability of the NREN community to resolve. Nevertheless, there are a number of key areas that advocate[s] for the NREN need to emphasize with legislators and others involved in public policy formulation.

This uncertainty is reflected in the recent literature, which reveals a range of policy issues that have been divided into 12 categories for the purposes of this review. The following discussion is neither complete nor exhaustive. Rather, it is intended to familiarize the reader with some of the major policy questions which preoccupy major NREN stakeholders. Figure 3-3 summarizes the key issues discussed below.

Design and Construction

The first category involves design and construction policy issues. Who should be involved in the design and construction of the network? In a recent memorandum to the Senate Subcommittee on Science, Technology, and Space, Gould noted that the planning process, currently in the hands of the Federal Research Internet Coordinating Committee, primarily includes representatives from other Federal departments and agencies (1989, p. 3). Other stakeholders, including the education, library, research, and development communities, telecommunications companies, and the private

Figure 3-3. Summary of Key Policy Issues

Design and Construction

- Which constituencies should be involved in the design and construction of the network?
- What role should users play in the design and construction of the NREN?

Size of the NREN

- How large should the network be?
- How many institutions and agencies should be connected to the NREN?

Access

- Should access to the NREN be open, or should there be restrictions on access to certain network services by certain classes of users?
- Should supercomputing, for example, be made available to as many network users as possible, allowing unlimited access to researchers based in other countries?
- Will scientists and researchers working in foreign countries on projects funded by their governments be allowed access to NREN services and resources?
- Will they be allowed to collaborate with colleagues in this country?
- If these scientists are not working on state-sponsored research, will they then be granted access to the NREN?

Equity and Fairness

- Should institutions be allowed to connect to the NREN regardless of their size and resources?
- If the smaller institutions cannot afford the costs of connection, who shall pay?

Transition from Existing Networks to the NREN

- How shall the transition be handled, and by whom?

Management Structure

- What type of management model should be employed to oversee the design, implementation, operation, maintenance, and improvement of the NREN?
- Who shall lead and who shall govern?

Maintenance and Operation

- To what extent should the daily management of the NREN be centralized?
- If the management structure is to remain under the aegis of the Federal government, what roles should academia and the private sector play?
- How will the routine performance of the network be monitored and its activities be measured?
- Who will be responsible for developing network standards which will allow fast, easy, and transparent communication across the NREN?

Figure 3-3. Summary of Key Policy Issues (continued)

Legal Issues

- What are the legal and regulatory barriers the NREN will have to face?
- Should the NREN be regulated? If so, should regulation be applied to the entire network in the same way or will different regulatory schemes be necessary?

Finances and Cost Recovery

- How should the NREN should be funded?
- How should charges be established for different types of users and for different services?
- Who should pay for use and who should not?

Transition to the Private Sector

- By what process will the NREN will be transformed from a government-managed operation to a private sector activity?
- Who will manage the transition?

Network Use

- How easy should the NREN be to use?
- Should there be guidelines defining acceptable use of the NREN? If so, who should set them?

User Education, Training, and Support

- Where does the responsibility for education and training reside; should it be handled at the Federal or the institutional level?
- Who should be responsible for creating and disseminating directories and other user support material?

Security and Privacy

- How can the NREN be protected from viruses and worms, and who should be responsible for doing so?
- What can be done to maintain the integrity of proprietary information that flows across the NREN?

Censorship

- Do users have the right to send any information they want to over the NREN or should there be some restrictions?
- If there are to be restrictions, should they be defined and imposed by the NREN management or should users practice self-censorship?

sector in general are not yet involved at the Federal level, although this involvement is called for in current legislation, such as S. 272 (Congress, Senate, 1991).

One suggestion is that a significant role should be provided for the regional and state networks that will eventually become part of the NREN. This would allow planners to more adequately address the coordination and management of user-to-user networking (Mandlebaum, in Congress, House, 1989a, p. 6). Another position is that the private sector should be brought into the design and construction process as quickly as possible (Bromley, in Congress, House, 1989a, p. 5; Kahn, 1988, p. 20; National Research Council, 1988b, p. 35; Office of Technology Assessment, 1987, p. 21). Finally, the Panel on Information Technology and the Conduct of Research strongly suggested that (1989, p. 52):

> Planning and development of this nationwide infrastructure should be guided by users of information technology in research, rather than by technical experts in information technology or hardware or software vendors. The Panel believes strongly that such a national network is too important to be left only to the technical experts.

Clearly, the successful development of the NREN will depend on the extent to which the major constituencies are brought into the planning and design process. A critical policy issue will be to determine who should be involved and the different levels of involvement necessary to ensure that all stakeholders' concerns are given adequate hearing and consideration.

Size

There are also questions about the NREN's size. How large should the network be? How many institutions and agencies should be connected? The 1987 OSTP plan suggested connecting 200 or 300 institutions in higher education, industry, and the Federal government. According to Gould, other interested parties have submitted proposals to the Federal government that advocate links to all 3,000 U. S. colleges and universities and the general industrial and research community (1989, p. 1). The Congressional Office of Technology Assessment's report, The Federal High Performance Computing Program (Appendix I), states that its goal is to "provide Na-

tional Research and Education access for every U. S. university and major laboratory . . . through a mid-level network" (1989a, p. 40).

S. 1976 stated that the NREN shall "provide computer users at more than one thousand universities, Federal laboratories, and industrial laboratories with access to supercomputers, computer databases, and other research facilities" (Congress, Senate, 1989a, p. 7). In current legislation, such as S. 272, there is no longer any language indicating the size of the network, other than referring to the NREN as national, nor is there language stipulating the number of institutions that are to be connected (Congress, Senate, 1991). There is a clear need for the major players in the development of the NREN to determine through open debate and decision making both the eventual size of the network and a reasonable plan to decide which types of institutions and agencies will connect to the network, how many of them will connect, and when they will connect.

Access

Should access to the NREN be open, or should there be restrictions on access to certain network services for certain classes of users? Should supercomputing, for example, be made available to as many network users as possible, as was suggested by Collins (in Congress, Senate, 1989d, p. 4) and Kahn (in Congress, Senate, 1988b, p. 40), allowing unlimited access to researchers based in other countries? The Panel on Information Technology and the Conduct of Research argued that "the national network . . . [should] be founded on the fundamental premise of open access to all qualified researchers/scholars" (1989, p. 53). A basic issue that must be resolved is the definition of a "qualified user."

The issue of access has not been resolved or even formulated clearly in NREN legislation. In Title III, Section 301(5) of the original version of S. 1067(Appendix B), one of the expectations of the NREN was that it would allow for international research collaboration (Congress, Senate, 1989b, p. 16). In Section 103(b)(1) of the version of S. 1067 that passed the Senate in 1990 (Appendix D), this language had been changed to read that the NREN and other information services would "support computer-based collaboration that allows researchers around the Nation to share information and instrumentation" (Congress, Senate, 1990b, p. 18).

Decisions must be made about international access to the NREN, especially given the international nature of research, the ability of telecommunications to cross political borders, the realities of current international network connections, and the multinational makeup of many R&D corporations. Some questions that arise are:

- Will scientists and researchers working in foreign countries on projects funded by their governments be granted access to NREN services and resources?
- Will such users be allowed to collaborate with colleagues in this country?
- If these scientists are not working on research sponsored by their governments, will they then be granted access to the NREN?

Policy decisions will be needed to determine the set of conditions under which scientists and researchers in foreign countries will have access to colleagues and to the resources and services provided by the NREN.

Equity

The assumption of open access also raises issues of equity. Users at smaller and less well-off institutions in this country may have their access to the NREN limited by their institutions' lack of resources (Collins, in Congress, Senate, 1989d, p. 4; Mandlebaum, in Congress, House, 1989a, p. 9). The provision of services to this constituency may be more costly than to other classes of users, but to restrict their access would prevent the NREN from becoming a "truly national network" (National Research Council, 1988a, p. 24). It would also reinforce the stratification of American science into a small, high-prestige elite and a larger group of scientists in smaller, poorly supported institutions. If the smaller institutions cannot afford the costs of connection, who shall pay?

Transition from Existing Networks to the NREN

A different type of policy issue related to the question of access involves the transition that must occur from existing networks to the NREN. The National Research Council report argued that "network technologies should not be developed from scratch where the technology base . . . [already] exists" (1988b, p. 30). However, Section 6(a) of S. 1976 required DoE to create a high-performance computer network to be known as the NREN, without indicating that it was to make use of existing networks and without explicitly involving any other agencies or departments in the development and implementation process (Congress, Senate, 1989a, p. 2). Section 6(a)(1) of S. 343, the 1991 version of S. 1976, retreated from this requirement, calling DoE's network the "Federal High-Performance Computer Network" (Congress, Senate, 1991a, p. 5). S. 343 still described this network in such a way as to allow DoE to compete with NSF. Section 6(a) of S. 272, on the other hand, required NSF in cooperation with the Department of Defense, the Department of Energy, the Department of Commerce, NASA, and other agencies to "provide for the establishment" of the NREN (Congress, Senate, 1991b, p. 12).

The 1989 OSTP report proposed that during the first stage of the program plan the Federal government would continue the development of the Internet, with participating agencies upgrading their networks to 1.5-megabit-per-second trunks (Office of Science and Technology Policy, 1989a, p. 33). Once this upgrade has been accomplished, these agencies will acquire a common set of 45-megabit-per-second transcontinental trunks which, during the second stage of the program plan, will become the Research Interagency Backbone (RIB) (p. 34). Some 200 to 300 research institutions will connect to the RIB, paving the way for the third stage, which would deliver a 1- to 3-gigabit-per-second networking service to selected research facilities, and 45-megabit-per-second networking to approximately 1,000 sites across the country (p. 32). Gould argued that the interim NREN was already emerging from a larger national computer network, the Internet, although it was, at that time, difficult to distinguish between the interim NREN and the Internet (1990b, p. 1).

Management Structure

There is an initial question about the type of management model that should be employed to oversee the design, implementation, operation, maintenance, and improvement of the NREN. Who shall lead, and who shall govern? This question is important because "the most pressing problems to be faced by network managers, science administrators and policy makers are likely to be organizational, rather than technical in nature" (Koch, 1989, p. 1).

In his 1988 Congressional testimony, Paul Huray, chair of the FCCSET Committee on Computer Research and Applications, stated that his committee had "not decided exactly what management model . . . [would] be used in operating a National Research

Network." The options that he outlined at that time included (Congress, Senate, 1988b, p. 32):

- A quasi-public organization
- A government-owned corporation
- Direct management by a Federal agency.

Gould argued that, whatever the model used, there would have to be "a high degree of cohesion and coordination." He contributed several more management options, including (1989, p. 2):

- Control by a single national association
- An industry/government consortium
- Decentralized control coupled with strict adherence to common standards. In his testimony, Mandlebaum added the possibilities of a (Congress, House, 1989c, p. 8):

  - A university consortium or not-for-profit corporation
  - A for-profit corporation
  - An independent public corporation.

He also stated that he supported the FRICC plan for the creation of a formal National Network Council (p. 7). This last option was strongly supported by Wulf, who claimed that once created the Council would have overall management responsibility for the development of the NREN (p. 5). There is strong support for making NSF the lead agency in the development of the NREN. This proposal has been endorsed by some (Office of Science and Technology Policy, 1989a, p. 35; Bloch, 1988, p. 12; Connolly, in Congress, Senate, 1988b, p. 87) and opposed by others (Wulf, in Congress, Senate, 1988b, p. 128).

S. 343 made the Department of Energy the lead agency for high-performance computing and network development, and stated that it "is the Federal agency having the greatest degree of expertise and knowledge in the research, development and use of high-performance computers, associated software, and networks" (Congress, Senate, 1991a, p. 2). In this legislation, DoE was directed to develop and implement a network similar to the NREN intended to serve almost the same user populations. DoE also received a mandate to take an active role in the interagency coordinating committee established to develop a Federal high-performance computing program (p. 9). If this bill were reintroduced and passed without change, the identity of the lead agency in the management of the

NREN would be clear, at least until 1996. How DoE would exercise its mandate, however, is not at all clear and requires further debate and consideration.

S. 272 named NSF the lead agency in the development of the NREN and assigned much of the responsibility for interagency coordination in relation to the national HPC program to FCCSET (Congress, Senate, 1991b, p. 9). DoE's role in this scenario would be minimized. If S. 272 should become law as written, the management question would be somewhat resolved, at least while the NREN is operated by the Federal government.

According to the National Research Council, no matter which model is chosen (1988b, p. 32):

> Competent management is absolutely essential for maximizing the effectiveness of the investment in an [NREN] . . . . It is a critical issue that requires early (and continuing) attention and action, and it is a non-trivial element of the total cost of providing network service. The overall problem is to engineer facilities and services to match demand, and tune them to the needs of users as expressed by users.

Serious consideration must be given to all of these options when determining the policies which will shape the management of the NREN.

Maintenance and Operation

There are other issues which must be related to the issue of management structures. First, to what extent should the management of the NREN be centralized? If the management structure is to remain under the aegis of the Federal government, what roles should academia and the private sector play? Once the management structure is determined, issues of operation and facilities management must be settled. The routine performance of the network must be monitored, and its performance evaluated. Monitoring, measurement, and evaluation procedures must be designed and implemented across the NREN in order to provide network managers with the information they need to maintain and upgrade the network (National Research Council, 1988b, p. 33). Also, the more transparent the network, the more difficult it will be to determine who is responsible for particular types of maintenance.

Network Standards

A set of network standards must be developed which will allow fast, easy, and transparent communication across the NREN (Kahn, 1988, p. 20) and coordination with interdependent institutional and mid-level networking (Office of Technology Assessment, 1989c, p. 31). According to the Panel on Information Technology and the Conduct of Research (1989, p. 37), the development of these standards "is painfully slow, and the process is intensely political." To further complicate this issue, networking technology is "developing faster than . . . [the] ability to define standards that make effective use" of it. Winkler agreed that standards are of "paramount importance" and suggested that they be created through government funding of advanced research and development and then be required in the specifications for procurements or for development projects (Congress, Senate, 1989e, p. 6).

Legal Issues

Mandlebaum raised a different issue in his comments on legal and regulatory barriers of importance to regional and mid-level networks (Congress, House, 1989b, p. 11). There may be problems of restraint of trade, the appearance of "anti-competitive collusion," or regulatory problems when the NREN is composed of a mix of not-for-profit and for-profit mid-level and regional networks. Should the NREN be regulated? If so, should regulation be applied to the entire network in the same way or will different regulatory schemes be necessary (Kahin, 1990)?

In a broader sense, these issues may reflect a need for a "clearly articulated national policy covering the movement of information" (Gabbard, in Congress, Senate, 1989e, p. 2). This is a critical policy issue because, as noted by OTA in a recent report on Federal scientific and technical information, the Federal government does not have an overall dissemination strategy or policy for scientific and technical information (1988). Indeed, the existing Federal STI policy system has been described as being in disarray (McClure, 1989).

Finances and Cost Recovery

Financial and cost recovery issues form another important area of policy concern. There is extensive debate over:

- How the NREN should be funded
- How charges should be established for different types of users and for different services
- Who should pay for use and who should not.

The Panel on Information Technology and the Conduct of Research argued that methods used for cost recovery can have "significant impacts on usage" patterns (1989, p. 36). In addition, OTA noted that a key issue concerns "the extent to which deliberate creation of a market should be built into network policy" (1989c, p. 32).

Collins argued that "the best way to get the job done is to turn to the private sector," which would own and operate the network (Congress, Senate, 1989d, p. 2). Kahn suggested the creation of an annually renewed, government-supported "infrastructure trust fund" for use by government agencies for research and development, a portion of which would be set aside to match funds provided by the private sector and the states (Congress, Senate, 1989c, p. 13). These monies would then be used to fund the construction and early operation of the NREN.

At the same hearings, Wulf stated that he preferred a mix of government subsidies to fund basic operations and user charges to support network services (p. 97). Kleinrock preferred to levy the heaviest user charges on industrial users (Congress, Senate, 1988b, p. 24), while Lucky preferred to use indirect government subsidies to support the network (Congress, Senate, 1989d, p. 8). He argued that funded research should include money specifically earmarked for supporting researchers' NREN activities. There seems to be general agreement that the NREN must have some strategy for charging users which will, according to OTA, probably involve some combination of "access/connectivity fees, and use-related fees . . . secured via a trust fund . . . or returned directly to operating authorities" (1989c, p. 32).

Transition to the Private Sector

If the Government is to relinquish control of the NREN eventually, a major issue involves how the NREN will be transformed from a government-managed operation to a private-sector operation. An examination of current NREN legislation indicated that this issue is far from settled, although the language that called for the NREN to be "phased out" has been deleted from the bill. For example, Section 6(b)(6) of S. 272 required that the NREN "be phased into commercial operation as commercial networks can meet the networking needs of American researchers and educators" (Congress, Senate, 1991, p. 13). Section 6(a)(7) of S. 1976 required that the NREN "be eliminated or sold to the private sector . . . when the networking needs provided by the NREN can be satisfied by other means" (Congress, Senate, 1990c, p. 2).

Kahn agreed with the goal of the commercialization of the NREN, arguing that the private sector, once it appreciates the profit potential of the network, will introduce competition into networking, giving researchers and other users the power of choice (Congress, Senate, 1988b, p. 36). The long-term result would be "a more powerful domestic information infrastructure" (p. 37). Wulf also discussed the "challenges of 'transitioning the network to commercial' service" (Congress, Senate, 1989d, pp. 8-9):

> The goal . . . is to move the [NREN] . . . as much out of the public sector as possible as soon as that is practical - that is as soon as the users are able to purchase the capability and connectivity they require. We believe that the market will grow due to this effort . . . and will intersect other developments underway in the communications industry sometime in the next five to ten years.

This effort will require considerable planning and effort to ensure that management and operating structures are in place, so that the transition to the private sector can proceed smoothly, without interrupting network traffic. There is no consensus on how migration from a publicly funded and operated network to a privately funded and operated network should occur. Further, there is no consensus if it should occur.

Network Use and Usability

Two related NREN issues are ease of use and determination of what will constitute its fair use if the network is viewed as a public infrastructure (Office of Technology Assessment, 1989c, p. 24). If network protocols and procedures are too complex, users will limit their involvement in networking. Kahn indicated that this problem already exists and questioned "whether the users themselves know how to use the full capacity of the networks effectively" (1988, p. 15).

Fuchs pointed out certain inconsistencies in usage guidelines of major academic networks and said that, assuming that users can acquire the skills necessary to work on networks, they still will face the problem that "what may be acceptable on one network may not be permitted on another" (1988, p. 47). He wondered whether a set of rules can be created which will apply across networks and suggested that policy makers may have to search for a common denominator among existing network rules and policies.

Dickinson, testifying as a working scientist, suggested that the computers and networking technology "that we have now and in the future must be made to be used by a wide variety of researchers and for this they must be made easy to use by scientists without very much special training beyond their scientific knowledge" (Congress, Senate, 1988b, p. 46). Although difficult to resolve, issues of network complexity are critical to the use of the NREN by the scientific and research community and other users, and these issues must be faced by policy makers, network designers, and network administrators.

User Education, Training, and Support

There has not been much comment in the literature on the need for user support and training, but those who have discussed this issue emphasize its importance to the success of the NREN. According to the Panel on Information Technology and the Conduct of Research, "the training and education necessary for using information technology are lacking" (1989, p. 39). It is not clear, however, where the responsibility for education and training will reside: Should it be handled at the Federal, regional, or institutional level?

Many researchers face a dilemma: They need considerable expertise to effectively utilize existing networks, but may lack the time or other resources, including inclination, to acquire the necessary knowledge and skills. Because the rate of change in information technology continues to increase, the learning and training process is continuous and time-consuming. In addition, very few directories are available, leaving users without access to information about network services and user addresses (Huray, in Congress, Senate, 1988b, p. 10).

Education and training issues must be given serious consideration in policy discussions about the NREN. Specifically referring to the High Performance Computing Program, Wulf argued that (Congress, Senate, 1988b, p. 93):

In the excitement over the hardware . . . people are too often overlooked. Our own experience with supercomputer support suggests that is a costly mistake . . . . With the next generation of parallel supercomputers, the investment in . . . training people in the new technology will be even more critical to the overall efficiency of the program, and hence to the quality of the science which emerges.

Kahn, testifying at the same hearing, agreed and commented that (1988, p. 36):

Actual network users need support for the kinds of equipment . . . that make it possible for them to use the network effectively, this will be especially important when we set about broadening our aspirations to other disciplines . . . . Many . . . research groups are not now outfitted in ways that will let them take advantage of networks from the point of view of equipment and software . . . . We are going to have to focus explicitly on helping those research communities learn to make effective use of networks . . . [and] learn what the power of them may be. It is an incremental process that must take place over time. We are going to have to support them in that . . . process as they begin to crawl . . . walk and then run.

The success of the NREN depends, in part, on the recognition of the importance of user education, training, and support in network use. The goal of linking several thousand institutions to the NREN means that the NREN user population will number in the thousands, and many of these users will need training and support so they can use the NREN effectively.

Security and Privacy

Network security has at least two components. The first involves the problem of computer worms and viruses. Leonard Kleinrock, chair of the National Research Network Review Committee, commented that his committee found that "computer viruses do pose a threat to research which would take place on a national research network." He minimized the significance of this threat, however, by suggesting

technical precautions that could be taken by network management to protect data and software (Congress, Senate, 1988b, p. 23). He was of the opinion that only "a small fraction of the research community would . . . be reluctant to hookup" to a national network because of the threat of viruses (p. 23). Kahn agreed, maintaining that "the benefits of an open national research network outweigh the occasional risks of misuse" (p. 42).

In contrast, the NRC adopted the position that "privacy and security in data communications have been under-appreciated and underprotected to date . . . [and that] propagation of failures and viruses . . . is a growing risk" (1988b, p. 33). These problems are exacerbated because of the scope of the proposed network, especially as the number of users and international connections increase (1988b, pp. 22-24). The problem for network managers will be to set policies that clearly delineate the rules and sanctions associated with unauthorized use of and possible damage to the NREN. A subsequent problem will be creating the means to enforce the policies and to effectively deal with violations and carrying out sanctions when necessary (Fuchs, 1988, p. 47).

The second component of security involves the nature of the information on the NREN. Problems of confidentiality and privacy must be resolved because of, for example, the ability to access, merge, and manipulate very large data sets, including data drawn from medical, insurance, tax, and other government records. This access underscores the conflict between the needs of researchers and government employees to generate and have access to information about individuals and the individual's right to privacy. Security issues also involve the problem of the proprietary nature of some information which will pass through the NREN. Kleinrock claimed that some "business organizations will . . . feel reluctant . . . [to hook up] due to the proprietary . . . and mission-critical nature of some of their data" (Congress, Senate, 1988b, p. 23). How can such sensitive information be protected? Should this type of information be allowed on the network at all?

Censorship

Censorship on the NREN, which may be prompted by privacy concerns, is also an issue. Should users have the right to send any information they want over the NREN, or should there be some restrictions? If there are to be restrictions, should they be defined and imposed by the NREN management, or should users practice self-censorship? To what extent should the flow of information be controlled or restricted by network managers and administrators?

Weingarten and Garcia argue that the increased access to information created by new information technologies will force policy makers to deal with issues of privacy and intellectual property (1988, p. 62). They also see conflicts arising between the norms of business and the norms of science (p. 66). They also discuss issues related to national security. Expressing a similar concern over issues of security, privacy, and censorship as they relate to networking, the Panel on Information Technology and the Conduct of Research recommended "the establishment of a body that will study and advise on these issues" (1989, p. 37).

THE NREN AND POLICY ISSUES

Clearly, the establishment of the NREN would give rise to a set of complex policy questions that must be resolved if the network is to be successful (see Figure 3-3). In order to resolve these issues in ways that will maximize effective use of the NREN, policy makers will require sound empirical evidence about the impacts of electronic networks on scientific research and communication and other uses. More specifically, they need information about the population of users who currently use networks, about future uses of the NREN, and about the new constituencies expected to become users of the NREN.

This chapter has reviewed key policy writings related to the design and implementation of the NREN. It has demonstrated that there is overwhelming support for the NREN in the Federal government, in academic and scientific research communities, and in the private sector. Many different stakeholders foresee a range of benefits and problems that would accompany the establishment of the NREN. A review of this policy literature, however, has revealed that this overwhelming support is based on little empirical evidence about the benefits of networking and a set of largely untested assumptions about the effects of networking, especially on scientific communication and productivity. Some of these assumptions are that:

- Typical users come to networks with considerable expertise, thereby obviating the concern for training and education.

- The next generation of users will acquire their skills as a matter of course during their education.
- Users will be able to maximize the benefits of the NREN if there is open access.
- The NREN will make scientific communication more wide spread and efficient.
- The NREN will increase scientific productivity, and scientists will want to integrate it into their research activities.
- The NREN will democratize science by increasing access to scientific resources and information for all qualified users.
- Definitions of acceptable use and qualified users will be unproblematic.
- The use of networks is "contagious," and the existence of the NREN will fuel demand, access, and use.

These assumptions may be accurate representations of the role that the NREN can be expected to play, but this must still be verified by empirical research.

The influence of these assumptions has persisted, in part, because questions of the impacts of electronic information networking technology on the productivity and quality of scientific research, on the research process, and on the other domains suggested by NREN proponents have yet to be carefully investigated. There are, then, several critical questions which define research problems concerned with the impacts of electronic networks on communication and productivity:

- How do scientists and other users actually use electronic networks?
- Do network use and its effects vary among scientific disciplines and across user communities?
- What are the main uses to which electronic networks are put by different user groups?
- From the perspective of the users, what are the significant ways in which network use changes their formal and informal communication patterns?
- From the perspective of the users, what are the significant ways in which network use changes their work routine and overall research productivity?
- Based on network users' and managers' experiences with electronic networks, what are some of the major benefits associated with network use? Are these the same benefits that are reported in the literature?

- Based on network users' and managers' experiences with electronic networks, what are some of the major problems or issues that the designers of the NREN should consider? Are these the same problems or issues that are reported in the literature?

Empirical research designed to investigate these questions is necessary if policy makers in the Federal government and network designers and managers are to make decisions that maximize the NREN's utility to all user groups.

A research perspective is beginning to emerge in several social science disciplines that can produce data about these and other concerns to policy makers. A description of this emerging perspective and its implications for the study of electronic networks in general, and the NREN in particular, is presented in Chapter 4. One example of a study using this approach to conduct a national study of users of high-speed computer networking is presented in Chapters 6 and 7.

Research on Computer-Mediated Communication and its Significance for the NREN

Chapter 4

This chapter examines the research literature of computer-mediated communication (CMC). The chapter has two main themes:

- There is an evolving research perspective that uses a variety of methodological approaches to investigate CMC in a variety of settings.
- In order to understand the social and behavioral factors critical to the successful use of high-speed electronic networks, such as the NREN, researchers should be aware of previous approaches and results.

The literature review presented in this chapter is selective and is not intended to be an exhaustive recounting of all research on CMC. Studies will be mentioned that illustrate the the chapter's two major themes.

For the purposes of this chapter, "CMC" refers to any exchange of messages through electronic media that involves the use of computers. This exchange can take place between two people, a person and a machine, or two machines. One common form of CMC is electronic mail, which can take the form of the private exchange of messages or public messaging, commonly called "computer conferencing," where many people send messages to a central address for distribution to other people who are on a centralized mailing list. Another form of CMC is asynchronous file transfer, where a user sends an electronic mail message to a remote location requesting a file, a copy of which is sent to the user at a later time. Other forms of CMC include the use of file and mail servers and interactive or synchronous communication.

CMC is a form of communication which is beginning to alter the ways in which people in governmental, academic, and private sector settings interact with one another in formal and informal ways. This is occurring because CMC, which does share some characteristics with other more traditional forms of communication also has novel characteristics. For example, the fact that the delivery of electronic mail messages is almost instantaneous means that the speed with which certain kinds of information is disseminated within a research community has increased markedly. Researchers who wish to make their work available to their colleagues rapidly can bypass traditional scientific journals and post their results on the network. Feedback from interested critics can be received the same day the results are posted. How will this phenomenon impact technology transfer and the rate of innovation among research communities with access to a high-speed broadband network like the NREN? The answer is not at all clear; according to Gould, "there is little empirical evidence on the nature of a network's ability to enhance the research process and increase productivity" (1990d, p. 12).

Academic researchers are becoming aware of the ability of CMC to alter communication behaviors, social interactions, and the routine activities of scientists, engineers, and educators. This is important because, until recently, much of the research on CMC has focused on the implementation and engineering aspects of computer networking and has largely ignored social and behavioral issues. There is, however, a research perspective emerging in several social science disciplines that focuses on the psychological, social, and cultural impacts of CMC on individuals, organizations, and society at large.

Researchers have investigated the social psychology of computer conferencing, electronic mail, and bulletin boards, focusing on the impacts of CMC on individuals and small groups; only a few studies have taken the organization as their unit of analysis, and even fewer have examined the effects on organizations whose members communicate with each other through CMC. With a few exceptions, these studies have been conducted in academic settings, using college students, faculty, or staff, or in industrial settings, focusing on managers and, occasionally, on other employees. Only a small number of researchers have examined the effects of CMC on the scientific community, and even fewer have focused specifically on how scientists make use of electronic networks in their research.

Within this literature, however, there is a developing research perspective that focuses on the relationships between the users of CMC and the networking technologies that allow them to communicate. It makes use of a variety of methods to examine the ways social interactions and social structures in different settings are affected by the ways in which people use CMC. Rather than concentrate on questions of system design and requirements, it seeks to investigate people's uses of systems, taking into account their understandings of the systems and networks they use. This perspective, informed by theories and methods from the social sciences, attempts to understand the impacts of CMC by focusing on the experiences of network users.

Some researchers with this user-based approach to the study of CMC are currently turning their attention to large-scale networks. Pilot and exploratory studies have begun to demonstrate that this perspective can be useful in the investigation of the impacts of CMC on organizations and individuals who use these networks. One of the underlying themes of this chapter is that research which uses this perspective to study national research and education networking will prove valuable to policy makers and others involved in NREN policy debates. This perspective also provides a methodological context for the study of the impact of high-speed networks on scientific communication and research reported in Chapters 6 and 7.

DEFINING THE RESEARCH TOPIC

The advent of CMC technologies has created new communication needs (Hellerstein, 1985, 1986) and has encouraged the emergence of patterns of communicative change which did not previously exist (Dunn, in press, p. 3; Love and Rice, 1985, p. 266). It is now possible for people who are widely dispersed to have regular and rapid communication with each other, one consequence of which is that remote collaborations are more likely to occur. Further, Muffo and Snizek (1987, p. 1) claimed that information networking technology engenders social and cultural changes "almost without notice by those most directly involved."

Althiede (1985) has argued that a communication medium and its formats will have significant effects on the social order because, for example, they provide a set of rules and practices which will define the ways in which communicative interactions can take place. According to Smilowitz, Compton, and Flint (1988, p. 311), as communications technology "changes the ways in which people interact, there may develop fundamental differences in the processes by which people accomplish their communications tasks." More specifically, the integration of computer and information networking technologies into complex organizations has created a new form of social interaction, CMC, which is changing the nature of social relations within and among organizations, the structure of communication, and the world of work (Harper, 1985; Rice and Love, 1987, p. 311; Schaefermeyer and Sewell, 1988, p. 113; Sullivan, 1989).

Given this research, it seems clear that the creation of the NREN will have significant effects upon the social environment of its users. One critical population will include those working in the world of scientific R&D. Several questions arise when considering the potential impacts of the NREN on this world:

- How will the daily routines of scientists and researchers be changed by the introduction of the NREN?
- How will the presence of the NREN affect patterns of formal and informal scientific communication?
- How will access to such a network affect the quality of R&D work and overall R&D productivity?
- What kinds of norms will emerge as scientists and researchers begin to integrate the NREN into their regular routines?

This chapter argues that there is a pressing need for research which attempts to answer these questions empirically.

The NREN, if implemented as proposed in current legislation such as S. 272 (Congress, Senate, 1991), will create a radically new environment and will alter scientific work and productivity in many ways. There is considerable discussion, both in the professional literature and the popular press, of the positive impacts of electronic networking and high-speed computing. A cursory examination of the literature reveals that many experts and commentators expect the NREN to:

- Improve researchers' access to colleagues, computing resources, and databases
- Increase the frequency with which researchers interact with each other in informal ways, such as through electronic mail, bulletin boards, and computer conferences
- Increase the frequency with which researchers interact with each other in formal ways, such as through teleconferencing and electronic publishing
- Change the ways in which scientific research is conducted, making it more efficient and productive
- Change the patterns of communication among scientists, extending their communication networks across disciplinary and organizational boundaries
- Greatly decrease the amount of time it takes to transfer technology from academic and government R&D environments to the private sector.

In general, a consensus seems to have been reached that the research process and patterns of scientific communication will be positively altered as national high-speed networking becomes a routine element of scientists' daily work activities.

As the authors and others have noted, however, the literature which discusses the positive impacts of the NREN is incomplete in that it offers little empirical evidence of how, specifically, scientific communication and research productivity have been or would be improved as a result of new communication technologies. Empirical evidence is difficult to gather, in part, because of the difficulties involved in defining and measuring R&D productivity. It is also difficult, in general, to study such complex communication systems.

Such studies typically focus on elite users, and their conclusions typically gloss over the problems of more representative users in order to arrive at claims for networking that are overwhelmingly positive. They do not adequately explain how institutional and individual characteristics influence the use of electronic information technologies by the R&D community. Finally, they do not adequately deal with the normative elements inherent in scientific activity and the impacts that these elements will have on NREN use.

Not all the literature on the effects of CMC on scientific work and productivity is subject to the problems outlined above. Hiltz and Turoff (1978) conducted extensive empirical investigations of network use by scientists. They found that, as networking becomes more pervasive, "scientists who engage in research along similar lines and who communicate intensively with one another" begin to form "invisible colleges" which are "internally stratified on the basis of productivity" (p. 19). Hiltz and Turoff state that scientists use CMC to set research agendas and reinforce the norms of scientific culture.

Other empirical studies, however, have concluded that electronic networks do not have positive effects on either scientific communication or productivity. Johansen, Degrasse, and Wilson (1978) conducted a 15-month study of the potential of computer conferencing for improving the productivity of scientists, the goals of which were to "get as close as possible to measures of research productivity . . . and the process of research communication" itself (p. 2). They found that there were variations in the ways in which scientists used computer conferencing and that changes in productivity were to be explained by both these different styles of interaction and by scientists' individual characteristics. The report de-emphasized the importance of the electronic networking as a factor in explaining increases in scientific productivity.

In a study of engineers' uses of electronic networks, Gerola and Gomory (1984, p. 16) argued that "the existence of an electronic linkage, powerful though it may seem, . . . [had] not, in fact altered the traditional methods of scientific work." They claimed that despite the upgrading of the electronic network at their research sites, "there was no apparent trend toward or improvement in collaboration between scientists" at remote locations (p. 16). This research did find, however, that there were some facets of scientific activity that were enhanced by network use. Their study showed that the most significant effects of networks could be found in applied research and the management of research projects, where communication became more efficient.

This body of research, while intriguing, is somewhat dated and inconclusive. It could not take into account the tremendous advances made in networking technology during the last decade, a period during which, for example, electronic mail and computer conferencing have become much more pervasive in academic, scientific, governmental, and industrial settings. Policy makers dealing with networking legislative and regulatory initiatives need current data on the use and effects of national high-speed networks on R&D communication and productivity.

Although conventional wisdom about the NREN holds that the benefits will far outweigh the drawbacks (see Chapter 3), it is possible that a national network could have negative impacts on the research process and scientific communication. According to Kahn, "we could end up spending a lot of money without any guarantee that a useful network for researchers will result" (1989, p. 14). He stated that those involved in the development, implementation, and management of the NREN must "think seriously about how . . . [to] make a national research network a really useful reality and not just a collection of technology and interfaces and communication lines connecting a bunch of sites" (p. 14). Clearly, this process must be supported by empirical research that examines network use from the perspectives of network users and managers. Such research should include both current and potential users of computer networks.

A significant problem that has hampered researchers, according to Kiesler, Siegel, and McGuire (1984, p.

1493), is that "the functions and impact of computer-mediated communication are still poorly understood." In Congressional testimony several years later, Wulf reiterated this point, stating that researchers cannot quantitatively measure the effects of networking on scientific work and productivity and cannot predict implications of networking (Congress, Senate, 1988b, p. 94).

Few studies have examined the impacts of networking on R&D user perspectives. All too often, research is conducted on the assumption that scientists, engineers, and educators will come to networks with a sophisticated knowledge base and set of skills that will allow them to effectively manipulate networks to accomplish their research agendas. As a result, the experiences of the "typical user" are left out or discounted. Considering the magnitude of the proposed NREN investment, policy decisions should not be made solely on the basis of anecdotal evidence about technically sophisticated users doing computationally intensive work at prestigious institutions. A new direction in research is needed that can gather, analyze, and present information about how scientists and engineers use networks in ways that will be useful to policy makers and system designers.

AN EXPANDED PERSPECTIVE ON CMC

In a 1986 review of the research literature on CMC, Steinfeld stated that many aspects of information networking technology have been extensively studied, but the major foci of this research have been design and implementation issues, the acceptance and rejection of CMC systems, systems applications, and system evaluations. Little research has been done on the social behaviors linked to the use of these systems (p. 197). He argued that such research was necessary so that system designers could create information networks that users would be able to exploit fully.

A report by the Panel on Information Technology and the Conduct of Research (1989, p. vii) found that: "The most superficial survey of researchers will reveal a wide range of capabilities in the use of information technology . . . in research. It will also reveal endemic frustration and dissatisfaction." The Panel also found that (p. 9):

> There is almost no systematic information on the users and uses of information technology. For example, the Panel cannot estimate how many or what proportion of scientists use

computers in different fields, how access to networks and computer facilities is distributed across disciplines, or to what extent useful applications are disseminated throughout the research community. Systematic collection of such information is essential to the development of intelligent policy. Researchers' experiences can help guide decisions about policy and resource allocation . . . . This process will continue to change the nature of scientific, engineering, and clinical research itself.

These comments reflect an emerging awareness both in the Federal government and in the academic and research communities that the development of the NREN must be accompanied by an extensive research program which focuses on current and potential users of national research and education networks.

The National Research Council (NRC) interviewed scientists who use electronic networks and discovered that, contrary to the common assumption that scientist and engineer users are highly skilled and motivated to use networks, researchers "are not a homogeneous community with uniform requirements for network support" and are "generally confused by the current state of network systems with which they must deal" (1988b, p. 9). This report also stated that the "research community at large does not offer the well-defined user behaviors assumed by planners of conventional data communications networks" (p. 13). The report implied that the underutilization of current networks could be explained, in part, by the tendency to plan and implement networks based on the conventional wisdom, rather than on empirical data, concerning network users. NRC called for extensive research designed to describe the community of researchers who are network users in terms of their actual networking activities, skills, and anticipated networking needs.

There is a growing body of research that uses a variety of methods to study CMC in a variety of organizational and experimental settings. The goals of this research include:

- Uncovering the ways in which CMC is used by different types of users
- Understanding how users' social interactions are affected by their use of information technologies

- Investigating the changes that are occurring in the processes of communication among different user populations
- Examining social and psychological impacts of the use of CMC on users' behaviors and attitudes.

This work, by and large, has not focused on R&D workers as network users, although this research could prove valuable to policy makers, planners, and others involved in the design and implementation of the NREN.

Studies of the Effects of CMC in Specific Organizational Settings

In a review of CMC research conducted during the 1970s, Rice (1980) found support for findings which claimed that the introduction and use of CMC in organizations changed the structure of existing communications networks, which became less rigid and had more lateral channels. He also argued that one consequence of the successful implementation of CMC systems was the decentralization of organizational structure.

Clifford Lynch (1980) examined factors critical to the acceptance and use of an electronic mail system at the University of California's Division of Library Automation. He presented a taxonomy of implementations intended to indicate the ways in which organizations established and integrated CMC systems. Lynch found that ease of use, accessibility of the terminals, reliability, and a "good human interface" were some of the key factors in successful implementation (p. 35). He also contended that the system worked, in part, because the users trained themselves; no training or support was provided by the organization. As users became more proficient in operating the system, their patterns of use changed, as did their perceptions of the system. On the other hand, Lynch also found that direct benefits were difficult to quantify.

Christie (1981) analyzed the sources of organizational resistance to the introduction of information technology and found that "individual and group inertia prevents changes in established procedures; it is not worth the effort to learn" (p. 228). Organizational resistance to the introduction of new technology was especially likely to occur, he argued, if it threatened to alter the organization's traditional decision-making procedures. However, in the event that these technologies could be successfully implemented and people began to use them in their work, "local changes affect the whole system" (p. 228).

In a study conducted in an academic setting, Rice and Case (1983, p. 133) found that people who used electronic message systems did not necessarily attribute greater benefits to CMC use as they gained experience with their systems. Their results indicate that, in this setting, CMC reduced some users' reliance on telephone- and paper-based messaging, although almost half of the users reported that they noticed no change in the ways in which they used traditional communication channels. Rice and Case concluded that electronic messaging could help to develop and sustain invisible colleges and could allow users to surmount resource allocation problems caused by status differences within and among organizations (p. 150).

Rafaeli (1986) studied the use of a computer bulletin board through a survey of users and an analysis of transaction logs and concluded that bulletin board use and impacts, although extensive, did not always validate the exaggerated claims of network advocates. Love and Rice (1985) and Rice and Love (1987) used network analysis, content analysis of message transcripts, and statistical inference to investigate social-psychological elements in electronic messaging and bulletin board use. They reported that approximately 30% of the communication on a CMC system will be "socio-emotional" (1987, p. 108), despite the fact that many in the field have long assumed that CMC channels effectively restrict messages to "less friendly . . . emotional, and more task-oriented" content (1985, p. 266). Recently, Boshier (1990) examined social-psychological factors in electronic networking by focusing on the ways in which users are affected by their use of the medium.

Grieve and McCabe (1986) looked at the implementation of an electronic mail system in the Department of Communications at The Ohio State University. They used user interviews and an analysis of quantitative frequency patterns of message exchanges provided by a system transaction file to study the characteristics that accompanied the successful implementation and use of the system. They argued that system success depended on the ability of users to quickly identify advantages in their daily routines that were clearly linked to their use of the system, and on the relative ease with which the system could be used. Hellerstein (1986) conducted an exploratory study of electronic messaging and conferencing and found that

users considered the "social uses" of CMC to be an important motivating factor in their continued use of the medium.

Sproull and Kiesler (1986) used questionnaire data, self-reports, interviews, and message transcripts to study electronic mail use in an organization. In this study, they developed and used operational measurements including message length in number of lines, the number of words used in the opening and closing of messages, and the number of words indicating positive and negative affect. They concluded that electronic mail speeded up the process of information exchange and led to the exchange of new information which would not have been sent using other, more traditional channels (p. 1500). They also found that CMC decreased the number of social cues available to participants as they communicated, producing a deregulating effect on communication behavior. This conclusion has been controversial among CMC researchers.

Safyeni, Lee, and MacGregor (1988) used interviews to compare managers' and employees' perceptions of two organizational electronic mail systems, one used by executives and one used by other employees. They concluded that the executives' system was perceived by both groups to be better and more efficient, although both systems were thought to contribute to organizational efficiency and productivity. In another study that examined electronic mail use within an organization, Sproull and Kiesler (1986) found that there was little difference in the messages sent from superiors to subordinates and from subordinates to superiors, a phenomenon that Rice called "access equalization" (1984, p. 134). Sullivan (1989) studied the impacts of the introduction of CMC into the Florida State Legislature and concluded that one of the significant consequences of the integration of electronic mail into the routines of the Legislature was "information empowerment."

In a study of CMC and organizational innovation conducted in a small government agency, Rice (1989, p. 67) argued that the introduction of CMC systems leads to changes in an organization's structures and processes, which, in turn, leads to "persistent, although malleable and non-revolutionary, differences" in the organization. CMC leads to boundary-spanning communication patterns, new forms of information acquisition, remote agenda setting, and desktop publishing. He argued that CMC supported such activities as:

- Information and opinion exchange
- Querying and responding
- Generating ideas
- Solving problems
- Resolving disagreements
- Staying in touch
- Getting to know others in the organization.

CMC did not facilitate persuasion, group decision making, or the exchange of confidential information. Rice found that electronic mail complemented rather than replaced print media, the use of which increased with the use of CMC. He concluded that the use of electronic mail "may generate more exchanges of facts, more short reports, more notes to process" and may result in more time being spent searching for information (1989, p. 182).

Figure 4-1 summarizes key findings from studies of the effects of CMC in organizational settings.

Laboratory Research on the Effects of CMC

Kiesler, Seigel, and McGuire (1984) used a social-psychological approach to compare face-to-face interaction, simultaneous electronic communication from remote locations, and electronic mail in a laboratory setting. They found distinct differences in styles of participation, decision making, and group interac-

tion depending upon the experimental condition. The electronic channels of communication were the verbal and non verbal cues which accompany face-to-face and voice interactions. One implication drawn from these findings was that the cuelessness of CMC could encourage "deindividuation," which could, in turn, lead to increased uninhibited behavior among users (p. 1132). It was this finding that was tested in later work (Sproull and Kiesler, 1986). Kiesler, Seigel, and McGuire also described CMC as "undeveloped culturally" and argued that there were not yet any strong norms to regulate its use, a finding which seems less true today.

Studies have also been conducted which have sought to uncover the impacts of CMC on arousal, feelings, and expressive behavior (e.g., Kiesler, Zubron, Moses, and Geller, 1985). Matheson and Zanna (1988) compared face-to-face interactions with CMC to investigate the ways in which the latter changed the nature of interpersonal communication. They found that subjects in the CMC trials experienced different levels of "private" and "public" self-awareness than did those in the face-to-face trials (p. 229). Subjects also exhibited an awareness of the social context of the communicative interaction, social and cultural standards, and personal norms, and displayed more uninhibited behavior. The latter finding seems to provide support for Kiesler, Seigel, and McGuire's

---

Figure 4-1. Summary Findings on the Effects of CMC in Specific Organizational Settings

- Users' actual behaviors when interacting through bulletin boards fall short of the claims of supporters of networking technology.
- As much as 30% of the message content in some computer conferences may be described as socio-emotional.
- As users' time on electronic networks increases, their patterns of use change as do their perception of the networks.
- It is very difficult to quantify the direct benefits that users and organizations gain from electronic networks.
- Successful implementation and use of networks may depend on the extent to which users can perceive clear advantages to their use and the relative ease with which the networks can be used in daily work routines.
- One significant factor which mitigates against the acceptance and use of networks in organizations is the lack of user training.
- CMC suppresses social cues, leading to more uninhibited or deregulated communicative behavior.
- Electronic networks may reduce status differences within organizations.
- CMC systems affect organizational structures and processes, increasing boundary spanning communication and creating more lateral communication channels.
- Use of CMC may lead to organizational decentralization.
- In academic settings, electronic networks are used to create and support invisible colleges and to promote resource sharing.

(1984) earlier finding that CMC encouraged deindividuation.

Smilowitz, Compton, and Flint (1988) replicated the famous Asch conformity studies to see if the presence of others would affect individual judgments when the individual communicated through a simulated computer conference. In the original study, a subject was placed in a situation where he or she had to choose between publicly giving an incorrect answer to a question, therefore conforming to the group consensus, or publicly contradicting the group by giving the correct answer. The replication was designed to test the effects of the presumed "egalitarian nature" of CMC (p. 313). The researchers found that people were less likely to conform to the consensus judgment of a group when making their decisions at a remote terminal than when they were in the physical presence of a group whose unanimous judgment was in direct opposition to theirs. Subjects in the CMC trials were also more willing to critically evaluate information (p. 320). The use of CMC, in this study, seemed to provide people with a setting more conducive to critical and non conforming decision making than did a face-to-face group setting.

Figure 4-2 is a summary of some of the key findings that have emerged from experimental studies of the effects of CMC on user behaviors. These findings, while provocative, must still be replicated in the field. They do, however, indicate that there are a range of social and psychological factors and effects which come into play when people use CMC. Laboratory studies have not thus far addressed the differences in these effects that might be felt by experienced rather than novice users.

Research on CMC and Scientific Communication

Several studies have examined the scientific research community's use of CMC. Hiltz and Turoff (1981) conducted an 18-month study of a sample drawn from five different research communities and gathered "detailed empirical evidence about changes in user behavior and preferences related to the features and capabilities of computer based communication systems as a function of experience" (p. 740). They found that these research communities were heavy users of networks for messaging and conferencing. Interviews with users revealed that they wanted CMC systems to provide group conferences, notebooks for text composition, self-defined commands, and simple messaging. Their analysis led them to observe that system designers should always base their planning on "feedback from the experiences of users in current systems" (p. 739).

Brotz (1983), writing about Laurel, a messaging network used by Xerox, claimed that he had discovered patterns of user behavior that apply to message systems in general by observing people as they used Laurel over a period of several months. After discussing five major problems that had occurred during the time he observed system use, Brotz (p. 181) offered some "biased suggestions about standards" that he believed would improve system effectiveness and reduce incidents of abuse.

Shapiro and Anderson (1985) wrote on the need for social norms that would regulate the quality and appropriateness of electronic communication. Their report was largely based on anecdotal evidence gathered during their experiences with an electronic

---

Figure 4-2. Summary Findings of Laboratory Studies on the Effects of CMC on User Behaviors

The use of electronic networks:

- Changes users' self-perceptions of public and private self-awareness
- Reduces users' awareness of the social context of communication
- Occurs within a context that lacks the social cues present in face-to-face and voice-only communication interactions
- May lead to deindividuation and uninhibited behavior among users
- May lead to increases in physiological and psychological arousal
- Makes users less likely to conform to the group and more likely to engage in nonconforming behavior when involved in group decision-making processes
- Encourages users to evaluate information more critically.

mail system in the Rand Corporation, and they did not present it as empirical research. Rather, their goal was to "accelerate the process by which social customs and behavior appropriate to electronic mail" and computer conferencing emerge, so that these media can be used effectively by the scientific community (p. iii). The report has value as a document representing two users' attempts to understand the evolution of patterns of communicative behavior over a computer network.

A recent study by Hesse, Sproull, Kiesler, and Walsh (1990, Draft) looked at the impacts that the use of computer networks has had on a specific scientific community. Setting out to examine the possible effects of network use on work and social structure in oceanography, they found that "traditional indices of success and status are recapitulated and reinforced, rather than usurped, by computer networks" (p. 21):

> Those who used the network frequently published more papers, knew more oceanographers, and received higher professional recognition scores than those who used the network infrequently . . . [P]roductive and professionally visible scientists used the network . . . for doing committee work, for discussing jointly produced manuscripts, and for transmitting reviews of manuscripts and proposals. Those scientists who reported being socially well-integrated within the community (who knew more oceanographers) indicated that they used the network to meet new people and monitor reports of new research techniques and projects.

This research team used multiple methodologies to study ocean scientists. They conducted interviews, administered a survey electronically over the network (SCIENCEnet) and collected network usage data. The research report made liberal use of the oceanographers' statements, clearly presenting the points of view of the users of SCIENCEnet.

In their conclusions, the team made explicit reference to the ways in which their work could be of value to policy makers. They maintained that policy makers must be sensitive to the ways in which changes in communication media may lead to changes in communication, work, and productivity and that one important goal of policy makers should be to develop mechanisms to support and encourage the widespread use of networks within scientific communities (p. 25).

Overall, some of the findings that have emerged from studies of CMC and scientific communication are that:

- Research communities will make use of electronic networks for messaging and conferencing.
- Network designers should always seek out user feedback.
- There is a need for social norms that will regulate user behavior on electronic networks.

The R&D community should receive more attention from CMC researchers. There is a pressing need for methodologically rigorous research that examines scientists' and engineers' use of CMC, particularly their use of high-speed electronic networks. The study of oceanographers is a good model of the way in which the emerging perspective on CMC can be used to investigate network use in a scientific community.

IMPLICATIONS OF THE EVOLVING RESEARCH PERSPECTIVE FOR THE NREN

It is clear that these findings, even when combined with the findings of field and laboratory research, do not provide an adequate account of typical users' experiences with electronic networks. Koch concurred and drew out one critical implication of this problem (1989, p. 16):

> It is difficult to translate [existing] findings into recommendations for how networks should be designed and managed . . . for several reasons . . . the research results are somewhat sketchy . . . most of the findings are descriptive . . . many of the studies provide snapshot characterizations of impacts, rather than longitudinal evidence; and . . . there is not a well-developed body of research specifically on scientific users of networks.

This literature does, however, represent a slowly developing interdisciplinary line of user-based research on CMC. It makes use of multiple research methods, employed in a variety of settings, to examine the ways in which CMC is being used and the ways in which a broad range of users are affecting and being affected by this new communication medium. See Figure 4-3 for a list of methods used in these studies.

Figure 4-3. Methods Used to Study CMC

Methods / Studies	Personal Observation	Interview	Survey	Content Analysis	Network Analysis	Statistical Inference	Self-Reports	Laboratory Experiment
Brotz (1983)	●							
Gerola and Gomory (1984)	●	●						
Grieve and McCabe (1986)		●				●		
Hellerstein (1985)		●	●					
Hesse, Sproull, Kiesler, and Walsh (1990)		●	●			●	●	
Hiltz and Turoff (1981)		●	●	●		●		
Johansen, Degrasse, and Wilson (1978)								●
Kiesler, Zubron, Moses, and Geller (1985)								●
Kiesler, Seigel, and McGuire (1984)								●
Love and Rice (1985)				●	●	●		
Lynch (1980)	●	●	●					
Matheson and Zanna (1988)								●
Rafaeli (1986)			●	●				
Rice (1989)		●	●	●		●		
Rice and Case (1983)		●	●	●	●	●	●	
Rice and Love (1987)				●	●	●		
Safyeni, Lee, and MacGregor (1988)		●						
Shapiro and Anderson (1985)	●	●						
Smilowitz, Compton, and Flint (1988)								●
Sproull and Kiesler (1986)		●	●	●			●	

There are a number of directions in which researchers have been moving, many of which will provide critical insights into the social and behavioral aspects of network use. Increasingly, studies have examined:

- The emergence of social norms governing CMC in different organizational settings and among different classes or categories of users
- The use of communications, psychological, social-psychological, and sociological theories to make sense of this emerging form of communication
- The effects of CMC in organizational settings, including academia, industry, and government
- The behaviors, perceptions, and attitudes of network users
- The social psychology of CMC
- The education, training, and support of CMC users.

The review of the research literature presented in this chapter is certainly not exhaustive. The intent of this presentation of selected research results has been to indicate that useful approaches to the study of CMC have been developed in the fields of communication studies, information science, sociology, and social psychology. Such approaches are of use because they seek to describe and explain the ways in which people actually use electronic networks, to describe the attitudes, beliefs, and feelings of users about the role of electronic networks in their lives, and to describe the practices and needs of users as they interact with each other over electronic networks.

A user-based approach is valuable because it seeks to gather, interpret, and present empirical information about many different social, psychological, and technical aspects of CMC use. Since the development, implementation, and operation of the proposed NREN represents a Federal investment of billions of dollars, it is imperative that policy makers, planners, and others make their decisions based on reliable data about existing and potential networking benefits. There is a real danger of developing a network which has procedures, resources, and services that do not fit the perceived needs of the populations expected to use them. The emerging perspective on the study of CMC discussed in this chapter is a theoretically and methodologically sound way to investigate the needs, wants, and skill levels of the populations of users expected to use the NREN. It can reveal existing use patterns, uncover the impacts networking has had on R&D

productivity and communication patterns, and indicate potential impacts of the NREN on the scientists, engineers, and educators who will use it. One example of a user-based study of networking in the R&D community is presented in Chapters 6 and 7. This work was conducted in order to provide policy makers with empirical data that would be useful in the development of policies related to the NREN.

ELECTRONIC NETWORKS AND SCIENCE*

CHAPTER 5

Scientists have been using electronic networks to communicate and share resources since the early 1970s (Quarterman and Hoskins, 1986; EDUCOM, 1988). During that time, networks have become central to the processes of science, and several networks dedicated to scientific and educational uses have been built. The Federal government is now considering plans to connect and upgrade these networks into an integrated network for research and education called the National Research and Education Network (NREN). While the goals and plans for this network are still being formulated, it is useful to review what is known about the effects of electronic networks on scientists and the processes of science. This chapter reviews the research literature on the impacts of electronic networks on science and explores the implications for network design, management, and operating policies. It then discusses the NREN in light of those implications.

Most of the literature on the impacts of electronic networks on science falls into one of two categories: empirical studies of impacts on individuals and organizations ("micro" impacts), and commentaries predicting impacts on science as a whole ("macro" impacts). Neither category of research seems to take the other much into account, leading to a situation in which the "micro" studies are well-grounded but difficult to generalize from, and the "macro" commentaries are policy-relevant but somewhat weakly supported. There is a dearth of research on how scientists are actually using electronic networks, indicating a need for more studies of scientists' time spent online -- the services they access, the tasks they accomplish, and the problems they encounter.

Many of the implications of recent research have more relevance to the concerns of science administrators and policy makers than to network managers. Findings about how the use of networks change decision-making patterns or the culture of scientific communities are likely to be of most concern to those responsible for scientists' work or for the overall output of the scientific community.

The literature reviewed in this chapter suggests that the most pressing problems to be faced by network managers, science administrators, and policy makers are likely to be organizational rather than technical in nature. The complexities of managing a network for the variety of users in science and education will require coordination among a great many public and private institutions, and conflicts will be reflected in disagreements over design plans,

* This chapter was written by Susan Koch, Department of Telecommunications, Indiana University, Bloomington, IN 47405.

costing procedures, management procedures, and operating policies.

As it is presently conceived, the NREN focuses on problems of capacity, interconnectivity, and technical network management. The research reviewed here indicates that several other factors will have to be taken into account if the utility of the NREN is to be maximized. These factors include:

- Availability of applications and services that fit within the cultures of research and education
- Development of a funding and cost charge-back system for network services
- Attainment of more widespread agreement on norms for communicating online and for sharing network facilities
- Availability of adequate user support
- Availability of well-organized and up-to-date directories of users and research facilities
- Availability of special support for academic communities that are interested in going online
- Continued opportunities for face-to-face meetings among scientists
- Availability of tools and procedures that give researchers control over their electronic environments
- A network management and administrative structure that is optimized for user service.

These and related considerations are discussed below.

IMPACTS OF ELECTRONIC NETWORKS ON SCIENCE

Although there is not an established literature devoted to the impacts of electronic networks on science, there are many threads of research that will help inform speculation about possible impacts. First, sociologists of science have examined the interaction patterns of scientists and the development and maintenance of scientific communities. These studies have helped clarify the nature of scientific communication, making it easier to see how electronic networks might change those interaction patterns. Second, psychologists, sociologists, and management scientists have examined the impacts of electronic networks on individuals and organizations, and some of their findings can be generalized to the research setting. Third, there is growing interest in the design of computerized tools to support collaborative work, with a significant portion of the design research

focusing on research collaborations. Finally, there are scattered studies, not yet well integrated, assessing the impacts of information technologies on science and the policy implications of those impacts.

The Processes of Science

Social studies of science examine the processes by which scientific knowledge is produced and scientific communities are generated and maintained (see Spiegel-Rosing and de Solla Price, 1977; Chubin, Porter, Rossini, & Connolly, 1986; Blau, 1973). Although a review of this literature is outside the scope of this chapter, the following two examples will illustrate its usefulness in understanding the impacts of electronic networks on science.

Recognition and Rewards

Significant attention has been paid to the system of rewards in science, which includes not only paychecks and advancement within one's organization, but the complex structure of prestige and recognition within the wider scientific community (see Mulkay, 1977, for review). Recognition by one's peers is an incentive for most scientists and is likely to lead to increased productivity (Cole and Cole, 1967). Increased recognition and productivity, in turn, earn a scientist more resources and more power within the scientific community. Some scientists eventually become members of an "invisible college," an elite group of high-performing colleagues, which, according to Davies (1977), "selects its own society, then shuts the door." According to Mulkay (1977, p. 103):

> Two clear conclusions emerge from these studies of the reward system of science. The first is that rewards are distributed by a social process of exchange, whereby valued information is made available to the research community in return for professional recognition. . . .
>
> The second is that this exchange process generates a self-reinforcing elite structure.

Understanding the interplay of recognition, motivation, and productivity in scientific communities will be helpful in predicting the possible impacts of electronic networks.

If electronic networks and the research capabilities they provide are allocated according to the existing "self-reinforcing elite structure," that means they are likely to be set up and used by the most prestigious institutions and researchers first. This process would reinforce the leadership role of those institutions and researchers and lead to little overall change in the elite structure of research disciplines, although perhaps a few "second-tier" researchers could use their access to networks to gain a toe-hold on the ladder to the invisible college.

There is also the possibility, however, that electronic networks would open up disciplinary dialogue so much that the elite structure would break down— invisible colleges would become more visible, and more people could take part in leading scientific discussions. Before predicting such an outcome, however, one would have to consider the many mechanisms in place to reinforce the existing structure (socialization in graduate schools, hiring, tenure, and admissions practices, funding systems, etc.). One would also want to consider the positive aspects of the invisible college, which performs a quality-control function within research disciplines and allows cutting-edge researchers to confer informally and make progress more quickly on their research efforts.

Collaborative Processes

Researchers have also studied how scientists work together in research projects. Kraut, Galegher, and Egido (1988) proposed a three-stage model of research collaboration -- initiation, execution, and public presentation -- and looked at the task and relational activities in each stage. They found that researchers put a great deal of effort into establishing and maintaining personal relationships with their collaborative partners during their research. They argue that (1988, p. 764):

> The challenge we see for information technology developers is to create tools that not only facilitate task completion but also support productive personal relationships. By contrast, the main technologies that have been developed so far to support group work focus primarily on task completion, and we believe, have been largely unsuccessful precisely because of this.

These researchers have studied the initiation phase of research, trying to isolate the factors that predict the likelihood that scientists will collaborate.

They find that proximity, by offering the opportunity for scientists to interact informally, makes it much more likely that they will develop a working relationship, even when similarity of research interests (which usually correlates with proximity) is controlled (Kraut, Egido, and Galegher, 1990). Allen's (1985) study of researcher communication found that about 25% of the engineers whose offices were next door to each other talked about technical topics at least once a week. If their offices were ten meters apart, the figure was 10%. The curve leveled off at 30 meters, indicating that, in any given week, people were as likely to talk to someone 30 meters away as to someone several miles away (with the same low probability of .04%). Studies such as this give us information with which to refine the claim that electronic networks will promote collaborations. Electronic networks may indeed provide a new form of "virtual proximity," or they may be unable to overcome the need for physical proximity in the initiation phase of collaboration.

In general, the research on collaboration suggests that the social dimension of research relationships is as important for their continuation and productivity as is the task dimension, and that it is important to support both dimensions. Knowing that unplanned interactions are a mainstay of collaboration, for example, has led software designers to come up with electronic equivalents of the chance hallway meeting. One such tool, "Cruiser," uses remote video and audio connections to allow users to "cruise" the hallways and offices of their remote colleagues (Root, 1988). This research also highlights the value of face-to-face communication in the formation of collaborative relationships.

Effects on Individual Researchers and Research Groups

Most of the empirical studies of electronic networks have looked at their effects on individuals and small groups. While many such effects have been isolated, most researchers agree that the impacts of the technology are mediated by how users use the systems; technology does not determine the outcomes directly (Poole, Homes, and De Sanctis, 1988; Blomberg, 1988). Researchers use electronic networks to communicate and transfer files, to conduct collaborative research, to access remote databases, and to share centralized computing resources (Jennings et al., 1986; Licklider and Vezza, 1988).

Levels of Acceptance and Use

Any potential impacts of electronic networks are preconditioned by scientists' acceptance and use of those networks. Several factors have been found to influence levels of acceptance and use, including attributes of available technology, communicators' needs, and attitudes toward networks (Steinfield, 1986). The cost of gaining access to electronic networks is an important factor for many users, as is the degree of interconnectivity among systems. In a study of an international scientific computer-based conference, Tombaugh (1984) found that technical issues were of most concern to scientists in developing countries, many of whom did not have easy access to terminal equipment or telecommunications connections. Scientists in industrialized countries were most concerned with organizational and social problems of computer conferencing, including lack of contributions from fellow researchers, the quality of information available on the system, and the lack of focus in some conferences.

One factor predicting levels of use of electronic networks is the type of service available on networks, and their usefulness to researchers. Hiltz (1984) summarized the service preferences of academic researchers on the Electronic Information Exchange System (EIES), as shown in Figure 5-1. While this list is indicative of one set of users' preferences, it is important to remember that usage patterns vary according to characteristics of users, their tasks, and the system itself, i.e., how specific features are designed (Allen, 1985).

Hiltz also found that users' preferences changed somewhat as they gained more experience with the system. Advanced users demanded features that facilitated group communication (as opposed to one-to-one communication); that allowed the user to tailor the system to his or her needs; that allowed the user to have more active control over the system (with command-driven, rather than menu-driven responses); and that supported the preparation of larger text documents.

Another important predictor of system usage is the quality of user groups' leadership. In Hiltz's (1984) study of six research-related computer conferences, she found that the group leaders accounted for between 11% and 24% of the total postings on the conferences. The amount of time that each group leader spent online was almost perfectly correlated with that group's rank in an overall measure of group success. Hiltz claimed that (1984, p. 81):

> In observing the conferences from week to week, it could be seen that if a group leader went on vacation or otherwise disappeared for

Figure 5-1. Reactions to Selected Features of the EIES System*

Feature	Extremely Valuable	Fairly Useful	Slightly Useful	Useless, Cannot Say
Private Messages	68%	22%	10%	1%
Text Editing	51	18	6	25
User Consultants	50	21	7	22
System Commands	40	27	7	26
Group Conferences	39	33	13	15
Group Messages	35	31	25	9
The Directory	34	35	17	14
Private Conferences	33	25	8	35
Retrieval	31	31	9	30
Searches	27	16	18	38
User-Defined Commands	21	15	5	59
Anonymity or Pen Name	10	13	16	61
Synchronous Discussions	9	12	16	63
Graphics Routines	7	5	2	86
Voting	2	12	7	79

*Selected from a more complete list presented in Hiltz, 1984, pp. 98-99.

more than a week at a time, the conference activity tended to become disorganized and then drop off sharply. The group conferences needed a strong, active leader to keep the discussion organized and moving in a way that was satisfying to the participants.

Such leadership activities may play an important role in communication and decision-making behavior.

Changes in Communication and Decision-Making Behavior

Most of the research on communication via electronic networks focuses on questions of how that communication differs from face-to-face interactions. Kiesler and Sproull and their colleagues have conducted numerous experiments comparing electronic and face-to-face communication and have begun to develop a theory to explain their results that emphasizes the absence of certain communicative cues in most electronic communication media (Sproull and Kiesler, 1986; Kiesler, Siegel, and McGuire, 1984; Dubrovsky, Kiesler, and Sethna, 1989).

They found that users of electronic mail tend to focus more on the content of their messages; feel a greater sense of anonymity, less empathy, less guilt, and less concern over how they compare with others; detect less individuality in others; and be less influenced by group norms (Kiesler, 1986). They also found that computer-mediated groups make slightly riskier decisions than do face-to-face groups, that they take longer to reach consensus, that members speak more uninhibitedly, that participants make more equal contributions to the discussions, and that the computer-mediated groups are more productive (Kiesler, 1986; Czajkowski and Kiesler, 1984; Finholt, Sproull, and Kiesler, 1990).

Hiltz, Turoff, and Johnson (1985), studying managers' use of computer conferencing, did not find the uninhibited behavior (frequent strident and off-color remarks) that Kiesler and her colleagues found. They explained Kiesler's findings as the result of using college students as subjects, and disagreed with the assumption that lack of nonverbal cues leads to "disinhibitive" behavior in electronic communication. They stressed the importance of group socialization in the development of electronic networks, and documented the emergence of group norms as users begin to form online communities (Hiltz, 1984). These

norms discouraged behavior that disrupts the communication within the community.

Several researchers have found an "equalization phenomenon" in which status differences in participation and influence are reduced when groups communicate electronically rather than face-to-face (Dubrovsky, Kiesler, and Sethna, 1989; Allen, 1985). In a study of electronic mail users, they found that most users knew the people with whom they conversed and could, therefore, supply much of the information about status, gender, age, etc., that nonverbal cues provide in face-to-face interactions (Sproull and Kiesler, 1986). Still, they found that messages from superiors and managers were not substantially different from messages from subordinates and non-managers. Rice (1984) showed a related "access equalization" afforded by electronic media that gave users contact with groups that they would not otherwise have had.

Information-Seeking Strategies

Library scientists have carried out a great deal of research on information seekers' strategies for formulating their information needs, locating potential sources of information, and accessing that information. Most studies have been carried out in libraries, and some have dealt specifically with database searches. Dervin (1987) drew several conclusions in her review of these studies:

- Users' skill levels are important determinants of whether their searches are successful.
- Successful searchers are those most like the message senders -- more educated, higher in income, and more aware of available services.
- The introduction of more elaborate or flexible technologies (such as computerized databases) has done little to change these success patterns.

These conclusions could be extended to suggest that electronic networks could reinforce existing inequalities among scientists. Dervin and others have called for more user-centered research on information-seeking strategies.

Scientists may face somewhat different constraints in their searches for information than other types of users. They have been trained in information-seeking and are usually familiar with sources of information within their disciplines. However, they often do not have the time to keep up with all the information that is available to them. Psychologists and software designers are experimenting with new ways of assisting users in their searches for information. Software is being developed that scans users' "electronic environment" -- their electronic mail, available computer conferencing systems, online databases, etc. -- and chooses materials of potential interest to the user (Malone et al., 1989). The trend is toward electronic "assistants" that are programmed to recognize what kinds of materials a user tends to access and are able to download that type of material automatically. Such assistants could eventually serve as filters for users who do not have time to wade through all the electronic messages they receive.

Sharing Centralized Facilities

With so much attention being given to the possible development of a national research and education network, it is surprising to find that there is almost no literature on how individual scientists actually use electronic networks to share centralized facilities. Quarterman and Hoskins (1986) hint at some of the problems that researchers face in their review of "notable" computer networks: nonstandard equipment, lack of common protocols, and the difficulty of learning multiple systems. McClure, Bishop, and Doty (1990) go further, documenting the frustrations of researchers attempting to use computing facilities outside their institution. After grappling with unfamiliar software and attempting to gain support from faceless (and sometimes unhelpful) systems administrators, many researchers just give up and learn to make do with their familiar facilities. The investment in time to set up a working relationship with a remote computing facility is more than some researchers can afford. Managing a network to maximize its utility to users has proven to be an extremely complex problem (Office of Technology Assessment, 1989a).

A workshop sponsored by the National Bureau of Standards (1984) found similar problems with the sharing of remote databases and listed several barriers to successful sharing:

- The difficulty of setting up electronic databases that are broad enough to meet the needs of a variety of scientists, yet particular enough to yield useful information
- The variety of formats in which scientific information can be stored and the difficulty of dealing with multiple formats

- The lack of standardization in terminology, which makes it difficult to catalogue data
- The difficulty of using scientific databases because of unwieldy interfaces and lack of documentation or support.

These points indicate that the improved productivity anticipated by sharing facilities via electronic communication will not be realized if these resources are not well managed. Databases have been set up in such a variety of formats that researchers cannot readily use what they need, even if they are able to find it (Panel on Information Technology and the Conduct of Research, 1989). It is sometimes difficult to get scientists to share their data, and even more difficult to set up databases that will be useful for a variety of unforeseen analyses (Fienberg, Martin, and Straf, 1985; Barinaga, 1989). There are few database administrators capable of controlling the quality of the data entered, and scientists are forced to spend significant time checking other scientists' work before they can proceed (Markoff, 1989c; Branscomb, 1983; Numerical Data Advisory Board, Committee on Data Needs, 1978).

Effects on Research Organizations

This section considers the same uses of electronic networks as did the previous section: communication and file transfer, collaborative research, access to remote databases, and the sharing of centralized computing facilities. Here, however, effects at the level of the organization, rather than the individual, will be discussed.

Emergence of New Organizational Groups

One of the most popular theses about the effects of electronic networks is that they will promote the growth of new groups, organized around common interests rather than proximity (Hiltz, 1984; Lederberg, 1978; Rice, 1984). Two characteristics of electronic communication make this growth likely. First, electronic communication makes remote communication easier, by eliminating "telephone tag" and by reducing the amount of work involved in producing some kinds of messages (Rice and Bair, 1983). Electronic communication also provides means for finding like-minded people in new ways -- through electronic bulletin boards and computer conferences. Users can scan lists of headings or do topical searches, and locate online discussion groups focused on their interests.

Hiltz's (1984) study of an academic computer communication network is probably the most detailed look at an "electronic community" to date. She found that users established significant ties to their peers on the network, occasionally to the exclusion of their face-to-face colleagues (see also Freeman, 1980). Often, however, users' network participation was a means of fulfilling their organizational duties, indicating that electronic networks will most likely make users members of additional communities without replacing their existing organizational ties (Markus, 1984; Lederberg, 1978). Indeed, some users in Hiltz's study became links between the online and offline communities, keeping both groups informed about the others' activities.

Many studies of the effects of electronic networks on group formation have been carried out in non-science organizations, but a quick summary of their findings might be instructive. Feldman (1987) found that electronic mail supports "weak ties" in organizations — ties between people who are very loosely connected to one another and who might not otherwise communicate. The ways that electronic networks support groups were also examined by Finholt and Sproull (1987), who found that 80% of one manufacturing firm's electronic mail messages were messages sent to distribution lists, and only 20% were messages from one individual to another. Eveland and Bikson (1988) found that groups using electronic communication were more likely to form subgroups and that their leadership patterns fluctuated more. The ease of setting up group aliases for electronic mailings probably encourages the formation of electronic subgroups but could also lead to an overload of messages sent to distribution lists.

Shifts in Channels of Communication

There has been a great deal of research on the impacts of information technologies on channels of communication and organizational structure. Crowston, Malone, and Lin (1988) reviewed this literature and found mixed reports regarding centralization and decentralization, some agreement that levels of management can be eliminated, and evidence that the overall amount of communication within organizations increases as a result of information technologies.

Besides allowing the formation of new groups within organizations, electronic networks make it possible to centralize or decentralize power and decision making in organizations (Attewell and Rule, 1988; Culnan and Markus, 1987). Managers can use the networks to maintain tighter control over work processes, or they can allow users to use the networks to take more responsibility in managing their own work (Allen, 1985). At least two studies have documented an increase in upward communication after the introduction of computer communication, one in a university and one in a software development firm (Conrath and Bair, 1974; Rice and Case, 1983).

Smith, Bozot, and Hill (in press) assessed the organizational consequences of electronic mail in an industrial research and development organization. They found that electronic mail was used most for administrative tasks rather than for sharing of direct research information, and that there were very few social messages. Most messages were sent within divisions, and 93% of the messages were within one organizational level, up or down. They found little evidence that the system was used to bypass the established chain of command.

Shifts in Types or Quality of Jobs

There is little empirical research on the effects of electronic networks on the types or quality of scientific jobs. Suggestions have been made, however, that the huge research projects made possible by supercomputers and electronic networks will lead to an increased division of labor in science, and perhaps to the emergence of a class of non-PhD technicians fulfilling functions that PhD candidates are now fulfilling (Alberts, 1985; Remington, 1988). Alternatively, graduate students might serve more and more as technicians, losing the opportunity to follow (or initiate) a project from start to finish because research programs are just too large, too long, and too costly (Spotts, 1987; Alberts, 1985). As administrative burdens increase, the number of science administrators could increase. These people could become more and more removed from ongoing research and could encounter difficulties evaluating personnel, equipment purchases, etc. (Alberts, 1985).

Recent literature on the impacts of computers on work quality can be found to both support and contest this claim. In a recent review, Attewell and Rule (1988) reported that while there is relative agreement that low-level clerical positions are often eliminated after computerization, the impacts on mid- and upper-level jobs are more mixed. Some researchers found increased job pressure and fragmentation as a result of computerization, while others report job enrichment and consolidation of tasks (Kraut, Dumais, and Koch, 1989). Factors that appear to affect which result occurs include the nature of the tasks involved, organizational size and level, and characteristics of the planning and implementation process.

Difficulties in Managing the Flow of Information

By making it easier to communicate across organizational boundaries, electronic networks make it more difficult for research organizations to control their proprietary information and to maintain internal security (Office of Technology Assessment, 1986, 1987). Most industrial research organizations have policies regarding the release of potentially valuable information, but the policies are hard to interpret and enforce when applied to the everyday, informal communication that goes on over networks. The fact that electronic bulletin board and computer conference postings are written and saved, and are available to readers unknown by the original poster, makes these forms of communication more vulnerable to borrowing than are more traditional forms of informal communication such as telephone calls and letters. Such postings are more like public speeches (except that they are easier to capture and reproduce), yet they do not have the formal, planned nature of speeches, and are thus more difficult for organizational administrators to manage.

Research organizations have to protect the security of their data and communication as well. The scientific and popular press have reported many incidents in which research organizations were forced to spend a great deal of time and money reconstructing files or file structures destroyed by computer viruses (Parker, 1983; McCain, 1987; Markoff, 1988b). Scientific networks may be particularly vulnerable to security breaches, due to the variety of users on the networks and scientists' needs for the widest possible access. The many benefits of electronic networks in science cannot be achieved if basic levels of security cannot be assured (National Research Council, 1988b).

Effects on Productivity

Pelz and Andrews (1976) found that scientists with more than average communication with colleagues were also the most productive scientists, even when organizational level was eliminated as a mitigating factor. It is reasonable to expect that any technology that makes communication easier will, therefore, improve productivity. Few researchers have demonstrated these improvements, however, partially because there are so many difficulties involved in measuring the productivity of scientists. Morell (undated) pointed out that what counts as quality varies from field to field and that social and psychological factors affect assessments of quality. It is also hard to assign economic value to factors like "increased contact with colleagues" and "faster turnaround of documents." The most obvious savings are seen in networks used to share remote facilities that are too expensive to be kept locally -- special printers and plotters, complex simulation equipment, large databases, supercomputers, etc. However, a few studies have attempted to quantify savings as a result of electronic networks.

In an assessment of a database of energy information for the U.S. Department of Energy, researchers assigned dollar values to estimated savings in time and equipment that resulted from having the information online. They suggested that the Department of Energy, by spending almost $6 million on the database, would yield a return of about $13 billion in savings to scientists and engineers who used the system (Department of Energy and King Research, 1982). In a study of electronic mail at a large computer manufacturing firm, managers estimated that using electronic mail saved them about seven hours per week by speeding up decision making (Crawford, 1982). Managers at a large financial information-processing company estimated that electronic mail saved them about three hours per week because they did not have to spend so much time playing telephone tag (Nyce and Groppa, 1983).

Effects on Scholarly Disciplines and Science as a Whole

Speculation about the effects of electronic networks on scholarly disciplines and science as a whole build upon the experience and opinions of experienced researchers and science administrators, and not usually on quantitative analyses.

Faster Advancements of Science

Some commentators have suggested that electronic networks have helped improve the efficiency and effectiveness of research activities, and are thus hastening scientific advancements (Brown, 1986). Researchers who used electronic networks and facsimile machines to help coordinate replication of Fleischmann and Pons' cold-fusion experiments, for example, were able to come to their scientific conclusions more quickly as a result of the technology (Markoff, 1989).

By linking researchers with engineers and developers, electronic networks might also be shortening the time lapse between scientific discovery and commercial development. The MOSIS system, for example, allows students and faculty to telemanufacture their designs for very large integrated circuits. Not only does this provide a valuable learning experience, but it also allows for the production of VLSI chips in a fraction of the time formerly required (Brown, 1986). Especially in the computer science and networking industries, government's investment in network research has led to great strides in commercial applications (Jennings et al., 1986).

Improved Access to Scientific Discussions

Electronic networks make it easier for scientists to communicate, and thus make it likely that scientists will have wider circles of colleagues (Branscomb, 1986). International networks, for example, are bringing researchers in contact with colleagues in other countries, which can lead to fruitful sharing of perspectives and/or to threats to U.S. competitiveness (Schrage, 1986).

There is mixed opinion as to whether electronic networks are breaking down barriers to participation in leading-edge scientific inquiry. A few of the studies reviewed in the section on "Effects on Individual Researchers and Research Groups" suggested that the absence of some contextual cues in electronic communication makes it more democratic, reducing race, sex, and status differences. In addition, the ability to access facilities remotely makes it more likely that researchers in smaller or under-funded institutions could participate in cutting-edge debates. Some of the research on the processes by which "invisible colleges" sustain and reproduce themselves challenged these claims, however, pointing out that access to the technological means of communication does not automatically break down other social, political, and economic barriers.

Increased Collaboration Across Disciplines

Wulf (1988) and Lederberg and Uncapher (1989) suggested the establishment of "collaboratories," electronic research institutions that would bring scientists together to work on joint problems in an interdisciplinary context. Electronic networks make it easier to establish links with researchers in other disciplines, but probably do not ameliorate some of the other barriers: divergent research histories and literatures, different vocabularies, and unfamiliar research procedures. Use of bulletin boards and computer conferences, however, brings scientists in contact with researchers from other disciplines, making possible the kind of informal communication that Kraut, Egido, and Galegher (1990) have found is a prelude to collaboration.

Changes in the Types of Research Undertaken

The rapid development of more powerful computers, and the electronic networks that make those computers accessible, allows scientists to explore research questions that were heretofore intractable (National Academy of Sciences, 1989; Congressional Research Service, 1986; Gerola and Gomory, 1984). For example, computers can monitor natural events remotely and generate graphic simulations that help bring the vast amounts of data within human comprehensibility. There is some disagreement over whether the new technologies are changing the questions that scientists ask, or are merely making existing questions easier to answer (Shields, in press).

Blurring of the Traditional Distinction Between Theoretical and Empirical

The fact that empirical observation is theory-laden is well recognized, but the explosion in computing power and the ability to use electronic networks and high-resolution graphics displays is further blurring the traditional distinction between theory and empirical observation (Brown, 1986; Branscomb, 1986). Scientific instruments and computer simulations are extending "experiments" beyond the merely empirical, with much of the "data" being provided from simulators based on particular theories.

New Forms of Information Dissemination

Scholarly publications and professional conferences play a central role in the maintenance of scientific communities and the progression of scientific thinking. Electronic networks make new forms of publication and communication possible, including electronic journals and computer conferences (Markoff, 1989; Congressional Research Service, 1986; Hiltz and Turoff, 1978). These could shorten the time between submission and publication, thereby making current reports more generally available.

The wider access to ongoing debates allowed by electronic media pose corresponding problems – information overload and a lack of quality control (Congressional Research Service, 1986; Lederberg, 1978). Refereed and unrefereed electronic journals are likely to supplement existing print journals even as researchers are struggling with information overload. Gelman claimed that news groups on the Internet produced about 4 million characters of new material a day in 1988, or about five average books. He also offered commentary on Internet traffic from two knowledgeable observers (1988, p. C1):

'You couldn't possibly read it all,' said James E. Cottrell III, a networking guru at the National Institute of Science and Technology. Then again, said Harvard's Clifford Stoll, you wouldn't want to: '90 percent of it is complete and utter trash.'

As scientific debates go online, will systems administrators or facilitators take the role of gatekeepers? If there are not gatekeepers of some sort, users will have to develop means of dealing with the overload, or the networks may prove to be too time-consuming for some users (Hiltz and Turoff, 1978).

Decreased Control Over Research Results

The ease of disseminating information electronically challenges existing norms about ownership and control of one's ideas and research results (Office of Technology Assessment, 1987). Tombaugh (1984), evaluating a scientific computer conference, found that 64% of the scientists felt that most participants were unwilling to share their ideas, and that 51% were reluctant to contribute information to the open conference. Crystallographers have exhibited a somewhat similar reluctance. Although a database has been set up to share information about DNA structures once they have been published, less than half of the published structures have actually been deposited in the database (Barinaga, 1989).

Reluctance to share information arises from several practical concerns. Publication and patenting have traditionally been the processes by which scientists' ideas are transferred to the greater scientific community, and recognition of scientific contributions is validated in publication and patenting. Scientists are then rewarded according to their publication and patent records. Because electronic publication is not yet recognized as a legitimate publication, scientists worry that they will not get credit for their ideas if they share them on public electronic networks. Even once findings have been published, the increased commercial significance of some sorts of data make scientists or their sponsoring institutions less willing to share that data publicly (Barinaga, 1989).

Increased Administrative and Political Burdens of Scientific Research

For the last several decades, commentators have been watching the rising costs and administrative burdens of large research projects and warning of their potential ill effects on the conduct of scientific research. According to Hagstrom (1965, p. 142):

Organizational activities lead to deviation from the norms of scientific conduct: articles are planned before findings are arrived at, the same findings are reported in several places, and trivial findings are given exaggerated importance.

While electronic networks certainly did not cause the increased cost of scientific research, their use (and attendant costs) are one element of today's "big science." Using the example of sharing particle accelerators in the 1960s, Hagstrom showed how scientists were forced to compete for scarce resources. This did not always lead to the most deserving projects getting the most accelerator time, because many nontechnical factors determined the outcome of the competition (Hagstrom, 1965). A similar situation is likely to emerge as scientists compete for access to electronic networks and the remote facilities to which they provide connections (Remington, 1988).

It is also likely that some scientists will have to pick up the increased administrative burden that will come with access to research networks. Records will be needed for charge-back and evaluation purposes, facilities will have to be allocated, and relations with other institutions and network coordinators will have to be maintained. To the extent that scientists become involved in these support activities, their time for research and information dissemination will be diminished.

Summary

The literature on the effects of electronic networks on science reveals a range of perspectives, methods, and findings. Sociologists of science show that the culture of science is structured into disciplines and tiers of notoriety and responsibility. Scientific and administrative practices -- tenure decisions, publication processes, funding systems, etc. -- serve to maintain disciplinary and status boundaries while remaining flexible to allow for change. Although most scientists share some underlying norms, values, and research practices, there is a great deal of variety among and within scientific disciplines, communities, and institutions.

Electronic networks are improving scientists' productivity by making their communication more efficient. Electronic communication can widen access to scientific discussions by allowing researchers to form more social ties and be members of more groups within and outside their organizations. These improvements, however, may be offset by problems of quality control and information overload. Use of electronic networks is also bringing one of the traditional norms of science, that of free and open exchange of ideas, into conflict with other concerns: national security, protection of proprietary information, and protection of data integrity.

Electronic communication (such as electronic mail and bulletin boards) that eliminates some social cues makes interactions more "democratic," with users displaying fewer status differences and participating more equally in decision making. The lack of social cues also appears to make some communicators more abrasive and irresponsible, however. Evidence of irresponsibility may be a result of inexperience or lack of identification with one's online partners. As users become more experienced with electronic networks and services, the ways that they use the systems change. They begin to see themselves as members of online communities. They also adopt more active information search and manipulation strategies, and use networks for more group-oriented communication.

Some of users' online communication is informal and non-task-related, and these interactions cement collaborative relationships and sometimes yield unexpected, task-related information. Online communication supplements face-to-face communication in most cases, and will probably not substitute for face-to-face interactions, especially in the developmental stages of collaborative relationships. Online communities are not likely to threaten users' loyalties to their traditional organizations, either, although they could make it more difficult for organizations to manage the flow of proprietary information and maintain internal security.

Technical access to electronic networks -- including factors like connectivity, ability to pay, and reliability -- is a necessary but not sufficient condition for network use. Sufficient conditions for use include the solution of several social/organizational issues, such as policies for data sharing, ensuring the quality of information, and promoting participation. Researchers who communicate electronically sometimes show a reluctance to share data. They also face difficulties in cataloging data for future use, and often lack adequate time and skills for database management and maintenance. Researchers who use networks to share remote facilities sometimes find it difficult to know what is available remotely, to establish online connectivity, and to locate documentation and live help.

The literature on electronic networks in science is not well integrated, and there is a need for further research that uses already-gathered empirical evidence to bolster and challenge the macro-level commentaries. In addition, there is very little research on how scientists are actually using electronic networks, yet such information is crucial if operational and policy decisions about science networks are to be made. For example, more studies are needed of online communities that cut across organizational boundaries. Studies are needed of scientists' time spent online, the services they access, the types of people they contact, and what they are accomplishing with that time. Case studies are also needed of scientists who are using networks to share remote facilities.

IMPLICATIONS FOR NETWORK DESIGN, MANAGEMENT, AND OPERATING POLICIES

The wide-ranging and sometimes conflicting research results reviewed in the first part of this chapter suggest that electronic networks will have positive and negative effects on the ways that scientists work and on the processes of science as a whole. Networks will make it easier for scientists to communicate with their peers, but may also cause them to be more cautious about the types of information they share. Networks will encourage the formation of groups of researchers with common interests, which could lead to more fruitful collaborations or to such a glut of information that scientists are forced to retreat from participation. The ability to collaborate with distant peers will probably hasten scientific advancement, but will raise new management and administrative challenges.

One potential value of these research findings is that they point to possible impacts of electronic networks while there is still time to affect those impacts. It is difficult to translate these findings into recommendations for how networks should be designed and managed, however, for several reasons:

- The research results are somewhat sketchy, scattered over a number of research topics and settings.
- Most of the findings are descriptive, and give little prescriptive guidance.
- Many of the studies provide snapshot characterizations of impacts, rather than longitudinal evidence.
- There is not a well-developed body of research specifically on scientific users of networks, and it is hard to know how those users compare to users in nonscience settings.

With these caveats in mind, this section will examine the implications of the research findings for network design, management, and operating policies. It will show that the demands on network managers and designers go far beyond technical and operational functions. They are more and more involved with questions of organizational design; management of relations with user institutions, scientific bodies, other networks, and government agencies; and policy setting.

In some cases, the challenges raised by electronic networks can be solved with "technological fixes" such as better tools for database searching or new encryption methods. More often, however, it appears that the "fixes" will be organizational and behavioral in nature, requiring fact-finding, negotiation, and compromise among the interested parties. Thus, network design and management have evolved into executive-level planning functions, similar to the evolution of financial management in previous decades.

Network Characteristics

A range of network characteristics will affect the degree to which electronic communication is an effective process as the proposed NREN is established. These characteristics include the following.

Connectivity and Interoperability

If electronic networks are to become a basic mode of communication for scientists, electronic connections will have to be ubiquitous and transparent. The nature of the network connections required will depend upon how they are to be used. For occasional file transfers or use of remote facilities, researchers are likely to be willing to invest some time in establishing connections and learning to use unfamiliar software. For everyday communication, like that required for research collaborations, however, scientists should be able to use their computer terminals as easily as they use the telephone. Electronic addresses should be readily available, and connections should appear seamless to the user. Penetration of electronic networks into other user communities has to increase so that users can assume that they will be able to make connections with any particular person they know of or hear about.

To attain this level of interconnectivity, network planners will have to continue their standardization and interconnection efforts. While most scientists at top research universities now have at least some level of access to computer networks, there are many universities and colleges and other institutions that have not yet been wired or that are not connected to a national network. As long as attention is focused on building higher-capacity connections among research universities, the benefits of a universal electronic network will not be realized.

As connections become prevalent enough that lack of electronic connections is not a barrier to access research facilities or scientific information, the interoperability of networks will also be improved.

This will require more standardization and/or translation between systems, especially in the human interfaces necessary to access remote facilities. Directory services will also be needed so scientists can find colleagues' electronic mail addresses. Using remote facilities should eventually become as easy, or easier, than going to the library to get information.

Capabilities

Use Tracking. Because science networks will be used by researchers from many different institutions, and with funding from a variety of sources, it may be necessary to keep track of who is using particular network resources. This information will be useful in planning network upgrades and the introduction of new services, and in tracing unauthorized uses. It could also be incorporated into a cost charge-back system to users. The gathering of use information will raise privacy issues, depending in part on the nature and level of detail of the information collected.

Access Control. Access to scientific networks will have to be controlled, and the levels of control and the means by which control is effected will have to be decided by network users and managers. Here the goal of opening access to the networks as much as possible comes into conflict with other pressures: the need to protect users' privacy and proprietary data, the need to share costs of the network fairly among users, the need to optimize network resources by planning and managing use, and the need to maintain the overall viability of the network in the face of security threats. The technical and operational ability to maintain access controls will be an important factor in scientists' willingness to use science networks.

User-Defined Resources. Scientists' uses of electronic networks vary from occasional electronic mail messages to huge projects involving the remote gathering and processing of data files with real-time graphic representations of output. There is likely to be demand, therefore, for dynamic allocation of networking resources, such that scientists can call upon (and pay for) network resources only when they use them. Such dynamic allocation will be most useful if the amount of time between requests and allocation, and the administrative tasks required to get access, are minimal.

Users should also be able to define features of the network to fit their specific needs. A basic set of network features and capacity, to which all users will be given access, is needed. The network can then provide additional features, and the means to alter those features, that users can choose to use. Such choice will allow the networks to fulfill the needs of a variety of users and will allow users' complements of features to evolve as their experience with networks grows.

Applications and Services

Network applications and services should assist scientists by:

- Making their electronic collaborations as easy as possible, as well as supporting their face-to-face interactions
- Supporting the social dimension of collaborations as well as the task dimension
- Helping them deal with information overload
- Making it easier for them to disseminate information electronically
- Giving them new means of controlling the dissemination of their ideas, and of tracking how and where their ideas are used
- Being responsive to the evolving needs of users as they become more experienced.

A few such applications have already been mentioned. The "Cruiser" attempts to provide spontaneous electronic interactions by allowing researchers to scan the halls, offices, and meeting spots of remote colleagues (Root, 1988). "Intelligent assistants" are software devices that filter users' incoming electronic messages and that eventually might go out into users' electronic environments looking for relevant information. With their complete record of past entries, computer conferences make it easier for users to trace the origins of group ideas. As the use of hypermedia becomes more common, there might be ways of keeping links between ideas and their origins, thereby establishing responsibility and credit for ideas as they evolve (Louie and Rubeck, 1989; Lederberg, 1978).

Training, Support, Documentation, and Facilitation

Means of supporting scientists as they use electronic networks should be considered as one of the networks' essential design elements. Because users will be of varying levels of sophistication, there will have to be help at a number of different levels. The need for well-written documentation, online help, and real-time user support is obvious, although it is often forgotten, especially when the user population is made up of sophisticated technicians. In some instances, scientists have had to do their own share of computer programming to make electronic networks work for them, especially in the remote use of sophisticated equipment. As the user community expands to include less experienced computer and network users, networks will have to provide new levels of support.

If network applications and support can be developed so that users will need minimal computing skills to access facilities remotely, scientists will be able to concentrate on their research tasks rather than on network problems. Building online help and problem diagnosis software are steps toward this goal, but it is unlikely that there will be a good substitute for experienced human help for some time. Networks can make it easy for inexperienced users to find and get help from experienced users, and support software could make it easier for experienced users to help newcomers.

Communities of scientific users will probably manage their own online discussions, but administrative procedures, tools, and training will be helpful in assisting these communities. This support can rest on top of individual support and could include guidance on planning new computer conferences, organizing a research community online, getting funding for particular applications, and maintaining and managing resources once they are in place.

Network Management

Another set of factors that have to be considered regarding the overall effectiveness of the proposed NREN are managerial and organizational in nature. These include the following.

Management and Decision-Making Structure

Many kinds of people and institutions will be involved in the design, use, and administration of electronic networks for science: scientists, students, science administrators, policy analysts, bureaucrats, network designers and technicians, schools, industrial research organizations, equipment manufacturers, software developers, government bodies, and professional associations. There is a great deal of variety within each of these categories. Setting up network management and decision-making structures that can adequately represent all of these constituen-

cies and still get anything done will be extremely difficult (Yavarkovsky, 1989).

The literature reviewed earlier gives little guidance as to how to set up a viable network management structure, except to caution that potential network users should be well-represented in the decision-making process (National Academy of Sciences, 1989). Research on organizational design and development is needed that would more directly address this challenge, as would research on implementation and planning processes.

Planning Network Evolution and New Services

The evolution of networks and the planning of new services will depend upon the goals with which network managers approach these tasks. Possible goals for scientific networks include: improving the efficiency of scientists (to attain faster advances, national competitiveness, or national security); leveraging scientific expenditures by providing access to shared scientific resources; equalizing opportunities across the research and education spectrum; and promoting upgrades of the communication facilities of the nation as a whole (by serving as a working demonstration and testbed).

A central question in considering network upgrades and new services concerns the categories of users to receive attention. Much of the activity regarding science networks concentrates on scientists and administrators in a rather small set of prestigious research institutions and industrial research firms. A quick glance at proceedings of networking conferences, Congressional hearings on science networks, or lists of recent National Science Foundation funding for network research tends to confirm this. While it is logical to assume that the prestigious universities and industrial labs are doing the best work on science networks, it is also reasonable to suspect that this research, especially when it bleeds into policy setting, network planning, and funding, might tend to focus on the needs of researchers in such leading institutions. Special attention to the needs of other potential users, including students, administrators, and teaching-oriented academicians, is also needed.

Arranging for Funding

The literature offers little guidance regarding potential funding of science networks. It does indicate that networks could make scientists more efficient, and therefore more productive, which provides an economic argument for the support of electronic networks. It also suggests that networks offer scientists the opportunity to interact in new ways and to carry out research heretofore impossible, making scientists not only more efficient, but more effective. Actually quantifying these benefits, however, is difficult and may be unreliable.

Operations Management

Electronic networks vary in their operational structure from networks with centralized management to decentralized networks in which each participating node handles a portion of the technical and administrative burdens. The strengths and weaknesses of potential users can constrain the options for a network's structure: If users (or their institutions) are technically proficient and willing to assume some technical and administrative tasks, for example, a decentralized approach is more viable than if users have little or no computer background.

The literature gives little guidance on the day-to-day operations of electronic networks for scientists, other than that scientists would prefer those operations to be as cheap and transparent as possible without compromising network viability, integrity, and security (National Research Council, 1988b). The discussion of operating policies below describes these characteristics in more detail.

Coordinating with User Institutions

The effectiveness with which network managers coordinate services with users and user institutions will be a key determinant of the success of science networks. Organizational fit, or the degree to which technical innovations are adapted to the circumstances of their implementing organization, is achievable only if network managers and users maintain an ongoing relationship of assessment, planning, and problem solving (Markus, 1983). The better that users' task demands, organizational position, and sociocultural circumstances are understood, the more likely it is that electronic networks and services can be established that will fit users' needs.

Electronic networks may change the way scientists work, which could have significant impacts for scientific institutions. For example, electronic networks will make it easier to maintain collaborative relationships with remote colleagues, and to share remote facilities. This could lead to strains on traditional means of funding and allocating costs to scientific projects, as it becomes more and more difficult to sort out which overhead costs are being used and borne by particular institutions. Increased remote collaboration will also make it harder for institutions to control the information flowing back and forth across their borders; for industrial research organizations, this will make it more difficult to protect proprietary data.

Coordination between network managers and user institutions can help address such problems as they arise. In some cases, there may be technical solutions, such as new means of data encryption. It is more likely, however, that compromises will have to be made -- that aspects of the network and of the organizations that are using it will have to change. The more that network managers can predict possible unforeseen effects of electronic networks and prepare their users for these consequences, the more likely it is that the network will be used productively.

Coordinating Network Design with Scientific Organizations

The literature indicates that networks are not only serving the institutions in which scientists work, but are also serving the larger scientific community. Scientific networks support research disciplines and interdisciplinary research, and coordination with these groups is needed. It is often at the level of the scientific discipline, perhaps through a professional association, that the decision is made to establish a shared resource, such as a database or electronic directory. Network managers will have to coordinate with representatives of the discipline in setting up such systems, and are likely to get involved in their nontechnical questions regarding access, security, data integrity, etc. As the applications evolve, network managers will be part of the process of planning new services.

Coordinating Network Design With Other Networks

Networks will require coordination among an increasingly large circle of network managers, as more and more networks are interconnected. Managers face common questions regarding access, security, standards, capacity, etc. They will also be responsible for facilitating remote use of facilities on their local system, which will probably require preparing documentation and providing help for users from other institutions. This may entail a change in the conception of local network management, from a local sense of responsibility to a national or international one.

Coordinating Network Design With Government Policy Makers and Funders

Electronic networks have policy implications that will draw network managers into contact with policy makers and government funders. For example, worries about the ability of electronic networks to protect users' data, or about the possibility that foreigners will gain valuable information and use it to the detriment of United States competitiveness, could limit the funding, use, or growth of networks if adequate solutions are not offered. Network planners will also play a role in government initiatives to promote or build science networks, which should help them have an impact on the policies that will, in turn, influence them.

Operating Policies

Many of the points in the preceding sections ultimately raise questions of operating policy. This section looks at four such policies, outlining some of the goals of these policies and problems that require resolution.

Access

Perhaps the most significant policy question regarding networks is the issue of access. To make the networks most useful for scientific collaboration and to hasten the advancement of science as a whole, the pool of participating scientists should be as large as possible. However, resource constraints and privacy and security concerns are limiting factors, dictating that difficult decisions will have to be made about who can gain access to specific networks.

If the goal of a specific network is to support scientists in a particular discipline, there are likely to be difficulties in defining the boundaries of that discipline and in determining which scientists are most in need of electronic support. If the goal is to hasten cutting-edge research advances, it is likely that individuals at teaching colleges, community colleges, and high schools will not be given priority in access. If

the goal is to speed up technology transfer, connections among universities, industrial labs, and manufacturing firms will have to be set up. These examples raise questions about funding sources and control of proprietary information, especially if government funds are being used to support the network or the research. Defense-related research raises even more problems because of security issues.

Many conflicts arise when considering policies for access to scientific networks. The research literature gives little guidance on how to resolve this issue, other than to point out the benefits of wide access and to highlight the cultural norm within science for open, unconstrained debate.

Charging For Services

How users are charged for access to and use of electronic networks helps determine how those networks are used. Planners will have to set rates for the various services available and decide the degree to which charges will be use-sensitive. If users are forced to be cost-conscious when deciding whether to use the network, especially for everyday uses like sending electronic mail or posting to computer conferences, it is likely that the services will suffer from lack of users or that only the most well-funded users will be able to participate.

Setting up a cost charge-back system that pays for system operations is likely to be further complicated by the funding mechanisms prevalent in scientific research. Network operations could be included in institutional overhead; such an approach would spread costs over a wide set of potential users, but might also disadvantage those not likely to use the system. Applications that make significant demands on network resources may necessitate some means of tracking use and charging back to specific researchers or research budgets. This function is not common in existing networks. Such a costing system not only raises access and fairness questions, but also privacy issues. Many users will be uncomfortable with a system that could track or trace their system use.

Security

Determining appropriate levels of network security involves tradeoffs between the cost and convenience of using the network, on the one hand, and the desire to protect information, on the other.

Users are likely to have somewhat different security needs, depending upon the nature of their work. However, the security of the entire system depends upon the security of its weakest link, so some minimum degree of security will have to be maintained throughout the system. When networks connect researchers in university dorm rooms, industrial laboratories, defense research centers, and government office buildings, it is difficult to establish security procedures that will satisfy, and be followed by, all users. The problem is exacerbated by the existence of dial-in ports and remote log-in capabilities, essential for collaboration and resource sharing, but a bane to security maintenance.

New technologies provide some assistance in this problem. New means of encrypting data, authenticating messages, and tracking unauthorized users provide some tools for implementing security policies that meet the varying needs of users (Parker, 1983). Perhaps more important, however, is the need to inculcate good security habits in network users so that susceptibility to misuse is reduced and losses, if they occur, are minimal.

Resource Sharing

Responsibility for coordinating the sharing of online resources, such as databases, computers, graphics displays, and other research equipment, may fall to network managers or to user groups. In either case, guidelines for the users' responsibilities will have to be established and enforced.

The maintenance of a centralized research database provides a good example. The database will be of most value to users if the data included are complete, verified, correctly catalogued, and well documented. The difficulties that crystalographers have had getting their colleagues to "donate" their data to a centralized database illustrates one problem: Users can be reluctant to share data, especially if the data have potential commercial value. Even if users are willing to share, a mechanism is needed to clean up donated data and prepare them for entry into the database. This is especially difficult if there is no agreement on how the data should be characterized and catalogued. Facilities and funding are necessary to keep up with contributions, especially in databases whose information is time-sensitive (National Academy of Sciences, 1978). Maintaining scientific databases and other such shared facilities requires skilled professional attention that is not likely to be within the

purview of most users, and subject expertise not typically found within the purview of most network managers.

SUMMARY

As suggested by the literature, the critical issues for network success are broader than those of technical network management. Many of the implications outlined above will be of special concern to users, science administrators, scientific leaders, and policy makers. The findings that online communication is more "democratic," or that online decision makers tend to make more risky decisions, for example, are probably going to be of more interest to managers in research organizations than to network managers. The possibility that electronic networks will further blur the distinction between the theoretical and the empirical in research is probably most interesting to philosophers of science. The research communities in some fields may be getting so far removed from actual empirical observation that they risk rendering themselves incapable of hearing when the empirical world tries to "talk back" to them. This could be a problem for those worried about the progress and viability of science, but it would tell a network manager little or nothing about how to build or run a network.

The implications also suggest that the most pressing problems for network managers, science administrators, and policy makers will be organizational in nature. Guidance on these problems is less likely to come from the technology impacts research reviewed here than from organizational studies of implementation, innovation, decision making, and organization design. While much of this literature does not consider technology, it does study the organizing processes and could help in understanding how scientific institutions and their members will adapt to electronic networks.

This discussion also suggests that the demands on network managers are so wide-ranging that the skills required for successful network management are beyond a traditional technical background. Network management is evolving into an organizational planning and coordination as well as technical function. Science administrators and policy makers will have to prepare network managers and give them the latitude and resources to deal with the multi-faceted challenges they will face.

IMPACT OF NETWORKS ON RESEARCH: RESULTS FROM AN EMPIRICAL STUDY

CHAPTER 6

As shown in previous chapters, much attention has been devoted recently to the Federal government's plans for the development of a three-gigabit-per-second National Research and Education Network (NREN). Such a network is envisioned as an electronic highway connecting researchers to each other and to computerized research tools. The government's rationale for this investment in the country's information technology infrastructure rests on projected increases in the efficiency of and return on investment from R&D in the United States and on anticipated improvements in technology transfer. The ultimate aim is to improve national competitiveness and the national welfare. Most government initiatives related to the NREN, however, focus on resolving technical problems and issues, giving little or no attention to social and behavioral issues that will have an important impact on the eventual adoption and use of the network.

There is little empirical evidence, for example, about how many researchers are regular users of the existing national network structure, what the vast majority of researchers use networks for, and about how networks affect R&D work. Few investigations have focused on both "high-profile" and other users of electronic research networks or on identifying the problems and issues faced by scientists and engineers who are network users or potential users.

This chapter reports on the authors' recently completed study of the impact of high-speed networks on scientific communication and research, which was sponsored by the U.S. Congress, Office of Technology Assessment. The study was exploratory and involved 136 subjects. The perspective taken in this study is that implementation of a national research network should not proceed according to technical specifications alone but should take into account the particular communication behaviors, information use patterns, and work environment of researchers.

The study sought answers to three research questions:

1. Are claims that networks change the modus operandi of researchers correct?
2. What evidence exists that networks have changed basic patterns of scientific communication?
3. What problems or issues do network users face?

Answers to these questions provide a basis for increased understanding of the role of a national research network and for policy recommendations that will increase the effectiveness of such a network.

The overall goal of the study was to help frame a strategy for national network design, implementation, and management. Thus, it combined policy research with empirical social science research methods: empirical data on the use of electronic networks by researchers were used to formulate policy recommendations. The study is also intended to demonstrate the richness and utility of qualitative data for the study of network use and for network policy analysis.

The research process and its epistemological foundations are relatively well understood (see, for example, Kaplan, 1964; and Kerlinger, 1986). The same is true for the process of scholarly communication (see, for example, Osburn, 1989; Garvey, 1979; and Crane, 1972). Substantial empirical research has been done on the behavior of information seekers and users, in general (see, for example, Saracevic et al., 1988; Saracevic and Kantor, 1988a, b; Belkin, Oddy, and Brooks, 1982; MacMullin and Taylor, 1984; Dervin and Nilan, 1986; and Taylor, 1986), on information needs and habits of scientists, scholars, and engineers, specifically (see, for example, Garvey, 1979; Federal Council for Science and Technology, 1965; Allen, 1985; Hagstrom, 1965; and Poole, 1985), and on the use of computer-mediated communication by people in a variety of settings (see Chapters 4 and 5). But there are few empirical studies that combine these perspectives to investigate the use of electronic networks by researchers (Hiltz, 1984; Feldman, 1987; and Foulger, 1990, are some exceptions). It is still unclear how the introduction of high-speed data communication networks has affected the research process and communication among researchers.

Network policy issues raised by study participants are discussed further in Chapter 8 and recommendations are presented in 9 (also see Parkhurst, 1990). The importance of the study reported in this chapter lies in its application of evidence gathered from network users to the analysis of major policy issues involved in the planning and implementation of a national research and education network. It represents one part of a small, but growing, effort toward assessing the significance of electronic networks for scholarly communication and research and toward considering policy strategies to promote the most effective and beneficial utilization of these networks.

STUDY DESIGN

For the purposes of the study, a research network was defined as any local- or wide-area electronic communications network used by researchers to exchange ideas or to conduct and disseminate the results of their work. A "researcher" was defined as a scientist, engineer, student, or other member of a team involved in R&D work in any social, behavioral, clinical, physical, computational, biological, or engineering discipline.

Methodological approaches to the study of computer-mediated communication systems (CMCS) have been reviewed by a number of authors and are summarized in Chapters 4 and 5. A variety of techniques have been used to investigate the uses and impacts of electronic networks. These include traditional social science methods such as case studies, interviews, and surveys, along with methods that rely on the information technology involved to collect and analyze data: the content analysis of network messages, the use of networks to distribute electronic questionnaires, and the analysis of network transaction logs to determine individuals' network use and the sociometric structure of communication networks. This study employed several of these data collection techniques.

The research questions suggested a two-phased methodological approach: (1) obtaining descriptive information (with surveys, questionnaires, and interviews or focus groups) about network use and the impacts of networks on scientific research and communication, and (2) analyzing that descriptive information in light of various policy issues. Multiple data collection strategies were used to collect descriptive, experiential, and evaluative data from researchers in different organizational settings. The data collected were largely qualitative, with the group discussions and interviews providing the richest data. Qualitative data were collected for several reasons. First, high-speed communication networks are relatively new, and users' behavior and needs patterns have not yet been firmly established, making traditional user studies inappropriate. Johnston (1989, pp. 494, 495) cites several other advantages of semi-structured interviews for studying CMCS:

> New technological capabilities constantly change the very character of CMCS and, therefore, its meaning for users. Even with stable systems, CMCS provide new ways of

communicating for users, and increasing use has the potential to alter users' entire conception of what communication is all about . . . . [T]he insights that came from some of the extended interviews captured dimensions of meaning that were unanticipated by the researchers at the beginning of the study.

Many CMCS studies rely on methods that produce purely quantitative data, such as that collected in surveys or transaction logs. These data are useful for describing certain aspects of network use but can fail to explain the meaning that a new technology has for a given community. In addition, anecdotal evidence is traditionally used in the context of policy analysis to give policy makers a better understanding of the views of particular stakeholder groups.

As noted in S. 1067 (Congress, Senate, 1989b) and H.R. 3131 (Congress, House, 1989b) of the 101st Congress, research networks serve to link researchers within and among at least three important settings:

- Private industry
- Academia
- Federal laboratories.

To understand the full and varied impact of networks on individual researchers and on science in general, the study investigated the impacts of networks in each of these different settings. While such settings have similarities, it was anticipated that each setting might also exhibit different network configurations and features, generate different issues, and be subject to different barriers to successful network implementation and use. One of the most difficult tasks in the development and implementation of a national network will be balancing the interests and concerns of these three major constituencies.

Within these three settings, data on the experiences and perceptions of several different populations are important: researchers who exhibit intensive use of networks, researchers who exhibit less intensive use of networks, and network managers. Both seasoned and novice network users were studied. Network users contributed their own "before and after" anecdotes about the impact of networks. Discussions with novice users served to balance the seasoned users' claims and provided clues to the barriers faced by all but the most technically-proficient researchers in the use of networks. Network managers were included in the study because they are an important source of descriptive data about network features, policies, and management issues. They also provided important information about trends in the evolution of research networks.

DATA COLLECTION ACTIVITIES

Figure 6-1 presents an overview of the study's data collection activities. It depicts the major facets of the research design. Data collection occurred during June-August 1989. The major data collection activities undertaken were focus groups, interviews, and mail and online surveys. These are described below.

As a preliminary activity, the study team arranged on-site meetings with network managers in each of the three sectors to be represented in the study: academia, the private sector, and a Federal laboratory. These meetings allowed the study team to assess the feasibility and desirability of conducting group data collection activities at these sites. They also allowed the study team to gather background data on the organizational climate and the technological environment of each site.

Focus Groups and Group Interview

The study relied heavily on focus groups for data collection. Focus groups are group discussions that center on topics of particular concern to both the participants in the group and the researcher. The researcher typically takes the role of moderator, and participants discuss a particular topic among themselves. Focus groups are currently used most often to conduct market research, although the technique has its origins in sociology.

The Focus Group Technique

Morgan (1988, p. 18) notes that "one advantage of group interviewing is that the participants' interaction among themselves replaces their interaction with the interviewer, leading to a greater emphasis on participants' points of view." Morgan, referring to Bellenger, also comments that "the give-and-take of interaction leads to . . . spontaneous responses from participants as well as producing a fairly high level of participant involvement" (pp. 17-18). In addition, focus groups possess a number of practical advantages: they are

Figure 6-1. Overview of Data Collection Activities

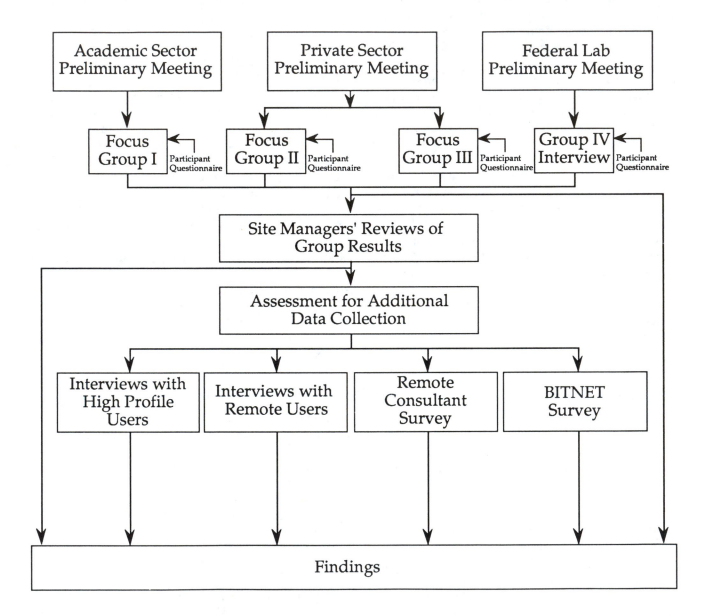

relatively easy to conduct and require minimal expenditures of time and money.

Focus groups can be used either as a self-contained technique or, as in this study, in conjunction with other data collection and analysis techniques such as individual interviewing, site observations, modeling, and surveys. The primary intent of focus groups is to promote self-disclosure, and "the permissive environment gives individuals license to divulge emotions that often do not emerge in other forms of questioning" (Krueger, 1988, p. 23). Another strength of focus groups is that the discussion and interactive format allows the respondents to define those topics and issues that are important to them. Because the study relied on gathering data about respondents' perceptions and experiences, it would have been counterproductive to constrain the freedom of respondents to direct the flow of the discussion. Therefore, the moderator tended to introduce general topics for discussion rather than pose specific questions to the focus group participants.

Selection of Group Sites and Participants

Based on the study's research questions and preliminary visits at a number of possible sites, the study team decided to collect data from the following groups[1]:

Group I: Researchers at an academic institution who regularly used local- and wide-area networks for "advanced" activities such as file transfer and supercomputer access. This institution is also the site of one of the national supercomputing centers.

Group II: Researchers at a private-sector R&D site who have limited experience with advanced information technologies and used local- and wide-area networks infrequently, primarily for electronic mail.

Group III: Researchers at the same private sector site who regularly use local- and wide-area networks for advanced activities.

Group IV: Managers at a Federal laboratory site who sit on a committee to plan for the development and integration of networks used by all staff at the laboratory.

Procedures for the identification and recruitment of individual participants were unique to each site. All potential participants in the three focus groups were briefed about the nature of the study and about why and how they were chosen to participate.

Group Discussion Topics

The topics introduced in the group discussions aimed to gather data about the impact of networks on scientific research and communication, existing network features, barriers to successful network use, and future scenarios for network and policy development. Questions were designed to stimulate group discussion and were modified to be appropriate for the characteristics of each particular group. Individual questions were grouped into discussion areas and proceeded from the general to the specific. In this way, participants were given every opportunity to raise various issues and points on their own and the moderators were able to pursue important, unexpected trails that emerged within each discussion topic.

The general discussion topics that were introduced with each focus group were:

- How do you use networks in connection with your research?
- How would you describe the impact of networks on the way you do research? At which stage of the research process do particular network functions have an impact?
- How would you characterize the impact of networks on your experiences with scholarly communication, both formal and informal?
- Have you or your colleagues experienced any barriers or problems in connection with network use?
- What recommendations can you offer about the future development of networks? How should they be managed? How can the problems you noted be solved?

The three focus groups were composed of individuals who considered their institutional role to be mainly that of researcher, so the same topics were introduced

---

[1]The first three group data collection activities were focus groups. Group IV is considered a group interview because it did not meet all the criteria for a focus group, e.g., the study team had little prior knowledge of participants' backgrounds.

with each of these groups. Some difference in emphasis occurred due to differences in the extent and nature of network use.

The Federal laboratory group interview followed a somewhat different format because participants were primarily information system managers, rather than researchers. An attempt was made to increase the validity of the responses by asking individuals to comment only on those topics clearly within the realm of their personal experience and interests. With this group, therefore, discussion centered on their use of networks and on policy issues related to the development and integration of internal and national networks.

An attempt was made to present topics in such a way that comparisons among respondents, both within and among groups, could be made. The data collected was used to explore network uses, barriers, and issue perspectives in light of organizational settings, organizational responsibilities, demographic characteristics, and other factors.

Group Questionnaires

All focus groups participants were asked to complete a short questionnaire. The type of background data elicited by the questionnaires is listed below:

- Demographic Characteristics: Age and sex
- Educational Background: Names, dates, institutions, and subjects of college degrees earned
- Research and Work Characteristics: Department, current position, key terms describing research areas, and percentage of time devoted to research
- Network-related Characteristics: Percentage of research time devoted to network use, network functions used and their frequency, source of training, and value to work.

The questionnaire completed by the Federal laboratory group members differed somewhat from those used in the focus groups. Federal laboratory respondents answered the same demographic and educational background questions, but the remaining questions centered on major job responsibilities and on the network use and training of the Federal laboratory researchers with whom they were familiar.

The data gathered from the groups' responses to the questionnaires were used to complement or verify comments made during the group discussions. The data also suggested trends and relationships associated with network users' experiences.

Models of Scientific Research and Communication

Two additional instruments were used to guide the discussion and collect data in the three focus groups. One was a model of the research process (Figure 6-2) and the other was a model of scholarly communication (Figure 6-3). They were derived from other models that have appeared in the literature (see, for example, Lin et al., 1970, pp. 29 and 42; Allen, 1985, p. 66) and were intended to be generic enough to be applicable to research and development in both "hard" and "soft" sciences. More general models of the scientific research and communication processes have been proposed by Kraut et al. (1991) and Lievrouw and Carley (in press). The models used in this study provided a common point of reference for participants throughout the study. They proved to be quite useful in helping group members give more specific responses to questions about the effects of networks on their work and communication patterns.

In addition, the model of the research process was used formally, to collect data from participants in the three focus groups. For Group I (advanced network users at the main academic site) and Group III (advanced network users at the private-sector site), a number of network functions were listed along the left side of the research process model. Participants were asked to indicate, by drawing or writing on the model, which network functions had the greatest impact on specific stages of their scientific work. For Group II (basic network users at the private sector site), the model included a list of the kinds of people with whom the researchers might communicate during the course of a research project. Participants were asked to record the types of people with whom they communicated (using electronic mail) at particular stages of a typical research project.

Administration of Group Data Collection Instruments

The participant questionnaires and models of the scientific research and communication processes were administered during group meetings that lasted between 90 and 120 minutes. Participants in the various focus groups were provided with an abstract of the study before the actual meeting dates. Each group discussion began with a general welcome, the

Figure 6-2. Model of the Research Process

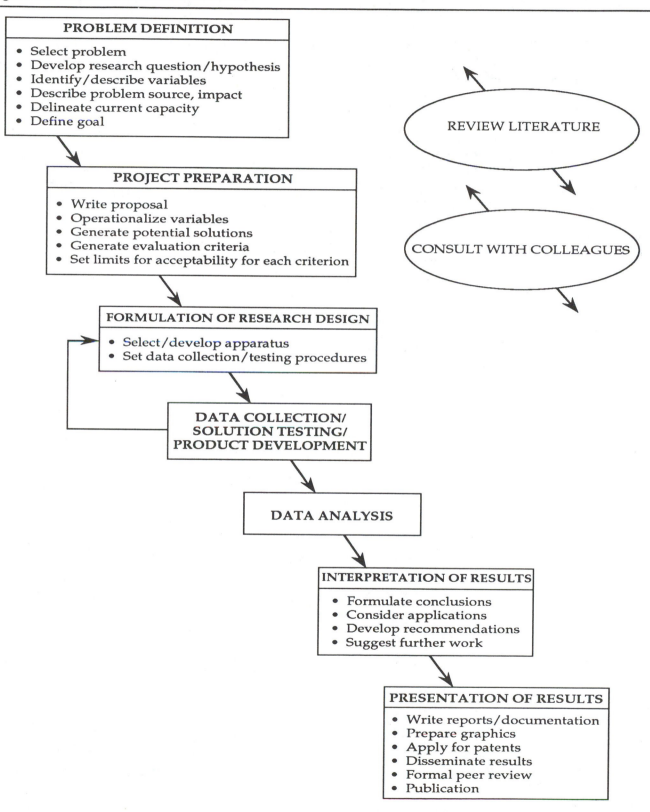

PROBLEM DEFINITION

- Select problem
- Develop research question/hypothesis
- Identify/describe variables
- Describe problem source, impact
- Delineate current capacity
- Define goal

PROJECT PREPARATION

- Write proposal
- Operationalize variables
- Generate potential solutions
- Generate evaluation criteria
- Set limits for acceptability for each criterion

FORMULATION OF RESEARCH DESIGN

- Select/develop apparatus
- Set data collection/testing procedures

DATA COLLECTION/ SOLUTION TESTING/ PRODUCT DEVELOPMENT

DATA ANALYSIS

INTERPRETATION OF RESULTS

- Formulate conclusions
- Consider applications
- Develop recommendations
- Suggest further work

PRESENTATION OF RESULTS

- Write reports/documentation
- Prepare graphics
- Apply for patents
- Disseminate results
- Formal peer review
- Publication

REVIEW LITERATURE

CONSULT WITH COLLEAGUES

Figure 6-3. Model of the System of Scholarly Communication

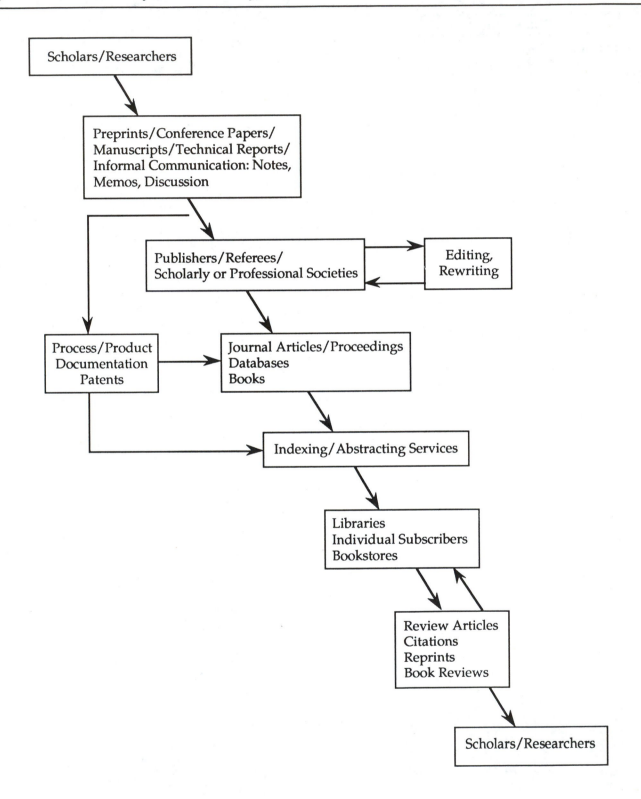

introduction of the study team (who served as the moderators), a general description of the study (with abstracts again distributed), and an outline of that session's agenda.

Questionnaires were then distributed to all participants and the participants were "walked through" the questionnaire. Each question was explained and, where necessary, key terms were clarified. Each group discussion began with a "round robin" question, e.g., "Who are you, and what do you do?," so that everyone could get acquainted and so that each person would have a chance to talk immediately. Next, the various general discussion topics were introduced and the models, where appropriate, were distributed and used for data collection. One way to improve the validity of data collected in focus groups is to ask participants to recall specific and recent occurrences of the phenomena under investigation. Therefore, it was suggested to group participants that they recall and report particular instances of recent benefits, problems, etc., associated with their own network use.

Once all of the pre-arranged topics had been addressed, the discussion groups concluded with the moderators asking for any final comments or questions. The role of the moderators was to guide the general direction of the discussion, to facilitate interaction among the groups' participants, and to encourage the participation of all group members. Moderators spoke as little as possible, especially avoiding any comments that might have seemed judgmental. The focus group sessions (Groups I-III) were audiotaped and later transcribed. All focus group participants were notified in advance that the sessions would be taped and were assured of the confidentiality of their spoken and written responses.

Site Manager Review of Group Results

At least one manager from each site was asked to review and comment upon a summary of that site's discussion. Although it was critical for the study team to be "in tune" with the group discussion participants, it was also considered important to validate and complement the group discussion data with the perceptions and expertise of managers in each setting. The study team distilled key points and issues from the group sessions and asked site managers to comment on them. The input from managers did not supersede or replace the opinions of the individuals interviewed. It served, rather, as a validity check on

technical matters such as access protocols, formal network policies, and network capacity. It also helped to clarify, to some extent, whether the perceptions of participants about organizational policies and norms were accurate. In addition, this approach helped the study team identify discontinuities between the users and managers of networks on selected issues.

Follow-Up Data Collection

After completing the group data collection activities, the study team assessed the feasibility and benefits of collecting follow-up data. The focus group sessions and the group interview raised several intriguing questions. The academic researchers who participated in the focus groups were not, for the most part, senior researchers who were involved in the conceptualization of research projects. Would senior researchers have different opinions about the impact of networks on their work and on scholarly communication? In order to explore this question, the study team conducted in-depth individual interviews with two high-profile users on the campus of the main academic site. A high-profile user program has been established by the national supercomputing center at that site to support and highlight the small group of researchers who are doing highly advanced, important, CPU-intensive work.

Another interesting question arose from the fact that the academic researchers who participated in the focus group were onsite users of one of the national supercomputing centers and that, as such, they experienced many advantages in terms of institutional resources and institutional commitment to networking and supercomputing. Would the experiences of remote users of that center shed a different light on the realities of networking, in general, and remote computing, specifically? Two follow-up data collection activities were undertaken to explore the phenomena of "remoteness" and "institutional support." Three researchers at another university who had recently attempted to access and use remotely the supercomputer at the main academic site participated in individual interviews that focused on the effect of an off-site location on one's ability to use networked computing facilities. In addition, a mail survey about network use and barriers was mailed to the 56 remote consultants of one of the national supercomputing centers. These individuals act as liaisons between the center and researchers at universities and laboratories around the country.

Finally, in order to increase the breadth of data gathered in the study, an online survey of BITNET (a widely used, not-for-profit, international academic network) users was conducted. Network users were presented with a brief description of the study's major research questions and were asked to reply with comments, anecdotes, or complaints about the impact of networks on their scholarly research and communication patterns. The procedures associated with each of the follow-up data collection activities are described in greater detail below.

Interviews with Individual High-Profile Users

A list of seven on-site high-profile users was supplied by the staff at the national supercomputing center. The first two users contacted agreed to participate in the study. Arrangements were made for them to be interviewed in their offices on the university campus by two members of the study team. The interviewers took extensive notes rather than taping the sessions. The interview format was modeled on the format of Focus Groups I and III, utilizing the same general discussion questions and questionnaire. The interviewees were shown the model of the research process as an aid to discussion but were not asked to "map" particular impacts. The interview format and setting made it possible to question them directly about specific points of impact and to record their responses. The interviews lasted 60 to 90 minutes.

Interviews with Remote Users

As noted above, another set of individual interviews concentrated on eliciting descriptions of barriers to network use from researchers at a university who had attempted, or were attempting, to access the national supercomputer center at the main academic site. Subjects came from several disciplines and had varying levels of computing and networking expertise. They had applied for supercomputer accounts, but their accounts revealed little or no activity. Three of the five candidates agreed to participate in interviews lasting about 45 minutes. These individuals also completed the same questionnaires as the participants in Focus Groups I and III and were shown the research process model only as an aid to discussion.

In addition to being asked generally about their use of information technology and its effect on their research and on their ability to communicate with colleagues, these individuals were asked to discuss, as specifically as possible, the circumstances surrounding their attempts to use the supercomputer remotely.

Remote Consultant Survey

A survey was developed, pre-tested, and mailed to the 56 remote consultants around the country who are employed to act as liaisons between remote researchers and one of the national supercomputer centers. The survey contained 19 questions, requiring responses in three formats: short answer, multiple choice, and Likert scale. The objective of the questionnaire was to obtain data on the following characteristics and topics:

- Demographic Characteristics: Name, sex, and age
- Educational Background: Name, date, place, and subject of college degrees earned
- Job Background: Current position, length of time as remote consultant, frequency of contact with clients, and frequency and mode of contact with the supercomputer center
- User Training and Services: Type of training offered for each networking/supercomputing function taught, marketing techniques employed, users' rating of documentation, personal ability to consult effectively, and effect of remoteness on supercomputer use
- Barriers to Supercomputer Use: Problems cited by network users, reasons more researchers do not use networks, and suggestions for overcoming the barriers noted.

Staff at the supercomputer center provided a list of the consultants and their addresses. In addition, the staff sent out an electronic mail announcement of the survey to the consultants and appended to it a statement of support for the study. Consultants were then mailed a copy of the survey along with a cover letter stressing the importance of the study and encouraging their participation, and an abstract describing the study. About eight days after the survey had been sent out, a follow-up electronic mail message was sent to all the consultants reminding them to complete and return their survey, if they had not already done so.

BITNET Survey

An online survey of researchers and network managers was conducted by broadcasting a message to the "futures" newsgroup on BITNET. BITNET has limited capabilities and its bylaws forbid commercial use. Therefore, it is used mainly by academic users for electronic mail and small file transfer. The "futures" newsgroup's subscribers are people who have an account on BITNET and are interested in the future of research networks. News items are seen by individuals occupying a variety of positions in a number of institutional settings in the United States and in other countries. Subscribers represent a full range of disciplines, research areas, and levels of computer expertise.

The news item broadcast by the study team was about a page in length and described the context of the study and its major research questions. Readers were asked to respond with an electronic mail message commenting on the impact of networks on science and scholarly communication and on particular issues and problems that they had encountered in their use of networks. They were invited to be as informal in their responses as they wished, and were assured that anecdotes, opinions, and complaints were all welcome.

DATA ANALYSIS AND REPORTING

The study generated evidence about a wide variety of users' and managers' experiences, attitudes, and activities. Data were collected and recorded in a variety of formats, such as audiotapes of discussions, written notes from interviews, electronic mail comments and anecdotes, and written questionnaire responses. Most of the data gathered for this study were qualitative in nature, consisting of oral or written responses to open-ended questions. Some questionnaire items, on the other hand, called for numerical (e.g., "number of years as consultant") or categorical (e.g., "Do you think remote users are at a major disadvantage/a slight disadvantage/no disadvantage compared to onsite users?") responses from subjects or asked them to produce lists of network features, services, uses, problems, etc. In the first stage of analysis, the major task was to summarize the responses resulting from each data collection activity. This was done mostly through content analysis of the open-ended responses (see, e.g., Krippendorff, 1980) and through tabulating the responses that lent themselves easily to this form of simple quantitative analysis.

Focus group data were analyzed in several ways. For each focus group, the analytic summaries prepared from session notes by individual members of the study team were integrated, and the consolidated version checked against the audio recordings and transcripts. The consolidated versions contain background information about participants, a summary of the group's comments, and the study team's analysis of the information, attitudes, and implications from the session. For each focus group, questionnaire responses were summarized quantitatively by manually tabulating the responses to each item on the questionnaire. Also tallied were the signs and symbols drawn by each set of focus group participants on their models of the research process. The data collected at the Federal laboratory group interview were analyzed in the same way as the focus group data, except that no audiotapes were produced, and the models of the research process were not used.

The individual interviews with high-profile users and remote users yielded data in the form of analytic summaries (produced by one member of the study team and reviewed by another) of each interview, questionnaire responses, and edited models from each subject. The questionnaire data from all the individual interviews were also tabulated manually.

The results of the consultant survey were analyzed in several different ways. Responses to demographic, educational, and numerical and categorical questions were tabulated manually. The open-ended questions on network publicity, users' problems (including those encountered specifically by remote users), and recommendations were subjected to content analysis. All responses to a particular question were read, and a rough typology based on the content of the responses was developed. Several iterations of this process occurred until the study team felt confident that the substance and tone of the responses were accurately represented by the categories. Once categories were established, the responses were analyzed and sorted into the typology that had been developed, and the number of responses in each category tabulated.

The electronic mail responses to the BITNET news group announcement were treated in two ways. On one level, the content of the responses (anecdotal reports, opinions, and complaints about the effect of networks on scholarly communication and the research process) was analyzed in the manner described above. On another level, the BITNET announcement was itself an experiment into the impact of electronic networks on scholarly communication and the research process. Responses were described and analyzed in terms of their contribution to the current study. The geographic location, institutional source, and profession of the respondents were recorded, and the number, length, and purpose of the messages tabulated.

Comments of individual participants in each activity (Groups I-IV; high-profile user interviews, remote user interviews, remote consultant survey, BITNET survey) were summarized and aggregated to obtain a set of data based on the group as a whole. In addition, the data were examined according to other criteria. To explore certain questions, the study team compared the responses of a few different groups. The availability of data from different stakeholder groups in three different settings led to results and conclusions that are a great deal more powerful than those produced by a less systematic, less comprehensive study.

The findings section of this chapter will report only selected data and analyses. Aggregated data on network uses from Groups I-IV and from the individual interviews will be presented. Data from key questions in the remote consultant survey will also be presented as will a summary of the BITNET survey responses. The data gathered could, of course, lend itself to other forms of analysis. In formulating conclusions and recommendations the study team considered all the data in its various forms.

FINDINGS

The data reported in this section were gathered using a variety of data collection techniques. The number of participants who took part in each collection activity are listed in Table 6-1.

Group Data Collection Activities and Interviews

Characterization of Participants

A total of 35 individuals participated in the face-to-face data collection activities and filled out a questionnaire: 7 in Group I (Academic/Expert), 6 in Group II (Private/Novice), 10 in Group III (Private/Expert), 7 in Group IV (Federal lab/Mixed), 2 in the high-profile user interviews (Academic/Expert), and 3 in the remote user interviews (Academic/Mixed). Participants identified their major work areas. Those areas and the number of participants citing each are given below:

Computing	13
Chemistry	11
Physics	4
Engineering	3
Management	1
Accounting	1
Geography	1
Animal Science	1

Participants in Groups I-III, the high-profile users, and the remote users were asked to estimate the amount of their work time devoted to research. Their responses

Table 6-1. Number of Study Participants, by Activity

Activity	No. of Participants/Respondents
Preliminary Site Meetings	16
Focus Group/Group Interview Sessions	31
Site Managers' Reviews of Group Results	4
BITNET Survey	46
Remote User Interviews	3
High-Profile User Interviews	2
Remote Consultant Survey	34
TOTAL	136

Table 6-2. Percent of Work Time Devoted to Research, by Group

	0-10%	11-25%	26-50%	51-75%	76-100%	TOTAL
Group I (Academic/Expert)	-	-	-	-	7	7
Group II (Private/Novice)	-	-	-	-	6	6
Group III (Private/Expert)	2	-	3	-	5	10
Strategic Users (Academic/Expert)	-	-	-	1	1	2
Remote Users (Academic/Mixed)	-	1	1	1	-	3
TOTAL	2	1	4	2	19	28

are depicted in Table 6-2. The number in each cell represents the number of participants who gave that response. The majority of participants in the group data collection activities spent between 75% and 100% of their work time on research.

Participants in the study's face-to-face data collection activities also estimated the percentage of their research time that was spent in network use. These responses are represented in Table 6-3. The participants in the group data collection activities were fairly well distributed between those who used networks heavily in their research and those who did not.

Network Use

The data on network use that were supplied by all those who filled out questionnaires were aggregated and are presented in Figure 6-4. The categories in both "frequency of use" and "value of work" are mutually exclusive, while respondents were allowed to choose more than one category under "source of

Table 6-3. Percent of Research Time Spent in Network Use, by Group

	0-10%	11-25%	26-50%	51-75%	76-100%	TOTAL
Group I (Academic/Expert)	2	1	1	1	2	7
Group II (Private/Novice)	3	2	1	-	-	6
Group III (Private/Expert)	-	3	3	-	4	10
Strategic Users (Academic/Expert)	2	-	-	-	-	2
Remote Users (Academic/Mixed)	2	-	1	-	-	3
TOTAL	9	6	6	1	6	28

Figure 6-4. Aggregated Data on Network Use

CHARACTERISTICS OF USE	FREQUENCY OF USE (N=35)			SOURCE OF TRAINING (N=28)				VALUE TO WORK (N=28)		
NETWORK FUNCTION	Daily	Weekly	Monthly or less	Self	Colleague	Academ. Course	Computing Staff	Critical	Import.	Useful
E-mail	**28**	4	1	**24**	9	1	4	**12**		
Bulletin Board	12	7	5	**13**	4	1	2	5		
File Transfer	**15**	12	5	**19**	7	1	2	**15**	6	
Searching Commercial Online Databases	0	5	**13**	2	**4**	0	**4**	1	**6**	3
Sharing Software	**14**	4	10	**17**	7	2	2	**12**	6	2
Accessing Remote Instruments and Data Sources	5	4	**14**	**6**	3	1	1	2	**5**	0
Accessing Computer Resources	**16**	8	5	**14**	7	2	3	**14**	3	4
Dissemination of Preliminary Results	2	4	**11**	**9**	4	1	0	4	**8**	4
Electronic Submission of	2	1	**8**	7	**9**	1	1	3	2	**4**
	0	**4**	3	**2**	1	0	1	**2**	1	2

* Values in each cell represent the number of participants who gave that response. Underlined numbers indicate the most common response for each characteristic.

training." Only the first "characteristic of use" has an N of 35 because the seven Group IV (Federal laboratory) participants could not supply specific information about the other two characteristics of use. The network functions listed for each group varied slightly, due to assumptions about the network activities of novice versus expert users. All subjects, however, were provided with an "other" option so that they could add functions that did not appear on their questionnaires.

The figure indicates that electronic mail is the most widely used network function, followed by accessing computer resources, transfering files, sharing software, and exchanging information on bulletin boards. The most valuable network functions, as noted by respondents, were file transfer, electronic mail, sharing software, and accessing computer resources.

Respondents relied, for the most part, on themselves and colleagues for network training. The Federal laboratory respondents also indicated that most researchers with whom they were familiar probably relied on themselves "a lot" or "somewhat" for learning how to use networks; 6 noted that colleagues and 4 noted that formal academic training were also relied on "a lot" or "somewhat." It is clear that the majority of the researchers and managers who took part in this study did not rely on any kind of formal training or assistance when learning how to use network resources and services.

Impact of Networks on the Research Process

The consensus among members in Focus Group I (Academic/Expert) was that the basic steps or components in the model of the research process have not, themselves, changed as a result of network use. Networks have, nonetheless, greatly facilitated the conduct of research. In terms of research productivity, the group saw itself as more _efficient_ as a result of networks and supercomputing, but not necessarily more _effective_. They indicated that the major productivity contribution was a reduction in both the number of "remedial and donkey work tasks" and the time committed to such tasks. Another important benefit noted by the group was that networks decreased the necessity for collaborators to be in one place.

The members of this group had difficulty articulating specific network impacts, but, on the other hand, they could not imagine working without networks. They noted that computers and networks had been

rapidly and completely integrated into their research lives. It should also be remembered that their model of the research process was largely that of the junior researcher, i. e., their research problems have been identified for them by their advisor or otherwise determined by existing research funds and groups. Thus, these study participants, by and large, were not at a point in their careers where they would be using the networks for generating new ideas, theory development, and related conceptual tasks. This situation is especially prevalent in large-scale collaborative projects, in which most of the participants were involved.

Focus Group II (Private/Novice) participants indicated that research networks had not contributed significantly to individual creativity and innovation but might in the future. This group agreed with the academic focus group that the basic steps or components in the model of the research process had not changed as a result of networks but that networks had made it easier to conduct research. A few "effectiveness" benefits were also cited. One researcher noted that by sharing his research report via electronic file transfer with another colleague (something he would not have done using other mechanisms), the colleague was able to reassess and clarify the data and offer new insights and conclusions. It was noted that the inability of the networks to handle chemical structures and scientific equations was a significant problem. These constitute the "language" of chemists and, if they cannot be easily transmitted over networks, the impact of networks on research in this discipline will remain limited.

Participants in Focus Group III (Private/Expert) also had great difficulty singling out particular impacts of networks on particular stages of the research process. The reasons behind this difficulty are significant for policy makers. One is that participants saw computers and networks as inextricably linked to "what science is." It was hard for them to pinpoint impact because they could not even imagine doing their research without advanced information technologies. The group was, in fact, dismayed by attempts to pinpoint impact by quantifying productivity gains. They felt that it was more important to understand that computers and networks changed the entire texture of what they did for the better. They felt that attempts to quantify benefits were, for the most part, misguided and of small utility. The group seemed to feel that network use had such a powerful and pervasive impact on research that computer literacy of some sort should be required of all scientists.

Focus Group III participants agreed that networks greatly reduced the amount of time needed to complete a given research project, particularly in the areas of project management and data analysis. Another way they expressed this was that networks greatly reduced the amount of time they needed to spend "away from research." This group felt more strongly than the other focus groups that networks had had a significant effect on all stages of the research process, perhaps in part because they themselves -- in contrast with the academic group -- were more often engaged in all stages of a research project. Participants placed more emphasis on the positive impact of networks in both the initial stage of problem definition and the final stages of interpreting and disseminating results than did other respondents. A great deal of discussion in this group centered on the importance of electronic bulletin boards. Participants said that news, comments, and advice placed on bulletin boards were valuable in generating new ideas and solving particular problems. The reliability and accuracy of bulletin boards' information were judged to be quite good. Care in accepting information, however, corresponded to the magnitude of the problem that would result if the information turned out to be flawed.

High-profile and remote users emphasized the impact of networks on data analysis. One remote user noted that his use of remote facilities stemmed from his need for a different kind of analysis and increased analytic speed than was available at his home institution. He noted that one great benefit of networking was the synergy it created, especially in data analysis -- it was especially important to exchange ideas and get feedback from colleagues quickly. Another remote user noted that his work and that of his students would not be possible without electronic networks and supercomputing analytic devices.

In summary, there was general agreement that networks were increasing the efficiency of research. The greatest impact on the research process, in the view of study participants, had been in the realm of data analysis, although several people also noted that networks had an impact on the interpretation, presentation, and dissemination of research results. Similarly, project design, preparation, and management were noted by several people as having been improved by the introduction of electronic networks. Comments on the impact of networks on the research process seemed, for the most part, to cut across sector and level of technical expertise, except that partici-

pants in Focus Group III (Private/Expert) indicated a greater breadth and depth of impact than did other participants.

Impact of Networks on Scholarly Communication

Most participants agreed that the basic steps or aspects of scholarly communication had not, in themselves, changed as a result of network use. Rather, network use facilitated scholarly communication in a number of ways. They felt that more researchers can better work together as a result of networking. Collaboration through networks is not location-driven or geography-sensitive, although, of course, it has not been purely location-driven for quite some time. Participants indicated that network use most easily facilitated collaboration which was based on previously established personal contacts. In other words, most researchers said that they felt more comfortable using networks to sustain relationships rather than initiate contacts. Study participants also noted the difficulty of ascertaining electronic mail addresses (except for people in their own research group and personal friends) and sending files with scientific notation or graphics. Novice users in all sectors were, not surprisingly, less convinced about the potential of networks to aid in collaborative work.

Virtually all participants felt that networks had greatly facilitated their research by allowing them to communicate much more easily with a broader range of colleagues. Electronic mail was widely used for personal and professional exhanges. Academic researchers noted that networks were used extensively to arrange sabbaticals, communicate with colleagues at one's home institution while traveling or on leave, help research group members share information and more easily deal with the logistical aspects of research, and organize international meetings. Those in the private sector and Federal laboratory remarked that networks facilitated communication of all kinds with remote researchers, vendors, customers, and others. Research workers in all three sectors noted that electronic bulletin boards allowed them to "lift ideas and information" from a broad range of contacts in such a way that everyone benefited from the transaction. Again, the more experience one had with electronic communication and file transfer, the more one extolled its virtues in facilitating scholarly communication. Novice networkers in the private sector generally agreed that increased external communication would "probably increase" researcher effectiveness and productivity, but, as a group, these researchers did not appear to believe that they were missing much by having little to no communication with researchers in academia, government, or other companies.

Some discussion centered on the comparison of characteristics of different media. Certain media were generally felt to be appropriate for certain types of scholarly communication. For example, many participants noted their preference for sending important, time-sensitive, graphic or specially formatted written materials via express mail or telefacsimile. A number of participants noted that one benefit of electronic mail was the elimination of certain social conventions that accompany face-to-face, written, or telephone communication; electronic mail messages could be very brief and informal. In addition, electronic mail was less intrusive than other media; message receivers were able to accept and respond to communications at their own convenience.

The use of electronic media for the exchange, dissemination, and publication of formal scholarly material was much less pervasive and also seemed much less palatable than informal communication to researchers in all sectors. The reasons for this were both technical and social. A number of participants had used the network to transmit preliminary results or reports to colleagues. Only a few mentioned the benefits of electronic access to formal publications through libraries and databases, although one novice networker in the private sector noted that "the creativity you have is influenced by the material you look at" -- if networks allow access to more scholarly material, perhaps researchers can be more creative.

Even fewer of the participants had tried or were particularly eager to try publishing in online journals. It was clear from their comments that the reward structure of science is based on formal publication history and that electronic publication does not enhance one's status or image; in fact, it may very well harm them. On the other hand, although only a few of the participants had experienced it, electronic submission of manuscripts for review and publication in print journals (in real time or by exchanging floppy disks or transmitting telefacsimiles) was seen as generally desirable, especially because of its potential to reduce delays and errors in the publication of articles. Real time electronic submission, however, was still seen as unreliable, partly because of the difficulties of retaining the formatting of the original paper. There was general contempt expressed for the "Fleischmann and

Pons Syndrome" (related to the infamous cold fusion experiment) i.e., using networks to circumvent the traditional peer review and publication process. This type of activity was condemned as being harmful to science.

Networking Problems

Generally speaking, participants in this study were pleased with electronic networks, glad that the networks were there, and recognized that networks facilitated research in a number of different ways. Despite this apparent general satisfaction with networks, specific conversations suggested problems. Participants in the study's group data collection activities and interviews identified several problems that limited their use of electronic networks or limited the beneficial impacts of networks on research. Technical problems were the easiest for people to identify and enumerate and there was wide agreement across sectors, job types, and levels of networking expertise about what those problems were. Participants also identified and addressed a variety of social and organizational barriers to network use.

Some of the most frequently mentioned technical problems were:

- Insufficient network capacity
- Insufficient transmission speed
- Lack of universal access
- Lack of standards
- Incompatibility among networks, hardware, and software
- Poor reliability of data transmission
- Lack of graphics capabilities
- Unknown, nonstandard, and complex addresses
- Lack of user-friendly interfaces.

Several participants also noted dissatisfaction with the operating system available to them and complained about degraded service during peak times. The difficulty of uploading and downloading files was mentioned by several participants. A few academic users noted the scarcity of software designed specifically for social science research. Several private-sector individuals noted problems due to the existence of network nodes that operate without human oversight and to the lack of good online diagnostics.

Perhaps the most commonly discussed nontechnical problem area was network training and support. Researchers noted that infrequent users expended an inordinate amount of effort to learn and relearn networking techniques. Both novice and expert users noted the need for better online and hard-copy documentation. Academic researchers who relied heavily on student assistants to support their networking activities said students currently receive little training in networking and supercomputing and have difficulty mastering the wide range of different network software packages. They also complained that computing consultants often operate as if researchers wanted to become computing and networking experts when, in fact, researchers want to concentrate on their research and only want to learn enough about computing to get their work done. In a similar vein, study participants stressed the importance of consultants' understanding the domain of researchers' work.

Study participants in all sectors discussed the general lack of networking training and support. Academic researchers seemed more or less satisfied with their ability to acquire whatever expertise they needed. Those in the Federal laboratory with a great deal of technical expertise saw this situation as natural and probably unavoidable, evincing little tolerance for researchers who were not "computer jocks." Private-sector researchers with minimal technical skills were satisfied with the support they received, although they admitted that their help line went unanswered and they experienced great difficulty with relatively simple tasks, such as file transfer. Technical experts in the same institution, ironically, complained that they received "no support" and that novice users were not afforded proper training and assistance.

Another common barrier to network use was the lack of a good means of keeping informed about available network resources, services, and activities. It was the network experts in all sectors who felt this need most acutely. Inexperienced network users seemed unaware of what they were missing. Most participants, while recognizing the importance of network security and confidentiality, did not seem very worried about these issues. They assumed that their network technicians were "handling it," and had great faith in the honesty of their fellow network users. A few network experts in the private sector, both researchers and managers, expressed some fear about their ability to control what goes into and comes out of their organization. One of the strategic users noted that in spite of all their "preaching" about technology transfer from academia and Federal laboratories to the private sector, the Department of

Defense and others deliberately limit the communication of their researchers with the outside world, even when the work in question is "nonsensitive." Participants also did not seem to be experiencing many difficulties with the electronic equivalent of "junk mail" personally, although they recognized that it could become a serious problem in the future and saw it as damaging to the scientific enterprise.

Many academic researchers noted the barrier presented by networking costs and the need to compete for computing resources. They noted that competition was becoming more intense and that funding was especially scarce in the social sciences and humanities. A number of problems unique to or exacerbated by remote use were also mentioned. Remote users had greater difficulty learning what resources and services were available and, in general, had trouble maintaining communications with central consultants. One remote user commented that the psychological barrier to interacting with people at a remote institution was very difficult to overcome, that he felt nervous and afraid every time he had to try a new computing procedure, even though he was very sophisticated technically.

Several instances of organizational conflict and problems with local network management were identified and discussed by study participants. Researchers in the private and academic sector lamented the lack of institutional incentives or rewards for acquiring networking expertise. One participant in the private sector observed that the speed of technological change demanded "reasonable migration strategies" so that organizations -- and the nation as a whole -- could minimize the cost and disruption of "going from one technology breakthrough to the next." Experienced network users recognized the benefit to their work, but it took time and patience to acquire needed expertise. Inexperienced users tended to feel that networking was simply a drain on time and resources that they should be devoting directly to their work. Researchers tended to dislike dealing with "systems people" and vice versa, and one strategic user was dismayed when colleagues became "so enamored of computers that they forget about science." Some junior researchers in academia who spent the majority of their research time online were afraid that they had been relegated to a "computer ghetto" and that their research careers were being jeopardized because they were cut off from conceptual work.

Corporate managers had trouble understanding the roles and benefits of networking and were, in some cases, suspicious of the potential for unfettered communication allowed by networks. Managers were not pleased when researchers' loyalty to colleagues in their online community seemed to exceed their institutional loyalty. Researchers grown used to networking resented any efforts on the part of management to constrain their communication behavior. Network managers in the Federal laboratory explained that lots of little network fiefdoms can exist at the institutional level with people creating their own systems and training their own users.

Problems of national network policy development were of little concern to most participants in this study. Researchers assumed that all their colleagues would continue to be responsible users of network resources and services and that everyone shared their beliefs about which kinds of network policies and activities would help science and which were harmful. Researchers did not expect that any government or industry power would ever be in a position to dictate network policy, but assumed that networks would be governed by the research community itself. Both of the high-profile users in this study emphasized their preference for ownership and control of their own computing and networking systems. They saw resource sharing on an institutional, regional, or national level as better than nothing, but looked forward to the time when they would have their own supercomputing work stations and, thus, total control over their own resources. These researchers saw the sharing of resources as an unfortunate impediment to the progress of their work.

Study participants in the Federal laboratory group were the most concerned with issues of national policy development, probably because the laboratory itself was engaged in research on networking technology and management. Some members of this group noted that difficulties in melding national and local networks remained an impediment to successful network communication. They focused on the difficulties of configuring an internal network (i.e., linking up a plethora of LANs and standardizing 300 individual machines so that all can reach the Federal backbone). They commented that this is "the other half of the national research network situation." How organizations manage this will have a direct impact on the success of a national research network. One study participant made the important observation that "we're talking about doing something of a scope and complexity that we've never done before. Local management issues don't necessarily scale up . . .

many of the technical and policy problems are still research areas." One new kind of problem brought about by national networking is the difficulty of determining the source of a technical problem and deciding who is responsible for fixing it.

Many of the social and behavioral issues presented here are discussed further in chapter 8.

Remote Consultant Survey

The purpose of the remote consultant survey was to collect data on the needs and problems of remote users of supercomputers. The survey, mailed to 56 remote user consultants employed by one of the NSF national supercomputing centers, was intended to identify remote user support mechanisms and particular problems associated with remote computing.

Thirty-four of the 56 remote consultants returned their questionnaires, a response rate of 61%. This rate compares favorably to that achieved by the supercomputer staff in its own surveys and to the expected rate of return for social science surveys, in general. The questionnaire was rather long (19 questions on two pages), and many of the questions were open-ended and required a considered response. The fact that so many questionnaires were returned suggests that issues related to the development of a national research network were of great concern to this particular group. Responses were received from consultants in academic and other settings, from both small and large organizations, and from all parts of the United States.

Twenty-four respondents were male, and ten were female. Three of the respondents had served as consultants for less than 6 months, 18 for 12 to 24 months, 11 for more than 24 months, and 2 respondents gave no indication of length of service. Most of the consultants were trained in the computational or natural sciences. This pattern reflects the educational background of most researchers who use advanced information technologies in their work.

The consultants were asked to report how they train and support researchers in the use of various network functions. Their responses are reported in Table 6-4, which is a copy of the chart filled out by the consultants. The number in each cell represents the number of consultants who indicated that they provide that type of service.

These results seem to support data on network use and problems that were collected in the focus groups and interviews. Networks were apparently used most

Table 6-4. Network Support Services Offered by Remote Consultants

NETWORK FUNCTION	TYPE OF SERVICE YOU PROVIDE					
	CONSULTING:			WORK-SHOPS	CLASSROOM INSTRUCTION	FORMAL AFFILIATION WITH A RESEARCH TEAM
	Telephone	E-Mail	In Person			
E-Mail	25	23	28	10	4	1
Bulletin Boards	7	8	7	3	2	0
File Transfer	27	24	30	6	5	1
Using Remote Software	15	15	22	5	2	2
Accessing Remote Research Instruments	5	6	10	1	0	0
Accessing Remote Data Sets	10	9	12	0	0	0
Accessing Supercomputer	28	28	31	11	6	3
Use of Online Help	23	22	24	6	3	0
Identification of Data Analysis Methods	14	11	16	4	2	2

often by remote users to access remote computing resources, transfer files, and send electronic mail. The data also suggest that users attempting even "simple" networking activities like electronic mail require support. The participation of consultants in the identification of data analysis methods suggests the importance of consultants' possessing some familiarity with the nature and substance of the work being done by researchers.

In order to evaluate the effects of remoteness, consultants were asked about the degree to which they thought their remote users were at a disadvantage compared to onsite supercomputer center researchers. Twenty-six percent of the respondents noted that their users were at a "major" disadvantage, about 50% said their users experienced "some" disadvantage, 18% considered the disadvantage to be "slight," and only 1 consultant (or 3%) felt that there was "no" disadvantage.

Possible causes of user disadvantage include the lack of skilled remote consultants. Thus, consultants were asked to evaluate their own ability to deal with users' problems. Most consultants were satisfied with their own technical and training background; 76% of the respondents noted that only 0-10% of their users' problems required additional assistance from the supercomputer center. Remote users are particularly dependent on network and computer documentation. The remote consultants estimated that researchers at their institutions generally rate the ease of use, clarity, availability, and overall quality of documentation as "good" or "fair." This suggests that supporting users of a national network will be a difficult task.

Respondents were asked to answer three questions related to barriers to remote computing. One question asked them to list reasons for remote users being at a disadvantage, another asked them to list barriers to remote computing cited by their users, and the third asked them to list reasons more researchers do not take advantage of remote computing. The consultants' responses to these three questions, as expected, overlapped to some extent. In each question, both technical and nontechnical problems were noted. Figure 6-5 summarizes the remote consultants'

Figure 6-5. Problems Associated with, and Reasons for Nonuse of, Remote Computing

---

Technical Problems

Insufficient connectivity
Difficulties with graphic processing
Slow, unreliable networks

Lack of desired operating systems
Lack of standards
Lack of compatible equipment at remote sites

Nontechnical Problems

Lack of need
Retraining requirements
Lack of awareness
Lack of local institutional support
Researchers lack time, money, motivation to
    adapt to new system
Proposal process too difficult, time-consuming,
    competitive

Few proficient consultants
Remote computing inconvenient, not user friendly
Distrust of remote computing
Local computing more convenient
Difficulty of remote training
Lack of documentation at remote sites
Lack of critical mass of users at remote sites
Lack of peer support
"Fear of the unknown"

---

responses to these three questions, with the problems noted most often in each group listed first.

As Figure 6-5 suggests, more consultants cited technical rather than nontechnical barriers, but they emphasized social and behavioral problems when reflecting specifically on lack of use. The most commonly cited technical problems were the lack of connectivity, reliability, and graphics processing capabilities. In terms of nontechnical problems, consultants seemed to feel that many researchers did not need supercomputers for their work. Even if they did, the effort, inconvenience, and frustration of getting an account at one of the national supercomputer facilities and learning how to use a new system remotely outweighed the benefits. One consultant said that there were no barriers to remote computing, while another reported that he "rarely hears of any problems."

Remote consultants noted that lack of awareness inhibited use. Thus, their methods for publicizing their services, listed in Table 6-5, are of interest. They chiefly used newsletters and online communications to promote network services.

Consultants made a number of recommendations for resolving problems related to remote networking and use of supercomputers. Technical improvements that were most often recommended were in the areas of network speed, reliability, capacity, and standards.

Table 6-5. Means of Publicizing Remote Supercomputing

Method cited	No. of Respondents
Distribution of literature (e.g., newsletters, brochures, fliers)	30
Online bulletin board, electronic mail announcements	15
Personal contact (e.g., letters, word of mouth)	13
Workshops, seminars, conferences, demonstrations	12
Physical bulletin boards	8
Announcements at supercomputing meetings and seminars	3
None	1

They also noted the inability of researchers at remote institutions to take full advantage of networks because of a simple lack of basic hardware, software, and network connections. Remote consultants noted that improvements were needed in the area of user support and training, and that researchers needed more discipline-specific, hands-on training, whether in workshops, individual instruction, or as a part of formal coursework. Consultants also said that improvements are needed in both hard-copy and online documentation. In terms of increasing potential users' awareness of available services, consultants noted that both local and national networking organizations need better mechanisms for reaching out to potential users and publicizing their services. It was recommended that network managers demonstrate more understanding of the demands, in terms of time and patience, that are currently placed on researchers who are trying to integrate networks into their work, and that they develop mechanisms for reducing the inconveniences currently faced by such people. Finally, consultants recommended that the financial burden currently faced by end users be reduced.

The problems noted by the remote consultants in the mail survey were quite similar to those discussed by researchers themselves in focus groups and interviews described above. Technical problems noted were virtually identical to those cited in the group data collection activities and interviews. Nontechnical problems were similar, but the consultants' perspective differed somewhat from that of the researchers. Consultants naturally focused on the realm of awareness, training, and support, while they appeared to be less aware of problems related to researchers' position in an organization or to their daily work life, such as lack of institutional rewards, disagreements with R&D managers over networking policies, and junk mail. Costs and competition for supercomputing and networking resources were mentioned by both groups, and the psychological barriers associated with remote use that were mentioned in interviews were also noted by remote consultants.

BITNET Survey

A message was posted to a BITNET newsgroup that asked researchers to comment on the impact of electronic networks on the research process and scholarly communication and any problems or issues that they had encountered with network use. Forty responses were received from the continental United States (14 from the Northeast, 9 from the South, 6 from the Midwest, and 9 from the West), and 2 from Hawaii. Two messages were from Canada, 1 from Denmark. The geographic locations of 3 of the respondents were unknown. Because BITNET serves primarily to link universities and colleges, most respondents (31) came from academic institutions. Also represented were Federal laboratories (4), private corporations (1), non-profit organizations (4), Federal agencies (1), and a graduate school connected with the armed services (1). Four responses came from institutions whose identities were unknown to the study team. Several responses were received by telephone or through the U.S. mail.

Responses ranged in length from a few lines to several pages. The purposes of the messages also varied. Most people responded directly to the questions posed. Some respondents, on the other hand, referred the study team to other sources of information (people, publications, and news items), provided documents of interest, offered procedural advice about certain aspects of the study, expressed approval or disapproval of the study, or expressed the desire to collaborate on future projects. Thus, the BITNET survey allowed the study team first-hand experience with the functions and value of remote network communication in the context of a research project.

The first BITNET question asked researchers to comment on the impact of electronic networks on their work. Five respondents reported that electronic networks had little or no impact on their research. One researcher said the changes networks caused were not fundamental, 1 said that the technology had not yet reached enough people for the overall impact to be very great, and 2 respondents noted that they had not experienced any change because they had always used networks in their research. Twenty-one respondents, on the other hand, identified 38 different examples of the positive impact of networks on the research process (see Table 6-6).

The second question posed to BITNET newsgroup readers asked them to comment on the impact electronic networks had on scholarly communication. Fifty-four individual comments on the impact of networks on scholarly communication were received. The largest number of comments dealt with the ability of networks to broaden (in terms of size and variety) the community of scholars with which any single researcher could interact. Researchers noted that networks allowed them to identify, contact, and keep in touch with many more colleagues than was previously possible. This, in turn, increased the number of people who could actively participate in a scholarly discussion, allowed one to keep track of important research developments, and increased the pool of knowledge available to any one researcher (see Table 6-7).

The final BITNET survey question asked researchers to comment on networking problems. Thirty-three separate comments were received on barriers and issues associated with the use of networks (see Table 6-8). The technical problems identified by the BITNET respondents were similar to those identified by other study respondents and published literature on national networking. People citing these problems argued that significant resources need to be committed to upgrading and enhancing the research network infrastructure. Non-technical problems and issues identified also paralleled other study responses.

Table 6-6. Impact of Networks on the Research Process

Impact cited	No. of Respondents
Promotion and facilitation of collaboration, especially internationally	12
Support of data collection and analysis as well as central processing:	
• Networks are necessary for real-time control of remote devices	3
• Networks support remote log-in, especially to supercomputers	3
• Networks allow design data to be shipped to a remote facility for fabrication	1
Reduction of negative effects of being at a remote or small institution	5
No change in conduct of research:	
• No fundamental change in the way I do research	1
• Networks do not change the way we think about problems	1
• No change because we have always used networks	2
• The technology has not yet reached the majority of colleagues	1
Improvement of researchers' ability to solve specific research problems:	
• Networks help provide answers to particular questions and resolve specific problems	3
• Network communication shares technical and procedural details not available in final report	1
Facilitation of resource sharing:	
• Networks allow the sharing of software	3
• Networks give access to online datasets	1
Effect upon conceptualization:	
• Greater communication level increases inspiration	1
• Networks facilitate conceptualization	1
• Networks change what research is contemplated	1
• Network use helps to prevent duplication of work	1
Increase in productivity	3
Improvement of project administration	2

Table 6-7. Impact of Networks on Scholarly Communication

Impact cited	No. of Respondents
Broadening of community of scholars:	
• Increase level of human resources available, tap into larger community's knowledge, increase the number of respondents in a discussion, and help to keep track of scholarly developments	9
• Can identify scholars with similar interests	3
• Reduce inertia in making and keeping contacts	2
• Make communication easier	4
• Can contact authors of papers	1
Facilitation and improvement of publication:	
• Electronic journals	1
• Journal preparation (refereeing, manuscript submission, international communication, and editing)	2
• Manuscript preparation (e.g., transmitting drafts)	7
• More accurate, better produced documents	1
Improvement of administration of scholarly activities:	
• Arrangements for visiting speakers	1
• Conference organization	4
• Processing grants	3
Assistance in document identification and provision	7
Distribution of scholarly announcements:	
• Meetings and conferences	2
• Calls for papers	1
• Grants	1
Facilitation of international communication:	
• Mitigate time differences	2
• Make community truly international	1
Decrease in communication costs	2

The responses from the BITNET survey provided a generally positive picture of the importance and role of networks in the research process. It should be remembered, however, that the respondents were self-selected and that BITNET is primarily an academic network. Furthermore, because of the mechanism used for data collection, it can be assumed that the respondents can be characterized as those more knowledgeable about computing and networks and generally more computer literate than the "typical" researcher.

CONCLUSIONS

Researchers view electronic networks as a tool for both information processing and communication. Network use is governed by a broad range of social and behavioral issues which frequently are more difficult to identify and resolve than technical issues.

This study focused on analyzing social and behavioral issues that have received inadequate attention in discussions about the NREN. Summary answers to the three questions guiding the study are presented below. Fuller discussion of a number of networking issues is presented in Chapters 7, 8, and 9.

Have Networks Changed the Modus Operandi of Researchers?

Regardless of the data collection technique employed, there were consistent responses to this research question. While specific aspects of the research process have been made more efficient or even more effective by networks, the basic components of the research process remain unchanged. The conduct of research continues much as it has in the past, although networks have greatly assisted in improving the process.

Table 6-8. Problems and Issues Related to Network Use

Problems and Issues	No. of Respondents
Technical problems:	
Reliability of networks and their links	5
Software not user-friendly	2
Incompatible e-mail formats	2
Difficulty with transmitting graphics	1
Nonstandard software	1
Saturation of network capacity	1
Insufficient speed	1
Communications not automated	1
Lack of universal connectivity	1
Nontechnical problems:	
Difficulty of determining e-mail addresses	5
Most people lack sufficient technical expertise	2
Lack of skilled personnel to manage information systems and resources	2
Difficulties with learning network skills may exceed benefits	1
Need cost-free access	1
Prices are subject to the whim of those who control networks	1
Hardware is expensive and requires long-range planning to acquire	1
Connections to a LAN, organizational network, and national network are expensive	1
The uninitiated in an organization think that networks are toys	1
Protection of free expression online may be problematic	1
Lack of network promotion and marketing	1
Few documents readily available in electronic format	1

There was little difference among the responses offered by subjects in the three sectors: academia, private sector, and Federal labs. Most respondents noted that networks have some impact on how they carry out their work, but have not really changed what they do or their understanding of what good research is. Networks are viewed as an important research tool, but one that, like any other, must be used within the traditional normative structure of the research enterprise (see Chapter 7).

Participants identified numerous specific examples at an individual level of how network use facilitates the research process. For example:

- Large data sets can be "crunched" in much less time by accessing supercomputers on the networks.
- Access to remote software can enhance data management and analysis.
- Collaboration among a number of participants who may be geographically dispersed is made easier.

Some respondents noted that they were able to ask and answer different kinds of questions because of the increased availability of sophisticated computational tools and instruments. Similar effects have been demonstrated elsewhere (e.g., Panel on Information Technology and the Conduct of Research, 1989; Hiltz, 1984; and Greif, 1988).

The study's findings also suggest that network use may provide researchers with a competitive advantage over researchers who are unable or unwilling to use high-speed research networks. Not only can researchers be more efficient by using electronic networks, but, in some cases, they can also be more effective and improve the quality of their work. For example, a researcher might use a supercomputer to conduct assessments of millions of alternative models as a means to determine which model has the greatest potential for exploring a research question. Applications that enhance the effectiveness of the researcher, however, appear to be limited thus far.

In addition, it appears that the majority of researchers have not been affected by networks; nor is it likely that, in the immediate future, electronic networks will affect the way all researchers work. Indeed, there appear to be a number of researchers who have been left behind in network development and use. These individuals have had limited training in the use of networks, are unconvinced that network use would facilitate their research activities, often see new information and computer technology as a barrier to their research, and generally continue to conduct research without extensive reliance on networks.

Have Networks Changed Basic Patterns of Scientific Communication?

Focus group participants and individual interviewees reviewed how networks have affected various phases of scientific communication. In addition, other data collection techniques provided evidence related to this research question.

Once again, the evidence suggests that the basic components of the scientific communication process have not changed significantly because of networks. Within those basic components, however, participants identified numerous ways in which networks have facilitated or otherwise enhanced the overall efficiency, and in some instances the effectiveness, of scientific communication. For example:

- Networks allow researchers, isolated through geography or lack of resources, to communicate with others who otherwise might not be contacted, e.g., one respondent commented that networks were her "lifeline" to the scientific community.
- Networks broaden the scope of the research community for all users, expanding the pool of human and bibliographic resources that may be tapped to keep abreast of current developments in the field or to solve particular problems, and networks allow the easier and broader dissemination of preliminary findings.
- Communication on the networks is more efficient than playing telephone tag with other researchers.
- Although uploading and downloading various types of messages still pose problems to some researchers, a broad range of information sources and documents can be transmitted over networks.
- Networks facilitate the planning and administration of research projects and arrangement of scholarly meetings.
- Networks can facilitate and improve various aspects of traditional print publishing, such as document editing and review, and general journal administration.

Networks seemed to be used more often to facilitate informal rather than formal communication. Electronic mail and electronic bulletin boards were frequently used to get information and resources to help solve particular research problems or to exchange ideas with peers. Networks were used less often to access libraries, send formal documents, or "publish" results. Researchers who were experienced network users were much more convinced of the potential benefits of informal network communication than were novice users or managers who were not experienced network users.

As might be expected, there were differences in the control placed on researchers' communication in the different sectors. Academics were the most free to communicate, although there are increasing restraints on communication, while researchers in the private sector are more heavily limited by proprietary and competitive concerns. Researchers in the Federal laboratory accept security constraints on their communication rather easily. An interesting issue arises, however, from the fact that more sophisticated network users are entering the ranks of management: Because they know the ins and outs of networking and the subterfuges used to circumvent communication restraints, will electronic communication be even more constrained in the future? Or will managers' familiarity with the benefits of networking decrease controls on network communication?

Overall, the study results, consistent with evidence from other studies, suggest that networks encourage researchers to communicate more often with a broader range of individuals and that electronic mail is, overwhelmingly, the most commonly used network function. There also is evidence to suggest that some network communication is of a personal nature and is not linked to specific research activities. This communication does contribute, however, to the social matrix in which science is done. The "law of the instrument" may also pertain here: messages and other material may be sent simply because it is easy and inexpensive to do so. Further, a number of the researchers commented that for some activities, such as brainstorming, networks cannot replace face-to-face communication.

Because of the difficulties of uploading and downloading documents and transmitting images and scientific characters, many researchers favored telefacsimile for the transmission of certain kinds of documents. Although electronic networks facilitate traditional print publishing and the informal dissemination of results among peers, networks do not seem to be used to any great extent for the formal publication and distribution of research results. Technical difficulties and normative restrictions both discourage this use of networks.

For those individuals who have not been affected by networks due to lack of appropriate technologies, lack of resources, limited knowledge about networks, or the belief that using the networks would provide little assistance to them, scientific communication will not change as a result of networks. They will be negatively affected, however, by the increased use of networks by others. Thus, the potential productivity gains from the use of networks, like network use itself, is likely to fall disproportionately across the scientific community.

What Problems Do Network Users Face?

A variety of barriers to network use were identified in this study by R&D workers and managers and by network managers and consultants. Many of the problems were technical. Prospective users lack the hardware, software, and connectivity needed to take advantage of national networking. Users complained that networks were unreliable, slow, and not standardized, and they lacked sufficient capacity for certain applications. Study respondents also detailed non-technical barriers to effective networking. Lack of training and support was noted by individuals in a variety of settings, as was the need to increase the awareness of available resources and services, and the increased competition for network resources as research networking gains in popularity. Problematic effects of networking on R&D organizations and on the research community were also mentioned.

A range of problems and barriers currently prevent the effective use of electronic networks. Barriers that were identified by network users, managers, and intermediaries included the following:

- **Complex or Unknown Procedures**. A frequent complaint from network users was that network managers or consultants indicate that a certain procedure, e.g., uploading a dataset to transmit over the network, is a very straightforward process. While the process may be straightforward for a network manager or consultant, this task is often perceived as too complex and burdensome by users.
- **Insufficient or Uneven Network Capacity**. A number of users commented that insufficient capacity, limited speed, or need for large bandwidths was a barrier for network use. Typically,

such users were high-profile users who had very sophisticated computing needs.

- **Insufficient Connectivity.** A major problem facing network users is connectivity among the various national networks and, often, within a single network. Some spoke of endless difficulties when attempting to send information from NSFNet, for example, to BITNET. Currently, connectivity among the networks is not well developed enough to be transparent to most users. On the other hand, extremely sophisticated users do not want system transparency for a number of reasons. For example, as one of the high-profile users put it: "If a [technical] problem occurs, how do you discover where it is, who's responsible for it, who fixes it, and who pays for fixing it?"

- **Unreliability of Data Transmission and Transformations.** Users commented that transmission of data that requires uploading or downloading, working with different kinds of application software, or similar procedures is likely to require significant editing and review after transmission. This problem was especially bothersome to naive network users who want only to download a text file and convert it into a particular word-processing format.

- **Lack of Technical Standards.** A major stumbling block for many users was the number of often conflicting protocols, commands, and procedures that must be understood if networks are to be used effectively. The lack of standards is compounded when users must work with different types of hardware and software.

- **Inadequate Training and Support.** Regardless of organizational setting, there is inadequate support for education and training of network users. Most users report that the knowledge necessary for using the network came from working with a colleague or "gutting it out" with a manual. Remote users of centralized computing resources are especially susceptible to lack of instititutional support.

- **Poor Documentation.** Other problems mentioned frequently by users were that (1) needed documentation may not be easily available, (2) documentation is frequently not user-friendly and requires someone else to "interpret it," and (3) the rapidly changing nature of networks requires constant updating of documentation. Users noted that online documentation was of little use when the procedures for obtaining that documentation were unclear, hard to obtain, or unknown.

- **Inadequate Directories of Users and Services.** There is inadequate descriptive information about available network services and few listings of individuals' electronic mail addresses. Users cannot make effective use of networks when they are unaware of the services that are available or are unable to contact others easily and reliably.

- **Technological Overkill.** For some users, rapid change in information technologies is, in and of itself, a barrier to effective network use. Many users commented that more technology and more applications are counterproductive when they are unable to use and understand the technology and applications they currently have.

- **Confusing and Dysfunctional Network Policies.** For a number of situations, the policies and procedures that govern uses of the network are unclear or simply not available. Users are unsure who or what has responsibility for particular types of network management tasks and from whom they should seek assistance in using networks.

- **Inadequate Control of Data.** Due perhaps to recent court cases involving public access to data files or backup tapes of electronic mail, there is some question about the degree to which individuals can be confident that (1) their electronic data are secure, (2) unknown backup systems that maintain copies of data will not be made public without consent, or (3) proprietary information will not escape from an organization onto the network.

- **Lack of User-based Systems and Applications.** The findings suggest that there is ineffective communication between network designers and managers and between these groups and network users. What network managers consider to be "user-based" system designs and procedures or "user-friendly" applications frequently are not considered as such by network users.

- **Cultural Differences Between Managers and Network Administrators and Researchers.** Researchers noted that their beliefs and concerns about network communication were frequently at odds with the beliefs of their managers and network administrators. Researchers claimed that managers and network administrators do not understand the nature and role of computing and communications in R&D; managers and network administrators claimed that researchers do not understand organizational constraints.

- **Increased Competition for Network Resources.** Many researchers reported that it was becoming more difficult to obtain network accounts and access to network resources. Some potential users find that costs outweigh potential benefits and that resources are being distributed unfairly.

These problems illustrate the range of barriers that users face in using electronic networks to support research. Unfortunately, many of these problems are ignored in discussions of the NREN and related initiatives because the importance of empirical, user-based research to policy development is relatively unrecognized. This list of problems also underscores the importance of communication to science: the long-term implications of research networks must be considered since they have great impact on the environment in which research is done. Finally, as discussed earlier, social and behavioral issues are of paramount importance in the adoption of information technologies and their integration into the working lives of researchers. It is impossible to develop tools to support research and education, such as the NREN, without understanding what workers in those fields are trying to achieve and what problems they face.

SCIENTIFIC NORMS AND THE USE OF ELECTRONIC RESEARCH NETWORKS

CHAPTER 7

With the United States poised to make an enormous additional investment in electronic networks, it becomes imperative to understand (1) the social context into which information technology is placed, and (2) how this social context affects and is affected by the use of electronic networks. Research discussed in Chapters 4, 5, and 6 has shown that social factors are as salient as technical factors in determining the adoption and use of information technology. If important social factors are not considered, national networking goals may not be met.

This chapter considers the relationship between the norms of science, perhaps the most important element of its social structure, and the use of electronic research networks. The relationship between the normative structure of science and the adoption and use of electronic networks by researchers is a topic that has not received a great deal of attention, although discussions of this topic in the scholarly and popular press are beginning to appear (Boesch, 1989; Lapidus, 1989). The aims of this chapter are to identify major issues, discuss the effects of scientific norms on the use of electronic research networks by researchers, consider possible implications of network use for the normative and reward structures of science, and suggest areas for further research.

This chapter provides a review of selected literature in the sociology of science. Several major facets of the normative structure of science are identified and discussed: social (or moral) norms, technical (or cognitive) norms, and the reward system of science. Some empirical findings on norms and networks will be discussed, and conclusions on the interaction between the normative structure of science and the use of networks by researchers will be offered. This chapter, however, is not intended to provide a definitive analysis of the relationship between the normative structure of the research enterprise and the use of electronic networks by scientists and engineers; rather, it should be seen as exploratory and as a source for stimulation of discussion.

Norms and Science as a Profession

Norms are, by their nature, prescriptive: they are meant to inform members of a social community and members of outside communities of expectations for behavior. Kolb (1964, p. 472) defined a norm as "a standard shared by the members of a social group to which the members are expected to conform, and conformity to which is enforced by positive and negative sanctions." Mitchell (1968, p. 132) defined norms as "the common standards or rules which guide members' responses in all established groups" and as "general precepts . . . internalized or accepted by individuals." Williams (1968, pp. 204 and 205) wrote that "norms are the standards by reference to which behavior is judged and approved or disapproved. A norm in this sense is . . . a cultural (shared) definition of desirable behavior." Williams also noted that "propriety or rightness traces back to some standard of value that is taken without further justification" (p. 205). Mann (1984, p. 266) offered a useful reminder: "A norm is not found within the personality of an individual, but can only be observed as a regularity in the behaviour of two or more people together."

The social role that scientific norms help define is that of the formally recognized profession of scientist or researcher. (See Pierce, 1987, which takes a standard approach in contrasting the "abstract" world of science with the "applied" world of the professions.) Social scientists have expended a great deal of effort in trying to delineate the characteristics that distinguish a profession from other kinds of activities, and much of their work is based on Weber's ideas about the professionalization and bureaucratization of modern social life. Storer (1966, pp. 17-19), Ritzer (1977, pp. 48-56), and others have sought to identify the major characteristics of a profession, and they have identified elements important to the overall normative structure of science: specialized knowledge and training governed by technical norms, the autonomy of the scientific community, and a unique reward system.

Social Norms of Science

In this section, views on the existence and nature of social norms in science are examined. These views range from the traditional belief in basic, idealistic norms, to views on the existence of counternorms, to more radical interpretations of the nature of social norms and their role in guiding the behavior of researchers. Understanding the nature of social norms in science and the degree to which they guide the behavior of researchers will help network policy makers and managers make decisions that increase the effectiveness of a national network.

Mertonian Norms: The Classical Ethos of Science

Robert Merton identified the ethos of science as "the emotionally toned complex of rules, prescriptions, mores, beliefs, values and presuppositions that are held to be binding upon the scientist" (1973, p. 258, n. 15), and based his work on the assertion that the fundamental aim of science is the accumulation of verified, empirical knowledge about the world, i.e., "the extension of certified knowledge." His first expression of the scientific ethos included four norms (1973, pp. 267-278):

- Universalism -- This norm asserts that scientists' claims to truth "are to be subjected to preestablished impersonal criteria: [i.e.,] consonant with observation and with previously confirmed knowledge" (p. 270). The source of these truth claims is to have no effect on the application of these impersonal criteria. Personal and social attributes of the person(s) making assertions of truth are not to influence decisions about the assertions, nor are they to influence the entry of individuals into science as a profession.

- Communism -- This norm asserts the common ownership of the results of research and that these results should be thought of as a "common heritage in which the equity of the individual producer is severely limited" (p. 273). This norm is based on the recognition that communication is essential to science, and Merton notes that "secrecy is the antithesis of this norm" (p. 273). Merton's views on this norm in relation to intellectual property and the reward structure of science is discussed below. The name of this norm was changed to "communalism" or "communality" by Barber (1952).

- Disinterestedness -- This norm is meant to characterize research as an institution, not individual behavior (see Wunderlich, 1974, on how Merton's thought on this point may have been misunderstood). The social institution of science, according to this norm, asserts social control over individuals by insisting on disinterested behavior. It is also asserted that "the dictates of socialized sentiment [disapproval of fraud and lack of acceptance of unverified claims] and of expediency largely coincide, a situation conducive to institutional stability" (p. 276).

- Organized Scepticism -- This norm involves the "temporary suspension of judgment and the detached scrutiny of beliefs in terms of empirical and logical criteria" (p. 277). This norm is both a "methodological and institutional mandate," and it insists on the critical, public nature of scientific knowledge (see Ziman, 1968, and Meadows, 1974).

These four norms, which support each other and are not mutually exclusive, constitute the "classical" ethos of science.

There have been additional norms suggested, but only two have been granted the same sort of fundamental status as Merton's. These were both suggested by Barber (1952):

- Rationality -- This norm involves the "moral, the emotional, the institutionalized . . . approval of . . . the critical approach to all the phenomena of human existence in the attempt to reduce them to ever more consistent, orderly, and generalized forms of understanding" (p. 62). Barber also said that "the modern world thinks the rule of reason more important than the rule of custom" (p. 63). This norm of science, according to Barber, results in the constant and dynamic inquiry that characterizes our society.
- Emotional Neutrality -- This norm is considered "an instrumental condition for the achievement of rationality" (p. 88). Emotional involvement is good for certain scientific purposes, especially in instilling the dedication needed to accept the other norms and to do good science, but, according to this normative injunction, emotion is out of place in the evaluation of knowledge claims.

Meadows (1974, p. 35) noted that "one can . . . define science as an activity ruled by a particular set of norms. A scientist is then a person whose conduct is governed by those norms."

It is primarily through the socialization process of specialized, disciplinary graduate education that these values and norms are internalized. According to the traditional Mertonian point of view, the budding scientist, through fear of sanctions and through the desire to emulate faculty and other role models, adopts scientific norms for two major reasons. In the first place, they are believed necessary for the development of scientific knowledge. Kolb (1964, p. 473) stressed this functional nature of norms -- "they are standards to which people are obligated to conform,

frequently because they are believed to be functional for the group in question." In addition, norms are moral injunctions for proper behavior. Mann (1984, p. 266) noted that "people come to feel moral commitment to the norms which define the rights and obligations of various roles within their social group." Merton (1973, p. 270) asserted the necessity of the norms as he has described them because they "possess a methodologic rationale . . . they are procedurally efficient . . . [and] they are believed right and good."

CounterNorms

Mitroff (1974b) investigated the occurrence of conflicting norms, which he identified and contrasted as norms and counternorms, among Apollo project scientists. The pairs of contrasted behavioral injunctions simultaneously supported by his subjects were rationality and nonrationality, emotional neutrality and emotional commitment, universalism and particularism, communality and solitariness, disinterestedness and interestedness, and organized scepticism and organized dogmatism. His study demonstrated the ability of participants in a social system, scientists in this case, to affirm and support conflicting codes of behavior. Mitroff concluded that standard norms apply to well-structured problems, while less-structured problems may demand counternorms. (See Ritzer, 1977, pp. 175-176, for another perspective on Mitroff's study.) As noted by Mitchell (1968, p. 132, citing Homans) "group norms may contradict each other and subsections of groups may employ different norms in the same situation."

Hiltz (1984), in her case studies on the introduction of networks into specific research groups, queried subjects on the degree to which attitudes of emotional neutrality as opposed to commitment, and universalism as opposed to particularism, prevailed among workers in their research specialties. She found that, generally, the counternorms of emotional commitment and particularity were thought to prevail, although some variation according to research specialty was evident. She found that counternorms were important to researchers and that they may help explain the adoption of information technologies.

Critiques of Merton: Nontraditional Approaches to the Study of Social Norms

The classical position, however, has not been without its critics. (See Zuckerman, 1988b, for a fairly comprehensive list.) Included among them are Barnes (1974) and Rothman (1972). These and other commentators have taken exception to a number of the characteristics of the classical Merton/Barber ethos of science. They have criticized, e.g.:

- The lack of attention to how personal interest and competitiveness affect the research process
- Disregarding the degree to which the Federal government and private business interests influence science by their funding practices
- The emphasis on the study of the social process of science without examining the epistemological foundations of scientific inquiry or the products (i.e., scientific knowledge claims) of this inquiry
- The identification of norms as moral injunctions related to specific and enforceable social sanctions
- The assertion that the classical ethos of science is necessary to the advancement of scientific knowledge and that lack of adherence to the norms in that ethos precludes the performance of good science.

Gibbs (1968, p. 211) gave a fruitful summary of the differences between the functionalists, a label that can be applied to Merton and his followers, and conflict sociologists, a term which can be applied to many of the critics of the Mertonian ethos. The functionalists believe that norms reflect consensus and a system of common values. For these sociologists, order in a social system is maintained through socialization and normatively defined reciprocity. The conflict sociologists, however, see norms as expressions of power. Since norms may be generated by dissensus and divergence of values among members of a social system, this school of thought emphasizes the role of coercion and sanctions in maintaining social order.

Mulkay (1976) flatly asserted that scientific norms are ideology and that the emergence of the ideal of pure science, protected and assured by scientists' adherence to the classical norms, simply serves scientists' political and social aims (also see Ritzer, 1977). (See Zuckerman, 1988b, p. 517, for a specific refutation of this claim.) Mitroff (1974b) noted that several of his respondents insisted that only the general public or beginning science students are naive enough to believe in the ideal of the pure scientist guided by the classical norms. The rhetoric exhibited by these researchers interviewed by Mitroff clearly emphasized the personal, contingent, "subjective" nature of the scientific enterprise.

More radical views on the nature of norms have led to the use of new methods for the study of the social component of research. Recent years have seen the emergence of ethnographic studies of the working life of researchers. These studies (e.g., Knorr-Cetina, 1981; Latour and Woolgar, 1979; Lynch, 1985), although not monolithic in their theoretical underpinnings, were conducted like anthropological field studies and drew attention to the personal, political, and other nonnormative factors that guide the behavior of researchers and the production of scientific knowledge. They argued that scientific knowledge is constructed by researchers in their laboratories from a multiplicity of possible facts and interpretations and that knowledge is the result of local negotiation and literary persuasion, not the result of strict adherence to scientific and technical norms. The production of legitimate, useful, and important results was seen as a rhetorical, rather than a technical, act.

Discourse analysis is another relatively new method used to investigate the link between norms and behavior. Gilbert and Mulkay (1984) drew attention to the multiplicity of meanings in research communication by treating the discourse of researchers as a topic of investigation, rather than as a resource that reveals what "really" happened in the laboratory or what really motivated researchers' behavior. They saw scientists, rather, as social actors who can characterize their beliefs and actions in different, often apparently incompatible ways, depending on the nature of the particular situation at the time their comments are made.

Expanding upon earlier work, Gilbert and Mulkay identified and characterized two main repertoires used by researchers to explain their behavior. The empiricist repertoire appears almost exclusively in the formal literature and is based on Mertonian norms and technical norms (discussed below). It "portrays scientists' actions and beliefs as following unproblematically and inescapably from the empirical characteristics of an impersonal natural world" (p. 56). The contingent repertoire, on the other hand, recognizes the existence of counternorms and personal, social, and political influences on the conduct of research. When operating within this mode of discourse, researchers portray their actions and beliefs as idiosyncratic, "heavily dependent on speculative insights, prior intellectual commitments, personal characteristics, indescribable skills, social ties and group membership" (p. 56). Thus, it seems that norms justify behavior rather than guide it in any simple way.

Mulkay (1980, p. 113) argued that the "basic Mertonian norms . . . have been used in such a loose and all-inclusive way . . . that any conceivable professional act on the part of research scientists has been classifiable, with a little ingenuity, within their frame of reference." Using specific statements related to the communication of research results that were made by a group of researchers in astronomy, Mulkay contrasted the simplicity of sociologists' version of the norm of communality with the complex and disparate formulations of the researchers. His examples demonstrated that one researcher can "apply to one action two or more rules which seem to be literally incompatible . . . without appearing to recognize any inconsistency" (p. 121). He concluded (pp. 123-124):

> [T]hat scientists have a complex repertoire of rules which can be brought to bear on their professional life; that the relationship between these rules and scientists' actions is highly problematic and little understood; . . . that scientists interpret and employ these rules in subtle and complex ways, making use of a variety of supplementary cultural resources and adapting the rules to the special characteristics of specific social situations; that there is no single, coherent code dominant in science, but rather a diverse variety of formulations which can easily be used by scientists to challenge any particular rule-based assertion; . . . that all rule-like formulations employed by scientists acquire their meaning through the interpretative work carried out by individuals in the course of social interaction in specific contexts.

In his view, norms are related to behaviors but not in a way that would allow prediction of the behavior of a researcher based on one's knowledge of normative rules alone.

Thus, there is considerable and fundamental controversy within the sociology of science about norms, their effects on behavior, and their role in science. Further, the identification, description, and interpretation of scientific norms by scientists and outsiders is problematic. The classical ethos of science presents a false choice between adherence to the norms, which assures the advance of science, and lack of adherence to the norms, which makes science

impossible. There is much evidence that indicates that this dichotomy is not real. Rather, scientists always adhere rhetorically to norms as moral injunctions, but their behavior is much more complex. For example, Etzkowitz (1989) gave a clear explanation of the transformation of academics' norms as they become entrepreneurs. Their choice is not between norms and normlessness; rather, they develop different kinds of behavior believed, by the researchers involved, to be allowable and even encouraged by the classical norms of science (see, for example, Shepard, 1954). Thus, the limited secrecy becoming more common in university research is seen by academic researchers as good, and researchers accept these and other limits on their communication imposed by the university or business and governmental sponsors relatively easily. Etzkowitz said that (1989, pp. 26 and 27):

> Entrepreneurship is thus made compatible with basic research through a legitimating theme that integrates the two activities . . . . New forms of behavior are allowed while traditional values are upheld . . . . Normative change rather than stigmatization of deviance is taking place.

A more fully realized example of normative development was given by Sutton (1984). His basic position was that "research norms and criteria of success are both situationally defined" (p. 197) and that professional norms are co-opted to achieve organizational research goals. His subjects, researchers in various groups at the Lawrence Livermore Laboratory (LLL), were faced with the dilemma of every researcher: How to balance organizational needs with professional norms (especially those assuring researchers' autonomy and independence). Researchers at the laboratory developed interpretations of their behavior which made them, in their eyes, closer to the ideal of research defined by the classical ethos than academic scientists are. Although Livermore's researchers' behavior was clearly well outside that expected by the majority of scientists, e.g., publication was relatively unimportant, funding was assured by "outside, secular" authority, and their problems were, to a large extent, determined by others, researchers at the laboratory still did good science and felt no major discrepancies between their behavior and the classical norms of science.

Several characteristics of LLL contributed to this particular research culture: the irrelevance of outside recognition to success at the laboratory and to funding decisions, the multidisciplinary nature of the research done there which fosters a clear division of labor and responsibility, the uniqueness of the technical problems studied, and an overall commitment to the organizational importance of the project goal (Sutton, 1984, pp. 206, 209, and 210). Thus, despite the lack of the usual control mechanisms, scientists at LLL developed their own normative mechanisms while they still used the classical ethos of science as the ultimate rhetorical standard of their behavior. This was especially true in their disdain for the mythology of the academic definition of research autonomy (p. 220).

Networks and Social Norms of Science

In summing up the relationship between social norms and behavior, Zuckerman (1988b, pp. 517 and 519) noted that:

> Commitment and conformity to norms are not the same; whether scientists do or do not conform in particular instances is quite distinct from whether they believe the norms are legitimate . . . . The ethos is neither consistently honored nor consistently flouted.

Scientific norms do not always guide behavior, nor do they always guide behavior in a particular way. In addition, both norms and counternorms are voiced by researchers, depending on which particular behaviors they are trying to explain or justify.

It would appear that, in a general way, researchers feel that science is a unique activity guided by its own set of rules. They see the autonomy of the research community as sacrosanct, synonymous with scientific progress (see Chapter 6). Thus, it seems likely that attempts to guide the use of networks by researchers with norms, goals, or policies that originate outside of the research community would meet with great resistance. Because communication is such an essential part of science, and because scientists insist on autonomous control of the means of scientific communication, researchers will not be anxious to use systems that obviously violate the social norms of science.

Whether norms actually determine behavior is uncertain; if they do influence behavior, the degree to which they do is also unclear. What is certain, however, is that norms perform essential rhetorical functions and that electronic networks must give rhetorical

support to the classical norms of science in order for researchers to feel comfortable using networks for normatively approved, formal functions. Further, unless the majority of researchers feel comfortable using networks, the objectives of national research networking initiatives will not be achieved. Because norms are important factors in the communication behavior of scientists, norms should be considered when designing and managing networks. Even if one accepts the functionalist view that norms have been clearly identified and that all researchers adhere to them, there are still difficulties with predicting network use based on norms, because norms can and will conflict.

As noted below, based on some of the data discussed in Chapter 6, researchers insisted that they would rely on scientists' adherence to normatively prescribed behavior (i.e., appropriate sharing of information, accurate allocation of credit, and "responsible network use") to dictate network policies. There are two interrelated difficulties with this point of view. The first is that computer networks are being used well beyond the computer subculture for whom they were originally intended (Greif, 1988, p. 16; and Quarterman, 1990). This subculture lives by rules that are inadequate for other users, e.g., there is "no strong etiquette . . . [about] how electronic communication should be used" (Kiesler et al., 1984, p. 661). In addition, research has shown that the cultural norms of computer professionals profoundly influence computer use and the development of networks so much that the assumptions about the adaptability and benefits of computer-mediated communication (CMC) outside that culture may need to be rethought (Kiesler et al., 1984, 661ff). There is little consensus among researchers, beyond the general moral content of normative statements, about the specifics of network use, although certain online communities are beginning to discuss and develop explicit codes of electronic conduct.

A second problem is that the "hacker" mentality, appropriate to the early days of computer networking, is clearly antithetical to normative science. As noted by Zuckerman (1988b, p. 521), research is based on scholars' "implicit trust" in each other, but invasive hackers compromise that trust. The case involving Cornell graduate student Robert Morris and the breaking into ARPANET in 1988 is one example of this conflict in mores. Stoll offered two other examples: his trailing and identifying a hacker responsible for breaking into Milnet and a subsequent hacker's targeting of Stoll for harassment and ridicule. Stoll lamented that "it's sad that people have these gun-slinger ethics" (Markoff, 1990a, p. A21), and he particularized the network user's dilemma: "Who wants to be eternally vigilant? . . . . We want to do science . . . . The cost is the people using these things are going to have to act responsibly" (Turner, 1990, p. A3). These examples indicate the kind of abuse to which electronic research networks are vulnerable. Researchers are afraid of this vulnerability.

A related problem is that the research done on social aspects of CMC seems to indicate that networks reduce the communication inhibitions of the people using them. For example, anger ("flaming"), sarcasm, "cute" remarks (Hiltz, 1984, p. 147), and junk mail are notable problems on electronic networks. While some electronic communities may have developed network norms, there seem to be no widely shared norms for electronic communication, and there appears to be no way of learning about them if they do exist (Kiesler et al., 1984; and Sproull and Kiesler, 1986). The general lack of consensus about rules and the occurrence of relatively uninhibited behavior threaten the use of networks for "normatively approved" scientific communication and any use beyond simple file transfer and data analysis.

Technical Norms of Science

In addition to social or moral norms, researchers also maintain technical or cognitive norms. Researchers must meet certain technical criteria, as defined by the research community, before their work will be accepted by that community. In On Being a Scientist (National Academy of Sciences, Committee on the Conduct of Science, 1989), young researchers are introduced to both the moral and technical criteria that must be met before "the limited, fallible work of individual scientists [can be] converted into the enduring edifice of scientific knowledge" (p. 1). It is useful, of course, to remember Mitroff's (1974b) comments about the naivete of students, young scientists, and the public at large in this context.

Implicitly and explicitly, researchers learn that "good" research depends on such technical skills as the ability to:

- Recognize and define important problems
- Use instruments correctly and secure accurate measurements
- Develop reasonable solutions and conclusions

- Accurately and appropriately report research results.

The demonstration of technical competence in these areas is thought to be linked to the production of legitimate, useful, and important results. This belief is based upon the assumption that adherence to these technical or cognitive norms, as well as to social or moral norms, is necessary for the advancement of science. Familiarity with technical standards for their work is part of the socialization process for all researchers. Technical standards such as those listed above are made explicit in graduate school training, by review criteria, and through technical writing instructions. Role models, both faculty members and other highly regarded professionals, are particularly important for this process (see, for example, Polanyi, 1966; Ziman, 1968; Wilson, 1983; and Pierce, 1987).

Technical Norms of Science, Informal Communication, and Electronic Networks

Networks facilitate both formal communication (e. g., the provision of published documents) and informal communication (e. g., communication through electronic mail) among researchers. They also allow researchers to access powerful tools for data collection and analysis. Because of these capabilities, networks seem to facilitate and improve problem recognition, the use of successful experimental procedures, and the development of solutions to research problems. Informal communication is particularly important to improving compliance with technical norms because it allows access to the craft knowledge and private versions of research that do not appear in the formal literature and yet are vital to the conduct of research.

The nature of informal communication and the conduct of research has been addressed from a sociological point of view. Most of this work is aimed at analyzing the production of knowledge and is basically inductive, arrived at by thinking about particular cases from history or personal experience. Informal communication is placed within the context of the practice of research, which is often described as an "art" or "craft" activity.

Ravetz (1971) presented perhaps the most complete analysis of the nature and importance of what he termed "craft knowledge" in R&D work, and of its conveyance through informal communication channels. He portrayed the researcher as a "craftsman" who (p. 75):

[W]orks with particular objects [including both material and intellectual constructs]; he must know their properties in all their particularity; and his knowledge of them cannot be specified in any formal account . . . . He must develop a personal, tacit knowledge of his objects and what he can do with them, if he is to produce good work.

Researchers must gain craft knowledge, through their own experience or through informal communication with more experienced researchers, to avoid pitfalls in their work and to satisfy the technical norms prevalent in their particular community for collecting and analyzing data and for assessing the adequacy of solutions to research problems.

According to Ravetz (1971, p. 77), one of the most important uses of craft knowledge is in the transferral of information about research methods:

The transmission of methods is accomplished almost entirely within the interpersonal channel, requiring personal contact and a measure of personal sympathy between the parties. What is transmitted will be partly explicit, but partly tacit; principle, precept, and example are all mixed together. There is no substitute for such personal communication; messages whose transmission requires a prior formulation and clarification of ideas (as even in a letter to a colleague), will necessarily be impoverished in their content of private craft knowledge.

An important issue is the degree to which informal electronic communication, such as that carried out using electronic mail or bulletin boards, shares the attributes of print media. Which characteristics does it share with both personal contact and a written letter to a colleague? Will it provide an adequate substitute for either of these media?

Ravetz (p. 179) summed up:

In conclusion, we may consider the two channels of communication and their contents as a pair of interpenetrating opposites. The one distributes and preserves the results of the work, while the other governs the work itself; one is public and explicit, while the other is informal and interpersonal. The contents of the public channel are in principle permanent, and exist independently of the circumstances or ultimate fate of the work which produced them; while the body of methods, bound to a very particular personal experience (both technical and social) directly control the future contents of the public channel. The results of scientific inquiry are in principle based on controlled experience and rigorous argument; but the methods governing the inquiry itself are a particularly subtle craft knowledge, different in nature from scientific knowledge.

Ravetz emphasized the importance of both social and technical factors in the conduct of research and, specifically, in research communication. His work acknowledged many philosophical antecedents. Polanyi's notion of "tacit knowledge" is one such source. Polanyi (1966) spoke of the reliance on tacit knowledge -- part experience, part intuition, part tactile sensation -- to accomplish a variety of activities, ranging from playing the piano to making a medical diagnosis.

Ziman wrote extensively on the nature of science as both a social and practical activity and the role of informal communication as part of this social fabric. He recognized that scientific investigation "is a practical art" that is "not learnt out of books, but by imitation and experience" (Ziman, 1968, p. 7). Like Ravetz, he contrasted the informality of interpersonal communication with the rhetorical nature of formal publications. He described a published research report as a "contrived document, with its logical teeth brushed and its observational trouser seams sharply creased. It is written in a curiously artificial 'impersonal' style, deliberately flat and unemotive, as from one calculating machine to another" (p. 34). The published report of an experiment, he noted, is "a long way indeed from that direct and strenuous wrestling with brute Nature that the individual reseacher experiences in his own laboratory" (p. 35). In the laboratory, science is "intuitive, uncertain, deeply felt and controversial . . . . romantic in its chaos" (pp. 72 and 73).

This characterization of research describes a context in which informal communication plays a significant role as a means of conveying the results of personal experience and intuition -- which, according to the norms of science, is barred from formal publications -- from one researcher to another. Ziman (p. 108) credited "unofficial channels" such as "private correspondence . . . conferences and meetings, interchange of manuscripts and data, sabbatical leaves, consulting visits, seminars, conversations around the coffee table" as "a grapevine of hints and ideas, observations and opinions." He concluded that "the informal system of scientific communication is quite as important as the formal system, although having a different function" (p. 116).

This view of research activity as a kind of chaos that requires all kinds of informal information for its accomplishment was also expressed, from a slightly different perspective, by Schon (1983), a management theorist. Schon (p. 170) described an important part of the process of science and technology as reflecting-in-action or constructing "a manageable problem from a problematic situation." Science is not the "after the fact presentation of knowledge of the sort usually found in the scientific journals but before the fact, apparently disorderly research of the kind sometimes described as 'the art of scientific investigation'" (p. 177). Thus, Schon, too, recognized the importance of informal knowledge in research work.

Beveridge (1957) produced a classic treatise on the art of scientific investigation. He proposed informal discussion as an important stimulus to the scientific mind. More specifically, he noted that the discussion of problems with colleagues may be helpful in several ways (p. 85):

- The other person may be able to contribute a useful suggestion.
- A new idea may arise from the pooling of information or ideas from two or more persons.
- Discussion provides a valuable means of uncovering errors.
- Discussion is usually refreshing, stimulating, and encouraging.
- Discussion helps one escape from an established habit of thought which has proved fruitless.

Thus, Beveridge's analysis also established a link between informal communication and the exchange of practical, how-to information.

The kinds of sociological investigations of the practice of research discussed above seem to prefigure some of the conclusions about the role of informal communication in research that were subsequently derived empirically. The literature of information science, psychology, and management contains research findings related to the importance of informal communication networks -- mostly human rather than electronic -- for research productivity. Informal communication is recognized as an important source of craft knowledge (and inspiration) for scientists and engineers and, thus, as a factor in improving R&D productivity.

Reviewing the literature on invisible colleges (i.e., human communication networks whose members are at the cutting edge of a particular research specialty), Cronin (1982, p. 225) noted that "informal communication is the lifeblood of scientific progress for both the physical and social sciences." He asserted that informal communication improves one's productivity and status because (p. 215):

> [I]t ensures that participants in (even loosely defined) networks are able to keep abreast of current developments (it also allows for the transmission of procedural or technical/ equipment-related data which cannot always be satisfactorily conveyed via the primary publication media), and . . . it reinforces the group's sense of identity and purpose.

What impact will electronic communication networks have on invisible colleges and on their function of facilitating the exchange of craft knowledge and the adherence to technical norms? Will computer networks extend these functions to more researchers and expand the number of members who may be associated with an invisible college?

Granovetter (1973) recognized a benefit of informal communication for both individuals and scientific progress as a whole, one that gains in import as research becomes increasingly interdisciplinary. He found that weak ties (i.e., communication among people who are not members of the same work group and may not even be formally acquainted with each other) facilitate more extensive communication flow and carry ideas across discipline boundaries. Electronic bulletin boards allow one to communicate with presumably trustworthy and knowledgeable strangers who share one's research interests. Thus, one benefit of universal electronic connectivity would be the extension of one's network of weak ties to a larger number of colleagues in other disciplines.

A number of researchers have looked at the informal communication behavior of scientists and engineers, but most of these studies of information sources, channels, and impacts were also conducted before the use of electronic networks became widespread. T.J. Allen (1985) found that personal contacts far outdistance literature as a source of potential engineering solutions, thus are more often the source of improved ideas and performance. In addition, he found that "unpublished reports" acquired "from colleagues" are the major source of printed information for (from Table 4.4 in Allen, 1985, on p. 81):

- The direct solution of a problem
- The determination of the results of related work performed by others
- The determination of procedures
- Learning a new specialty or broadening areas of attention
- Browsing that results in significant discovery
- Verifying reliability of an answer
- Aiding in definition of the operational environment.

Allen did not, however, derive explicit impacts on the research process from informal communication per se (as opposed to informal publications).

Garvey (1979), on the other hand, did specifically examine uses and benefits of interpersonal communication with colleagues. He found that informal communication was used most for (from Figure 4 on p. 266):

- Aiding problem definition
- Selecting a design for data collection
- Selecting a data gathering technique
- Designing equipment or apparatus
- Choosing a data analysis technique
- Enabling full interpretation of data.

These tasks, again, are those that are usually associated with the transmission of craft knowledge and the ability of researchers to comply with technical norms.

This literature suggests that informal communication channels are important not only for cementing the social structure of science, but also for improving researchers' ability to produce technically competent work. Wilson and Farid (1979, p. 130, following Ziman, 1968, pp. 34-35) noted that "behind the public story finally formulated and presented to the world lies the private story of what went wrong as well as what went right, of successive attempts and corrected versions, of mistakes and lucky guesses, of detours and discouragements." Gilbert and Mulkay (1984, p. 53) reported that "scientists stressed that carrying out experiments is a practical activity requiring craft skills, subtle judgements, and intuitive understanding."

In addition to this literature, some newer online information systems (e.g., BIONET and ACTIS) are developed by and for particular research communities include both formal (databases) and informal (electronic mail, newsletter, research-in-progress databases) components. This new type of system seems to verify the importance and practicality of using networks not only to access formal information resources, but also to exchange informal research communications of a craft nature. Cronin (1982, p. 229) asserted that "developments in information technology will bring about changes in the way in which scientists communicate informally, but it is hard to see how these changes will radically affect the kinds of interactions which are recorded." He predicted, in other words, that traditional communication patterns and norms would prevail, regardless of technological advances. This statement, on the one hand, validates the importance of further investigation of the nature and purpose of informal research communication for predicting the effects that the new communication technologies will have on the working lives of researchers. On the other hand, the truth of this prediction has yet to be thoroughly tested in connection with the use of CMC by researchers.

The Reward Structure of Science

As a social and historical enterprise, science has developed a complex reward structure in which communication (formal publication and informal exchanges), scientific norms, and rewards are inextricably linked. In fact, Storer (in Merton, 1973, p. 281) correctly identified "the heart of the Mertonian paradigm [as] the powerful juxtaposition of the normative structure of science with its institutionally distinctive reward system." Reward takes the general form of recognition of the value of particular work to the advancement of knowledge, but this recognition can also entail financial gain, career advancement, and the ability to garner more resources to support one's research. Granting recognition presupposes an ability to identify the individual contributions of researchers or teams of researchers, to assess the merits of their contributions, and to sort out claims of priority through formally recognized channels. Formal publication in the peer-reviewed, open literature is seen as the primary vehicle through which the reward system operates. While the informal exchange of knowledge also leads to rewards, one needs access to the information channels used by researchers to communicate with each other in order to participate in this type of activity.

This section of the chapter discusses a number of topics related to the reward structure of science: the general nature of rewards in science, the exchange system of science, the Matthew Effect (defined below), and the concept of the invisible college. It concludes with a brief analysis of the highly problematic relationship between formal publication and the use of electronic networks.

Rewards in Science

Recognition and reward in science can take many forms. Figure 7-1 presents those rewards which, in today's environment, a researcher might expect to receive for network communication, e.g., for making one's results available "online," for acting as an information gatekeeper, or for helping other network users solve particular research problems. All of these rewards could also be obtained without participating in network activities. Figure 7-2 presents rewards not likely to be given to a researcher because of network use.

The rewards noted in Figure 7-1, except the ability to participate in invisible colleges, would probably be of less significance to most researchers than would the rewards in Figure 7-2. The rewards listed in the first figure are also not likely to contribute directly to the more significant forms of award in the second. It must be noted, however, that the various forms of recognition and reward listed in both figures are not universally or equally desired by all researchers, their funders, or their organizational superiors.

Exchange System of Science

The scientific enterprise can be seen as a system of exchange. There are several kinds of mechanisms for exchange that involve the transmission of knowledge. For example, individuals exchange information, and both parties benefit. Another kind of exchange involves the granting of concrete rewards, such as prizes or career advancement, for important contributions to the common fund of knowledge. Since networks function as a primary channel for the exchange of information for a number of researchers, the attitudes of researchers towards this channel as an exchange mechanism must be examined.

Storer (1966) took the ethos of science promulgated by Merton and Barber and developed it further through an extended analysis of science as a formal

---

Figure 7-1. Rewards that May Accrue from the Use of Research Networks

Personal satisfaction from others' recognition of the value of one's work

Membership on editorial boards, funding review committees, and blue-ribbon panels

Appointment as moderator of online bulletin board or editor of online journal

Opportunity to serve as coordinator of a conference

Appointment as formal reviewer of peers' work

Invited lectures, presentations, and speeches

Professional celebrity

Citation in the literature

Increased interaction with elite of one's own and other disciplines (i.e., participation in important invisible colleges)

Consulting opportunities

Figure 7-2. Rewards Not Likely to Accrue from the Use of Research Networks

Professional society honors

Journal, monograph, and conference proceedings editorship

Intellectual property awards

Career advancement, including academic tenure and promotion

Most financial gains (in terms of salary and promotion)

Awards or prizes

General celebrity

Recognition in political spheres and appointment as formal or informal advisor to governmental officials

Increased and more reliable research funding

Eponymous identification of period, process, or phenomenon (e.g., the Copernican Revolution)

Entrepreneurial ventures and endorsements

social system. He noted that Talcott Parsons, Merton's teacher, identified mutual reward as an essential part of any social system (p. 32), and Storer developed a well-reasoned functionalist argument identifying the major commodity (or medium of exchange) of the scientific exchange and reward system. That commodity is "competent response" (p. 84). It is this commodity that is the social engine of research. The aim of all science, according to Storer's hypothesis, is to guarantee competent response from one's peers to the products of one's creative efforts. Gibbs (1968, p. 211) concluded that one of the most important factors in keeping order in any social system is reward obtained through normatively defined reciprocity. Hagstrom (1965) also noted that scientists make their contributions to the common fund of knowledge in order to be rewarded with the recognition of their peers.

Ouchi (1980) discussed the concepts of reciprocity and social exchange, but he did so in terms of organizational structure and behavior. He said that "a norm of reciprocity underlies all exchange mechanisms" (p. 138) and that a period of apprenticeship and socialization supports the coincidence of personal and organizational goals in many situations. In addition, each participant in any exchange must be aware that

reciprocity is assured -- if any party involved in social exchange is not certain that reciprocity is met, the entire transaction is in jeopardy, and transaction costs increase. This model can be applied to the scientific enterprise, and it fits in well with both functionalist and anti-functionalist conceptions of scientific norms. Other "economic" accounts of science consistently stress the exchange of recognition and reward for access to other resources and for the continued opportunity to excel (see, for example, Zuckerman, 1988b; and Meadows, 1974). Latour and Woolgar (1979) characterize this exchange as that of credibility for other resources.

Formal publication, especially in the journal literature, is a major element in the exchange system of science. Storer (1966, p. 71) said that "'the literature' of science is extremely important because it supports each scientists's assumption that his colleagues know or can know what he knows." This presumption, even if inaccurate, of one's colleagues' state of knowledge makes science more cohesive and also reassures the individual scientist that creative efforts will be appreciated and rewarded. In his description of the literature, Storer also continued an argument made in Merton (1973, p. 464):

With the advent of printing . . . findings could be permanently secured, errors in the transmission of precise knowledge greatly reduced, and intellectual property rights registered in print.

Storer (p. 157) took the argument one step further by referring to the fact that publication grants access to a guaranteed, competent audience, the major reward exchanged by scientists.

Many commentators have provided evidence of the reliance of science upon formal, peer-reviewed publication for the operation of the reward structure. For example, Gaston (1978, p. 133) stated that "scientific recognition can be explained almost entirely by the amount [sic] of publications scientists produce." While other factors, discussed below, also are of major importance in determining status in the social structure of science, it is quite clear that publication is foremost. Yet it is here that the gap between the ideal of the Mertonian ethos and the reality of social practice becomes clear. Chase (1970; see also Zuckerman, 1970, p. 249) analyzed criteria for publication in certain journals and found that there is significant reliance on "extra-rational" factors, i.e., nonnormative according to the classical ethos of science, in the evaluation of manuscripts submitted for publication. The classical Mertonian ethos of science is called into doubt if publication, the major vehicle for the reward and exchange systems of science, exhibits nonnormative characteristics.

The norm of reciprocity is also important in understanding the nature of rewards accumulated through informal communication. One major reward is the ability to adhere to technical norms. Electronic mail and electronic bulletin boards give researchers access to a wide pool of competent colleagues. It is assumed that, in the long run, reciprocity will obtain and those benefiting from the knowledge and experience of others will also contribute, in time, to the solution of others' problems.

As discussed above, publication in the open, peer-reviewed, journal literature is most often the foundation for the reward system of science which, in turn, supports the normative structure. As access to electronic networks proliferates, and as researchers are increasingly threatened by information overload, there will be continuing suggestions for electronic alternatives to the traditional scientific journal. Such suggestions are problematic for a number of reasons (see, for example, Piternick, 1989; and Meadows, 1974):

- Ergonomics: electronic media pose significant problems with reading cues, print size, portability, physical access, reliable source of electric power, and related issues.
- Economics: there are few rewards for publishing electronically, and professional societies which produce print journals might lose both the considerable financial support offered by journals and a major membership perquisite.
- Technical considerations: limited network capacity, incompatibiltiy of hardware and software, and inability to reproduce sophisticated graphics inhibit electronic publication.
- Social factors: electronic have-nots may be increasingly distanced from mainstream science.
- Mores of scientific communication: the difficulty of assuring adequate peer review and general quality control, and uncertainty about the archival record of science, are significant obstacles.

The Matthew Effect

One of the ideas developed by Merton and further explored by others is what he identified as the Matthew Effect, based on a theme expressed in the Gospel of Saint Matthew: For comparable work, recognized researchers get disproportionately greater credit than do less well-known researchers. This phenomenon has also been expressed as "the rich get richer and the poor get poorer" (Merton, 1973, especially pp. 440-459; Merton, 1988; and Zuckerman, 1988b, p. 532). This effect especially compromises the norm of universalism because attributes such as the reputation of individuals and institutions, available resources, site of graduate training, and demographic characteristics (e.g., age, sex, and race) influence the distribution of scientific recognition and other rewards. Chase's (1970) work, based to some extent on research done by Crane in 1967, also discussed the Matthew Effect.

Merton noted that the publication explosion is exacerbating the Effect, especially in the allocation of resources and in access to journal publication (1973, pp. 449, 457, and 481). The differences among individuals and institutions in access to scientific opportunity of all kinds has been well-documented by Merton elsewhere (1988) and others, including Allison and Stewart (1974), Zuckerman (1970 and 1988b), Storer (1966), Cronin (1982), and Rothman (1972). This work is predicated on the awareness of the inequitable distribution of scientific resources and scientific reward, in clear defiance of the ideal of the Merton/ Barber ethos.

Crane's investigation (1965) of the effects of institutional placement on the reputations of and rewards granted to academic scientists showed that researchers at "major" universities have considerable advantage in accumulating the resources necessary to ensure high recognition and reward in science. This result is not surprising, given the wealth of data demonstrating the Matthew Effect in a number of situations. What is surprising, however, is that Crane asserted that position in a specific institution is more important than productivity, as measured by publication (p. 710). Such a conclusion differed markedly from the general consensus that publication and productivity are the prime determinants of recognition (see, for example, Cole and Cole, 1973).

Gaston (1978, p. 122) maintained that, while the Matthew Effect is dysfunctional for some individuals, it may be functional for science as a whole because it helps scientists discriminate among all of the information vying for their attention. This assertion is based, however, on Gaston's assumptions that talent will eventually tell, that "real" contributions will eventually be recognized, and that contributions and researchers unfairly ignored because of the Matthew Effect are outweighed by the time and effort that scientists gain by being selective in their use of information. This interpretation is inherent, to some extent, in some of Merton's own research. Cole and Cole argued "that accumulative advantage may result from giving each scientist his due, and that the resulting social inequities may be highly functional for scientific progress" (Allison and Stewart, 1974, p. 598).

A major issue is whether electronic networks will solidify or erode the social stratification, of which the Matthew Effect is one symptom. As discussed by Zuckerman (1988b, p. 526), "individuals, groups, laboratories, institutes, universities, journals, fields and specialities, theories, and methods are incessantly ranked and sharply graded in prestige." The stratification exists both across and within institutions. The authors' earlier work (see Chapter 6) also presented some special stratification effects with regard to electronic research networks, e.g., access, training, institutional support, and disciplinary differences. Hiltz (1984, p. 11) noted that "a computerized conferencing system might increase equality of opportunity among researchers . . . . However, competitive pressures might make users unwilling to help

out their peers." Will electronic networks increase or decrease this sort of stratification? The answer, of course, is uncertain.

The Invisible College

One of the major symptoms of the Matthew Effect is the dominance of invisible colleges by "rich" individuals, disciplines, and institutions. The term "invisible college" was first used to describe the informal scientific groups predating the Royal Society of London in 1660. The idea of the invisible college was resurrected by Derek de Solla Price (1961), and this topic has experienced a number of phases of "popularity" with regard to social scientists' opinions of its explanatory power. Most work emphasizes that invisible colleges are highly selective, relatively small groups of elite scientists working on the hot topics of the day. Such groups often are characterized by personal acquaintance, intense informal communication, and the relatively free exchange of information and other resources.

Merton (1973, p. 331, and 1988, p. 615) emphasized the important role that information plays in the invisible college. Those in the invisible college are at "strategic nodes in the networks of scientific communication" and benefit greatly from it. Those not in the invisible college experience great anxiety and exhibit more intense competition with their peers because of this exclusion. Because some researchers maintain that "informal communication is the lifeblood of scientific progress" (Cronin, 1982, p. 225), exclusion from the invisible college in one's field is tantamount to being relegated to second-class status.

The Matthew Effect clearly is important in the composition and workings of invisible colleges. Cronin (p. 229) also noted that it is very difficult for younger researchers or those in less prestigious institutions to get access to invisible colleges. Network expertise can provide greater participation in the important invisible colleges, and networks can ameliorate the Matthew Effect. At the same time, however, the growth in electronic research networks can also intensify the Matthew Effect and make invisible colleges more inaccessible.

Reward Structure of Science and Electronic Networks

It is ordinarily believed that the norms of science and the reward system work in tandem. Scientific rewards, including recognition by one's peers, are supposedly allocated <u>within</u> normative channels <u>for</u> normative behavior. Mulkay (1979, p. 69) and others, however, gave numerous examples of significant rewards granted for behavior clearly outside the limits set by the classical ethos of science. Because norms are often defined by the sanctions which carry forbidding rewards to those who defy the norms, many sociologists have concluded that the rewarding of non-normative behavior demonstrates the lack of norms in science.

In a more general way, since science depends upon exchange, researchers cannot fully participate in science without physical access to the channel used for exchange. At this time, prestigious, high-tech institutions virtually monopolize both network capacity and higher network functions. On the other hand, full participation and reward in science are not guaranteed by access to the channels of communication alone; therefore, simple access to research networks will not assure equitability in the allocation of resources and reward nor any change in social status for researchers at less prestigious institutions or in less prestigious disciplines.

Networks, of course, have the potential to ameliorate or exacerbate the Matthew Effect. If network access is made universal, more researchers will be able to participate in invisible colleges and to get access to important tools. If network access and support remain exclusive, however, those researchers who do have access will move even farther ahead of their less fortunate colleagues in terms of prestige and resources. Policy makers should consider the implications of this aspect of national network implementation.

A related issue is that researchers in all settings show increasing signs of entrepreneurship (see, for example, Shenhav, Lunde, and Goldberg, 1989; Etzkowitz, 1989; and Rothman, 1972) and a concomitant concern with keeping data and other information secret. Electronic networks make sharing much easier and faster, while researchers are becoming warier about sharing. Thus, the very ease and speed of electronic communication becomes a threat to some scientists, rather than a boon. Hedrick (1985) clearly illustrated that the costs and benefits of sharing data are not evenly distributed. She (pp. 124-143) and the Committee on National Statistics (1985, pp. 15-24) gave lists of benefits and costs of data sharing, which are summarized in Figure 7-3.

Cecil and Griffin (1985, p. 148) stated quite clearly that "few of the benefits and most of the burdens [of data sharing, especially electronically] fall to the possessor of a data set." Thus, networks exist in a context where it is not easy to overcome researchers' reluctance to assume the considerable costs of data sharing. A particular example is given in Barinaga (1989), where she discussed researchers' unwillingness to share full information, including X-rays, about published molecules. Ceci (1988) described researchers' attitudes toward data sharing and some of their main objections to it, while Zuckerman (1988a) discussed the emergence of new claimants, especially universities, to scientific data.

Also, the dissemination of research results electronically does not "count" as formal publication. Network communications do not have the same legitimacy as print communication in terms of resolving disputes regarding priority of discovery or intellectual property. Network communications do not have the status to resolve questions involving scientific reward. Therefore, there are very strong disincentives for using electronic networks to broadcast the results of research. In addition, some disciplines and organizations stigmatize members for "overactive" network participation.

The increased use of electronic networks in all phases of research poses serious questions to the present reward system of science, given that the "essence of science" is communication and that recognition and reward are based on formal publication. Characteristics of electronic, interactive media that appear threatening to the normative structure of science are the:

- Inherent volatility of the medium
- Difficulty of assuring an accurate, complete archival record
- The need for document authentication
- Speed of communication
- Ease with which thousands of domestic and global communicants are reached
- Inability to assure secure, confidential communication at an acceptable cost
- Possible democratization of access to information and communication channels leading to a possible decrease in the value of communication, increase in information load, and circumvention of already developed and sophisticated organizational communication patterns

- Matthew Effect whereby privileged researchers, institutions, and disciplines operate at great advantage with regard to communication and analytical tools.

Policy makers must carefully consider the implications of any decisions related to these characteristics, both in regard to national networking initiatives and in a broader context. These characteristics might be seen as the opposite side of the positive effects of electronic networks, but they are rarely discussed in the policy literature dealing with the NREN and related projects. At the same time, these characteristics have considerable influence on the behavior of individual scientists and upon science as a social community. The relative neglect of these topics might be attributed to a desire to stress the positive effects of networks and the powerful functions they offer to users, a political concern with justifying the financial and policy investment in national networks, and the general inability of information professionals and organizational analysts to deal with the topics. De-

Figure 7-3. Cost and Benefits of Data Sharing *

COSTS

- Technical obstacles, e.g., hardware and software incompatibility
- Need to provide data documentation, e.g., details of data collection procedures
- Poor communication
- Storing and transferring data
- Exposure of errors to criticism
- Loss of priority
- Necessity for rebuttal of misinterpretation
- Recognition and proprietary concerns of primary researchers
- Loss of control of data
- Costs to subsequent analysts, e.g., massaging of data set, conversion of records, and error correction
- Contribution to the costs of data sharing
- Concern about the qualifications of data requesters
- National security considerations
- Data with special problems, including personal data with identifiers and data which result from a researcher's unique, life's work
- Administrative inconvenience and cost

BENEFITS

- Reinforcement of open scientific inquiry
- Verification, refutation, or refinement of original results
- Replications with multiple data sets
- Exploration of new questions
- Reductions in the incidence of faked and inaccurate results
- Reduction of respondent burden
- Promotion of new research and creation of new data sets by connecting existing data
- Encouraging more appropriate use of empirical data in policy formulation and evaluation
- Improvements of measurement and data collection methods
- Development of theoretical knowledge and knowledge of analytic techniques
- Encouragement of multiple perspectives
- Provision of resources for training in research
- Protection against faulty data

* After Hedrick (1985) and Committee on National Statistics (1985)

spite such factors, these areas must be explained and made accessible to the general public and to policy makers.

One specific difficulty is that electronic media pose special problems for the intellectual property system (see, for example, Office of Technology Assessment, 1986; Zuckerman, 1988b; and Doty, 1989). Among these problems are an inability to identify specific contributions of individuals in the production of knowledge and the inability of the major intellectual property regimes (patents, copyrights, trademarks, and unfair competition) to adjust to the increased pace of technological change. The success of national networking initiatives will be diminished because of researchers' doubts about the protection of their intellectual property rights in an electronic environment. Miller and Blumenthal (1986, p. 229) put the matter succinctly:

> Today, the value of information is no longer dependent on or even tied to tangible, fixed expression of the information . . . . [I]f someone buys a book . . . both tangible and intangible property are transferred. It is easy to see that a property transfer has taken place. In contrast, if someone buys computerized information, enjoys it, and wants to share it with someone else, he generally need not give up his own "copy." It is more difficult to see that a property transfer has taken place. Technology makes it vastly more difficult to prove that an infringement has occurred, even if the proper legal remedies exist.

Zuckerman (1988a, p. 8) asserted, stating an opinion shared by many sociologists of science, that property rights in science are particularly paradoxical because of the normative mandates for both humility/disinterestedness <u>and</u> proper allocation of credit. The paradox is made even more complex by the threats to intellectual property posed by electronic information technologies.

EMPIRICAL DATA ON NORMS AND NETWORKS

This section reports on a re-analysis of some of the data gathered in a study funded by the U.S. Congress, Office of Technology Assessment (OTA) and reported in Chapter 6. Re-analyzing comments made by participants in the study provided an empirical assessment of the degree to which subjects' use of networks seemed to be influenced by the kinds of norms discussed in the first part of this chapter.

Social Norms

Although the normative structure of science was not an explicit area of investigation in the earlier study, many subjects seemed to base their remarks about network use, their views of appropriate network behavior, and their recommendations for network policies firmly within the context of scientific norms. Many of their remarks indicated that the social context of research, along with the prevailing reward structure of the research enterprise, profoundly influenced the research community's use of electronic networks. It was respondents' comments, in fact, that drew the authors' attention to the potential importance of the relationship between networks and the normative structure of science.

Subjects' responses alerted the study team to the fact that norms of science play an important role in researchers' expectations about networks, about other researchers' use of networks, and about network design and management strategies. For example, the study respondents made numerous comments related to the social norms of science and its reward structure:

- Network access should be as broad as possible.
- The early distribution of results facilitates science.
- Network censorship, regulation, and policing must be avoided.
- Researchers regulating themselves can lead to the scientific and technical elite becoming "resource hogs."
- National network police may be necessary.
- Junk mail can be a problem.
- Commercial traffic has no place on the network.
- We [a private sector corporation] cannot communicate on BITNET because we're commercial.
- Reputation depends upon formal publication, so don't "publish" on the net.
- Unless network submissions are credited to their publication record, people won't contribute to electronic journals.
- The agendas of systems get in the way of research.
- Students and junior researchers do most of the computing on networks.
- Management doesn't understand [research] computing needs and benefits.
- Researchers don't understand computing benefits.

- Proprietary information must be protected on the networks.
- Peer pressure regulates the quality of software disseminated over networks.

This list gives an indication of researchers' and research managers' attitudes toward the use of electronic networks and some indication of the normative content of these attitudes. The respondents' replies also give an indication of some of the major areas of controversy and conflict between the use of research networks and the norms of science, e.g., the appropriability of intellectual property on the networks, the problems posed by uninhibited network behavior (flaming and junk mail) and a hacker mentality, and the inherent volatility of the electronic medium.

A number of issues important to both network users and managers in the development of a national research network were also mentioned by study participants:

- Access
- Definition of qualified users
- Definition and operationalization of acceptable network use
- Costs and fees associated with network use
- Security and privacy of information
- Intellectual property and ownership of network information
- Electronic publishing.

Scholars and researchers who participated in the study have deeply ingrained attitudes and behaviors concerning these issues. Specifically, they tend to define the possible resolution of these issues in terms of the normative structure that governs their particular work group or institution. Network managers and policy makers, on the other hand, approach these issues with their own set of criteria for acceptable solutions. They frequently fail to consider prevailing organizational and scientific norms in the design and operation of networks. In general, policy makers, network designers and network managers, and research and other organizational managers tend to limit their attention to short-term, financial, and technical problems. This limited vision will severely undermine the ability of national networking initiatives to achieve their long-range goals.

Technical Norms

The connection between the use of networks and the ability of researchers to comply with technical norms was made by both expert and novice network users in all three sectors and across disciplines. In addition, both junior and senior researchers seemed to seek outside ideas, resources, and expertise during the course of their research. The quotations listed in Figure 7-4 are representative of the kinds of comments made and illustrate the links between networks and technical norms that were mentioned by the researchers who participated in the study. The comments are reported verbatim.

Researchers often use electronic mail to exchange behind-the-scenes information, both with colleagues who are already known to them and with researchers, students, faculty members, and others, whom they have never met. Engineers also rely on information from vendors, customers, and other project or firm members to improve the technical quality of their work. Again, much of this information may be transmitted on networks. Many researchers describe the benefits derived from networks in terms of increased access to a larger pool of knowledgeable colleagues and to the kind of expertise needed to solve the day-to-day problems that confront them in the workplace.

By consulting experts, some researchers use networks to gain access to the craft knowledge that normally comes with experience. Thus, they are able to improve their adherence to technical norms and, ultimately, the quality of their work and their status in the research community. Moreover, their status is also improved if they use networks to become acquainted with the more influential and prestigious members of the research community. Mulkay (1979, pp. 75 and 90) referred to the tacit component of scientific knowledge and the need for personal contact for successful sharing of that knowledge. Networks may not be a completely suitable mechanism for the transmission of

Figure 7-4. Electronic Networks and Technical Norms: Comments Made by Researchers on the Use of Networks to Improve Research Quality

- My work is influenced by the ideas of other researchers that I respect. The main way I obtain these ideas is not through reading their papers or talking with them at conferences, but by discussing or hearing about their ideas via net messages. These net messages are from both personal correspondence and news groups.

- Community Knowledge: Regardless of external impressions, we do not work in an ivory tower that is insolated from trivial, bothersome, day-to-day details. Recently I was typesetting a paper and I wanted to have the references look a certain way. I had never typeset references in this way before, and I didn't know how to go about doing so. I . . . [posted] a message to a mailing list and let someone who already [knew] how to do it tell me.

- One of the professors in my lab . . . really needed a certain kind of tool to progress much further . . . I told him . . . I'd do some "shopping on the net" . . . . Within three hours I had found a public domain version of the tool . . . ported it to my machine, and shown the professor how to use the tool.

- I have used BITNET to ask questions of researchers in the fields on the current state of problems.

- Essentially, what is happening is the "walk down the corridor to ask an easy question" is being replaced with "post a notice to ask an easy question." The advantage, of course, is a greater pool of expertise that even smaller or isolated departments can draw upon, and a greater range of "easy question."

- The conferences (or "hotlines") routinely carry debates about concepts and theory, requests for assistance in data analysis or in finding other resources, or requests for conducting cooperative research.

- [Networks have changed the way we do research] somewhat in techniques -- the whole NSF supercomputer initiative is an example of how the network makes resources available to researchers.

- The development of survey instruments, software for the experiments . . . were all coordinated via BITNET . . . . Now particularly when a technical problem is encountered for which there doesn't seem to be an easy solution, one can send out a HELP message on an appropriate bulletin board to see if someone else has encountered and/or solved it already. As a result, "expertise" is being shared not only more widely and quickly, but in ways that did not occur before. Lots of the practical ins and outs of research do not end up included in journals or even presentations at professional meetings since they are not defined as part of the valued products of research despite their fundamental importance to the conduct of good research . . . . Finally, networks change what research is even contemplated.

- I am able to design custom CMOS and GaAs chips locally, and submit them electronically to MOSIS foundries for fabrication. In addition, I am able to keep in touch with my colleagues on key developments in the field. Finally, with new library services like CARL in Colorado, I am able to look up the latest references and order recent articles. These three developments make it possible to do leading research at any location.

- I don't have access to statistics or computer consultants on campus, and the small size of our academic departments limits the breadth of expertise represented in many areas. The discussion lists enable me to converse with specialists who would not otherwise be easily accessible. In addition, I'm made aware of new statistical techniques, software packages, and literature references by monitoring the general discussions. Many of the benefits that I would expect to accrue from regular personal interactions with a large body of scholars result from interactions via computer networks.

Figure 7-4. Electronic Networks and Technical Norms: Comments Made by Researchers on the Use of Networks to Impove Research Quality (continued)

- [I]t is not uncommon for a researcher to post a request for help on an experimental method or for access to materials and receive several responses from various sites around the world within a day.

- [A]nd what is helpful to do is, in our lab, we write . . . these current awareness reports . . . where people talk about what they're doing and share in their data . . . this fellow [e-mailed] me a note, asking me what I meant, what I was saying [in my current awareness report]. He said "Is what you're saying in here really what you believe?" and I said "Yeah." So he said, "Well, maybe I can help you out with the problem you're having," so I sent him the raw data that I'd collected . . . and he analyzed it and said "Yeah, I know how to get you out of your problem."

- [Networking aids in problem definition because] you don't engage in defining a problem in a vacuum . . . . You've got ideas as the result of a discussion.

- You have no idea what it means to be without [networks] . . . to be disconnected from the world. Reading articles is not the same . . . If you read only the paper, you have no possibility of asking. In the paper, everything is nice and easy, but when you start to do it . . . .

the tacit knowledge necessary to do science; neither can they completely take the place of face-to-face contact with colleagues (see, for example, Kraut, Egido, and Galagher, 1991; and Kraut, Galagher, and Egido, 1988). Informal network messages such as those typically transmitted via electronic mail and bulletin boards appear to be, however, better at conveying the lore of science than is the formal, archival, published literature.

Networks can facilitate the exchange of craft knowledge, thus improving the ability to conform to certain technical norms, without directly threatening any of the classical social norms. The relationship of networks to the appropriate formulation and accurate reporting of research results, however, is problematic. Networks support informal communication and access to the literature about the content or format of research reports. Networks can also be used to transmit drafts of reports among collaborators for their revisions, to reviewers for their comments, or to publishers for typesetting, although not without some technical problems. Networks are not commonly used, however, for the actual publication of formal research papers because scientists perceive this as circumventing the established review process, as detrimental to the reputation of the researcher, and as largely unrewarded behavior.

Figure 7-5 lists some observations of the study team about the relationship between the social norms

of science, the technical norms of science, and the reward structure of science on the one hand, and the use of electronic research networks on the other based upon remarks given by the study respondents. These conclusions, while only tentative, offer some insight into the complex of issues related to these topics and to areas for future research.

The following general conclusions about norms and networks can be offered:

- Norms are used to justify and condemn network policies and behavior.
- Norms seem to play some role in guiding the use of networks by researchers. In other words, the reaction of researchers to some network policies and services might be predicted, but with extreme caution.
- Scientific norms permeate the R&D community, i.e., they span institutional boundaries, disciplines, and levels of technical expertise.
- It may be difficult to reconcile certain network policies, services, and practices with existing scientific norms.

The re-analysis of the data suggests that scientific norms are playing a role in the use of electronic networks and that they are likely to affect future uses and applications of a national network in ways which may not be well understood at this time. It seems

Figure 7-5. Observations on Subjects' Normative Comments

- Variations in views do not always occur along expected boundaries (e.g., both academic and industrial researchers espouse classic norms).

- For researchers across sectors and disciplines, rewards associated with network use are perceived to depend, to a large extent, on the degree to which networks allow one to "do better and more research" within a traditional framework.

- Computer scientists, not surprisingly, are more likely to experience rewards that are attributable to network use per se.

- Conflicts exist in assertions within one norm (e.g., "Network access should be as broad as possible" vs. "Commercial traffic should not be allowed on the network").

- Conflicts exist between norms (e.g., "Using networks to evade peer review is bad science" vs. "Prepublication distribution of results facilitates science").

- Electronic journals challenge the traditional reward structure of the research community.

- Institutions, as well as individuals, experience both rewards and disincentives associated with network use. Networks can greatly increase the amount of information flowing into an organization and have the potential to enhance the productivity of an organization's R&D workers. On the other hand, organizations must cope with new problems such as network security and increased information overload.

- With regard to the social structure of the research community, networks are apparently used mainly by junior colleagues. This is true in all sectors.

- Many junior colleagues, however, appear to use networks to advance their status by tapping into a variety of resources, including communication with more senior researchers.

- Electronic mail and bulletin boards seem adaptable to the work life of most researchers; it can be used for informal, nonintrusive communication of both a personal and research-related nature.

- The integration of networks into organizations can be dysfunctional, i.e., it can upset traditional communication patterns, control mechanisms, and status relationships.

- Loyalties to and reliance on one's own group of peers often takes precedence over institutional loyalty, because the research community feels itself to be largely autonomous and free from many organizational restrictions.

clear that the introduction of new information technologies into the research community should not be attempted without first considering the social environment of science, and its fundamental reliance on communication, the sharing of information, and collaboration.

CONCLUSIONS

Sociologists of science have examined the normative structure of science in a number of ways. One is the functionalist perspective which asserts that the classical ethos expresses the way that science "is." Another is the approach taken by those who posit the existence and value of norms diametrically opposed to those suggested by Merton and his followers (the so-called counternorms). Another perspective is the antifunctionalist approach which maintains that the classical norms and the counternorms are used only to maintain scientists' social power and autonomy in a way similar to other professions' protection of their occupational status and prerogatives.

Research Networks and the Norms of Science

The literature in computer-mediated communication (CMC) (see Chapter 4) clearly demonstrates the preeminence of social factors in determining the successful adoption and use of information technologies. Likewise, sociologists of science have been able to identify several of the major characteristics of science as a social structure, especially its norms.

The power of norms exists in the sense that virtually all researchers espouse them. This common rhetoric is the glue that holds the social fabric of science together and gives researchers their deep sense of community. It also provides researchers with a coherent and idealistic explanation of their behavior to offer to outsiders. Certain network designs and policies that unequivocally and explicitly flout norms will likely deter researchers from using networks, and, thus, limit the success of national networking initiatives.

For example, if network access were expressly limited to institutions or individuals who met criteria based strictly on prestige or the availability of extensive funds, many researchers might seek out more universal channels of communication. In addition, researchers will have a great deal of difficulty accepting, on principle, network policies that are imposed by nonresearchers. BITNET's electronic Policy-l discussion list has featured heated debate on the rights of local, regional, or national network managers to impose policies on users. Some users argued that rules and policy decisions should be arrived at by user consensus or that, minimally, users should have the opportunity to vote at meetings where policies are decided.

Normative differences among researchers in academia, Federal laboratories, and industry may not be of critical importance in determining network use, but closer examination of the question may lead to a different conclusion. Researchers in all sectors explain their behavior by referring to the same norms, while at the same time recognizing the validity of organizational constraints on their actions. Researchers, for example, would not be tempted to release proprietary information in order to conform to the norm of communality. In addition, researchers in all sectors exhibit behavior that is becoming more similar, for reasons discussed earlier.

The normative structure of science appears to play a significant role in guiding network use, but researchers possess a great deal of flexibility in complying with norms. The ambiguity and mutability of norms suggests that, while network policies should attempt to reflect norms in a very broad way, policies may not be able to prescribe or punish specific behaviors regardless of individual situations.

For the most part, networks will be assimilated into the prevailing normative structure. Certain behaviors will not be tolerated because they violate scientific norms. For example, the sabotage of network hardware, introduction of computer viruses, distribution of junk mail, and use of memory- or bandwith-intensive games all threaten the free flow of communication and the ability of networks to provide effective service to researchers. Stealing proprietary information or compromising the confidentiality or reliability of research data would also be condemned by researchers. Damage to the archival record of formal or informal communication upon which the distribution of rewards is based and the use of networks for gross commercial activity would also not be tolerated.

On the other hand, scientific norms will themselves also change, in the sense that the range of behaviors justified by norms will expand as the use of electronic networks increases. The absolute reliance on formal publication to establish priority of claims and distribute rewards and the absolute equation of formal publication with print media will probably change, albeit slowly and painfully. For example, online journals seem finally to be gaining some degree of acceptance. The astute editor of an online psychology newsletter, in soliciting electronic contributions in the form of "skywriting" (current research ideas and preliminary results) from researchers, explicitly addressed researchers' concerns about rewards, priority of discovery, and similar topics. The current use of networks to gain access to prestigious researchers is additional evidence of the ability of norms to change. Further, it seems clear that, once the number of network users reaches a certain threshhold, uninhibited electronic communication may be circumscribed (by users themselves or by others) so that researchers will not be inundated by unwanted messages. In addition, many researchers will have to change their old normative assumptions about fees and information sharing in order to conform to certain legal and financial realities of network communication.

In conclusion, it is important to remember that a user perspective is essential to the success of any information product, service, or system. In addition, this perspective entails awareness of users' individual characteristics, including tasks and goals, and awareness of the social structure within which the user works. It seems clear that the normative structure of science, as a major facet of the social matrix within which research is done, does and will play a role in scientists' use of electronic research networks. Policy makers and network designers and managers should consider that structure in the planning and implementation of networks. At the same time, however, the exact nature of the influence of norms on network use is not clear, for a number of reasons discussed throughout the chapter. Additional research into this topic would be of use to policy makers, scholars interested in the sociology and communication patterns of science, and to research and network managers.

Several chapters in this book suggest the importance of a user perspective in understanding both the attitudes and behavior of those in the R&D community. Clearly, a number of research questions and issues require additional attention before the nature of scholarly communication and the research process in an electronic environment can be fully appreciated. A key theme of this chapter, however, is that the role of scientific norms in the use of electronic networks is one particular issue that has yet to receive adequate

attention by the designers of the proposed NREN and other research networks.

Indeed, one might argue that the overall effectiveness and efficiency of the NREN might be significantly affected by the degree to which the network espouses and reinforces existing scientific norms. As suggested earlier in this chapter, when researchers' norms are placed in conflict with information systems and expected behaviors, the norms typically take precedence. Of course, this situation is largely attributable to the rhetorical nature of norms and their status as ultimate arbiters of conflict. In any case, if researchers are expected to access or use the NREN in prescribed ways, and that behavior is in conflict with normative prescriptions, the effectiveness of the network may be reduced.

Although there is inadequate understanding of the relationship of norms and electronic networks, network designers must continue to make decisions on how best to develop electronic networks. Thus, designers and proponents of the NREN have two basic policy options to consider regarding scientific norms: design the NREN to consider and support existing scientific norms or ignore scientific norms in the design and development of the NREN. The first alternative would have to occur by intent, but the second could occur either by intent or by default. Designers of the NREN and other research networks must attempt to understand users' attitudes and perceptions and the possible effects of community norms on researchers' behavior and use of electronic networks. They must also understand how norms are transformed by organizational imperatives. This book provides a basis for policy makers and others concerned with research networks to consider design, implementation, management, and evaluation strategies which will take account of the relationship between existing scientific norms and researchers' use of electronic networks.

For example, regarding the norm of universalism, network designers might wish to:

- Ensure that all sectors of the scientific and research community have access to the network and that certain constituency groups do not receive special services or favored status
- Develop costing and user fee structures that do not inhibit the have-not institutions from participating on the network

- Provide gateways within the network through which users could easily access a range of other information resources, e.g., online bibliographic databases, university library catalogues, and government agency databases.

To support communality, the NREN might:

- Establish linkages and protocols that allow users to move easily and quickly among various research groups or other individuals studying similar phenomena
- Eliminate or at least tightly regulate the degree to which commercial information and junk mail are distributed
- Provide indexing and filtering systems to help users control their files.

Regarding disinterestedness, network design might:

- Ensure that users are guaranteed complete privacy and security for their transmissions, files, and other communication on the network
- Allow participants to make proposals and vote on matters related to network use and management.

With regard to organized skepticism, the network could:

- Promote opportunities for peer review of ideas, discussions, papers, etc.
- Provide mechanisms for network managers to receive ongoing feedback on the manner in which the network is used and managed.

The NREN might:

- Establish means by which network users' institutions could provide direct and tangible rewards for participation on the network; e.g., if refereeing journal articles is one criterion by which professional achievement is judged, individuals could be recognized for reviewing papers or other intellectual work on the network
- Establish means by which the network itself can provide formal means of reward and recognition of contributions made, especially those contributions using the network itself or improving the overall effectiveness of the network.

These strategies are illustrative only. Additional analysis is needed to identify appropriate strategies that support and espouse scientific norms for network development. The point, however, is that specific strategies for network use and development can be derived from further analysis of scientific norms.

A second policy option is to ignore the relationships between scientific norms and network uses and applications. If this alternative were consciously chosen, it is likely that a number of conflicts and dysfunctions will occur between the system and the users, among various users, and between users and network managers. Three scenarios might be forecast if this option were chosen.

A first scenario is that ongoing conflicts and dysfunctions involving system operations and scientific norms would frustrate some users to the point that they stop using the network and find alternative communication mechanisms or techniques to conduct research. Typically, those who will be most easily frustrated will be those least knowledgeable about the network and those with the least amount of technical and financial support. Thus, it is possible that those remaining on the network will be experts who have overcome or who ignore those aspects of the system that conflict with their norms.

A second scenario is that, regardless of the network design and operating procedures developed, the scientific norms of users would change system operations and procedures over time. This scenario suggests that, if for no other reason than by default, the norms themselves will direct and affect the development of the network. This, of course, is an optimistic scenario that assumes that scientific norms can "overpower" inappropriate system design characteristics.

A third scenario is that norms themselves will change over time and in certain institutional situations. What this means is that, while the classical ethos will still be publicly espoused by researchers, the behaviors it is used to justify and explain will change. This possibility is likely even if NREN designers and operators choose to take norms into consideration in the design and management of the network.

These policy alternatives and possible scenarios are speculative, but they consider real normative influences on the overall performance, impact, and use of networks. To some degree, scientific norms may act as factors that will drive network uses and operations regardless of how the network is designed -- much as supply and demand drive an open market system. There may not be wide agreement that all norms contribute to the effectiveness or success of scholarly communication and the research process.

Nonetheless, there has been increased recognition that the successful evolution of the NREN will require greater efforts to provide the kinds of network services and products that are needed by and appropriate to the culture of network customers, i.e., researchers (Mandelbaum, 1990, p. 11):

> A major problem with our current networking structure lies in the lack of or failure of basic feedback mechanisms within all tiers and at the tier interfaces . . . . Our fundamental failure is our inability to make the transition from a research network [i.e., one that is merely a conduit of information] to a production network [i.e, one that offers service and products generated from the network]. We have not found a way to substitute the incentives driving service-industry providers for those driving the researcher, to change from an engineering-driven approach to a customer-driven approach.

A similar injunction was recently voiced on BITNET's online Policy-l discussion group by a network manager: "If particular networks don't start paying attention to what users want and need, those users will just go elsewhere." As incentives are changed and as the NREN evolves toward this customer-driven approach, considerations of the impacts of scientific norms on network use will take on increased importance.

The current debates and discussions about the development of the NREN typically ignore social and behavioral issues that are likely to have significant impacts on national network use and effectiveness. Additional consideration by policy makers and network designers of the norms that prevail in the research community is essential if a national network is to provide an infrastructure that effectively supports the science and technology policy goals of the United States.

USER PERSPECTIVES ON ELECTRONIC NETWORKS

CHAPTER 8

This chapter discusses topics that emerged from discussions with groups and individuals during the research reported in Chapters 6 and 7. The chapter is arranged as a series of broad social and behavioral issue areas related to national networking. The ultimate success of a national research network will depend on the degree to which these user-oriented issues are understood by network policy makers and administrators.

The comments reported here are intended to indicate the range of users' opinions, beliefs, and assessments about electronic networking. As such, the views of the study participants do not cover all the possible topics and issues related to electronic networking, but they do offer a user-oriented perspective on the development of a national research and education network. Reported within each issue area are both actual comments from users and the study team's interpretation of users' views. The tone of this chapter is casual, in keeping with the tenor of the original remarks from which it is drawn.

MANAGING A NATIONAL NETWORK

Most researchers who participated in the study had given little thought to the management of a national network. They assumed that all network users would act responsibly, in accord with shared norms, and that little or no outside interference from the government or other management bodies would be needed. Some individuals seemed very comfortable with the notion that the people in the forefront of network use would continue to define "reasonable solutions" to networking problems. Participants saw a national network as primarily a technical and physical entity, not a logical, social, or political entity. The idea that national goals should drive network development or that Federal programs should be concerned with regulating access and assuring appropriate use was clearly foreign to the study respondents and considered by them to be quite distant from any connection to their work.

One user voiced the common opinion that "I have absolutely no idea how things are currently run and managed [either at the institutional, national, or international level], but they work. It's remarkable what we can do." He did not want or feel competent to comment, either as a user of research networks or as a citizen, on possible network models or management strategies for national networking initiatives. He did refer to the political paradox of trying to justify major investments in information technology for only a few users, while encouraging many users will only degrade machine speed and performance.

Network managers pointed out that the existing research base of information on network management is minimal and that, for questions such as control and management of a national research network, no one knows what might be best and what types of management models are appropriate and effective. The scope and complexity of integrating the management of existing networks or managing a national network are significant. Network managers emphasized that experience with local networks or the current ad hoc national networks may not be adequate preparation for the management of a more fully integrated national network. One stated that "we're talking about doing something of a scope and complexity that we've never done before. Local management issues don't necessarily scale up . . . . Many of the technical and policy problems that we've been discussing are still [unexplored] research areas." He concluded, as had the researchers who participated in the study, that most decisions about network management at all levels are now done by mutual agreement and peer contact.

DEFINING THE CONCEPT OF A NATIONAL RESEARCH AND EDUCATION NETWORK

When the study team introduced the topic of the development of a national research and education network, a number of participants responded that "we already have a national research network and use it every day." This response suggests that the NREN envisioned by the Office of Science and Technology Policy (OSTP), the National Science Foundation (NSF), the Coalition for Networked Information (CNI), and others is not well understood by users. Further, it was unclear to most study participants how a national network such as the NREN would be different from existing networks or how the use of the NREN would differ from the use of current networks. If the NREN is to receive wide support from network users, it is essential that its promoters better operationalize the intended design, services, and uses of such a network.

Some participants saw a national network as a single network with a main trunk line that everyone would use, while others saw it more as a "connector" among existing national and regional networks. Explaining the latter position, one individual said that, given the past history of networks, "the national

network" would best be conceived and developed as a linking or connecting mechanism among existing networks and as a means to standardize information exchange and other functions, rather than as a replacement or new network.

WHO WILL CONTROL THE NETWORKS?

This question raised much interest among the participants, although some respondents did not feel comfortable discussing the issue of control. Some participants clearly had never thought about the issue before. Generally, the view expressed was that there were already sufficient controls on network use: Researchers can be trusted, they understand the responsibilities inherent in a cooperative model of resource sharing, and increasing costs for network use filters out some uses and users anyway. The participants' belief in self-regulation was based on faith in a shared ethic of responsibility among researchers.

The metaphor of electronic networks as a public utility, analogous to telephone companies and other common carrier services, was offered -- someone would provide the utility, and then researchers should be free to use it in virtually any way that they see wanted. The majority of respondents supported this public utility model of network management, which they interpreted as being equivalent to free, easy, open, multipurpose access to the network for qualified researchers who would all follow some inherent code of responsible use. Many felt that peer pressure would be a successful alternative to centralized control, which no one thought was desirable. The users did not see any connection between their complaints about too many people trying to access resources like supercomputers and the need for rules or regulations to control this problem. The study participants seemed to believe that some control at the organizational level was probably unavoidable, but that it should be kept to a minimum and should be implemented as a technical solution, i.e., passwords for system access should be required. Study participants identified several models for network control:

- Pluralistic Coordination: The members of the network resolve management issues among themselves. This is basically a user-driven or peer-based model of management in which there is policy development by default.

- Elitist Coordination: The best and the brightest of the network users and managers resolve management issues among themselves; they tell the users how it will be.
- Centralized Direction: Some agency (Federal or non-Federal) takes responsibility for the management of the network. Typically, this would be the agency that is funding the development of the network.
- Public Utility Model: A corporate model of public utility management could provide some centralized control and still give the "public" (in this case the users) a great deal of freedom and flexibility.

The comment was made that currently there appears to be little strategic or even systematic network management rather, much present network management occurs by evolution, user input, and default.

Whatever the model suggested by participants, there was strong consensus that control of the network should not disrupt existing norms of scientific behavior and communication and that researchers should not forfeit their voice in control of networks -- although it was unclear how much actual control users had in the development and management of networks.

In considering a model for the development of a national research network, study respondents noted that flexibility and adaptability were important. The network would have to accommodate:

- The needs and norms of different scientific disciplines in terms of the conduct of research (e.g., reliance on graphic images by geologists or molecular structures by chemists)
- A broad range of skill levels among users
- A range of institutional, governmental, and network security levels.

Thus, criteria advocated for assessing the appropriateness of network control mechanisms and determining acceptable use are likely to vary, depending on researchers' backgrounds and specific institutional situations.

TECHNICAL CONSIDERATIONS IN NETWORK MANAGEMENT

An issue that was noted with some interest by network users was the difficulty of dealing with technical problems. As one participant noted, "If a problem occurs, how do you discover where it is? Who's responsible for it? Who fixes it and who pays for fixing it?" Most users said that they did not want to get involved in solving technical problems. The most common attitude was summed up by one respondent:

> I don't know how networks work, and I don't care. I'm perfectly satisfied with things the way they are and I don't see the need for any changes. Just leave well enough alone . . . and make sure I get enough funding to do my work.

An analogy to the postal system was made by one study participant: people just need to know how to address and stuff envelopes; they do not need to understand the intricacies of what happens to their letter once they put it in the mailbox. Generally, users did not want to be concerned with technical problems or issues.

On the other hand, highly sophisticated users do not like transparent systems. There are several reasons for this phenomenon:

- Sophisticated users' jobs often demand that they solve technical, formatting, and other computing and networking problems; transparency makes that job more difficult.
- Sophisticated users are proud of their expertise and ability to control systems, and their communities of immediate peers (local and remote) often determine status by technical criteria. Surrendering control, through the use of transparent systems, means surrendering status.
- Less sophisticated users, as one respondent put it, "just want to get the job done." Their use of the electronic media is most often simply instrumental. Even these users, however, are beginning to use networking expertise as one criterion to determine status.

These remarks give some idea of the complexity of this issue it will not be resolved by simply supporting both menu-driven and command-driven modes on the NREN.

ACCESS

Most researchers expressed the view that universal, free access is "essential" for all researchers, especially for those in the social sciences who lack the financial support given to the computational and natural sciences. One respondent noted that networks should be like libraries: "There could be and have been some abuses, but we must be careful with restrictions . . . . Policies should be put in place to encourage a broad base of users." At the same time, he said that "everybody and his brother can't use the network." This is only one example of how the issues of fees, access, acceptable use, and qualified users were not resolved in the minds of most study participants.

COMMUNICATION BETWEEN PRIVATE SECTOR AND OTHER USERS

The often tangled relationships between individual private corporations and universities add another confounding factor to the establishment of a national network. Users commented that the sponsorship of research in certain areas, and confidentiality and intellectual property agreements, make policy here especially complex. But specific strategies for improving private-sector relationships with others were not suggested (see the section below on organizational conflict resulting from network use).

Some users in a private-sector setting said that they were subtly discouraged from using networks to collaborate with scientists outside their company. The "not invented here" syndrome (where organizations believe that they alone can develop useful and trustworthy products, processes, etc.), the proprietary nature of some research, and the difficulty of obtaining clearance to share research findings all discourage the sharing of scientific ideas. One private-sector researcher said that his company, like many other organizations, seemed to want to be, in his words, a "data sink." In other words, organizations recognize the benefits of acquiring scientific and technical information from various sources, but none wants to fulfill the mutual obligations of quid pro quo, i.e., sharing information in order to gain information. Many company scientists must publish or informally communicate some of their results in order to gain credibility with their peers outside their companies. Lack of credibility leads to lack of access to important information. Several study participants suggested the

formation of some kind of "communication consortium," that would allow a company to pre-approve communication links with other institutions and individuals. This was seen as one way to allow free communication among researchers while reducing organizational security concerns.

Participants in one private-sector site noted, however, that in recent years there seemed to be greater freedom for researchers at their institution to access and disseminate technical information. The amount of freedom, however, varied significantly with the particular nature of the researchers' work. Those doing research in sensitive areas or areas having immediate impact on company profits are, naturally, much more constrained than others. Some participants were a bit surprised to discover, during study interviews, that it was easier to share or discuss research in some other departments than in their own. It became apparent that certain laboratories are typically required to wait at least two years before publishing their research results in order to guarantee that the company is able to maximize the commercial value of such research, while other researchers can discuss their work with external colleagues almost immediately upon beginning a line of inquiry.

SECURITY

Network security and the need to protect proprietary information exchanged on the network were discussed by all of the study participants. Most, however, seemed relatively unconcerned about these issues, although they recognized their importance. As discussed elsewhere, they felt that the scientific community could almost always be depended upon to act ethically and that, in those institutions where security and protecting information are critical, "someone must be ensuring that appropriate standards and polices are followed." Private-sector participants emphasized that these were issues for which each researcher must assume individual responsibility.

Private-sector respondents also noted that their institutions had a number of security controls in place to protect proprietary information. For example, they cannot directly log onto their work computers from home; they must call the company, and then the computer will call back. The sense of these participants, however, was that network use offered little danger to organizational security. These respondents explained that only individual responsibility and personal awareness of security can prevent the disclosure of proprietary or secure information. All employees must sign at least one security agreement. If researchers wanted to divulge important information, they could do so whether networks are in place or not. Major security concerns arose chiefly from the fear that outsiders would break into corporate files.

The consensus of private-sector researchers and managers on security issues was summed up by a simile used by one of the group members: "Just like you wrap a piece of china up when you send it through the mail, you do what you have to do to protect your data." There was some discussion of the remarkable speed of computer crime and of the lack of evidence that usually characterizes such crimes. A national network was seen by some, in this light, as a threat as well as an advantage.

Security of the networks from viruses and similar threats was also discussed with all participants. Generally, the researchers believed that recent abuses, such as the intrusion of a virus into ARPANET in October 1988, were uncommon events and that, even if such things were to happen again, "everyone has backups and could recover without too much difficulty." This attitude was even expressed by researchers in such fields as physics, where research is often focused on unique, nearly irreplicable events. If backups are behind or are not being made, years of research and considerable capital might be lost because of a virus or system failure.

It was noted that the "bad network etiquette" demonstrated by data thieves, intrusive advertisers, and others would lead people to sever electronic ties with them. But once again, there was no consensus on how exactly this should be done or how to decide when it should be done. There was little interest in answering such questions as: Must you sacrifice the connection to major network resources and services because of a few problems? Should there be warning and grievance procedures with formal appeals before bad electronic citizens, whether individual or institutional, can be thrown off major networks? Who would make such decisions?

In summary, the study team posed a number of questions related to security of information on networks and found less concern for security issues than had been anticipated. While researchers are aware of the need for security, they seemed to believe that it is not a key problem or issue in conducting research in an electronic environment. There was little fear that highly sensitive information would be divulged to the outside world or that research data were susceptible to threats from hackers. General network security was assumed to be adequate.

ELITISM

Electronic networks were originally designed and used by computer scientists and electronic communications researchers. The vision of a national research network to improve research productivity across institutions and disciplinary boundaries is very different from the original concept of a network employed only by cutting-edge computer science researchers in prestigious institutions. The expanded vision requires the democratization of network services, universal access, the provision of user-friendly systems, and comprehensive programs for network training, support, and marketing. Aside from the technical elitism expressed by some study participants (i.e., only technically proficient researchers deserve access to networks), there is a sense in the research community itself that it is an elite group whose contributions to society depend upon its remaining free from government and other external controls.

A number of study participants had always worked in a research environment characterized by high-speed research networks and supercomputing. They considered this the norm and acted surprised at the suggestion that such resources were not available everywhere. These researchers expressed the belief that their access to networks and supercomputers did not give them a competitive advantage over less privileged or sophisticated colleagues.

The network managers participating in one group interview showed a limited understanding of and concern for user needs. Their sentiments were "If they [users] have to ask for assistance, then they shouldn't be using the network." The elitism expressed by these network administrators seemed to arise because they were technically literate and found it difficult to sympathize with those who did not posses a similar degree of technical competence.

In many instances, participants expressed the opinion that certain institutions were better able to exploit the networks and were more likely to contribute to science by being better connected and supported than other institutions. Indeed, some participants raised concerns about users in "second rate" institutions and in less computationally intensive disciplines clogging up the network with "unimportant or inappropriate use." But even within particular institutions, elitism was a problem between the senior and the junior scientists, graduate assistants and professors, and network managers and network users. In many instances participants were quite emphatic about the importance of their work and its demand for electronic networking. Yet they all believed that others not using electronic networks and supercomputing "probably were doing leading-edge science." These views suggest the importance of scientific norms and the impact of these norms on network use (see Chapter 7).

ORGANIZATIONAL CONFLICT RESULTING FROM NETWORK USE

Study participants identified several ways in which network use led to conflicts within their organizations. Conflicts most often arose between managers and researchers on issues related to resource allocation and the nature of scientific communication. Extraorganizational communication was natural and important to researchers. This type of communication, however, was problematic for management in terms of justifying costs and controlling proprietary information.

The process of obtaining clearance to present private-sector research findings, as mentioned above, is often time-consuming and discourages outside collaboration. Approval for outside collaboration or sharing of information must come from upper levels of management. At these levels, however, there is often less understanding of the sharing ethic of research communication and of the research work itself. Researchers felt that there were unnecessary and counterproductive restrictions on, and uninformed decision making about, communication with people outside the corporation. The sense of some private-sector participants was that the corporate rule of thumb was "when in doubt [about granting approval], don't let it out."

In one group session, an argument developed between two people about a private-sector organization's gateway to external networks. One network manager argued that the gateway was merely a cost-accounting and security device, while the other manager maintained that the gateway was a mechanism for exerting undue control over (i.e., for "spying on") researchers' communication with others.

One theme that arose in a number of sessions was the feeling of divided loyalty experienced by many researchers who said that they often feel a greater sense of loyalty to, colleagues in other institutions than to their own organization. For example, one private-sector participant noted that he spent a fair amount of his work time and resources using electronic networks to help people in an academic computer center where he used to work. This comment alarmed one of the other network administrators in the group. This experience of divided loyalty is consistent with the findings of other investigators of scientific collaboration and may be typical of pre-network behavior patterns, but network use further encourages it.

Several people said that networks can be used to circumvent management control generally. Participants also noted that ways can be found to circumvent attempts to control network use and external communication. A number of researchers in one group said that they used someone else's computer when they wanted to perform network functions which their computers, by management design, were not able to perform. Judging by a number of comments, it seems that most managers do not understand the impact of networks on their organizations. It may turn out in the future that managers are much more savvy about computer and network use. If this happens, will managers crack down on or encourage network use and access to remote peers?

Many participants remarked that there did not seem to be any comprehensive plan for managing network development at their institutions. This leads to frustration and uncertainty for network users. It was also noted that network support staff seemed to be viewed as "overhead" by management. One private-sector user consultant wondered how serious the company could really be about user support services if "there is only one of me" for such a large and heterogeneous organization. This situation implies a lack of understanding on the part of management of the importance of information technology for today's researcher and an underestimation of the importance of adequate support even to the most sophisticated users. Many participants stated explicitly that upper management was out of touch in both these respects. Moreover, management, especially in the private sector, is most concerned with management information systems (MIS) and automated data processing (ADP) applications of information technology as opposed to network use for research tasks and scientific communication. There is, therefore, little management understanding of and support for research networking.

THE SKEWED DISTRIBUTION OF NETWORK EXPERTISE

There is a wide gulf between those few researchers who consider themselves expert users of networks and the majority of researchers who have little knowledge of what information technology can do for them, what resources are available, and how to use them. These two groups, obviously, have different expectations concerning networks, different motivations for network use, and different training and interface needs. Further, there are a number of skill levels between these two extremes.

One recommendation from a group of interviewees was to have two levels of interaction modes in any national network: one menu-driven and "idiot-proof," the other command-driven. The question was posed about whether the national network should serve the "five or ten thousand" who could and would use it most fully or the "hundreds of thousands" who use it infrequently and do not have the time or the inclination to become computing or networking experts.

Experienced and novice users who participated in the study seemed to have different opinions about the quality and adequacy of existing user support services. Novice users seemed almost universally pleased with available support services, saying they were "excellent" and required no changes. These subjects also noted, however, that sometimes no one answered the designated computing help line and that they had given up on trying to do even simple file transfers. Expert users, on the other hand, complained that there was "no support." Their expectations about the potential value of computer networks to their work were much higher and, consequently, their demands for service and support much higher. This finding runs counter to the common wisdom that high-end users need virtually no support.

More technology, better hardware, moving to a 3-gigabit-per-second transmission speed, or increasing bandwidth will not be of much benefit to less skilled users. They are unable to apply the existing technologies and have yet to catch up with a number of previous "new generations" of hardware and software development. The development of user-friendly software for networks and customized training are likely to have more impact on network use than continued emphasis on new high-end tools.

One user noted that he and others were not taking full advantage of present network capabilities. This

awareness already displays a level of sophistication far beyond that of many researchers. The real novices do not know how little they know; they may be satisfied with a relatively low level of service because they are not aware of the immense potential of networking.

SCIENTIFIC NORMS AND NETWORK USE

Many participants placed network use and policy issues firmly within the context of prevailing scientific norms (see Chapter 7). Network policies and practices that were thought to have a detrimental effect on science were heartily condemned. All participants were highly socialized into the norms of science and of their particular disciplines, especially the fact that peer-reviewed publications are the primary component of a good scientific reputation. All participant groups generally asserted that sending research results out on the network "cheapens" the status of the researcher. High status in one's scientific community and other rewards, are based in part on publications. The participants who were not computing or networking researchers or administrators understand this and have internalized the situation as "correct." Subjects who were more sophisticated in network use, especially computing and networking researchers, however, were members of communities which appreciated and rewarded networking activity.

All groups gave evidence (both implicit and explicit) to support the idea that networks did not alter prevailing norms of research. Participants felt that an individual's own ingrained sense of scientific ethics, along with peer pressure, defined and evaluated network activity according to the same attitudes and practices that make up the general culture of science.

One very experienced user was quite offended by the notion of junk mail on the network, although he had never experienced any problems with it. "It should be outlawed," he said, as an invasion of privacy and a waste of time. He said that much electronic junk mail was the result of commercial enterprises' interference with science. On the other hand, he was firmly against any form of censorship of communications. He emphasized that there must be other, perhaps economic, strategies for limiting undesirable traffic by making an analogy with the Postal Service: "If they would stop giving 4th class rates, we wouldn't have so much junk mail." He concluded that perhaps the complaints of junk mail recipients, followed up by actual enforcement of penalties on the senders of such mail, should be the only policing of networks.

IMPACT OF INFORMATION TECHNOLOGY ON RESEARCH AND PRODUCTIVITY

Study participants had conflicting views on the appropriate place of information technology in their work. In general, respondents saw themselves as researchers first; network use was subsumed into their larger research and professional goals. But attitudes toward computers and networks seemed to vary according to the participants' research specialty, organizational position and status, and network experience. These differing attitudes appeared to affect researchers' motivation to use research networks, the kinds of network uses they think are appropriate, and the benefits they expect from networking. It is important that network designers, managers, and user consultants realize that researchers have very strong feelings about the appropriate role of information technology in their work. Unwillingness to become expert in the workings of networks does not necessarily mean that a researcher is afraid of the technology, unable to use it, or contemptuous of those who do use it. It may reflect, rather, the researcher's view that time and other resources would be better invested elsewhere.

In one academic setting, junior researchers who were experienced networkers felt that there was a substantial gap between themselves and their senior professors in terms of network and supercomputer literacy. Most junior researchers, however, did not resent this gap but saw it as a natural division of labor. They noted that it was the responsibility of the senior faculty to obtain research funding and recognized that it would be impossible for senior faculty to stay current with the latest developments since they did not use networks regularly.

In one focus group, there was an interesting interplay between a senior researcher and some of the junior chemists. The senior chemist obviously had difficulty with the operation of computers and networks and used them only "when forced to do so." The junior scientists had a much more positive attitude. At times, when the senior scientist said that a certain network procedure was problematic and never worked out correctly, one of the junior scientists suggested how to complete the procedure or described ways to resolve the problem. Generally, the senior chemist appeared to leave the meeting unconvinced

that there really were "easy" ways to accomplish network tasks.

In general, some researchers see use of computer networks as being in <u>competition</u> with research time while others saw network use as an <u>investment</u> in their research activities. Many of the individuals who participated in the study used network technology and resources only when necessary, or in some cases, if forced to do so. These people represent the scientists "in the trenches" who cannot possibly spend all the time needed to stay up to date on new versions of software, new equipment, and so forth. Much of the literature related to the NREN suggests that networks will greatly increase research productivity and overall national competitiveness. But many comments from researchers suggest an opposite perspective: networks are putting researchers in "technical bondage," and may, in fact, restrict their productivity.

One researcher described computer networks as just another tool, like a chisel to a sculptor, and a debate developed whether the changes effected by networks represented only a difference in degree (more efficient research) or a difference in kind (the research process is different). Most of the researchers saw a tug-of-war between users, most of whom want to know only as much as they need to know about networks, and computing support staff, who users say get carried away in their enthusiasm for the tools and expect all users to want to become experts.

Another impact of networks appears to be the creation of a research underclass or "computer ghetto" in some academic settings. Junior researchers, because of previous training and expertise, are often relegated to computer and networking tasks <u>only</u>, at the expense of participation in the more conceptual aspects of research. This is a self-perpetuating cycle that many young researchers see as a serious threat to their careers -- a paradox wherein increased computing and networking skills dooms a researcher to virtual network clerical status.

Some participants remarked that their institutions seem ready to buy information technology "at the drop of a hat," but that other purchases are much harder to get approved. Often respondents felt that they might have to choose between the purchase of information technology and other more specific research equipment (e.g., distillation apparatus). In addition, it appears that support, training, and the integration of the technology into job applications have been largely overlooked by network and R&D managers.

One participant said that it seemed hard to motivate researchers to use information technology if they were not already so inclined, noting that one could cite the virtues, benefits, and advantages of using computers and networks, but it would not seem to make much of an impression. One participant made an analogy between networks and microwave ovens: "People are either dying to have one, or they couldn't care less." Thus network impact appears to be limited by the difficulty of attracting new users.

One senior academic researcher said that he would take on any student well-grounded in science (either chemistry or physics) who wanted to be a part of his research team. He noted that computing is something anyone can learn and that, if certain computing and networking tasks are beyond him and his researchers, he hires programmers or other technicians to handle them. Programmers are also hired to train the researchers, who then develop all their own software and "do the actual science." Programming was described as something that a scientist "is a slave to and would rather shake off." He sympathized with the computer ghetto syndrome, and reiterated that he hired technicians to do computing and networking and researchers to do science. He was chagrined whenever any of his researchers became so involved in computing that they went on to jobs in that arena: "When that happens, I feel like I've done something wrong."

The impact of computer networks on research and the scientific enterprise is a complicated phenomenon. Comments made by study participants suggest that simply providing new technology to researchers will not guarantee increases in productivity.

NETWORK TRAINING AND SUPPORT

As noted in Chapter 6, there are discontinuities between the values and expectations of network managers and those of network users, especially novice users. Technical experts must understand that researchers want to do research, not become expert in computing or networking as such. Network trainers and administrators, along with R&D administrators, must ensure that the time and effort that researchers spend in network training are tied specifically to the accomplishment of users' research goals. This can be achieved only through planning, a clear understanding of users' goals and information use habits, and a fundamentally sound marketing and public relations program.

The fact that networking has spread well beyond the computer science and network research communities also has profound implications for training. Computing and networking experts have relied on colleagues, manuals, and online experimentation to learn about networking, but it may not be realistic to expect other kinds of users to be able to use such techniques successfully. Formal training programs must explicitly recognize the ignorance of non-users and new users about networking and their inability to "gut out" procedures regarded as simple by experts.

Similarly, education and training must also help users develop:

- Realistic expectations of network costs and benefits

- An understanding of the organizational, resource, and other limitations under which network administrators and trainers operate.

Such concerns are not meant to imply, however, that trainees should be overwhelmed by detail, whether technical, financial, or otherwise.

CONCLUSIONS

Overall, the studies described in Chapters 6 and 7 provided a rich and robust set of comments regarding electronic networking and the development of the NREN. Researchers' and managers' remarks reflect a broad range of views, assumptions, opinions, and beliefs on national networking issues, even though most subjects were not familiar with the intricacies of the policy debates surrounding NREN development. Many of the more elite, experienced users thought that the development process was moving along well. Novice users, on the other hand, knew little about the range of network resources, services, and benefits cited by their more experienced colleagues.

This chapter highlights some of the "meta-issues" brought to light by network users and potential users. It is important to remember that these user issues are of significance in the development of the NREN and to other national networking initiatives, but that there is little empirical evidence about many of them beyond what is discussed in this book. The needs, views, and opinions of users must be investigated further, especially because they form the basis of some of the policy issues, discussed in Chapter 9, which must become part of the public debate about NREN.

ISSUES, RECOMMENDATIONS, AND PROSPECTS

CHAPTER 9

The preceding chapters suggest that the development and design of the NREN will require much public debate, careful analysis, and additional research. Indeed, if such a network is to be successful, additional debate, analysis, and research is essential. The purpose of this chapter is to help frame this debate, offer an analysis and perspective on selected topics, and identify key areas requiring additional research.

The first section provides the authors' synthesis of key issues related to the development of the NREN. The next section offers recommendations for increasing the likelihood that the NREN will meet user information needs and contribute to improved scientific communication and productivity. The chapter closes with a brief overview of current activities and initiatives regarding NREN development as 1991 begins, and it provides a perspective regarding likely future developments.

KEY ISSUE AREAS

Based on the comments offered by participants in the study discussed in Chapters 6, 7, and 8, and a review of the literature, the authors identified a number of underlying issue areas related to the design, implementation, and management of a national research network. These issue areas are especially important because of:

- Their overarching effects on the adoption and use of networks by researchers
- The failure of managers, network administrators, and systems analysts to recognize and address them in the design, implementation, and support of networks and related technologies
- Their relative neglect by policy makers and commentators.

Social and policy issues are in some ways more intractable than technical ones, but steps can be taken to understand and resolve them. Their interrelationships make them difficult to assess and analyze individually, and they are discussed as separate areas here only to aid comprehension and analysis. These issues are summarized in Figure 9-1.

Figure 9-1. Summary of Key Issues

Education, Training, and Support

- Who should take responsibility for network users' training and support? Who should pay for it?
- How can users and managers justify the individual and discipline-specific educational support that is needed?
- Are there mechanisms for effective user support that would be less costly but still as effective as discipline- and problem-specific documentation and online help?

Scientific and Social Norms

- How do scientific and social norms vary in different sectors?
- How do norms influence network use?
- Should network policies conform to prevailing norms within and among the different sectors? If they should, how can they?
- Do networks alter the social stratification of science?
- Can the existing scholarly publication and reward system accommodate network communications?

Generation, Occupation, and Situation Gaps

- In considering network use, what gaps in individuals' skills, needs, tasks, habits, attitudes, and goals exist? Where do they occur? What impacts will they have?
- How can network training keep up with the continuing gap between network experts and novices?
- How do networks affect organizational structure and goals? How can managers increase their awareness of network impacts?
- How can the NREN bridge gaps among individuals with quite different levels of skills, needs, and goals?

Role of Information Technology in Research Work

- Are networks a special research tool or a part of a wider information infrastructure?
- What implications arise from the fact that most researchers note that networks contribute to research efficiency rather than change the nature of the science done?
- What information or information processing capacity is needed at each stage of research work? What is the role of networks as the source of information or the channel of information processing at each stage?

Access

- Which aspects of access are most critical in encouraging network use? How can all important aspects of access be facilitated at the individual, organizational, and national levels?
- Access is currently often correlated with the "importance" of a research area to national economic, social, and security goals. What are the implications of this situation?
- Will networks increase or reduce the Matthew Effect in science?

Figure 9-1. Summary of Key Issues (continued)

Remoteness

- Which solutions are the most effective in dealing with the barriers between remote users and resources?
- Should the resource provider or the user's home institution be responsible for meeting the needs of remote users? What are the implications of either answer?

Sector Differences and Relationships

- How will a national research network operate given the differences among the various sectors' attitudes towards security and confidentiality?
- How will acceptable use be determined?
- Who will resolve conflicts that arise in network access and use because of sector differences?

Network Design and Management

- To what extent should and can researchers' beliefs about appropriate network behavior be incorporated into network policy?
- How can conflict among opinions about network management be resolved?
- What should the role of the private sector be in the design of the NREN?
- What should the relationship be between the public and private sectors in providing support and maintenance for the NREN?
- If it is determined that the NREN should begin as a public enterprise and evolve into a private one, how will that change be accomplished?
- What implications does this evolution hold for users in all sectors with regard to (1) fees for access, telecommunications, and related costs, and (2) network access?

Difficulty of Measuring Productivity Increases and Other Benefits

- How will the NREN be evaluated? How will the results of such evaluation be used to increase the effectiveness of network services?
- Who will provide policy makers, Federal and otherwise, with practicable, reliable criteria for assessing the NREN?

Networks Magnify Existing Tendencies, Patterns, and Preferences

- In what ways can or should the NREN alter the nature of scientific work?
- If networks reinforce existing patterns and tendencies, how should this affect network promotion, training, policies, and expectations of benefits?

Figure 9-1. Summary of Key Issues (continued)

Technophoria

- How can high-level policy attention be directed to social, behavioral, and other problems beyond the technical realm?
- On an institutional level, how can network managers be made more aware of social and behavioral factors related to network adoption and use?

Elitism

- Are elitist attitudes restricting network use?
- Do elitist attitudes have a negative effect on network policy development?
- How can the negative effects of elitist attitudes be mitigated?

Education, Training, and Support

It appears that a large proportion of the researchers at the sites visited were not aware of the existence or capabilities of existing networks, did not take full advantage of networks, did not know how to use desired network functions, or did not use networks at all. One major reason for this seems to be the lack of formal training and adequate user technical support at the institutional level. Most researchers learn to use networks by "brute force." They learn about networks and about how to use networks on an ad hoc basis, either from their colleagues or by themselves. Formal academic courses and computer staff training were not generally relied upon for training. The study's findings indicate that this situation is common to all sectors and cuts across individual levels of expertise.

Network training, when associated with complex functions such as data collection or analysis, requires an inordinate time investment for researchers who may need to accomplish the task at hand in connection with only one particular project. The distribution of all network users appears to be bimodal; users are either very sophisticated or are relative novices. General training appears to put the user only into the "novice" group. The model for network training and support that appears best suited for making novices into experts is the network "consultant." Consultants not only actively market networks to a particular research group and offer technical assistance with communications and computer technology, but they also understand the researcher's work well enough to

offer application-specific training and one-on-one "hand-holding."

Improvement in the extent, level, and effectiveness of network education, training, and support is critical for leveraging the investment in a national network. Currently, the number of network users and the ability of researchers to exploit networks in their work are severely limited by the lack of adequate attention to these areas.

Scientific and Social Norms

Like all professions, science is governed by norms and has a social structure. Networks may prove dysfunctional to the scientific enterprise if network policies and practices do not fit into that prevailing social structure. Much previous research has focused on the nature and importance of scientific norms and the social practices and environment of scientific work (Merton, 1973; Mitroff, 1974a, 1974b; Crane, 1972; Zuckerman, 1986; Kuhn, 1970; Cole and Cole, 1973; and Barnes, 1974). Scientific discourse and communication have also been dealt with in this context, but this research has generally not considered formal and informal electronic communication (Garvey, 1979; Allen, 1985; and Gilbert and Mulkay, 1984). The study team's findings indicate, not surprisingly, that the way researchers use networks and the way they envision network policies are influenced by prevailing scientific and social norms. Further, the norms of the research community seem to vary somewhat according to the organizational goals and constraints associated with each of the three major sectors (private, governmental, and academic).

Researchers in all sectors contended, either explicitly or implicitly, that network use is governed by, and must support, the traditional scientific norms (Merton, 1973, pp. 267-278) of <u>communality</u> (free communication of ideas), <u>organized skepticism</u> (testing others' research results), <u>disinterestedness</u> (evaluating research on the basis of its intrinsic merit), and <u>universalism</u> (ignoring origin in the evaluation of research). For example, researchers were appalled by the notion that a "competitive advantage" resulted from network access to information and other resources, by the suggestion that their network communication might be censored, and by the use of networks to circumvent the usual "quality control" and peer-review processes of research (e.g., the "Fleischmann and Pons syndrome"). See Merton (1973, pp. 309-316 and 321-322) on such "deviant behavior." Also, reputation, publication, and reward are inextricably interwoven in the scientific community. Norms may profoundly affect network behavior, and, at the same time, networks may not be subsumable into extant norms. Current intellectual property laws and scientific reward structures may be significantly challenged if the NREN is fully developed.

Generation and Occupation Gaps

Gaps in network attitudes and skills exist along several dimensions: between older and younger researchers, between researchers and network administrators and managers, between people in different sectors, between researchers from different disciplines, and between researchers working on different kinds or different stages of problems. Gaps in network skill among users will not disappear with the attrition of older researchers because technology is constantly evolving. There will always be a gap between those very few researchers who are the current information technology experts and their colleagues. Networks will always have to serve, and training will always have to meet the needs of, those very sophisticated users, those unsophisticated users, and everyone in between.

Managers frequently do not understand the extent of impact that network implementation can have on their organizations. When organizational and scientific norms conflict and when (typically older) managers are not astute about the technical possibilities of electronic communication, researchers sometimes use

networks to circumvent management control of their work activities. Gaps in attitudes and skills must be reduced if network use is to become more universal and well integrated. Such gaps also cause organizational discord.

Role of Network Technology in Research Work

If the NREN is intended to improve research productivity, it is important to understand how information technology is viewed and adopted by researchers. Many researchers view science as a zero-sum enterprise in which there is a finite amount of time, money, and institutional support available. Thus, some people consider computing and research to be in competition for resources. A potentially significant variation on this theme is that some junior researchers interviewed feared that their network expertise would relegate them to a "computer ghetto," in which they no longer participate in the conceptual aspects of research. Some senior researchers, on the other hand, are afraid of losing talented, discipline-trained researchers to general computing jobs in such lucrative areas as software development.

These and like-minded researchers view networks simply as a tool to facilitate science and emphasize the primacy of good science over any particular tool. For such researchers, computing and networks are essential; but others view these tools as resource-devouring toys or inappropriate and annoying, even ultimately counterproductive and dysfunctional for science. As noted above, although many parts of the research process have been affected by network use, it seems that conceptual aspects are the least altered. Thus, productivity gains will be bounded. Scientific "breakthroughs" from a national network seem most likely to occur in research areas where there has been a lack of computing power.

Access

Previous research has shown that degree of access to networks is associated with degree of use (Hiltz, 1984, and Attewell and Rule, 1988). The concept of access, however, has often been restricted to the notions of proximity and availability (Do researchers have a network connection on their desks? Do they have to share it with other people?). The findings of this study suggest that the concept of access must be broadened to include other aspects as well, such as the potential user's:

- Awareness of available information and technology resources: Do researchers even know of the network functions and capabilities available to them?
- Organizational culture: Does the organizational culture of the researcher permit and actively support networking?
- Attitude toward information and communication technologies: Do researchers perceive information and communication technologies as a benefit or barrier to their investigations? Do they expect improvements in their work from the use of such technologies?
- Available technical expertise: Do researchers themselves have sufficient skill and training to use networks? Do they have sufficient access to sources of expertise that may be needed to support their work on an ongoing basis?
- Financial resources: Do researchers have sufficient resources to use networks when and how they want to?

On a national level, the results of this study indicate that network access, especially as defined above, is far from universal. Many institutions have:

- No physical connection to the network
- Inadequate hardware, software, and facilities
- Inadequate institutional support for and interest in the marketing of networks
- Limited user interest in and knowledge of network services
- Unequal support for all disciplines (i.e., the physical and computational sciences receive the most support).

Many people fear that the Matthew Effect (i.e., the rich get richer) will govern the distribution of network support of various kinds and that the distinction between the information rich and the information poor will be exacerbated by the increasing need for expensive technology and technical expertise to do science. Researchers with network support will most likely obtain the greatest share of the resources and reputation needed to engage in significant scientific work.

Remoteness

Many people assert that the Matthew Effect in science will be mitigated by networks. This assertion appears to be true to some extent. BITNET survey respondents from small, remote institutions noted that networks allowed them access to research resources that were absolutely essential to their work and gave them their only chance to participate in their field on an equal footing with their colleagues. Thus, in some cases, networks are helping the "poor" get "richer."

On the other hand, problems associated with lack of access may be exacerbated by remoteness from centrally located or controlled resources. Psychological barriers associated with using remote resources are very difficult for researchers to overcome (see Kiesler et al., 1984; Sproull and Kiesler, 1986; Short, Williams and Christie, 1976; and Daft and Lengel, 1984). One psychological barrier is related to the principle of least effort. Information seekers will use tools and sources that they know are inferior if such information resources require less physical and mental effort to access than those of higher quality (Culnan, 1985; see also Zipf, 1965). Lack of institutional support and personal attention also discourages remote users. The fear and embarrassment that an inexperienced user might feel about requesting help with networks are accentuated if the user must turn to an outsider, especially to support staff at some other institution. Finally, the kinesthetic element in learning to use technology is reduced if one must rely on online, written, or telephone rather than personal assistance.

Sector Differences and Relationships

As noted earlier, the proposed NREN is intended to serve researchers and other users in three major sectors: private corporations, academia, and Federal laboratories. While network users in these three sectors share some characteristics (e.g., levels of expertise, goals of network use, and other attributes), there are also significant differences among them. NREN design and policy must recognize both the similarities and differences among these three sectors if it is to be the universally accessed electronic highway envisioned by its proponents.

In a very basic way, the three sectors have different goals and different standards by which the success or failure of an institution or researcher is measured. Academic institutions' primary reason for being, despite all the more "realistic" and economic reasons, is the advancement of knowledge; Federal laboratories exist in order to make discoveries that will advance human understanding and contribute to the military, economic, and social well-being of the nation; and private-sector organizations exist for profit. Although this characterization is simplistic, it indicates areas of potential conflict among these users of a national research network. In the private-sector site, for example, there was a subtle but real influence that discouraged researchers from collaborating with researchers outside the corporation.

Organizational culture often determines acceptance of innovation, so consideration of cultural factors must be included in the design and operation of a national network. In addition, disregard of sector differences will result in less national coordination and collaboration and more conflict among the different sectors.

Network Design and Management

Very few of the researchers who participated in this study had given any extended thought to future network policy development. They assumed that the status quo would always be maintained, i.e., that there would never be any restrictions placed on their network activities beyond voluntary compliance with general guidelines on acceptable use that had been developed by their own community. Researchers apparently appreciate neither the constraints under which managers operate nor the difficulty of resolving conflicts among users, especially across sectors.

Study respondents worried about the imposition of any kind of control, such as external standards, communication monitoring or censoring, and network fees. They were particularly concerned about the ability of an "outsider" (e.g., the government, telephone company, or centralized network council) to interfere directly with their activities. Specifically, most researchers in the study maintained that:

- Self-regulation by researchers in accord with the norms of science should continue as the only form of network control
- The government should support network development without imposing control
- In principle, universal access should be guaranteed to "qualified users."

Researchers stated, in no uncertain terms, that any form of restriction on communication was abhorrent to science and detrimental to scientific productivity.

Difficulty Of Measuring Productivity Increases and Other Network Benefits

Many of the researchers who took part in the study emphasized that it is more important to recognize that networks changed the entire texture of what they did than to try to quantify any specific productivity gains. Respondents at all skill levels commented that the effect of information technologies is so powerful and pervasive that computer literacy should be required of all researchers. Such an opinion might be attributable to the assumptions that the benefits and importance of networks are so obvious that evaluation is not necessary or that only scientists' peers can judge the value of scientific work and networks' part in it. It was quite clear to the study team, however, that these assumptions did not prompt the respondents' replies.

This observation underscores some conceptual difficulties in evaluating the success of the NREN. These difficulties arise from the nature of information itself and of the scientific enterprise, e.g.:

- There is no validated, agreed upon method for determining the value of information in general, and information gained from networks specifically.
- We do not have the conceptual tools to measure the impact of a "good idea."
- It is virtually impossible to measure the benefit of broadening one's community, one of the major positive effects of electronic networks.

These conceptual difficulties indicate that the expectation of easily measurable productivity gains from the implementation of an NREN may be unrealistic -- unrealistic because such an expectation does not match the way science is actually done and because productivity is not easily defined or determined. The researchers, therefore, insisted that the NREN should be considered as an investment in infrastructure. In addition, such an investment in the infrastructure may take 10 or 15 years or more to pay dividends.

There is consistent difficulty in convincing policy makers, institutional and Federal, of the importance of the above observations. Many expect immediate and measurable results from the NREN. There is also considerable concern in some quarters that serious public discussion of these issues will compromise the possibility of and funding for the NREN. Evaluation of the NREN, of course, is vital to its success, but reliance on the vague concept of "productivity gains" may not be realistic.

Networks Magnify Existing Tendencies, Patterns, and Preferences

Networks do not seem to alter existing organizational cultures or patterns of resource allocation, nor do they seem to change peoples' attitudes toward technology or their current levels of technical expertise (Hiltz, 1984). Some of our respondents were adamant about their aversion to investing much time and energy in information technologies, while, at the other end of the spectrum, respondents with highly sophisticated network skills and knowledge welcomed developments in information technology as a further opportunity to demonstrate their organizational, professional, and personal value.

Electronic networks are not introduced into a social, personal, or organizational vacuum. The study's findings suggest that networks do not so much alter existing inclinations, attitudes, and behaviors as support, magnify, or extend them. For example, most researchers claimed that networks facilitated, rather than changed the nature of, their work. It seems that many researchers incorporate networks into their existing communication and research styles and existing scientific norms.

Technophoria

As noted throughout this report, the benefits to be gained from a truly national research network could be substantial. The only way to maximize benefits of the NREN, however, is with a realistic and careful look at some of the technical, social, and policy issues involved in such an enterprise. One of these issues might be labeled "technophoria," i.e., a blind belief in the beneficial effects of technology and an identification of technology as the panacea for all kinds of problems. Just as with its counterpart, technophobia, the major difficulty with technophoria is its absolute character -- all technology is good, all problems have technical solutions, the only important problems are those that can be solved with technology, and technical experts should be the first and final arbiters of all conflicts.

Technophoria is especially pernicious because it can cause policy makers, the general public, and network users to develop unrealistic expectations about the power and benefits of networks. This leads to neglect of social and behavioral problems, of any problem beyond the technical and financial. The immense benefits of an NREN can be realized only by curbing technophoria and addressing the wider social issues noted throughout this book.

Elitism

Currently, elites are in control of networks. High-status researchers have access to more resources, including information technology resources, in most organizations. Researchers (1) with significant technical expertise, (2) at major research institutions, and (3) in certain highly supported natural and computational science disciplines are at a significant advantage socially as well as professionally when compared to other scientists or nonusers of networks. While it is comforting to believe that merit alone determines the distribution of scientific resources, social and geographic factors noted play a significant role in determining "who gets what." One of the primary reasons for the establishment of the NREN is to ensure a level playing field for researchers so that all available expertise is brought to bear on research problems. Attention to technical and financial problems alone will not ensure full NREN participation by the vast majority of U.S. researchers.

A number of the study participants knew only a research process based on high-speed research networks and supercomputing, and they considered this the normal state of affairs for other researchers. These researchers also believed that they have no competitive advantage in their careers because of their network expertise and that the money and resources that they enjoyed would continue to be available.

On a national level, high-profile users are best able to manipulate networks to achieve high professional and personal status, and they often dictate the agenda for network development. For example, EDUCOM, a major stakeholder in the development of the NREN, is made up of major and influential research universities, and the national collaboratory conference held at Rockefeller University (Lederberg and Uncapher, 1989) was attended primarily by representatives of influential, elite private and public organizations. Such groups, including others with connections to the "grand challenges" of research and other Big Science projects, effectively determine which questions about networks are useful to ask and how they shall be answered.

Elitist practice leads to elitist versions of network management strategies, e.g., networks should be managed and used only by technical experts, and network policy should be decided by councils of prestigious scientists. This elitist practice also contributes to technophoria. Those with the greatest scientific reputation and technical expertise have effectively determined which issues related to network development issues should be addressed. In addition, such high-profile users often do not explicitly recognize their elite status, but, at the same time, they are often unwilling to relinquish this unique position and status. A fully integrated and accessible national network must overcome these attitudes in order to realize the greatest benefit from the national investment in such a project.

RECOMMENDATIONS

Given the study's findings and the identification of key issues, a number of recommendations can be offered to reduce the problems and barriers faced by users and help resolve the issues. This section is intended to answer the question: What implications do the study's findings hold for the design and implementation of a national research and education network?

Conduct Survey of Existing Network Users/Policies

As discussed in several chapters in this book, there currently is limited knowledge available about national patterns of existing network uses, applications, and policies. Policy makers and network designers need to have national data that identify and describe, minimally:

- The number of network users
- The demographics of network users
- Equipment currently being used with/for network access and applications
- The types and frequency of network use
- The nature of the information and communication needs that networks satisfy
- The existing policies and procedures governing the operation and management of various networks.

As it is, the only data available are localized for a specific network, or, typically, for individual institutional settings. It is essential that such national data be collected and analyzed. The key policy issues related to the actual implementation of the NREN cannot be properly framed without such a context. Further, the data could provide support to specific funding requests and add credibility to proposals for the design

of the NREN. Without such data, policy makers and system designers will make decisions based on opinion and "guesstimates," will be unaware of evolving trends and uses, and are likely to ignore user information needs.

Design the NREN in Light of User Information Needs and Behavior

As more information is transmitted over and stored in electronic networks, careful thought and consideration must be given to how the <u>user</u> approaches these systems. Borgman (1989, p. 237) concluded that "users of information retrieval systems are not created equal." Users are heterogeneous in terms of their skills in using a particular system and the demands they place upon that system. Successful information systems are those designed to respond to these heterogeneous user needs and demands.

While it is clear that networks must meet a broad range of goals, they cannot meet those goals unless they are designed to accommodate user information needs. In publications dealing with network development and information policy alternatives, the role and importance of the user seems to have been set aside. The authors have detailed elsewhere selected research findings on information systems design and information gathering and use behaviors that are frequently ignored in the design of information dissemination and retrieval systems (McClure, Bishop, and Doty, 1989, pp. 67-69). As the nation continues the design of the NREN, decision makers <u>and</u> policy makers must make certain that spokespersons for users and the manner in which users actually gather and use information contribute to the design of such services and policies.

Require Direct Support for Network Training

Policy should be developed that requires the NREN to allocate a certain percentage of its resources for training and education purposes. Thus, if the NREN is budgeted at $400 million, the law might indicate that 8% of that total budget must be dedicated to education and training. The disposition of these funds could also help to assure a level playing field, maximize national investment in R&D, and limit network elitism.

A number of interviewees commented that if the Federal government did not require resources to be spent on training, institutions would not engage in meaningful programs of user education. Indeed, the key here is the need for <u>programs</u> of education and training. Having one or two individuals who will respond to demand does not constitute an educational program. Educational programs tend to be most successful in one-on-one learning situations with hands-on, proactive training techniques. New information technologies have little impact if the majority of users are unable to apply these technologies to specific problems and research activities for want of adequate training.

Obtain Greater Involvement from the Library Community

To date, there has been minimal consideration of the role of libraries and areas for involvement by the library community in the NREN. Indeed, recent NREN reports by OSTP, OTA, and the National Academy provide little attention to how the library community could be involved. This situation is somewhat paradoxical given that community's experiences with bibliographic utilities such as OCLC, online databases, and other national networking applications. More specifically, the involvement of the nation's libraries in the NREN could take a number of directions, for example:

- Provision of network access to selected bibliographic utilities
- Provision of personalized electronic reference services to researchers
- Development of directories and indexes of network services
- Promotion of and training for network use.

These are only a few of the possibilities. Library leaders knowledgeable about the NREN and electronic networks should be actively and immediately involved in a range of planning activities.

Provide Better Documentation and Directories

Significant improvements in the use and impact of the NREN can result from improving documentation for the range of network uses and applications available. Such documentation should be written from a problem-solving perspective rather than from a technical perspective. In addition, directories of the broad range of available information resources and services, access techniques, and individuals involved

in networking are also needed to increase the usefulness of networks.

Many users are less interested in why something works than in how to make it work. Technically intensive and detailed documentation, print or online, is often counterproductive. Also, existing knowledge about graphic presentations, integrating text with graphics, and producing high-impact publications or online information, paradoxically, frequently fails to find its way into the production of network documentation.

Establish a Lead Federal Agency for NREN Development

Currently, there are a number of Federal agencies (e.g., Office of Science and Technology Policy, National Science Foundation), educational institutions, and other groups (e.g., EDUCOM, the National Academy, and FCCSET) who are key players in the development of an NREN. It is unclear how the activities of these various groups are being coordinated. It is also unclear how these groups (or other interested groups) are designing strategy to justify the necessary expenditures or otherwise advising Congress on how best to proceed with the design of the NREN.

For the short term and, perhaps, in transition from Federal funding to other types of funding and governance for the NREN, the Office of Science and Technology Policy (OSTP) and/or the National Science Foundation (NSF) might be considered as candidates for the lead agency status. Regardless of the identity of the appropriate agency, there is an immediate need to better coordinate the activities of the various stakeholders interested in the development of the NREN.

Plan for the Management of the NREN

There are a number of stakeholders with an interest in how the NREN should be organized and managed. These stakeholders include elected officials, educational institutions, private-sector R&D firms, telecommunications firms, Federal labs, scientists, libraries, network engineers and managers, and other individual users. Each of these groups has a vested interest in determining how an NREN is managed, who or what makes policy and procedural decisions, and the manner in which the NREN enforces or makes certain that policy and procedures are followed.

Two major management policy issues which must be addressed during the planning stages of the NREN are:

- Who shall be identified as a "qualified user"? How will that identification be made? By whom? There is a general assumption among researchers, policy makers, and proponents of the NREN that only "qualified users" will be eligible to use the network, but there is no mention of how such a category will be defined. This issue has the potential for intense controversy.
- A related problem is that of acceptable use of the network -- How will acceptable use be defined? Who will define it? What sanctions, if any, will be employed to govern acceptable use? This issue, too, will require negotiation and flexibility among stakeholders.

There is little evidence that these questions have been asked, and less evidence to suggest that they have been answered. Whatever model of network management is implemented, these questions must be addressed.

Develop Mechanisms to Improve Communication Between Network Engineers/Managers and Network Users

The evidence from the study suggests that there are two very different perspectives on how networks should be used, how they should be designed, and how they might be managed. Generally, network engineers and managers have a technical, hardware perspective while users tend to be oriented more to applications and problem solving. Unfortunately, there is oftentimes little effective communication between these two groups.

Findings from the study suggest that network engineers, managers, and support personnel are perceived by the users as "out of touch" with users' computing needs and fixated on technology. Users are often perceived by the engineers and managers as being unwilling or unable to learn and use the new technologies. Users are seen as naive about the constraints under which networks are designed and managed, while users say that network engineers and managers do not understand the process of integrating technology into research and scientific communication. The successful development of electronic networks in support of research and scientific communi-

cation, as well as other uses, will require regular and effective communication between network users and network engineers and managers.

Conduct Additional Research

The current political context for decision making regarding the NREN is inadequate as a basis for designing the network. As noted earlier, there are a number of questions which suggest the need for additional empirical research. Some of the more important research questions to be answered are:

- Is there a competitive advantage for scientists who use electronic networks?
- Do electronic networks exacerbate inequalities between the information "haves" and "have-nots"?
- What are the strengths, weaknesses, and benefits of particular management models for administering the NREN?
- What user-based factors should be taken into consideration in the design and operation of networks?
- Who will bring network resources under bibliographic control (i.e., organizing, describing, and providing access points) to make them available to all kinds of users?
- How should the network be organized?
- What types of educational programs, delivery techniques, and topics are most important for specific types of users?
- How can data transfer across networks and application packages be accomplished more easily and reliably?
- How are scientists' attitudes toward scientific norms related to their actual network behavior?

As suggested earlier, there is much more speculation and "opinionating" about the use, design, impact, benefits, and roles of an NREN than there is empirically based evidence. If policy makers determine that the NREN should be supported, they should also support (1) research to aid in the design of the network, and (2) ongoing evaluation and research into the network's performance.

CURRENT DEVELOPMENTS AND PROSPECTS

It is clear that more debate about the development of the NREN will occur in the future. Less clear, however, is how that debate will evolve, who the key players will be in the debate, and the key issues that will frame the debate. The <u>High Performance Computing Act of 1990</u> (S. 1067) passed the Senate but not the House in the closing hours of the 101st Congress. But the version passed by the Senate did not include key provisions in the original bill related to information services and training. Indeed, some members of the library and education community were relieved that the bill did not pass in its final form.

Previous chapters in this book have offered a perspective on the background, key issues, and recommendations regarding a national electronic networking initiative. As this book is completed in early 1991, a number of developments are taking place that will affect the development of the NREN. This section provides a brief overview of some of those developments.

Non-Federal Network Developments

It would be a mistake to conclude that, because S.1067 did not pass the 101st Congress, development of the NREN is not proceeding. While space does not permit a detailed account of the many initiatives currently underway, an overview of some of the more interesting and important ones is offered in this section.

In June 1990, the National Science Foundation awarded the Corporation for National Research Initiatives (CNRI, a nonprofit organization) $15.8 million to "oversee the research on setting up five separate networks and experimenting with new hardware and software technology" (Markoff, 1990b, p. F-1). Robert E. Kahn, president of the corporation, is especially concerned about designing an infrastructure to support high-speed computing and national electronic networking (p. F-3):

> Dr. Kahn cites as an example the creation of a library system that would be computerized and connected but would not exist in one centralized computer. Instead, the nation's information would be located in widely separated specialized databases, which would range from yellow-page-type information stored in phone company computers, say, to geological fault figures stored in an oil-company or university mainframe.

The infrastructure needed to support such a system is, at this time, unclear. Research efforts, however,

currently in progress at CNRI are likely to have significant impact on the development of the NREN and national electronic computing.

Another significant development is the formation of Advanced Network Services, Inc. (ANS). The not-for-profit company was organized and is supported by Merit, Inc. (a consortium of state-supported universities in Michigan), IBM Corporation, and MCI Communications Corporation. The goals of ANS, as outlined by Allen H. Weis, its President and CEO are to ("Advanced Network Services, Inc.," 1990, p. 43):

- Assist in the expansion of the existing national network so that it broadly serves the research and education communities
- Increase the speed and capability of the network, maintaining it as the leading edge of technology
- Provide the highest quality network and services in helping to advance research and education.

Initially, ANS will manage and operate the Federally funded National Science Foundation Network (NSFNET).

A number of observers have raised questions as to the degree to which ANS intends to be "not-for-profit" because ANS intends to develop and provide a broad range of information services to researchers, educators, and government officials, and others as appropriate ("Advanced Network Services, Inc.," 1990, p. 46).

Fees that are charged to ANS subscribers, together with contributions from industrial companies such as IBM and MCI, could help reduce the financial burden of the Federal government in its initiative to provide the nation with a high-speed computer network.

Many of ANS' activities and objectives are similar to those proposed in NREN legislation. Moreover, the support of IBM and MCI for ANS is considerable and is likely to have significant impact on national networking developments.

The evolution of ANS will be especially interesting to watch in light of the development of national electronic networking initiatives such as that of Performance Systems International, Inc. (PSI) and its PSINet ("National Network Expansion," 1990, p. 1):

> PSINet is a reliable and multi-functional wide area network (WAN) system and service. It spans the continental U.S. from its customer's premises to its "core nodes" placed at intersecting fiber optic paths. Its combination of hardware, software and communications

facilities represents a substantial deployment of components. . . . Our national infrastructure is built in secure facilities that are leased from telephone companies, providing privacy, high reliability, direct access to fiber optic facilities, and professional, on-site maintenance -- a unique and unmatched capability.

Individuals and institutions can subscribe to PSINet, obtain immediate connectivity to national networks, and use a range of services available from PSI as well as other network vendors.

While PSI is a national initiative, there are also a number of regional networks that are evolving and providing a range of connectivity and service options. One example is NYSERNet, the New York State Education and Research Network -- a nonprofit corporation "whose mission is to advance science, technology, and education through access to high-speed data computer networking" (NYSERNet User, 1990, p. 2).

NYSERNet is a good example of an aggressive, expanding, and user-based regional network that is increasing connectivity throughout a range of institutions. By more than simply providing connectivity to national networking, this regional is initiating a range of network services and educational programs (e.g., K-12 educational projects) that suggest future directions in networking services and applications. Moreover, NYSERNet is consciously courting the library community for involvement and participation in the network.

The developments reported in this section suggest that, despite the failure to pass S. 1067, considerable work has been done on a range of national networking initiatives. In fact, these developments suggest the degree to which Federal, public, and private sector divisions are being blurred as electronic networks and services are scrambling for support, development, and subscribers. These examples suggest that national electronic networking initiatives will continue to expand, regardless of a Federal proposal and regardless of the existing policy vacuum in national electronic networking.

The Coalition for Networked Information

The Coalition for Networked Information (CNI) was organized in Spring 1990 by the Association of Research Libraries (ARL), CAUSE, and EDUCOM. ARL is an organization of the major research libraries in the United States and Canada. CAUSE is the association for the management of information technology in higher education and has been very interested in issues of networking and telecommunications in higher education. EDUCOM is a nonprofit consortium of colleges, universities, and other institutions founded in 1964 to facilitate the introduction, use, and management of information technology in higher education.

CNI has become an important and articulate participant in the policy debates regarding the NREN. Material released by CNI says that (Coalition for Networked Information, 1990, Section 2, p. 1):

- The mission of the Coalition for Networked Information is to promote the creation of and access to information resources in networked environments in order to enrich scholarship and to enhance intellectual productivity.
- The Coalition pursues its mission by seeking to realize the information distribution and access potential of existing and proposed high performance computers and networks that support the research and education activities of a wide variety of institutions and organizations.
- The Coalition accomplishes this realization by undertaking activities, on its own and in partnership with others, that formulate, promulgate, evaluate, and promote policies and protocols that enable powerful, flexible, and universal access to networked information resources.
- The Coalition directs the combined intellectual, technological, professional, and financial resources of its members according to a shared vision of how the nature of information management is changing and will continue to change through the end of the 20th century and into the beginning of the 21st.

It is quite likely that CNI will work to enhance and extend the "E" (education) aspects of NREN legislation. Moreover, the Coalition represents a significant group of organizations and will be a key player in NREN policy debates.

At the Coalition's Fall 1990 meeting, seven working groups were organized to address specific topics and issue areas (Coalition for Networked Information, 1990, Section 2):

- Noncommercial publishing
- Commercial publishing
- Architectures and standards
- Legislation, codes, policies, and practices

- Directories and resource information services
- Teaching and learning
- Management and professional and user education.

These working groups will develop vision statements and positions for their respective particular areas. One can anticipate that these vision statements will provide direction to CNI's lobbying efforts.

CNI also appears to be evolving into a voice for many of the issues and concerns of interest to the library community. It is most likely that the library community will become increasingly involved in NREN issues during 1991 and beyond (Arms, 1990; Nielson, 1990). Some people in the library community are only now recognizing the significance and impact of electronic computing on the design of library information services, information systems, and the role of professional librarians: "It is especially important that the library community, with its skills and knowledge of users and meeting user information needs, becomes actively involved in the decision making for the design and operation of the NREN" (McClure et. al., 1990, p. 32). National electronic networking and the development of the "virtual library" may be the single most important issue to the library community in the 1990s.

Given the complexity of the issues, the increasing interest in NREN by educational institutions aligned with CNI, the limited resources that might be available from the Federal government, and the need for some agreement about goals and activities for a national network, it is likely that public debate about the NREN will continue to grow. Moreover, the focus of the debate is likely to shift more from developing the NREN for the research community into its possible role in enhancing the nation's educational infrastructure.

The Harvard Information Infrastructure Conference

In late November and early December 1990, Information Infrastructure for the 1990s, a workshop/ symposium, was held at Harvard University's John F. Kennedy School of Government. The overall purpose of the conference was to explore public policy related to the NREN and to the national "information infrastructure" in general. There were about one hundred participants in the workshop, and they were drawn from a number of important stakeholder groups: the National Science Foundation, economists, librarians, lawyers, hardware and software designers, private-

sector information providers, scientists, network administrators, government at all levels, and other groups.

Although there may have been some hope to use the workshop to provide recommendations about national networking, especially the NREN, it became clear that the hope was ill-founded. There were several, fundamental differences among the conference participants which were not easily reconcilable, and that some attendees considered intractable. These included differences along several dimensions:

- Goals – the NREN should be for elite, high-end users in cutting-edge research vs. the NREN should allow more scientists to participate in leading-edge research, and, further, the NREN should be used, in a way similar to universal telephone service, to permit the ordinary citizen to benefit from the enormous national investment in networking.
- Federal role -- the Federal government should invest heavily in the NREN and other networking R&D as a matter of course vs. the government should not invest in NREN, or it should only after its users, costs, and payoffs are clearly identified.
- Models for management -- the NREN should eventually be managed by private, for-profit enterprises which will guarantee the "most efficient" use of the service vs. the NREN should remain in public hands.
- Network capacity-- the NREN should have only "light fiber," i.e., network capacity should match demand and be parceled out only sparingly to qualified users with a substantiated need for high-capacity networks vs. the NREN should have "dark fiber," i.e., excess capacity available which will support all kinds of uses by all kinds of users.
- Fees -- fees, however applied, will ensure a "clear pipe" for those that really need the capacity vs. access should be universal and free, if possible.
- Regulation -- NREN and other national networking initiatives should be used to decrease the amount of Federal telecommunications regulation vs. NREN should be the means by which more and/or different Federal communication regulations are effected.
- Means to determine the values of NREN -- Economics, efficiency, and rational modeling techniques vs. social equity, economic externality, subsidy, and other arguments.

- Traffic -- bits and bytes (a computer science, traffic, mechanistic model) vs. functions and applications (an information service, user support model).
- Measurement of NREN -- NREN should be thought of as a high-speed, i.e., gigabits/second, network vs. NREN should be considered as a high-capacity network.

Many of these issues are variations on themes identified earlier in this book -- users, goals, and finance. There were other major issues discussed, but the list above gives a flavor of the primary themes about which there were considerable differences of opinion.

Many issues, of course, were not discussed at any length, despite their importance to NREN and any national information infrastructure: network management; the heterogeneity of scientific, high-end users; social or behavioral factors in network development and use; the nature of information; how information infrastructures and networks differ from other kinds of networks and infrastructures; intellectual property; the archiving, storage, and retrieval of massive amounts of information; collaborative technologies; and some fundamental epistemological topics. Some of the papers presented discussed issues related to these issues, and posed interesting questions, e.g., what models of cognition and communication are inherent in these kinds of communication tools? Might we want to develop other kinds of models? Do such systems merely share information, or do they facilitate the mutual construction of meaning?

There were some fundamental problems which did receive a fair amount of attention and were almost universally identified as important:

- The necessity of moving away from an engineering and computer science perspective when discussing national networks and towards a customer-oriented, applications-driven perspective
- The importance of the needs of end users and helping them to solve their problems
- The inappropriateness of the voice metaphor to advance telecommunication networks and its technical limitations, especially for the enablement of the end user
- Problems of scaling up from present networks to a truly integrated national networking infrastructure
- Need for human intermediaries to act as effective catalysts between the technology and available resources on the one hand and end users on the other

- Subsidies for users should be considered as opposed to continued subsidies for service providers
- The necessity of tapping the experience of present intermediaries, especially their ability to provide information about information, i.e., meta-information.

Many of the stakeholder groups present at the conference agreed on the importance of these areas.

As noted above, not only was consensus not reached about recommendations for the NREN and other national networking initiatives, there was great dissensus about the identity of some of the most important issues which must be addressed. The overall feeling at the end of the conference was that this was not a coming together for the proposal of recommendations; rather, it was the beginning of a long and difficult process of identifying issues, considering alternatives, and making policy decisions. While everyone at the conference clearly supported national investments in networking and related technologies, it was also clear that the NREN and other national networking infrastructure initiatives raised some fundamental political, social, and legal issues which must be addressed before design, implementation, and evaluation of truly national systems can take place.

An important product of this conference was the various position papers and issue briefs that were developed for participants. A number of these papers are exceptionally useful as background information and in defining/understanding the complexity of the issues surrounding the development of the NREN. A compilation of these papers, perhaps with additional material, is scheduled for publication by the Kennedy School early in 1991.

Office of Technology Assessment Project

The Congressional Office of Technology Assessment (OTA) is completing a study (as of February 1991) that will identify and assess key issues related to the NREN and offer policy recommendations for the design and implementation of such a national network. The study began in 1989, and it is anticipated that the final report, tentatively titled Networking the Nation, will be issued in early Summer 1991.

As part of that project, a number of contract reports were written. Chapters 5, 6, and 7 of this book are revised versions of such reports. Additional contractor reports related to this project will be incorporated into the final report. As part of this overall project, OTA issued High Performance Computing & Networking for Science: Background Paper in 1989. That report is included as Appendix K of this book. Also issued was Seeking Solutions: High Performance Computing for Science (1991), included as Appendix Q.

As part of this project, OTA held a workshop on December 11, 1990 in Washington, DC entitled "Access to the NREN," with invited participants from the government, private, and educational communities. The sense of the workshop was similar to that at the Harvard Conference, i.e., there was still considerable debate about identifying and defining key issues. Interestingly, this particular group of participants were very concerned about emphasizing the education aspects of the NREN and discussing possible issues to expand the scope of S. 1067 into electronic education. Specific ideas and suggestions for resolving issues and developing policy recommendations lagged considerably behind understanding and defining key issues.

Another interesting aspect of the OTA project is its use of an electronic conference to discuss a range of issues related to the proposed NREN. This electronic conference is being conducted using CAUCUS software on the Internet. The discussions have been extensive, but once again, participants are largely at the stage of identifying and discussing issues -- not at proposing specific policy initiatives.

Discussions on the electronic conference and additional workshops will be used as input for the OTA final report. The appearance of the OTA report from this project in the Summer 1991 could be a significant step contributing to identifying and defining the key policy issues. Perhaps more importantly, the study may provide a framework for policy initiatives that could be incorporated into any new legislation such as S. 272 (Appendix E) and S. 343 (Appendix O), introduced into the 102nd Congress.

The High Performance Computing Act of 1991

In late January 1991, Senator Gore introduced S. 272, "The High Performance Computing Act of 1991" (Congress, Senate, 1991) (see Appendix E). A similar version of the bill, H.R. 656, was introduced by Representative Brown in the House of Representatives. In his introductory comments, Gore stated (Gore, 1991, pp. S. 1198-1190):

This legislation provides for a multi-agency high performance computing research and development program to be coordinated by the White House Office of Science and Technology (OSTP). . . . . This bill will roughly double funding for high performance computing at NSF and NASA during the next 5 years. Additional funding -- more than $1 billion during the next 5 years -- will also be needed to expand research and development programs at DARPA and DOE. . . . With this bill we can help shape the future -- shape it for the better. This is an investment in our national security and our economic security, which we cannot afford not to make.

With the introduction of this bill, the debates and discussions as to how best to implement the NREN are likely to continue throughout 1991. Moreover, S. 343, "Department of Energy High-Performance Computing Act of 1991" (see Appendix O) was also introduced. It described an NREN initiative for the Department of Energy, authorizing the Department to establish a multi-gigabit-per second network to "link Government, Industry, and the higher education community" ("Department of Energy High-Performance Computing Act," 1991, p. S 1560). Those interested in the NREN will need to track the progress of S. 272, S. 343, and H.R. 656.

Moreover, the introduction of a High Performance Computing Act of 1991 insures that the various stakeholders will have another chance to shape the legislation. The range of stakeholders, however, with an interest in this legislation is broad. It will indeed be very interesting to see how the bills develop as they progress through the 102nd Congress.

Competition for Federal Funds

Competition for Federal funds has always been spirited, but as the United States enters 1991, the competition is likely to increase and be especially fierce. The competing issues requiring attention by the 102nd Congress are also significant: an emerging national recession, conflict in the Middle East, expenses related to the savings and loan bail-out, clean-up of toxic waste-sites, and other issues. Where high-performance computing and the NREN will fit in relative to these and other issues remains unclear. The size of the Federal funds that could be made available to support NREN initiatives also is unclear.

In February 1991, the administration proposed a High Performance Computing and Communications Program (HPCC) (Appendix P). It had the goals of extending U.S. technological leadership in high-performance computing and computer communications, providing wide dissemination and application of the technologies, and spurring gains in U.S. productivity and industrial competitiveness by making high-performance computing and networking technologies an integral part of the design and production process. The program has four key component areas (Office of Science and Technology Policy, 1991):

- High-performance computing systems
- Advanced Software Technology and Algorithms
- National Research and Education Network
- Basic Research and Human Resources.

The program details goals and strategies for each of these areas and has a cost of $638 million. Of special interest is the program's approach of distributing responsibility for managing these components across a number of Federal agencies. The 102nd Congress is likely to carefully review this program proposal as well as the various legislative initiatives.

In the past, Congress has been hesitant to provide funding for large-scale projects such as the NREN when there is little consensus among key stakeholder groups as to the purpose, management, operation, and benefits from the initiative. As 1991 begins, this consensus has yet to form around the NREN, suggesting that significant and additional public debate will be necessary to forge such a consensus. But if the past is any harbinger of the future, Congress will want more information, greater agreement among stakeholders, and better detailing of benefits and impacts before large-scale funding, in the range proposed in S. 272 or in the High Performance Computing and Communications program, is provided.

ADDRESSING THE CHALLENGE

The primary challenge in national electronic networking is to design the NREN so that it accomplishes a range of national, institutional, and individual objectives; serves a spectrum of uses in various settings; and meets the diverse needs of these users. In addressing this challenge, there are several concerns:

- Defining exactly what the NREN is and how such a network is related to existing networks
- Establishing an educational and instructional infrastructure to support the NREN
- Ensuring that the development of the NREN adequately considers users' information and communication needs and behavior and is designed to meet those needs
- Determining who or what will be responsible for managing the NREN and specifying the administrative responsibilities of that agency
- Promoting the development of a level playing field where access to the NREN is widely available to the larger scientific and research community and other users
- Securing adequate resources for nontechnological expenditures, e.g., support for educating network users and promoting research to assess the impact and effectiveness of the NREN.

Any legislation that supports the establishment of the NREN should address these challenges in very specific terms. Suggestions provided in this book are intended to help to address these concerns.

Currently, the very title "NREN" is a bit of a misnomer. The "National" aspects of the network may have significantly different connectivity and access impacts depending on the geographic location of the user. The "Research" component may assist primarily elite institutions and high-profile individuals. Some have argued that the "Education" component has yet to be fully developed and little attention was given it in S. 1067. And the "Network," or at least "networks," already exist, and are providing services and connectivity.

Despite the fact that "the Internet environment offers a unique environment for the development of a coherent system of networked information resources," (Lynch and Preston, 1990, p. 269), the expectation that everyone can be a better scientist, researcher, or educator as a result of the NREN may not be realistic. The claims of significant increases in productivity and enhanced national competitiveness must be tempered by an appreciation of the range of social and behavioral issues yet to be addressed and resolved. Indeed, the technical problems and issues associated with the design of the NREN are likely to be easier to resolve than the social and behavioral problems discussed throughout the book.

A range of policy issues, some of which have been identified in this book, require additional debate and

study. Indeed, virtually no empirical research has
been done on some of these topics and still less has
been done that is user-oriented rather than technically
oriented. Identifying, studying, debating, and resolving these issues, however, can contribute significantly
to the positive effects of a national research and
education network on research and national competitiveness. User-based perspectives on electronic
networking are essential if such networks are to
successfully accomplish their goals and increase both
the user's and the nation's overall productivity and
competitiveness.

BIBLIOGRAPHY

Sources Cited

Advanced Network Services, Inc., formed to expand national supercomputer highway. (1990, November). Information Today, 7(10), 43.

Alberts, Bruce. (1985). Limits in science: In biology, small science is good science. Cell, 41, 337-338.

Allison, P. and Stewart J. (1974). Productivity differences among scientists: Evidence for accumulative advantage. American Sociological Review, 39, 596-606.

Allen, Brenda J. (1989). Computer-Mediated Communication: Purposes and Correlates of Use of an Intraorganizational Electronic Mail System. Dissertation. Howard University.

Allen, T. J. (1985). Managing the Flow of Technology: Technology Transfer and the Dissemination of Technological Information within the R&D Organization. Cambridge, MA: The MIT Press.

Althiede, David L. (1985). Keyboarding as a social form. Computers and the Social Sciences, 1, 97-106.

American Library Association. (1990a, March, 28). Resolution on a national research and education network. Information Packet on the Proposed National Research and Education Network. Chicago, IL: Library and Information Technology Association.

_____. (1990b, January 10). Telecommunications - NREN. ALA Washington Newsletter, 42(3), 4-5.

Arms, Caroline. (1990, September). A new information infrastructure. Online, 14(5), 15-22.

Association of Research Libraries, CAUSE, and EDUCOM. (1989, March 16). ARL, CAUSE, and EDUCOM announce the Coalition for Networked Information. Press Release.

Attewell, Paul and Rule, James. (1988). Computing and organizations: What we know and what we don't know. In Irene Grief (Ed.), Computer Supported Cooperative Work: A Book of Readings. San Mateo, CA: Morgan Kaufman Publishers, 557-579.

Barber, B. (1952). Science and the Social Order. Glencoe, IL: Free Press.

Barinaga, Marcia. (1989, September 15). The missing crystallography data. Science, 24, 1179-1181.

Barnes, Barry. (1974). Scientific Knowledge and Sociological Theory. London: Kegan and Paul.

Belkin, N., Oddy, R., and Brooks, H.M. (1982). ASK for information retrieval: Part I. Journal of Documentation, 38, 61-71.

Bell, C. Gordon. (1988, February). Gordon Bell calls for a U.S. research network. IEEE Spectrum, 25(4), 54-57.

Beveridge, W. I. B. (1957). The Art of Scientific Investigation. NY: Vintage Books.

Blau, Peter. (1973). The Organization of Academic Life. NY: Wiley.

Bloch, Erich. (1988, Summer/Fall). A national network: Today's reality, tomorrow's vision, Part 1. <u>EDUCOM Bulletin</u>, <u>23</u>,(2/3), 11-13.

Blomberg, Jeannette. (1988). The variable impact of computer technologies on the organization of work activities. In Irene Grief (Ed.), <u>Computer Supported Cooperative Work: A Book of Readings</u>. San Mateo, CA: Morgan Kaufman Publishers, 771-781.

Boesch, Frank T. (1989). Ethics in scientific research via networking. In Carol C. Gould (Ed.), <u>The Information Web: Ethical and Social Implications of Computer Networking</u>. Boulder, CO: Westview Press, 147-160.

Borgman, Christine L. (1989). All users of information systems are not created equal: An exploration into individual differences. <u>Information Processing and Management</u>, <u>25</u>, 237-251.

Boshier, Roger. (1990, January-March). Social psychological factors in electronic networking. <u>International Journal of Lifelong Education</u>, <u>9</u> (1), 49-64.

Branscomb, Lewis. (1983, October 14). Improving R&D productivity: The federal role. <u>Science</u>, <u>222</u>, 133.

_____. (1986, November-December). Science in 2006. <u>American Scientist</u>, <u>74</u>, 650-658.

Britten, William A. (1990, February). BITNET and the Internet: Scholarly networks for librarians. <u>College and Research Library News</u>, <u>51</u>(2), 103-107.

Brotz, Douglas K. (1983, April). Message system mores: Etiquette in Laurel. <u>ACM Transactions on Office Systems</u>, 1(2), 179-192.

Brown, John Seeley. (1986, September 10-12). The impact of the information age on the conduct and communication of science. In <u>Science Policy Task Force: Hearings on the Impact of the Information Age on Science</u>. Washington, DC: GPO.

Brownrigg, Edwin. (1990). Developing the information superhighway: Issues for libraries. In Carol A. Parkhurst, (Ed.), <u>Library Perspectives on the NREN: National Research and Education Network</u>. Chicago, IL: Library and Information Technology Association, 55-63.

Ceci, S. (1988). Scientists' attitudes toward data sharing. <u>Science, Technology, & Human Values</u>, <u>13</u>, 45-52.

Cecil, J. S. and Griffin, E. (1985). The role of legal policies in data sharing. In S. Fienberg, M. Martin, and M. Straf (Eds.), <u>Sharing Research Data</u>. Washington DC: National Academy Press, 148-198.

Chase, J. (1970). Normative criteria for scientific publication. <u>The American Sociologist</u>, <u>5</u>, 262-265.

Christie, Bruce. (1981). <u>Face to File Communication: A Psychological Approach to Information Systems</u>. Chichester, UK: John Wiley and Sons.

Chubin, Darly, Porter, Alan, Rossini, Frederick, and Connolly, Terry (Eds). (1986). <u>Interdisciplinary Analysis and Research</u>. Mt. Airy, MD: Lomond.

Cline, Nancy. (1990, Summer). Information resources and the national network. <u>EDUCOM Review</u>, 25(2), 30-34.

Coalition for Networked Information. (1990). <u>Resources Binder: Fall, 1990 Meeting</u>. Washington, DC: Coalition for Networked Information.

Cole, S. and Cole, J. R. (1967, June). Scientific output and recognition. <u>American Sociological Review</u>, <u>32</u>, 377-390.

_____. (1973). <u>Social Stratification in Science</u>. Chicago, IL: University of Chicago Press.

Committee on National Statistics. (1985). Report of the Committee on National Statistics. In S. Fienberg, M. Martin, and M. Straf, (Eds.), <u>Sharing Research Data</u>. Washington DC: National Academy Press, 3-36.

Congress. (1986, August 21). <u>National Science Foundation Authorization Act for Fiscal Year 1987</u>. (P. L. 99-383). Washington, DC: GPO.

Congress. House. (1989a, October 3) <u>High Performance Computing . . . Hearings</u>. Washington, DC: GPO.

_____. (1989b, August 3). <u>The National High Performance Computer Act of 1989</u>. (H. R. 3131). Washington, DC: GPO.

_____. (1990a, March 21). <u>American Technology Preeminence Act</u>. (H. R. 4329). Washington, DC: GPO.

_____. (1991). <u>High-Performance Computing Act of 1991</u>. (H.R. 656). Washington, DC: GPO.

_____. Committee on the Judiciary. (1990b, June 14). <u>American Technology Preeminence Act</u>. Report 101-481, Part 2. Washington, DC: GPO.

_____. Committee on Space, Science, and Technology. (1990c, May 10). <u>American Technology Preeminence Act</u>. Report 101-481, Part 1. Washington, DC: GPO.

_____. Subcommittee on Science, Research, and Technology. (1990d, March 14). <u>Hearings on The National High Performance Computer Act of 1990</u>. Washington, DC: GPO.

_____. (1989c, June 20). <u>The U.S. Supercomputing Industry . . . Hearings</u>. Washington, DC: GPO.

Congress. Senate. (1986, June 24). <u>The Supercomputer Network Study Act of 1986</u>. (S. 2594). Washington, DC: GPO.

_____. (1988a, October 19). <u>The National High-Performance Computer and Technology Act of 1988</u>. (S. 2918). <u>Congressional Record</u>, 134 (149), S 16897-16901. Washington, DC: GPO.

_____. (1989a, November 21). <u>Department of Energy High Performance Computing Act of 1989</u>. (S. 1976). Washington, DC: GPO. [Appendix G]

_____. (1989b, May 18). <u>The National High-Performance Computer and Technology Act of 1989</u>. (S. 1067). Washington, DC: GPO. [Appendix B]

_____. (1990a, April 4). <u>High-Performance Computing Act of 1990</u> (S. 1067). Working draft as reported out of the Commerce Committee. Washington, DC: GPO. [Appendix C]

_____. (1990b, October 24). <u>High-Performance Computing Act of 1990</u>. (S. 1067). Version passed by the Senate. Washington, DC: GPO. [Appendix D]

_____. (1991a, February). Department of Energy High-Performance Computing Act of 1991. (S. 343). Washington, DC: GPO. [Appendix O]

_____. (1991b, January 25). High-Performance Computing Act of 1991. (S. 272). Washington, DC: GPO. [Appendix E]

_____. Committee on Commerce, Science, and Transportation. (1990c, July 23). High Performance Computing Act of 1990. Report 101-387. Washington, DC: GPO. Appendix F]

_____. (1990d). Section-By-Section Analysis of S. 1067, The National High-Performance Computing Act of 1990. Mimeo. Washington, DC: GPO.

_____. Committee on Energy and Natural Resources. (1990e, July 19). Department of Energy High Performance Computing Act of 1990. Report 101-377. Washington, DC: GPO. [Appendix H]

_____. Subcommittee on Science, Technology, and Space. (1988b, August 11). Computer Networks and High Performance Computing . . . Hearing. Washington, DC: GPO.

_____. (1989c, September 15). Computer Technology and the New Age of Information . . . Hearing. Washington, DC: GPO.

_____. (1989d, June 21, July 26, September 15). National High Performance Computer Technology Act of 1989 . . . Hearing. Washington, DC: GPO.

_____. (1989e, June 21). S. 1067 -- Supercomputing and Information Superhighways . . . Hearing. Washington, DC: GPO.

_____. (1989f, July 26). S. 1067 -- Visualization, Artificial Intelligence, and Advanced Computer Software . . . Hearing. Washington, DC: GPO.

Congressional Research Service. (1986, September). The Impact of Information Technology on Science. For the Committee on Science and Technology, U.S. House of Representatives. Washington, DC: GPO.

Conrath, D. W. and Bair, James. (1974). The computer as an interpersonal communication device. Proceedings of the Second International Conference on Computer Communications. Stockholm, Sweden.

Crane, Diane. (1972). Invisible Colleges: Diffusion of Knowledge in Scientific Communities. Chicago, IL: University of Chicago Press.

_____. (1965). Scientists at major and minor universities: A study of productivity and recognition. American Sociological Review, 30, 699-714.

Crawford, Albert. (1982). Corporate electronic mail -- A communication-intensive application of information technology. MIS Quarterly, 6, 1-14.

Cronin, B. (1982). Invisible colleges and information transfer. Journal of Documentation, 38, 212-236.

Crowston, K., Malone, T., and Lin, F. (1988). Cognitive science and organizational design: A case study of computer conferencing. Human Computer Interaction, 3, 59-85.

Culnan, Mary J. (1985). The dimensions of perceived accessibility to information: Implications for the delivery of information systems and services. <u>Journal of the American Society for Information Science</u>, <u>36</u>, 302-306.

_____ and Markus, M. Lynne. (1987). Information technologies. In Frederic Jablin et al. (Eds.), <u>Handbook of Organizational Communication</u>. Newbury Park, CA: Sage Publications, 420-443.

Czajkowski, Alex and Kiesler, Sara. (1984). Computer-mediated communication, or the new next best thing to being there. <u>National Forum</u>, <u>64</u> (3), 191-34.

Daft, R. and Lengel, R. (1984). Information richness: A new approach to managerial behavior and organization design. <u>Research in Organizational Behavior</u>, <u>6</u>, 191-233.

Davies, J. (1977). The National Foundation for Educational Research in England and Wales Information Service. <u>Education Libraries Bulletin</u>, <u>20</u>(50), 9-23.

DeCandido, GraceAnne A. and Rogers, Michael. (1990, April 15). "Virtual library" promulgated by library/education coalition. <u>Library Journal</u>, <u>115</u>, 14.

Denning, P. (1985). The science of computing: Computer networks. <u>American Scientist</u>, <u>73</u>, 127-129.

Department of Energy and King Research. (1982, March 31). <u>Value of the Energy Database</u>. Washington, DC: Department of Energy.

Department of Energy High-Performance Computing Act. (1991, February 5). <u>Congressional Record</u>. (S 1559-1564). Washington, DC: GPO.

Dervin, Brenda. (1987, September 8). <u>Categorization of Communication Users</u>. Office of Technology Assessment Contractor Report, Communication and Information Technologies Program. Mimeograph.

_____ and Nilan, Michael S. (1986). Information needs and uses. In M. Williams (Ed.), <u>Annual Review of Information Science and Technology</u>, <u>21</u>. Chicago, IL: Knowledge Industry Publications, 3-33.

Doty, Philip. (1989). Federal research and development (R&D) as intellectual property. In Charles R. McClure and Peter Hernon (Eds.), <u>U.S. Scientific and Technical Information Policies: Views and Perspectives</u>. Norwood, NJ: Ablex, 139-171.

Dubrovsky, Vitaly, Kiesler, Sara, and Sethna, Beheruz. (1989, July). <u>The Equalization Phenomenon: Status Effects in Computer-Mediated and Face-to-Face Decision-Making Groups</u>. Unpublished Manuscript.

Dunn, John A., Jr. (in press). Electronic media and information sharing. In P. Ewell (Ed.). <u>Improving the Linkage Between Information and Decision</u>. San Francisco, CA: Jossey-Bass.

Ebbinghouse, Carol. (1990, November/December). Legislative Update -- the demise of NREN legislation for 1990. <u>Research and Education Networking</u>, <u>1</u> (2), 2-3.

EDUCOM. (1988, February, March). Special Issue on National Network. <u>EDUCOM Bulletin</u>, <u>23</u>.

Etzkowitz, H. (1989). Entrepreneurial science in the academy: A case of the transformation of norms. <u>Social Problems</u>, <u>36</u>, 14-29.

Eveland, J.D. and Bikson, T.K. (1987). Evolving electronic communication networks: An empirical assessment. Office: Technology and People, 3, 103-128.

_____. (1988). Work group structures and computer support: A field experiment. In Proceedings of the Conference on Computer-Supported Cooperative Work, 324-343.

Federal Library and Information Center Committee. (1990a, January). National Research and Education Network: Special Report 90-2. Washington DC: Library of Congress.

_____. (1990b, Winter). Bill on National Network Being Redrafted. FLICC Newsletter, 151, 4.

Federal Council for Science and Technology. Committee on Scientific and Technical Information. (1965). Recommendations for National Document Handling Systems in Science and Technology. 3 vols. Washington, DC: Federal Council for Science and Technology. NTIS, AD-624-560.

Feldman, Martha S. (1987). Electronic mail and weak ties in organizations. Office: Technology and People, 3, 83-101.

Fienberg, Stephen, Martin, Margaret, and Straf, Miron, (Eds.). (1985). Sharing Research Data. Washington, DC: National Academy Press.

Finholt, Tom and Sproull, Lee. (1987, November 13). Electronic Groups at Work. Unpublished manuscript. Carnegie Mellon University.

_____ and Kiesler, Sara. (1990). Communication and performance in ad hoc task groups. In Jolene Galagher, Robert E. Kraut, and Carmen Egido (Eds.), Intellectual Teamwork: Social and Technical Foundations of Cooperative Work. Hillsdale, NJ: Lawrence Erlbaum, 291-325.

Foulger, Davis A. (1990). Medium as Process: The Structure, Use, and Practice of Computer Conferencing on IBMP PBMPC Computer Conferencing Facility. Unpublished Dissertation. Temple University.

Freeman, L. (1980). Q-Analysis and the structure of friendship networks. International Journal of Man-Machine Studies, 12(3), 367-378.

Fuchs, Ira. (1988). Research networks and acceptable use. EDUCOM Bulletin, 23(2/3), 43-48.

Garvey, W. D. (1979). Communication: The Essence of Science. Oxford, UK: Pergamon Press.

Gaston, J. (1978). The Reward System in British and American Science. NY: Wiley and Sons.

Gelman, Barton. (1988, November 20). The computer heard 'round the nation. The Washington Post, 111(351), A1.

Gerola, Humberto and Gomory, Ralph E. (1984, June 6). Computers in science and technology: Early indications. Science, 225(4657), 11-18.

Gibbs, J. (1968). The study of norms. International Encyclopedia of the Social Sciences. Volume 11. NY: Macmillan, 208-213.

Gilbert, G. N. and Mulkay, Michael. (1984). Opening Pandora's Box: A Sociological Analysis of Scientists' Discourse. Cambridge, UK: Cambridge University Press.

Gore, Albert Jr. (1991, January 24). The High Performance Computing Act of 1991. <u>Congressional Record</u>. S 1198-1203.

_____. (1989, November). The Information superhighways of tomorrow. <u>Academic Computing</u>, <u>4</u>(3), 30-31.

Gould, Stephen. (1989, June 6). <u>The National Research and Education Network, Memorandum to the Senate Subcommittee on Science, Technology, and Space</u>. Washington, DC: Congressional Research Service, Library of Congress.

_____. (1990a). An intellectual utility for science and technology: The national research and education network. <u>Government Information Quarterly</u>, <u>7</u> (2), <u>7</u>(4), 415-425.

_____. (1990b, November 8). <u>Building the National Research and Education Network: Updated November 8, 1990</u>. CRS Report for Congress. Washington, DC: Congressional Research Service, Library of Congress. [Appendix N is an earlier version.]

_____. (1990c, July 26). <u>The Federal Research Internet and the National Research and Education Network: Prospects for the 1990s</u>. CRS Report for Congress. Washington, DC: Congressional Research Service, Library of Congress. [Appendix M]

_____. (1990d, January 11). <u>High Performance Computing: An Overview</u>. CRS Issue Brief. Washington, DC: Congressional Research Service, Library of Congress.

_____. (1990e, December 18). <u>High Performance Computing: An Overview; Updated December 18, 1990</u>. CRS Issue Brief. Washington, DC: Congressional Research Service, Library of Congress. [Appendix L]

Granovetter, M. (1972). The strength of weak ties. <u>American Journal of Sociology</u>, <u>78</u>, 1360-1380.

Greif, Irene. (Ed.). (1988). <u>Computer-Supported Cooperative Work: A Book of Readings</u>. San Mateo, CA: Morgan Kaufmann Publishers.

Grieve, Shelley and McCabe, Barbara G. (1986). E-mail use in a university department of communication. In Julie M. Hurd (Ed.), <u>ASIS '86: Proceedings of the 49th Annual Meeting of the American Society for Information Science</u>. Medford, NJ: Learned Information, 96-101.

Hagstrom, Warren. (1965). <u>The Scientific Community</u>. Carbondale, IL: Southern Illinois Press.

Hancock, E. M. (1988, Summer/Fall). The strategic importance of a national network. <u>EDUCOM Bulletin</u>, <u>23</u>(2/3), 3-7.

Harper, Dean. (1985). Computer technology and social relations. <u>Computers and the Social Sciences</u>, <u>1</u>, 127-132.

Hedrick, T. (1985). Justifications for and obstacles to data sharing. In S. Fienberg, M. Martin, and M. Straf, (Eds.), <u>Sharing Research Data</u>. Washington, DC: National Academy Press, 123-147.

Hellerstein, Laurel Nan. (1985). The social use of electronic communication at a major university. <u>Computers and the Social Sciences</u>, <u>1</u>, 191-197.

_____. (1986). Electronic messaging and conferencing with an emphasis on social use: An exploratory study. Paper presented at the Annual Meeting of the International Communication Association, Chicago, IL.

Henderson, Carol. (1990a, June). Federal development of a national research and education network: A chronology of significant events and library community involvement. In Carol Parkhurst (Ed.), <u>Library Perspectives on NREN: The National Research and Education Network</u>. Chicago, IL: Library and Information Technology Association, 7-14.

_____. (1990b). National Research and Education Network legislation: S. 1067 and H. R. 3131. In Carol Parkhurst (Ed.), <u>Library Perspectives on NREN: The National Research and Education Network</u>. Chicago, IL: Library and Information Technology Association, 3-6.

Hesse, Bradford, Sproull, Lee, Kiesler, Sara, and Walsh, John P. (1990, July 25). <u>Computer Network Support for Science: The Case of Oceanography</u>. Unpublished draft.

Hiltz, Starr Roxanne. (1984). <u>Online Communities: A Case Study of the Office of the Future</u>. Norwood, NJ: Ablex.

_____ and Turoff, Murray. (1978). <u>The Network Nation: Human Connection via Computer</u>. Reading, MA: Addison Wesley.

_____ (1981, November). The evolution of user behavior in a computerized conference system. <u>Communications of the ACM</u>, <u>24</u>(11), 738-751.

_____ Turoff, Murray, and Johnson, K. (1985). Disinhibition, deindividuation, and group process in computerized conferences. Paper presented at the International Communication Association Annual Convention, Honolulu, Hawaii.

Horwitt, Elizabeth. (1989, August). Science to take the high-speed route. <u>Computerworld</u>, <u>23</u>(1), 104.

Huray, Paul G. and Nelson, David B. (1990, Summer). The Federal High Performance Program. <u>EDUCOM Review</u>, <u>25</u>(2), 17-24.

Jennings, Dennis M., Landweber, Lawrence, Fuchs, Ira, Farber, David, and Adrion, Richard. (1986, February 28). Computer networking for scientists. <u>Science</u>, <u>231</u>, 943-950.

Johansen, Robert, DeGrasse, Robert Jr., and Wilson, Thaddeus. (1978, February). <u>Group Communication through Computers: Vol. 5: Effects on Working Patterns</u>. (Report R-1). Menlo Park, CA: Institute for the Future.

Johnston, Jerome. (1989). Commentary on issues and concepts in research on computer-mediated communication systems. In J. Anderson (Ed.), <u>Communications Yearbook/12</u>. Newbury Park, NJ: Sage Publications, 490-497.

Kahin, Brian. (1990, April 30). <u>Toward a Public Information Infrastructure: Information Policy and the Internet</u>. Report prepared for Office of Technology Assessment.

Kahn, Robert E. (1988, Summer/Fall). A national network: Today's reality, tomorrow's vision, part 2. <u>EDUCOM Bulletin</u>, <u>23</u>(2/3), 14-21.

Kaplan, Abraham. (1964). <u>The Conduct of Inquiry</u>. San Fransisco, CA: Chandler.

Kerlinger, F. N. (1986). <u>Foundations of Behavioral Research.</u> 3rd ed. NY: Holt, Rinehart, and Winston.

Kiesler, Sara. (1986, January/February). Thinking ahead: The hidden messages in computer networks. Harvard Business Review, 64(1), 46-60.

_____, Zubron, David, Moses, Anne Marie, and Geller, Valerie. (1985). Affect in computer-mediated communication: An experiment in synchronous terminal-to-terminal discussion. Human-Computer Interaction, 1(1), 77-104.

_____, Siegel, Jane and McGuire, Timothy W. (1984, October). Social psychological aspects of computer-mediated communications. American Psychologist, 39(10), 1123-1134.

King, Kenneth M. (1988, Summer/Fall). The national network: Where do we go from here? EDUCOM Bulletin, 23(2/3), 2.

Knorr-Cetina, K. (1981). The Manufacture of Knowledge: An Essay on the Constructivist and Contextual Nature of Science. NY: Pergamon Press.

Koch, Susan E. (1989). How Electronic Networks are Changing Science: Implications for a National Research and Education Network. Final Report Submitted to the Office of Technology Assessment.

Kolb, W. (1964). Norms. A Dictionary of the Social Sciences. NY: The Free Press of Glencoe, 472-473.

Kraut, Robert, Dumais, Susan, and Koch, Susan. (1989). Computerization, productivity, and quality of work life. Communications of the ACM, 32(2), 220-238.

_____, Galegher, Jolene, and Egido, Carmen. (1988). Relationships and tasks in scientific collaboration. Human-Computer Interaction, 3, 31-58.

_____. (Draft, 1989). Informal Communication in Scientific Work. Mimeo.

_____, Egido, Carmen, and Galegher, Jolene. (1990). Patterns of contact and communication in scientific research collaborations. In Jolene Galagher, Robert E. Kraut, and Carmen Egido (Eds.), Intellectual Teamwork: Social and Technical Foundations of Cooperative Work. Hillsdale, NJ: Lawrence Earlbaum, 149-172.

Krueger, R. A. (1988). Focus Groups: A Practical Guide for Applied Research. Newbury Park, CA: Sage.

Krippendorf, Klaus. (1980). Content Analysis: An Introduction to its Methodology. Beverly Hills, CA: Sage.

Kuhn, Thomas. (1970). The Structure of Scientific Revolutions. 2nd ed., enlarged. Chicago, IL: University of Chicago Press.

Lapidus, I. Richard. (1989). Ethics and the practice of science in a computer networked environment. In Carol C. Gould (Ed.), The Information Web: Ethical and Social Implications of Computer Networking. Boulder, CO: Westview Press, 119-146.

LaQuey, Tracy. (1989, November). Networks for academics. Academic Computing, 4(3), 32-39 and 65.

Larsen, Ronald. (1990, February). The colibratory: The network as testbed for a distributed electronic library. Academic Computing, 4(5), 22-23, 35-37.

Latour, B. and Woolgar, S. (1979). Laboratory Life: The Social Construction of Scientific Facts. Beverly Hills, CA: Sage.

Lederberg, Joshua. (1978). Digital communications and the conduct of science: The new literacy. Proceedings of the IEEE, 66(11), 1314-1319.

_____ and Uncapher, Keith. (1989). Towards a National Collaboratory: Report of an Invitational Workshop At The Rockefeller University. New York, NY, March 17-18. Mimeo.

Licklider, J. C. R. and Vezza, Albert. (1988). Applications of information networks. In Irene Grief (Ed.), Computer Supported Cooperative Work: A Book of Readings. San Mateo, CA: Morgan Kaufman Publishers, 143-183.

Lievrouw, L.A. and Carley, K. (in press). Changing patterns of communication among scientists in an era of "telescience." Technology in Society, 12(4).

Lin, N., Garvey, W. D., and Nelson, C. E. (1970). A study of the communication structure of science. In C. E. Nelson and D. K. Pollack (Eds.), Communication among Scientists and Engineers. Lexington, MA: Heath Lexington Books, 23-60.

Link Letter: The Merit/NSFNET Backbone Project. (1990a, September). Merit, IBM, MCI Form New Company, 3(4). 1.

_____. (1990b, December). Initial T3 Deployment in Place on the NSFNET, 3(5). 1.

Louie, Steven and Rubeck, Robert. (1989, May). Hypertext publishing and the revitalization of knowledge. Academic Computing, 3(9), 20-23.

Love, Gail and Rice, Ronald E. (1985). Electronic emotion: A content analysis and role analysis of a computer-mediated communication network. In Carol A. Parkhurst (Ed.), ASIS '85: Proceedings of the 84th Annual Meeting of the American Society for Information Science, Vol. 22. Medford, NJ: Learned Information, 266-270.

Lynch, Clifford A. (1980). Practical electronic mail through a centralized computing facility. In Carol A. Parkhurst (Ed.), Communicating Information: Proceedings of the 43rd ASIS Annual Meeting, Vol. 17. NY: Knowledge Industry, 34-37.

_____ and Preston, Cecilia M. (1990). Internet access to information resources. In Martha E. Williams (Ed.), Annual Review of Information Science and Technology. Vol. 25. NY: Elsevier Science Publishers, 263-312.

Lynch, M. (1985). Art and Artifact in Laboratory Science: A Study of Shop Work and Shop Talk in a Research Laboratory. London: Routledge and Kegan Paul.

MacMullin, Susan and Taylor, Robert. (1984). Problem dimensions and information traits. The Information Society, 3, 91-111.

Malone, Thomas W., Grant, Kenneth R., Lai, Kum-Yew, Rao, Ramana, and Rosenblitt, David A. (1989). The information lens: An intelligent system for information sharing and coordination. In Margarethe Olson (Ed.), Technological Support for Work Group Collaboration. Hillsdale, NJ: Lawrence Erlbaum, 65-88.

Mandelbaum, Richard. (1990, Spring). Free-market networking EDUCOM Review, 25(1), 10-13.

Mann, M. (Ed.). (1984). The International Encyclopedia of Sociology. NY: Continuum.

Markoff, John. (1988a, December 29). A supercomputer in every pot. The New York Times, 1 and 38.

_____. (1988b, November 4). Virus in military computers disrupts systems nationwide. <u>The New York Times</u>, A1.

_____. (1989a, May 16). Computer's strength is in Numbers. <u>New York Times</u>, D8.

_____. (1989b, February 19). New Satellite Channel Opens Computer Link to the Soviets. <u>New York Times</u>, A1 and A38.

_____. (1989c, June 4). Scientists share data at speed of light. <u>The New York Times</u>, 4-6.

_____. (1990a, March 21). Caller says he broke into U.S. computers to taunt experts. <u>New York Times</u>, A1 and A21.

_____. (1990b, September 2). Creating a giant computer highway. <u>The New York Times</u>, Section 3, 1 and 6.

Markus, M. Lynne. (1983). Power, politics, and MIS implementation. <u>Communications of the ACM</u>, <u>26</u>, 430-444.

_____. (1984). <u>Systems in Organizations: Bugs and Features</u>. Marshfield, MA: Pitman Press.

Matheson, Kimberly and Zanna, Mark P. (1988). The impact of computer-mediated communication on self-awareness. <u>Computers in Human Behavior</u>, <u>4</u>(3), 221-233.

McAdams, Alan K., Vietorisz, Thomas, Dougan, William L., and Lombardi, James T. (1988, Summer/Fall). Economic benefits and public support of a national education and research network. <u>EDUCOM Bulletin</u>, <u>23</u> (2/3), 63-71.

McCain, Mark. (1987, May 19). Computer users fall victim to a new breed of vandals. <u>New York Times</u>, A1.

McClure, Charles R. (1989). Increasing Access to U.S. Scientific and Technical Information: Policy Implications. In Charles R. McClure and Peter Hernon (Eds.), <u>U.S. Scientific and Technical Information Policies: Views and Perspectives</u>. Norwood, NJ: Ablex, 319-354.

_____, Bishop, Ann, and Doty, Philip. (1989). Federal information policy development: The role of the Office of Management and Budget. In Charles McClure, Peter Hernon, and Harold C. Relyea (Eds.). <u>United States Government Information Policies: Views and Perspectives</u>. Norwood, NJ: Ablex, 51-76.

_____. (1990). <u>Impact of High Speed Networks on Scientific Communication and Research</u>. Report to the U.S. Congress, Office of Technology Assessment.

McClure, Charles R., and Hernon, Peter. (Eds.). (1989). <u>United States Scientific and Technical Information Policies: Views and Perspectives</u>. Norwood, NJ: Ablex.

_____ and Relyea, Harold. (Eds.). (1989). <u>United States Government Information Policies: Views and Perspectives</u>. Norwood, NJ: Ablex.

Meadows, A.J. (1974). Communication in Science. London: Butterworths.

Merton, Robert. (1973). <u>The Sociology of Science</u>. Edited by N. W. Storer. Chicago, IL: University of Chicago Press.

_____. (1988). The Matthew Effect in science, II: Cumulative advantage and the symbolism of intellectual property. ISIS, 79, 606-623.

Miller, N. and Blumenthal, C. (1986). Intellectual property issues. In A. Branscomb, (Ed.) Toward a Law of Global Communications Networks. NY: Longman, 227-237.

Mitchell, G. D. (Ed.). (1968). A New Dictionary of the Social Sciences. NY: Aldin Publishing.

Mitroff, Ian. (1974a). The Subjective Side of Science. Amsterdam, The Netherlands: Elsevier.

_____. (1974b). Norms and counter-norms in a select group of the Apollo moon scientists: A case study of the ambivalence of scientists. American Sociological Review, 34, 579-595.

Morgan, D. (1988). Focus Groups as Qualitative Research. Newbury Park, CA: Sage.

Morrell, Jonathan. (Undated). The Impact of Information Technology on Research: An Agenda for Social Science Investigation. Unpublished Manuscript. Ann Arbor, MI: Industrial Technology Institute.

Muffo, John A. and Snizek, William E. (1987). Planning for the social disruption of the microcomputer revolution in academe. Paper presented at the SAIR-SCUP Conference, New Orleans, LA.

Mulkay, Michael J. (1976). Norms and ideology in science. Social Science Information, 15, 637-656.

_____. (1977). Sociology of the scientific research community. In A. Spiegel-Rosing, and Derek de Solla Price (Eds.), Science, Technology and Society. Beverly Hills, CA: Sage Publications, 93-148.

_____. (1979). Science and the Sociology of Knowledge. London: George Allen and Unwin.

_____. (1980). Interpretation and the use of rules: The case of the norms of science. In T. Gieryn, (Ed.), Science and the Social structure: A Festschrift for Robert K. Merton. Transactions of the New York Academy of Sciences. Series III, Volume 39. NY: New York Academy of Sciences, 111-125.

National Academy of Sciences. Committee on the Conduct of Research. (1989). On Being a Scientist. Washington, DC: National Academy Press.

_____. Numerical Data Advisory Board. Committee on Data Needs. (1978). National Needs for Critically Evaluated Physical and Chemical Data. Washington, DC: National Academy Press.

National Bureau of Standards (1984). The Effect of Computers on the Generation and Use of Technical Data: Report of a Workshop. Gaithersburg, MD: National Bureau of Standards.

"National Network Expansion." (1990). The PSI Connection, 1. Reston, VA: Performance Systems, Inc.

National Research Council. (1988a). The National Challenge in Computer Science and Technology. Washington, DC: National Academy Press.

_____. (1988b). Toward a National Research Network. Washington, DC: National Academy Press.

New York State Library and the Nelson A. Rockefeller Institute of Government. (1989, February). Technology and the Research Environment of the Future: The Impact of the Information Science Revolution on the Research

Environment of the Future, (Research report). Albany, NY: Authors.

Newell, Allen and Sproull, Robert F. (1982, February). Computer networks: Prospects for scientists. Science, 215, 843-852.

Nielson, Brian. (1990, October). Finding it on the Internet: The next challenge for librarianship. DATABASE, 13(5), 105-107.

Numerical Data Advisory Board, Committee on Data Needs. (1978). National Needs for Critically Evaluated Physical and Chemical Data. Washington, DC: National Academy Press, 1.

Nyce, H. Edward and Groppa, Richard. (1983, May). Electronic mail at MHT. Management Technology, 65-72.

NYSERNet User, 1 (Fall/Winter, 1990), Syracuse, NY: NYSERNet, Inc., 2.

Office of Science and Technology Policy. (1987). A Research and Development Strategy for High Performance Computing. Washington, DC: GPO.

_____. (1989). The Federal High Performance Computing Program. Washington, DC: GPO. [Appendix I]

_____. Federal Coordinating Council for Science, Engineering, and Technology. Committee on Physical, Mathematical, and Engineering Sciences (1991). Grand Challenges: High Performance Computing and Communications, The FY 1992 U.S. Research and Development Program. Washington, DC: OSTP. [Appendix P]

Office of Technology Assessment. (1986). Intellectual Property Rights in the Age of Electronics and Information. Washington, DC: GPO.

_____. (1987). Defending Secrets, Sharing Data. OTA-CIT-310. Washington, DC: GPO.

_____. (1988, October). Informing the Nation: Federal Information Dissemination in an Electronic Age. Washington, DC: GPO.

_____. (1989a). High-Performance Computing and Networking for Science. OTA-BP-CIT-59. Washington, DC: GPO.

_____. (1989b). High Performance Computing and Networking. (Draft Interim Paper). Washington, DC: GPO.

_____. (1989c) High Performance Computing and Networking for Science: Background Paper. OTA-CIT-302. Washington, DC: GPO.

Olsen, Florence. (1989, April). NSF expects to outgrow backbone net. Government Computer News, 8(1), 100.

Osburn, C.B. (1989, May). The structuring of the scholarly communication system. College and Research Libraries, 50, 277-286.

Ouchi, W. (1980). Markets, bureaucracies, and clans. Administrative Science Quarterly, 25, 129-141.

Panel on Information Technology and the Conduct of Research. (1989). Information Technology and the Conduct of Research: The User's View. Washington, DC: National Academy Press.

Parker, Donn B. (1983). <u>Fighting Computer Crime</u>. NY: Charles Scribner's Sons.

Parkhurst, Carol A. (Ed.). (1990a). <u>Library Perspectives on NREN: The National Research and Education Network</u>. Chicago, IL: Library and Information Technology Association.

_____. (1990b, June). LITA information packet on the proposed National Research and Education Network: Introduction and contents. <u>Information Packet on the Proposed National Research and Education Network</u>. Chicago, IL: Library and Information Technology Association.

Pelz, Donald and Andrews, Frank. (1976). <u>Scientists in Organizations</u>. Ann Arbor, MI: University of Michigan Press.

Peters, Paul Evan. (1990, November). Update and Commentary on Senate Bill 1067. Posted on Listserv.

Pierce, S. (1987). Characteristics of professional knowledge structures: Some theoretical implications of citation studies. <u>Library and Information Science Research</u>, <u>9</u>, 143-171.

Piternick, A. (1989). Attempts to find alternatives to the scientific journal. <u>The Journal of Academic Librarianship</u>, <u>15</u>, 260-266.

Polanyi, Michael. (1966). <u>The Tacit Dimension</u>. Chicago, IL: University of Chicago Press.

Poole, H.L. (1985). <u>Theories of the Middle Range</u>. Norwood, NJ: Ablex.

Poole, Marshall Scott, Homes, Michael, and De Sanctis, Gerardine. (1988, September). Conflict management and group decision support systems. <u>Proceedings of the Conference on Computer-Supported Cooperative Work</u>, ACM.

Price, Derek de Solla. (1961). <u>Science Since Babylon</u>. New Haven, CT: Yale University Press.

Quarterman, John S. (1990). <u>The Matrix: Computer Networks and Conferencing Systems Worldwide</u>. Bedford, MA: Digital Press.

_____ and Hoskins, Josiah. (1986). Notable computer networks. <u>Communications of the ACM</u>, <u>29</u>(10), 932-971.

Rafaeli, Sheifaz. (1986). The electronic bulletin board: A computer-driven mass medium. <u>Computers and the Social Sciences</u>, <u>2</u>(3), 123-136.

Ravetz, J.R. (1971). <u>Scientific Knowledge and its Social Problems</u>. NY: Oxford University Press.

Remington, John A. (1988). Beyond big science in America: The binding of inquiry. <u>Social Studies of Science</u>, <u>18</u>, 45-72.

Ricart, Glenn. (1989, November). Slowing the big bang of computer networking. <u>Academic Computing</u>, <u>4</u>(3), 28-29 and 53-55.

Rice, Ronald E. (1980). The impacts of computer-mediated organizational and interpersonal communication. <u>Annual Review of Information Science and Technology</u>, Vol. 15. NY: Knowledge Industry, 221-249.

_____. (1984). Mediated group communication. In R.E. Rice and Associates (Eds.), <u>The New Media: Communication, Research, and Technology</u>. Beverly Hills, CA: Sage Press, 129-154.

_____. (1989). Outcomes associated with new media use are contingent on task characteristics. In Jeffrey Katzer and Gregory B. Newby (Eds.), <u>Managing Information Technology: ASIS '89. Proceedings of the 52nd Annual Meeting of the American Society for Information Science</u>. Medford, NJ: Learned Information, 177-182.

_____ and Bair, James. (1983). Conceptual role of new communication technology in organizational productivity. In R.F. Vondran et. al. (Eds.), <u>Productivity in the Information Age: Proceedings of the American Society for Information Science 46th Annual Meeting</u>. White Plains, NY: Knowledge Industry, 4-8.

_____ and Case, Donald. (1983, Winter). Electronic message systems in the university: A description of use and utility. <u>Journal of Communication</u>, <u>33</u> (1), 131-152.

_____ and Love, Gail. (1987, February). Electronic emotion: Socio-emotional content in a computer-mediated communication network. <u>Communication Research</u>, <u>14</u>(1), 85-108.

Ritzer, George. (1977). <u>Working: Conflict and Change</u>. 2nd ed. Englewood Cliffs, NJ: Prentice-Hall.

Roberts, Michael M. (1989, Winter). The NREN and commercial services. <u>EDUCOM Review</u>, <u>24</u>(4), 10-11.

Root, Robert. (1988, September). Design of a multi-media vehicle for social browsing. <u>Proceedings of the Conference on Computer-Supported Cooperative Work</u>. Portland, OR, 25-38.

Rothman, R.A. (1972). A dissenting view on the scientific ethos. <u>British Journal of Sociology</u>, <u>23</u>, 102-108.

Safyeni, F., Lee, E., and MacGregor, J. (1988). An empirical investigation of two electronic mail systems. <u>Behavior and Information Technology</u>, <u>7</u>(4), 361-372.

Saracevic, Tefko et al. (1988, May). A study of information seeking and retrieving. I, Background and methodology. <u>Journal of the American Society for Information Science</u>, <u>39</u>(3), 161-176.

_____ and Kantor, Paul. (1988a, May). A study of information seeking and retrieving. II, User, questions, and effectiveness. <u>Journal of the American Society for Information Science</u>, <u>39</u>(3), 177-196.

_____. (1988b, May). A study of information seeking and retrieving. III, Searchers, searches, overlap. <u>Journal of the American Society for Information Science</u>, <u>39</u>(3), 197-216.

Schaefermeyer, Mark J. and Sewell, Edward H., Jr. (1988). Communicating by electronic mail. <u>American Behavioral Scientist</u>, <u>32</u>(2), 112-123.

Schon, David. (1983). <u>The Reflective Practitioner: How Professionals Think in Action</u>. NY: Basic Books.

Schrage, Michael. (1986, May 27). U.S. seeking to limit access of Soviets to computer data. <u>The Washington Post</u>, <u>109</u>(173), A1.

Shapiro, Norman Z. and Anderson, Robert H. (1985, July). <u>Towards an Ethics and Etiquette for Electronic Mail</u>. (Report prepared for the National Science Foundation). Santa Monica, CA: Rand Corporation.

Shenhav, Y., Lunde, T., and Goldberg, A. (1989). External effects on research endeavors: Conceptual framework and empirical examination. <u>Human Relations</u>, <u>5</u>, 403-421.

Shepard, H. (1954). The value system of a university group. <u>American Sociological Review</u>, <u>19</u>, 456-462.

Shields, Mark. (in press). Technological innovation in higher education: A case study of academic computing. In Jonathan Morell and Mitchell Fleischer (Eds.), <u>Advances in the Implementation and Impact of Computer Systems</u>. Greenwich, CT: JAI Press.

Short, J., Williams, E., and Christie, B. (1976). <u>The Social Psychology of Telecommunications</u>. NY: Wiley.

Smilowitz, Michael, Compton, D. Chad, and Flint, Lyle. (1988). The Effects of CMC on an individual's judgement: A study based on the methods of Asch's social influence experiment. <u>Computers in Human Behavior</u>, <u>4</u>(4), 311-322.

Smith, Nancy, Bozot, Elizabeth, and Hill, Thomas. (in press). Use of electronic mail in a research and development organization. In Jonathan Morrell and Mitchell Fleisher (Eds.), <u>Advances in the Implementation and Impact of Computer Systems</u>. Greenwich, CT: JAI Press.

Special Libraries Association. (1990, June 9). <u>Resolution Supporting the National Research and Education Network</u>. Pittsburgh, PA: Special Libraries Association.

Spiegel-Rosing, A., and de Solla Price, Derek (Eds.), (1977). <u>Science, Technology and Society</u>. Beverly Hills, CA: Sage Publications.

Spotts, Peter N. (1987, September 4). "Big science" trend worries experts. <u>The Christian Science Monitor</u>, <u>79</u>(198), 3-4.

Sproull, Lee and Kiesler, Sara. (1986, November). Reducing social context cues: Electronic mail in organizational communication. <u>Management Science</u>, <u>32</u> (11), 1492-1512.

Steinfield, Charles W. (1986). Computer-mediated communication systems. In Martha E. Williams (Ed.), <u>Annual Review of Information Science and Technology</u>, Vol. 21. NY: Knowledge Industry, 167-202.

Storer, N. (1966). <u>The Social System of Science</u>. NY: Holt, Rinehart, and Winston.

Sullivan, Christopher. (1989). Electronic mail and information empowerment: The impact of computer-mediated communication in the Florida State Legislature. Paper presented at the Annual Telecommunications Policy Research Conference, Warrenton, VA.

Sutton, J. (1984). Organizational autonomy and professional norms in science: A case study of the Lawrence Livermore Laboratory. <u>Social Studies of Science</u>, <u>14</u>, 197-224.

Taylor, Robert S. (1986). <u>Value-Added Processes in Information Systems</u>. Norwood, NJ: Ablex.

Tombaugh, Jo W. (1984). Evaluation of an international scientific computer-based conference. <u>Journal of Social Issues</u>, <u>40</u>(3), 129-144.

Turner, J. A. (1990, April 4). A $.75 discrepancy propels astronomers into a maze of computer networks and onto a best-seller list. <u>The Chronicle of Higher Education</u>, <u>36</u>(29), 3.

Walgren, Douglas. (1988, Summer/Fall). Towards a higher education network. <u>EDUCOM Bulletin</u>, <u>23</u>(2/3), 8-10.

Weingarten, Fred W. and Garcia, D. Linda. (1988). Public policy concerning the exchange and distribution of scientific information. In M. Aborn (Ed.), <u>Telescience: Scientific Communication in the Information Age (Special Issue)</u>. <u>The Annals of the American Academy of Political and Social Science</u>, <u>495</u>, 61-72.

Wenk, E. (1986). <u>Tradeoffs: Imperatives of Choice in a High-Tech World</u>. Baltimore, MD: The Johns Hopkins University Press.

Williams, Robin. (1968). The concept of norms. <u>International Encyclopedia of the Social Sciences</u>. Volume 11. NY: Macmillan, 204-208.

Wilson, P. (1983). <u>Second-Hand Knowledge: An Inquiry into Cognitive Authority</u>. Westport, CT: Greenwood Press.

_____ and Farid, Mona. (1979). On the use of the records of research. <u>Library Quarterly</u>, <u>49</u>, 127-145.

Wintsch, Susan. (1989, Winter). Toward a National Research and Education Network. <u>MOSIAC</u>, <u>20</u>(4), 32-42.

Wulf, William. (1988, December 20). <u>The National Collaboratory: A White Paper</u>. Unpublished manuscript. Washington, DC: National Science Foundation.

Wunderlich, R. (1974). The scientific ethos: A clarification. <u>British Journal of Sociology</u>, <u>25</u>, 373-377.

Yavarkovsky, Jerome. (1989, February). <u>Technology and the Research Environment of the Future</u>. Unpublished Manuscript. The Nelson A. Rockefeller Institute of Government, State University of New York, and The New York State Library.

Ziman, J. (1968). <u>Public Knowledge: An Essay Concerning the Social Dimensions of Science</u>. Cambridge, UK: Cambridge University Press.

Zipf, G.K. (1965). <u>Human Behavior and the Principle of Least Effort</u>. NY: Hofner Publishing Co.

Zuckerman, H. (1970). Stratification in American science. <u>Sociological Inquiry</u>, <u>40</u>, 235-257.

_____. (1986). Patterns of name-ordering among authors of scientific papers: A study of social symbolism and its ambiguity. <u>American Journal of Sociology</u>, <u>74</u>, 276-291.

_____. (1988a). Introduction: Intellectual property and diverse rights of ownership in science. <u>Science, Technology, and Human Values</u>, <u>13</u>, 7-16.

_____. (1988b). The sociology of science. In Neil J. Smelser, (Ed.), <u>Handbook of Sociology</u>. Beverly Hills, CA: Sage Publications, 511-574.

Additional Sources

Arms, Caroline. (1990, September). Using the national networks: BITNET and the Internet. <u>Online</u>, <u>14</u>(5), 24-29.

ARL, CAUSE, and EDUCOM announce the Coalition for Networked Information. (1990). Press release, March 16.

Belkin, N., Oddy, R., and Brooks, H.M. (1982). ASK for information retrieval: Part II. <u>Journal of Documentation,</u> <u>38</u>, 145-164.

<u>The Catalyst</u>. (1990, Summer). <u>1</u>, 1.

Federal Research Internet Coordinating Committee. (1989, January). <u>Program Plan for the National Research</u> <u>Network</u>. Draft. Washington, DC: GPO.

Fraser, A. G. (1985). Opportunities and obstacles for a national research network. <u>EDUCOM Bulletin,</u> <u>23</u>(2/3), 22-31.

Gore, Albert. (1990, Summer). Remarks on the NREN. <u>EDUCOM Review</u>, 25(2), 12-16.

_____. (1989a, May 16). Computer's strength is in numbers. <u>The New York Times</u>.

Gould, Stephen. (1989b, June 15). <u>Commercialization of the National Research and Education Network,</u> <u>Memorandum to the Senate Subcommittee on Science, Technology, and Space</u>. Washington, DC: Congressional Research Service, Library of Congress.

_____. (1989c, June 9). <u>Issues Relating to the National Research and Education Network, Memorandum to</u> <u>the Senate Subcommittee on Science, Technology, and Space</u>. Washington, DC: Congressional Research Service, Library of Congress.

McClure, Charles R., Bishop, Ann Peterson, Doty, Philip, and Rosenbaum, Howard. (1990). Realizing the promise of NREN: Social and behavioral considerations. In Carol Parkhurst (Ed.), <u>Library Perspectives on NREN</u>. Chicago, IL: American Library Association, 23-32.

National Bureau of Standards. (1984, March 19-20). <u>The Effect of Computers on the Generation and Use of</u> <u>Technical Data: Report of a Workshop.</u> Gaithersberg, MD.

NYSERNet (New York State Education and Research Network). (1988). <u>Market and Economic Impact Study,</u> <u>Report 2: Lessons from Four Networks</u>. NY: NYSERNET.

Office of Technology Assessment. (1989). <u>Federal Scientific and Technical Information: Opportunities and</u> <u>Challenges of Electronic Dissemination</u>. Draft. Washington, DC: GPO.

Rogers, Susan M. (1990, Summer). Educational Applications of the NREN. <u>EDUCOM Review</u>, 25(2), 25-29.

Smith, P. (1990, September). Merit, IBM, MCI form new company. <u>LINK Letter</u>, <u>3</u>, 4.

Smith, Sheldon B. and Bollentin, Wendy Rickard. (Eds.). (1988, Summer/Fall). <u>National Net '88 Double Issue:</u> <u>Public and Private Initiatives to Create a National Education and Research Network</u>. EDUCOM Bulletin, <u>23</u>.

CONTRIBUTORS TO THE BOOK

Ann P. Bishop is a doctoral candidate at Syracuse University, School of Information Studies, Syracuse, NY 13244. She has conducted systems, behavioral, and policy research in the areas of scientific and technical information (STI) transfer and the organization and use of information resources. With Charles R. McClure and Philip Doty she recently co-authored <u>Federal Information Inventory/Locator Systems: From Burden to Benefit</u> (Syracuse, NY: ERIC Clearinghouse, 1990). She has also co-authored papers on the design of an STI transfer center, the development of information systems for technology transfer, and the history of Federal STI policies and systems, and the analysis of book index features and quality.

Philip Doty is a doctoral candidate at Syracuse University, School of Information Studies, Syracuse, NY 13244. His research interests include scientific and technical information and communication, intellectual property, Federal information policy, art and geoscience information systems, and the sociology of science. He has worked with Ann P. Bishop and Charles R. McClure on a number of projects funded by the U.S. Congress, Office of Technology Assessment and the Office of Management and Budget. Some of his more recent papers include "Federal Research and Development as Intellectual Property" (1989) and "Federal Information Resources Management (IRM): A Policy Review and Assessment" (1989).

Susan Koch is a Visiting Lecturer in the Department of Telecommunications at Indiana University, Bloomington, IN 47405. She received her Ph.D. from the University of Texas in speech communication. Her current research is on the relationship between telecommunications and economic development, focusing on rural community development. She has also worked at the U.S. Congress, Office of Technology Assessment, at Bell communications Research, and as an independent consultant.

Charles R. McClure is a Professor at Syracuse University, School of Information Studies, Syracuse, NY 13244. He completed his Ph.D. from Rutgers University and teaches courses in the areas of Federal Information Resources Management, Federal Information Policies, Planning and Evaluation of Library and Information Services. He has served as principal investigator for a number of studies funded by the U.S. Congress, Office of Technology Assessment, the National Science Foundation, the Government Printing Office, and the Office of Management and Budget. He recently co-edited the books <u>U.S. Government Information Policies</u> and <u>U.S. Science and Technical Information Policies</u>, both published by Ablex (1989). With Ann P. Bishop and Philip Doty, his co-authored study "Electronic Networks, the Research Process, and Scholarly Communication," received the Jesse H. Shera award for the best research paper in library/information science in 1990 by the American Library Association. McClure is Editor of <u>Electronic Networking: Research, Applications, and Policies</u>, and also serves as Associate Editor for <u>Government Information Quarterly</u>.

Howard Rosenbaum is a doctoral candidate at Syracuse University, School of Information Studies, Syracuse, NY 13244. His research interests include telecommunications networking, scientific and technical information policy, Federal information policies, computer-mediated communication, and the intersection of sociology and information science. He has published on information flows in educational organizations (1987), Federal information policies concerning access to Japanese Scientific and Technical Information (1988), and computer-mediated communication as an emerging form of human communication (1990).

APPENDICES

A.   Federal Development of a National Research and Education Network: A Chronology of Significant Events

B.   S. 1067, <u>National High-Performance Computing Technology Act of 1989</u>, U.S. Congress, Senate, 101st Congress, May 18, 1989 [Identical House Bill is H.R. 3131, introduced August 3, 1989].

C.   S. 1067, <u>High-Performance Computing Act of 1990</u>, U.S. Congress, Senate, 101st Congress, April 4, 1990 working draft [version as reported out of the Commerce Committee].

D.   S. 1067, <u>High-Performance Computing Act of 1990</u>, U.S. Congress, Senate, 101st Congress, October 25, 1990 [version passed by the Senate].

E.   S. 272, <u>High-Performance Computing Act of 1991</u>, U.S. Congress, Senate, 102nd Congress, January 24, 1991.

F.   <u>High-Performance Computing Act of 1990</u>, U.S. Congress, Senate, Senate Committee on Commerce, Science and Transportation. Report 101-387.

G.   S. 1976, <u>Department of Energy High-Performance Computing Act of 1989</u>, U.S. Senate, 101st Congress, November 21, 1989.

H.   <u>Department of Energy High-Performance Computing Act of 1990</u>, U.S. Congress, Senate, Committee on Energy and Natural Resources. Report 101-377.

I.   <u>The Federal High-Performance Computing Program</u>, U.S. Executive Office of the President, Office of Science and Technology Policy, September 8, 1989.

J.   "Executive Summary," in <u>Information Technology and the Conduct of Research: The User's View</u>, Washington, DC: National Academy Press, 1989, pp. 1-5.

K.   <u>High-Performance Computing & Networking for Science: Background Paper</u>, U.S. Congress, Office of Technology Assessment, 1989.

L.   <u>High-Performance Computing: An Overview</u>, U.S. Congress, Congressional Research Service, December 18, 1990.*

M.   <u>The Federal Research Internet and the National Research and Education Network: Prospects for the 1990s</u>, U.S. Congress, Congressional Research Service, July 26, 1990.*

N.   <u>Building the National Research and Education Network</u>, U.S. Congress, Congressional Research Service, January 7, 1991.*

APPENDICES (continued)

O.   S. 343, <u>Department of Energy High-Performance Computing Act of 1991</u>, U.S. Congress, Senate, Committee on Energy and Natural Resources, February 5, 1991.

P.   <u>Grand Challenges: High Performance Computing and Communications, the FY 1992 U.S. Research and Development Program</u>, Committee on Physical, Mathematical, and Engineering Sciences, Federal Coordinating Council for Science, Engineering, and Technology, and Office of Science and Technology Policy, 1991.

Q.   <u>Seeking Solutions: High-Performance Computing for Science</u>, U.S. Congress, Office of Technology Assessment, 1991.

R.   Glossary

*   Congressional Reserach Service issue briefs are updated regularly and more recent versions of these reports may be available.

APPENDIX A

FEDERAL DEVELOPMENT OF A NATIONAL RESEARCH AND EDUCATION NETWORK*
A Chronology of Significant Events

August 21, 1986

Legislation introduced by Senator Albert Gore, Jr. (D-TN) required the office of Science and Technology Policy to provide Congress with an analysis of the networking needs of academic and federal research computer and supercomputer programs, and "the benefits and opportunities that an improved computer network would offer for electronic mail, file transfer, and remote access and communications for universities and Federal research facilities in the United States." The provision became law on August 21, 1986, as part of the National Science Foundation Authorization Act for FY 1987 (P.L. 99-383, 100 Stat. 816).

November 20, 1987

The Office of Science and Technology Policy (OSTP), in compliance with PL 99-383, issued *A Research and Development Strategy for High Computing*, developed by the Federal Coordinating Council for Science, Engineering, and Technology (FCCSET) Committee on Computer Research and Applications. The report recommended: "U.S. government, industry, and universities should coordinate research and development for a research network to provide a distributed computing capability that links the government, industry, and higher education communities."

August 11, 1988

The Senate Commerce, Science, and Transportation Subcommittee on Science, Technology, and Space concluded hearings to examine new developments in computing and computer networking.

October 19, 1988

Sen. Gore, chairman of the Science, Technology, and Space Subcommittee, introduced S. 2918, National High-Performance Computer Technology Act of 1988. The bill included title II, National Research Computer Network, and title III, National Information Infrastructure.

December 5-7, 1988

The Library of Congress Network Advisory Committee (on which ALA is represented) held a joint meeting with EDUCOM on "Connecting the Networks" (Proceedings published in 1989 by LC as #18, *Network Planning Papers*). The proposed NREN was a major focus. The two groups agreed on a joint statement: "Our common effort must recognize our shared mission of service to the information user. These users can best be served through interconnected networks. The members of NAC and EDUCOM will work together in a coalition whose purpose is to achieve this common vision."

*This chronology is an updated and expanded version based on that developed by Carol C. Henderson, published under the same title and appearing in <u>Library Perspectives on NREN: The National Research and Education Network</u>, edited by Carol Parkhurst (Chicago: American Library Association, 1990), pp. 7-12.

January, 1989	The ALA Legislation Committee was informally alerted to S. 2918 shortly after its introduction, but the NREN appeared as a formal Committee agenda item for the first time at the 1989 Midwinter Meeting. NREN developments have continued to be a regular agenda item.
May 18, 1989	Sen. Gore introduced S. 1067, the National High-Performance Computer Technology Act of 1989, an updated version of S. 2918 from the previous Congress. Title II was revised and called the National Research and Education Network. In introductory remarks, Sen. Gore said: "Libraries, rural schools, Minority institutions, and vocational education programs will have access to the same national resources -- databases, supercomputers, accelerators -- as more affluent and better known institutions" (May 18, 1989, *Congressional Record*, p. S5689). He envisioned the National Information Infrastructure of title III as a "National Digital Library."
June, 1989	The ALA Washington Office began coverage of legislation to establish the NREN in the *ALA Washington Newsletter* and the *Legislative Report of the ALA Washington Office* (distributed widely at ALA conferences, including to ALA Council). Coverage continues regularly in these publications as well as in the *ALA Washington Newsline* on the ALANET electronic mail system.
June 20, 1989	Rep. Doug Walgren (D-PA) chairs a hearing of the Subcommittee on Science, Research, and Technology of the House Science, Space, and Technology Committee on the "U.S. Supercomputer Industry."
June 21, 1989 July 26, 1989	The Senate Commerce, Science, and Transportation Subcommittee on Science, Technology, and Space held hearings on S. 1067.
August 3, 1989	Rep. Doug Walgren (D-PA), then chairman of the Science, Research and Technology Subcommittee, and ranking minority member Sherwood Boehlert (R-NY); Rep. Robert Roe (D-NY), chairman of the parent Science, Space, and Technology Committee; and several other members introduced HR 3131, the National High-Performance Computer Technology Act of 1989, an identical companion measure to S. 1067.
September, 1989	The congressional Office for Technology Assessment issued *High Performance Computing and Networking for Science -- Background Paper* (OTA-BP-CIT-59, GPO), with a detailed discussion of NREN issues.
September 8, 1989	D. Allan Bromley, President Bush's new science advisor and director of the Office of Science and Technology Policy, issued a development plan for the NREN in *The Federal High Performance Computing Program*. The report was written by representatives of more than a dozen agencies working with OSTP. "Education" was included in the name of the network in explicit recognition of the importance of the interrelationships between the network, research, and education, according to this report. At congressional hearings on September 15, Dr. Bromley testified that the Administration preferred to address this high-priority initiative through administrative action rather than through separate legislation.

September 15, 1989	The Senate Commerce, Science, and Transportation Subcommittee on Science, Technology, and Space held hearings on S. 1067. Witnesses included Librarian of Congress James Billington accompanied by Henriette Avram, LC assistant librarian for processing services; and Daniel Masys, director of Lister Hill National Center for Biomedical Communications, National Library of Medicine. Dr. Billington said that high-capacity data networks could allow LC to become a "library without walls" providing scholars nationwide with access to its materials, and expanding far beyond its traditional role of providing bibliographic information.
October 3, 1989	The House Science, Space, and Technology Subcommittee on Science, Research, and Technology held a hearing on High Performance Computing, including the NREN.
October 4, 1989	The House Energy and Commerce Subcommittee on Telecommunications and Finance held a hearing on the nation's telecommunications infrastructure and the "network of the future." Subcommittee chairman Edward Markey (D-MA) is a cosponsor of HR 3131.
November 21, 1989	Sen J. Bennett Johnston (D-LA) and Sen. James McClure (R-ID), chairman and ranking minority member of the Energy and Natural Resources Committee, and Sen. Albert Gore, Jr., introduced S. 1976, the Department of Energy High-Performance Computing Act of 1989. S. 1976 would define and authorize the DOE portion of the multi-agency program proposed in S. 1067.
January, 1990	The Administration's budget request submitted for fiscal year 1991 proposed the use of $469 million for the High Performance Computing Program (an increase of 5 percent over the 1990 allocation). Since there was no crosscut in the budget document, this increase could not be tied to any particular agency programs in the budget document.
January 9, 1990	The National Telecommunications and Information Administration (NTIA) in the Commerce Department initiated a study of the domestic telecommunications infrastructure (55 Federal Register 800-818). The numerous issues on which NTIA sought public comment included the NREN.
January 10, 1990	The American Library Association Council passed a Resolution on a National Research and Education Network (1989-90 CD #54), endorsing the concept of the NREN and resolving to "work to improve legislative and other proposals to increase opportunities for all types of library participation and leadership in, and contributions to, the National Research and Education Network." The resolution originated with ALA's Library and Information Technology Association.

February 1, 1990	A coooperative library working group drafted proposed amendments to the ongoing Senate staff revision of S. 1067. Library organizations represented included the American Library Association, the Association of Research Libraries, the Chief Officers of State Library Agencies, the Special Libraries Association, and the U.S. national Commission on Libraries and Information Science. The amendments and supporting rationale, designed to strengthen library linkages to the NREN, were discussed with staff of the Senate Science, Technology, and Space Subcommittee on February 1. Most of these suggestions were incorporated into the revised bill subsequently approved by the parent Commerce, Science, and Transportation Committee. The amendments were also discussed with House subcommittee staff.
March, 1990	EDUCOM's Networking and Telecommunications Task Force issues a revised policy paper which represents a collective vision on policy regarding NREN goals, funding, management, etc.
March 6, 1990	The Senate Energy and Natural Resources Subcommittee on Energy Research and Development held hearings on S. 1976.
March 14-15, 1990	The House Science and Technology Subcommittee on Science, Research, and Technology held hearings on HR 3131. On March 15, Paul Gherman, Director of Libraries at Virginia Polytechnic Institute and State University, testified in support of HR 3131 on behalf of the American Library Association and the Association of Research Libraries.
March 15, 1990	Sen. Gore's keynote speech on the NREN introduced the National Net '90 Conference, the third annual meeting organized by EDUCOM which cosponsors groups to forge a strategic partnership among education, government, and industry in pursuit of the NREN. A library session on "Information Resources and the National Network" was organized by the Association of Research Libraries Telecommunications Task Force.
March 16, 1990	The formation of the Coalition of Networked Information was announced by the Association of Research Libraries, CAUSE, and EDUCOM. CNI will promote the provision of information resources on existing networks and on proposed interconnected networks.
March 21, 1990	D. Allan Bromley, the President's science advisor and director of OSTP, addressed the Forum on Federal Information Policies, sponsored by the Federal Library and Information Center Committee at the Library of Congress. He listed four current priorities of OSTP: education, economic competitiveness, global change, and high-performance computing, the last include building the NREN. He said: "Imagine how the role of libraries will change when most American homes are connected to them over local networks via a wide band width channel....Individuals would be able to search their local library or other repositories electronically to select and retrieve text and picture, rent and view a movie, or research specific needs...all of these are technically feasible today."

March 21, 1990	Chairman Robert Roe, ranking minority member Robert Walker (R-PA), Rep. Tim Valentine (who had just days before become chairman of the Science, Research, and Technology Subcommittee), and a majority of members of the Science, Space, and Technology Committee introduced HR 4329, the American Technology Preeminence Act. The Committee approved the bill the same day and issued its report (H. Rept. 101-481, Part I) on May 10, when HR 4329 was refereed to the Judiciary Committee. This omnibus technology bill includes as title VII, the National High Performance Computer Technology Program, the plan for which is to include establishment of the NREN. HR 4329 would incorporate elements of HR 3131, but without any specific authorization of funds.
April 3, 1990	S. 1067 was favorably reported by the Senate Commerce, Science, and Transportation Committee with an amendment in the nature of a substitute, which included a number of library community recommendations. The Committee's report on S.1067 was issued on July 23.
April 5, 1990	The ALA Washington Office submitted comments on behalf of ALA in response to NTIA's notice of inquiry and request for comments on a Comprehensive Study of Domestic Telecommunication Infrastructure. ALA recommended support of NREN development with public access through the nation's libraries. Representatives of several ALA units reviewed a draft of the ALA comments.
April 24, 1990	Sen. Gore spoke about S. 1067 and his vision of the NREN at the morning briefing for participants at the 16th Annual National Library Week Legislative Day, sponsored by the American Library Association, the D.C. Library Association, and the Special Libraries Association. Briefing materials prepared by the ALA Washington Office included background and status information on NREN legislation. More than 550 library supporters from 48 states and D.C. visited congressional offices to discuss library issues, including S. 1067 and HR 3131.
May 10, 1990	The House Science, Space, and Technology Committee issued its report (H. Rept. 101-481) on HR 4329, the American Technology Preeminence Act, which incorporates the NREN interagency planning element.
June, 1990	The Library and Information Technology Association, a division of ALA, issued *LITA Information Packet on the Proposed National Research and Education Network*, to bring information about the NREN before a broad library audience.
June 8, 1990	The National Science Foundation announced that NSF and the Defense Advanced Research Projects Agency will provide $15.8 million for a three-year research project to develop the technology to enable networks and computers to support multi-gigabit/second speeds. A number of communications and high-tech companies will also make financial commitments and participate in the joint project. The research to be conducted by national laboratories, universities, supercomputer centers, and companies will be overseen by the Corporation for National Research Initiative in Reston, Virginia, which received the grant.

June 27, 1990	The Senate Energy and Natural Resource Committee ordered reported S. 1976, the Department of Energy High-Performance Computing Act of 1990, with a substitute amendment.
June 27, 1990	Richard M. Dougherty, in his inaugural speech as ALA President, said that the debate now underway about how the national electronic network should look and whom it should serve is "one in which we as librarians have a national responsibility to participate." He pledged to devote his year as ALA President to support "a national electronic network that serves all of us, that serves the democratic aims of our society, that empowers the citizenry in the ways that only information literacy can empower."
July, 1990	The Association of Research Libraries issued *Linking Researchers and Resources: The Emerging Information Infrastructure and the NREN Proposal* (ARL Briefing Package No. 4).
July 10, 1990	The Subcommittee on Defense Industry and Technology of the Senate Armed Services Committee approved the Defense Department authorization with an additional $30 million for a high-performance computing initiative at the Defense Advanced Research Projects Agency (DARPA).
July 11, 1990	The House by a vote of 327-93 passed a revised version of the American Technology Preeminence Act. Title IV of HR 4329 includes the National High Performance Computer Technology Program, which would require the President to submit a five-year plan to support the development of the NREN. The bill contains no authorization of funds for the NREN.
July 15, 1990	In "Networking the Future," in the *Washington Post*, Sen. Gore described the high-capacity information network as the "on-ramp to tomorrow," needed to make the most of high-performance computers. "If we had the information superhighways we need, a school child could plug into the Library of Congress...and explore a universe of knowledge..." For a lay audience, Sen. Gore's article underscored his broad vision for the NREN and its far-reaching implications. It was inserted in the July 16 *Congressional Record*, pp. S9762-63.
July 19, 1990	The Senate Energy and Natural Resources Committee issued its report (S. Rept. 101-377) on S. 1976, the Department of Energy High-Performance Computing Act of 1990. As (rather unexpectedly) revised by the Committee, the bill would replace NSF with the Department of Education (DOE) as the agency to develop and manage the NREN, with users expected to include industry, the higher education community, researchers, librarians, federal agencies, and information service providers. Negotiations began between the Senate energy and science committees on a compromise bill to combine S. 1067 and S. 1976.

July 23, 1990	The Senate Commerce, Science, and Transportation Committee issued its report (S. Rept. 101-387) on S. 1067 as revised and approved by the Committee on April 3. Among the revisions approved by the Committee: Purposes now include federal support for making information services available over the network. Coordination among federal agencies involved in a national high-performance computing plan would include the Department of Education, the Library of Congress, the National Agricultural Library, and the National Library of Medicine, all of which are to encourage the distribution of library and information resources through the NREN. Libraries and schools are to be provided access to the NREN and its resources. Network services are to include orientation and training of users. Library and information science would be added to the research and education title.
September 5, 1990	A set of joint recommendations on S. 1067, developed by the American Library Association Washington Office, was delivered to the Senate Commerce, Science, and Transportation Committee and the Senate Energy and Natural Resources Committee. The document recommended certain changes to the joint Senate Energy-Commerce Committee staff drafted August 13. The recommendations were jointly sponsored by ALA and the American Association of Law Libraries, the Association of Research Libraries, the Coalition for Networked Information, the Chief Officers of State Library Agencies, EDUCOM, the Special Libraries Association, and the U.S. National Commission on Libraries and Information Science.
October 23, 1990	S. 1067 passes the Senate unanimously. The House was unable to act on the bill before adjournment, thus, S.1067 failed to be passed out of the 101st Congress. The version passed by the Senate had a number of changes from the version reported out of Committee. Some of these changes were not supported by the Coalition for Networked Information and other groups.
January 24, 1991	S. 272, "The High Performance Computing Act of 1991," is introduced by Senator Gore. The bill provides for a multiagency high-performance computing research and development program to be coordinated by the Office of Science and Technology. A similar bill, H.R. 656, is introduced in the House by Representative George Brown.
February 5, 1991	S. 343, "The Department of Energy High Performance Computing Act of 1991," is introduced by Senator Johnston. The purposes of the bill are to (1) promote the research and development of high-performance computers and associated software, and (2) create a multi-gigabit-per-second nationwide computer network for use by the Department of Energy and other Federal departments and agencies.
February, 1991	The administration proposes the High Performance Computing and Communications (HPCC) program, a $638 million initiative in the areas of high-performance computing systems, advanced software technology and algorithms, the national research and education network (NREN), and basic research and human resources. The program is outlined in the report Grand Challenges: High Performance Computing and Communications, authored by the Committee on Physical, Mathematical and Engineering Sciences.

B

S. 1067,

National High-Performance Computing Technology Act of 1989,
**U.S. Congress, Senate, 101st Congress, May 18, 1989
[Identical House Bill is H.R. 3131, introduced August 3, 1989].**

IN THE SENATE OF THE UNITED STATES

MAY 18 (legislative day, JANUARY 3), 1989

Mr. GORE (for himself and Mr. JEFFORDS) introduced the following bill; which was read twice and referred to the Committee on Commerce, Science, and Transportation

---

A BILL

To provide for a coordinated Federal research program to ensure continued United States leadership in high-performance computing.

1 *Be it enacted by the Senate and House of Representa-*

2 *tives of the United States of America in Congress assembled,*

3 SECTION 1. This Act may be cited as the "National

4 High-Performance Computer Technology Act of 1989".

5 SEC. 2. (a) Congress finds and declares the following:

6   (1) Advances in computer science and technology

7 are vital to the Nation's prosperity, national security,

8 and scientific advancement.

1   (2) The United States currently leads the world in
2 development and use of high-performance computer
3 technology for national security, industrial productivity,
4 and science and engineering, but that lead is being
5 challenged by foreign competitors.

6   (3) Further research and improved computer re-
7 search networks are necessary to maintain United
8 States leadership in the field of high-performance com-
9 puting.

10 (b) It is the purpose of Congress in this Act to ensure
11 the continued leadership of the United States in high-per-
12 formance computer technology. This requires that the United
13 States Government—

14   (1) expand Federal support for research, develop-
15   ment, and application of high-performance computing
16   technology in order to—

17   (A) establish a high-capacity national re-
18   search and education computer network;

19   (B) develop an information infrastructure of
20   data bases, services, and knowledge banks which
21   is available for access over such a national net-
22   work;

23   (C) promote the more rapid development and
24   wider distribution of computer software;

1   (D) stimulate research on artificial intelli-

2   gence;

3   (E) accelerate the development of computer

4   systems; and

5   (F) invest in basic research and education;

6   and

7   (2) improve planning and coordination of Federal

8   research and development on high-performance com-

9   puting.

10   TITLE I—NATIONAL HIGH-PERFORMANCE

11   COMPUTER TECHNOLOGY PROGRAM

12   SEC. 101. The National Science and Technology Policy,

13 Organization, and Priorities Act of 1976 (42 U.S.C. 6601 et

14 seq.) is amended by adding at the end the following new title:

15 "TITLE VI—NATIONAL HIGH-PERFORMANCE

16   COMPUTER TECHNOLOGY PROGRAM

17   "FINDINGS

18   "SEC. 601. (a) Congress finds and declares the follow-

19 ing:

20   "(1) In order to strengthen America's computer

21   industry and to assist the entire manufacturing sector,

22   the Federal Government must provide leadership in the

23   development and application of high-performance com-

24   puter technology. In particular, the Federal Govern-

25   ment should support the development of a high-capac-

1 ity, national research and education network; facilitate

2 the development of software for research, education,

3 and industrial applications; continue to fund basic re-

4 search; and provide for the training of computer scien-

5 tists and computational scientists.

6 "(2) Several Federal agencies have ongoing high-

7 performance computer technology programs. Improved

8 interagency coordination, cooperation, and planning

9 could enhance the effectiveness of these programs.

10 "(3) A recent report by the Office of Science and

11 Technology Policy outlining a research and develop-

12 ment strategy for high-performance computing provides

13 a framework for a multiagency computer technology

14 program.

15 "NATIONAL HIGH-PERFORMANCE COMPUTER TECHNOLOGY

16 PLAN

17 "SEC. 602.(a)(1) The President, through the Federal

18 Coordinating Council for Science, Engineering, and Technol-

19 ogy (hereafter in this title referred to as the 'Council'), shall

20 develop and implement a National High-Performance Com-

21 puter Technology Plan (hereafter in this title referred to as

22 the 'Plan') in accordance with the provisions, findings, and

23 purpose of this Act. Consistent with the responsibilities set

24 forth under subsection (c) of this section, the Plan shall con-

25 tain recommendations for a five-year national effort, to be

26 submitted to Congress within one year after the date of en-

1 actment of this title and to be revised at least once every two

2 years thereafter.

3   "(2) The Plan shall—

4   "(A) establish the goals and priorities for a Feder-

5   al high-performance computer technology program for

6   the fiscal year in which the Plan (or revised Plan) is

7   submitted and the succeeding four fiscal years;

8   "(B) set forth the role of each Federal agency and

9   department in implementing the Plan;

10   "(C) describe the levels of Federal funding and

11   specific activities, including education, research activi-

12   ties, hardware and software development, and acquisi-

13   tion and operating expenses for computers and comput-

14   er networks, required to achieve such goals and prior-

15   ities; and

16   "(D) consider and use, as appropriate, reports and

17   studies conducted by Federal agencies and depart-

18   ments, the National Research Council, or other

19   entities.

20   "(3) The Plan shall address, where appropriate, the rel-

21 evant programs and activities of the following Federal agen-

22 cies and departments—

23   "(A) the National Science Foundation;

24   "(B) the Department of Commerce, particularly

25   the National Institute of Standards and Technology

1 and the National Oceanic and Atmospheric Administra-

2 tion;

3 "(C) the National Aeronautics and Space Admin-

4 istration;

5 "(D) the Department of Defense, particularly the

6 Defense Advanced Research Projects Agency, the

7 Office of Naval Research, and, as appropriate, the

8 National Security Agency;

9 "(E) the Department of Energy;

10 "(F) the Department of Health and Human Serv-

11 ices, particularly the National Institutes of Health; and

12 "(G) such other agencies and departments as the

13 President or the Chairman of the Council considers

14 appropriate.

15 "(b) The Council shall—

16 "(1) serve as lead entity responsible for develop-

17 ment and implementation of the Plan;

18 "(2) coordinate the high-performance computing

19 research and development activities of Federal agencies

20 and departments and report at least annually to the

21 President, through the Chairman of the Council, on

22 any recommended changes in agency or departmental

23 roles that are needed to better implement the Plan;

24 "(3) prior to the President's submission to Con-

25 gress of the annual budget estimate, review each

1   agency and departmental budget estimate in the con-

2   text of the Plan and make the results of that review

3   available to each agency and department and to the

4   appropriate elements of the Executive Office of the

5   President, particularly the Office of Management and

6   Budget;

7   "(4) work with Federal agencies, with the Nation-

8   al Research Council and with academic, State, and

9   other groups conducting research on high-performance

10   computing; and

11   "(5) consult with actual and potential users of

12   such research by establishing an advisory board, which

13   shall include representatives from universities and

14   industry.

15   "(c)(1) The Plan shall take into consideration, but not be

16 limited to, the following missions and responsibilities of agen-

17 cies and departments:

18   "(A) The National Science Foundation shall con-

19   tinue to be responsible for basic research in all areas of

20   computer science, materials science, and computational

21   science. The Foundation shall continue to solicit grant

22   proposals and award grants by merit review for re-

23   search in universities, nonprofit research institutions,

24   and industry. The National Science Foundation shall

25   also be responsible for providing researchers with

access to supercomputers and providing for the establishment, by 1996, of a three-gigabit-per-second national computer network, as required by section 201 of the National High-Performance Computer Technology Act of 1989. Additional responsibilities include development of an information infrastructure of services, data bases, and knowledge banks connected to such computer network; facilitation of the validation of software and distribution of that software over such computer network; and promotion of science and engineering education.

"(B) The National Institute of Standards and Technology shall be responsible for ensuring interoperability between computer networks run by different agencies of the Federal Government and for establishing, in conjunction with industry, benchmark tests and standards for high-performance computers and software. Pursuant to the Computer Security Act of 1987 (Public Law 100–235; 100 Stat. 1724), the National Institute of Standards and Technology shall continue to be responsible for developing standards and guidelines for Federal computer systems, including standards and guidelines needed to assure the cost-effective security and privacy of sensitive information in Federal computer systems.

1   "(C) The National Oceanic and Atmospheric Ad-

2 ministration shall continue to observe, collect, commu-

3 nicate, analyze, process, provide, and disseminate data

4 about the Earth, its oceans, atmosphere, and space en-

5 vironment. It shall improve the quality and accessibil-

6 ity of the environmental data stored at the four Nation-

7 al Oceanic and Atmospheric Administration data cen-

8 ters. In addition, the National Oceanic and Atmospher-

9 ic Administration shall perform research and develop

10 technology to support its data handling role.

11   "(D) The National Aeronautics and Space Admin-

12 istration shall continue to conduct basic and applied re-

13 search in high-performance computing, particularly in

14 the field of computational science, with emphasis on

15 aeronautical applications and remote sensing data

16 processing.

17   "(E) The Department of Defense, through the

18 Defense Advanced Research Projects Agency, the

19 Office of Naval Research, and other agencies, shall

20 continue to conduct basic and applied research in high-

21 performance computing, particularly in computer

22 networking, semiconductor technology, and large-scale

23 parallel processors. Pursuant to the Stevenson-Wydler

24 Technology Innovation Act of 1980 (15 U.S.C. 3701

25 et seq.), the Department shall ensure that unclassified

1   computer technology research is readily available to

2   American industry. The National Security Agency,

3   pursuant to the Computer Security Act of 1987 (Public

4   Law 100–235; 100 Stat. 1724), shall continue to pro-

5   vide, where appropriate, technical advice and assist-

6   ance to the National Institute of Standards and Tech-

7   nology for the development of standards and guidelines

8   needed to assure the cost-effective security and privacy

9   of sensitive information in Federal computer systems.

10   "(F) The Department of Energy and its national

11   laboratories shall continue to conduct basic and applied

12   research in high-performance computing, particularly in

13   software development and multiprocessor supercom-

14   puters. Pursuant to the Stevenson-Wydler Technology

15   Innovation Act of 1980 (15 U.S.C. 3701 et seq.), and

16   other appropriate statutes, the Department of Energy

17   shall ensure that unclassified computer technology re-

18   search is readily available to American industry.

19   "(2) The Plan shall facilitate collaboration among agen-

20   cies and departments with respect to—

21   "(A) ensuring interoperability among computer

22   networks run by the agencies and departments;

23   "(B) increasing software productivity, capability,

24   and reliability;

25   "(C) promoting interoperability of software;

1   "(D) distributing software among the agencies and

2   departments; and

3   "(E) distributing federally funded, unclassified

4   software to industry and universities.

5   "(d)(1) Each Federal agency and department involved in

6 high-performance computing shall, as part of its annual re-

7 quest for appropriations to the Office of Management and

8 Budget, submit a report identifying each element of its high-

9 performance computing activities, which—

10   "(A) specifies whether each such element (i) con-

11   tributes primarily to the implementation of the Plan or

12   (ii) contributes primarily to the achievement of other

13   objectives but aids Plan implementation in important

14   ways; and

15   "(B) states the portion of its request for appro-

16   priations that is allocated to each such element.

17   "(2) The Office of Management and Budget shall review

18 each such report in light of the goals, priorities, and agency

19 and departmental responsibilities set forth in the Plan, and

20 shall include, in the President's annual budget estimate, a

21 statement of the portion of each agency or department's

22 annual budget estimate that is allocated to each element of

23 such agency or department's high-performance computing ac-

24 tivities. The Office of Management and Budget shall ensure

25 that a copy of the President's annual budget estimate is

1 transmitted to the Chairman of the Council at the same time

2 as such budget estimate is submitted to Congress.

3 "ANNUAL REPORT

4 "SEC. 603. The Chairman of the Council shall prepare

5 and submit to the President and Congress, not later than

6 March 1 of each year, an annual report on the activities con-

7 ducted pursuant to this title during the preceding fiscal year,

8 including—

9 "(1) a summary of the achievements of Federal

10 high-performance computing research and development

11 efforts during that preceding fiscal year;

12 "(2) an analysis of the progress made toward

13 achieving the goals and objectives of the Plan;

14 "(3) a copy or summary of the Plan and any

15 changes made in such Plan;

16 "(4) a summary of agency budgets for high-

17 performance computing activities for that preceding

18 fiscal year; and

19 "(5) any recommendations regarding additional

20 action or legislation which may be required to assist in

21 achieving the purposes of this title.".

22 TITLE II—NATIONAL RESEARCH AND

23 EDUCATION NETWORK

24 SEC. 201. (a) The National Science Foundation shall, in

25 cooperation with the Department of Defense, the Department

26 of Energy, the Department of Commerce, the National Aero-

1 nautics and Space Administration, and other appropriate
2 agencies, provide for the establishment of a national three-
3 gigabit-per-second research and education computer network
4 by 1996, to be known as the National Research and Educa-
5 tion Network, which shall—

6   (1) link government, industry, and the higher edu-
7   cation community;

8   (2) be developed in close cooperation with the
9   computer and telecommunications industry;

10   (3) be designed and developed with the advice of
11   potential users in government, industry, and the higher
12   education community;

13   (4) have accounting mechanisms which allow
14   users or groups of users to be charged for their usage
15   of the network, where appropriate; and

16   (5) be phased out when commercial networks can
17   meet the networking needs of American researchers.

18 Sec. 202. In addition to other agency activities associ-
19 ated with the establishment of the National Research and
20 Education Network, the following actions shall be taken:

21   (1) The Federal Coordinating Council for Science,
22   Engineering, and Technology shall—

23   (A) establish a National Network Advisory
24   Committee to provide technical and policy advice
25   from all the interests involved in the Network

program, including (i) researchers from university, industry, and Federal laboratories who will use the Network; (ii) university and college educators; (iii) librarians involved in electronic data storage and retrieval; (iv) industrial organizations that develop and provide relevant technology and services; (v) managers of regional computer networks; and (vi) experts in networking and computer science who can provide technical guidance;

(B) submit to Congress, within one year after the date of enactment of this Act, a report describing and evaluating effective mechanisms for providing operating funds for the long-term maintenance and use of the Network, including user fees, industry support, and continued Federal investment; and

(C) allow recipients of Federal research grants to use grant moneys to pay for computer networking and other telecommunications expenses.

(2) The Department of Defense, through the Defense Advanced Research Projects Agency, shall be responsible for research and development of advanced fiber optics technology, switches, and protocols needed

1   to develop a gigabit computer network essential for the

2   Network.

3   (3) The National Institute of Standards and Tech-

4   nology shall develop, in cooperation with the National

5   Security Agency and other relevent agencies, a

6   common set of standards to provide interoperability,

7   common user interfaces to systems, and enhanced secu-

8   rity for the Network.

9   (4) The National Telecommunications and Infor-

10   mation Administration shall determine to what extent

11   current Federal telecommunications laws and regula-

12   tions hinder or facilitate private industry participation

13   in the data transmission field. Within one year after

14   the date of enactment of this Act, the Administration

15   shall report such determination to the Congress.

16   SEC. 203. In addition to such sums as may be author-

17 ized to be appropriated to the National Science Foundation

18 by other law, there are authorized to be appropriated to the

19 National Science Foundation for the research, development,

20 and implementation of the National Research and Education

21 Network, in accordance with the purposes of this title,

22 $50,000,000 for fiscal year 1990, $50,000,000 for fiscal year

23 1991, $100,000,000 for fiscal year 1992, $100,000,000 for

24 fiscal year 1993, and $100,000,000 for fiscal year 1994.

TITLE III—NATIONAL INFORMATION INFRASTRUCTURE

SEC. 301. The National Science Foundation shall coordinate, in close cooperation with the Department of Commerce (in particular the National Oceanic and Atmospheric Administration, the National Institute of Standards and Technology, and the Bureau of the Census), the Department of Defense, the National Aeronautics and Space Administration, and other relevant agencies, the development of a national science and technology information infrastructure of data bases and knowledge banks accessible through the National Research and Education Network referred to in title II of this Act. The infrastructure shall include, but not be limited to—

> (1) a directory of network users;

> (2) provision for access to unclassified Federal scientific data bases, including weather data, census data, economic data, and remote sensing satellite data;

> (3) rapid prototyping of computer chips and other devices using centralized facilities connected to the network;

> (4) data bases and knowledge banks for use by artificial intelligence programs; and

> (5) provision for international collaboration among researchers.

TITLE IV—SOFTWARE

Sec. 401. (a) The Office of Science and Technology Policy, as indicated in the National High-Performance Computer Technology Plan (hereinafter referred to as the "Plan") developed and implemented under title VI of the National Science and Technology Policy, Organization, and Priorities Act of 1976, as added by section 101 of this Act, shall oversee the cooperative efforts of Federal departments and agencies in the research and development of high-performance computer software, including projects focused on astrophysics, engineering, materials, biochemistry, plasma physics, and weather and climate forecasting.

(b) The National Science Foundation shall establish clearinghouses to validate and distribute unclassified software developed by federally funded researchers and other software in the public domain, including federally funded educational and training software. Such clearinghouses shall—

    (1) maintain libraries of programs;

    (2) provide funding to researchers to improve and maintain software they have developed;

    (3) help researchers locate the software they need;

    (4) make software available through the National Research and Education Network; and

    (5) promote commercialization of software where possible.

S 1067 IS

1   (c)(1) The National Science Foundation shall place spe-

2 cial emphasis on the development of artificial intelligence and

3 shall establish joint research programs among government,

4 industry, and the higher education community to develop ar-

5 tificial intelligence applications.

6   (2) for purposes of this section, the term "artificial intel-

7 ligence" means software and hardware which can be used for

8 computer systems that learn, exhibit knowledge of them-

9 selves and their environment, make logical inferences, display

10 creativity, or mimic other aspects of human intelligence, and

11 such term includes expert systems, neural networks, natural

12 language processing programs, translation programs, and

13 higher level programming languages.

14   (d) The National Institute of Standards and Technology

15 shall develop standards for software programs purchased or

16 developed by the Federal Government that promote develop-

17 ment of interoperable software systems that can be used on

18 different computer systems with different operating systems.

19   (e) Procurement regulations at the Defense Department

20 and other departments or agencies shall be changed so that

21 contractors providing software to the Federal Government no

22 longer are required to forfeit the proprietary software devel-

23 opment tools that they used to develop the software.

24   SEC. 402. There are authorized to be appropriated to

25 the Office of Science and Technology Policy for distribution

1 to the National Science Foundation, the Department of De-
2 fense, the Department of Energy, the National Aeronautics
3 and Space Administration, and other relevant agencies for
4 computer software research and development, in accordance
5 with the purposes of this title, $50,000,000 for fiscal year
6 1990, $100,000,000 for fiscal year 1991, $150,000,000 for
7 fiscal year 1992, $200,000,000 for fiscal year 1993, and
8 $250,000,000 for fiscal year 1994.

9 TITLE V—COMPUTER SYSTEMS

10 SEC. 501. The National Science Foundation shall
11 ensure that the national supercomputer centers in the United
12 States continue to have the most advanced, commercially
13 available supercomputers produced by United States manu-
14 facturers.

15 SEC. 502. Where appropriate, Federal agencies shall
16 procure prototype or early production models of new high-
17 performance computer systems and subsystems to stimulate
18 hardware and software development in the American high-
19 performance computer industry. Particular emphasis shall be
20 given to promoting development of advanced display technol-
21 ogy, alternative computer architectures, advanced peripheral
22 storage devices, and very-high-speed communication links.

23 SEC. 503. Within sixty days following the date of enact-
24 ment of this Act, the Secretary of Commerce shall review
25 export controls that hinder the development of foreign mar-

1 kets for United States manufacturers of supercomputers and

2 other high-performance computer technology, and report to

3 the Congress the results of such review.

4   SEC. 504. There are authorized to be appropriated to

5 the Office of Science and Technology Policy, for distribution

6 to appropriate agencies and departments as specified in the

7 Plan, for research in computational science and engineering,

8 $30,000,000 for fiscal year 1990, $60,000,000 for fiscal year

9 1991, $90,000,000 for fiscal year 1992, $120,000,000 for

10 fiscal year 1993, and $150,000,000 for fiscal year 1994.

11 TITLE VI—BASIC RESEARCH AND EDUCATION

12   SEC. 601. The Office of Science and Technology Policy

13 shall, in cooperation with relevant departments and

14 agencies—

15   (1) support basic research on computer technolo-

16   gy, including research on advanced semiconductor chip

17   designs, new materials for chips, improved chip fabrica-

18   tion techniques, photonics, and superconducting com-

19   puters;

20   (2) create technology transfer mechanisms to

21   ensure that the results of basic research are readily

22   available to United States industry;

23   (3) promote basic research in computer science,

24   computational science, electrical engineering, and ma-

25   terial science; and

220

1   (4) educate and train more researchers in com-

2   puter science and computational science.

3   SEC. 602. To expand its traditional role in supporting

4   basic research in universities and colleges, and in training

5   scientists and engineers in computer science, computational

6   science, and electrical engineering, there are authorized to

7   be appropriated to the National Science Foundation,

8   $10,000,000 for fiscal year 1990, $20,000,000 for fiscal year

9   1991, $30,000,000 for fiscal year 1992, $40,000,000 for

10 fiscal year 1993, and $50,000,000 for fiscal year 1994.

○

C

S. 1067,
High-Performance Computing Act of 1990,
U.S. Congress, Senate, 101st Congress,
April 4, 1990 working draft
[version as reported out of the Commerce Committee].

To provide for a coordinated Federal research program to ensure continued
United States leadership in high-performance computing.

IN THE SENATE OF THE UNITED STATES

MAY 18 (legislative day, JANUARY 3), 1989

Mr. GORE (for himself, Mr. JEFFORDS, Mr. DURENBERGER, Mr. PELL, Mr.
KASTEN, Mr. CONRAD, Mr. PRESSLER, Mr. LOTT, Mr. WIRTH, Mr.
SASSER, Mr. KOHL, Mr. BRYAN, Mr. GRAHAM, Mr. KERREY, Mr. ROBB,
Mr. GORTON, Mr. REID, Mr. KERRY, Mr. CRANSTON, Mr. BOSCHWITZ, Mr.
BINGAMAN, Mr. BREAUX, and Mr. HEINZ) introduced the following bill;
which was read twice and referred to the Committee on Commerce, Science,
and Transportation

JULY 23, (legislative day, JULY 10), 1990

Reported by Mr. HOLLINGS, with an amendment

[Strike out all after the enacting clause and insert the part printed in italic]

A BILL

To provide for a coordinated Federal research program to
ensure continued United States leadership in high-performance computing.

1   *Be it enacted by the Senate and House of Representa-*

2 *tives of the United States of America in Congress assembled,*

2

SECTION 1. This Act may be cited as the "National High-Performance Computer Technology Act of 1989".

SEC. 2. (a) Congress finds and declares the following:

(1) Advances in computer science and technology are vital to the Nation's prosperity, national security, and scientific advancement.

(2) The United States currently leads the world in development and use of high-performance computer technology for national security, industrial productivity, and science and engineering, but that lead is being challenged by foreign competitors.

(3) Further research and improved computer research networks are necessary to maintain United States leadership in the field of high-performance computing.

(b) It is the purpose of Congress in this Act to ensure the continued leadership of the United States in high-performance computer technology. This requires that the United States Government—

(1) expand Federal support for research, development, and application of high-performance computing technology in order to—

(A) establish a high-capacity national research and education computer network;

1 ~~(B) develop an information infrastructure of~~
2 ~~data bases, services, and knowledge banks which~~
3 ~~is available for access over such a national net-~~
4 ~~work;~~
5 ~~(C) promote the more rapid development and~~
6 ~~wider distribution of computer software;~~
7 ~~(D) stimulate research on artificial intelli-~~
8 ~~gence;~~
9 ~~(E) accelerate the development of computer~~
10 ~~systems; and~~
11 ~~(F) invest in basic research and education;~~
12 ~~and~~
13 ~~(2) improve planning and coordination of Federal~~
14 ~~research and development on high-performance com-~~
15 ~~puting.~~
16 ~~TITLE I—NATIONAL HIGH-PERFORMANCE~~
17 ~~COMPUTER TECHNOLOGY PROGRAM~~
18 ~~SEC. 101. The National Science and Technology Policy,~~
19 ~~Organization, and Priorities Act of 1976 (42 U.S.C. 6601 et~~
20 ~~seq.) is amended by adding at the end the following new title:~~
21 ~~"TITLE VI—NATIONAL HIGH-PERFORMANCE~~
22 ~~COMPUTER TECHNOLOGY PROGRAM~~
23 ~~"FINDINGS~~
24 ~~"SEC. 601. (a) Congress finds and declares the follow-~~
25 ~~ing:~~ 225

1   "~~(1) In order to strengthen America's computer~~

2   ~~industry and to assist the entire manufacturing sector,~~

3   ~~the Federal Government must provide leadership in the~~

4   ~~development and application of high-performance com-~~

5   ~~puter technology. In particular, the Federal Govern-~~

6   ~~ment should support the development of a high-capac-~~

7   ~~ity, national research and education network; facilitate~~

8   ~~the development of software for research, education,~~

9   ~~and industrial applications; continue to fund basic re-~~

10   ~~search; and provide for the training of computer scien-~~

11   ~~tists and computational scientists.~~

12   "~~(2) Several Federal agencies have ongoing high-~~

13   ~~performance computer technology programs. Improved~~

14   ~~interagency coordination, cooperation, and planning~~

15   ~~could enhance the effectiveness of these programs.~~

16   "~~(3) A recent report by the Office of Science and~~

17   ~~Technology Policy outlining a research and develop-~~

18   ~~ment strategy for high-performance computing provides~~

19   ~~a framework for a multiagency computer technology~~

20   ~~program.~~

21 "~~NATIONAL HIGH-PERFORMANCE COMPUTER TECHNOLOGY~~

22   ~~PLAN~~

23   "~~SEC. 602.(a)(1) The President, through the Federal~~

24 ~~Coordinating Council for Science, Engineering, and Technol-~~

25 ~~ogy (hereafter in this title referred to as the 'Council'), shall~~

26 ~~develop and implement a National High-Performance Com-~~

1 puter Technology Plan (hereafter in this title referred to as

2 the 'Plan') in accordance with the provisions, findings, and

3 purpose of this Act. Consistent with the responsibilities set

4 forth under subsection (c) of this section, the Plan shall con-

5 tain recommendations for a five-year national effort, to be

6 submitted to Congress within one year after the date of en-

7 actment of this title and to be revised at least once every two

8 years thereafter.

9   "(2) The Plan shall—

10   "(A) establish the goals and priorities for a Feder-

11   al high-performance computer technology program for

12   the fiscal year in which the Plan (or revised Plan) is

13   submitted and the succeeding four fiscal years;

14   "(B) set forth the role of each Federal agency and

15   department in implementing the Plan;

16   "(C) describe the levels of Federal funding and

17   specific activities, including education, research activi-

18   ties, hardware and software development, and acquisi-

19   tion and operating expenses for computers and comput-

20   er networks, required to achieve such goals and prior-

21   ities; and

22   "(D) consider and use, as appropriate, reports and

23   studies conducted by Federal agencies and depart-

24   ments, the National Research Council, or other

25   entities.

1 "(3) The Plan shall address, where appropriate, the rel-

2 evant programs and activities of the following Federal agen-

3 cies and departments—

4 "(A) the National Science Foundation;

5 "(B) the Department of Commerce, particularly

6 the National Institute of Standards and Technology

7 and the National Oceanic and Atmospheric Administra-

8 tion;

9 "(C) the National Aeronautics and Space Admin-

10 istration;

11 "(D) the Department of Defense, particularly the

12 Defense Advanced Research Projects Agency, the

13 Office of Naval Research, and, as appropriate, the

14 National Security Agency;

15 "(E) the Department of Energy;

16 "(F) the Department of Health and Human Serv-

17 ices, particularly the National Institutes of Health; and

18 "(G) such other agencies and departments as the

19 President or the Chairman of the Council considers

20 appropriate.

21 "(b) The Council shall—

22 "(1) serve as lead entity responsible for develop-

23 ment and implementation of the Plan;

24 "(2) coordinate the high-performance computing

25 research and development activities of Federal agen-

1   cies and departments and report at least annually to

2   the President, through the Chairman of the Council, on

3   any recommended changes in agency or departmental

4   roles that are needed to better implement the Plan;

5   "(3) prior to the President's submission to Con-

6   gress of the annual budget estimate, review each

7   agency and departmental budget estimate in the con-

8   text of the Plan and make the results of that review

9   available to each agency and department and to the

10   appropriate elements of the Executive Office of the

11   President, particularly the Office of Management and

12   Budget;

13   "(4) work with Federal agencies, with the Nation-

14   al Research Council and with academic, State, and

15   other groups conducting research on high-performance

16   computing; and

17   "(5) consult with actual and potential users of

18   such research by establishing an advisory board, which

19   shall include representatives from universities and

20   industry.

21   "(c)(1) The Plan shall take into consideration, but not be

22   limited to, the following missions and responsibilities of agen-

23   cies and departments:

24   "(A) The National Science Foundation shall con-

25   tinue to be responsible for basic research in all areas of

1 computer science, materials science, and computational

2 science. The Foundation shall continue to solicit grant

3 proposals and award grants by merit review for re-

4 search in universities, nonprofit research institutions,

5 and industry. The National Science Foundation shall

6 also be responsible for providing researchers with

7 access to supercomputers and providing for the estab-

8 lishment, by 1996, of a three-gigabit-per-second na-

9 tional computer network, as required by section 201 of

10 the National High-Performance Computer Technology

11 Act of 1989. Additional responsibilities include devel-

12 opment of an information infrastructure of services,

13 data bases, and knowledge banks connected to such

14 computer network; facilitation of the validation of soft-

15 ware and distribution of that software over such com-

16 puter network; and promotion of science and engineer-

17 ing education.

18 "(B) The National Institute of Standards and

19 Technology shall be responsible for ensuring interoper-

20 ability between computer networks run by different

21 agencies of the Federal Government and for establish-

22 ing, in conjunction with industry, benchmark tests and

23 standards for high-performance computers and soft-

24 ware. Pursuant to the Computer Security Act of 1987

25 (Public Law 100–235; 100 Stat. 1724), the National

1 Institute of Standards and Technology shall continue
2 to be responsible for developing standards and guide-
3 lines for Federal computer systems, including standards
4 and guidelines needed to assure the cost-effective secu-
5 rity and privacy of sensitive information in Federal
6 computer systems.

7 "(C) The National Oceanic and Atmospheric Ad-
8 ministration shall continue to observe, collect, commu-
9 nicate, analyze, process, provide, and disseminate data
10 about the Earth, its oceans, atmosphere, and space en-
11 vironment. It shall improve the quality and accessibil-
12 ity of the environmental data stored at the four Nation-
13 al Oceanic and Atmospheric Administration data cen-
14 ters. In addition, the National Oceanic and Atmospher-
15 ic Administration shall perform research and develop
16 technology to support its data handling role.

17 "(D) The National Aeronautics and Space Admin-
18 istration shall continue to conduct basic and applied re-
19 search in high-performance computing, particularly in
20 the field of computational science, with emphasis on
21 aeronautical applications and remote sensing data
22 processing.

23 "(E) The Department of Defense, through the
24 Defense Advanced Research Projects Agency, the
25 Office of Naval Research, and other agencies, shall

1 continue to conduct basic and applied research in high-
2 performance computing, particularly in computer
3 networking, semiconductor technology, and large-scale
4 parallel processors. Pursuant to the Stevenson–Wydler
5 Technology Innovation Act of 1980 (15 U.S.C. 3701
6 et seq.), the Department shall ensure that unclassified
7 computer technology research is readily available to
8 American industry. The National Security Agency,
9 pursuant to the Computer Security Act of 1987 (Public
10 Law 100–235; 100 Stat. 1724), shall continue to pro-
11 vide, where appropriate, technical advice and assist-
12 ance to the National Institute of Standards and Tech-
13 nology for the development of standards and guidelines
14 needed to assure the cost-effective security and privacy
15 of sensitive information in Federal computer systems.

16 "(F) The Department of Energy and its national
17 laboratories shall continue to conduct basic and applied
18 research in high-performance computing, particularly in
19 software development and multiprocessor supercom-
20 puters. Pursuant to the Stevenson–Wydler Technology
21 Innovation Act of 1980 (15 U.S.C. 3701 et seq.), and
22 other appropriate statutes, the Department of Energy
23 shall ensure that unclassified computer technology re-
24 search is readily available to American industry.

1   "(2) The Plan shall facilitate collaboration among agen-

2 cies and departments with respect to—

3   "(A) ensuring interoperability among computer

4 networks run by the agencies and departments;

5   "(B) increasing software productivity, capability,

6 and reliability;

7   "(C) promoting interoperability of software;

8   "(D) distributing software among the agencies and

9 departments; and

10   "(E) distributing federally funded, unclassified

11 software to industry and universities.

12   "(d)(1) Each Federal agency and department involved in

13 high-performance computing shall, as part of its annual re-

14 quest for appropriations to the Office of Management and

15 Budget, submit a report identifying each element of its high-

16 performance computing activities, which—

17   "(A) specifies whether each such element (i) con-

18 tributes primarily to the implementation of the Plan or

19 (ii) contributes primarily to the achievement of other

20 objectives but aids Plan implementation in important

21 ways; and

22   "(B) states the portion of its request for appro-

23 priations that is allocated to each such element.

24   "(2) The Office of Management and Budget shall review

25 each such report in light of the goals, priorities, and agency

1 and departmental responsibilities set forth in the Plan, and

2 shall include, in the President's annual budget estimate, a

3 statement of the portion of each agency or department's

4 annual budget estimate that is allocated to each element of

5 such agency or department's high-performance computing ac-

6 tivities. The Office of Management and Budget shall ensure

7 that a copy of the President's annual budget estimate is

8 transmitted to the Chairman of the Council at the same time

9 as such budget estimate is submitted to Congress.

10 "ANNUAL REPORT

11 "SEC. 603. The Chairman of the Council shall prepare

12 and submit to the President and Congress, not later than

13 March 1 of each year, an annual report on the activities con-

14 ducted pursuant to this title during the preceding fiscal year,

15 including—

16   "(1) a summary of the achievements of Federal

17   high-performance computing research and development

18   efforts during that preceding fiscal year;

19   "(2) an analysis of the progress made toward

20   achieving the goals and objectives of the Plan;

21   "(3) a copy or summary of the Plan and any

22   changes made in such Plan;

23   "(4) a summary of agency budgets for high-

24   performance computing activities for that preceding

25   fiscal year; and

1 "(5) any recommendations regarding additional

2 action or legislation which may be required to assist in

3 achieving the purposes of this title.".

4 TITLE II—NATIONAL RESEARCH AND

5 EDUCATION NETWORK

6 SEC. 201. (a) The National Science Foundation shall, in

7 cooperation with the Department of Defense, the Depart-

8 ment of Energy, the Department of Commerce, the National

9 Aeronautics and Space Administration, and other appropriate

10 agencies, provide for the establishment of a national three-

11 gigabit-per-second research and education computer network

12 by 1996, to be known as the National Research and Educa-

13 tion Network, which shall—

14   (1) link government, industry, and the higher edu-

15   cation community;

16   (2) be developed in close cooperation with the

17   computer and telecommunications industry;

18   (3) be designed and developed with the advice of

19   potential users in government, industry, and the higher

20   education community;

21   (4) have accounting mechanisms which allow

22   users or groups of users to be charged for their usage

23   of the network, where appropriate; and

24   (5) be phased out when commercial networks can

25   meet the networking needs of American researchers.

1   SEC. 202. In addition to other agency activities associ-

2 ated with the establishment of the National Research and

3 Education Network, the following actions shall be taken:

4   (1) The Federal Coordinating Council for Science,

5   Engineering, and Technology shall—

6   (A) establish a National Network Advisory

7   Committee to provide technical and policy advice

8   from all the interests involved in the Network

9   program, including (i) researchers from university,

10   industry, and Federal laboratories who will use

11   the Network; (ii) university and college educators;

12   (iii) librarians involved in electronic data storage

13   and retrieval; (iv) industrial organizations that de-

14   velop and provide relevant technology and serv-

15   ices; (v) managers of regional computer networks;

16   and (vi) experts in networking and computer sci-

17   ence who can provide technical guidance;

18   (B) submit to Congress, within one year after

19   the date of enactment of this Act, a report de-

20   scribing and evaluating effective mechanisms for

21   providing operating funds for the long-term main-

22   tenance and use of the Network, including user

23   fees, industry support, and continued Federal

24   investment; and

1   ~~(C) allow recipients of Federal research~~

2   ~~grants to use grant moneys to pay for com-~~

3   ~~puter networking and other telecommunications~~

4   ~~expenses.~~

5   ~~(2) The Department of Defense, through the De-~~

6   ~~fense Advanced Research Projects Agency, shall be re-~~

7   ~~sponsible for research and development of advanced~~

8   ~~fiber optics technology, switches, and protocols needed~~

9   ~~to develop a gigabit computer network essential for the~~

10   ~~Network.~~

11   ~~(3) The National Institute of Standards and Tech-~~

12   ~~nology shall develop, in cooperation with the National~~

13   ~~Security Agency and other relevent agencies, a~~

14   ~~common set of standards to provide interoperability,~~

15   ~~common user interfaces to systems, and enhanced se-~~

16   ~~curity for the Network.~~

17   ~~(4) The National Telecommunications and Infor-~~

18   ~~mation Administration shall determine to what extent~~

19   ~~current Federal telecommunications laws and regula-~~

20   ~~tions hinder or facilitate private industry participation~~

21   ~~in the data transmission field. Within one year after~~

22   ~~the date of enactment of this Act, the Administration~~

23   ~~shall report such determination to the Congress.~~

24   ~~SEC. 203. In addition to such sums as may be author-~~

25 ~~ized to be appropriated to the National Science Foundation~~

1 by other law, there are authorized to be appropriated to the

2 National Science Foundation for the research, development,

3 and implementation of the National Research and Education

4 Network, in accordance with the purposes of this title,

5 $50,000,000 for fiscal year 1990, $50,000,000 for fiscal year

6 1991, $100,000,000 for fiscal year 1992, $100,000,000 for

7 fiscal year 1993, and $100,000,000 for fiscal year 1994.

8 TITLE III—NATIONAL INFORMATION

9 INFRASTRUCTURE

10 SEC. 301. The National Science Foundation shall co-

11 ordinate, in close cooperation with the Department of Com-

12 merce (in particular the National Oceanic and Atmospheric

13 Administration, the National Institute of Standards and

14 Technology, and the Bureau of the Census), the Department

15 of Defense, the National Aeronautics and Space Administra-

16 tion, and other relevant agencies, the development of a na-

17 tional science and technology information infrastructure of

18 data bases and knowledge banks accessible through the Na-

19 tional Research and Education Network referred to in title II

20 of this Act. The infrastructure shall include, but not be

21 limited to—

22   (1) a directory of network users;

23   (2) provision for access to unclassified Federal sci-

24   entific data bases, including weather data, census data,

25   economic data, and remote sensing satellite data;

1   (3) rapid prototyping of computer chips and other

2   devices using centralized facilities connected to the

3   network;

4   (4) data bases and knowledge banks for use by ar-

5   tificial intelligence programs; and

6   (5) provision for international collaboration among

7   researchers.

8   TITLE IV—SOFTWARE

9   SEC. 401. (a) The Office of Science and Technology

10 Policy, as indicated in the National High-Performance Com-

11 puter Technology Plan (hereinafter referred to as the "Plan")

12 developed and implemented under title VI of the National

13 Science and Technology Policy, Organization, and Priorities

14 Act of 1976, as added by section 101 of this Act, shall over-

15 see the cooperative efforts of Federal departments and agen-

16 cies in the research and development of high-performance

17 computer software, including projects focused on astrophys-

18 ics, engineering, materials, biochemistry, plasma physics, and

19 weather and climate forecasting.

20   (b) The National Science Foundation shall establish

21 clearinghouses to validate and distribute unclassified software

22 developed by federally funded researchers and other software

23 in the public domain, including federally funded educational

24 and training software. Such clearinghouses shall—

25   (1) maintain libraries of programs;

1   (2) provide funding to researchers to improve and

2   maintain software they have developed;

3   (3) help researchers locate the software they need;

4   (4) make software available through the National

5   Research and Education Network; and

6   (5) promote commercialization of software where

7   possible.

8   (c)(1) The National Science Foundation shall place spe-

9   cial emphasis on the development of artificial intelligence and

10   shall establish joint research programs among government,

11   industry, and the higher education community to develop ar-

12   tificial intelligence applications.

13   (2) for purposes of this section, the term "artificial intel-

14   ligence" means software and hardware which can be used for

15   computer systems that learn, exhibit knowledge of them-

16   selves and their environment, make logical inferences, dis-

17   play creativity, or mimic other aspects of human intelligence,

18   and such term includes expert systems, neural networks, nat-

19   ural language processing programs, translation programs,

20   and higher level programming languages.

21   (d) The National Institute of Standards and Technology

22   shall develop standards for software programs purchased or

23   developed by the Federal Government that promote develop-

24   ment of interoperable software systems that can be used on

25   different computer systems with different operating systems.

240

1 ~~(c) Procurement regulations at the Defense Department~~

2 ~~and other departments or agencies shall be changed so that~~

3 ~~contractors providing software to the Federal Government no~~

4 ~~longer are required to forfeit the proprietary software devel-~~

5 ~~opment tools that they used to develop the software.~~

6 ~~SEC. 402. There are authorized to be appropriated to~~

7 ~~the Office of Science and Technology Policy for distribution~~

8 ~~to the National Science Foundation, the Department of De-~~

9 ~~fense, the Department of Energy, the National Aeronautics~~

10 ~~and Space Administration, and other relevant agencies for~~

11 ~~computer software research and development, in accordance~~

12 ~~with the purposes of this title, $50,000,000 for fiscal year~~

13 ~~1990, $100,000,000 for fiscal year 1991, $150,000,000 for~~

14 ~~fiscal year 1992, $200,000,000 for fiscal year 1993, and~~

15 ~~$250,000,000 for fiscal year 1994.~~

16 ~~TITLE V—COMPUTER SYSTEMS~~

17 ~~SEC. 501. The National Science Foundation shall~~

18 ~~ensure that the national supercomputer centers in the United~~

19 ~~States continue to have the most advanced, commercially~~

20 ~~available supercomputers produced by United States manu-~~

21 ~~facturers.~~

22 ~~SEC. 502. Where appropriate, Federal agencies shall~~

23 ~~procure prototype or early production models of new high-~~

24 ~~performance computer systems and subsystems to stimulate~~

25 ~~hardware and software development in the American high-~~

1 performance computer industry. Particular emphasis shall be

2 given to promoting development of advanced display technol-

3 ogy, alternative computer architectures, advanced peripheral

4 storage devices, and very-high-speed communication links.

5 SEC. 503. Within sixty days following the date of enact-

6 ment of this Act, the Secretary of Commerce shall review

7 export controls that hinder the development of foreign mar-

8 kets for United States manufacturers of supercomputers and

9 other high-performance computer technology, and report to

10 the Congress the results of such review.

11 SEC. 504. There are authorized to be appropriated to

12 the Office of Science and Technology Policy, for distribution

13 to appropriate agencies and departments as specified in the

14 Plan, for research in computational science and engineering,

15 $30,000,000 for fiscal year 1990, $60,000,000 for fiscal year

16 1991, $90,000,000 for fiscal year 1992, $120,000,000 for

17 fiscal year 1993, and $150,000,000 for fiscal year 1994.

18 TITLE VI—BASIC RESEARCH AND EDUCATION

19 SEC. 601. The Office of Science and Technology Policy

20 shall, in cooperation with relevant departments and

21 agencies—

22 (1) support basic research on computer technolo-

23 gy, including research on advanced semiconductor chip

24 designs, new materials for chips, improved chip fabrica-

1 ~~tion techniques, photonics, and superconducting com-~~
2 ~~puters;~~

3 ~~(2) create technology transfer mechanisms to~~
4 ~~ensure that the results of basic research are readily~~
5 ~~available to United States industry;~~

6 ~~(3) promote basic research in computer science,~~
7 ~~computational science, electrical engineering, and ma-~~
8 ~~terial science; and~~

9 ~~(4) educate and train more researchers in com-~~
10 ~~puter science and computational science.~~

11 ~~SEC. 602. To expand its traditional role in supporting~~
12 ~~basic research in universities and colleges, and in training~~
13 ~~scientists and engineers in computer science, computational~~
14 ~~science, and electrical engineering, there are authorized to~~
15 ~~be appropriated to the National Science Foundation,~~
16 ~~$10,000,000 for fiscal year 1990, $20,000,000 for fiscal year~~
17 ~~1991, $30,000,000 for fiscal year 1992, $40,000,000 for~~
18 ~~fiscal year 1993, and $50,000,000 for fiscal year 1994.~~

19 *SECTION 1. This Act may be cited as the "High-Per-*
20 *formance Computing Act of 1990".*

21 *SEC. 2. (a) The Congress finds and declares the*
22 *following:*

23 *(1) Advances in computer science and technology*
24 *are vital to the Nation's prosperity, national and eco-*
25 *nomic security, and scientific advancement.*

1　　　　　　(2) The United States currently leads the world

2　　　in development and use of high-performance computing

3　　　for national security, industrial productivity, and sci-

4　　　ence and engineering, but that lead is being challenged

5　　　by foreign competitors.

6　　　　　　(3) Further research, improved computer research

7　　　networks, and more effective technology transfer from

8　　　government to industry are necessary for the United

9　　　States to fully reap the benefits of high-performance

10　　　computing.

11　　(b) It is the purpose of Congress in this Act to help

12　ensure the continued leadership of the United States in high-

13　performance computing and its applications. This requires

14　that the United States Government—

15　　　　　　(1) expand Federal support for research, develop-

16　　　ment, and application of high-performance computing

17　　　in order to—

18　　　　　　　　(A) establish a high-capacity national re-

19　　　　　search and education computer network;

20　　　　　　　　(B) expand the number of researchers, edu-

21　　　　　cators, and students with training in high-per-

22　　　　　formance computing and access to high-perform-

23　　　　　ance computing resources;

24　　　　　　　　(C) develop an information infrastructure of

25　　　　　data bases, services, access mechanisms, and re-

1   *search facilities which is available for use through*

2   *such a national network;*

3   *(D) stimulate research on software tech-*

4   *nology;*

5   *(E) promote the more rapid development and*

6   *wider distribution of computer software tools and*

7   *applications software;*

8   *(F) accelerate the development of computer*

9   *systems and subsystems;*

10   *(G) promote the application of high-perform-*

11   *ance computing to Grand Challenges; and*

12   *(H) invest in basic research and education;*

13   *and*

14   *(2) improve planning and coordination of Federal*

15   *research and development on high-performance com-*

16   *puting.*

17   Sᴇᴄ. *3. As used in this Act, the term—*

18   *(1) "North American company" means a compa-*

19   *ny or other business entity in which majority owner-*

20   *ship or control is held by individuals who are citizens*

21   *of the United States, or citizens of Canada, or a com-*

22   *bination of United States and Canadian citizens,*

23   *except that such term includes a company owned or*

24   *controlled by Canadian citizens only if, in the judg-*

25   *ment of the Secretary of Commerce, the company is*

1 *not acting, with respect to the joint venture concerned,*

2 *as an agent or intermediary for a third-country compa-*

3 *ny or foreign government; and*

4 *(2) "Grand Challenge" means a fundamental*

5 *problem in science and engineering, with broad eco-*

6 *nomic and scientific impact, whose solution will re-*

7 *quire the application of high-performance computing*

8 *resources.*

9 *TITLE I—NATIONAL HIGH-PERFORMANCE*

10 *COMPUTING PROGRAM*

11 *SEC. 101. The National Science and Technology*

12 *Policy, Organization, and Priorities Act of 1976 (42 U.S.C.*

13 *6601 et seq.) is amended by adding at the end the following*

14 *new title:*

15 *"TITLE VI—NATIONAL HIGH-PERFORMANCE*

16 *COMPUTER TECHNOLOGY PROGRAM*

17 *"FINDINGS*

18 *"SEC. 601. (a) The Congress finds and declares the*

19 *following:*

20 *"(1) In order to strengthen America's computer*

21 *industry and to assist the entire manufacturing sector,*

22 *the Federal Government must provide leadership in the*

23 *development and application of high-performance com-*

24 *puting. In particular, the Federal Government should*

25 *support the development of a high-capacity, national*

1 *research and education network; make information*

2 *services available over the network; facilitate the devel-*

3 *opment of software for research, education, and indus-*

4 *trial applications; continue to fund basic and applied*

5 *research; and provide for the training of computer sci-*

6 *entists and computational scientists.*

7 *"(2) Several Federal agencies have ongoing high-*

8 *performance computing programs. Improved inter-*

9 *agency coordination, cooperation, and planning could*

10 *enhance the effectiveness of these programs.*

11 *"(3) A 1989 report by the Office of Science and*

12 *Technology Policy outlining a research and develop-*

13 *ment strategy for high-performance computing provides*

14 *a framework for a multiagency high-performance com-*

15 *puting program.*

16 *"NATIONAL HIGH-PERFORMANCE COMPUTING PLAN*

17 *"SEC. 602. (a)(1) The President, through the Federal*

18 *Coordinating Council for Science, Engineering, and Tech-*

19 *nology (hereafter in this title referred to as the 'Council'),*

20 *shall develop and implement a National High-Performance*

21 *Computing Plan (hereafter in this title referred to as the*

22 *'Plan') in accordance with the provisions, findings, and pur-*

23 *pose of this Act. Consistent with the responsibilities set forth*

24 *under subsection (d) of this section, the Plan shall contain*

25 *recommendations for a five-year national effort, to be submit-*

26 *ted to the Congress within one year after the date of enact-*

1 *ment of this title and to be revised at least once every two*

2 *years thereafter.*

3   *"(2) The Plan shall—*

4   *"(A) establish the goals and priorities for a Fed-*

5 *eral high-performance computing program for the fiscal*

6 *year in which the Plan (or revised Plan) is submitted*

7 *and the succeeding four fiscal years;*

8   *"(B) set forth the role of each Federal agency and*

9 *department in implementing the Plan;*

10   *"(C) describe the levels of Federal funding for*

11 *each agency and specific activities, including educa-*

12 *tion, research activities, hardware and software devel-*

13 *opment, and acquisition and operating expenses for*

14 *computers and computer networks, required to achieve*

15 *such goals and priorities; and*

16   *"(D) consider and use, as appropriate, reports*

17 *and studies conducted by Federal agencies and depart-*

18 *ments, the National Research Council, or other*

19 *entities.*

20   *"(3) The Plan shall address, where appropriate, the rel-*

21 *evant programs and activities of the following Federal agen-*

22 *cies and departments—*

23   *"(A) the National Science Foundation;*

24   *"(B) the Department of Commerce, particularly*

25 *the National Institute of Standards and Technology,*

1   *the National Oceanic and Atmospheric Administration,*

2   *and the National Telecommunications and Information*

3   *Administration;*

4   *"(C) the National Aeronautics and Space Admin-*

5   *istration;*

6   *"(D) the Department of Defense, particularly the*

7   *Defense Advanced Research Projects Agency and, as*

8   *appropriate, the National Security Agency;*

9   *"(E) the Department of Energy;*

10   *"(F) the Department of Health and Human Serv-*

11   *ices, particularly the National Institutes of Health;*

12   *"(G) the Department of Education;*

13   *"(H) the Library of Congress, the National Li-*

14   *brary of Medicine, and the National Agricultural Li-*

15   *brary; and*

16   *"(I) such other agencies and departments as the*

17   *President or the Chairman of the Council considers*

18   *appropriate.*

19   *"(b) The Council shall—*

20   *"(1) serve as lead entity responsible for develop-*

21   *ment and implementation of the Plan;*

22   *"(2) coordinate the high-performance computing*

23   *research and development activities of Federal agencies*

24   *and departments and report at least annually to the*

25   *President, through the Chairman of the Council, on*

1   *any recommended changes in agency or departme*

2   *roles that are needed to better implement the Plan;*

3   *"(3) prior to the President's submission to*

4   *Congress of the annual budget estimate, review e*

5   *agency and departmental budget estimate in the con*

6   *of the Plan and make the results of that review av*

7   *able to the appropriate elements of the Executive Of*

8   *of the President, particularly the Office of Mana*

9   *ment and Budget;*

10   *"(4) work with Federal agencies, with the Natic*

11   *al Research Council, and with academic, State, indi*

12   *try, and other groups conducting research on hig*

13   *performance computing.*

14   *"(c) The Office of Science and Technology Policy sho*

15 *establish a High-Performance Computing Advisory Pan*

16 *consisting of representatives from industry and academia*

17 *provide the Council with an independent assessment of (*

18 *progress made in implementing the Plan, (2) the need i*

19 *revise the Plan, (3) the balance between the components of th*

20 *Plan, (4) whether the research and development funded unde*

21 *the Plan is helping to maintain United States leadership i*

22 *computing technology, and (5) other issues identified by th*

23 *Director of the Office of Science and Technology Policy.*

1   *"(d)(1) The Plan shall take into consideration, but not*

2 *be limited to, the following missions and responsibilities of*

3 *agencies and departments:*

4   *"(A) The National Science Foundation shall con-*

5 *tinue to be responsible for basic research in computer*

6 *science and engineering, computer technology, and*

7 *computational science. The Foundation shall continue*

8 *to solicit grant proposals and award grants by merit*

9 *review for research in universities, nonprofit research*

10 *institutions, and industry. The National Science*

11 *Foundation shall also provide researchers with access*

12 *to supercomputers and have primary responsibility for*

13 *the establishment, by 1996, of a multi-gigabit-per-*

14 *second national computer network, as required by sec-*

15 *tion 201 of the High-Performance Computing Act of*

16 *1990. Prior to deployment of a multi-gigabit-per-second*

17 *national network, the National Science Foundation*

18 *shall maintain, expand, and upgrade its existing com-*

19 *puter networks. Additional responsibilities include pro-*

20 *moting development of information services and data*

21 *bases available over such computer networks; facilita-*

22 *tion of the documentation, evaluation, and distribution*

23 *of research software over such computer networks; en-*

24 *couragement of continued development of innovative*

1   *software by industry; and promotion of science and en-*

2   *gineering education.*

3   *"(B) The National Institute of Standards and*

4   *Technology shall be responsible for developing, through*

5   *the open standards setting process, standards, guide-*

6   *lines, measurement techniques, and test methods for the*

7   *interoperability of high-performance computers in net-*

8   *works and for common user interfaces to systems. In*

9   *addition, the National Institute of Standards and*

10   *Technology shall be responsible for developing bench-*

11   *mark tests and standards, through the open standards*

12   *setting process and in conjunction with industry, for*

13   *high-performance computers and software. Pursuant to*

14   *the Computer Security Act of 1987 (Public Law 100–*

15   *235; 100 Stat. 1724), the National Institute of Stand-*

16   *ards and Technology shall continue to be responsible*

17   *for adopting standards and guidelines needed to assure*

18   *the cost-effective security and privacy of sensitive infor-*

19   *mation in Federal computer systems. These standards*

20   *and guidelines shall be developed through the open*

21   *standards setting process and in conjunction with*

22   *industry.*

23   *"(C) The National Oceanic and Atmospheric Ad-*

24   *ministration shall continue to observe, collect, commu-*

25   *nicate, analyze, process, provide, and disseminate data*

1 *about the Earth and its oceans, atmosphere, and space*

2 *environment. The National Oceanic and Atmospheric*

3 *Administration shall improve the quality and accessi-*

4 *bility of the environmental data stored at its four data*

5 *centers and shall perform research and develop technol-*

6 *ogy to support its data handling role.*

7   *"(D) The National Aeronautics and Space Ad-*

8 *ministration shall continue to conduct basic and ap-*

9 *plied research in high-performance computing, particu-*

10 *larly in the field of computational science, with empha-*

11 *sis on aeronauticals and the processing of remote sens-*

12 *ing data.*

13   *"(E) The Department of Defense, through the De-*

14 *fense Advanced Research Projects Agency and other*

15 *agencies, shall continue to conduct basic and applied*

16 *research in high-performance computing, particularly*

17 *in computer networking, semiconductor technology, and*

18 *large-scale parallel processors. Pursuant to the Steven-*

19 *son-Wydler Technology Innovation Act of 1980 (15*

20 *U.S.C. 3701 et seq.) and other appropriate Acts, the*

21 *Department shall ensure that unclassified computing*

22 *technology research is readily available to United*

23 *States industry. The National Security Agency, pur-*

24 *suant to the Computer Security Act of 1987 (Public*

25 *Law 100–235; 100 Stat. 1724), shall continue to pro-*

1 *vide, where appropriate, technical advice and assist-*

2 *ance to the National Institute of Standards and Tech-*

3 *nology for the adoption of standards and guidelines*

4 *needed to assure the cost-effective security and privacy*

5 *of sensitive information in Federal computer systems.*

6 *"(F) The Department of Energy and its national*

7 *laboratories shall continue to conduct basic and applied*

8 *research in high-performance computing, particularly*

9 *in software development and multiprocessor supercom-*

10 *puters. Pursuant to the Stevenson-Wydler Technology*

11 *Innovation Act of 1980 (15 U.S.C. 3701 et seq.), and*

12 *other appropriate Acts, the Department of Energy shall*

13 *ensure that unclassified computer research is readily*

14 *available to North American companies.*

15 *"(G) The Department of Education, pursuant to*

16 *the Library Services and Construction Act (20 U.S.C.*

17 *351 et seq.) and the Higher Education Act of 1965*

18 *(20 U.S.C. 1060 et seq.), shall encourage the distribu-*

19 *tion of library and information resources, through li-*

20 *brary linkages to the National Research and Educa-*

21 *tion Network and through other means.*

22 *"(H) The Library of Congress, the National Li-*

23 *brary of Medicine, and the National Agricultural Li-*

24 *brary, as national libraries of the United States, shall*

25 *continue to compile, develop, and maintain electronic*

1 *data bases in appropriate areas of expertise and pro-*

2 *vide for dissemination of, access to, and use of these*

3 *data bases and other library resources through the*

4 *Network.*

5 *"(2) The Plan shall facilitate collaboration among agen-*

6 *cies and departments with respect to—*

7   *"(A) ensuring interoperability among computer*

8 *networks run by the agencies and departments;*

9   *"(B) increasing software productivity, capability,*

10 *and reliability;*

11   *"(C) encouraging, where appropriate, agency co-*

12 *operation with industry in development of software;*

13   *"(D) promoting interoperability of software;*

14   *"(E) distributing software among the agencies*

15 *and departments; and*

16   *"(F) distributing federally-funded, unclassified*

17 *software to State and local governments, industry, and*

18 *universities.*

19 *"(e)(1) Each Federal agency and department involved*

20 *in high-performance computing shall, as part of its annual*

21 *request for appropriations to the Office of Management and*

22 *Budget, submit a report identifying each element of its high-*

23 *performance computing activities, which—*

24   *"(A) specifies whether each such element (i) con-*

25 *tributes primarily to the implementation of the Plan or*

1 *(ii) contributes primarily to the achievement of other*

2 *objectives but aids Plan implementation in important*

3 *ways; and*

4 *"(B) states the portion of its request for appro-*

5 *priations that is allocated to each such element.*

6 *"(2) The Office of Management and Budget shall*

7 *review each such report in light of the goals, priorities, and*

8 *agency and departmental responsibilities set forth in the*

9 *Plan, and shall include, in the President's annual budget*

10 *estimate, a statement of the portion of each agency or depart-*

11 *ment's annual budget estimate that is allocated to each ele-*

12 *ment of such agency or department's high-performance com-*

13 *puting activities. The Office of Management and Budget*

14 *shall ensure that a copy of the President's annual budget*

15 *estimate is transmitted to the Chairman of the Council at the*

16 *same time as such budget estimate is submitted to Congress.*

17 *"ANNUAL REPORT*

18 *"SEC. 603. The Chairman of the Council shall prepare*

19 *and submit to the President and the Congress, not later than*

20 *March 1 of each year, an annual report on the activities con-*

21 *ducted pursuant to this title during the preceding fiscal year,*

22 *including—*

23 *"(1) a summary of the achievements of Federal*

24 *high-performance computing research and development*

25 *efforts during that preceding fiscal year;*

1   *"(2) an analysis of the progress made toward*

2 *achieving the goals and objectives of the Plan;*

3   *"(3) a copy or summary of the Plan and any*

4 *changes made in such Plan;*

5   *"(4) a summary of agency budgets for high-*

6 *performance computing activities for that preceding*

7 *fiscal year; and*

8   *"(5) any recommendations regarding additional*

9 *action or legislation which may be required to assist in*

10 *achieving the purposes of this title.".*

11 Sec. 102. (a) Section 102(a)(6) of the National Sci-

12 ence and Technology Policy, Organization, and Priorities

13 Act of 1976 (42 U.S.C. 6602(a)(6)) is amended to read as

14 follows:

15   *"(6) The development and implementation of long-*

16 *range, interagency research plans to support policy de-*

17 *cisions regarding identified national and international*

18 *concerns, and for which a sustained and coordinated*

19 *commitment to improving scientific understanding will*

20 *be required.".*

21 *(b)(1) Section 401 of the National Science and Tech-*

22 *nology Policy, Organization, and Priorities Act of 1976 (42*

23 *U.S.C. 6651) is amended to read as follows:*

24   *"FUNCTIONS OF COUNCIL*

25   *"Sec. 401. (a) The Federal Coordinating Council for*

26 *Science, Engineering, and Technology (hereinafter referred*

1 *to as the 'Council') shall consider problems and developments*

2 *in the fields of science, engineering, and technology and relat-*

3 *ed activities affecting more than one Federal agency, and*

4 *shall recommend policies and other measures designated to—*

5   *"(1) provide more effective planning and adminis-*

6   *tration of Federal scientific, engineering, and techno-*

7   *logical programs;*

8   *"(2) identify research needs, including areas re-*

9   *quiring additional emphasis;*

10   *"(3) achieve more effective utilization of the scien-*

11   *tific, engineering, and technological resources and fa-*

12   *cilities of Federal agencies, including the elimination*

13   *of unwarranted duplication; and*

14   *"(4) further international cooperation in science,*

15   *engineering, and technology.*

16   *"(b) The Council may be assigned responsibility for de-*

17 *veloping long-range and coordinated plans for scientific and*

18 *technical research which involve the participation of more*

19 *than two Federal agencies. Such plans shall—*

20   *"(1) identify research approaches and priorities*

21   *which most effectively advance scientific understanding*

22   *and provide a basis for policy decisions;*

23   *"(2) provide for effective cooperation and coordi-*

24   *nation of research among Federal agencies; and*

●S 1067 RS

1   *"(3) encourage domestic and, as appropriate,*

2   *international cooperation among government, industry,*

3   *and university scientists.*

4   *"(c) The Council shall perform such other related advi-*

5 *sory duties as shall be assigned by the President or by the*

6 *Chairman of the Council.*

7   *"(d) For the purpose of carrying out the provisions of*

8 *this section, each Federal agency represented on the Council*

9 *shall furnish necessary assistance to the Council. Such as-*

10 *sistance may include—*

11   *"(1) detailing employees to the Council to perform*

12   *such functions, consistent with the purposes of this sec-*

13   *tion, as the Chairman of the Council may assign to*

14   *them; and*

15   *"(2) undertaking, upon request of the Chairman,*

16   *such special studies for the Council as come within the*

17   *scope of authority of the Council.*

18   *"(e) For the purpose of developing interagency plans,*

19 *conducting studies, and making reports as directed by the*

20 *Chairman, standing committees and working groups of the*

21 *Council may be established.".*

22   *(2) Section 207(a)(1) of the National Science and*

23 *Technology Policy, Organization, and Priorities Act of 1976*

24 *(42 U.S.C. 6616(a)(1)) is amended by striking "established*

25 *under Title IV".*

1   *TITLE II—NATIONAL RESEARCH AND*

2   *EDUCATION NETWORK*

3   *Sec. 201. The National Science Foundation shall, in*

4 *cooperation with the Department of Defense, the Department*

5 *of Energy, the Department of Commerce, the National Aero-*

6 *nautics and Space Administration, and other appropriate*

7 *agencies, provide for the establishment of a national multi-*

8 *gigabit-per-second research and education computer network*

9 *by 1996, to be known as the National Research and Educa-*

10 *tion Network, which shall—*

11   *(1) link government, industry, and the education*

12   *community;*

13   *(2) provide computer users with access to super-*

14   *computers, computer data bases, and other research*

15   *facilities;*

16   *(3) provide users of libraries and other education-*

17   *al institutions with access to the Network and informa-*

18   *tion resources;*

19   *(4) be developed in close cooperation with the com-*

20   *puter, telecommunications, and information industry;*

21   *(5) be designed and developed with the advice of*

22   *potential users in government, industry, and the higher*

23   *education community;*

24   *(6) be established in a manner which fosters and*

25   *maintains competition and private sector investment in*

●S 1067 RS

1 *high speed data networking within the telecommunica-*

2 *tions industry;*

3   *(7) where technically feasible, have accounting*

4 *mechanisms which allow, where appropriate, users or*

5 *groups of users to be charged for their usage of the Net-*

6 *work and copyrighted materials available over the Net-*

7 *work; and*

8   *(8) be phased out when commercial networks can*

9 *meet the networking needs of American researchers.*

10   *SEC. 202. In addition to other agency activities associ-*

11 *ated with the establishment of the National Research and*

12 *Education Network, the following actions shall be taken:*

13   *(1) The Federal Coordinating Council for Sci-*

14 *ence, Engineering, and Technology shall—*

15   *(A) establish a Federal Networking Advisory*

16 *Committee to provide technical advice from the in-*

17 *terests involved in existing Federal research net-*

18 *works and the National Research and Education*

19 *Network; and*

20   *(B) submit to the Congress, within one year*

21 *after the date of enactment of this Act, a report*

22 *describing and evaluating effective mechanisms*

23 *for providing operating funds for the maintenance*

24 *and use of the Network, including user fees, in-*

25 *dustry support, and continued Federal investment,*

1   *and containing a plan for the eventual commer-*

2   *cialization of the Network.*

3   *(2) The National Science Foundation, the Na-*

4   *tional Aeronautics and Space Administration, the De-*

5   *partment of Energy, the Department of Defense, the*

6   *Department of Commerce, the Department of the Inte-*

7   *rior, the Department of Agriculture, the Department of*

8   *Health and Human Services, and the Environmental*

9   *Protection Agency shall allow recipients of Federal re-*

10   *search grants to use grant monies to pay for computer*

11   *networking expenses.*

12   *(3) The Department of Defense, through the De-*

13   *fense Advanced Research Projects Agency, shall have*

14   *the primary responsibility for research and develop-*

15   *ment of advanced fiber optics technology, switches, and*

16   *protocols needed to develop a multi-gigabit computer*

17   *network.*

18   *(4) The National Institute of Standards and*

19   *Technology shall, in consultation with the National*

20   *Science Foundation. the National Security Agency,*

21   *other relevant agencies, and industry, adopt a common*

22   *set of standards and guidelines, developed through an*

23   *open standards setting process, to provide interoperabil-*

24   *ity, common user interfaces to systems, and enhanced*

25   *security for the Network.*

1   *(5) The National Telecommunications and Infor-*

2   *mation Administration shall determine to what extent*

3   *current State and Federal telecommunications laws*

4   *and regulations hinder or facilitate private industry*

5   *participation in the data transmission field. Within*

6   *one year after the date of enactment of this Act, the*

7   *Administration shall report such determination to the*

8   *Congress.*

9   *TITLE III—INFORMATION SERVICES*

10   *SEC. 301. The National Science Foundation, with as-*

11 *sistance from the Department of Commerce (in particular the*

12 *National Oceanic and Atmospheric Administration, the Na-*

13 *tional Institute of Standards and Technology, the National*

14 *Technical Information Service, and the Bureau of the*

15 *Census), the Department of Defense, the National Aeronau-*

16 *tics and Space Administration, the Department of Energy,*

17 *the National Institutes of Health, the Library of Congress,*

18 *the United States Geological Survey, the Department of Ag-*

19 *riculture, and other agencies identified by the Director of the*

20 *Office of Science and Technology Policy, shall promote de-*

21 *velopment of information services over the National Research*

22 *and Education Network established under section 201 of this*

23 *Act. These services shall include, but not be limited to—*

24   *(1) directories of users of networks;*

1   *(2) directories of data bases available over the*

2 *Network;*

3   *(3) identifying, cataloguing, and providing for*

4 *access to unclassified Federal scientific data bases, in-*

5 *cluding weather data, census data, economic data, and*

6 *remote sensing satellite data, and providing data bases*

7 *and knowledge banks for use by artificial intelligence*

8 *programs;*

9   *(4) digital libraries to video programming, books,*

10 *and journals stored in electronic form and other com-*

11 *puter data;*

12   *(5) orientation and training of users of data bases*

13 *and networks;*

14   *(6) commercial information services to researchers*

15 *using the Network;*

16   *(7) rapid prototyping of integrated circuits and*

17 *other devices using centralized facilities connected to*

18 *the Network; and*

19   *(8) technology to support computer-based collabo-*

20 *ration that allows researchers around the Nation to*

21 *share information and instrumentation.*

22   *SEC. 302. Within one year after the date of enactment*

23 *of this Act, the Office of Science and Technology Policy shall*

24 *report to the Congress on—*

(1) how commercial information service providers could be charged for access to the National Research and Education Network in order to defray some of the Network operating expenses;

(2) the technological feasibility of allowing commercial information service providers to use the Network and other federally-funded research networks;

(3) how Network users could be charged for such commercial information services;

(4) how best to protect the copyrights of authors whose work may be distributed over the Network; and

(5) appropriate policies to ensure the security of resources available on the Network and protect the privacy of users of networks.

TITLE IV—SOFTWARE

SEC. 401. (a) The Office of Science and Technology Policy, as indicated in the National High-Performance Computing Plan (hereinafter referred to as the "Plan") developed and implemented under title VI of the National Science and Technology Policy, Organization, and Priorities Act of 1976, as added by section 101 of this Act, shall oversee the cooperative efforts of Federal departments and agencies in the research and development of high-performance computer software, including projects focused on astrophysics, geophysics,

1 *engineering, materials, biochemistry, plasma physics, and*

2 *weather and climate forecasting.*

3 *(b)(1) The National Science Foundation and the Na-*

4 *tional Aeronautics and Space Administration shall define*

5 *several Grand Challenges and provide for the research and*

6 *development of the high-performance computer software and*

7 *hardware needed to address such Grand Challenges.*

8 *(2) The Grand Challenges to be addressed by the*

9 *National Science Foundation under paragraph (1) could*

10 *include—*

11 *(A) prediction of global change, with the goal to*

12 *understand the coupled atmosphere, ocean, biosphere*

13 *system in enough detail to be able to make long-range*

14 *predictions about its behavior and determine its re-*

15 *sponse to human-caused releases of carbon dioxide,*

16 *methane, chlorofluorocarbons, and other gases;*

17 *(B) materials science, with the goal to use high-*

18 *performance computing to improve our understanding*

19 *of the atomic nature of materials, leading to the design*

20 *and production of improved semiconductors, supercon-*

21 *ductors, ceramics, and other materials;*

22 *(C) computer vision, with the goal to develop*

23 *vision systems for computers and robots;*

24 *(D) ocean sciences, with the goal to develop a*

25 *global ocean model incorporating temperature, chemical*

1   *composition, circulation, and coupling of the ocean and*

2   *atmosphere; and*

3   *(E) astronomy, with the goal to develop the com-*

4   *puter systems and algorithms needed to process and*

5   *analyze the very large volume of data generated by*

6   *radio telescopes such as the Very Large Array and*

7   *other astronomical facilities.*

8   *(3) The Grand Challenges to be addressed under para-*

9   *graph (1) by the National Aeronautics and Space Adminis-*

10 *tration could include—*

11   *(A) turbulence, with the goal to better understand*

12   *turbulence to allow engineers to more accurately model*

13   *the aerodynamic behavior of airplanes, spacecraft,*

14   *ships, submarines, trucks, automobiles, and other*

15   *vehicles;*

16   *(B) transportation, with the goal to use computer*

17   *models in the design of air and land vehicles in order*

18   *to improve their stability, performance, and life-cycle;*

19   *(C) prediction of global change, with the goal to*

20   *understand the coupled atmosphere, ocean, biosphere*

21   *system in enough detail to be able to make long-range*

22   *predictions about its behavior and determine its re-*

23   *sponse to human-caused releases of carbon dioxide,*

24   *methane, chlorofluorocarbons, and other gases; and*

1   *(D) speech, with the goal to develop computer sys-*

2   *tems that can understand normal human speech.*

3   *(4) The National Science Foundation and the National*

4   *Aeronautics and Space Administration shall support collabo-*

5   *rative research groups consisting of scientists and engineers*

6   *concerned with a particular Grand Challenge, software and*

7   *systems engineers, and algorithm designers, and provide*

8   *them with—*

9   *(A) computational and experimental facilities, in-*

10   *cluding supercomputers for numerical modeling;*

11   *(B) access to the National Research and Educa-*

12   *tional Network and other computer networks; and*

13   *(C) access to and technology for effectively utiliz-*

14   *ing scientific data bases.*

15   *(c) The National Science Foundation shall support the*

16   *development of software tools and components to accelerate*

17   *development of software for computers, especially supercom-*

18   *puters. Support shall be provided for research on fundamen-*

19   *tal algorithms, models of computation, program analysis, and*

20   *new programming languages. Particular emphasis shall be*

21   *given to development of programming languages, compilers,*

22   *operating systems, and software tools for parallel computer*

23   *systems.*

24   *SEC. 402. The National Science Foundation shall es-*

25   *tablish clearinghouses to improve, document, evaluate, and*

1 *distribute unclassified public-domain software developed by*

2 *federally-funded researchers and other software, including*

3 *federally-funded educational and training software. Such*

4 *clearinghouses shall—*

5   *(1) maintain libraries of programs;*

6   *(2) provide funding to researchers to improve and*

7 *maintain software they have developed;*

8   *(3) help researchers locate the software they need;*

9   *(4) make software available through the National*

10 *Research and Education Network; and*

11   *(5) promote commercialization of software where*

12 *possible.*

13   *SEC. 403. The National Institute of Standards and*

14 *Technology shall adopt standards, developed under an open*

15 *standards setting process and in conjunction with industry,*

16 *for software programs purchased or developed by the Federal*

17 *Government. The purpose of these standards shall be to pro-*

18 *mote development of interoperable software systems that can*

19 *be used on different computer systems with different operat-*

20 *ing systems.*

21   *SEC. 404. (a) The Secretary of Commerce shall con-*

22 *duct a study to—*

23   *(1) evaluate the impact of Federal procurement*

24 *regulations which require that contractors providing*

25 *software to the Federal Government share the rights to*

1 *proprietary software development tools that the contrac-*

2 *tors used to develop the software; and*

3   *(2) determine whether such regulations discourage*

4 *development of improved software development tools*

5 *and techniques.*

6 *(b) The Secretary shall, within one year after the date*

7 *of enactment of this Act, report to the Congress regarding the*

8 *results of the study conducted under subsection (a).*

9   *TITLE V—COMPUTER SYSTEMS*

10   *Sec. 501. The National Science Foundation shall pro-*

11 *vide for research and development on all aspects of high-*

12 *performance computer systems, including processors, memory*

13 *and mass storage devices, input/output devices, and associat-*

14 *ed systems software.*

15   *Sec. 502. Where appropriate, Federal agencies shall*

16 *procure prototype or early production models of new high-*

17 *performance computer systems and sub-systems to stimulate*

18 *hardware and software development in North American com-*

19 *panies. Particular emphasis shall be given to promoting de-*

20 *velopment of advanced display technology, alternative com-*

21 *puter architectures, advanced peripheral storage devices, and*

22 *very high-speed communication links.*

23   *Sec. 503. Within 120 days following the date of enact-*

24 *ment of this Act, the Secretary of Commerce, in consultation*

25 *with the Department of State, the Department of Defense, the*

1 *Central Intelligence Agency, the National Security Agency,*

2 *and other appropriate agencies, shall review export controls*

3 *that hinder the devlopment of foreign markets for supercom-*

4 *puter and other high-performance computer technology made*

5 *by North American companies, and report to the Congress*

6 *the results of such review.*

7 *TITLE VI—BASIC RESEARCH AND EDUCATION*

8 SEC. 601. *The Office of Science and Technology Policy*

9 *shall oversee and coordinate efforts of the relevant depart-*

10 *ments and agencies to—*

11 *(1) support basic research on computer technology;*

12 *(2) create technology transfer mechanisms to*

13 *ensure that the results of basic research are readily*

14 *available to North American companies;*

15 *(3) promote basic research in computer science,*

16 *computational science, library and information sci-*

17 *ences, electrical engineering, and materials science;*

18 *and*

19 *(4) educate and train more researchers in com-*

20 *puter science and computational science.*

21 *TITLE VII—AUTHORIZATION OF*

22 *APPROPRIATIONS*

23 SEC. 701.(a) *There are authorized to be appropriated to*

24 *the National Science Foundation for the research, develop-*

25 *ment, and implementation of the National Research and*

1 *Education Network, in accordance with the purposes of title*

2 *II, $15,000,000 for fiscal year 1991, $25,000,000 for fiscal*

3 *year 1992, $55,000,000 for fiscal year 1993, $50,000,000*

4 *for fiscal year 1994, and $50,000,000 for fiscal year 1995.*

5 *(b) There are authorized to be appropriated to the Na-*

6 *tional Science Foundation for the purposes of titles III, IV,*

7 *and V of this Act, $23,000,000 for fiscal year 1991,*

8 *$53,000,000 for fiscal year 1992, $77,000,000 for fiscal*

9 *year 1993, $107,000,000 for fiscal year 1994, and*

10 *$131,000,000 for fiscal year 1995.*

11 *(c) To expand its traditional role in supporting basic*

12 *research in universities and colleges, and in training scien-*

13 *tists and engineers in computer science, computational sci-*

14 *ence, library and information sciences, and electrical engi-*

15 *neering, there are authorized to be appropriated to the Na-*

16 *tional Science Foundation, $8,000,000 for fiscal year 1991,*

17 *$10,000,000 for fiscal year 1992, $13,000,000 for fiscal*

18 *year 1993, $15,000,000 for fiscal year 1994, and*

19 *$18,000,000 for fiscal year 1995.*

20 *SEC. 702. There are authorized to be appropriated to*

21 *the National Aeronautics and Space Administration for the*

22 *purposes of titles II, III, IV, V, and VI of this Act,*

23 *$22,000,000 for fiscal year 1991, $45,000,000 for fiscal*

24 *year 1992, $67,000,000 for fiscal year 1993, $89,000,000*

25 *for fiscal year 1994, and $115,000,000 for fiscal year 1995.*

1   SEC. 703. *The amounts authorized to be appropriated*

2   *under sections 701 and 702 are in addition to any amounts*

3   *that may be authorized to be appropriated under other laws.*

D

S. 1067,
High-Performance Computing Act of 1990,
U.S. Congress, Senate, 101st Congress, October 25, 1990
[version passed by the Senate].

IN THE HOUSE OF REPRESENTATIVES

OCTOBER 25, 1990

Referred to the Committee on Science, Space, and Technology

AN ACT

To provide for a coordinated Federal research program to ensure continued United States leadership in high-performance computing.

1   *Be it enacted by the Senate and House of Representa-*

2 *tives of the United States of America in Congress assembled,*

3 **SECTION 1. SHORT TITLE.**

4   This act may be cited as the "High-Performance Com-

5 puting Act of 1990".

6 **SEC. 2. FINDINGS AND PURPOSE.**

7   (a) The Congress finds the following:

1   (1) Advances in computer science and technology

2 are vital to the Nation's prosperity, national and eco-

3 nomic security, and scientific advancement.

4   (2) The United States currently leads the world in

5 the development and use of high-performance comput-

6 ing for national security, industrial productivity, and

7 science and engineering, but that lead is being chal-

8 lenged by foreign competitors.

9   (3) Further research, improved computer research

10 networks, and more effective technology transfer from

11 government to industry are necessary for the United

12 States to fully reap the benefits of high-performance

13 computing.

14   (4) Several Federal agencies have ongoing high-

15 performance computing programs, but improved inter-

16 agency coordination, cooperation, and planning could

17 enhance the effectiveness of these programs.

18   (5) A 1989 report by the Office of Science and

19 Technology Policy outlining a research and develop-

20 ment strategy for high-performance computing provides

21 a framework for a multi-agency high-performance com-

22 puting program.

23 (b) It is the purpose of Congress in this Act to help

24 ensure the continued leadership of the United States in high-

1 performance computing and its applications. This requires

2 that the United States Government—

3   (1) expand Federal support for research, develop-

4   ment, and application of high-performance computing

5   in order to—

6   (A) establish a high-capacity national re-

7   search and education computer network;

8   (B) expand the number of researchers, educa-

9   tors, and students with training in high-perform-

10   ance computing and access to high-performance

11   computing resources;

12   (C) develop an information infrastructure of

13   data bases, services, access mechanisms, and re-

14   search facilities which is available for use through

15   such a national network;

16   (D) stimulate research on software tech-

17   nology;

18   (E) promote the more rapid development and

19   wider distribution of computer software tools and

20   applications software;

21   (F) accelerate the development of computer

22   systems and subsystems;

23   (G) provide for the application of high-per-

24   formance computing to Grand Challenges; and

S 1067 RFH

1   (H) invest in basic research and education;

2   and

3   (2) improve planning and coordination of Federal

4   research and development on high-performance com-

5   puting.

6 **SEC. 3. DEFINITIONS.**

7   As used in this Act, the term—

8   (1) "Director" means the Director of the Office of

9   Science and Technology Policy; and

10   (2) "Council" means the Federal Coordinating

11   Council for Science, Engineering, and Technology

12   chaired by the Director of the Office of Science and

13   Technology Policy.

14 **SEC. 4. MISCELLANEOUS PROVISIONS.**

15   (a) Except to the extent the appropriate Federal agency

16 or department head determines, the provisions of this Act

17 shall not apply to—

18   (1) programs or activities regarding computer sys-

19   tems that process classified information; or

20   (2) computer systems the function, operation, or

21   use of which are those delineated in paragraphs (1)

22   through (5) of section 2315(a) of title 10, United States

23   Code.

24   (b) Where appropriate, and in accordance with Federal

25 contracting law, Federal agencies and departments may pro-

1 cure prototype or early production models of new high-per-

2 formance computer systems and subsystems to stimulate

3 hardware and software development.

4   (c) Nothing in this Act or in any amendment made by

5 this Act limits the authority or ability of any Federal agency

6 or department to undertake activities, including research, de-

7 velopment, or demonstration, in high-performance computing

8 or computer network applications or technologies.

9   (d) Nothing in this Act shall be deemed to convey to any

10 person, partnership, corporation, or other entity immunity

11 from civil or criminal liability under any antitrust law or to

12 create defenses to actions under any antitrust law. As used in

13 this section, "antitrust laws" means those Acts set forth in

14 section 1 of the Clayton Act (15 U.S.C. 12), as amended.

15 TITLE I—THE HIGH-PERFORMANCE COMPUTING

16   ACT OF 1990

17 **SEC. 101. NATIONAL HIGH-PERFORMANCE COMPUTING PRO-**

18   **GRAM.**

19   The National Science and Technology Policy, Organiza-

20 tion, and Priorities Act of 1976 (42 U.S.C. 6601 et seq.) is

21 amended by adding at the end the following new title:

"TITLE VII—NATIONAL HIGH-PERFORMANCE COMPUTING PROGRAM

"NATIONAL HIGH-PERFORMANCE COMPUTING PLAN

"SEC. 701. (a)(1) The President, through the Federal Coordinating Council for Science, Engineering, and Technology (hereafter in this title referred to as the 'Council'), shall, in accordance with the provisions of this title—

"(A) develop a National High-Performance Computing Plan (hereafter in this title referred to as the 'Plan'); and

"(B) provide for interagency coordination of the Federal high-performance computing program established by this title.

The Plan shall contain recommendations for a five-year national effort and shall be submitted to the Congress within one year after the date of enactment of this title. The Plan shall be resubmitted upon revision at least once every two years thereafter.

"(2) The Plan shall—

"(A) establish the goals and priorities for a Federal high-performance computing program for the fiscal year in which the Plan (or revised Plan) is submitted and the succeeding four fiscal years;

1   "(B) set forth the recommended role of each Fed-

2   eral agency and department in implementing the Plan;

3   and

4   "(C) describe the levels of Federal funding for

5   each agency and department and specific activities, in-

6   cluding education, research activities, hardware and

7   software development, and acquisition and operating

8   expenses for computers and computer networks, re-

9   quired to achieve the goals and priorities established

10   under subparagraph (A).

11   "(3) The Plan shall address, where appropriate, the rel-

12 evant programs and activities of the following Federal agen-

13 cies and departments:

14   "(A) the National Science Foundation;

15   "(B) the Department of Commerce, particularly

16   the National Institute of Standards and Technology,

17   the National Oceanic and Atmospheric Administration,

18   and the National Telecommunications and Information

19   Administration;

20   "(C) the National Aeronautics and Space Admin-

21   istration;

22   "(D) the Department of Defense, particularly the

23   Defense Advanced Research Projects Agency;

24   "(E) the Department of Energy;

1   "(F) the Department of Health and Human Serv-

2   ices, particularly the National Institutes of Health and

3   the National Library of Medicine;

4   "(G) the Department of Education;

5   "(H) the Department of Agriculture, particularly

6   the National Agricultural Library; and

7   "(I) such other agencies and departments as the

8   President or the Chairman of the Council considers ap-

9   propriate.

10   "(4) In addition, the Plan shall take into consideration

11 the present and planned activities of the Library of Congress,

12 as deemed appropriate by the Librarian of Congress.

13   "(5) The Plan shall identify how agencies and depart-

14 ments can collaborate to—

15   "(A) ensure interoperability among computer net-

16   works run by the agencies and departments;

17   "(B) increase software productivity, capability,

18   portability, and reliability;

19   "(C) encourage, where appropriate, agency coop-

20   eration with industry in development and exchange of

21   software;

22   "(D) distribute software among the agencies and

23   departments;

24   "(E) distribute federally-funded software to State

25   and local governments, industry, and universities;

1   "(F) accelerate the development of high perform-

2   ance computer systems, subsystems, and associated

3   software;

4   "(G) provide the technical support and research

5   and development of high-performance computer soft-

6   ware and hardware needed to address Grand Chal-

7   lenges in astrophysics, geophysics, engineering, materi-

8   als, biochemistry, plasma physics, weather and climate

9   forecasting, and other fields; and

10   "(H) identify agency rules, regulations, policies,

11   and practices which can be changed to significantly im-

12   prove utilization of Federal high-performance comput-

13   ing and network facilities, and make recommendations

14   to such agencies for appropriate changes.

15   "(6) The Plan shall address the security requirements

16 and policies necessry to protect Federal research computer

17 networks and information resources accessible through Fed-

18 eral research computer networks. Agencies identified in the

19 Plan shall define and implement a security plan consistent

20 with the Plan.

21   "(b) The Council shall—

22   "(1) serve as lead entity responsible for develop-

23   ment of, and interagency coordination of the program

24   under, the Plan;

1   "(2) recommend ways to coordinate the high-per-

2   formance computing research and development activi-

3   ties of Federal agencies and departments and report at

4   least annually to the President, through the Chairman

5   of the Council, on any recommended changes in agency

6   or departmental roles that are needed to better imple-

7   ment the Plan;

8   "(3) review, prior to the President's submission to

9   the Congress of the annual budget estimate, each

10   agency and departmental budget estimate in the con-

11   text of the Plan and make the results of that review

12   available to the appropriate elements of the Executive

13   Office of the President, particularly the Office of Man-

14   agement and Budget; and

15   "(4) consult and coordinate with Federal agencies,

16   academic, State, industry, and other appropriate groups

17   conducting research on high-performance computing.

18   "(c) The Director of the Office of Science and Technolo-

19   gy Policy shall establish a High-Performance Computing Ad-

20   visory Panel consisting of prominent representatives from in-

21   dustry and academia who are specially qualified to provide

22   the Council with advice and information on high-performance

23   computing. The Panel shall provide the Council with an inde-

24   pendent assessment of—

25   "(1) progress made in implementing the Plan;

1   "(2) the need to revise the Plan;

2   "(3) the balance between the components of the

3   Plan;

4   "(4) whether the research and development

5   funded under the Plan is helping to maintain United

6   States leadership in computing technology; and

7   "(5) other issues identified by the Director.

8   "(d)(1) Each appropriate Federal agency and depart-

9   ment involved in high-performance computing shall, as part

10   of its annual request for appropriations to the Office of Man-

11   agement and Budget, submit a report to the Office identifying

12   each element of its high-performance computing activities,

13   which—

14   "(A) specifies whether each such element (i) con-

15   tributes primarily to the implementation of the Plan or

16   (ii) contributes primarily to the achievement of other

17   objectives but aids Plan implementation in important

18   ways; and

19   "(B) states the portion of its request for appro-

20   priations that is allocated to each such element.

21   "(2) The Office of Management and Budget shall review

22   each such report in light of the goals, priorities, and agency

23   and departmental responsibilities set forth in the Plan, and

24   shall include, in the President's annual budget estimate, a

25   statement of the portion of each appropriate agency or de-

1 partment's annual budget estimate that is allocated to each
2 element of such agency or department's high-performance
3 computing activities.

4 "(e) As used in this section, the term 'Grand Challenge'
5 means a fundamental problem in science and engineering,
6 with broad economic and scientific impact, whose solution
7 will require the application of high-performance computing
8 resources.

9 "ANNUAL REPORT

10 "SEC. 702. The Chairman of the Council shall prepare
11 and submit to the President and the Congress, not later than
12 March 1 of each year, an annual report on the activities con-
13 ducted pursuant to this title during the preceding fiscal year,
14 including—

15 "(1) a summary of the achievements of Federal
16 high-performance computing research and development
17 efforts during that preceding fiscal year;

18 "(2) an analysis of the progress made toward
19 achieving the goals and objectives of the Plan;

20 "(3) a copy and summary of the Plan and any
21 changes made in such Plan;

22 "(4) a summary of appropriate agency budgets for
23 high-performance computing activities for that preced-
24 ing fiscal year; and

1   "(5) any recommendations regarding additional

2   action or legislation which may be required to assist in

3   achieving the purposes of this title.".

4 **SEC. 102. NATIONAL RESEARCH AND EDUCATION NETWORK.**

5   (a) The National Science Foundation, the Department of

6 Defense, the Department of Energy, the Department of

7 Commerce, the National Aeronautics and Space Administra-

8 tion, and other appropriate agencies shall provide for the es-

9 tablishment of a national multi-gigabit-per-second research

10 and education computer network by 1996, to be known as

11 the National Research and Education Network (hereinafter

12 referred to as the "Network"), which shall link government,

13 industry, and the education community.

14   (b) The Network shall provide—

15   (1) computer users with appropriate access to su-

16   percomputers, computer data bases, and other research

17   facilities; and

18   (2) users of libraries and other educational institu-

19   tions with appropriate access to the Network and infor-

20   mation resources.

21   (c) The Network shall—

22   (1) be developed in close cooperation with the

23   computer, telecommunications, and information indus-

24   tries;

1 (2) be designed and developed with the advice of

2 potential users in government, industry, and the higher

3 education community;

4 (3) be established in a manner which fosters and

5 maintains competition and private sector investment in

6 high speed data networking within the telecommunica-

7 tions industry;

8 (4) be established in a manner which promotes re-

9 search and development leading to deployment of com-

10 mercial data communications and telecommunications

11 standards;

12 (5) where technically feasible, have accounting

13 mechanisms which allow, where appropriate, users or

14 groups of users to be charged for their usage of the

15 Network and copyrighted materials available over the

16 Network; and

17 (6) be phased into commercial operation as com-

18 mercial networks can meet the metworking needs of

19 American researchers and educators.

20 (d) The Department of Defense, through the Defense

21 Advanced Research Projects Agency, shall support research

22 and development of advanced fiber optics technology,

23 switches, and protocols needed to develop the Network.

1   (e) Within the Federal Government, the National Sci-

2 ence Foundation shall have primary responsibility for con-

3 necting colleges, universities, and libraries to the Network.

4   (f)(1) The President, through the Council, shall, within

5 one year after the date of the enactment of this Act, establish

6 an entity or entities to carry out the functions set forth in

7 paragraph (2).

8   (2) Consistent with the Plan developed under section

9 701 of the National Science and Technology Policy, Organi-

10 zation and Priorities Act of 1976 (42 U.S.C. 6601 et seq.),

11 as added by section 101 of this Act, the entity or entities

12 established under paragraph (1) shall—

13   (A) develop goals, strategy, and priorities for the

14   Network;

15   (B) identify the roles of Federal agencies and de-

16   partments implementing the Network;

17   (C) provide a mechanism to coordinate the activi-

18   ties of Federal agencies and departments in deploying

19   the Network;

20   (D) oversee the operation and evolution of the

21   Network;

22   (E) manage the connections between computer

23   networks of Federal agencies and departments;

24   (F) develop conditions for access to the Network;

25   and

1   (G) identify how existing and future computer net-

2 works of Federal agencies and departments could con-

3 tribute to the Network.

4   (3) The President shall report to Congress within one

5 year after the date of the enactment of this Act on the imple-

6 mentation of this subsection.

7   (g) In addition to other agency activities associated with

8 the establishment of the Network, the following actions shall

9 be taken:

10   (1) The Council shall submit to the Congress,

11   within one year after the date of enactment of this Act,

12   a report describing and evaluating effective mecha-

13   nisms for providing operating funds for the mainte-

14   nance and use of the Network, including user fees, in-

15   dustry support, and continued Federal investment, and

16   containing a plan for the eventual commercialization of

17   the Network.

18   (2) The National Institute of Standards and Tech-

19   nology shall adopt a common set of standards and

20   guidelines to provide interoperability, common user

21   interfaces to systems, and enhanced security for the

22   Network.

23   (h) Within one year after the date of enactment of this

24 Act, the Director, through the Council, shall report to the

25 Congress on—

1   (1) how commercial information service providers

2 could be charged for access to the Network;

3   (2) the technological feasibility of allowing com-

4 mercial information service providers to use the Net-

5 work and other federally-funded research networks;

6   (3) how Network users could be charged for such

7 commercial information services;

8   (4) how to protect the copyrights of material dis-

9 tributed over the Network; and

10   (5) appropriate policies to ensure the security of

11 resources available on the Network and to protect the

12 privacy of users of networks.

13   (i) Nothing in this section confers upon the entity or

14 entities established under subsection (f) any authority to

15 direct a Federal agency's or department's computer network-

16 ing activities.

17 **SEC. 103. ROLE OF THE NATIONAL SCIENCE FOUNDATION.**

18   (a) The National Science Foundation shall provide fund-

19 ing to enable researchers to access supercomputers. Prior to

20 deployment of the Network, the National Science Foundation

21 shall maintain, expand, and upgrade its existing computer

22 networks. Additional responsibilities include promoting devel-

23 opment of information services and data bases available over

24 such computer networks; facilitation of the documentation,

25 evaluation, and distribution of research software over such

1 computer networks; encouragement of continued develop-

2 ment of innovative software by industry; and promotion of

3 science and engineering education.

4   (b)(1) The National Science Foundation shall, and other

5 agencies and departments may, promote development of in-

6 formation services that could be provided over the Network

7 established under section 102. These services shall include,

8 but not be limited to, the provision of directories of users and

9 services on computer networks, databases of unclassified

10 Federal scientific data, training of users of data bases and

11 networks, access to commercial information services to re-

12 searchers using the Network, and technology to support com-

13 puter-based collaboration that allows researchers around the

14 Nation to share information and instrumentation.

15   (2) The Federal information services accessible over the

16 Network shall be provided in accordance with applicable law.

17 Appropriate protection shall be provided for copyright and

18 other intellectual property rights of information providers and

19 Network users, including appropriate mechanisms for fair re-

20 muneration of copyright holders for availability of and access

21 to their works over the Network.

22   (c) The National Science Foundation shall expand ef-

23 forts to improve, document, evaluate, and help distribute un-

24 classified public-domain software developed by federally-

25 funded researchers and other software, including federally-

1 funded educational and training software. Such efforts

2 shall—

    (1) maintain libraries of programs;

    (2) provide funding to researchers to improve and
    maintain software they have developed;

    (3) help researchers locate the software they need;

    (4) make software available through the Network;
    and

    (5) promote commercialization of software where
    possible.

11 (d)(1) There are authorized to be appropriated to the

12 National Science Foundation for the research, development,

13 and support of the Network, in accordance with the purposes

14 of section 102, $15,000,000 for fiscal year 1991,

15 $25,000,000 for fiscal year 1992, and $55,000,000 for fiscal

16 year 1993.

17 (2) There are authorized to be appropriated to the Na-

18 tional Science Foundation for the purposes of this title,

19 $31,000,000 for fiscal year 1991, $63,000,000 for fiscal year

20 1992, and $90,000,000 for fiscal year 1993.

21 (3) The amounts authorized to be appropriated under

22 this subsection are in addition to any amounts that may be

23 authorized to be appropriated under other laws.

1 **SEC. 104. THE ROLE OF THE NATIONAL AERONAUTICS AND**

2 **SPACE ADMINISTRATION.**

3   (a) The National Aeronautics and Space Administration

4 shall continue to conduct basic and applied research in high-

5 performance computing, particularly in the field of computa-

6 tional science, with emphasis on aeronautics and the process-

7 ing of remote sensing and space science data.

8   (b) There are authorized to be appropriated to the Na-

9 tional Aeronautics and Space Administration for the purposes

10 of this Act, $22,000,000 for fiscal year 1991, $45,000,000

11 for fiscal year 1992, and $67,000,000 for fiscal year 1993.

12   (c) The amounts authorized to be appropriated under

13 subsection (b) are in addition to any amounts that may be

14 authorized to be appropriated under other laws.

15 **SEC. 105. ROLE OF THE DEPARTMENT OF COMMERCE.**

16   (a) The National Institute of Standards and Technology

17 shall adopt standards and guidelines, and develop measure-

18 ment techniques and test methods, for the interoperability of

19 high-performance computers in networks and for common

20 user interfaces to systems. In addition, the National Institute

21 of Standards and Technology shall be responsible for devel-

22 oping benchmark tests and standards for high performance

23 computers and software. Pursuant to the Computer Security

24 Act of 1987 (Public Law 100–235; 100 Stat. 1724), the Na-

25 tional Institute of Standards and Technology shall continue

26 to be responsible for adopting standards and guidelines

1 needed to assure the cost-effective security and privacy of
2 sensitive information in Federal computer systems.

3   (b)(1) The Secretary of Commerce shall conduct a study
4 to—

5   (A) evaluate the impact of Federal procurement
6   regulations which require that contractors providing
7   software to the Federal Government share the rights
8   to proprietary software development tools that the con-
9   tractors used to develop the software; and

10   (B) determine whether such regulations discourage
11   development of improved software development tools
12   and techniques.

13   (2) The Secretary shall, within one year after the date
14 of enactment of this Act, report to the Congress regarding
15 the results of the study conducted under paragraph (1).

SEC. 106. FUNCTIONS OF THE FEDERAL COORDINATING COUN-
CIL FOR SCIENCE, ENGINEERING, AND TECH-
NOLOGY.

19   (a) Section 102(a)(6) of the National Science and Tech-
20 nology Policy, Organization, and Priorities Act of 1976 (42
21 U.S.C. 6602(a)(6)) is amended to read as follows:

22   "(6) The development and implementation of
23   long-range, interagency research plans to support
24   policy decisions regarding identified national and inter-
25   national concerns, and for which a sustained and co-

1 ordinated commitment to improving scientific under-

2 standing will be required.".

3 (b) Section 401 of the National Science and Technology

4 Policy, Organization, and Priorities Act of 1976 (42 U.S.C.

5 6651) is amended to read as follows:

6 "FUNCTIONS OF COUNCIL

7 "SEC. 401. (a) The Federal Coordinating Council for

8 Science, Engineering, and Technology (hereinafter referred

9 to as the 'Council') shall consider problems and developments

10 in the fields of science, engineering, and technology and re-

11 lated activities affecting more than one Federal agency, and

12 shall recommend policies and other measures designed to—

13 "(1) provide more effective planning and adminis-

14 tration of Federal scientific, engineering, and techno-

15 logical programs;

16 "(2) identify research needs, including areas re-

17 quiring additional emphasis;

18 "(3) achieve more effective utilization of the scien-

19 tific, engineering, and technological resources and fa-

20 cilities of Federal agencies, including the elimination of

21 unwarranted duplication; and

22 "(4) further international cooperation in science,

23 engineering, and technology.

24 "(b) The Council may be assigned responsibility for de-

25 veloping long-range and coordinated plans for scientific and

1 technical research which involve the participation of more

2 than two Federal agencies. Such plans shall—

3   "(1) identify research approaches and priorities

4   which most effectively advance scientific understanding

5   and provide a basis for policy decisions;

6   "(2) provide for effective cooperation and coordi-

7   nation of research among Federal agencies; and

8   "(3) encourage domestic and, as appropriate,

9   international cooperation among government, industry,

10   and university scientists.

11 "(c) The Council shall perform such other related advi-

12 sory duties as shall be assigned by the President or by the

13 Chairman of the Council.

14 "(d) For the purpose of carrying out the provisions of

15 this section, each Federal agency represented on the Council

16 shall furnish necessary assistance to the Council. Such assist-

17 ance may include—

18   "(1) detailing employees to the Council to perform

19   such functions, consistent with the purposes of this sec-

20   tion, as the Chairman of the Council may assign to

21   them; and

22   "(2) undertaking, upon request of the Chairman,

23   such special studies for the Council as come within the

24   scope of authority of the Council.

1 "(e) For the purpose of developing interagency plans,
2 conducting studies, and making reports as directed by the
3 Chairman, standing committees and working groups of the
4 Council may be established.".

5 "(c) Section 207(a)(1) of the National Science and Tech-
6 nology Policy, Organization, and Priorities Act of 1976 (42
7 U.S.C. 6616(a)(1)) is amended by striking "established under
8 Title IV".

9 TITLE II—DEPARTMENT OF ENERGY HIGH-
10 PERFORMANCE COMPUTING ACT OF 1990

11 **SEC. 201. SHORT TITLE AND DEFINITIONS.**

12 (a) This title may be cited as the "Department of
13 Energy High-Performance Computing Act of 1990".

14 (b) For the purposes of this title, the term—

15 (1) "Secretary" means the Secretary of Energy;

16 (2) "Department" means the Department of
17 Energy;

18 (3) "Federal laboratory" means any laboratory, or
19 any federally-funded research and development center,
20 that is owned or leased or otherwise used by a Federal
21 agency or department and funded by the Federal Gov-
22 ernment, whether operated by the Government or by a
23 contractor;

24 (4) "national laboratory" means any Federal labo-
25 ratory that is owned by the Department of Energy;

1   (5) "educational institution" means a degree

2   granting institution of at least a Baccalaureate level;

3   and

4   (6) "software creation" means any innovation or

5   preparation of new computer software of whatever kind

6   or description whether patentable or unpatentable, and

7   whether copyrightable or non-copyrightable.

8 **SEC. 202. DEPARTMENT OF ENERGY HIGH-PERFORMANCE**

9   **COMPUTING PROGRAM.**

10   (a) The Secretary, acting in accordance with the author-

11 ity provided by the Federal Nonnuclear Energy Research

12 and Development Act of 1974 (42 U.S.C. 5901 et seq.) and

13 subject to available appropriations, shall establish a High-

14 Performance Computing Program (hereinafter referred to as

15 the "HPC Program").

16   (b) Within one year after the date of the enactment of

17 this Act, the Secretary shall establish a management plan to

18 carry out HPC Program activities. The plan shall—

19   (1) be developed in conjunction with the Direc-

20   tor's overall efforts to promote high-performance com-

21   puting;

22   (2) summarize all ongoing high-performance com-

23   puting activities and resources at the Department that

24   are not classified or otherwise restricted;

1   (3) describe the levels of funding for each aspect

2   of high-performance computing that are not classified

3   or otherwise restricted;

4   (4) establish long range goals and priorities for re-

5   search, development, and application of high-perform-

6   ance computing at the department, and devise a strate-

7   gy for achieving them; and

8   (5) ensure that technology developed pursuant to

9   the HPC Program is transferred to the private sector

10   in accordance with applicable law.

11 SEC. 203. DEPARTMENT OF ENERGY HIGH-PERFORMANCE

12   COMPUTING PROGRAM ACTIVITIES.

13   (a)(1) The Secretary shall provide for a high-perform-

14 ance computer network (the "Department of Energy Net-

15 work") to link the government, research, industry, and edu-

16 cation constituencies of the Department.

17   (2) The Secretary may create networks or make use of

18 existing networks (including the Network established under

19 section 102), to carry out the requirements of paragraph (1).

20   (b) The Secretary shall promote education and research

21 in high-performance computational science and related fields

22 that require the application of high-performance computing

23 resources by making the Department's high performance

24 computing resources more available to undergraduate and

1 graduate students, post-doctoral fellows, and faculty from the

2 Nation's educational institutions.

3 (c) The Secretary shall establish at least two Collabora-

4 tive Consortia, and as many more as the Secretary deter-

5 mines are needed to carry out the purposes of this Act, by

6 soliciting and selecting proposals.

7 (1) Each Collaborative Consortium shall—

8 (A) undertake basic research and develop-

9 ment of high-performance computing hardware

10 and associated software technology;

11 (B) undertake research and development of

12 advanced prototype networks;

13 (C) conduct research directed at scientific

14 and technical problems whose solutions require

15 the application of high performance computing re-

16 sources;

17 (D) promote the testing and uses of new

18 types of high-performance-computing and related

19 software and equipment;

20 (E) serve as a vehicle for computing vendors

21 to test new ideas and technology in a sophisticat-

22 ed computing environment; and

23 (F) disseminate information to Federal de-

24 partments and agencies, the private sector, educa-

25 tional institutions, and other potential users on the

1 availability of high-performance computing
2 facilities.

3   (2) Each Collaborative Consortium shall be com-
4 prised of a lead institution, which has responsibility for
5 the direction and performance of the consortium, and
6 participants from industry, Federal laboratories or
7 agencies, educational institutions, and others, as may
8 be appropriate.

9   (3) Each lead institution shall be a national labo-
10 ratory which has the experience in research on prob-
11 lems that require the application of high-performance
12 computing resources.

13   (4) Industrial participants in each consortium shall
14 not be reimbursed for costs associated with their own
15 involvement, though the consortium may fund research
16 and development associated with prototype computing
17 technology.

18 (c) The provisions of the National Cooperative Research
19 Act of 1984 (15 U.S.C. 4301–4305) shall apply to research
20 activities taken pursuant to this section.

21 (d) Each Collaborative Consortium may be established
22 by a Cooperative Research and Development Agreement as
23 provided in section 12 of the Stevenson-Wydler Technology
24 Innovation Act of 1980 (15 U.S.C. 3710a).

1   (e) The Secretary shall report annually to the Commit-

2 tee on Energy and Natural Resources of the Senate and the

3 Committee on Science, Space, and Technology of the House

4 of Representatives regarding the HPC Program.

5 **SEC. 204. GOVERNMENT AND PRIVATE SECTOR COOPERATION.**

6   In accordance with applicable law, the Secretary may

7 cooperate with, solicit help from, provide funds to, or enter

8 into contracts with private constractors, industry, govern-

9 ment, universities, or any other person or entity the Secre-

10 tary deems necessary in carrying out the provisions of this

11 Act to the extent appropriated funds are available.

12 **SEC. 205. OWNERSHIP OF INVENTIONS AND CREATIONS.**

13   (a) Except as otherwise provided by the National Com-

14 petitiveness Technology Transfer Act of 1989 (103 Stat.

15 1674) and any other applicable law, title to any invention or

16 software creation developed under this title shall vest in the

17 United States and shall be governed by the provisions of sec-

18 tion 9 of the Federal Nonnuclear Energy Research and De-

19 velopment Act of 1974 (42 U.S.C. 5908).

20   (b) Trade secrets and commercial or financial informa-

21 tion that is privileged and confidential and which is obtained

22 from a non-Federal party participating in research or other

23 activities under this title may be withheld in accordance with

24 section 552(b)(4) of title 5, United States Code.

1   (c) The Secretary, for a period of up to 5 years after the

2 development of information that results from research and

3 development activities conducted under this title and that

4 would be a trade secret or commercial or financial informa-

5 tion that is privileged or confidential, under the meaning of

6 section 552(b)(4) of title 5, United States Code, if the infor-

7 mation had been obtained from a non-Federal party, may

8 provide appropriate protection against the dissemination of

9 such information, including exemption from subchapter II of

10 chapter 5 of title 5, United States Code.

11 **SEC. 206. AUTHORIZATION.**

12   In addition to existing authorizations that may be used

13 to carry out this title, there is authorized to be appropriated

14 for the purposes of this title $65,000,000 for fiscal year

15 1991, $100,000,000 for fiscal year 1992, and $135,000,000

16 for fiscal year 1993.

    Passed the Senate October 25 (legislative day, Octo-
ber 2), 1990.

    Attest: WALTER J. STEWART,

Secretary.

E

S. 272,
High-Performance Computing Act of 1991,
U.S. Congress, Senate, 102nd Congress, January 24, 1991.

To provide for a coordinated Federal research program to ensure continued
United States leadership in high-performance computing.

IN THE SENATE OF THE UNITED STATES

JANUARY 24 (legislative day, JANUARY 3), 1991

Mr. GORE (for himself, Mr. HOLLINGS, Mr. KENNEDY, Mr. PRESSLER, Mr. FORD, Mr. BREAUX, Mr. BINGAMAN, Mr. ROBB, Mr. KERRY, Mr. KASTEN, Mr. GLENN, Mr. JEFFORDS, Mr. KERREY, Mr. REID, Mr. DURENBERGER, Mr. HATFIELD, Mr. KOHL, Mr. CONRAD, and Mr. RIEGLE) introduced the following bill; which was read twice and referred to the Committee on Commerce, Science, and Transportation

---

A BILL

To provide for a coordinated Federal research program to ensure continued United States leadership in high-performance computing.

1   *Be it enacted by the Senate and House of Representa-*

2 *tives of the United States of America in Congress assembled,*

3 **SECTION 1. SHORT TITLE.**

4   This Act may be cited as the "High-Performance com-

5 puting Act of 1991".

6 **SEC 2. FINDINGS AND PURPOSE.**

7   (a) The Congress finds the following:

1   (1) Advances in computer science and technology

2   are vital to the Nation's prosperity, national economic

3   security, and scientific advancement.

4   (2) The United States currently leads the world in

5   the development and use of high-performance comput-

6   ing for national security, industrial productivity, and

7   science and engineering, but that lead is being chal-

8   lenged by foreign competitors.

9   (3) Further research, improved computer research

10   networks, and more effective technology transfer from

11   government to industry are necessary for the United

12   States to fully reap the benefits of high-performance

13   computing.

14   (4) Several Federal agencies have ongoing high-

15   performance computing programs, but improved inter-

16   agency coordination, cooperation, and planning could

17   enhance the effectiveness of these programs.

18   (5) A 1989 report by the Office of Science and

19   Technology Policy outlining a research and develop-

20   ment strategy for high-performance computing provides

21   a framework for a multiagency high-performance com-

22   puting program.

23   (b) It is the purpose of Congress in this Act to help

24   ensure the continued leadership of the United States in high-

1 performance computing and its applications. This requires

2 that the United States Government—

    3   (1) expand Federal support for research, develop-

    4   ment, and application of high-performance computing

    5   in order to—

    6   (A) establish a high-capacity national re-

    7   search and education computer network;

    8   (B) expand the number of researchers, educa-

    9   tors, and students with training in high-perform-

    10   ance computing and access to high-performance

    11   computing resources;

    12   (C) develop an information infrastructure of

    13   data bases, services, access mechanisms, and re-

    14   search facilities which is available for use through

    15   such a national network;

    16   (D) stimulate research on software technolo-

    17   gy;

    18   (E) promote the more rapid development and

    19   wider distribution of computer software tools and

    20   applications software;

    21   (F) accelerate the development of computer

    22   systems and subsystems;

    23   (G) provide for the application of high-per-

    24   formance computing to Grand Challenges; and

1   (H) invest in basic research and education;

2   and

3   (2) improve planning and coordination of Federal

4   research and development on high-performance com-

5   puting.

6 **SEC. 3. DEFINITIONS.**

7   As used in this Act, the term—

8   (1) "Director" means the Director of the Office of

9   Science and Technology Policy; and

10   (2) "Council" means the Federal Coordinating

11   Council for Science, Engineering, and Technology

12   chaired by the Director of the Office of Science and

13   Technology Policy.

14 **SEC. 4. MISCELLANEOUS PROVISIONS.**

15   (a) Except to the extent the appropriate Federal agency

16 or department head determines, the provisions of this Act

17 shall not apply to—

18   (1) programs or activities regarding computer sys-

19   tems that process classified information; or

20   (2) computer systems the function, operation, or

21   use of which are those delineated in paragraphs (1)

22   through (5) of section 2315(a) of title 10, United States

23   Code.

24   (b) Where appropriate, and in accordance with Federal

25 contracting law, Federal agencies and departments shall pro-

1 cure prototype or early production models of new high-per-

2 formance computer systems and subsystems to stimulate

3 hardware and software development.

4 **SEC. 5. NATIONAL HIGH-PERFORMANCE COMPUTING PRO-**

5   **GRAM.**

6   The National Science and Technology Policy, Organiza-

7 tion, and Priorities Act of 1976 (42 U.S.C. 6601 et seq.) is

8 amended by adding at the end the following new title:

9   "TITLE VII—NATIONAL HIGH-PERFORMANCE

10   COMPUTING PROGRAM

11   "NATIONAL HIGH-PERFORMANCE COMPUTING PLAN

12   "SEC. 701. (a)(1) The President, through the Federal

13 Coordinating Council for Science, Engineering, and Technol-

14 ogy (hereafter in this title referred to as the 'Council'), shall,

15 in accordance with the provisions of this title—

16   "(A) develop and implement a National High-Per-

17   formance Computing Plan (hereafter in this title re-

18   ferred to as the 'Plan'); and

19   "(B) provide for interagency coordination of the

20   Federal high-performance computing program estab-

21   lished by this title.

22 The Plan shall contain recommendations for a five-year na-

23 tional effort and shall be submitted to the Congress within

24 one year after the date of enactment of this title. The Plan

1 shall be resubmitted upon revision at least once every two

2 years thereafter.

3   "(2) The Plan shall—

4   "(A) establish the goals and priorities for a Fed-

5   eral high-performance computing program for the fiscal

6   year in which the Plan (or revised Plan) is submitted

7   and the succeeding four fiscal years;

8   "(B) set forth the role of each Federal agency and

9   department in implementing the Plan; and

10   "(C) describe the levels of Federal funding for

11   each agency and department and specific activities, in-

12   cluding education, research activities, hardware and

13   software development, establishment of a national giga-

14   bits-per-second computer network, to be known as the

15   National Research and Education Network, and acqui-

16   sition and operating expenses for computers and com-

17   puter networks, required to achieve the goals and pri-

18   orities established under subparagraph (A).

19   "(3) The Plan shall address, where appropriate, the rel-

20 evant programs and activities of the following Federal agen-

21 cies and departments:

22   "(A) the National Science Foundation;

23   "(B) the Department of Commerce, particularly

24   the National Institute of Standards and Technology,

25   the National Oceanic and Atmospheric Administration,

1 and the National Telecommunications and Information
2 Administration;

3   "(C) the National Aeronautics and Space Admin-
4 istration;

5   "(D) the Department of Defense, particularly the
6 Defense Advanced Research Projects Agency;

7   "(E) the Department of Energy;

8   "(F) the Department of Health and Human Serv-
9 ices, particularly the National Institutes of Health and
10 the National Library of Medicine;

11   "(G) the Department of Education;

12   "(H) the Department of Agriculture, particularly
13 the National Agricultural Library; and

14   "(I) such other agencies and departments as the
15 President or the Chairman of the Council considers ap-
16 propriate.

17 "(4) In addition, the Plan shall take into consideration
18 the present and planned activities of the Library of Congress,
19 as deemed appropriate by the Librarian of Congress.

20 "(5) The Plan shall identify how agencies and depart-
21 ments can collaborate to—

22   "(A) ensure interoperability among computer net-
23 works run by the agencies and departments;

24   "(B) increase software productivity, capability,
25 portability, and reliability;

1 "(C) expand efforts to improve, document, and
2 evaluate unclassified public-domain software developed
3 by federally funded researchers and other software, in-
4 cluding federally funded educational and training soft-
5 ware;

6 "(D) cooperate, where appropriate, with industry
7 in development and exchange of software;

8 "(E) distribute software among the agencies and
9 departments;

10 "(F) distribute federally funded software to State
11 and local governments, industry, and universities;

12 "(G) accelerate the development of high perform-
13 ance computer systems, subsystems, and associated
14 software;

15 "(H) provide the technical support and research
16 and development of high-performance computer soft-
17 ware and hardware needed to address grand challenges
18 in astrophysics, geophysics, engineering, materials, bio-
19 chemistry, plasma physics, weather and climate for-
20 casting, and other fields;

21 "(I) provide for educating and training additional
22 undergraduate and graduate students in software engi-
23 neering, computer science, and computational science;
24 and

S 272 IS

1   "(J) identify agency rules, regulations, policies

2   and practices which can be changed to significantly im-

3   prove utilization of Federal high-performance comput-

4   ing and network facilities, and make recommendations

5   to such agencies for appropriate changes.

6   "(6) The Plan shall address the security requirements

7 and policies necessary to protect Federal research computer

8 networks and information resources accessible through Fed-

9 eral research computer networks. Agencies identified in the

10 Plan shall define and implement a security plan consistent

11 with the Plan.

12   "(b) The Council shall—

13   "(1) serve as lead entity responsible for develop-

14   ment of the Plan and interagency coordination of the

15   program established under the Plan;

16   "(2) coordinate the high-performance computing

17   research and development activities of Federal agencies

18   and departments and report at least annually to the

19   President, through the Chairman of the Council, on

20   any recommended changes in agency or departmental

21   roles that are needed to better implement the Plan;

22   "(3) review, prior to the President's submission to

23   the Congress of the annual budget estimate, each

24   agency and departmental budget estimate in the con-

25   text of the Plan and make the results of that review

1 available to the appropriate elements of the Executive

2 Office of the President, particularly the Office of Man-

3 agement and Budget; and

4   "(4) consult and coordinate with Federal agencies,

5 academic, State, industry, and other appropriate groups

6 conducting research on high-performance computing.

7 "(c) The Director of the Office of Science and Technolo-

8 gy Policy shall establish a High-Performance Computing Ad-

9 visory Panel consisting of prominent representatives from in-

10 dustry and academia who are specially qualified to provide

11 the Council with advice and information on high-performance

12 computing. The Panel shall provide the Council with an inde-

13 pendent assessment of—

14   "(1) progress made in implementing the Plan;

15   "(2) the need to revise the Plan;

16   "(3) the balance between the components of the

17 Plan;

18   "(4) whether the research and development

19 funded under the Plan is helping to maintain United

20 States leadership in computing technology; and

21   "(5) other issues identified by the Director.

22 "(d)(1) Each appropriate Federal agency and depart-

23 ment involved in high-performance computing shall, as part

24 of its annual request for appropriations to the Office of Man-

25 agement and Budget, submit a report to the Office identifying

1 each element of its high-performance computing activities,

2 which—

>"(A) specifies whether each such element (i) con-
tributes primarily to the implementation of the Plan or
(ii) contributes primarily to the achievement of other
objectives but aids Plan implementation in important
ways; and

>"(B) states the portion of its request for appro-
priations that is allocated to each such element.

"(2) The Office of Management and Budget shall review each such report in light of the goals, priorities, and agency and departmental responsibilities set forth in the Plan, and shall include, in the President's annual budget estimate, a statement of the portion of each appropriate agency or department's annual budget estimate that is allocated to each element of such agency or department's high-performance computing activities.

"(e) As used in this section, the term 'Grand Challenge' means a fundamental problem in science and engineering, with broad economic and scientific impact, whose solution will require the application of high-performance computing resources.

"ANNUAL REPORT

"SEC. 702. The Chairman of the Council shall prepare and submit to the President and the Congress, not later than March 1 of each year, an annual report on the activities con-

1 ducted pursuant to this title during the preceding fiscal year,

2 including—

3   "(1) a summary of the achievements of Federal

4   high-performance computing research and development

5   efforts during that preceding fiscal year;

6   "(2) an analysis of the progress made toward

7   achieving the goals and objectives of the Plan;

8   "(3) a copy and summary of the Plan and any

9   changes made in such Plan;

10   "(4) a summary of appropriate agency budgets for

11   high-performance computing activities for that preced-

12   ing fiscal year; and

13   "(5) any recommendations regarding additional

14   action or legislation which may be required to assist in

15   achieving the purposes of this title.".

16 **SEC. 6. NATIONAL RESEARCH AND EDUCATION NETWORK.**

17   (a) In accordance with the Plan developed under section

18 701 of the National Science and Technology Policy, Organi-

19 zation and Priorities Act of 1976 (42 U.S.C. 6601 et seq.),

20 as added by section 5 of this Act, the National Science Foun-

21 dation, in cooperation with the Department of Defense, the

22 Department of Energy, the Department of Commerce, the

23 National Aeronautics and Space Administration, and other

24 appropriate agencies, shall provide for the establishment of a

25 national multi-gigabit-per-second research and education

1 computer network by 1996, to be known as the National

2 Research and Education Network (hereinafter referred to as

3 the "Network"), which shall link government, industry, and

4 the education community.

5 (b) The Network shall provide users with appropriate

6 access to supercomputers, computer data bases, other re-

7 search facilities, and libraries.

8 (c) The Network shall—

9 (1) be developed in close cooperation with the

10 computer, telecommunications, and information indus-

11 tries;

12 (2) be designed and developed with the advice of

13 potential users in government, industry, and the higher

14 education community;

15 (3) be established in a manner which fosters and

16 maintains competition and private sector investment in

17 high speed data networking within the telecommunica-

18 tions industry;

19 (4) be established in a manner which promotes re-

20 search and development leading to deployment of com-

21 mercial data communications and telecommunications

22 standards;

23 (5) where technically feasible, have accounting

24 mechanisms which allow, where appropriate, users or

25 groups of users to be charged for their usage of the

1 Network and copyrighted materials available over the

2 Network; and

3   (6) be phased into commercial operation as com-

4 mercial networks can meet the networking needs of

5 American researchers and educators.

6 (d) The Department of Defense, through the Defense

7 Advanced Research Projects Agency, shall be lead agency

8 for research and development of advanced fiber optics tech-

9 nology, switches, and protocols needed to develop the Net-

10 work.

11 (e) Within the Federal Government, the National Sci-

12 ence Foundation shall have primary responsibility for con-

13 necting colleges, universities, and libraries to the Network.

14 (f)(1) The Council, within one year after the date of en-

15 actment of this Act and consistent with the Plan developed

16 under section 701 of the National Science and Technology

17 Policy, Organization, and Priorities Act of 1976 (42 U.S.C.

18 6601 et seq.), as added by section 5 of this Act, shall—

19   (A) develop goals, strategy, and priorities for the

20   Network;

21   (B) identify the roles of Federal agencies and de-

22   partments implementing the Network;

23   (C) provide a mechanism to coordinate the activi-

24   ties of Federal agencies and departments in deploying

25   the Network;

1   (D) oversee the operation and evolution of the
2   Network;

3   (E) manage the connections between computer
4   networks of Federal agencies and departments;

5   (F) develop conditions for access to the Network;
6   and

7   (G) identify how existing and future computer net-
8   works of Federal agencies and departments could con-
9   tribute to the Network.

10 (2) The President shall report to Congress within one
11 year after the date of enactment of this Act on the implemen-
12 tation of this subsection.

13 (g) In addition to other agency activities associated with
14 the establishment of the Network—

15   (1) the national Institute of Standards and Tech-
16   nology shall adopt a common set of standards and
17   guidelines to provide interoperability, common user
18   interfaces to systems, and enhanced security for the
19   Network; and

20   (2) the National Science Foundation, the National
21   Aeronautics and Space Administration, the Department
22   of Energy, the Department of Defense, the Depart-
23   ment of Commerce, the Department of the Interior,
24   the Department of Agriculture, the Department of
25   Health and Human Services, and the Environmental

1   Protection Agency are authorized to allow recipients of

2   Federal research grants to use grant moneys to pay for

3   computer networking expenses.

4   (h) Within one year after the date of enactment of this

5 Act, the Director, through the Council, shall report to the

6 Congress on—

7   (1) effective mechanisms for providing operating

8   funds for the maintenance and use of the Network, in-

9   cluding user fees, industry support, and continued Fed-

10   eral investment;

11   (2) plans for the eventual commercialization of the

12   Network;

13   (3) how commercial information service providers

14   could be charged for access to the Network;

15   (4) the technological feasibility of allowing com-

16   mercial information service providers to use the Net-

17   work and other federally funded research networks;

18   (5) how Network users could be charged for such

19   commercial information services;

20   (6) how to protect the copyrights of material dis-

21   tributed over the Network; and

22   (7) appropriate policies to ensure the security of

23   resources available on the Network and to protect the

24   privacy of users of networks.

SEC. 7. ROLE OF THE NATIONAL SCIENCE FOUNDATION.

(a) The National Science Foundation shall provide funding to enable researchers to access supercomputers. Prior to deployment of the Network, the National Science Foundation shall maintain, expand, and upgrade its existing computer networks. Additional responsibilities may include promoting development of information services and data bases available over such computer networks; facilitation of the documentation, evaluation, and distribution of research software over such computer networks; encouragement of continued development of innovative software by industry; and promotion of science and engineering education.

(b)(1) The National Science Foundation shall, in cooperation with other appropriate agencies and departments, promote development of information services that could be provided over the Network established under section 6. These services shall include, but not be limited to, the provision of directories of users and services on computer networks, data bases of unclassified Federal scientific data, training of users of data bases and networks, access to commercial information services to researchers using the Network, and technology to support computer-based collaboration that allows researchers around the Nation to share information and instrumentation.

(2) The Federal information services accessible over the Network shall be provided in accordance with applicable law.

1 Appropriate protection shall be provided for copyright and

2 other intellectual property rights of information providers and

3 Network users, including appropriate mechanisms for fair re-

4 muneration of copyright holders for availability of and access

5 to their works over the Network.

6   (c)(1) There are authorized to be appropriated to the

7 National Science Foundation for the purposes of this Act,

8 $46,000,000 for fiscal year 1992, $88,000,000 for fiscal year

9 1993, $145,000,000 for fiscal year 1994, $172,000,000 for

10 fiscal year 1995, and $199,000,000 for fiscal year 1996.

11   (2) Of the moneys authorized to be appropriated in sub-

12 section (c)(1), there is authorized for the research, develop-

13 ment, and support of the Network, in accordance with the

14 purposes of section 6, $15,000,000 for fiscal year 1992,

15 $25,000,000 for fiscal year 1993, $55,000,000 for fiscal year

16 1994, $50,000,000 for fiscal year 1995, and $50,000,000 for

17 fiscal year 1996.

18   (3) The amounts authorized to be appropriated under

19 this subsection are in addition to any amounts that may be

20 authorized to be appropriated under other laws.

21 **SEC. 8. THE ROLE OF THE NATIONAL AERONAUTICS AND**

22   **SPACE ADMINISTRATION.**

23   (a) The National Aeronautics and Space Administration

24 shall continue to conduct basic and applied research in high-

25 performance computing, particularly in the field of computa-

1 tional science, with emphasis on aeronautics and the process-

2 ing of remote sensing and space science data.

3   (b) There are authorized to be appropriated to the Na-

4 tional Aeronautics and Space Administration for the purposes

5 of this Act, $22,000,000 for fiscal year 1992, $45,000,000

6 for fiscal year 1993, $67,000,000 for fiscal year 1994,

7 $89,000,000 for fiscal year 1995, and $115,000,000 for

8 fiscal year 1996.

9   (c) The amounts authorized to be appropriated under

10 subsection (b) are in addition to any amounts that may be

11 authorized to be appropriated under other laws.

12 **SEC. 9. ROLE OF THE DEPARTMENT OF COMMERCE.**

13   (a) The National Institute of Standards and Technology

14 shall adopt standards and guidelines, and develop measure-

15 ment techniques and test methods, for the interoperability of

16 high-performance computers in networks and for common

17 user interfaces to systems. In addition, the National Institute

18 of Standards and Technology shall be responsible for devel-

19 oping benchmark tests and standards for high performance

20 computers and software. Pursuant to the Computer Security

21 Act of 1987 (Public Law 100–235; 101 Stat. 1724), the Na-

22 tional Institute of Standards and Technology shall continue

23 to be responsible for adopting standards and guidelines

24 needed to assure the cost-effective security and privacy of

25 sensitive information in Federal computer systems.

1   (b)(1) The Secretary of Commerce shall conduct a study

2 to—

3   (A) evaluate the impact of Federal procurement

4   regulations which require that contractors providing

5   software to the Federal Government share the rights

6   to proprietary software development tools that the con-

7   tractors used to develop the software; and

8   (B) determine whether such regulations discourage

9   development of improved software development tools

10   and techniques.

11   (2) The Secretary shall, within one year after the date

12 of enactment of this Act, report to the Congress regarding

13 the results of the study conducted under paragraph (1).

○

F

High-Performance Computing Act of 1990,
U.S. Congress, Senate, Senate Committee on Commerce, Science and Transportation. Report 101-387.

Calendar No. 710

101st Congress *2d Session*	SENATE	Report 101–387

HIGH-PERFORMANCE COMPUTING
ACT OF 1990

Mr. Hollings, from the Committee on Commerce, Science, and Transportation, submitted the following

R E P O R T

OF THE

SENATE COMMITTEE ON COMMERCE, SCIENCE, AND TRANSPORTATION

ON

S. 1067

July 23 (legislative day, July 10), 1990.—Ordered to be printed

---

U.S. GOVERNMENT PRINTING OFFICE

39-010   WASHINGTON : 1990

326

101st Congress 2d Session	SENATE	Report 101–387

HIGH-PERFORMANCE COMPUTING ACT OF 1990

July 23 (legislative day, July 10), 1990.—Ordered to be printed

Mr. Hollings, from the Committee on Commerce, Science, and Transportation, submitted the following

REPORT

[To accompany S. 1067]

The Committee on Commerce, Science, and Transportation, to which was referred the bill (S. 1067) to provide for a coordinated Federal research program to ensure continued United States leadership in high-performance computing, having considered the same, reports favorably thereon with an amendment in the nature of a substitute and recommends that the bill as amended do pass.

Purpose of the Bill

The primary objective of the legislation is to accelerate research, development, and application of high-performance computing in research, education, and industry. High-performance computing is the most advanced computing technology—the most sophisticated computer chips, the fastest computers with the largest memories, the fastest algorithms, and the fastest computer networks.

This bill authorizes Federal funding for the development and use of new supercomputers, advanced software, and a National Research and Education Network (NREN), a computer network capable of transmitting billions of bits (gigabits) of data per second. In total, the bill authorizes $650 million for the National Science Foundation (NSF) and $338 million for the National Aeronautics and Space Administration (NASA) for fiscal years (FY) 1991–95.

The bill also establishes a National High-Performance Computing (HPC) Program involving NSF, NASA, the Department of Energy (DOE), and the Defense Advanced Research Projects Agency (DARPA) of the Department of Defense (DOD), as well as

39–010

other agencies. This program would be planned and coordinated by the White House Office of Science and Technology Policy (OSTP).

Background and Needs

Importance of Computing

In the last 30 years, computer technology has transformed American science and industry. Today, computers are indispensable tools found in almost every laboratory, office, and factory. They have enabled researchers to solve previously unsolvable problems; have transformed the way products are designed, manufactured, and marketed; have changed the way offices are operated; and have given teachers a new, powerful educational tool.

The last five years have seen a rapid increase in the use of supercomputers in science and engineering. Supercomputers are commonly defined as the most powerful computers available at any given time. They usually cost $1–$20 million and are 1,000 to 100,000 times more powerful than a typical personal computer. Today's supercomputers are capable of making billions of mathematical calculations per second, which is about 50 to 100 times faster than the fastest computers available just ten years ago. Using complex computer "models," researchers now can simulate and test the behavior of advanced aircraft designs, proposed new drugs, and new manufacturing techniques. Scientists have used supercomputer models to understand better the Earth's climate and weather, the Nation's economy, the evolution of our galaxy, and even the voting patterns of Members of Congress.

To facilitate communication among researchers, students, and educators, and to promote the use of advanced computers, NSF and other Federal agencies have established fiber optic computer networks, which link researchers around the country to supercomputers, to other computing facilities, and to each other. Unlike copper telephone wires, fiber optic cable is capable of carrying the billions of bits of data generated every second by supercomputers. Such high data rates are needed because, for many types of computer models, scientists need sophisticated "visualization" techniques to sort out their results. Computer graphics allow researchers to decipher data sets so large that they could fill hundreds of pages of computer printouts. Unfortunately, most computer networks operate at speeds of 1.5 million bits (megabits) per second or less, and thus network users cannot utilize supercomputers fully.

Faster networks also will allow researchers to retrieve huge volumes of data (e.g., satellite images) from data bases and to share their own data with others. Multi-gigabit networks would allow scientists and engineers to control and collect data from research facilities (e.g., particle accelerators and radio telescopes) from thousands of miles away, reducing the need for expensive, time-consuming travel. These high-speed networks would allow researchers around the country to collaborate over the network as effectively as they could face-to-face, leading to the creation of what has been termed a National Collaboratory.

In recent years, support has been growing for a large increase in Federal funding for high-performance computing. A November 1985, White House Science Council report, "Research in Very High

Performance Computing," states: "The bottom line is that any country which seeks to control its future must effectively exploit high-performance computing. A country which aspires to military leadership must dominate, if not control, high-performance computing. A country seeking economic strength in the information age must lead in the development and application of high-performance computing in industry and research." At a July 21, 1989, committee hearing on his nomination to his current position, Dr. Allan Bromley, the President's Science Advisor and Director of OSTP, stated that high-performance computing must be "a very high priority" because "it has a catalytic effect on just about any brand of research and development" and "will, eventually, transform industry, education, and virtually every sector of our economy, bringing higher productivity and enhanced competitiveness." In a similar vein, a 1989 OSTP report, written by representatives from over a dozen Federal agencies, calls for new funding to "maintain and extend U.S. leadership in high-performance computing."

CONGRESSIONAL ACTION

Similar interest has been shown in both houses of Congress. In order to spur development of faster computer networks and more advanced supercomputers, in 1986, the Committee reported legislation authorizing NSF programs, which included legislation introduced by Senator Gore, to require OSTP to provide Congress with an analysis of the computer networking needs of American researchers and the benefits and opportunities that a national high-speed fiber optic network for computers and supercomputers would provide. That legislation was enacted into law as part of the NSF Authorization Act for FY 1987 (P.L. 99–383, 100 Stat. 816).

As required by the legislation, OSTP released a report in December 1987 entitled "A Research and Development Strategy for High Performance Computing," which outlined an ambitious, comprehensive research program in supercomputing and computer networking, and proposed that the Federal Government spend an additional $1.74 billion over the next five years on high-performance computing. This report was followed in September 1989 by an implementation plan for the program, "The Federal High Performance Computing Program," which was developed by more than a dozen agencies working with OSTP. While that report presented a five-year funding profile for a high-performance computing program, the President has yet to endorse the additional funding needed to implement it. However, there are reports that the Administration is preparing a major initiative in this area for FY 1992. The high-performance computing program outlined in the OSTP reports has four elements: high-performance computers; software technology and algorithms; networking; and basic research and human resources.

In 1988, S. 2918 was introduced by Senator Gore to create a National HPC Program, similar to that outlined in the 1989 OSTP report. The following year, Senator Gore introduced S. 1067 authorizing funds for high-performance computing at NSF, NASA, DOE, and DARPA. As introduced and as reported this bill differs from the OSTP reports in several ways: it places more emphasis on providing access to scientific data; it seeks to increase industry involvement in a Federal HPC program; it emphasizes more the role of high-performance computing in education; and it specifies funding levels for the different agencies in the program.

The first title of the reported bill provides for coodination between the Federal agencies involved in high-performance computing through the Federal Coordinating Council for Science, Engineering, and Technology (FCCSET), which is chaired by the Director of OSTP. In recent years, FCCSET has provided critically-needed, high level interagency coordination of research in a number of areas, most notably global change. The second title of the bill mandates creation, by 1996, of the NREN, a national fiber optic network capable of transmitting billions of bits of data per second from coast to coast. The third title gives NSF responsibility for promoting development of data bases and other information services, which would be available over the NREN. The fourth title provides for development of improved software for supercomputers and other computers. The fifth title funds research and development on new, more advanced supercomputers and related systems. The sixth title calls for more basic research in computing and expanded efforts to educate and train computer scientists and computational scientists (users of high-performance computing). The seventh and final title provides authorizations for NSF and NASA for their contributions to the National HPC Program.

To fully reap the benefits of high-performance computing, the Federal Government needs to implement a comprehensive research and development program similar to that provided for in S. 1067. Because the components of the program are all closely linked, progress in high-performance computing will be hindered if the pace of development in any one area is not as fast as in other areas. For instance, if a national high-speed computer network were established, but if faster, more powerful supercomputers were not developed to handle the data that would flow across such a network, the result would be missed opportunities and wasted resources. Similarly, the development of faster supercomputers, without the development of software needed to utilize them effectively and of networks to access them, would be a poor investment of research funds. Clearly, there is a need for a balanced, comprehensive approach.

BENEFITS OF S. 1067

Most of the funding authorized in S. 1067 is in support of basic research. There is broad agreement on the general need for the Federal funding of basic research—basic research has been shown repeatedly to be a good investment. For example, in a soon-to-be published study, Dr. Edwin Mansfield of the University of Pennsylvania estimated that the annual rate of return on Federal investments in academic research is approximately 28 percent.

The return on investments in basic research on high-performance computing may be even higher. On July 26, 1989, in testimony before the Science, Technology, and Space Subcommittee, Dr. James H. Clark, Chairman and Founder of Silicon Graphics Computer Systems, told how a single $12 million DARPA research grant which Dr. Clark and his colleagues received while he was a professor at Stanford from 1979 to 1982 led directly to the creation of SUN Microsystems, Silicon Graphics Computer Systems, and MIPS Computer Systems. Today, just eight years later, these three computer companies have combined total revenues of almost $2.5 billion per year and an average annual growth rate of 60 percent.

In addition, because high-performance computing represents an enabling technology which can increase greatly the productivity not only of computer scientists, but also of researchers in almost all fields of science and engineering, the returns are likely to be greater than the average return on investments in basic research. This research will lead to faster, more powerful computers than can tackle previously unsolvable problems; faster networks that can provide easier access to data and promote collaboration between researchers; and better software that can reduce the time spent computing the solution to a particular problem and thus allow researchers time to explore more facets of a problem.

The investment proposed by S. 1067 would provide needed tools for federally-funded researchers and enhance greatly their productivity. At a June 21, 1989, hearing of the Science, Technology, and Space Subcommittee, Dr. William Wulf, then Assistant Director of NSF's Directorate for Computer and Information Science and Engineering, testified that supercomputing and high-speed networking can increase the productivity of many American researchers by 100 percent, 200 percent, or more. Given that the Federal Government invests approximately $70 billion a year in research and development, such a productivity gain could produce enormous benefits and more than pay for the approximately $2 billion total cost of funding the National HPC Program for the next five years.

High-performance computing will allow researchers to tackle previously unsolvable problems, with huge benefits to society. For instance, better models of global climate change would lead to better policies to address global warming, policies which could have trillion-dollar impacts. Supercomputing could lead to a better understanding of AIDS, cancer, and genetic diseases, leading to breakthroughs impossible without more computing power.

Just as important as the benefits to American researchers are the benefits for American industry. Supercomputers are routinely used by automobile companies, both to design and to "crash test" cars; energy companies use them to analyze seismic data and prospect for oil; and even financial markets now utilize them to get real-time analyses of market behavior. On June 21, 1989, Mr. John Rollwagen, Chief Executive Officer of Cray Research Inc., testified before the Science, Technology, and Space Subcommittee that ARCO used a Cray supercomputer to determine how to increase production of its Prudhoe Bay oil field by two percent, which translates into an additional $2 billion in profits. The engines on Boeing's new 737 airplane were designed using a supercomputer and, as a result, are 30 percent more efficient than earlier models. ALCOA used supercomputer models to reduce the amount of aluminum needed to produce a soda can by 10 percent, resulting in millions of dollars in reduced materials, production, and transportation costs.

In the United States, the most extensive use of supercomputers has been for defense and aerospace applications. The National Security Agency (NSA) relies heavily on the fastest supercomputers for signal processing and breaking codes. Supercomputers are essential for anti-submarine warfare and for the design of new weapons systems. The Strategic Defense Initiative and other military research and development projects rely heavily on supercomputer modeling. NASA has several supercomputers devoted to modeling the aerodynamics of aircraft and spacecraft. These supercomputers can be used to replace or complement expensive wind tunnel tests.

In the future, high-performance computing will be utilized increasingly by the education and library communities. Supercomputers can store and sort through huge quantities of data, and with optical disk storage systems it is possible to store entire libraries of information electronically and retrieve them in seconds. The Library of Congress and other libraries are starting to develop the technology needed for "digital libraries" of books, journals, images, music, and videos—all stored in digital form and accessible over computer networks. Title III of S. 1067 as reported would provide for expanded efforts to develop such digital libraries.

In addition, title III provides for existing Federal data sets, like weather satellite data and census data, to be available on the NREN. At present, a great deal of scientific and economic data is stored in electronic form, but much of it, especially remote-sensing satellite data, is almost inaccessible to researchers and other users. The bill would make data sets like those at the Earth Resources Observation System (EROS) Data Center accessible over the NREN and other networks, thus greatly enhancing the usefulness of these data sets and ensuring that the United States maximizes the return on its investment in the collection of that data.

One of the most far-reaching impacts of the bill would be in the area of high-speed, fiber-optic telecommunications technology. Fiber-optic cable can transmit billions and even trillions of bits of data per second, thousands of times more than long-distance copper telephone cables. Scientists and engineers are using this new capability to develop technology for teleconferencing, for using supercomputers and other research equipment remotely, and for improving communication and collaboration among computer users. By creating a national, high-speed computer network, this bill would provide a demonstration of the potential of high-speed fiber optic computer networks.

Under this bill, the Federal Government would fund creation of a national multi-gigabit network and development of applications that use it. The technology and standards developed will be available publicly and will be applied quickly by private companies building commercial multi-gigabit networks. At present, the private sector is reluctant to make the multi-billion-dollar investments needed to build a national multi-gigabit network, in part because the technology has not been demonstrated and the market has not been proven. The Federal funding called for in this bill will demonstrate the benefits of a high-speed national network and lead to development of standards for such a network, this stimulating private-sector investment in multi-gigabit networking. At an October 4, 1989, hearing of the House Energy and Commerce Subcommittee on Telecommunications and Finance, John Edwards from Northern Telecom testified that Federal funding authorized by this bill could accelerate the creation of a national, multi-gigabit network by 5 to 10 years. Like the interstate freeway system and other types of infrastructure, such a network would provide untold benefits to all sectors of the American economy.

HPC AND U.S. COMPETITIVENESS

The development of HPC will have a significant impact on U.S. technology competitiveness, particularly given the efforts of other countries to develop a supercomputing capability. The Japanese and other foreign competitors have been quick to recognize the benefits of supercomputing and fiber optic networks. In fact, the Japanese have targeted the world supercomputer market and are now producing some of the fastest supercomputers available. In April 1990, Japan announced a major research program to accelerate research and development on parallel processing supercomputers. Similarly, other countries are making massive investments in high-speed fiber optic networks. Japan's Nippon Telegraph and Telephone Corporation has announced that it intends to invest $126 billion to install a national fiber optic network which would reach every home, office, and factory in Japan by the year 2015 and be capable of transmitting hundreds of millions of bits of data per second. The Europeans are developing initiatives to build their own high-speed networks as part of EC 92.

Without additional Federal and private-sector investment in supercomputing, the United States risks losing the $2.4 billion world supercomputer market, and more importantly, it risks having to rely upon foreign suppliers for an essential tool in improving research and development, in increasing American competitiveness, and in enhancing U.S. national security. The funding authorized by S. 1067 would help the United States maintain its lead in the development and application of supercomputers.

NEED FOR ADDITIONAL HPC FUNDING

To provide supercomputing services to American researchers, the NSF created five supercomputer centers in the mid-1980s. For FY 1991, NSF is requesting $59.59 million to fund the centers. Other Federal agencies, including NASA and DOE, also maintain large supercomputers for use by Federal and academic scientists.

The science agencies also fund several computer networks, including NSF's NSFNET, NASA's NASNET and SPAN (Space Physics Analysis Network), DOE's MFENET and HEPNET, and DOD's MILNET. Together with many State-funded or for-profit regional networks, several of these networks are linked by the Internet, which consists of over 2,000 interconnected networks. While it is not known exactly how many computers communicate via Internet, most estimates are that well over 100,000 computers are linked in this way.

However, present supercomputing and networking programs are not adequate to meet the needs of researchers. The supercomputers at the NSF centers are chronically over-subscribed. DARPA and other agencies which fund development of new supercomputers lack the money to fund more than a small fraction of the promising proposals for new types of machines, which can cost from $10 million to $500 million to prototype. Furthermore, researchers are often frustrated by the lack of useful research software for supercomputers which stems from the lack of adequate funding for supercomputer software development.

Perhaps even more importantly, inadequate funding levels would result in a delay in the establishment of the NREN. The NREN would be capable of transmitting gigabits (billions of bits) of data per second, and by 1996 would link up to 1,300 institutions and about a million researchers nationwide. The NREN would be about 2,000 times faster than the current NSFNET. While this nationwide computer network links over 500 institutions in all 50 States its data rate is only 1.5 million bits per second, more than a thousand times slower than the proposed NREN. Even after NSFNET is upgraded to 45 million bits per second this year, researchers will be unable to utilize fully the supercomputers and data bases connected to it. Since use of NSFNET is growing at a rate of 20 to 30 percent each month, its new capacity will not be enough to accommodate the increased usage expected in the next two or three years. For FY 1991, NSF has requested $22.04 million for NSFNET. Additional funding for both NSF and DARPA will be needed to develop a multi-gigabit NREN.

The multi-gigabit NREN is needed if researchers are to use the new networking technology being developed in laboratories around the country. The first computer networks, built in the late 1960s, enabled computers to exchange data at rates of a few thousand bits of data a second (a single page of double-spaced text represents about 10,000 bits of data). Today, there are experimental computer networks that can transmit billions of bits of data a second, enabling computer users to share computer graphics and huge volumes of data in a few seconds. At a billion bits a second, the entire Encyclopedia Brittanica could be transmitted to any computer on the network in less than a second. Unfortunately, these experimental networks are limited, connecting only a few computers. More research and development will be needed before the NREN, which will connect thousands of computers, can be built.

According to the President's FY 1991 budget request (p. 85, "Budget of the United States Government)," in FY 1990, the Federal Government spent $448 million on high-performance computing, and for FY 1991, the President is requesting $469 million, an increase of five percent, which barely covers inflation. Without additional funding, researchers will not have access to the supercomputing resources they need; the NREN will be delayed; development of new, more powerful machines will be delayed; supercomputer software development will slow; and insufficient numbers of scientists and engineers will be trained to use supercomputers.

The funding authorized by S. 1067 would roughly double funding for supercomputing at NSF and NASA over the next five years, and would roughly triple NSF's networking budget. These funding increases parallel those outlined in the 1987 OSTP report and the follow-up report released in September 1989, "The Federal High Performance Computing Program."

LEGISLATIVE HISTORY

On May 18, 1989, Senator Gore introduced S. 1067, legislation similar to S. 2918, which Senator Gore had introduced in October 1988. S. 1067 is cosponsored by Senators Jeffords, Durenberger, Pell, Kasten, Conrad, Pressler, Lott, Wirth, Sasser, Kohl, Bryan, Graham, Kerrey, Robb, Gorton, Reid, Kerry, Cranston, Boschwitz, Bingaman, Breaux, and Heinz.

The Subcommittee on Science, Technology, and Space held three hearings on S. 1067. The first hearing, on June 21, 1989, focused on the NREN. The second hearing, on July 26, 1989, considered the development and application of advanced software and visualization, and the third one, held on September 15, 1989, examined present and future technology for managing and distributing electronic data. Witnesses at the hearings included several leading computer scientists, representatives of computer, supercomputer, and telecommunications companies, and representatives of NSF, DARPA, the U.S. Geological Survey, and the National Library of Medicine (NLM). Witnesses testified on the many new applications of supercomputing, and enthusiastically endorsed the idea of a NREN. Dr. William Wulf, testifying for NSF, stated that the Administration endorses the goals of the legislation, but that it opposes S. 1067 because the funding authorized by the legislation had not been requested in the President's budget. In addition, the Administration believes that a five-year budget for research funding should not be made, because this field is evolving so rapidly.

At its April 3, 1990, executive session, the Commerce Committee considered in open session and adopted without objection an amendment in the nature of a substitute for S. 1067. As introduced, S. 1067 provided funding for DOE and DOD, as well as NASA and NSF. Because DOE and DOD programs are not generally authorized by the Commerce Committee, the substitute provides funding for only NASA and NSF.

Authorizations for the DOE high-performance computing program are contained in S. 1976, the DOE High-Performance Computing Act, introduced on November 21, 1989, by Senator Johnston and cosponsored by Senators Gore and McClure. The Senate Energy Committee held a hearing on S. 1976 on March 6, 1990, and ordered the bill reported on June 27, 1990. When it was introduced, the sponsors of S. 1976 indicated their intention to have S. 1067 and S. 1976 considered together by the full Senate once each was reported. Funding for the portion of the HPC program to be conducted by DOD's DARPA is expected to be provided in the DOD FY 1991 authorization bill.

SUMMARY OF MAJOR PROVISIONS

As reported, S. 1067 would authorize a five-year program roughly doubling Federal funding for research and development on supercomputers, advanced computer software, and computer networks. The major provisions are as follows.

1. Title I establishes an interagency National HPC Program involving NSF, NASA, DOE, DOD, and other relevant agencies. Interagency coordination and planning for the program would be

provided by OSTP's FCCSET, which is to work closely with industry.

2. Title II requires NSF to work with other agencies to establish a multi-gigabit NREN by 1996. This network would be capable of transmitting several billions of bits of data per second and would link hundreds of thousands of researchers in government, industry, and universities around the country.

3. Title III makes NSF the lead agency for ensuring that federally-funded data bases and network services can be accessed over the network.

4. Title IV calls for expanded software research and development, especially on software for supercomputers. Most of the funding would go to scientists, engineers, and computer scientists using high-performance computing to solve so-called "Grand Challenges," fundamental problems in science and engineering, examples of which are provided in the bill as reported.

5. Title V provides for research on supercomputers and encourages development of new supercomputing technology by the private sector.

6. Title VI requires OSTP to oversee and coordinate Federal programs for basic research in computer technology and for the education of computer scientists, computational scientists, information scientists, and electrical engineers.

7. Title VII authorizes $338 million to NASA for FY 1991–95 for the purposes of the bill. For FY 1991–95, the bill authorizes for NSF $195 million to establish the network, $64 million for basic research and education, and $391 million for the other purposes of titles III, IV, and V. The total authorization for NASA and NSF for FY 1991 is $68 million.

ESTIMATED COSTS

In accordance with paragraph 11(a) of rule XXVI of the Standing Rules of the Senate and section 403 of the Congressional Budget Act of 1974, the Committee provides the following cost estimate, prepared by the Congressional Budget Office:

U.S. CONGRESS,
CONGRESSIONAL BUDGET OFFICE,
Washington, DC, April 27, 1990.

Hon. ERNEST F. HOLLINGS,
Chairman, Committee on Commerce, Science, and Transportation,
U.S. Senate, Washington, DC.

DEAR MR. CHAIRMAN: The Congressional Budget Office has prepared the attached cost estimate for S. 1067, the High-Performance Computing Act of 1990.

If you wish further details on this estimate, we will be pleased to provide them.

Sincerely,

ROBERT D. REISCHAUER,
Director.

CONGRESSIONAL BUDGET OFFICE COST ESTIMATE

1. Bill number: S. 1067.
2. Bill title: The High-Performance Computing Act of 1990.

3. Bill status: As ordered reported by the Senate Committee on Commerce, Science, and Transportation, April 3, 1990.

4. Bill purpose: S. 1067 would require the Federal Coordinating Council on Science, Engineering, and Technology (FCCSET) to develop and implement a National High-Performance Computing Plan. It would also mandate that the National Science Foundation (NSF), in conjunction with the Department of Defense (DOD), the National Aeronautics and Space Administration, and other relevant federal agencies, establish a national network of high speed computers, which would be known as the National Research and Education Network (NREN).

The requirements of S. 1067 would affect numerous federal agencies as developers and users of the NREN. For example, the bill would requires the NSF and NASA to help develop software for the types of computer used in the network; the National Institute of Standards and Technology, a part of the Department of Commerce, would be charged with developing government-wide standards for computer networks; and the DOD, through the Defense Advanced Research Projects Agency (DARPA), would have primary responsibility for research and development on technology needed for the network. The FCCSET would have the general responsibility for overseeing and coordinating the work of the agencies involved in this project.

To fund development of the network, the bill would authorize appropriations to the NSF and NASA of nearly $1 billion over five years. The bill would also authorize NSF to charge a fee for use of the system.

5. Estimated cost to the Federal Government:

[By fiscal year, in millions of dollars]

	1991	1992	1993	1994	1995
Specific athorizations:					
National Science Foundation	46	88	145	172	199
NASA	22	45	67	89	115
Subtotal, specific authorizations	68	133	212	261	314
Estimated authorizations	12	13	13	14	14
Total authorization level	80	146	225	275	328
Estimated outlays	45	107	180	241	295

The costs of this bill would be in budget functions 250 and 370.

Basis of estimate: This estimate assumes that the full amounts authorized would be appropriated for each fiscal year. Based on information provided by the Department of Commerce, CBO estimates that the cost of research and studies required by the bill but not specifically authorized would be roughly $12 million per year beginning in 1991; this amount, with adjustments for inflation, is shown as the estimated authorization level in the table above. The estimated outlays are based on historical spending patterns.

CBO expects that fees for use of the network would be phased in once the network is operating, which would probably be in 1993 or 1994. Receipts from these fees could ultimately provide a significant offset to the operating costs of the network. Nevertheless, we do not expect that receipts would be significant during the five-year period covered by this estimate.

6. Estimated cost to State and local governments: None.

7. Estimate Comparison: None.

8. Previous CBO estimate: None.

9. Estimate Prepared by: Doug Criscitello and Michael Sieverts.

10. Estimate approved by: James L. Blum, Assistant Director for Budget Analysis.

Regulatory Impact Statement

In accordance with paragraph 11(b) of rule XXVI of the Standing Ruels of the Senate, the Committee provides the following evaluation of the regulatory impact of the legislation, as reported.

NUMBER OF PERSONS CONVERED

This legislation provides additional funding for research and development in high-performance computing. This will not result in new regulations, because the additional funding provided by the legislation would be distributed according to existing regulations regarding NSF research grants and NASA contracts. These regulations would apply only to those persons and companies choosing to apply for this funding.

ECONOMIC IMPACT

This legislation authorizes $988 million in additional Federal spending for FY 1991–95. By providing for improved inter-agency coordination, this legislation should improve the effectiveness of Federal research and development on high-performance computing.

This legislation also requires the National Institute of Standards and Technology (NIST) within the Department of Commerce (DOC) to develop guidelines and standards: (1) to provide for interoperability of Federal computer networks, and (2) to promote the use of "open systems software" which can run on several different computer systems. These guidelines should be cost-effective in increasing the usefulness of Federal networks and software purchased by the Federal Government.

PRIVACY

This legislation will not have any adverse impact on the personal privacy of individual Americans. The creation of the NREN and associated databases will make existing Federal scientific data bases (including economic data and census data) more accessible to users throughout the country, but personal data already protected by rules and regulations (e.g., tax returns and individual census forms) will remain confidential.

PAPERWORK

This legislation requires FCCSET to submit an annual report to the President and the Congress on the National HPC Program. The National Telecommunications and Information Administration (NTIA) within DOC is to report to Congress on whether State and

Federal telecommunications laws and regulations hinder or facilitate private industy participation in the data transmission field. OSTP shall report to Congress on options for charging users of the NREN and the databases connnected to it. DOC is to report to Congress on whether Federal procurement regulations discourage the development of better software development tools and on whether export controls hinder the development of foreign markets for North American manufacturers of high-performance computer systems.

Section-by-Section Analysis

Section 1.—Short Title

This section states that the bill may be cited as the "High-Performance Computing Act of 1990".

Section 2.—Findings and Purposes

This section contains the Congressional findings and purposes of the Act. Under subsection (1), Congress finds, among other things, that advances in computer technology are vital to the propsperity, national and economic security, and scientific advancement of the United States. Under subsection (b), to maintain leadership in computer technology and its applications, and to reap the benefits of high-performance computing, the reported bill calls for expanding Federal support for research, development, and application of high-performance computing, and improving planning and coordination of Federal research and development on high-performance computing. Subsection (b) states that this legislation is intended to help establish a high-capacity national research and education computer network; expand the numbers of researchers, educators and students with training in and access to high-performance computing; develop a system of data bases and other services available through such a network; accelerate development of more powerful supercomputers and other advanced computer systems; stimulate research and development of better software for both supercomputers and other computers; promote application of high-performance computing to "Grand Challenges" of science and engineering; and provide for basis research in high-performance computing.

Section 3.—Definitions

Definitions of "North American Company" and "Grand Challenge" are provided in Section 3.

Several provisions in this bill are designed to assist U.S. industry. However, the recently signed Free Trade Agreement between the United States and Canada is to encourage economic cooperation between the two nations and reduce economic barriers. Therefore, the term "North America company" is used to allow Canadian and U.S.-Canadian joint ventures to benefit from these provisions.

A "Grand Challenge" is a fundamental problem in science and engineering, with broad economic and scientific impact, whose solution will require the application of high-performance computing resources. Examples of Grand Challenges include modeling of global change, designing of new materials and drugs, and deciphering of the human genome.

TITLE I

SECTION 101.—NATIONAL HIGH-PERFORMANCE COMPUTING PROGRAM

This section amends the National Science and Technology Policy, Organization, and Priorities Act of 1976 (42 U.S.C. 6601 et seq., hereinafter referred to as "the Science Act") in order to establish a National HPC Program coordinated by OSTP. This section would add a new title VI to the Science Act, with the following sections:

New section 601 contains findings similar to those in section 2 of the reported bill.

New section 602 mandates a National HPC Plan, which under subsection (a)(1) is to be developed and implemented by FCCSET. FCCSET is chaired by the Chairman of OSTP, who is traditionally also the President's Science Advisor. It is currently charged with addressing research issues and coordinating research programs that involve more than one Federal agency. For instance, in recent years, FCCSET has done an exemplary job of providing high-level coordination on global change research. The National Global Change Research Program can serve as a model for the National HPC Program. As with global change research, high-performance computing involves several agencies, and there is no one agency with the expertise, breadth, and facilities to oversee all Federal efforts in the field. FCCSET provides a mechanism for building on existing agency programs, preventing duplication of effort, and identifying previously unaddressed problems, without establishing a new bureaucratic entity. In addition, building on existing agency programs, rather than creating a separate agency for high-performance computing, would ensure that new developments in high-performance computing are utilized by individual agencies to accomplish their different missions.

Under subsection (a)(2) of new section 602, the plan is to establish the goals and priorities for a National HPC Program, to set forth the roles and computer research budgets of the agencies involved, and to include the results of studies by Federal agencies and departments, the National Research Council (NRC), and other entities. The Committee expects that the plan would be similar to the 1989 OSTP report, "The Federal High-Performance Computing Program," except that it also would include a budget showing the level of funding for each of the activities undertaken in support of the program by each of the agencies involved and provide a comprehensive inventory of what high-performance computing programs are currently underway throughout the Federal government that could contribute to the National HPC Program.

Under subsection (a)(3), the plan would summarize the activities of NSF, DOC, NASA, DOD, DOE, the Department of Health and Human Services (HHS), the Department of Education, the Library of Congress, the NLM, the National Agricultural Library, and other relevant agencies.

Subsection (b) of new section 602 provides that FCCSET will have the lead in developing and implementing the plan. At least once a year, the Chairman of FCCSET will report to the President on how to improve implementation of the plan.

Working through the Executive Office of the President, and especially with the Office of Management and Budget (OMB), FCCSET should provide the high-level coordination needed to direct and implement effectively the National HPC program. Coordination between OMB and FCCSET will be critical to the success of the program. Under subsection (b)(3), prior to the submission of the President's annual budget request, FCCSET will review each agency and department's budget estimate to determine how it contributes to the implementation of the HPC program. This review is intended to guide OMB in determining each agency's budget for high-performance computing.

In addition, FCCSET will work with Federal agencies, the NRC, and other groups involved in high-performance computing to formulate and implement the plan. To receive advice from industry and academia, OSTP is directed under subsection (c) of new section 602 to establish an HPC Advisory Panel which will consider issues pertaining to the program and evaluate its progress, focus, and direction. This panel primarily should provide advice on policy decisions regarding the National HPC Program. The Committee realizes that additional funding will be necessary for this panel and encourages the Administration and the Appropriations Committees to increase funding for OSTP accordingly.

This new section in subsection (d) also describes the existing missions of ten of the agencies that will contribute to the National HPC Program. By summarizing the agenices' existing roles, the Committee intends to ensure that existing agency programs are incorporated into the National HPC Program. The inclusion of current research roles is not intended to limit agency responsibilities or to interfere otherwise with the flexibility that will be required by FCCSET to develop and implement a comprehensive national research program. The Committee expects agency responsibilities to evolve over time, as the challenges associated with high-performance computing change and the technology advances. In addition, this subsection requires the agencies to work together to connect their computer networks and to improve, share, and distribute computer software they have developed.

As outlined in the 1989 OSTP report, the four key agencies in the National NPC Program are NSF, DARPA, NASA, and DOE. NSF will continue to fund university research and development in high-performance computing and provide researchers with access to state-of-the-art supercomputers. In addition, NSF is to implement the NREN. DARPA's first priorities will be to develop the multi-gigabit network technology needed to build the NREN and to fund development of future generations of supercomputers and other advanced computer systems. DARPA will fund development of new advanced conventional and massively-parallel supercomputers. DARPA also will work with and provide technical support to the high-performance computing research programs within the Army, the Navy, the Air Force, the National Security Agency, and other parts of DOD. NASA will continue to conduct basic and applied research on high-performance computing, with particular emphasis on the development of applications for supercomputing in areas like aeronautics and the processing of remote-sensing data. DOE will continue to conduct basic and applied research in high-performance computing, particularly in software development and development and use of parallel-processing supercomputers.

Concerns have been expressed in the past that technology developed at DOE has not been transferred effectively to the private sector. As part of the National HPC Program, DOE and other agencies will ensure that unclassified computer research is readily available to North American companies. This provision should not be interpreted as barring foreign firms from access to high-performance computing technology developed with Federal funding, but simply requires that special emphasis should be given to encouraging technology transfer to North American firms, which often have been slower to utilize federally-funded research and development than their foreign competitors.

While the amount of funding provided for NIST for its part of the National HPC Program is a small fraction of that provided to the four key agencies, NIST has a critical role to play in developing the standards and guidelines needed to ensure compatibility of different computer systems and networks. In conjunction with the NSA, NIST has important responsibilities in the area of computer security. The privacy of network users and the integrity of data bases connected to the network must be protected. In addition, under section 403 of this bill, NIST will play a key role in promoting use by the Federal Government of "open systems software," which can be easily transported from one type of computer system to another. It is anticipated that additional funding requests for high-performance computing programs at NIST will be needed.

The National Oceanic and Atmospheric Administration (NOAA), responsible for managing much of the earth science data collected by Federal programs, has an important role to play in the National HPC Program, both as a user of advanced computer systems and networks, and as a supplier of data to users for the NREN and others. NOAA has huge archives of remote-sensing satellite data, such of which has not been analyzed thoroughly. The NREN and the supercomputers developed as part of this program will help researchers make better use of existing NOAA data and of data that will be collected in the future.

Other agencies involved in the National HPC Program will play important roles, epecially in developing applications for supercomputing and networking for use in both the research community and beyond. In particular, the Committee encourages the DOE, through its library programs, to initiate and fund projects that promote linkages between existing library and information science networks and the NREN. The benefits of this enhanced resource sharing among networks are improved end user document delivery, improved interlibrary resource sharing and electronic interlibrary loans, and improved communication between users in the NREN and users outside the NREN.

The three national libraries—the Library of Congress, the National Agriculture Library, and the NLM—have long been at the leading edge of automation of library functions, creation and standardization of bibliographic and information data bases, and electronic transmittal of information about their holdings to libraries across the county via library networks. All three libraries are now experimenting with electronic formats for entire portions of their collections, including some use of the Internet. The advent of the NREN will permit new opportunities for the research and academic communities to benefit from these information resources in performing research and in the creation of new knowledge that will improve the U.S. economic competitiveness.

The Committee is particularly interested in the work being done at the NLM, and elsewhere, to use national computer networks for the sharing of biomedical research information. For instance, the NLM's Medline system provides references and abstracts from medical literature to doctors throughout the country, providing an invaluable service, especially to doctors in rural areas as far from major libraries. Ongoing research at NLM is providing the technology needed for doctors thousands of miles apart to share X-ray images, CAT scans, PET scans, and other medical imagery. In this way, a general practitioner will be able to obtain advice from specialists anywhere in the country.

A biomedical community clearly has much to gain from advances in high-performance computing and the use of computer networks, and should be encouraged to take advantage of this technology. Unfortunately, relatively few laboratory-based biomedical researchers at universities, and almost no clinical researchers or health care practitioners, use the current Internet. At the same time, it is clear that new computer-based technologies, such as clinical imaging, are essential to accurate diagnosis and treatment and to the conduct of biomedical research. Improved methods of communications among health care practitioners and life sciences researchers will facilitate basic and clinical research, and accelerate the search for cures of many human diseases.

Therefore, it is envisioned that within HHS, the National Institutes of Health (NIH) and the NLM will establish the appropriate mechanisms to ensure the development of a biomedical component of the NREN and promote and facilitate the use of the NREN by the biomedical research community. The NREN will serve as an invaluable testbed for development of networking applications for the health care community since most Federal health care agencies (e.g., NIH and NLM) will be connected to NREN as will many university medical centers, hospitals, and other medical facilities. The medical community will help spur the development of high-speed commercial computer networks as doctors become more and more dependent upon medical imaging and as they recognize the potential of high-speed networking technology.

Finally, under new section 602(e), each Federal agency and department involved in high-performance computing, as part of its annual request to OMB for appropriations, is to submit a report to OMB identifying its high-performance computing activities. OMB is to review each such report in light of the HPC Plan and shall include in the President's budget each agency or department's budget allocation to high-performance computing activities.

New section 603 mandates that the Chairman of FCCSET submit an annual report to the President and the Congress on the National NPC Program. The report shall summarize, among other things, the progress made by the program, detail the agency budgets for high-performance computing, and recommend any additional action or legislation which may be required to assist in achieving the purposes of the legislation.

SECTION 102.—AMENDMENTS TO THE SCIENCE ACT

This section would amend section 102(a) of the Science Act, which identifies the principles that form the basis for national science and technology policy. The list of principles would be expanded to emphasize the need for comprehensive long-term planning of research to address complex scientific issues of national and international concern. The purpose of such planning would be to ensure a scientific basis for policy decisions.

This section, in subsection (b), also amends section 401 of the Science Act, which defines the responsibilities of FCCSET. Section 401 also provided for FCCSET's initial creation. However, during a 1977 reorganization, FCCSET was abolished, its functions were transferred to the President, and it was later reestablished under executive order. Section 401(a), as amended, simply restates the responsibilities of FCCSET under the Science Act, reflecting that reorganization.

Section 401(b), as amended, would provide FCCSET with new authority to develop and coordinate interagency research. FCCSET would formulate plans that would identify critical research needs and provide for cooperation among government, industry, and academic scientists in the United States and overseas. Section 401(c) and (d), as amended, address FCCSET's authority to perform advisory duties assigned by the President or its chairman and the requirement that Federal agencies represented on FCCSET furnish necessary assistance to FCCSET. Also section 401(e), as amended, would add the development of interagency plans to the purposes for which FCCSET committees and working groups may be formed.

TITLE II—NATIONAL RESEARCH AND EDUCATION NETWORK

SECTION 201.—FUNCTIONS OF THE NETWORK

This section requires NSF to work with DOD and other relevant agencies to establish a national computer network capable of transmitting more than two billion bits of data (gigabits) per second. Such a network would connect more than half a million computers and their users at more than 1,000 colleges, universities, Federal laboratories, industry laboratories, libraries, and other institutions in all fifty States. This would provide access to supercomputers, computer data bases, and other research facilities.

The NREN would be developed in close cooperation with the computer and telecommunication industries and with potential users in government, industry, and the higher education community, including researchers, librarians, educators, and information services providers. The network is to be established in a manner that fosters competition and private-sector investment in high-speed data networking within the telecommunications industry.

One way to meet these goals is to develop and operate the NREN in much the same way as NSF's NSFNET, a national computer network connecting the five NSF supercomputer centers and over 500 colleges and universities. NSF funds NSFNET's high-speed (1.5 million bits per second), interstate "backbone" which connects the supercomputer centers and other facilities. Regional networks, both private or non-profit, connect the backbone to individual colleges and universities which in turn have their own local campus networks. The NSFNET backbone has been built and managed by MERIT, a consortium of Michigan universities, in cooperation with MCI Telecommunications and IBM, which provide fiber optic phone lines and computer hardware as well as technical expertise. This kind of industry-government-academia partnership provides for the rapid development of networking technology and its rapid dissemination.

In order to ensure that the NREN does not compete unfairly with commercial high-speed networks, paragraph (8) provides that it is to be phased out when national commercial high-speed networks can meet the networking needs of American researchers, by providing a cost-effective alternative to the NREN. To provide for a smooth transition to commercial service, mechanisms shall be established under paragraph (7) for charging network users or their institutions for their use of the network. Otherwise, if networking is provided free to the user, networking resources will be wasted, and it will be very difficult to phase out the NREN and replace it with commercial networks.

In addition under paragraph (7), mechanisms for charging for the use of copyrighted material available over the NREN shall be implemented, where technically feasible. These mechanisms should not be implemented without due consideration of both the rights of authors and the rights of users of copyrighted material. Specifically, provision needs to be made for the fair use of copyrighted works for teaching, scholarship, or research.

The development and implementation of pricing schemes for users of the NREN likely will be technically difficult when gigabit networking technology is in its infancy. The inability to implement such schemes, however, should not delay the deployment of a gigabit network.

SECTION 202.—AGENCY RESPONSIBILITIES

This section requires under paragraph (1) that FCCSET establish a Federal Networking Advisory Committee to provide technical advice to FCCSET from the interest involved in existing Federal research networks and the NREN. In contrast to the HPC Advisory Panel established under title I, in new section 602(c) of the Science Act, this advisory committee is not intended to provide advice on broad policy issues, but instead will address technical problems encountered in establishing the NREN. In addition, FCCSET is to submit to Congress, within one year of enactment of this bill, a report on how best to fund and commercialize the NREN.

Under paragraph (2), NSF and all other Federal agencies which provide research grants shall allow grantees to use grant monies to pay for use of computer networks. Although policies vary with each agency, today most recipients of Federal research grants cannot use grant money for any type of telecommunications expenses. Providing funding for computer networking would increase the productivity of researchers, who are increasingly dependent upon computers and computer networks to manipulate, search, store, and share their data.

DARPA shall have primary responsibility under paragraph (3) for developing the gigabit networking technology needed to create the NREN. Under paragraph (4) NIST, in cooperation with other agencies, shall adopt government-wide networking standards and guidelines to enable government networks to be linked together. These standards will be adopted with the advice and comment of private industry, will provide common user interfaces to systems, and will provide enhanced security for the NREN. It is expected that, in addition, work being done at NIST, such as measurement research and development needed to develop advanced optical fibers and optoelectronic components for high-performance optical fiber communications, will contribute to the National HPC Program.

Within one year of enactment, NTIA under paragraph (5) shall report to Congress on whether State and Federal telecommunications laws and regulations hinder or facilitate private industry participation in the data transmission field. In particular, the report should focus on development of data transmission systems, using high-speed fiber optic networks.

TITLE III—INFORMATION SERVICES

SECTION 301.—DATA SERVICES

This section gives NSF responsibility for working with other relevant Federal agencies to promote development of several information services over the NREN. In particular, NSF shall provide for a directory of users of the NREN and other networks. It also shall provide directories of the different data basis available over the NREN. In addition, it is to identify and provide for access to Federal scientific data bases (e.g., whether data, satellite data, economic data, and other research data) and provide data bases and knowledge banks for use by artificial intelligence (AI) programs. AI experts have developed computer programs called "know-bots" which can search data bases and knowledge banks for the information users need. Knowledge banks consist of textbook knowledge stored in computer-based form so that AI programs can access and use it.

This section also requires NSF to help provide access to "digital libraries" of video programming, books and journals stored in electronic form, and other computer data. It is expected that NREN users will have access to commercial information services like Lexis-Nexis and Dialog, with appropriate mechanisms for charging customers of these services. NSF also shall provide for orientation and training of users of networks and data bases, by providing training software on the networks they use and by providing experts to guide and teach users of those networks.

The NREN also will provide access to research facilities like radio telescopes, seismometers, and manufacturing facilities. A particularly noteworthy example of such a manufacturing facility is one operated by DARPA. Called MOSIS (for Metal Oxide Semiconductor Implementation System), it allows integrated circuit designers to send their designs electronically over a network to an integrated circuit foundry where the design can be turned into hardware in only a few weeks. This rapid turn-around time compares to typical turn-around times of several months. Several other federally-funded programs, including DOD's CALS and MANTECH (Manufacturing Technology) programs, DOC's Product Design Electronic Specification (PDES), and NIST's Manufacturing Technology Centers programs, are using visualization and electronic specifications ("electronic blueprints") to improve the productivity and flexibility of American manufacturers.

SECTION 302.—OSTP REPORTS TO CONGRESS

This section requires that, within one year of enactment of the legislation OSTP shall report to Congress on several issues, including mechanisms for charging information service providers for access to the NREN, the technology needed to charge users of such services for their use of them, and charge-back mechanisms and other ways to pay copyright holders royalties for use of their material by NREN users. In addition, the Committee has become increasingly concerned by the growing number of reports of computer viruses and unauthorized use of government and university computer systems. Therefore, OSTP is to report on appropriate policies to ensure the security of data bases and other resources available on the NREN and protection of the privacy of NREN users. In developing this report, OSTP should work closely with OMB, which is involved in establishing many aspects of government information policy.

TITLE IV—SOFTWARE

SECTION 401.—THE GRAND CHALLENGES

This section instructs OSTP in subsection (a) to coordinate and oversee research and development of software for high-performance computer systems. Under subsection (b), this software is to be developed, in particular, to address so-called Grand Challenges of sciences and engineering, complex problems of great economic and scientific importance whose solution requires the use of the most advanced computer systems and software. This subsection lists several examples of Grand Challenges to be addressed by NSF and NASA, including prediction of global change, accurate modelling of turbulence, and processing of the huge volumes of data produced by telescopes and other astronomical facilities. The Grand Challenges listed in this section are merely examples and are not meant to limit the scientific problems that might be addressed. Some other potential Grand Challenges are in the fields of molecular biology, superconductivity, the human genome, theoretical physics, nuclear fusion, and oil and gas exploration. An appendix to the 1989 OSTP report summarizes twenty Grand Challenges. Both NSF and NASA shall provide support to interdisciplinary groups of scientists, engineers, computer scientists, and computational scientists to develop the high-performance computer systems and software needed to address the Grand Challenges.

DOE has funded several such groups, including University of Tennessee/Oak Ridge National Laboratory Joint Institute for Computational Science, which has focused on development of computational tools for massively-parallel supercomputers needed to address a number of Grand Challenges, and the National Supercomputing Center for Energy Research at the University of Nevada, Las Vegas (UNLV), which is using high-performance computing to study radioactive waste management, among other issues. These DOE programs bring together resources from the Federal Government, universities, and industry, and can serve as models for similar cooperative efforts at other agencies.

In addition to addressing Grand Challenges, NSF will support, under subsection (c), basic research on software and development of tools and techniques for accelerating the development of software, especially for supercomputers. Such tools and techniques are essential if supercomputing is to become a routinely-used research tool. This is particularly true for massively-parallel supercomputers, which often can be used for only a limited set of problems because existing software does not allow for use of the full capabilities of the systems.

SECTION 402.—SOFTWARE CLEARINGHOUSE

This section instructs NSF to establish and maintain clearinghouses of research software. Too often, scientists and engineers supported by Federal research grants develop new computer programs for a particular project on which they are working, and then, after they have completed the project, they set aside these programs, never to be used again. Later, another researcher working on a similar project has to develop new software because there is no way of knowing that the needed software is already available elsewhere.

These clearinghouses would allow researchers to deposit voluntarily their research software at the clearinghouse where it would be catalogued and made available to others. Staff at the clearinghouse could make such software easier to use and accessible to other researchers over the NREN. In addition, the clearinghouse would provide funding to researchers to upgrade and document their software so that other researchers would be able to use it more easily and more broadly. The clearinghouses are to promote the commercialization of particularly popular and useful software, always respecting the intellectual property rights of the researchers who originally created the software. The committee believes that the NSF Supercomputer Centers are well-equipped to serve as clearinghouses for software for both supercomputers and less powerful computers.

SECTION 403.—SOFTWARE STANDARDS

NIST will develop, in conjunction with industry, standards that will promote the Federal Government's use of so-called "open systems software," which can be used on many different computer systems. Such software can reduce greatly the time and effort required to shift software from one system to another and thus increase the productivity of computer users.

SECTION 404.—COMMERCE DEPARTMENT REPORTS

This section requires that, within one year of enactment of this Act, the Secretary of Commerce (Secretary) shall report to Congress on the impact of Federal procurement regulations which require that contractors share the rights to proprietary software development tools and on whether Federal procurement regulations discourage the development of better software development tools and techniques. It is expected that this report will be written in consultation and cooperation with DOD, NASA, and other agencies which contract for large amounts of customized software. At present, in most agencies, if a contractor sells software to the government, that contractor must not only provide the software itself, but also must provide the software used to develop it. Today, many software companies use proprietary software tools to streamline software development, and these tools can require more money and manpower to make than the software that they are used to produce. Because of anachronistic procurement regulations, companies are discouraged from developing better, easier-to-use software tools, and if they do develop them, they do not use them to produce government software, resulting in the government paying higher prices for lower-quality software.

TITLE V—COMPUTER SYSTEMS

SECTION 501.—RESEARCH ON COMPUTER SYSTEMS

This section requires NSF to provide for research and development on high-performance computer systems. Such research is not to be limited only to supercomputers, but shall include work on input/output devices, memory and mass storage devices, communication devices, and the systems software required to make for the operation of supercomputers.

SECTION 502.—PROCUREMENT OF PROTOTYPE MODELS OF SUPERCOMPUTERS

In the 1970s, several Federal agencies, including DOE, DOD, and NSA, purchased prototype or early production models from American computer manufacturers. Such purchases gave fledging companies, like Cray Research, Inc., the money they needed to become viable companies. Equally important, Cray and other companies were able to have their machines tested by scientists and engineers working on real problems. The first Cray 1 was installed at Los Alamos National Laboratory before Cray had been able to complete the systems software for the new machine. Input from DOE scientists helped make Cray the work leader in the supercomputer industry.

Unfortunately, in recent years, many agencies have been discouraged from making purchases of prototypes by regulations stemming from the so-called "Brooks Act" and other laws regulating Federal purchases of computer equipment. Although this was not the intent of the Brooks Act, regulations resulting from that Act make it very difficult for an agency to contract to buy a supercomputer before it is in production. Unfortunately, without such pre-production contracts, a fledging supercomputer company is unlikely to survive.

This section makes clear that Federal agencies can and should buy prototype and early production models of leading-edge, high-performance computer systems and subsystems. Such purchases provide critically-needed opportunities to test new design concepts and can be particularly effective in promoting commercialization of leading-edge technologies. This section also provides that particular emphasis is to be given to promoting development of advanced display technology (which will be needed for high-definition television (HDTV) and subsequently digital TV), supercomputers with alternative architectures, advanced storage devices, and very high-speed (multi-gigabit-per second) communications links.

SECTION 503.—REPORT ON EXPORT CONTROLS

This section requires the Secretary, within 120 days of date of enactment, to review and report to Congress on, export controls that hinder the development of foreign markets for North American manufacturers of high-performance computer systems. Supercomputer technology is advancing so quickly that export restrictions often become out-dated in a few years. Export controls imposed 10 years ago would prohibit export to many countries of most personal computers available today. Therefore, it is essential that export controls be reviewed frequently so that North American supercomputer manufacturers are not at a disadvantage relative to foreign competitior operating under more relaxed export controls. This section also requires that any review is to be conducted in consultation with the Department of State, DOD, the Central Intelligence Agency, NSA, and other appropriate agencies, in order to take into account national security and other concerns.

TITLE VI—BASIC RESEARCH AND EDUCATION

SECTION 601.—BASIC RESEARCH AND EDUCATION

This section requires OSTP to oversee and coordinate efforts of the relevant agencies and departments to support basic research on computer technology and create technology transfer mechanisms to ensure that the results of such basic research are readily available to North American companies. These provisions should not be interpreted as barring foreign companies from access to federally-funded technology. In addition, under this section ASTP is to coordinate efforts to promote basic research in computer science and engineering, computational science, library and information sciences, electrical engineering, and materials science, and to train more researchers in computer science and computational science. "Computational scientists" come from all disciplines of science and engineering, but all use high-performance computing to find solutions to the problems they are studying.

NSF traditionally has had a large role in funding basic research and education in colleges and universities. However, other agencies have a role as well. According to the 1989 OSTP report, NSF, NASA, DOE, and DARPA are planning to allocate at least ten percent of their budgets for high-performance computing to basic research and education.

TITLE VII—AUTHORIZATIONS

For FY 1991–95, the reported bill authorizes $338 million to NASA for the purposes of titles II, III, IV, V, and VI. This is in addition to funds authorized in other legislation. To maximize the President's flexibility in implementing the high-performance computing program, the funding for NASA's part of the program has not been divided among the various components of the program.

Authorizations for NSF for the purposes of titles III, IV, and V total $391 million. Of that amount, the Committee expects that between 10 and 15 percent shall be allocated for the purposes of title III. In addition, there is authorized to NSF $195 million to establish the network and $64 million for basic research and education. The separate authorizations to NSF for the NREN and for basic research are to highlight the importance of those two activities. These authorizations are in addition to those made in the NSF Authorization Act of 1988 (P.L. 100–570), which authorized funding for NSF for FY 1989–93. Since that legislation was enacted, the use of high-performance computing in research has become more widespread, and it has become clear that additional funding is required to expand NSF's high-performance computing program.

The authorizations provided in this legislation do not include monies for DARPA and DOE, the other two principal agencies in the National HPC Program. DOE, and in particular its national laboratories, has on-going high-performance computing programs that would be expanded as part of the national program. The authorization of funding for DOE's part of the National HPC program is provided in S. 1476, which the Senate Committee on Energy and Natural Resources ordered reported on June 27, 1990. Funding for DARPA's high-performance computing program is expected to be authorized in the DOD FY 1991 reauthorization bill.

AUTHORIZATIONS IN S. 1067

[In millions of dollars]

	Fiscal year—					Total
	1991	1992	1993	1994	1995	
For NSF:						
Networking	15	25	55	50	50	195
Information Services, Software, and Computer Systems	23	53	77	107	131	391
Basic Research and Education	8	10	13	15	18	64
Total	46	88	145	172	199	650
For NASA	22	45	67	89	115	338

CHANGES IN EXISTING LAW

In compliance with paragraph 12 of rule XXVI of the Standing Rules of the Senate, changes in existing law made by the bill, as reported, are shown as follows (existing law proposed to be omitted is enclosed in black brackets, new material is printed in italic, existing law in which no change is proposed is shown in roman):

NATIONAL SCIENCE AND TECHNOLOGY POLICY, ORGANIZATION, AND PRIORITIES ACT OF 1976

Section 102 of That Act

DECLARATION OF POLICY

SEC. 102. (a) PRINCIPLES.—In view of the foregoing, the Congress declares that the United States shall adhere to a national policy for science and technology which includes the following principles:

(1) through (5) * * *

[(6) The recognition that, as changing circumstances require periodic revision and adaptation of title I of this Act, the Federal Government is responsible for identifying and interpreting the changes in those circumstances as they occur, and for effecting subsequent changes in title I as appropriate.]

(6) The development and implementation of long-range, interagency research plans to support policy decisions regarding identified national and international concerns, and for which a sustained and coordinated commitment to improving scientific understanding will be required.

(b) through (c) * * *

Section 207 of That Act

ADDITIONAL FUNCTIONS OF THE DIRECTOR: ADMINISTRATIVE PROVISIONS

SEC. 207. (a) The Director shall, in addition to the other duties and functions set forth in this title—

(1) serve as Chairman of the Federal Coordinating Council for Science, Engineering, and Technology [established under Title IV]; and

(2) serve as a member of the Domestic Council—

(b) through (c) * * *

Section 401 of That Act

[ESTABLISHMENT AND FUNCTIONS

[SEC. 401. (a) There is established the Federal Coordinating Council for Science, Engineering, and Technology (hereinafter referred to as the "Council").

[(b) The council shall be composed of the Director of the Office of Science and Technology Policy and one representative of each of the following Federal agencies: Department of Agriculture, Department of Commerce, Department of Defense, Department of Health, Education, and Welfare, Department of Housing and Urban Development, Department of the Interior, Department of State, Department of Transportation, Veterans' Administration National Aeronautics and Space Administration, National Science Foundation, Environmental Protection Agency, and Energy Research and Development Administration. Each such representative shall be an official of policy rank designate by the head of the Federal agency concerned.

〔(c) The Director of the Office of Science and Technology Policy shall serve as Chairman of the Council. The Chairman may designate another member of the Council to act temporarily in the Chairman's absence as Chairman.

〔(d) The Chairman may (1) request the head of any Federal agency not named in subsection (b) of this section to designate a representative to participate in meetings or parts of meetings of the Council concerned with matters of substantial interest to such agency, and (2) invite other persons to attend meetings of the Council.

〔(e) The Council shall consider problems and developments in the fields of science, engineering, and technology and related activities affecting more than one Federal agency, and shall recommend policies and other measures designed to—

〔(1) provide more effective planning and administration of Federal scientific engineering, and technological programs,

〔(2) identify research needs including areas requiring additional emphasis,

〔(3) achieve more effective utilization of the scientific, engineering, and technological resources and facilities of Federal agencies, including the elimination of unwarranted duplication, and

〔(4) further international cooperation in science, engineering, and technology.

〔(f) The Council shall perform such other related advisory duties as shall be assigned by the President or by the Chairman.

〔(g) For the purpose of carrying out the provisions of this section, each Federal agency represented on the Council shall furnish necessary assistance to the Council. Such assistance may include—

〔(1) detailing employees to the Council to perform such functions, consistent with the purposes of this section, as the Chairman may assigned to them, and

〔(2) undertaking, upon request of the Chairman, such special studies for the Council as come within the functions herein assigned.

〔(h) For the purpose of conducting studies and making reports as directed by the Chairman, standing subcommittees and panels of the Council may be established. Among such standing subcommittees and panels of the Council shall be the Subcommittee on Food, Agriculture, and Forestry Research. This subcommittee shall review Federal research and development programs relevant to domestic and world food and fiber production and distribution, promote planning and coordination of this research in the Federal Government, and recommend policies and other measures concerning the food and agricultural sciences for the consideration of the Council. The subcommittee shall include, but not be limited to, representatives of each of the following departments or agencies; the Department of Agriculture, the Department of State, the Department of Defense, the Department of the Interior, the Department of Health and Human Services, the National Oceanic and Atmospheric Administration, the Department of Energy, the National Science Foundation, the Environmental Protection Agency, and the Tennessee Valley Authority. The principal representatives of the

Department of Agriculture shall serve as the chairman of the sub-committee.]

Sec. 401. (a) The Federal Coordinating Council for Science, Engineering, and Technology (hereinafter referred to as the "Council") shall consider problems and developments in the fields of science, engineering, and technology and related activities affecting more than one Federal agency, and shall recommend policies and other measures designed to—

(1) Provide more effective planning and administration of Federal scientific, engineering, and technological programs;

(2) identify research needs, including areas requiring additional emphasis;

(3) achieve more effective utilization of the scientific, engineering, and technological resources and facilities of Federal agencies, including the elimination of unwarranted duplication; and

(4) further international cooperation in science, engineering, and technology.

(b) The Council may be assigned responsibility for developing long-range and coordinated plans for scientific and technical research which involve the participation of more than two Federal agencies. Such plans shall—

(1) identify research approaches and priorities which most effectively advance scientific understanding and provide a basis for policy decisions;

(2) provide for effective cooperation and coordination of research among Federal agencies; and

(3) encourage domestic and, as appropriate, international cooperation among government, industry, and university scientists.

(c) The Council shall perform such other related advisory duties as shall be assigned by the President or by the Chairman of the Council.

(d) For the purpose of carrying out the provisions of this section, each Federal agency represented on the Council shall furnish necessary assistance to the Council. Such assistance may include—

(1) detailing employees to the Council to perform such functions, consistent with the purposes of this section, as the Chairman of the Council may assign to them; and

(2) undertaking, upon request of the Chairman, such special studies for the Council as come within the scope of authority of the Council.

(e) For the purpose of developing ingeragency plans, conducting studies, and making reports as directed by the Chairman, standing committees and working groups of the Council may be established.

New Title VI of That Act

TITLE VI—NATIONAL HIGH-PERFORMANCE COMPUTING PROGRAM

FINDINGS

SEC. 601. The Congress finds and declares the following:

(1) In order to strengthen America's computer industry and to assist the entire manufacturing sector, the Federal Government must provide leadership in the development and application of high-performance computing. In particular, the Federal Government should support the development of a high-capacity, national research and education network; make information services available over the network; facilitate the development of software for research, education, and industrial applications; continue to fund basic and applied research; and provide for the training of computer scientists and computational scientists.

(2) Several Federal agencies have ongoing high-performance computing programs. Improved interagency coordination, cooperation, and planning could enhance the effectiveness of these programs.

(3) A 1989 report by the Office of Science and Technology Policy outlining a research and development strategy for high-performance computing provides a framework for a multi-agency high-performance computing program.

NATIONAL HIGH-PERFORMANCE COMPUTING PLAN

SEC. 602. (a)(1) The President, through the Federal Coordinating Council for Science, Engineering, and Technology (hereafter in this title referred to as the "Council"), shall develop and implement a National High-Performance Computing Plan (hereafter in this title referred to as the "Plan") in accordance with the provisions, finding, and purpose of this Act. Consistent with the responsibilities set forth under subsection (d) of this section, the Plan shall contain recommendations for a five-year national effort, to be submitted to the Congress within one year after the date of enactment of this title and to be revised at least once every two years thereafter.

(2) The Plan shall—

(A) establish the goals and priorities for a Federal high-performance computing program for the fiscal year in which the Plan (or revised Plan) is submitted and the succeeding four fiscal years;

(B) set forth the role of each Federal agency and department in implementing the Plan;

(C) describe the levels of Federal funding for each agency and specific activities, including education, research activities, hardware and software development, and acquisition and operating expenses for computers and computer networks, required to achieve such goals and priorities; and

(D) consider and use, as appropriate, reports and studies conducted by Federal agencies and departments, the National Research Council, or other entities.

(3) The Plan shall address, where appropriate, the relevant programs and activities of the following Federal agencies and departments—

(A) the National Science Foundation;

(B) the Department of Commerce, particularly the National Institute of Standards and Technology, the National Oceanic and Atmospheric Administration, and the National Telecommunications and Information Administration;

(C) the National Aeronautics and Space Administration;

(D) the Department of Defense, particularly the Defense Advanced Research Projects Agency and, as appropriate, the National Security Agency;

(E) the Department of Energy;

(F) the Department of Health and Human Services, particularly the National Institutes of Health;

(G) the Department of Education;

(H) the Library of Congress, the National Library of Medicine, and the National Agricultural Library; and

(I) such other agencies and departments as the President or the Chairman of the Council considers appropriate.

(b) The Council shall—

(1) serve as lead entity responsible for development and implementation of the Plan;

(2) coordinate the high-performance computing research and development activities of Federal agencies and departments and report at least annually to the President, through the Chairman of the Council, on any recommended changes in agency or departmental roles that are needed to better implement the Plan;

(3) prior to the President's submission to the Congress of the annual budget estimate, review each agency and departmental budget estimate in the context of the Plan and make the results of that review available to the appropriate elements of the Executive Office of the President, particularly the Office of Management and Budget;

(4) work with Federal agencies, with the National Research Council, and with academic, State, industry, and other groups conducting research on high-performance computing.

(c) The Office of Science and Technology Policy shall establish a High-Performance Computing Advisory Panel consisting of representatives from industry and academia to provide the Council with an independent assessment of (1) progress made in implementing the Plan, (2) the need to revise the Plan, (3) the balance between the components of the Plan, (4) whether the research and development funded under the Plan is helping to maintain United States leadership in computing technology, and (5) other issues identified by the Director of the Office of Science and Technology Policy.

(d)(1) The Plan shall take into consideration, but not be limited to, the following missions and responsibilities of agencies and departments:

(A) The National Science Foundation shall continue to be responsible for basic research in computer science and engineering, computer technology, and computational science. The Foundation shall continue to solicit grant proposals and award grants by merit review for research in universities, non-profit re-

search institutions, and industry. The National Science Foundation shall also provide researchers with access to supercomputers and have primary responsibility for the establishment, by 1996, of a multi-gigabit-per-second national computer network, as required by section 201 of the High-Performance Computing Act of 1990. Prior to deployment of a multi-gigabit-per-second national network, the National Science Foundation shall maintain, expand, and upgrade its existing computer networks. Additional responsibilities include promoting development of information services and data bases available over such computer networks; facilitation of the documentation, evaluation, and distribution of research software over such computer networks; encouragement of continued development of innovative software by industry; and promotion of science and engineering education.

(B) The National Institute of Standards and Technology shall be responsible for developing, through the open standards setting process, standards, guidelines, measurement techniques, and test methods for the interoperability of high performance computers in networks and for common user interfaces to systems. In addition, the National Institute of Standards and Technology shall be responsible for developing benchmark tests and standards, through the open standards setting process and in conjunction with industry, for high performance computers and software. Pursuant to the Computer Security Act of 1987 (Public Law 100–235; 100 Stat. 1724), the National Institute of Standards and Technology shall continue to be responsible for adopting standards and guidelines needed to assure the cost-effective security and privacy of sensitive information in Federal computer systems. These standards and guidelines shall be developed through the open standards setting process and in conjunction with industry.

(C) The National Oceanic and Atmospheric Administration shall continue to observe, collect, communicate, analyze, process, provide, and disseminate data about the Earth and its oceans, atmosphere, and space environment. The National Oceanic and Atmospheric Administration shall improve the quality and accessibility of the environmental data stored at its four data centers and shall perform research and develop technology to support its data handling role.

(D) The National Aeronautics and Space Administration shall continue to conduct basic and applied research in high-performance computing, particularly in the field of computational science, with emphasis on aeronautics and the processing of remote sensing data.

(E) The Department of Defense, through the Defense Advanced Research Projects Agency and other agencies, shall continue to conduct basic and applied research in high-performance computing, particularly in computer networking, semiconductor technology, and large-scale parallel processors.-Pursuant to the Stevenson-Wydler Technology Innovation Act of 1980 (15 U.S.C. 3701 et seq.) and other appropriate Acts, the Department shall ensure that unclassified computing technology research is readily available to United States industry. The National Secu-

rity Agency, pursuant to the Computer Security Act of 1987 (Public Law 100–235; 100 Stat. 1724), shall continue to provide, where appropriate, technical advice and assistance to the National Institute of Standards and Technology for the adoption of standards and guidelines needed to assure the cost-effective security and privacy of sensitive information in Federal computer systems.

(F) The Department of Energy and its national laboratories shall continue to conduct basic and applied research in high-performance computing, particularly in software development and multi-processor supercomputers. Pursuant to the Stevenson-Wydler Technology Innovation Act of 1980 (15 U.S.C. 3701 et seq.) and other appropriate Acts, the Department of Energy shall ensure that unclassified computer research is readily available to North American companies.

(G) The Department of Education, pursuant to the Library Services and Construction Act (20 U.S.C. 351 et seq.) and the Higher Education Act of 1965 (20 U.S.C. 1060 et seq.), shall encourage the distribution of library and information resources, through library linkages to the National Research and Education Network and through other means.

(H) The Library of Congress, the National Library of Medicine, and the National Agricultural Library, as national libraries of the United States, shall continue to compile, develop, and maintain electronic data bases in appropriate areas of expertise and provide for dissemination of, access to, and use of these data bases and other library resources through the Network.

(2) The Plan shall facilitate collaboration among agencies and departments with respect to—

(A) ensuring interoperability among computer networks run by the agencies and departments;

(B) increasing software productivity, capability, and reliability;

(C) encouraging, where appropriate, agency cooperation with industry in development of software;

(D) promoting interoperability of software;

(E) distributing software among the agencies and departments; and

(F) distributing federally-funded, unclassified software to State and local governments, industry, and universities.

(e)(1) Each Federal agency and department involved in high-performance computing shall, as part of its annual request for appropriations to the Office of Management and Budget, submit a report identifying each element of its high-performance computing activities, which—

(A) specifies whether each such element (i) contributes primarily to the implementation of the Plan or (ii) contributes primarily to the achievement of other objectives but aids Plan implementation in important ways; and

(B) states the portion of its request for appropriations that is allocated to each such element.

(2) The Office of Management and Budget shall review each such report in light of the goals, priorities, and agency and departmental responsibilities set forth in the Plan, and shall include, in the Presi-

dent's annual budget estimate, a statement of the portion of each agency or department's annual budget estimate that is allocated to each element of such agency or department's high-performance computing activities. The Office of Management and Budget shall ensure that a copy of the President's annual budget estimate is transmitted to the Chairman of the Council at the same time as such budget estimate is submitted to the Congress.

ANNUAL REPORT

SEC. 603. The Chairman of the Council shall prepare and submit to the President and the Congress, not later than March 1 of each year, an annual report on the activities conducted pursuant to this title during the preceding fiscal year, including—

(1) a summary of the achievements of Federal high-performance computing research and development efforts during that preceding fiscal year;

(2) an analysis of the progress made toward achieving the goals and objectives of the Plan;

(3) a copy or summary of the Plan and any changes made in such Plan;

(4) a summary of agency budgets for high-performance computing activities for that preceding fiscal year; and

(5) any recommendations regarding additional action or legislation which may be required to assist in achieving the purposes of this title.

○

G

S. 1976,
Department of Energy High-Performance Computing Act of 1989,
U.S. Senate, 101st Congress, November 21, 1989.

101ST CONGRESS
1ST SESSION
S. 1976

To provide for continued United States leadership in high-performance computing.

IN THE SENATE OF THE UNITED STATES

NOVEMBER 21 (legislative day, NOVEMBER 6), 1989

Mr. JOHNSTON (for himself, Mr. GORE, and Mr. McCLURE) introduced the following bill; which was read twice and referred to the Committee on Energy and Natural Resources

---

A BILL

To provide for continued United States leadership in high-performance computing.

1   *Be it enacted by the Senate and House of Representa-*

2 *tives of the United States of America in Congress assembled,*

3 That this Act may be referred to as the "Department of

4 Energy High-Performance Computing Act of 1989".

5   FINDINGS AND PURPOSES

6   SEC. 2. (a) The Congress finds and declares the

7 following:

8   (1) In the last twenty years, computing technol-

9   ogy has transformed America's research laboratories,

361

1 factories, and offices, and become indispensable to our

2 way of life.

3   (2) Rapid advances in computing technology have

4 resulted in uses for computers unimaginable only five

5 or ten years ago. Many of these advances are a result

6 of research and development on supercomputers, ad-

7 vanced computer software, and other aspects of high-

8 performance computing technology.

9   (3) High-performance computing is a powerful

10 tool to increase productivity in industrial design and

11 manufacturing, scientific research, communications, and

12 information management.

13   (4) The United States currently leads the world in

14 the development and use of high-performance comput-

15 ing. However, that lead is increasingly being chal-

16 lenged, and American firms share of the multi- bil-

17 lion-dollar world market for both high-performance

18 computer systems and other computers is shrinking.

19   (5) In order to strengthen America's computer in-

20 dustry and to assist the entire manufacturing sector,

21 the Federal Government must provide leadership in the

22 development and application of high-performance com-

23 puter technology. In particular, the Federal Govern-

24 ment should create a National High-Performance Com-

25 puting Program to support the development of a high-

1   capacity, national research and education computer

2   network; facilitate the development of software for re-

3   search, education, and industrial applications; continue

4   to fund basic research; and provide for the training of

5   computer scientists and computational scientists.

6   (6) Several Federal agencies have ongoing high-

7   performance computing research and development pro-

8   grams which can contribute to a National High-Per-

9   formance Computing Program. Such a program would

10   provide additional funding for these existing programs,

11   create new research and development programs, and

12   improve coordination between the various agency

13   programs.

14   (7) A September 1989 report by the Office of Sci-

15   ence and Technology Policy entitled "The Federal

16   High Performance Computing Program" outlining a

17   research and development plan provides a framework

18   for such a program.

19   (8) The Department of Energy, in order to fulfill

20   its mission to conduct energy research and direct the

21   Nation's nuclear weapons program, has established

22   several high-performance computing research and de-

23   velopment programs. High-energy physics, materials

24   sciences, fusion energy research, human genetics re-

25   search, oil and gas exploration, nuclear reactor design,

1 and nuclear weapons design all rely heavily on high-

2 performance computing.

3 (9) The Department of Energy has extensive

4 high-performance computing facilities and has played a

5 key role in developing software and applications for su-

6 percomputers. It has funded research in mathematical

7 and computational sciences, has developed new designs

8 for supercomputers, and has established advanced com-

9 puter networks for connecting supercomputers and

10 other computers throughout the country.

11 (10) By building upon existing Department of

12 Energy high-performance computing research and de-

13 velopment programs, the Department of Energy can

14 play a key role in a National High-Performance Com-

15 puting Program.

16 (b) PURPOSE.—It is the purpose of the Congress in this

17 Act to authorize the Secretary of Energy to—

18 (1) develop a long-range strategy for research,

19 development, and application of high-performance

20 computing;

21 (2) implement that strategy in conjunction with

22 other Federal agencies as part of a National High-

23 Performance Computing Program; and

1   (3) ensure the appropriate transfer of high-

2 performance computing technology to United States

3 industry.

4   (c) DEFINITIONS.—

5   (1) "Secretary" means the Secretary of Energy.

6   (2) "Department" means the Department of

7 Energy.

8 DEPARTMENT OF HIGH-PERFORMANCE COMPUTING PLAN

9   SEC. 3. (a) The Secretary is authorized to immediately

10 develop and implement long-range plan for high-performance

11 computing at the Department of Energy. The Secretary shall

12 develop the plan within one year after the date of enactment

13 of this Act. The plan shall cover the fiscal year the plan is

14 implemented and at least the next four years. The plan shall

15 thereafter be updated annually.

16   (b) The plan shall—

17   (1) summarize ongoing high-performance comput-

18 ing programs at the Department of Energy;

19   (2) detail the Department of Energy's contribution

20 to a National High-Performance Computing Program

21 to expand Federal support for research, development,

22 and application of high-performance computing technol-

23 ogy in order to—

24   (A) establish a high-capacity national re-

25 search and education computer network;

1   (B) develop data bases, services, and re-

2   search facilities which would be available for

3   access over such a national network;

4   (C) stimulate research on software tech-

5   nology;

6   (D) promote the more rapid development and

7   wider distribution of computer software;

8   (E) accelerate the development of computer

9   systems; and

10   (F) invest in basis research and education.

11 (3) establish the goals and priorities for research,

12 development, and application of high-performance com-

13 puting at the Department of Energy for the time

14 period covered by the plan;

15 (4) describe the levels of funding for each aspect

16 of high-performance computing, including basic re-

17 search, hardware and software development, education,

18 acquisition and operating expenses for computers and

19 computer networks, and education;

20 (5) define the role of each of the Department of

21 Energy's national laboratories involved in research, de-

22 velopment, and application of high-performance com-

23 puting technology; and

24 (6) set a timetable for creation and implementa-

25 tion of technology transfer mechanisms to ensure that

1   the results of research funded under the plan are read-

2   ily available to United States industry.

3   THE NATIONAL RESEARCH AND EDUCATION NETWORK

4   SEC. 4. (a) As part of a National High-Performance

5 Computing Program, the Secretary shall, in cooperation with

6 the Director of the National Science Foundation, the Secre-

7 tary of Defense, the Secretary of the Department of Com-

8 merce, the Administrator of the National Aeronautics and

9 Space Administration, and other appropriate agencies, pro-

10 vide for the establishment of a national multi-gigabit-per-

11 second research and education computer network by 1996, to

12 be known as the National Research and Education Network

13 (NREN).

14   (b) The network shall—

15   (1) link government, industry, and the higher edu-

16   cation community;

17   (2) provide computer users at more than one thou-

18   sand universities, Federal laboratories, and industrial

19   laboratories with access to supercomputers, computer

20   data bases, and other research facilities;

21   (3) be developed in close cooperation with the

22   computer and telecommunications industry;

23   (4) be designed and developed with the advice of

24   potential users in government, industry, and the higher

25   education community;

(5) be established in a manner which fosters and maintains competition in high speed data networking within the telecommunications industry;

(6) have accounting mechanisms which allow users or groups of users to be charged for their usage of the network, where appropriate; and

(7) be phased out when commercial networks can meet the networking needs of American researchers.

(c) The Department of Energy shall—

(1) provide networking support for the energy research community;

(2) provide for interconnection of existing computer networks run by the Department and other agencies, where appropriate;

(3) participate, with other Federal agencies, in the development and testing of advanced prototype networks;

(4) conduct research and development of advanced networking technology, particularly for supercomputers;

(5) develop technology to support computer-based collaboration that allows researchers around the Nation to share information and instrumentation using computer networks; and

1   (6) take an active role in the interagency coordi-

2   nating committees established to develop the National

3   Research and Education Network.

4   (d) There is authorized to be appropriated to the Secre-

5 tary for the purposes of this title, $10,000,000 for fiscal year

6 1991, $15,000,000 for fiscal year 1992, $20,000,000 for

7 fiscal year 1993, and $25,000,000 for fiscal year 1994, and

8 $30,000,000 for fiscal year 1995.

9   SOFTWARE

10   SEC. 5. (a) In accordance with the plan outlined in sec-

11 tion 3, the Secretary shall provide for research and develop-

12 ment of high-performance computer software for application

13 in high-energy physics, fusion energy research, engineering,

14 materials sciences, astrophysics, climate modeling, genetics,

15 and other fields. The Secretary shall also provide for the de-

16 velopment of improved software tools and components to fa-

17 cilitate the development of software for high-performance

18 computer systems.

19   (b) The Secretary shall define and provide advanced

20 software technology support to research groups collaborating

21 to address so-called Grand Challenge problems in science and

22 engineering. A Grand Challenge is a fundamental problem in

23 science and engineering, with broad economic and scientific

24 impact, whose solution will require the application of the

25 high-performance computing resources.

1   (1) The Grand Challenges to be addressed include

2 by are not limited to—

3   (A) PREDICTION OF GLOBAL CHANGE.—The

4 goal is to understand the coupled atmosphere,

5 ocean, biosphere system in enough detail to be

6 able to make long-range predictions about its be-

7 havior and determine its response to man-caused

8 releases of carbon dioxide, methane, chlorofluoro-

9 carbons, and other gases.

10   (B) MATERIALS SCIENCES.—The goal is to

11 use high-performance computing technology to

12 improve our understanding of the atomic nature of

13 materials, enabling the design and production of

14 improved semiconductors, superconductors, ceram-

15 ics, and other materials.

16   (C) HUMAN GENOME.—The goal is to use

17 high-performance computing technology to ana-

18 lyze, store, and disseminate data on the molecular

19 structure of the DNA that expresses the tens of

20 thousands of genes carried by each human being.

21 Identification of these genes would lead to a

22 better understanding and possibly treatment of ge-

23 netic diseases, cancer, and other diseases.

24   (D) NUCLEAR FUSION.—The goal is to use

25 supercomputer models to understand the physics

1 of plasmas at the very high temperature required

2 for nuclear fusion.

3   (E) ENERGY EFFICIENCY.—The goal is to

4 use supercomputer models to better understand

5 combustion in order to design more efficient en-

6 gines and furnaces.

7   (F) ENHANCED OIL AND GAS RECOVERY.—

8 The goal is to use supercomputer models to locate

9 and better exploit oil and gas fields.

10 (2) The Secretary shall focus research on those

11 Grand Challenges that are of greatest importance to

12 the Nation, will benefit most from the application of

13 high-performance computing, and are most consistent

14 with the mission of the Department of Energy.

15 (3) The Secretary shall establish collaborative re-

16 search groups consisting of scientists and engineers

17 concerned with a particular Grand Challenge, software

18 and systems engineers, and algorithm designers, and

19 provide them with—

20   (A) computational and experimental facilities,

21 including supercomputers for numerical modeling;

22   (B) access to the National Research and

23 Educational Network and other computer net-

24 works, and;

1   (C) access to and technology for effectively

2   utilizing scientific data bases.

3   (d) The Secretary shall establish programs to develop

4 software tools and components to accelerate development of

5 software for computers, especially supercomputers. Such pro-

6 grams would fund research on fundamental algorithms,

7 models of computation, program analysis, and new program-

8 ming languages. Particular emphasis should be given to de-

9 velopment of programming languages, compilers, operating

10 systems, and software tools for parallel computer systems.

11   (e) The Secretary shall establish high-performance com-

12 puting research centers to accelerate the development and

13 application of new generations of high-performance comput-

14 ing technology by enabling researchers to explore applica-

15 tions of this new technology.

16   (1) Most of these centers would be located within

17   existing computer research organizations funded by the

18   Department of Energy;

19   (2) These centers could facilitate research on the

20   Grand Challenges and other applications;

21   (3) Both new and existing Department of Energy

22   supercomputers centers shall help provide the national

23   research community with access to supercomputers be-

24   cause researchers developing algorithms, software

1 tools, and operating systems require access to new

2 generation technology; and

3   (4) These centers shall provide access to a variety

4 of different high-performance computer systems with

5 different computer architectures.

6 (f) There is authorized to be appropriated to the Secre-

7 tary for research and development on scientific Grand Chal-

8 lenges, development of advanced software technology, and

9 creation of high-performance computing research centers, in

10 accordance with the purposes of this section, $30,000,000 for

11 fiscal year 1991, $45,000,000 for fiscal year 1992,

12 $60,000,000 for fiscal year 1993, $75,000,000 for fiscal year

13 1994, $90,000,000 for fiscal year 1995.

14   HIGH-PERFORMANCE COMPUTER SYSTEMS

15 SEC. 6. (a) In accordance with the plan required in sec-

16 tion 3, the Secretary shall provide for support of research and

17 development of high-performance computer systems. Funding

18 shall be provided for—

19   (1) research and development in the national lab-

20 oratories, universities, and industry on all aspects of

21 high-performance computer systems including proces-

22 sors, memory, mass storage devices, input/output de-

23 vices, and associated system software;

24   (2) increased research in—

25   (A) computer science,

26   (B) parallel computer architectures,

1   (C) optoelectronics, and

2   (D) mass storage technology; and

3   (3) development of tools for the rapid design, pro-

4   totyping, and integration of high-performance comput-

5   ing systems.

6   (b) In addition, the Department of Energy shall pur-

7 chase early market and production model computer systems

8 and subsystems for use both in high-performance computing

9 research centers and for other research programs within the

10 Department. Such purchases will—

11   (1) stimulate hardware and software development

12   by reducing the research and development risk of

13   United States manufacturers developing high-perform-

14   ance computer systems;

15   (2) provide manufacturers with valuable tests of

16   their new systems.

17   (c) There is authorized to be appropriated to the Secre-

18 tary for research and development, procuring, and testing of

19 high-performance computer systems, $15,000,000 for fiscal

20 year 1991, $25,000,000 for fiscal year 1992, $35,000,000

21 for fiscal year 1993, $45,000,000 for fiscal year 1994, and

22 $55,000,000 for fiscal year 1995.

23   BASIC RESEARCH AND EDUCATION

24   SEC. 7. (a) In order to address the long-term national

25 need for high-performance computing, the Secretary shall—

1   (1) support basic research on computer technol-
2   ogy, including research on advanced semiconductor
3   computer chip designs, new materials for integrated
4   circuits, improved integrated circuit fabrication
5   techniques, photonics, and superconducting computer
6   components;

7   (2) support basic research on computing technolo-
8   gy, including basic research on algorithms, software
9   languages and tools, architectures, systems software,
10   networks, distributed computing, and symbolic
11   processing;

12   (3) create technology transfer mechanisms to
13   ensure that the results of basic research are readily
14   available to United States industry;

15   (4) promote basic research in computer science,
16   computational science, electrical engineering, and ma-
17   terials sciences; and

18   (5) educate and train more researchers in comput-
19   er science and computational science by—

20   (A) making the national laboratories avail-
21   able to senior graduate students, postdoctoral fel-
22   lows, and faculty from the Nation's universities;

23   (B) expanding summer science programs for
24   high school students;

   (C) providing computer facilities to universities throughout the country; and

   (D) establishing more cooperative research programs with the academic computational science community.

(b) There is authorized to be appropriated to the Secretary for the purposes of this section, $10,000,000 for fiscal year 1991, $15,000,000 for fiscal year 1992, $20,000,000 for fiscal year 1993, $25,000,000 for fiscal year 1994, and $30,000,000 for fiscal year 1995.

GOVERNMENT AND PRIVATE SECTOR COOPERATION

SEC. 8. (a) The Secretary may cooperate with, solicit help from, provide funds to, or enter into contracts with private contractors, industry, government, universities, or any other person or entity the Secretary deems necessary in carrying out the Provisions of this Act.

(b) The Secretary shall cooperate with other Federal agencies in carrying out the provisions of this Act, particularly the National Science Foundation, the Department of Commerce (particularly the National Institute of Standards and Technology), the National Aeronautics and Space Administration, the Department of Defense, and the Office of Science and Technology Policy.

REPORT REQUIREMENT

SEC. 9. The Secretary shall within one year after the date of enactment of this Act, report to the Congress regard-

1 ing the implementation of this Act, and thereafter, provide

2 annual reports to the Congress.

○

H

Department of Energy High-Performance Computing Act of 1990, U.S. Congress, Senate, Committee on Energy and Natural Resources. Report 101-377.

Calendar No. 700

101ST CONGRESS *2d Session*	SENATE	REPORT 101–377

DEPARTMENT OF ENERGY HIGH-PERFORMANCE COMPUTING ACT OF 1990

JULY 19 (legislative day, JULY 10), 1990.—Ordered to be printed

Mr. JOHNSTON, from the Committee on Energy and Natural Resources, submitted the following

REPORT

[To accompany S. 1976]

The Committee on Energy and Natural Resources, to which was referred the bill (S. 1976) to provide for continued United States leadership in high-performance computing, having considered the same, reports favorably thereon with an amendment and recommends that the bill, as amended, do pass.

The amendment is as follows:

Strike out all after the enacting clause and insert in lieu thereof the following:

SEC. 1. SHORT TITLE.

This Act may be referred to as the "Department of Energy High-Performance Computing Act of 1990".

SEC. 2. FINDINGS.

The Congress finds that—

(a) over the last twenty years high-performance computing has transformed America's research laboratories, industries and offices, and has become indispensable to our way of life;

(b) national security, economic competitiveness, productivity and the quality of life are increasingly dependent on high-performance computing;

(c) the United States currently leads the world in the development and use of high-performance computing, but that lead is increasingly being challenged;

(d) the Federal Government must provide leadership in the research, development and application of high-performance computing technology through collaboration with industry, educational institutions, government laboratories and others; and

(e) for high-performance computing to have its greatest impact, the Federal Government must coordinate and make better use of existing Federal high-performance computing resources.

SEC. 3. PURPOSES.

The purposes of this Act are—

39–010

379

(a) to authorize and direct the Secretary of Energy to establish a High-Performance Computing Program consisting of—

(1) a National Research and Educational Network; and

(2) Collaborative Consortia to undertake basic research and development of high-performance computing hardware and software, and to engage in research directed at the solutions to scientific and engineering problems which require the application of high-performance computing resources; and

(b) to establish a Federal Interagency High-Performance Computing Task Force.

SEC. 4. DEFINITIONS.

For the purposes of this Act the term—

(a) "Secretary" means the Secretary of Energy;

(b) "Department" means the Department of Energy;

(c) "Federal laboratory" means any laboratory that is owned by the Federal Government, whether it is operated by the Government or by a contractor;

(d) "national laboratory" means any Federal laboratory that is owned by the Department of Energy;

(e) "software creation" means any innovation or preparation of new computer software of whatever kind or description whether patentable or unpatentable, and whether copyrightable or noncopyrightable; and

(f) "educational institution" means a degree granting institution of at least a Baccalaureate level.

SEC. 5. DEPARTMENT OF ENERGY HIGH-PERFORMANCE COMPUTING PROGRAM.

(a) The Secretary, acting in accordance with the authority provided by the Federal Non-Nuclear Research and Development Act of 1974 (42 U.S.C. 5901 et. seq.) and subject to available appropriations, shall establish a High-Performance Computing Program ("HPC Program").

(b) Within one year after the date of the enactment of this Act, the Secretary shall establish a management plan to carry out HPC Program activities. The plan shall—

(1) be developed in conjunction with the Federal Government's overall efforts to promote high-performance computing;

(2) summarize all ongoing high-performance computing activities and resources at the Department of Energy that are not classified or otherwise restricted;

(3) describe the levels of funding for each aspect of high-performance computing that are not classified or otherwise restricted;

(4) establish long range goals and priorities for research, development and application of high-performance computing at the department, and devise a strategy for achieving them; and

(5) ensure that technology developed pursuant to the HPC Program is transferred to the private sector in accordance with applicable law.

SEC. 6. DEPARTMENT OF ENERGY HIGH-PERFORMANCE COMPUTING PROGRAM ACTIVITIES.

(a) The Secretary shall create a high-performance computer network to be known as the National Research and Education Network ("NREN"). The NREN shall—

(1) have a multi-gigabit-per-second data transmission capacity;

(2) enable government, industry, educational institutions and others to link together, as may be appropriate;

(3) be developed with the advice of potential users;

(4) have mechanisms that allow users to be charged appropriately for the use of the NREN;

(5) be subject to such terms, conditions, charges and limitations as the Secretary deems reasonable and appropriate;

(6) be operational by not later than the end of 1996; and

(7) be eliminated or sold to the private sector, in accordance with applicable law, when the networking needs provided by the NREN can be satisfied by other means.

(b) The Secretary shall promote education and research in high-performance computational science and related fields that require the application of high-performance computing resources by making the Department's high performance computing resources more available to undergraduate, graduate students, post-doctoral fellows and faculty from the Nation's educational institutions.

3

(c) The Secretary shall establish at least two Collaborative Consortia, and as many more as the Secretary determines are needed to carry out the purposes of this Act, by soliciting and selecting proposals.

    (1) Each Collaborative Consortium shall—

        (A) undertake basic research and development of high-performance computing hardware and associated software technology;

        (B) undertake research and development of advanced prototype networks;

        (C) conduct research directed at scientific and technical problems whose solutions require the application of high performance computing resources;

        (D) promote the testing and uses of new types of high-performance-computing and related software and equipment;

        (E) serve as a vehicle for computing vendors to test new ideas and technology in a sophisticated computing environment; and

        (F) disseminate information to Federal agencies, the private sector, educational institutions and other potential users on the availability of high-performance computing facilities.

    (2) Each Collaborative Consortium shall be comprised of a lead institution, which has responsibility for the direction and performance of the consortium, and participants from industry, Federal laboratories or agencies, educational institutions, and others, as may be appropriate.

    (3) Each lead institution shall be a national laboratory which has the experience in research on problems that require the application of high-performance computing resources.

    (4) Industrial participants in each consortium shall not be reimbursed for costs associated with their own involvement, though the consortium may fund research and development associated with prototype computing technology.

(d) The provisions of the National Cooperative Research Act of 1984 (15 U.S.C. 4301–4305) shall apply to research activities taken pursuant to this section.

(e) Each Collaborative Consortium may be established by a Cooperative Research and Development Agreement as provided in 15 U.S.C. 3710a, the National Competitiveness Technology Transfer Act of 1989.

(f) The Secretary shall report yearly to Congress regarding the HPC Program.

SEC. 7. FEDERAL INTERAGENCY HIGH-PERFORMANCE COMPUTING TASK FORCE.

(a) There is hereby established a Federal Interagency High-Performance Computing Task Force ("Task Force").

(b) The purposes of the Task Force are—

    (1) to develop a government-wide high-performance computing strategy;

    (2) to bring about the maximum efficient use of available Federal high-performance computing resources by Federal agencies; and

    (3) to coordinate Federal agencies' policies and activities with respect to this section.

(c) The Task Force shall be composed of the Secretary of Energy, the Secretary of Commerce, the Secretary of Defense, the Administrator of the National Aeronautics and Space Administration, the Director of the National Science Foundation, and the heads of other Federal agencies that the Chairman of the Task Force may find appropriate.

(d) The Task Force shall be chaired by the Secretary and shall report to the Director of the Office of Science and Technology Policy.

(e) The Task Force shall develop a comprehensive, government-wide high-performance computing strategy that—

    (1) establishes how the high-performance computing activities of Federal agencies and departments should be coordinated to carry out the strategy;

    (2) establishes the goals and priorities for Federal high-performance computing;

    (3) identifies the role of each Federal agency and department in implementing the strategy;

    (4) recommends the level of Federal funding needed to carry out the strategy for each agency;

    (5) determines which Federal high-performance computing facilities are under-utilized and why they are under-utilized, and makes recommendations to such agencies for appropriate actions;

    (6) identifies agency rules, regulations, policies and practices which unduly limit the maximum efficient utilization of Federal high performance computing and network facilities, and makes recommendations to such agencies for appropriate changes;

4

(7) determines who outside of the Federal Government should have access to Federal high-performance computing facilities, if anyone, and the appropriate terms and conditions for such access;

(8) identifies hardware and software needed for the maximum efficient utilization of existing facilities; and

(9) disseminates information to Federal agencies, corporations, educational institutions and others, as may be appropriate, on the availability of Federal high-performance computing facilities, and the means by which access can be obtained.

(f) The Chairman of the Task Force shall establish a private sector advisory panel of persons eminent in the field of high-performance computing from the educational establishment, corporations, the private sector and from elsewhere as the Chairman finds appropriate, which shall advise the Task Force.

(g) The Task Force shall issue an annual report which shall review progress made in carrying out the provisions of this section, including activities taken by Federal agencies, describe plans for carrying out the requirements of this Act in the future, and make such recommendations as may be appropriate.

(h) The Task Force and the private sector advisory panel shall not be considered an advisory Committee within the meaning of 5 U.S.C. appendix 3(2), the Federal Advisory Committee Act.

SEC. 8. GOVERNMENT AND PRIVATE SECTOR COOPERATION.

In accordance with applicable law, the Secretary may cooperate with, solicit help from, provide funds to, or enter into contracts with private contractors, industry, government, universities, or any other person or entity the Secretary deems necessary in carrying out the provisions of this Act to the extent appropriated funds are available.

SEC. 9. OWNERSHIP OF INVENTIONS AND CREATIONS.

(a) Except as otherwise provided by law, title to any invention or software creation shall vest in the United States and shall be governed by the provisions of 42 U.S.C. 5908, the Federal Non-Nuclear Research and Development Act of 1974.

(b) No trade secrets or commercial or financial information that is privileged or confidential, under the meaning of 5 U.S.C. 552(b)(4), which is obtained from a non-Federal party participating in research or other activities under this Act shall be disclosed.

(c) The Secretary, for a period of up to five years after the development of information that results from research and development activities conducted under this Act and that would be a trade secret or commercial or financial information that is privileged or confidential, under the meaning of 5 U.S.C. 552(b)(4), if the information had been obtained from a non-Federal party, may provide appropriate protection against the dissemination of such information, including exemption from subchapter II of chapter 5 of title 5, United States Code.

SEC. 10. AUTHORIZATION.

In addition to existing authorizations that may be used to carry out this Act, there is authorized to be appropriated for the purposes of this Act $65,000,000 for fiscal year 1991, $100,000,000 for fiscal year 1992, $135,000,000 for fiscal year 1993, $170,000,000 for fiscal year 1994, and $205,000,000 for fiscal year 1995.

PURPOSE OF THE MEASURE

The purpose of S. 1976, as reported by the Committee, is to help the United States maintain preeminence in high-performance computing and to make supercomputing power available to larger segments of the United States.

To accomplish these objectives, the bill would require the Secretary of Energy to establish a program to carry out basic research and development in high-performance computing through collaborative research and development consortia. The Secretary would also be required to establish a National Research and Education Network ("NREN") to make the Nation's data and computing resources available to more segments of society. The bill also establishes a high-performance computing task force that, under the direction of the Secretary of Energy, would design and implement a national high-performance computing strategy to coordinate the Federal Government's overall efforts in high-performance computing.

BACKGROUND AND NEED

Background

High-performance computing, a definition

A common definition of a supercomputer is simply "the most powerful computer available at any given time." However, the definition of "power" is inexact and depends on many factors, including processor speed, memory size, user skill, the type of job being performed and the type of software used.

Today, supercomputers cost anywhere from $1 million to $30 million and have 1,000 to 100,000 times more power than a typical personal computer. These supercomputers make billions of mathematical calculations per second, which is 50 to 100 times faster than the supercomputers available ten years ago.

The more general term, "high-performance computing," refers to the whole field of advanced computing technologies. These technologies include all types of supercomputers: the traditional types, such as parallel or vector processors, and the experimental types, such as large scale parallel processors, neural nets and optoelectronics. These technologies also include components of supercomputers that have great impact on the power of the computer: memory, storage devices, input/output devices and software. Computer networks are often linked under the category of high-performance computing because it is through networks that supercomputers are accessed. Furthermore, the networks themselves require sophisticated computing technology.

No one really knows what the high-performance computers of tomorrow will look like. The two most common types of high-performance computer hardware in use today are parallel processors and vector processors. Parallel processors use several very sophisticated and powerful processors to analyze different pieces of a problem at the same time. Today's large high-performance computers, such as those offered by Cray or IBM, have anywhere from two to eight processors. However, this assumes that a problem may be broken into large independent pieces. Vector processing produces a series of similar calculations in an assembly line fashion, which does not require that the problem be broken down into separate pieces.

Other types of specialized systems have appeared that are largely experimental. They use fundamentally different types of hardware architecture to obtain gains in computational power. For example, some try to gain increases in computing speed by hooking together hundreds or even thousands of simpler and slower processors. Many experts think that any large increases in computational power must grow out of experimental systems such as these.

The personal computers of tomorrow will rival the high-performance computers of today. Since the dawn of computing technology, computer performance has improved one million times. Improvements in computer design, chips and software allow today's personal computers to approach the power of the supercomputers used in the 1970s. The rapidly evolving nature of computing technology will permit the personal computers of the near future to approach the power of today's supercomputers.

Historical development of high-performance computing

The United States invented high-performance computing and continues to lead the world in the development of high-performance computing. The biggest single factor accounting for the development of high-performance computing has been large computational demands required by defense research, particularly in the area of nuclear weapons design.

Historically, the Department of Energy and its predecessor agencies played the lead role in the development of high-performance computing, particularly the supercomputer. Supercomputing originated with the "Los Alamos problem", the design of the first atomic bomb. In 1945, Los Alamos researchers used the first large-scale electronic computer, the ENIAC, to help solve the Los Alamos problem. Subsequent collaborations with supercomputer vendors, such as IBM, Univac (now Unisys), Control Data and Cray Resarch, have continued to this day, enabling the United States to become the leader in computational science.

In fact, Cray Research would not exist without the Los Alamos National Laboratory of the Department of Energy. In 1976 Cray offered its first supercomputer to the Los Alamos laboratory without software or an operating system if the laboratory would develop the technologies needed to operate the machine. The Department of Energy and the Los Alamos laboratory were crucial in getting the first Cray supercomputer to work. Today, Cray is the biggest manufacturer of supercomputers in the world, and the Los Alamos National Laboratory is the most powerful scientific computing center in the world, serving more than 8,000 researchers throughout the nation via a computer network.

Much of the Department's research, such as nuclear weapons design or research in high-energy physics, requires the most powerful computers available. In order to carry out the research, DOE has often accelerated the development of high-performance computers by undertaking cooperative activities involving its national laboratories and computer manufacturers, universities and other Federal agencies. The Department has shaped high-performance computing by acquiring early market and production-model computing systems for its research programs.

The Department's laboratories have become the world's most demanding, sophisticated and experienced users of supercomputers. Manufacturers of high-performance computers routinely send new prototype computers to the national laboratories for testing. The laboratories help the manufacturer identify problems, find solutions for them and write the unique software packages supercomputers require.

Today, the Department of Energy remains the biggest user of supercomputers. The Department has 33 unclassified supercomputers. The Department of Defense has 20 unclassified supercomputers. These two agencies account for three-fourths of the federal government's unclassified supercomputers.

7

Need

Benefits of supercomputers

Many scientific endeavors would not be possible without the use of supercomputers. For example, the data we collect from outer space can only be understood and visualized by a supercomputer. The superconducting supercollider will require supercomputers to understand the data it produces. Weather forecasting becomes more accurate the more powerful the supercomputer. The United Kingdom more accurately predicts the weather than the United States because of supercomputers. The human genome project is possible only because of high-performance computers.

It has only been recently that supercomputers have been able to graphially visualize the outcome of experiments. The ability to see the results visually in graphic form is a major step forward in scientific analysis. Without the ability to graphically visualize the results, the researcher must analyze hundreds of pages of computer printouts, a painstakingly slow process.

Most of the data this country generates from its scientific endeavors goes unused. Researchers simply do not have the computing resources to analyze all of the data that exists. For example, the data used to discover the ozone hole had existed for ten years. A researcher looking through that data while working on an unrelated problem inadvertently discovered the ozone hole.

According to Dr. William Wulf, the former Assistant Director of the National Science Foundation's Directorate for Computer and Information Science and Engineering, supercomputing and high-speed networking can increase the productivity of many American researchers by up to 200 percent. Such an increase in productivity would increase the benefits from the $70 billion a year the Federal Government spends on research and development.

Important policy questions depend on high-performance computing. Better models of global climate change would lead to better policies to address global warming. In fact, today's supercomputers are inadequate for some global studies that have been designed. The studies are waiting for sufficiently powerful supercomputers. The outcome of these studies could lead to important policy decisions with substantial implications for the world.

American industry has discovered the benefits of high-performance computers. When Airbus, a European consortium, started using supercomputers to help design more efficient airplanes, Boeing and McDonald Douglass was forced to follow. Boeing then used a supercomputer to design a 30-percent more efficient airplane. This savings offset the cost of the supercomputer and helped Boeing to remain competitive.

ARCO used a Cray supercomputer to increase production of its Prudhoe Bay oil field resulting in an additional $2 billion in profits. ALCOA used supercomputing modeling to reduce the amount of aluminum needed in its aluminum cans by 25 percent. This reduction saved billions of dollars from reduced materials, production, and transportation costs.

The most extensive user of supercomputers has been for defense applications. The National Security Agency requires the fastest supercomputers available for signal processing and breaking codes.

The Strategic Defense Initiative relies heavily on supercomputers. The nuclear weapons program within the Department of Energy remains the single biggest consumer of supercomputers.

Benefits of computer networks

Research users were the first to link computers into networks for the purpose of sharing information and broadening remote access to computing resources. The Defense Advanced Research Project Agency created ARPANET in the 1960s to advance networking and data communications and to develop a robust communications network that would support the data-rich conversations of computer scientists. Other federal agencies soon followed with their own specialized networks for their research communities. Academic and industry users not served by the agency sponsored networks developed their own networks.

Today, there are thousands of computer networks in the United States. These networks range from temporary linkages between desk top computers over common carriers to institution-wide area networks, to regional and national networks. Some of the services are amateur and poorly maintained, while others are mature information organizations with well-developed services.

Recently, some agencies have pooled funds to support a shared national backbone called the Internet to connect existing networks. The need for connecting the users of the networks has been the primary reason for the Internet. Just as telephones would be of little use if only a few people had them, a network's usefulness comes from the ability of each network to reach the desks, labs, and homes of its users. Networks expand access to computing resources, data, and instruments and allow users to communicate with each other. The payoff comes from connecting people, information, and resources.

Technologies developed through research networks have enhanced the productivity of all economic sectors. Today's federally supported networks resulted in frontier-breaking network research leading to advances in data-networking technologies. Packet-switching technology developed for the ARPANET has resulted in multi-billion dollar data handling for business and financial transactions.

This legislation would create a National Research and Education Network (NREN) with the capability of transmitting billions of bits of data per second. Such a network will bring substantial benefits. Today's networks transmit data at the rate of 1.5 million bits per second, more than a thousand times slower than the proposed NREN. The NSF announced this year it was upgrading its NSFNET to 45 million bits per second. Yet, this rate is slow in computer speed. The supercomputers and data bases connected to NSFNET is growing at the rate of 20 to 30 percent per month, the new capacity will soon be saturated.

High data rates are needed to carry out even the most basic scientific studies. Today, if a scientist wants to study global warming, the data must be physically carried to a supercomputer, processed and then physically returned. A high-speed network would allow that same scientist to transmit the data in seconds, process the data and graphically see the results as the computer is carrying out the study. The scientist could easily change variables in the data and rerun the program as he gains feedback and understanding from the computer.

Other countries have also recognized the benefits of high-speed networks. Japan's Nippon Telegraph and Telephone Corporation has announced that it intends to invest $126 billion to install a national fiber optic network which will reach every home, office, and factory in Japan and be capable of transmitting data at the rate of hundreds of millions of bits per second. The Europeans have launched their own initiative to build a high-speed network. Other countries have launched national initiatives. The Unites States has yet to follow.

Government support for applied research can decrease risk, create markets for network technologies and services, trascend economic and regulatory barriers, and accelerate early technology development and deployment. A Federal commitment to build a national research and education network would accelerate its creation by 5 to 10 years. This would not only bolster U.S. science and education, but would fuel industry R&D and support the market competitiveness of the U.S. network and information services industry.

United States leadership in high-performance computing is being challenged

While the United States continues to lead the world in the development of high-performance computing, that lead is being challenged. Some estimate that the Japanese will dominate the supercomputer market in the early 1990s. Yet, the Japanese did not enter the field of high-performance computing until 1983. Today, outside of the United States, Japan is the single biggest market for and supplier of supercomputers. American supercomputers account for less than one-fifth of all supercomputers sold in Japan.

Japan's three supercomputer manufacturers, NEC, Hitachi and Fujitsu, have made rapid advances in high performance computing technology. In 1989, NEC announced the development of a supercomputer with processor speeds up to eight times faster than Cray Research's fastest machine at the time of NEC's announcement.

European countries are also catching up with the United States. West Germany, France, England, Denmark, Spain, Norway, the Netherlands, Italy, Finland, Switzerland and Belgium all have supercomputers. The United States remains the biggest consumer of supercomputer, but only because the Federal Government purchases 65 percent of all supercomputer installed in the United States. In Japan, industry consumes the biggest share of supercomputers.

Other countries have launched national efforts to undertake research and development in high-performance computing and promote its use. The United Kingdom began implementing a national high performance computing plan in 1985. The European Community just completed Phase I of its "European Strategic Programme for Research in Information Technology (Esprit)". Phase one, which lasted for 5 years, received $3.88 billion in funding and concentrated on research and development in information related technologies. Phase II calls for the commercialization of Phase I technologies. An estmated $4.14 billion will be provided for Phase II.

The U.S. Government currently spends $500 million a year directly on high-performance computing. The spending occurs through uncoordinated efforts of individual agencies working on individual projects. While this benefits select companies and specific technologies, the Government's overall efforts have been lacking and American industry cannot meet the challenge singlehandedly.

Though IBM is now trying to reenter the high-performance computing market after a 20-year hiatus, Cray Research remains the United States' only supercomputer manufacturer that can sell the most powerful supercomputers available. Other companies have been formed to develop new types of high-performance computers. For example, the Convex computer company took the approach of developing so-called "minisupercomputers" that rival the power of the Cray computer of a few years ago. These minisupercomputers enjoy remarkable success in this country and abroad because of their relatively low cost.

Other experimental designs are in the process, and some prototypes have been built. For example, the Thinking Machines Corporation developed a prototype supercomputer containing 65,536 processors. However, these experimental designs face large obstacles in becoming viable products in the marketplace. Because of the high capital costs associated with high-performance computers, it is difficult to develop new supercomputers, to build them, and to convince companies to spend anywhere from one to thirty million dollars to purchase one.

One year ago, Cray's only American competition in the general-purpose supercomputer market, Control Data Corporation, closed its subsidiary, ETA Systems. Control Data invested over $400 million in its supercomputer subsidiary. The company's investment and technology contribution have been lost, including the nation's only automated supercomputer manufacturing company.

Control Data's inability to sell its supercomputer to the government contributed to the company's failure. Cray Research has enjoyed success largely because the Department's laboratories have helped Cray improve its supercomputers and the software for them. Armed with proven supercomputers and the software to run them, Cray has had a much easier time convincing private industry to invest in their supercomputers.

Because of changes in the procurement process, federal laboratories and agencies have become reluctant to purchase new prototype computers. Faced with this new policy and Cray's established position as industry leader, companies such as Control Data have difficulty entering the supercomputer market.

This bill would provide a strong support base for the development of high performance computing activities, particularly supercomputers. The collaborative research and development consortia established by the bill will help stimulate development of supercomputers by reducing the risk of research and development to United States manufacturers.

The need for immediate action

The White House Science Council Committee on Research in Very High-Performance Computing in its November 1985 report came to the following conclusion:

The bottom line is that any country which seeks to control its future must effectively exploit high performance computing. A country which aspires to military leadership must dominate, if not control, high performance computing. A country seeking economic strength in the information age must lead in the development and application of high performance computing in industry and research.

Dr. Allan Bromley, the President's Science Advisor and Director of the White House Office of Science and Technology Policy (OSTP), stated that high-performance computing must be "a very high priority" because "it has a catalytic effect on just about any brand of research and development" and "will, eventually, transform industry, education, and virtually every sector of our economy, bringing higher productivity and enhanced competitiveness."

In response to a 1986 request by Congress, the OSTP prepared a report on options for high-performance computing. This report has since been revised into a national high-performance computing initiative released in September 1989, entitled a "Federal High Performance Computing Program". The initiative calls for an ambitious research and development program in high-performance computing systems, advanced software and algorithms, a National Research and Education Network (NREN) and long term support for human resources. The OSTP report emphasizes the need for coordination, stable funding, broadened goals, integrated management and increased private sector involvement.

Congress' own Office of Technology Assessment released its interim report on high-performance computing in September 1989. The report calls for immediate and coordinated Federal action to bring together the high-performance computing activities of the Federal Government. The report cites the importance of high-performance computing to our economic security, national security and the scientific community.

Congress, the Executive branch, the research community and the private sector all recognize the wisdom of devoting substantially more resources to high-performance computing for its own sake and for the Federal Government to assume a leadership role in such an effort. Issues related to high performance computing have been subjected to extensive studies over the last decade. Many committees have been formed, and reports released, all calling for immediate action. The Federal Government should commit itself to a national high-performance computing initiative.

While the OSTP plan sets out a national initiative, it has yet to be implemented. In fiscal year 1990, the Federal Government spent $448 million on high-performance computing. The President's fiscal year 1991 budget request calls for the Federal Government to spend $469 million, a 5 percent increase. While a 5 percent increase does correct for inflation, it falls short of the recommendations of the President's OSTP report, which calls for a funding increase of $2 billion over current levels, spread over 5 years. Furthermore, the organization chosen by the OSTP report to coordinate the Federal Government's activities lacks sufficient authority to do so.

The OSTP report would use as the primary vehicle to implement the national initiative the Federal Coordinating Council for Science, Engineering and Technology (FCCSET). FCCSET has been instrumental in helping to formulate a national strategy and bringing awareness of the importance of this issue. FCCSET developed the initiative through informal interagency committees. The OSTP report would continue the informal nature of the FCCSET process to implement the initiative. FCCSET is ill-equipped to operate a major Federal program. FCCSET has neither the authority nor resources to effectively integrate the activities of the various Federal agencies to implement a national high-performance computing strategy.

For the initiative to move forward the Federal Government must commit itself to action and give sufficient authority, direction and resources to its agencies to carry out the initiative. The initiative needs a lead agency capable of operating the program. Congress must formally establish the roles FCCSET and the other Federal agencies will play, their responsibilities, and the national goals to be achieved. Without such direction and commitment by Congress the overall effort in high-performance computing will be unwieldy, unfunded, uncoordinated and slow.

For example, Federal leadership and funding brought together a wide base of university commitment, national laboratory and academic expertise, and industry interest and technology in creating the Internet. Each of the networks forming the Internet was created individually. The patchwork nature of the current myriad of networks has resulted in some networks of high quality, others of low speed, poor quality and limited accessibility. The patchwork nature limits the effectiveness of the Internet.

The rapidly growing demand for services provided by the Internet has already saturated the network's capabilities. Demand overburdens the informal administrative arrangements between agencies to operate the Internet. Expanded capability will require a strengthened Federal management role as well as substantial technological innovation and investment.

The vehicle being used today to operate the Internet in the Federal Research Internet Coordinating Committee (FRICC), which is a subcommittee of FCCSET. The OSTP report recommends that FRICC coordinate the creation of the NREN. FRICC is an informal committee that grew out of agencies' shared interest in coordinating related network activities and avoiding duplication of resources. While FRICC has achieved remarkable progress to date, the future of the NREN can no longer depend on an informal arrangement of agencies. None of these agencies has funding authority to create the NREN. Management of a sophisticated, heavily used network cannot be based on loose policy guidelines from FRICC. Individual agency priorities and budget fortunes should not dictate what the future of the NREN is to be. Under the status quo, continued progress in achieving a national network remains uncertain.

The OSTP report also leaves important policy issues regarding the NREN unresolved. It calls for commercialization, but fails to specify how that will take place. It does not address cost recovery or access the NREN. All networks require standards at some common denominator. What standards should be imposed? To what extent should industry participate?

FRICC can discuss these issues, but as an informal interagency committee it lacks the authority to implement decisions. The achievements of FRICC resulted from voluntary participation by federal agencies. With the scaling up of the network, more formal mechanisms, with sufficient authority, are needed to deal with larger budgets, to more tightly coordinate further development, and to decide the important policy issues that will come up as the NREN develops. Even if FRICC has the authority to create the NREN, the future of the NREN will be uncertain. Since FRICC is an interagency committee, no one agency is solely responsible. Each agency will vie for its own individual agendas through FRICC. No one agency has the authority or responsibility to resolve the interagency conflicts and demands. The tough choices that will have to be made will more likely be deferred than resolved. A single lead agency with sole responsibility is needed to take charge of the NREN.

FRICC placed the National Science Foundation as the lead agency in deploying and operating the network. Other agencies were not considered for this role because it was assumed NSF would be the lead agency. The NSF created the backbone for the Internet. NSF also asked FRICC to prepare the NREN program plan, and FRICC is chaired by NSF. Furthermore, under the OSTP plan NSF's role as a lead agency is weakened by the need to work through FRICC.

Other agencies such as the Department of Energy were not considered. FCCSET or OSTP did not select DOE to undertake the NREN as it is not directly related to DOE's core missions. Nonetheless, DOE is well equipped to assume such a leadership role. DOE has extensive experience in creating computer networks, the resources to establish the NREN and the management structure and experience to operate the NREN. Because of these resources, DOE has no need to act through an interagency committee as FRICC.

The Committee believes that DOE management will bring accountability, stability, and freedom from interagency politics and budget uncertainty. As the NREN develops and the DOE gains feedback DOE can immediately implement a course correction. As the agency with sole responsibility DOE will decisively resolve the issues and not defer them to the FRICC process.

DOE will move much more quickly than the FRICC process. DOE, unlike the NSF, is familiar with the particular issues that confront a large agency in developing a computer network that is open to users outside of the agency. DOE has the expertise to develop uniform standards for the NREN. DOE has the technological experience to link together the vast array of existing networks. DOE has the resources and expertise to provide the decisive leadership needed to develop the NREN.

The success of a national high-performance computing initiative also depends ultimately on the management structure placed upon it, and not on the spending levels. The Committee believes that a Federal interagency high-performance computing task force can integrate the components among Federal agencies, and ensure participation from the private and academic sector. This formal alliance between government, academia and industry will provide guidance in integrating the program. But, the program must be managed by a lead agency experienced in technology development and program operation. That agency is DOE. Under DOE leadership, the Federal Government should commit to a national high-performance computing initiative that will consolidate and fortify agency plans, devote substantially more resources, and catalyze a broader national involvement.

LEGISLATIVE HISTORY

Senator Johnston, with Senators McClure and Gore as cosponsors, introduced S. 1976 on November 21, 1989. The bill was referred to the Committee on Energy and Natural Resources. On March 6, 1990, the Subcommittee on Energy Research and Development held a hearing on the bill.

A similar bill, S. 1067, was introduced by Senator Gore on May 18, 1989, and referred to the Committee on Commerce, Science, and Transportation. The Subcommittee on Science, Technology, and Space held three hearings on S. 1067 on June 21, July 26, and September 15, 1989. On April 3, 1990, the Commerce, Science and Transportation Committee ordered S. 1067 favorably reported with an amendment in the nature of a substitute.

H.R. 3131, a companion bill to S. 1067, was introduced on August 8, 1989, and referred to the Committee on Science, Space, and Technology. On March 14, 1990, the Subcommittee on Science, Research and Technology held a hearing on the bill.

At a business meeting on June 27, 1990, the Senate Energy and Natural Resources Committee ordered S. 1976 favorably reported with an amendment in the nature of a substitute.

COMMITTEE RECOMMENDATIONS AND TABULATION OF VOTES

The Senate Committee on Energy and Natural Resources, in open business session on June 27, 1990, by a unanimous vote of a quorum present, recommends that the Senate pass S. 1976, if amended as described herein.

The rollcall vote on reporting the measure was 19 yeas, 0 nays, as follows:

YEAS	NAYS
Mr. Johnston	
Mr. Bumpers [1]	
Mr. Ford	
Mr. Bradley	
Mr. Bingaman [1]	
Mr. Wirth	
Mr. Conrad	
Mr. Heflin	
Mr. Rockefeller [1]	
Mr. Akaka [1]	
Mr. McClure	
Mr. Hatfield [1]	
Mr. Domenici [1]	
Mr. Wallop	
Mr. Murkowski [1]	

Mr. Nickles [1]
Mr. Burns
Mr. Garn
Mr. McConnell

[1] Indicates voted by proxy.

COMMITTEE AMENDMENTS

The Committee adopted an amendment in the nature of a substitute to S. 1976.

S. 1976 as introduced required the Secretary of Energy to develop a long-range plan for high-performance computing within the Department. The plan required the Secretary to establish a National Research and Education Network (NREN), carry out research and development of software and high-performance computing technology, and to educate and train more researchers in computer science and related fields. Specific authorization levels for each activity were provided.

The amendment authorizes the same activities but restructures the program under which the Secretary carries out those activities. Also, the specific responsibilities associated with each activity were expanded in some cases and narrowed in others.

High-performance computing program

The amendment directs the Secretary to establish a High-Performance Computing Program (the "Program") subject to available appropriations. The establishment of the Program will elevate the importance of high-performance computing within the Department from an activity used to support other Department missions, to being a mission of the Department. The Secretary will implement the Program through a management plan.

The amendment requires the Secretary to develop the management plan in conjunction with the Federal Government's overall efforts in high-performance computing. A successful high-performance computing initiative by the Federal Government requires cooperation between all Federal agencies with each agency contributing to the initiative from their respective areas of expertise.

As part of the Program, the amendment directs the Secretary to undertake three major activities. The amendment requires that the Secretary establish a National Research and Education Network (NREN); it requires the Secretary to promote education and research in high-performance computational science and related fields; and it requires the Secretary to establish collaborative research and development consortia.

National Research and Education Network (NREN)

The amendment requires the Secretary to make the NREN operational by 1996. The NREN will enable government, industry, educational institutions and others to link together as may be appropriate.

The amendment directs the Secretary to develop the NREN in close cooperation with all potential users. Potential users of the NREN include the computer and telecommunication industries, the higher education community, researchers, librarians, Federal agencies and information service providers.

The Internet has only been possible through the cooperation of Federal agencies as coordinated by FRICC. The amendment selects the Department as the lead agency to develop the NREN. This ensures a formal mechanism with the necessary authority and resources needed to deal with the larger budgets, to more tightly coordinate further development and decide important policy issues as the NREN develops.

Management of the NREN should be stable enough to survive political and budgetary changes, but flexible enough to allow for accountability, feedback, and course correction. It should promote cost efficiency and provide incentives for commercial networks. The selection of the DOE, with its extensive resources and networking experience, as the lead entity will bring this management structure into the NREN.

In carrying out its role as the lead agency, DOE will work with other Federal agencies through the Federal Interagency High-Performance Computing Task Force established by the bill. Though DOE has sole authority and responsibility to establish the NREN, the Task Force allows the Secretary to coordinate research efforts between DOE and other agencies, such as DARPA, to gain input from the other agencies and the Task Force's private sector advisory panel. Such input will be instrumental in helping the Secretary resolve important policy issues that will confront the Secretary as the NREN develops.

The amendment addresses some, but not all of these policy issues. For example, to what extent should industry participate in the development of the NREN? The amendment requires that the NREN be eliminated or sold to the private sector when the networking needs provided by the NREN can be met by other means. The Secretary will establish the NREN in a manner that fosters competition and investment in high speed networking within the telecommunications industry. The amendment requires that user fees be charged when appropriate. However, the Secretary, through the Task Force, could decide the extent to which user fees are charged as the users of the NREN, and the extent of such use becomes apparent.

The amendment does not provide when commercialization will occur. Though the NREN will be operational by 1996, its make-up will be largely unknown. Once operational, the NREN will continue to grow in size, both in terms of the services the NREN provides and the number and kinds of users. Because of these uncertainties, the amendment gives the Secretary the flexibility to decide when and the extent to which commercialization or elimination of the NREN will occur.

The Secretary may eventually sell all of the NREN to the commercial sector, or the Secretary may only turn over part of the NREN because the commercial sector can only partially provide the services offered by the NREN. The Secretary could use a consortium of universities and private companies to build the NREN. Such a government-industry-academia partnership leads to an easy transition to full commercialization.

To deal with these unresolved issues, the amendment gives the Secretary broad authority in establishing the NREN. The amendment directs that the NREN be subject to such terms, conditions, charges and limitations as the Secretary deems reasonable and appropriate.

Collaborative research and development consortia

The amendment directs the Secretary to establish at least two collaborative research and development consortia (CRDCs) between industry, Federal laboratories or agencies, educational institutions and others as may be appropriate.

The exact number depends on the number needed to carry out the purposes of this Act, the cost of each and the amount of funding available. As the Secretary gains experience with the CRDCs, the Secretary has the flexibility to create more CRDCs and change the structure or activities of them. The CRDCs will directly support the goals of the bill by helping to shape high-performance computing technology, and by putting more useful computing power into the hands of U.S. industry, higher education and broader segments of the population.

Building on current models

DOE and its laboratories are in a position to help the U.S. maintain its leadership, strengthen the U.S. computing industry, and encourage deployment of high-performance computing in analysis, design, concurrent engineering, and manufacturing for U.S. industry. In the past, the Department accomplished this role almost entirely with the financial support of the nuclear weapons, research, development and testing program. That is no longer appropriate, nor possible, today. The Department's contributions now extend to a much broader spectrum from the human genome project to enhanced oil recovery. From these new applications the Department can continue to shape high-performance computing.

The Department of Energy's Advanced Computing Laboratory (ACL) at Los Alamos National Laboratory provides a prototype CRDC. The ACL acts as a catalyst by collaborating with industry to conduct research in three key technology areas: real-time visualization, high-speed networking and software for sophisticated scientific computer programs.

The ACL also serves as the primary interface for Los Alamos laboratory participation in several other activities: the DOE/Applied Mathematical Sciences Advanced Computing program, the NSF Science and Technology Center for Research on Parallel Computation (a consortium of Rice University, Caltech, Los Alamos, and Argone), and the Gigabit National test bed.

The need to solve a broad spectrum of applications drives the activities of the ACL. Los Alamos' ACL provides an excellent example of an existing center of excellence in high-performance computing that is positioned to participate in the development of computing technology through the High-Performance Computing Program.

CRDC structure

The amendment allows virtually all of the required activities to be carried out through the CRDC's. For example, the amendment requires the Secretary to promote education and research in high-performance computational science and related fields. The CRDC's may meet this requirement by providing opportunities to graduate students to work and study at the CRDC's through fellowships.

The CRDC's may also involve university faculty and students to address computational problems that may result in new approaches to high-performance computing hardware, software and algorithms. Such collaboration will help raise a new generation of computer scientists.

The CRDC's could help to establish the NREN required by the amendment. The CRDC's could undertake research and development of advanced prototype networks in helping to establish the NREN. Since the NREN will require sophisticated software applications, CRDC's would be an excellent resource in helping to write the software. Furthermore, both hardware and software development are specific activities the amendment requires the CRDC's to undertake.

The amendment requires that the Secretary establish each CRDC by soliciting and selecting proposals. This will establish a competitive atmosphere generating a number of proposals for the Secretary to select from.

A lead institution will lead each CRDC. The amendment specifies that each lead institution be a Department of Energy national laboratory with experience in research problems requiring the application of high-performance computing resources. The use of a DOE national laboratory as a lead institution and the requirement for experience with high-performance computing builds and expands upon the knowledge and experience of the Department's national laboratories.

While the lead institution has responsibility for the direction and performance of the consortium, the other participants from industry, universities, and the Federal sector may carry out CRDC activities. Thus, not all of the many activities the CRDC will perform will necessarily take place at the geographic location of the lead institution. Most likely, the participants will be spread out through the country. Each of the participants will have their own specific task assigned to them. Geographically distributed participants allow the CRDC's to develop advanced prototype networks, promote technology transfer, and involve more individuals from diverse backgrounds.

Just as with the activities of the ACL, the need to solve a broad spectrum of applications will determine the activities of each CRDC. The amendment requires that each CRDC conduct research directed at scientific and technical problems whose solutions require the application of high-performance computing resources. In the same way that the DOE laboratories have provided the "pull" for high-performance computing technology from the computing industry in the past because of the intense computational demands of the nuclear research program, the CRDC's will challenge high-performance computing vendors to continue pushing the state of the art through other computation-intensive scientific problems.

CRDC activities

The amendment requires that the CRDC's are to undertake basic research and development of high-performance computing hardware and associated software technology. S. 1976 as introduced illustrated the kinds of high-performance computing hardware systems envisioned: processors, input/output devices, parallel computer architectures, optoelectronics and mass storage technology. Also illustrated were kinds of computer technology associated with high-performance computing systems, such as advanced semiconductor computer chip designs, new materials for integrated circuits, improved integrated circuit fabrication techniques, photonics, and superconducting computer components. Types of software and algorithms were also mentioned.

The amendment intentionally leaves silent the types of technology to be supported. The list set out in S. 1976 as introduced was illustrative only. In setting out such a list many other kinds of computing technology were left out: neural nets, distributed data storage systems, advanced ceramic materials for electronic packaging and various kinds of software technology. The amendment remains silent on the kinds of technology supported in order to avoid leaving out any kind of computing technology that exists today or that has yet to be invented.

By remaining silent, no one technology gains more importance over any other. This gives the Secretary the needed flexibility to adapt to the rapidly changing nature of computing technology. The Administration supports the goals and purposes of a high-performance computing initiative, but the Administration felt S. 1976 locked in funding levels for specific kinds of technology denying it the flexibility it needs to meet the rapidly changing environment of high-performance computing. The Committee believes that the reported bill provides the needed flexibility.

The amendment requires that the CRDC's serve as vehicles for testing new technology in a sophisticated computing environment. Los Alamos' ACL illustrates how a CRDC can serve as such a vehicle. The ACL has helped Thinking Machines, Inc., develop a second generation Connection Machine. Scientific problems requiring intense computational resources test the Connection Machine's performance.

This collaboration between the laboratories and industry will help computing vendors understand what products will be needed next, and help industrial users to learn what high-performance computers can do for them.

The amendment does not subsidize industry. The amendment prohibits industrial participants from being reimbursed for costs associated with their own involvement. The Secretary has flexibility in establishing to what extent industry should share in the cost.

For example, a company may detail one or more employees to a CRDC in order to help the CRDC study that company's latest product. The company would not be reimbursed for the expenses associated with that employee. However, the company may sell the product to the consortium. Some companies may sell their product at cost or even offer the use of the machinery at no cost to a CRDC. Companies stand to gain substantial benefits from improvement the CRDC's may make to the product. A CRDC will improve the company's product giving that company an incentive to allow a CRDC to use it at little or no cost.

However, a CRDC may wish to fund a particular type of prototype computing technology, which any one company cannot undertake by itself. The amendment authorizes the CRDC's to fund research and development of prototype computing technology. The CRDC's may pay full cost, or may only pay partial cost. The competitive forces of the selection process may well establish the allocation of costs between the Secretary and the CRDC participants under the general principle that industry will pay its own way.

The technology developed through the CRDC's will be rapidly disseminated to vendors as well as users. The collaboration between industry, universities and the Federal Government will accomplish this goal. The Secretary may establish each CRDC as a Cooperative Research and Development Agreement (CRDA) as provided for in the National Competitiveness Technology Transfer Act of 1989 (15 U.S.C. 3710a). The reference to this Act makes it clear that the CRDC's may be established as a CRDA, and not that they have to be. This gives the Secretary the flexibility to choose the technology transfer mechanisms most appropriate for each of the CRDC's.

The Secretary may devise new types of technology transfer mechanisms, such as an industrial user program. For example, high-performance capabilities might be made available through high-speed networks to industries who have been reluctant to make use of high-performance computers. Demonstration programs of the value of high-performance computing to businesses, schools and universities might also be utilized.

To belay the fears of companies of potential antitrust problems, the amendment expressly affords the protection offered by the National Cooperative Research Act of 1984 (15 U.S.C. 4301–4305) to research activities carried out under the amendment.

Federal Interagency High-Performance Computing Task Force

The amendment establishes in law a Federal Interagency High-Performance Computing Task Force (the "Task Force") as the appropriate vehicle to carry out a national high-performance computing initiative and gives it the appropriate authority to do so. The same agencies that are involved in the high-performance computing effort through FCCSET are on the Task Force. Many of the recommendations made by the OSTP report will be adopted by the Task Force. Enacting legislation establishing this Task Force offers many advantages.

The amendment mandates that the Task Force develop a national strategy, and then to coordinate Federal agencies' policies and activities in implementing that strategy. The OSTP's recommended national program merely recommends a course of action. Agency participation in fashioning a national initiative under the OSTP initiative would be voluntary. For the initiative to move forward a high degree of coordination between the agencies is necessary.

FCCSET's informal agency arrangements cannot achieve that level of coordination.

All those interested in the initiative will have input into the Task Force. Non-Federal parties have not been adequately represented by FCCSET. The amendment establishes a private sector advisory panel to represent all non-Federal parties interested in the initiative.

The high-performance computing initiative will be the Task Force's only responsibility. FCCSET has broad responsibility to coordinate scientific activities of federal agencies in general. An entity with its only charge being the creation and implementation of a national high-performance computing initiative will be free from other duties and responsibilities which might otherwise slow down the process.

The Secretary of Energy is to chair the Task Force. Because of the significant responsibilities the Secretary plays in the national high-performance computing initiative, the amendment requires that the Task Force be chaired by the Secretary. For example, in developing the NREN, other Federal agencies cooperation with the Secretary of Energy is essential in creating the network. The collaborative research and development consortia established by the amendment also involve extensive cooperation with other agencies in carrying out research and other activities.

Finally, there will be significant oversight by Congress in the implementation of the initiative. With the Secretary of Energy chairing the Task Force, there will be one spokesperson for the initiative. It would be difficult under FCCSET for Congress to assert its oversight authority.

Ownership of Inventions and Creations

The amendment requires that title to any invention or software creation, a defined term, to vest in the United States and be governed by the provisions of 42 U.S.C. 5908, unless otherwise provided by law. The amendment does not change or effect the myriad of intellectual property laws that exist today. Rather, the provision addresses a gap in the law.

The only protection afforded to inventors of software is a copyright. However, under current law the government may not obtain protection through the copyright laws. Without an express provision dealing with title, who owned software developed under the amendment may not be clear. The amendment closes this gap by investing title to "software creations" in the government. The amendment then grants the generic authority provided under 42 U.S.C. 5908 to the Secretary in dealing with intellectual property rights. However, to the extent another law would specifically govern title or the allocation of property rights to inventions, that other law would apply.

For example, the CRDC's may well be established as a Cooperative Research and Development Agreement under the National Competitiveness Technology Transfer Act of 1989 (15 U.S.C. 3710a), which has its own patent protection provision. To the extent that those provisions, or any other law, may be applied, they should be.

The amendment also prohibits the disclosure of trade secrets, or commercial or financial information. Without this protection, non-Federal parties are reluctant to participate in research activities with the Federal Government. The amendment prohibits disclosure of information brought in by the non-Federal parties as well as information that is developed as a result of the research activities.

For example, a CRDC may develop a new type of software. Though the first part of this section would vest title in the government, current law requires the government to disclose the blueprint for that software. A company would be reluctant to help create the software if information the company brought in or information related to the creation of that software was then given out to its competitors.

However, information created as a result of the research activities under the amendment may be withheld from disclosure only up to 5 years. This gives the Secretary the flexibility and the discretion to decide how long the disclosure protection should be given.

Authorization

S. 1976 as originally introduced specified the level of funding for each activity authorized: basic research in hardware and software, the NREN, and education. The Administration supports a high-performance computing initiative, but objected to the specific funding levels assigned by the bill as this would restrict flexibility in an area of rapidly changing technologies.

Besides the elimination of specific references to kinds of technologies, the amendment addressed these concerns in two other ways. First, the authorization levels were combined into one general authorization section, giving the Administration flexibility to change funding levels regarding specific activities and technologies. Second, the amendment makes clear that the authorized funding levels are in addition to current levels of authority.

SECTION-BY-SECTION ANALYSIS

Section 1 establishes the short title, "The Department of Energy High-Performance Computing Act of 1990".

Section 2 contains the findings of Congress. High-performance computing has become an indispensable tool to our national security, economic competitiveness, productivity and our overall quality of life. Though the United States currently leads the world in high-performance computing, that lead is increasingly being challenged. In order to ensure that lead and obtain the greatest benefits from high-performance computing, the Federal Government must provide leadership in the research, development and application of high-performance computing technology through collaboration with industry, educational institutions and government laboratories.

Section 3 states that the purposes of the bill are to create a high-performance computing program within the Department of Energy, and to establish a Federal Interagency High-Performance Computing Task Force.

Section 4 contains definitions of terms used in the bill. The term "software creation" is defined for purposes of vesting title to software in secton nine.

Section 5 establishes a high-performance computing program within the Department of Energy. The Secretary is directed to establish a management plan to carry out program activities.

Section 6 establishes the program activities. The Secretary is to create a National Research and Education Network. The Secretary is to promote education and research in fields in and related to high-performance computing. The Secretary is to establish at least two Collaborative Consortia to undertake basic research and development of high-performance computing hardware, software and networks. Also, the Consortia are to promote the testing and uses of new types of high-performance computing, and to disseminate information on the availability of high-performance computing facilities.

Each Consortium is to be formed as collaborations between the federal laboratories, industry, universities, and others. Each Consortium is to be headed by a Department of Energy national laboratory that has experience in high-performance computing. Industrial participants are not to be reimbursed for costs associated with their own involvement.

Each consortium may be established as a Cooperative Research and Development Agreement as provided by title 15 U.S.C. section 3710a. The National Cooperative Research Act of 1984 also applies to research activities undertaken by the consortia.

Section 7 establishes a Federal interagency high-performance computing task force composed of the Secretary of Energy, the Secretary of Commerce, the Secretary of Defense, the Administrator of the National Aeronautics and Space Administration, and the Director of the National Science Foundation.

The task force is to develop a government-wide high performance computing strategy designed to: bring about the maximum efficient use of available Federal high-performance computing resources by Federal agencies; coordinate Federal agencies' high-performance computing roles, polices and activities; establish the level of federal funding needed to carry out the strategy for each agency; disseminate information to federal agencies, corporations, and educational institutions on the availability of federal high-performance computing facilities, and the means by which access can be obtained.

A private sector advisory panel to advise the Task Force would be composed of persons eminent in the field of high-performance computing from the educational establishment and the private sector.

Section 8 authorizes the Secretary, in accordance with applicable law, to cooperate with and enter into contracts with the privide sector and other Federal agencies to carry out the Act.

Section 9 establishes that title to inventions or creations (a defined term which essentially deals with software) vests in the United States in accordance with 42 U.S.C. section 5908. Trade secrets or commercial or financial information obained from non-federal parities is given protection from disclosure.

Section 10 authorizes $65,000,000 for fiscal year 1991, $100,000,000 for fiscal year 1992, $135,000,000 for fiscal year 1993,

170,000,000 for fiscal year 1994 and $205,000,000 for fiscal year 1995.

The following estimate of the cost of this measure has been provided by the Congressional Budget Office:

U.S. CONGRESS,
CONGRESSIONAL BUDGET OFFICE,
Washington, DC, July 5, 1990.

Hon. J. BENNETT JOHNSTON, Jr.,
Chairman, Committee on Energy and Natural Resources,
U.S. Senate, Washington, DC.

DEAR MR. CHAIRMAN: The Congressional Budget Office has prepared the attached cost estimate for S. 1976, the Department of Energy High-Performance Computing Act of 1990.

If you wish further details on this estimate, we will be pleased to provide them.

Sincerely,

ROBERT D. REISCHAUER,
Director.

1. Bill number: S. 1976.
2. Bill title: Department of Energy High-Performance Computing Act of 1990.
3. Bill status: As ordered reported by the Senate Committee on Energy and Natural Resources, June 27, 1990.
4. Bill purpose: The bill would authorize a High-performance Computing (HPC) Program within the Department of Energy (DOE) and would establish a Federal Interagency HPC Task Force.

S. 1976 would require DOE to develop and implement a plan to carry out HPC program activities, including coordination with other agencies for creating a national network of high-speed computers, which would be known as the National Research and Education Network (NREN). Under S. 1976, DOE also would establish two or more collaborative consortia to undertake basic research and development or HPC hardward, asssociated software, and prototype computer networks.

The bill would establish a Federal Interagency HPC Task Force to develop a government-wide HPC strategy, encourage efficient use of availabale HPC resources within the government, and coordinate federal agencies' HPC activities.

To find HPC activities by DOE and the Interagency Task Force, S. 1976 would authorize appropriations of $675 million over five years. The bill also would authorize DOE to charge fees for use of the proposed NREN system.

5. Estimated cost to the Federal Government:

[By fiscal year, in millions of dollars]

	1991	1992	1993	1994	1995
Authorization level	65	100	135	170	205
Estimated outlays	26	73	110	145	181

The costs of this bill fall within budget functions 050, 250, and 270.

Basis of estimate: This estimate assumes that the full amounts authorized would be appropriated for each fiscal year, and that spending will occur at historical rates for similar federal activities.

The bill would require DOE to establish the NREN as an operational system by the end of 1996. CBO expects that fees for use of the network would be phased in once the system is operating. Ultimately, such fees could provide a significant offset to the operating costs of the network, but we do not expect the government to collect any significant amount of receipts during the 1991–1995 period.

6. Estimated cost to State and local governments: None.

7. Estimate comparison: None.

8. Previous CBO estimate: On April 27, 1990, CBO provided a cost estimate for S. 1067, the High-Performance Computing Act of 1990, as ordered reported by the Senate Committee on Commerce, Science, and Transportation, on April 3, 1990. S. 1076 would authorize nearly $1 billion over five years for HPC activities by the National Science Foundation and the National aeronautics and Space Administration. S. 1067 would not authorize any funds for the DOE activities that S. 1976 would authorize.

9. Estimate prepared by: Perter Fontaine.

10. Estimate approved by James L. Blum, Assistant Director for Budget Analysis.

REGULATORY IMPACT EVALUATION

In compliance with paragraph 11(b) of Rule XXVI of the Standing Rules of the Senate, the Committee makes the following evaluation of the regulatory impact which would be incurred in carrying out S. 1976.

The bill is not a regulatory measure in the sense of imposing government-established standards or significant economic responsibilities on private individuals and businesses. The bill contains authorizations for a national research and education network, a research and development program within the Department of Energy, a federal interagency high-performance computing task force and directives to the Secretary of Energy with respect to the operation of these activities. Any involvement of private firms and individuals in these activities is voluntary.

No personal information would be collected in administering the program. Therefore, there would be no impact on personal privacy from the bill.

Little, if any, additional paperwork would result from the enactment of S. 1976.

EXECUTIVE COMMUNICATIONS

On December 6, 1989, the Committee on Energy and Natural Resources requested legislative reports from the Office of Science and Technology Policy, the Department of Energy, the National Science Foundation, the Department of Defense, the Department of Commerce, the National Aeronautics and Space Administration, and the Office of Management and Budget setting forth executive views on S. 1976.

The pertinent legislative report received by the Committee from the Department of Defense setting forth executive agency recommendations relating to S. 1976 is set forth below. No other legislative reports from the other agencies had been received at the time of filing this report. When the reports become available, the Chairman will request that they be printed in the Congressional Record for the advice of the Senate.

GENERAL COUNSEL OF THE
DEPARTMENT OF DEFENSE,
Washington, DC, May 23, 1990.

Hon. J. BENNETT JOHNSTON,
Chairman, Committee on Energy and Natural Resources,
U.S. Senate, Washington, DC.

DEAR MR. CHAIRMAN: This is in response to your request for the views of the Secretary of Defense on S. 1976, 101st Congress, a bill "To provide for continued United States leadership in high-performance computing."

S. 1976 would provide funds to the Department of Energy to engage in research and development in networking, software, high-performance computing systems, and basic research. Total funding to be authorized is $675M over five years.

The Department of Defense has reservations regarding this bill. In September 1989, the Office of Science and Technology Policy (OSTP) presented the Federal High Performance Computing Program, which was developed by the Federal Coordinating Council on Science, Engineering, and Technoplogy (FCCSET). The Department of Defense participated in the development of the OSTP program plan and supports it. There are, however, problems with the implementation approach embodied in S. 1976.

The Federal High Performance Computing Program presents a balanced plan involving four principal agencies, which are the National Science Foundation (NSF), the Department of Energy (DOE), the National Aeronautics and Space Administration (NASA), and the Defense Advanced Research Projects Agency (DARPA) of the Department of Defense. These agencies, with support from OSTP and the other agencies involved in the FCCSET process, have developed a coordination plan with assigned roles and responsibilities.

This balanced plan provides a means for effectively responding to the long-term high performance computing needs of the mission agencies, including DOE, DoD, and NASA, and for ensuring continued United States leadership in a technology area critical for national security.

As part of the plan development process, agencies agreed to take on leadership roles consistent with their strengths and capabilities. In particular, it has been agreed that the NSF is to take the lead in deployment of the National Research and Education Network, that DARPA is to take the lead in research for gigabit capacity networks, that NASA is to coordinate the software and algorithms efforts, and that DARPA is to take the lead in research in support of future high performance computing systems.

The Department of Defense has the following reservations regarding the bill:

1. The bill provides for the participation of one agency without regard to the contributions of the other agencies, whose participation is indicated above is essential in order to ensure success of the Program in meeting the long-term computing needs and in sustaining U.S. leadership.

2. The bill is inconsistent with lead agency assignments and budgets as developed through FCCSET coordination process and as agreed to by the participating agencies, including the Department of Energy. For example, the budget levels contained in the bill for the National Research and Education Network should be authorized primarily ot the NSF and DARPA.

The Office of Management and Budget advises that, from the standpoint of the Administration's program, there is no objection to the presentation of this report for the consideration of the Committee.

Sincerely,

TERRENCE O'DONNELL.

CHANGES IN EXISTING LAW

In compliance with paragraph 12 of Rule XXVI of the Standing Rules of the Senate, the Committee notes that no changes in existing law are made by the bill S. 1976, as reported.

O

I

The Federal High-Performance Computing Program,
U.S. Executive Office of the President, Office of Science
and Technology Policy, September 8, 1989.

THE FEDERAL
HIGH PERFORMANCE COMPUTING
PROGRAM

Executive Office of the President
Office of Science and Technology Policy
September 8, 1989

The Federal High Performance Computing Program

High Performance Computing Systems
Research for Future Generations

System Design Tools

Advanced Prototype Development

Evaluation of Early Systems

Advanced Software Technology and Algorithms
Support for Grand Challenges

Software Components and Tools

Computational Techniques

High Performance Computing Research Centers

National Research and Education Network
Interagency Interim NREN

Gigabits Research and Development

Deployment of Gigabits NREN

Structured Transition to Commercial Service

Basic Research and Human Resources

In November 1987, my predecessor, William R. Graham, transmitted to Congress A Research and Development Strategy for High Performance Computing. That report laid out a five-year strategy for federally supported R&D on high performance computing, including hardware for state-of-the-art supercomputers, software, computer networks, and supporting infrastructure. It was written with the assistance of the Committee on Computer Research and Applications under the OSTP Federal Coordinating Council for Science, Engineering, and Technology (FCCSET). This strategy document was to be followed by a detailed program plan.

I am pleased to transmit to Congress that program plan -- the result of an intense interagency effort by a special task force within the Committee on Computer Research and Applications. Following the general organizational structure of the 1987 strategy report, it lays out a broad R&D policy and program plan designed to advance U.S. leadership in high performance computing. This plan calls for a federally coordinated government, industry, and university collaboration to accelerate the development of high speed computer networks and to accelerate the rate at which high performance computing technologies -- both hardware and software -- can be developed, commercialized, and applied to leading-edge problems of national significance.

High performance computing is a vital and strategic technology, exerting strong leverage on the rest of the computer industry and other cutting-edge areas. However, U.S. leadership and diversity in the supercomputer industry itself has declined dramatically; and history shows that a scant 15 years separates the first appearance of a top-of-the-line supercomputer from the appearance of that same computing power in the higher end of the personal computer market. A future national high speed computer network could have the kind of catalytic effect on our society, industries, and universities that the telephone system has had during the twentieth century.

We cannot afford to cede our historical leadership in high performance computing and in its applications. We need to encourage the dynamism of the U.S. computer industry and, hence, our economy. I would ask all of the federal agencies with research programs in high performance computing to work toward implementing the recommendations in this report.

D. Allan Bromley
Director

Foreword

High Performance Computing is a powerful tool to increase productivity in industrial design and manufacturing, scientific research, communications, and information management. It represents the leading edge of a multi–billion dollar world market, in which the U.S. is increasingly being challenged. A strong, fully competitive domestic high performance computer industry contributes to U.S. leadership in critical national security areas and in broad sectors of the civilian economy, including the technical base for many national economic and military security needs. For this reason we are initiating the preliminary planning to address this important U.S. technology.

GOALS

Accordingly, the goals of the Federal High Performance Computing (HPC) Program are to:

- Maintain and extend U.S. leadership in high performance computing, and encourage U.S. sources of production;

- Encourage innovation in high performance computing technologies by increasing their diffusion and assimilation into the U.S. science and engineering communities; and

- Support U.S. economic competitiveness and productivity through greater utilization of networked high performance computing in analysis, design, and manufacturing.

COMPONENTS

The HPC Program is implemented through four complementary, closely coordinated, multidisciplinary Components:

- High Performance Computing Systems;
- Advanced Software Technology and Algorithms;
- The National Research and Education Network; and
- Basic Research and Human Resources.

POLICY

The Federal High Performance Computing (HPC) Program features increased cooperation between business, academia and government. While each of these sectors will retain its current role, the success of this Program will depend in large part on an effective transition from R&D to commercialization—an outcome of successful cooperation among the above sectors.

The measure of success of this Program in the area of R&D will be an increased rate of development of new computing concepts, systems, and architectures. A longer term measure of success will be the rate at which this technological progress shows up in commercialized products. The HPC Program will be consistent with the traditional roles of government, business and academia.

Specifically:

- The government will provide R&D support for HPC and will coordinate R&D among its agencies;

- Business will be the decision maker and source of capital investment for commercialization of HPC technology in response to its assessment of market opportunities; and

- Universities and Federal laboratories will be the primary institutions receiving government funding under this Program.

The government will, in addition, foster a number of mechanisms for increased collaboration and interaction among government, business and universities. Specifically:

- The government will continue to serve as a market for commercial prototypes and for commercial products. This particularly will be the case in the defense sector. These markets will exist in U.S. laboratories, Federal agencies, university centers of excellence and industrially led consortia;

- The government will assist in the development of industrially-led consortia in cases where appropriate (an existing example is SEMATECH); and

- The government will promote centers of excellence, jointly funded and staffed by government, academia, and industry. Technology transfer to industry from government and academia will happen automatically as a result of this ongoing collaboration.

Foreign policy objectives will be supported through existing or future international science and technology agreements. "Symmetry and reciprocity," protection of U.S. proprietary interests, and enforcement of intellectual property rights will continue to be guiding principles.

The Federal High Performance Computing Program will ensure the broadest possible national benefit by addressing:

- Many problems susceptible to computational solution;

- A wide geographic and demographic distribution; and

- The inclusion of government, academia and industry.

STRATEGY

To achieve the policy goals of the HPC Program, our strategy is to:

- Support computational advances through R&D effort to address U.S. scientific and technical challenges;

- Reduce the uncertainties to industry for development and use of this technology though increased cooperation among government, industry and academia and the continued use of government and government-funded facilities as a market for HPC prototypes and commercial products;

- Support the underlying research, network and computational infrastructures on which U.S. high performance computing technology is based; and

- Support the U.S. human resource base to meet needs of industry, academia and government.

ROLE OF FEDERAL, ACADEMIC AND INDUSTRIAL SECTORS

Federal agencies

- Funding for the Program will come from agencies their annual appropriations;

- User agencies will continue to define their respective missions and goals, though guided by the High Performance Computing Program goals and objectives; and

- OSTP, through its Federal Coordinating Council on Science, Engineering, and Technology (FCCSET) Committee on Computer Research and Applications, will assist the agencies as part of its continuing responsibility for coordination and policy guidance. OSTP will also assist by recommending special computational opportunities. However, final priority setting will reside with the respective agencies.

Academia

Universities and colleges will participate in the HPC Program in the following ways:

- Responding to agency program announcements;

- Forming consortia with government and industry;

- Focusing research capabilities on specific areas of computational science;

- Enhancing curricula to take advantage of new generations of computing technologies, attracting additional manpower into various disciplines of computational science; and

- Bringing the Program to the attention of State leaders for potential leveraging of Federal funds.

Industry

- Private industry will develop hardware, software, and networks in response to the Program. Commercialization will be at the initiative and discretion of private industry;

- Industry will join and help finance university or government laboratory R&D activities (at its choosing) to obtain access to expertise and government funded facilities. As a result of these collaborative relationships, the partnership will supply industry with R&D and technology information;

- A broadly representative industry body will assist in making long-range demand and robustness projections for: high capacity research networks; the spectrum of computer architectures; the adequacy of software development; and the level of the manpower pool. This body will help assure a smooth transition between successive generations of high performance computing systems; and

- Private industry suppliers will provide the network services to Federal agencies in the first two stages of the National Research and Education Network. Industry should plan to operate the NREN fully as soon as feasible.

FUNDING OF THE HPC PROGRAM

The magnitude of the program envisioned by this Program will require major new Federal R&D investment. It is assumed that existing Federal base funding for computer and information science and technology research and development, roughly $500 million annually, will continue. Preliminary planning estimates suggest that the first year of the program would require an augmentation of $150 million, which would then grow to an incremented annual level of $600 million by the fifth year.

MANAGEMENT OF THE HPC PROGRAM

The components of the Program will be managed by existing Federal agencies.

Oversight of the HPC Program will be the responsibility of the Office of Science and Technology Policy with the assistance of the FCCSET Committee on Computer Research and Applications and the help of a High Performance Computing advisory panel which will report to the Director of OSTP:

- The HPC advisory panel will interact regularly with the FCCSET Committee on Computer Research and Applications; and

- The HPC advisory panel will have representation from all sectors and will monitor the progress of the Program for cross-sector balance, breadth of applicability, network security, competitiveness versus international cooperation, and technology transfer effectiveness.

SCOPE OF THIS REPORT

This report is designed for agency-level planning purposes and does not represent the Administration's approval or support of any program not included in the President's budget requests. Programs discussed in this document are subject to budget constraints and Administration approval.

TABLE OF CONTENTS

1. Executive Summary

High Performance Computing * is a pervasive and powerful technology for industrial design and manufacturing, scientific research, communications, and information management. A strong U.S. high performance computer industry contributes to our leadership in critical national security areas and competitiveness in broad sectors of the civilian economy.

The goals of the High Performance Computing Program are to:

Goals

- Maintain and extend U.S. leadership in high performance computing, and encourage U.S. sources of production;

- Encourage the pace of innovation in high performance computing technologies by increasing their diffusion and assimilation into the U.S. science and engineering communities; and

- Support U.S. economic competitiveness and productivity through greater utilization of networked high performance computing in analysis, design, and manufacturing.

Strategy

These goals will be accomplished through Federally coordinated government, industry, and university collaboration to:

- Support computational advances through a more vigorous R&D effort to expedite solutions to U.S. scientific and technical challenges;

- Reduce the uncertainties to industry for R&D and use of this technology through increased cooperation between government, industry and academia and the continued use of government and government–funded facilities as a market for HPC early commercial products;

- Support the underlying research, network and computational infrastructures on which U.S. high performance computing technology is based; and

- Support the U.S. human resource base to meet needs of industry, academia and government.

* *High performance computing* refers to the full range of advanced computing technologies including existing supercomputer systems, special purpose and experimental systems, and the new generation of large scale parallel systems.

1. Executive Summary

The HPC Program

The Program will consist of four complementary, coordinated components in each of the key areas of high performance computing. The components are planned carefully to produce not only long term results but a succession of intermediate national benefits. Figure 1 shows the relationship of the components of the Program. The High Performance Computing Program will build on those programs already in place, providing additional funds in carefully selected areas to meet its goals. Selected computational challenges, which will have significant effect on national leadership in science and technology, will be used as focal points for these efforts.

High Performance Computing Systems: The United States' leadership in supercomputing is increasingly being challenged. We have developed new, more powerful supercomputing architectures based on innovations. Particularly in parallel processing, we must capitalize on these innovations. To do this, a long range effort involving Federal support will be required for basic research on high performance computing technology and the appropriate transfer of research and technology to U.S. industry, consisting of efforts in the following areas:

- Research for future generations of computing;

- System design tools;

- Advanced prototype development; and

- Evaluation of early systems.

Advanced Software Technology and Algorithms: Historically, software improvements have increased computational performance much more than hardware investments. Yet software productivity is generally poor, and existing software can seldom be re-used without modification. In computing systems for industrial, scientific and military applications, software costs have exceeded those of hardware more than fivefold. Advances in software will be critical to the success of high performance computers with massively parallel architectures. To improve software productivity, an interagency effort will support joint research among government, industry and universities to improve basic software tools, data management, languages, algorithms, and associated computational theory with broad applicability for the *Grand Challenge** problems. These complex problems will require advances in software that have widespread applicability to computational problems in science and technology.

---

* A *Grand Challenge* is a fundamental problem in science or engineering, with broad economic and scientific impact, that could be advanced by applying high performance computing resources.

1. Executive Summary

Effort in this component focuses on:

- Support for Grand Challenges;

- Software components and tools;

- Computational techniques; and

- High performance computing research centers.

National Research and Education Network: For the past decade technology developed by the U.S. has been available to eliminate distance as a factor in computer access and in collaborations among high technology workers. To maintain our leadership, the U.S. government, together with industry and universities, will jointly develop a high–speed research network to provide a distributed computing capability linking government, industry and higher education communities. This network will serve as a prototype for future commercial networks which will become the basis for a distributed industrial base. This component will consist of:

- An interagency effort to establish an interim National Research and Education Network;

- Research and development for a billions of bits per second (gigabits) network adequate to support national research needs;

- Deployment of the gigabits National Research and Education Network; and

- Structured transition to commercial service.

Basic Research and Human Resources: U.S. universities are not meeting the expanding needs of industry for trained workers in computer technology. There is not an adequate number of high quality computer science departments in this country, and many industrial and Federal laboratories have inadequate research capabilities. Furthermore, existing university, government, and industrial groups do not collaborate effectively enough, and their interdisciplinary activities are too limited. To correct these deficiencies a long term effort to support basic research in computer science and engineering (creating computing systems) will be established by building upon existing programs. This component will also establish industry, university, and government partnerships to improve the training and utilization of personnel and to expand the base of research and development personnel in computational science and technology (using computers).

Organization

Leadership of the Program is the responsibility of the Office of Science and Technology Policy, through the Federal Coordinating Council on Science, Engineering and Technology (FCCSET) Committee on Computer Research and Applications, whose members include representatives of the key agencies that fund R&D in high performance computing. Duties and responsibilities of the Committee include:

- Interagency planning and coordination;

- Technology assessment;

- Policy recommendations to OSTP; and

- Formal annual reports of progress to OSTP.

A High Performance Computing Advisory Panel will be formed, consisting of eminent individuals from government, industry, and academia. Members of the Advisory Panel will be selected by and will report to the Director of OSTP. The Panel will provide the Director and the Committee on Computer Research and Applications with an independent assessment of:

- Progress of the Program in accomplishing its objectives;

- Continued relevance of the Program goals over time;

- Overall balance among the Program Components; and

- Success in strengthening U.S. leadership in high performance computing, and integration of these technologies into the mainstream of U.S. science and industry.

This implementation plan was prepared by the FCCSET Committee on Computer Research and Applications under the leadership of the Office of Science and Technology Policy. It represents a broad spectrum of government, industrial and university interests. The Committee has established subcommittees that will be responsible for planning, organizing, monitoring and coordinating the components of the Program.

SCOPE OF THIS REPORT

This report is designed for agency-level planning purposes and does not represent the Administration's approval or support of any program not included in the President's budget request. Programs discussed in this document are subject to budget constraints and Administration approval.

Enables
US Competitiveness

High Performance Computing Technology

Enables
Grand Challenges

Advanced Software and Algorithms

Support for Grand Challenges

Software Components and Tools

Computational Techniques

HPC Research Centers

Enables
Advanced Software

High Performance Computing Systems

Research for Future Generations

System Design Tools

Advanced Prototype Development

Evaluation of Early Systems

Enables
Resource Sharing

National Research & Education Net

Interagency Interim NREN

R&D for Gigabits Network

Deploy Gigabits NREN

Transition to Commercial Service

Basic Research and Human Resources

Fig. 1 – Relationship of HPC Program Components

2. Introduction

Purpose and Scope of Report

The purpose of this document is to provide the initial implementation plan for the U.S. High Performance Computing Program. This plan encompasses the first five year period and provides for periodic reviews to be conducted by the Federal Coordinating Council on Science, Engineering and Technology (FCCSET) with the participation of government, industry, and university representatives.

This document discusses:

- National economic and technical issues associated with high performance computing;

- Goals and strategy of this Program;

- Plans for synergistic government, industrial, and university participation;

- Organizational structure to coordinate, manage and review the Program program;

- Economic and technical benefits of the Program; and

- Proposed budget for the first five years of the Program.

This implementation plan was prepared by the FCCSET Committee on Computer Research and Applications under the leadership of the Office of Science and Technology Policy. It represents a broad spectrum of government, industrial, and university interests. This report is designed for agency-level planning purposes and does not represent the Administration's approval or support of any program not included in the President's budget request. Programs discussed in this document are subject to budget constraints and Administration approval.

Background

The Federal Coordinating Council on Science, Engineering and Technology (FCCSET), chartered by the Office of Science and Technology Policy (OSTP), coordinates Federal interagency activities of broad national interest. The FCCSET Committee on Computer Research and Applications serves as the forum for developing a national agenda for computing technology needs, opportunities, and trends.

This FCCSET Committee has examined the scientific, technological and economic effects of high performance computing. The Committee issued reports as early as 1983

2. Introduction

that assessed the status of high performance computing and possible supporting government activities. These studies have consistently demonstrated the need for a strategy to coordinate high performance computing related activities in the government, industrial and university sectors. Dramatic increases in foreign investments in computer related technology have been noted, which challenge the world leadership of the U.S. computing industry. The studies also emphasized that advances in critical areas of national security and broad sectors of the civilian economy depend strongly on high performance computing technology.

The unprecedented power of high performance computing systems has created a new mode of scientific research: computational investigations that complement the traditional modes of experiment and theory. Computational research is being applied to a wide range of scientific and engineering problems called Grand Challenges. *A Grand Challenge is a fundamental problem in science or engineering, with potentially broad economic, political, and/or scientific impact, that could be advanced by applying high performance computing resources.* While the Grand Challenges are already being addressed to some extent using existing supercomputers, progress is often severely limited by current computer speeds and memory capacities. Examples of Grand Challenges are:

(1) Computational fluid dynamics for the design of hypersonic aircraft or efficient automobile bodies and recovery of oil.

(2) Computer based weather and climate forecasts, and understanding of global environmental changes.

(3) Electronic structure calculations for the design of new materials such as chemical catalysts, immunological agents and superconductors.

(4) Plasma dynamics for fusion energy technology and for safe and efficient military technology.

(5) Calculations to improve our understanding of the fundamental nature of matter, including quantum chromodynamics and condensed matter theory.

(6) Machine vision to enable real-time analysis of complex images for control of mechanical systems.

The sample Grand Challenge areas provided in Appendix A are representative of the science and technology areas that will be affected by application of leading edge computational resources and supporting systems. Figure 2 illustrates some of the Grand Challenges that can be adequately addressed through existing high performance computing technology and problems that could be attacked much more successfully with a thousandfold increase in performance.

2. Introduction

Agency Activities: In the early 1980's, Federal agencies initiated programs that provide the basis for the opportunities described in this Program. The NSF established the National Supercomputer Centers to provide high performance computers to the science and engineering community and interconnected them with the research community via the NSFNET. The centers and network have stimulated the development of innovative computational approaches to a wide range of scientific and engineering problems related to the Grand Challenges. NSF also reorganized to create a new Directorate of Computer and Information Science and Engineering (CISE) with increased emphasis and funding for computer and computational disciplines, with a focus on computer networking as a tool for scientific and engineering research.

DARPA initiated the Strategic Computing program to accelerate development of an alternate approach to building high performance computer systems. This program focuses on large scale parallel systems, custom VLSI and associated software, including symbolic processing for the advanced functionality characterized by artificial intelligence. Strategic Computing stimulated the first generation of commercially available scalable parallel computer systems using conservative components and packaging. Early production models of these systems were acquired by several agencies for experimental use. A second generation of these systems is being developed, using custom VLSI. The military services have participated in this program, providing applications focus and technical consultation.

The Office of Naval Research, Air Force Office of Scientific Research, and Army Research Office have separately sponsored important research and development in basic research for advanced computing.

The DOE expanded the National Magnetic Fusion Computer Center and its MFE Network to serve all energy research users in national laboratories, universities, and industry. Several of the National Laboratories have formed computational groups to experiment with novel high performance computers and to develop algorithms that exploit the power of those computers. Special funding was provided to enable university, industry, laboratory collaborations with the national laboratories to acquire parallel computer prototypes to test ideas for advanced high performance computing architectures.

NASA upgraded the computational capability at several of its research and flight centers and established a data network to link them together. At the Ames Research Center, the Numerical Aerodynamics Simulation (NAS) was set up to provide a focused attack on computational aerodynamics employing the highest powered computers available surrounded by data reduction and visualization systems.

HPC Strategy: In 1986 Congress requested that OSTP conduct a study of the critical problems and options for communication networks that support the U.S. high

2. Introduction

performance computing environment. The charter of the FCCSET Committee on Computer Research and Applications was broadened to include the technical aspects of this study. A number of working groups were formed to ensure a perspective that spanned all aspects of the U.S. high performance computing environment. In addition a consortium of government, industry and university experts focused on national infrastructure requirements for high performance computing.* The FCCSET study is documented in "A Research and Development Strategy for High Performance Computing" also known as the *High Performance Computing Strategy (HPC Strategy)*, published by the Office of Science and Technology Policy (included as Appendix B). It provides the foundation for this Program.

The *HPC Strategy* findings were:

- A strong domestic high performance computer industry contributes to maintaining U.S. leadership in critical national security areas and in broad sectors of the civilian economy.

- Research progress and technology transfer in software and applications must keep pace with advances in computing architectures and microelectronics.

- The U.S. faces serious challenges in networking technology which could become a barrier to the advance and use of computing technology in science and engineering.

- Federal research and development funding has established laboratories in universities, industry, and government which have become the major sources of innovation in the development and use of computing technology.

The recommendations of the *HPC Strategy* form the basis for the four components of the High Performance Computing Program.

Four National Research Council reports issued in the period following publication of the *HPC Strategy* have confirmed its findings and emphasized the need to carry out its recommendations: *Toward a National Research Network* (1988), *The National Challenge in Computer Science and Technology* (1988), *Global Trends in Computer Technology and Their Impact on Export Control* (1988), and *Information Technology and the Conduct of Research* (1989).

In December 1988, the Office of Science and Technology Policy charged the FCCSET Committee on Computer Research and Applications to develop this implementation plan for the High Performance Computing Program. The goals, strategy, and actions to implement the Program are discussed in the following sections.

---

* *A National Computing Initiative*,
Society for Industrial and Applied Mathematics, Philadelphia, PA 1987.

What is High Performance Computing?

High Performance Computing refers to a productive computing environment that includes high performance components, system and applications software, networking, and the underlying research and human resource infrastructure.

High performance computing systems are those at the forefront of the computing field in terms of computational power, storage capability, input/output bandwidth, and software. These systems include high speed vector and pipeline machines, special purpose and experimental systems, scalable parallel architectures, and associated mass storage systems, input/output units, and systems software. Underlying these advanced systems are microelectronics, optoelectronics, logic devices, and storage technologies.

Advanced software technology and algorithms includes general–purpose operating systems for high performance computer systems and tools and utilities, such as compilers, analysis tools, debuggers, and data management systems. Mathematical algorithms and other general purpose libraries facilitate the use of high performance computers for science and engineering. Software tools will allow high performance computing systems to be embedded transparently in a distributed environment which includes applications specific software and other specialized methods and algorithms. The technology base required to build such environments includes software engineering and data management tools, and basic research in high–level languages and algorithms. Improving these capabilities will greatly enhance scientific and engineering software productivity.

Computer network technology consists of communications and switching capable of providing a very high speed backbone on which the high performance computing environment is distributed. Internetworking and feeder network technology connects local or mid–level high speed networks to the national high speed network. User services such as directories are also essential components of an effective networking environment. Advanced networks will provide improved access to high performance computing systems and increased collaboration opportunities for universities, industry, and government.

Development of high performance computing environments requires a long term, continuing investment in basic research over a wide spectrum of computer and computational science and engineering. A basic infrastructure of knowledge, research, computing facilities, and people are required to create and exploit high performance computing technology.

Why is High Performance Computing Important to the U.S.?

During the last two decades computing has become an important complement to experimental and theoretical research. Computer aided design and engineering

2. Introduction

techniques are replacing manual ones. Computer assisted and automated manufacturing is increasing productivity and improving the value and reliability of industrial products, while reducing the time required for engineering and manufacturing cycles. New knowledge and new industries are increasingly dependent upon computing.

Most of these advances in computing have originated in the United States. However, many of them have been most successfully applied in other countries, where their use has eroded the competitive edge that the U.S. had previously enjoyed. This Program is intended to maintain the U.S. edge by focusing our research advantage in high performance computing toward applications with high value to our economy and national security. Fortunately, current U.S. leadership in high performance computing offers a strategic opportunity to maintain our industrial momentum. The HPC Program provides a way to do this.

The national economic benefits of a strong high performance computing industry are recognized and pursued by other countries. Those nations have formed and funded collaborations between their private and public sectors. Their successes constitute vigorous competition for technological and economic leadership in high performance computing. Foreign computing industries benefit tremendously from government support. To retain our leadership, domestic industrial efforts must be encouraged by a strategy that shares the economic risk of innovation in this capital–intensive field.

National economy: High performance computing is by definition the leading edge of computing technology, which in turn supports many areas of science and technology. Computing constitutes a significant portion of the U.S. economy. For example, in 1988 the U.S. computing industry accounted for 10% of GNP, and almost 10% of all capital investment.* The pace of innovation that it sets pervades the domestic computing industry technology and economics. In terms of capability, today's supercomputer is tomorrow's desk-top workstation and the following day's classroom tool. Thus, U.S. competitive success in the world computing market is supported by leadership in high performance computing.

National security: High performance computing technology is used in critical national security areas. Examples include advanced computer systems architectures, computer network communication technology, and signal processing techniques. Continued acceleration of this technology, including availability of U.S. sources of production, is important to U.S. national security.

Science and technology: High performance computing provides a basis for other innovative scientific and engineering efforts. The pace of rapidly developing technologies, such as robotics, artificial intelligence, communications, high definition

---

* *The National Challenge in Computer Science and Technology,*
National Academy Press, Washington, D.C., 1988, p. 7.

2. Introduction

television (HDTV), campus network applications, semiconductor design, superconductivity, transportation, speech recognition, and data visualization are all dependent on a strong and innovative high performance computing industry.

Manufacturing: High performance computing constitutes an important tool for many industries. Its use in simulation and design improves the productivity of large industries such as aircraft production and automobile manufacturing and is rapidly being extended to other industries. Recent vigorous growth in use of high performance computing in electronics, energy, chemical and pharmaceutical industries illustrates the role of computing in the long term strength of the U.S. economy.

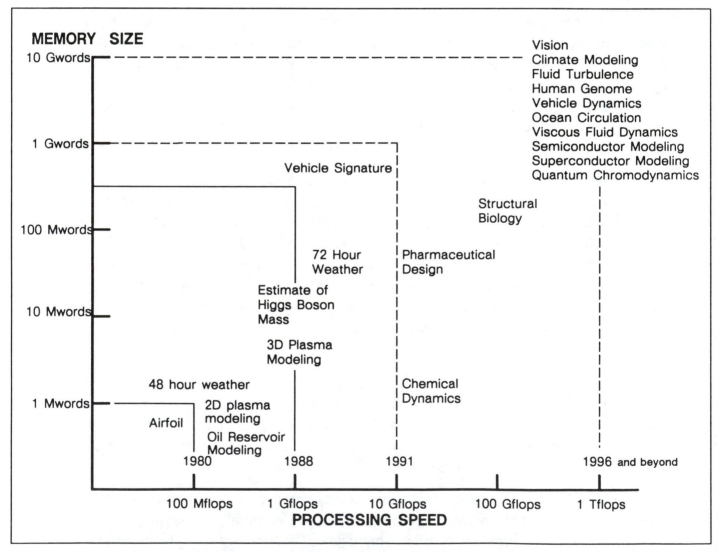

Fig. 2 – Some Grand Challenges and their Projected Computational Requirements

3. Program Plan

Introduction

The goals of the High Performance Computing Program are to:

- Maintain and extend U.S. leadership in high performance computing, and encourage U.S. sources of production;

- Encourage innovation in high performance computing technologies by increasing their diffusion and assimilation into the U.S. science and engineering communities; and

- Support U.S. economic competitiveness and productivity through greater utilization of networked high performance computing in analysis, design, and manufacturing.

To achieve these goals, a strategy has been established to:

- Support computational advances through R&D efforts to address U.S. scientific and technical challenges;

- Increase the use of this technology by reducing the uncertainties to industry for R&D and by increasing cooperation among government, industry, and academia;

- Continue use of government and government–funded facilities as a market for HPC early commercial products;

- Support the underlying research, network and computational infrastructures on which U.S. high performance computing technology is based; and

- Support the U.S. human resource base to meet needs of industry, academia and government.

The HPC Program is composed of four coordinated program components: High Performance Computing Systems, Advanced Software Technology and Algorithms, the National Research and Education Network, and Basic Research and Human Resources. Each of the four program components stimulates the development of progressively more advanced products for use throughout computing technology. The four areas build upon each other and upon the existing research base, as illustrated in Figure 1. Each component carries out a recommendation of the November 20, 1987 *HPC Strategy* (see Appendix C.)

Although the program components are described separately, they are interdependent, so that success of the Program depends on balanced support for all of them. For example, the development of high performance computing systems depends on development of advanced software technology and algorithms, because algorithm and software requirements largely determine the corresponding architecture of successful

3. Program Plan

computing systems. Similarly, as the new computing systems become available, new algorithms and software systems are required to take advantage of their capabilities and allow the systems to be used in practical ways.

The High Performance Computing Program requires an unprecedented level of coordination among agencies of the Federal government that are involved in high performance computing. The agencies involved have already begun cooperation to meet this challenge in order to mount a sufficiently comprehensive program in support of U.S. competitiveness.

The remainder of this section describes the goals for each of the four components of the Program, the actions that will be taken to achieve these goals, and the responsibilities of each of the participating federal agencies. Although the Program builds on the existing research base, its goals extrapolate significantly from those of the base and will require significant additional funding. This funding is presented in Table 1 at the end of the plan, with the funding elements keyed to each component and action of the Program.

High Performance Computing Systems

Recommendation: The U.S. Government should establish a long range strategy for Federal support for basic research on high performance computer technology and the appropriate transfer of research and technology to U.S. industry. [*HPC Strategy*, 1987]

Goals

High performance computing systems consist of processors, memory, mass storage, input/output, and associated system software. The systems are characterized in this report by overall sustained performance on large problems. They will be designed so that memory capacities, storage sizes and input/output rates scale to provide sustained performance in proportion to processing.

The goal is to support the development of high performance computing systems which will be capable of sustaining trillions of operations per second on significant problems. The program builds upon present government supported efforts which have established U.S. leadership in developing large scale computer systems and the underlying component technologies. However, achieving and effectively exploiting this thousandfold improvement in performance will require developing a new technology base through a program of research in computer architectures, microelectronics and packaging, and associated systems software .

A primary objective of the plan is to assist the continued viability of domestic sources of high performance computers and their critical components that meet the requirements of U.S. industry and Federal programs, both civil and defense. The plan will focus Federally funded research and promote transfer of results between Federally–funded research programs and U.S. industry. This requires close collaboration of researchers in the nation's universities and government laboratories with industrial scientists and engineers. Government funding will also assist risk reduction in critical areas and will complement private capital in the computer market.

To date Federal investment in high performance computing systems has taken two forms: (1) purchase of early market and production model systems and (2) research and development which has the led to commercial high performance systems. In both cases Federal funding has reduced the R&D risk of the high performance computing systems for U.S. manufacturers. Because many foreign computer manufacturers are willing to accept greater R&D risk due to their financial environment, the Federal strategy has been important in maintaining U.S. technical leadership in high performance computing systems.

Early purchase has served several critical functions. It has often provided essential financial assistance and early technical feedback to manufacturers during production of their first model of a new high performance computing system. The substantial computational resources provided by these early purchases have maintained the rapid technological advance of the U.S. in both civil and defense sectors, thereby supporting the nation's economic and military security. Early users have devised efficient ways of exploiting the capabilities of new systems, providing a performance characterization of the design. They have also furnished significant new concepts to be incorporated in the designs of succeeding generations. This information has often led to improvements leading to more viable commercial products.

For example, NASA and DOE encouraged industry to develop a more advanced supercomputer to meet their research needs, which resulted in the Cray 2 supercomputer. This powerful new machine with greatly expanded memory might not have achieved market acceptance without the identified high performance computing requirement and subsequent acquisition by these Federal agencies. DOE and NASA acquired the first Cray 2 systems, and their early experience showed the broader market for computational research the importance of memories of hundreds of million words and provided valuable feedback that led to engineering changes for better performance.

Federal research and development investment has facilitated advanced research partnerships between industrial firms and university researchers. Industry provides practical knowledge and advanced manufacturing technology to produce high performance computing systems, while universities have developed new concepts and experimental systems. The results of these partnerships have often been significant in supporting the U.S. economy and national security.

The DARPA Strategic Computing program, DOE, and NASA have funded industry/university partnerships which have established U.S. leadership in scalable, highly parallel, high performance computing systems. Unlike the present generation of supercomputers, the resulting systems employ hundreds to thousands of processors. These architectures are generally scalable to higher levels of parallelism and, in the future, can exploit higher performance components and packaging with corresponding increases in sustained performance. This program has produced very promising results: the first generation of scalable parallel systems are now commercially available and have demonstrated high performance in both numeric and non-numeric applications. The second generation of this class of high performance computers is now emerging and scientific, engineering, defense, and business users are preparing for their arrival. Additional results include enhanced performance for workstations, personal computers, mass storage, graphics and input/output systems.

This Component of the HPC Program will build on recent experience in coordinated funding by different agencies of high performance computing systems research and development. For example, the Strategic Computing program at DARPA invested in R&D for an advanced parallel computer which was subsequently commercialized by

Thinking Machines Corporation. DARPA then collaborated with DOE and NASA to facilitate early use of this system in their research laboratories. The NSF recently funded a Science and Technology Center at Rice University, California Institute of Technology, Argonne National Laboratory, and Los Alamos National Laboratory which will consider more effective applications of this and other parallel architectures.

Action Plan

The focused high performance computing systems projects in this plan will be undertaken in cooperation with the software development projects. The systems also must be coordinated with advances in networking to ensure that their potential performance is available to remote users via the National Research and Education Network. The advanced research tasks provide excellent training grounds for the next generation of computer and computational scientists and engineers. Collaboration among these components is essential to the success of the Program.

Research for future generations of computing: Research in computer science, scalable parallel computer architectures, high density packaging technology, VLSI technology and optoelectronics will be increased. New packaging and component technologies will be developed together with associated design, analysis, simulation, and testing tools to enable their use in implementing larger scale computer architectures. This includes creating and extending models of computation, together with sufficient efforts in adaptation of fundamental algorithms, operating systems, and programming languages. These systems–specific activities complement the more generic and applications–focused software described in Advanced Software Technology and Algorithms where the emphasis is to develop the full potential of the new architectures.

System design tools: Support for rapid design, prototyping, and integration is essential to reach the capabilities needed for the Program. Progress in research, development and manufacturing of high performance computing systems is presently limited by lack of adequate automated design and analysis tools. A new generation of design tools and techniques will be developed for integrated, computer–assisted design and manufacturing of high performance computing systems from functional specifications through full systems. The tools will be developed so as to provide rapid prototyping in support of research, interfaced with the latest advances in automated manufacturing so as to boost U.S. industrial capabilities in addition to increasing research and development productivity. These facilities will make use of the latest high–density packaging technology which will be required to create systems at the targeted level of performance.

Transfer of technology to stimulate advanced prototypes: Cooperative university/industry high–risk research and development projects will provide rapid technology transfer from research results to working prototypes. Revolutionary concepts are emerging from the frontiers of research in computer science and engineering, innovative computer architectures, mass storage systems, input/output systems, high density packaging, Very Large Scale Integration (VLSI) and optoelectronics. Government funds will be invested where opportunities exist for leverage to accelerate the transfer of the Federally–funded computing technology to American industry and vice versa. Advanced application–specific integrated circuits (ASICs) will be utilized where appropriate in these general purpose high performance computing systems. Joint projects in high risk areas will be pursued on a cost sharing basis with industry in close collaboration with government laboratories and academia. The focus of these projects will be to accelerate transition of high risk, revolutionary concepts from research laboratories into the commercial market while encouraging a domestic means of production for all critical components.

By the mid 1990s, it is expected that commercial advanced prototypes will be capable of sustaining two or three orders of magnitude better performance than today's systems for complex science, engineering, and defense applications, and for other problems of national importance. System software, including operating systems, programming languages, and software analysis tools, will be developed to determine the computational potential of the commercial systems. Performance analysis and measurement tools will be improved to enable the design and configuration of heterogeneous systems.

Evaluation of Early Systems: Evaluation of early production models of new high performance computing systems will be undertaken using representative problems. These systems will be acquired at the smallest scale that can evaluate their potential performance. The resulting evaluations will form a basis for decisions to develop the associated generic software and specific large scale applications in the Advanced Software Technology and Algorithms component. Needs of the Grand Challenges will be considered fully, and some early production models of high performance computers may be utilized in one or more of the Grand Challenges, at the sites performing this research.

This component of the HPC Program does not include acquisition of full scale systems. Some of these will be acquired under the High Performance Computing Research Centers in the Advanced Software Technology and Algorithms component; others will be purchased by Federal agencies to fulfill their missions. This investment will sustain the U.S. competitive edge and must be protected by ensuring appropriate export controls.

Rationale

Improvements in materials and component technology are advancing computer capability rapidly. Memory and logic circuits are continuing to improve in speed and density, but as fundamental physical limits are approached, advances are being sought through improved computer architectures, custom components, and software and algorithms. Application–specific integrated circuits, such as for real–time signal processing, are being incorporated into special purpose computing systems. Computer architectures have begun to evolve into large scale parallel systems. Scalable architectures provide a uniform approach that enables a wide range of capacity, from workstations to very high performance computers.

At current performance levels our ability to model many important science, engineering, and economic problems is still limited. Computational models which have been developed for these problems require for realistic solutions speeds of trillions of operations per second and corresponding improvement in memory size, mass storage, and input/output systems. *Achievement of this performance level in the next five years is feasible, based on extrapolations of processor capability, demonstrated architectures, number of processors, and improved software performance.*

Responsibilities

NSF, NASA, DOE and DOD share responsibility for long–range research on the foundations of high performance systems. Within the DOD this responsibility will rest with DARPA, the Army Research Office (ARO), the Office of Naval Research, (ONR) and the Air Force Office of Scientific Research (AFOSR). These agencies have all been involved in this area and have considerable knowledge of the status and opportunities.

DARPA will carry the prime responsibility for high–risk research and development leading to commercialization of highly parallel high performance computing systems and will work with ARO, ONR, and AFOSR to achieve this end. DARPA will also have the lead responsibility for supporting research facilities for rapid design, prototyping, and integration of these systems, using advanced components and packaging. DARPA's unique style of managing high risk, large scale projects is particularly effective for transfering technology in joint university and industrial efforts.

The DOE, NASA and DARPA will continue to acquire first production models of high performance computing systems. The diversity of interests represented by these agencies has been important to the broad range of systems developed by industry in the U.S.. This healthy arrangement will continue.

NIST will expand its program for development of measurement techniques and performance modeling for high performance computer systems, and will support transfer of this technology to industry.

Advanced Software Technology and Algorithms

Recommendation: The U.S. should take the lead in encouraging joint research with government, industry, and university participation to improve basic tools, languages, algorithms, and associated theory for the scientific Grand Challenges with widespread applicability. [*HPC Strategy*, 1987]

Goals

Sustained improvements in computing hardware performance and sophistication have resulted in a shift from hardware and architecture to software and algorithms as the primary determiners of the power, flexibility, and reliability of major computing systems. Today the ability to exploit computing technology to address scientific and technological problems of competitive and national importance is determined primarily by software capability.

Breakthroughs in software technology enable computer solutions to problems whose scale, complexity or evolving nature previously inhibited any organized approach. Breakthroughs in algorithm design improve problem solving performance by orders of magnitude, making tractable computational solutions in problem areas where previously no solutions of any sort, or only traditional analytical or experimental methods, were available.

The goal for the Software Technology and Algorithms component of the High Performance Computing Program is to develop a base of software technology and algorithms that (1) will enable solution of Grand Challenge application problems in science and engineering, and that (2) will have broad national impact on software productivity and on systems capability and reliability.

The approach taken is to develop the advanced algorithms and software technology required to address applications problems on the scale of Grand Challenges, while ensuring that the generic technology developed can be applied to a broad range of computational problems. This investment may lead to the development of commercial products, but only after the new concepts have been illustrated and their feasibility demonstrated. Therefore, specific investments will be made to reduce the risks associated with the transition and adoption of these advanced technologies.

The U.S. lead in many areas of science and technology will be closely linked to advances made on important fundamental problems identified as Grand Challenges. Grand Challenges come from many fields from basic science to applied technology. Their solutions will have significant, national–level impact across diverse fields of interest to many Federal agencies. Appendix A describes several Grand Challenges and the agencies concerned with their solutions.

Improvements in algorithm design and implementation are as important to total "user realized" system performance as are performance improvements in the computer systems in which these algorithms will be executed. High performance computing offers scientists and engineers the opportunity to simulate conditions that are difficult or impossible to create and measure. This new paradigm of computational science and engineering offers an important complement to traditional theoretical and experimental approaches, and it is already having major impact in many areas. New approaches combining numeric and symbolic methods are emerging. Development of new instruments and data generation methods in fields as diverse as genetics, seismology, and materials is accelerating demand for computational power. As problems grow to the size and complexity of Grand Challenges, and as computer architectures grow more complex in order to provide increased computing power, the software and algorithms challenge becomes significantly greater.

Effective exploitation of the performance potential of the emerging parallel systems poses a special challenge both to software technology and to algorithm design. The required software technology has many dimensions, ranging from systems software, advanced compilers, and languages, to programming environments for developing and adapting software, to large scale distributed data repositories. Also included are techniques for analyzing and constructing software with high reliability and numerical accuracy, design of high performance algorithms for solving generic problems on specific architectures, and development of algorithmic and software architectural approaches specific to solving the Grand Challenges.

Research in fundamental parallel algorithms is needed to provide a sufficient base of algorithms for high performance architectures. The characteristics of the generic algorithms are often strongly dependent on the computational model embodied in a particular machine architecture. Various models of parallelism yield different algorithms, as do heterogeneous systems configurations involving hybrid computational models.

Networking technology will also have significant influence on the design of algorithms for distributed systems. Fundamental algorithms must be specialized and combined to provide application–specific algorithms appropriate for the Grand Challenges. Algorithm design, development, optimization, and validation requires substantial resources and collaboration. Experimental facilities are a critical tool for developing and demonstrating applications and systems software, computer architectures, and networks.

Action Plan

Support for Grand Challenges: A principal focus of activity will be providing advanced software technology support to research groups collaborating to address the Grand Challenges. The purpose of this is not to provide sustaining support for this research, but rather to provide a means to reduce the risks assumed by Grand Challenge researchers when adopting innovative high performance computing technologies.

3. Program Plan:
Advanced Software Technology and Algorithms

Collaborative groups will include scientists and engineers concerned with Grand Challenge areas, software and systems engineers, and algorithm designers. These groups will be supported by shared computational and experimental facilities, including professional software engineering support teams, linked together by the National Research and Education Network. Groups may also create a central administrative base, which can be located anywhere on the network. Experimental facilities, often called testbeds, are included in the network in order to provide real-time access to data streams and support for rapid validation of computational models.

Technical contributions arising from this investment will include development of application-specific codes for innovative high performance computing systems, design and analysis of algorithms for Grand Challenge problems, and architecture and performance assessment as it relates to specific applications.

Agencies will select Grand Challenge applications to be included in this Program on the basis of the national importance of the specific area and the extent of cost-sharing from sources directly concerned with the specific scientific and engineering applications. An additional consideration will be the leveraging potential in other areas, in particular the commercial domain. Investment related to high performance computing will complement the traditional sources of support for Grand Challenge research by enabling exploratory use of advanced computational techniques.

Software components and tools: The Grand Challenge applications groups will have common needs in many areas of software technology including programming environments for code development and adaptation, advanced compiler technology. Also needed will be tools for optimization and parallelization, data management and interoperability, analysis and performance measurement, user interaction and visualization, debugging, and instrumentation. Advances in these generic software technology areas will have broad national impact, beyond the immediate scope of the Grand Challenge applications.

In order to provide these tools in a manner that is responsive to the needs of the applications researchers, collaborative groups will be formed that cut across the Grand Challenge areas in order to coordinate and share supporting software technology. This will enable multiple applications groups to sustain more easily a fast pace of innovation in the underlying software technology. These groups will include industrial, academic, and government researchers. Innovative approaches will be used to provide incentive for industry to participate and share costs.

A major focus of systems design and engineering will be developing advanced software applications that exploit the high capacity of the National Research and Education Network to provide new capabilities to researchers. An important example is a distributed operating system that permits high capacity interactions among programs at multiple network sites. This capability will enable a researcher to develop applications that may involve several high performance computers located at diverse sites to work

3. Program Plan:
Advanced Software Technology and Algorithms

together effectively. Other applications include distributed shared data and program libraries, research report dissemination systems, and advanced user interaction and visualization systems. For example, security support and data interoperability are required to enable distributed databases that exploit the National Research and Education Network.

Computational techniques: Developing software tools and components is basic to fundamental research in computational technology. It is this research that yields the fundamental algorithms, models of computation, new approaches to program analysis, and language approaches that provide fundamental generational advances.

Research in computational techniques includes the areas of parallel algorithms, numerical and mathematical analysis, parallel languages, and program refinement techniques. Also included are models of computation, formal methods for high assurance, theoretical and empirical techniques for algorithm analysis, and related areas.

Results in design and theory of algorithms are as important to breaking down computational scaling barriers as are performance improvements in computing hardware. Algorithm breakthroughs continue to be made on even fundamental problems such as linear algebra that are often assumed to be well understood. Breakthroughs can yield thousandfold speedup factors above and beyond hardware advances, as illustrated in Figure 3.

Parallel computing is the principal source of opportunity to improve computational performance. There are many differences among the models of computation embodied in parallel computers, and all of these differ from the purely sequential model that dominated the first half-century of computing. Algorithm theory has already yielded scalable parallel solutions to many computational problems that were assumed by most practitioners to be inherently sequential. In order to realize the potential for performance and scaling implicit in the parallel computer technology, research in the design of algorithms will be supported.

The evolution of parallel computing technology has also stimulated renewed activity in the area of high level programming languages. Languages that have inherently sequential semantics force programmers to make unnecessary and undesirable computational commitments that must, in any case, be undone by optimizing compilers. Efforts will be funded to develop higher level languages that will enable computational scientists to consider separately the abstract computational problem being solved and the specific implementation approach. This will also enable use of emerging programming tools that integrate program transformation and optimization with analysis to yield implementations with higher assurance and predictable numerical characteristics.

High performance computing research centers: The HPC Program will support deployment of innovative high performance computing architectures to computational scientists and engineers working on Grand Challenge applications, and to other computer scientists and engineers. Centers will be established to accelerate transition to new generations of high performance computing technology by enabling researchers to explore applications of this new technology.

Information gained from evaluating prototypes of new architectures as part of the High Performance Computing Systems Component will aid the choice of architectures to support the Grand Challenges. As the risks associated with application of innovative systems diminishes in individual Grand Challenges, the costs associated with the facilities will be transferred to the interested sponsors of the applications research. In this component we include computing hardware, network access to the operating systems of scientific instrumentation, and operational support for the Grand Challenge cooperative groups.

Facilities will also be provided to researchers in computing technology in order to support a more rapid transition to the new technology base. Researchers in areas such as algorithms, software environments, and operating systems require experimental access to new generation hardware. For example, there are a number of theoretical models for parallel computation in general use among algorithm designers, but only through empirical work can these models by adjusted to reflect more faithfully the models embodied in the parallel systems. Crucial systems parameters, for example, the relation of processing time to communications time and memory speed, interact with algorithm design parameters in ways that can best be explored empirically.

It is expected that many of the facilities allocated as part of Advanced Software Technology and Algorithms component will be used to facilitate transition of Grand Challenge applications to the new high performance computing systems. The remaining portion will be provided to computing technology researchers in order to support the development of generic algorithms and software technology. These facilities are in addition to those which will be provided as part of the High Performance Computing Systems component of the Program as a means to accelerate the transition from prototypes into products.

Responsibilities

DOE, NASA, NSF, NOAA and **DARPA** share responsibility for clearly defining the computational requirements of the Grand Challenges. They will select Grand Challenge applications areas in which collaborative groups are to be formed, and are responsible for providing advanced software technology support to the research groups collaborating to address the Grand Challenges applications in their domains.

NASA will carry lead responsibility for organizing and chairing the Federal Advanced Software, Technology and Algorithms Coordinating Committee. DOE, NSF, DARPA and other DOD research activities will be among the agencies participating in this committee.

3. Program Plan:
Advanced Software Technology and Algorithms

NASA, DARPA, NSF and **DOE** will support development of software tools and standard components for use across the spectrum of the Grand Challenges. DOE and NASA share responsibility for exploiting the nearer term potential for commercialization of these software developments.

DOE, NASA, NSF and **DARPA** will incorporate early production models of the high performance computing systems into high performance computing laboratories. These high performance computing laboratories will include the advanced software tools and components, innovative computational techniques and the application-specific algorithms and experimental code for the Grand Challenges. These facilities will support the required integrated research, and will be available to users through the National Research and Education Network.

NSF, DOE, NOAA and **NASA** will build on their existing supercomputer centers which will provide the facilities for several high performance computing research centers, accessible to the national research community.

NOAA will be responsible for organizing the coordination of R&D in data management, and will play a lead role in supporting basic research in tools and techniques required for management and analysis of large-scale scientific data bases and distributed data handling.

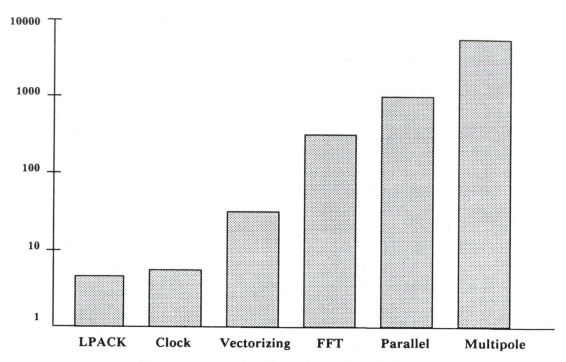

Factors in Computational Speedup
Examples using vectors of length n=4096 (2¹²)

Method	Type	Order	Speedup
LAPACK: BLAS1–>BLAS3 {Dongarra, et al.}	Algorithm & Software	constant	4
Hardware Clock Speed {1976 to 1989}	Microelectronics	12ns–>2 ns	6
Vectorizing Compilers {CFT, VAST, KAP}	Algorithm & Software	32*scalar	32
Fast Fourier Transform {Cooley and Tukey}	Algorithm	$O(n2)$–>$O[n*ln(n)]$	340
Parallel Processors {Gustafson, Montry and Benner}	Algorithm & Architecture	Linear in nr. of processors	1000
Fast Multipole Method {Greengard & Rokhlin}	Algorithm	$O(n2)$–>$O(n)$	4000

Fig. 3 – Speedup Due to Advances in Algorithms

The National Research and Education Network

Recommendation: U.S. Government, industry and universities should coordinate research and development for a research network to provide a distributed computing capability that links the Government, industry, and higher education communities. [*HPC Strategy*, 1987]

Introduction

The United States must develop a National Research and Education Network (NREN) to support communication between persons and organizations involved in open research and scholarly pursuits in the United States. This need has become increasingly obvious to the research community, especially among those who have experienced the benefits of electronic mail and database access, exchange of files between computers, and remote access to specialized and high–performance computing systems. As networking technology grows in power, network–based collaboration continues to allow substantive improvements in research effectiveness. These themes are well expressed in the recent National Research Council report *Toward a National Research Network* (1988). In developing the plan for this component the growing importance of the interrelationships between the network, the research components of the Program, and the U.S. academic community became increasingly clear. *Education* has been included in the name of the network in explicit recognition of this importance.

Today, all major organizations and government agencies use computer networking to some extent, and those with the most progressive and demanding missions have organized major transcontinental networks. A number of these networks are interconnected, notably those of the National Science Foundation (NSFNET), the Department of Defense (ARPANET and MILNET), the Department of Energy (ESNET), and the National Aeronautics and Space Administration (NASA Science Internet). These and many other commercial and regional networks collectively form the Internet, which currently supports a large portion of the U.S. science and engineering research community.

Today's Internet is far from uniform in the type and quality of service provided, and it does not yet reach the entire research community. Even so, expanding the Internet and enhancing its performance as far as technology allows will fall far short of what can and should be accomplished. The goal of this component is to create a new NREN which operates at rates of gigabits per second nationwide. This tremendous challenge is within the grasp of the United States in the next ten years. A network with this level of performance will provide another major improvement in the effectiveness of the national research community and their resulting ability to contribute to U.S. competitiveness.

3. Program Plan:
The National Research and Education Network

Availability of the NREN will provide an environment which enhances collaboration both for software technology development and for basic research and scholarship nationally. In return the development of the NREN will benefit from advances in software technology, particularly in the area of network services.

The eventual impact of the NREN on national competitiveness may well extend beyond such gains in research productivity. The NREN should be the prototype of a new national information infrastructure which could be available to every home, office and factory. Wherever information is used, from manufacturing to high–definition home video entertainment, and most particularly in education, the country will benefit enormously from deployment of this technology.

Stages of the NREN: The stages of NREN development as articulated in the *HPC Strategy* are:

The *first stage* involves an upgrade of the existing Internet to 1.5 megabit per second trunks. (This process is underway.)

The *second stage* will deliver upgraded network services to 200 to 300 research installations, using a shared backbone network with 45 megabit per second capacity.

The *third stage* will deliver one to three gigabit per second networking service to selected research facilities, and 45 megabit per second networking to approximately 1000 sites nationwide.

The stages of the NREN are illustrated in Figure 4.

Government/Industry/University roles: The Federal government plays a dual role in the development of computer networking. Federal funding has supported networking research and technology development in academic, industrial, and (to a lesser degree) government laboratories. The government also supports operational networks and network services. These are expected eventually to create a commercially viable market whose needs can be supplied by the private sector. In this latter role, the government has supplied networks as value–added services on communication circuits leased from the common carriers, and has subsidized their use by segments of the scholarly and research communities.

Universities play a major research role in advanced networking technology. Whereas most of the improvements in *communications* technology have come from industry, many of the most important *networking* technologies have been developed by universities. Educational institutions are also the primary users of networking nationwide, both for access to high performance computing and for collaboration among themselves and with government and industry.

To date, the role of industry has mostly been to provide communications links and produce equipment for networking. This situation is changing and in fact must be radically altered in order to develop the high speed networks of the future. At data rates of gigabits per second the switching elements of the network need to be integrated with the communications links within the facilities of the communications industry. Applications of networks within and between industrial groups should also increase to support a more competitive U.S. industrial posture.

It is anticipated that the government will continue to fund networking research in partnership with academia and industry, and will continue to support parts of the national research networking infrastructure which do not yet have a sizable market. This will be necessary both to build the market for private offerings as well as other commercial goals. It also will be necessary for those government agencies sponsoring development of advanced networking to coordinate the work of multiple government laboratories, industrial, and university groups.

Action Plan

The Federal Research Internet Coordinating Committee (FRICC), a collaboration of the NSF, DARPA, DOE, NASA, and the Department of Health and Human Services (HHS), has begun transforming the present day Internet toward the goal of an NREN. This is being accomplished through sharing communications circuits, network access points, and even entire networks, leading to streamlined operations and reduced costs. The FRICC has established coordinating members in other agencies and national networking organizations and has developed a program plan for implementing the NREN. While these activities have provided a healthy start for the NREN, an additional effort will be necessary to achieve the ultimate goals of the High Performance Computing Program. FRICC, while not formally a part of the FCCSET structure of OSTP, works closely with the Committee on Computer Research and Applications and conducts its activities consistent with the policy guidance of the HPC Program.

Interagency effort to produce an interim NREN. Coordinating an interagency project as large as the NREN will not be easy. It is clear that a unified focus for management is necessary. It is equally clear that the project will not be fully supported by the diverse agencies involved unless they have a decisive role in shaping the project, and are kept in constant, close communication so that the resulting network fills their needs.

In *Stage 1* the agencies will continue to upgrade their networks to 1.5 megabit per second (T1) trunks. This effort is already well underway. In addition, DARPA project known as the *Research Internet Gateway (RIG)* is acquiring a prototype platform for development of "policy–based routing" mechanisms which will allow interconnection of these trunks. Also the FRICC has plans to develop enhanced capabilities such as directory services in support of network users.

As the Internet expands, issues of *network security* have become a source of increasing concern. Recent incidents have demonstrated the vulnerability of computers attached to national networks. A significant effort in implementing the NREN will be development and implementation of mechanisms to enhance the security of the connected computing systems, and mechanisms to protect the networks themselves. These mechanisms will rely on policy-based routing capabilities, and also on recent advances in public-key cryptography.

In *Stage 2* the agencies are planning to acquire a common set of 45 megabit per second transcontinental trunks, the *Research Interagency Backbone (RIB)*. The ability to share backbone trunks, resulting in lower costs and improved service for all agencies, will be enabled by gateways with policy-based routing capabilities. When the RIB is fully operational, it will be interconnected with the NSFNET backbone; the result will be the interim NREN. Another equally important result will be the stage 2 technologies, which will provide a base from which commercial providers can offer compatible networking services nationally.

Research and development for billions of bits per second (gigabits) net. The ultimate structure of the *Stage 3* network will not become clear until this research effort is complete. However, it is clear that fiber-optic trunks now being installed by communications carriers will become increasingly important, new switching systems and network protocols must be developed, new high-speed interconnections to workstations and supercomputers will be needed, and some form of interconnection with the Stage 2 network will be needed. An additional goal of stage 3 is to support such advanced capabilities as remote interactive graphics, nationwide data files, and network-based high definition displays for education. Managing the dynamics of these activities will be a major challenge, but the payoff for success in terms of national capabilities will be enormous in terms of research productivity and, subsequently, in the form of technologies and services available from commercial sources.

Deployment of gigabits NREN. Stage 3 culminates in an operational national network with gigabits trunks. Deployment is not expected to begin until the middle to late 1990's.

Structured transition to commercial service: Mid-level networks organized on a regional basis or by other limited constituencies have sprung up indigenously (for example BITNET and several state-funded networks). Other mid-level networks have been formed with seed funding from NSF, NASA, and DARPA. These have become, in varying degrees, part of the existing Internet. They provide an important vehicle for the economic participation of state and local governments and of industry by providing access to the national network and by giving these other sectors a stake in its operation, thus reducing the funding burden on the Federal government. Moreover, each of these networks is typically a private and autonomous (although possibly subsidized) business entity; thus elements of the emerging national network have already become part of the private sector. Continuation of this trend will result in opportunities for many companies to become involved in leading-edge data communications.

By the end of Stage 2, it is expected that every university and major laboratory will be connected to the NREN through a mid-level network. Present regional offerings vary widely in reliability and scope. To provide homogeneous and universal networking service, interaction of the Federal government with mid-level networks must increase. It is also to be expected that competition and other market forces will come into play between these networks.

Each of the services developed for the NREN must become available commercially at the earliest practical time. The intention is that networking infrastructure should be a commercial offering nationwide. The government and its contractors would then purchase network connections from companies which would provide service to subscribers in general.

Eventually, computer networking should be as pervasively available as telephone service is today. The corresponding ease of inter-computer communication will then provide the benefits associated with the NREN to the entire nation, improving the productivity of all information-handling activities. To achieve this end, the deployment of the Stage 3 NREN will include a specific, structured process resulting in transition of the network from a government operation to a commercial service.

Agency Responsibilities

NSF will be the lead agency for deploying the operating NREN within the HPC Program. NSF has assumed responsibility for supporting a backbone for the NREN, and will coordinate collaboration among Federal agencies in this area. The NSF role of support and coordination will expand as the NREN grows; NSF will upgrade and extend the operational network, providing advanced network services, and collaboration technology. NSF will also support and participate in the interagency networking testbed.

DARPA will be the lead agency for the Program's advanced networking technology research and development. DARPA's research leading to the advanced networking technology for gigabit speeds (Stage 3) will take place within its Command, Control, and Communications programs as the primary contribution of the Department of Defense to the NREN. DARPA will also create a testbed, jointly funded with other participating agencies, for advanced network technology and inter-agency collaboration.

DOE will provide networking support for the energy research community and participate in the interagency networking testbed.

NASA will provide networking support for the aerospace research community, participate in the interagency testbed, and support research on aerospace applications and technology with a focus on telescience research and development.

3. Program Plan:
The National Research and Education Network

DARPA, NSF, DOE and NASA will continue their active roles in governance of the Internet, and will expand these roles by providing representatives on the council which sets policy for the NREN.

NOAA will provide networking in support of the climate and global change research community and will participate in the interagency testbed.

NIST will participate by establishing networking standards, with particular emphasis on protocols and security standards. NIST will continue its traditional role of coordinating developing technologies such as Broadband ISDN with service providers, computer manufacturers, telecommunication manufacturers, system integrators and end users through the standards process.

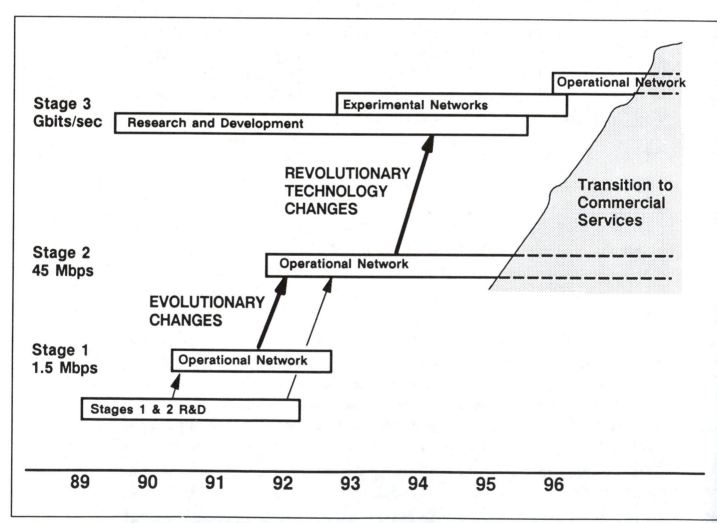

Fig. 4 – Timetable for the National Research and Education Network

Basic Research and Human Resources

Recommendation: Long term support for basic research in computer science should be increased within available resources. Government, industry, and universities should work together to improve the training and utilization of personnel to expand the base of research and development in computational science and technology. [*HPC Strategy*, 1987]

Goals

This component of the High Performance Computing Program addresses longer term national needs for high performance computing. The rapid growth of computing technology and computational science and engineering has created extraordinary demands for more rapid innovation, significantly increased manpower, and accelerated transfer of technology. The basic research community plays a major role in addressing these needs.

We must sustain a rapid pace of innovation in computer science and in computational science by investing in long term basic research.

Proprietary control is difficult to retain in an industry that is characterized by periodic major structural innovations, such as the shift now in progress from central timeshared computing to distributed networked workstations. Because of this, industry has little incentive to invest in long term approaches unless costs and risks are shared. For this reason, most of the major breakthroughs in computing have been the result of basic research activity. Examples include timesharing, local and national networks, VLSI design technology, personal computing, parallel computing, artificial intelligence, and many others. Each of these breakthroughs has had an enormous impact in the marketplace.

Increased numbers of qualified people are needed both in computational science and engineering, and in computer science and engineering. Universities are beginning to create new academic programs in areas of computational science and engineering that develop skills in both computer technology and in specific areas of science and engineering. The rapid evolution of this technology requires practitioners with a broad range of generic skills.

There is a need to reduce risk to industry in adapting and applying new technology. Technology is transferred rapidly from research into practice when the research community is an active participant in the process and when there is consensus in the research community on basic technical issues. The diversity of parallel computing models and algorithmic approaches now emerging provides unusual opportunity for application. The rapid pace of technology development in computing and computational science demands active participation of basic researchers in accomplishing transfer of the emerging technologies.

3. Program Plan:
Basic Research and Human Resources

Support for basic research must be supported in several respects. The High Performance Computing Program addresses this need through direct basic research support, improved infrastructure to increase research productivity, and facilitation of collaboration. The goals of this component of the Program are:

- **Basic research.** Ensure an adequate level of basic research activity to produce the next generation of innovative results in computing technology.

- **Human resources.** Support basic research, education, and training in order to meet the needs of research, personnel, and transition support in both computing technology and in computational science and engineering.

- **Support for collaboration.** Promote collaborations involving the basic research community, industry, and government to allow attacks on larger scale problems and accelerate dissemination of results.

- **Infrastructure.** Supprt the effectiveness of the research community by providing facilities and research infrastructure, including experimental high performance computers, networks, associated systems software, and applications software components.

The Basic Research Enterprise. Basic research programs already underway and supported by current Federal funding provide a base from which many computing applications goals can be achieved, but this base is already under great pressure even without the demands of important new thrusts[1]. The pace of expansion of computing technology and its applications greatly exceeds the rate of expansion of basic research, with consequent strain on the basic research community[2].

Effectively integrating new high performance computing technology into the US technological and scientific mainstream will require sustained research effort across the spectrum of computing technology. Some examples are microsystems component technology and packaging, computer architecture, fundamental algorithms and complexity, software engineering languages and tools, networking and distributed computing, artificial intelligence, numerical algorithms, and applications–specific algorithms.

Human Resources. Several studies in the past 10 years have documented the human resources challenges to the continued development and exploitation of computer technology[3]. A particular focus of these studies has been the severe undersupply of computer scientists and computer engineers at advanced degree levels. Computational scientists and engineers are in even shorter supply.

1. *The National Challenge in Computer Science and Technology*, Computer Science and Technology Board of the National Research Council, National Academy Press, Washington, 1988.
2. Gries, D., et al. *Imbalance Between Growth and Funding in Academic Computer Science: Two Trends Colliding*, Communications of the Association for Computing Machinery, 29(9), Sept 1986.

3. Program Plan:
Basic Research and Human Resources

Addressing the Grand Challenge applications requires large scale collaborative effort involving diverse groups of scientists, engineers, and mathematicians. The manpower shortage in computing technology and in computational science and engineering is hindering progress in these areas.

Collaboration. Interactions among multiple research teams and potential technology recipients contribute significantly to reducing the risks associated with transfer of major technologies into production. Collaboration can be facilitated in the basic research community by ensuring a high level of access to the network applications software based on the National Research and Education Network and by involving basic research groups in Grand Challenge applications.

The network support software will include capabilities for activities such as rapid distribution and sharing of research results, software distribution and configuration management support mechanisms, high-capacity interaction support for remote computers, access to instrumentation in remote experimental laboratories, rapid search and retrieval in distributed library databases, and so on.

Infrastructure. Scarcity of funds in computing technology research has hindered modernization of university computing research and education facilities. A rapid pace of technological innovation requires aggressive investment to ensure that universities remain at the forefront. Networked access to high performance computing with advanced software support is important for training computational scientists and engineers. The potential for using networks to disseminate results and conduct collaborative research at all educational levels is just beginning to be realized.

Basic infrastructure for computer research has been a concern for some years. Several agencies have programs that support the needs of the HPC Program. The Institutional Infrastructure Program at NSF has helped to equip approximately 25 computer science and computer engineering departments in the past eight years. DARPA for many years has been instrumental in building a core research base at major universities. The University Research Instrumentation program of the Department of Defense has provided important equipment and research support. The DOE research program has provided modern parallel computer facilities to several of its national laboratories and universities to promote basic research in high performance computing and to provide training facilities for graduate students and young faculty in all the disciplines involved in computational sciences. NASA maintains several research institutes and centers of excellence to interface with universities.

3. Gries, *op. cit.;* Feldman, Jerome A. and William R. Sutherland. *Rejuvenating Experimental Computer Science.* Comm. ACM 22, 9 (Sept. 1979), 497–502.; Kosaraju, S. Rao., et al. *Meeting the Basic-Research Needs of Computer Science,* Study report of the NSF CCR Advisory Committee, December, 1986; *Profiles -- Computer Science: Human Resources and Funding,* National Science Foundation report 88-324, February, 1989.

3. Program Plan:
Basic Research and Human Resources

Action Plan

Several specific approaches are taken to address the goals. These approaches will, in most cases, be implemented as possible expansions of existing research funding programs.

Expand basic research. Increase basic research activity in computing technology areas that influence high performance computing, including algorithms, software languages and tools, architectures, systems software, microsystems, networks, distributed computing, and symbolic processing.

Attain a level of 1000 computer science Ph.D.s per year by 1995. Strengthen the human resource infrastructure for basic research. Support university risk investment in computational science and engineering degree programs. This should be done by expanding the number of universities capable of providing high quality advanced education in computer and computational science and engineering.

Promote at least 10 computational science and engineering degree programs. Sponsor interdisciplinary programs in universities to accelerate the maturing of computational science and engineering subdisciplines.

Upgrade 10 university computer science departments toward the standards of current 10 best. Include facilities for research in high performance computing. Also, upgrade an additional 25 computer science departments to nationally competitive quality.

Provide National Research and Education Network access for every U.S. university and major laboratory. Every university and major laboratory will be connected to the National Research and Education Network through a mid-level network.

Improve facilities available to support basic research and advanced education. High performance computing facilities currently available to researchers are in such demand that there is only limited availability for educational usage in computational science and engineering degree programs. The effective introduction of computational science and engineering techniques into industry requires students to receive exposure to high-performance machines.

Improve ties between computing technology and other disciplines. Many breakthroughs in computational science and engineering applications result from interactions with computer scientists. Correspondingly, computer science, through exposure to the needs of computational science and engineering, is producing technology to address future needs. Funding will be directed to promote these interactions.

Provide access to professional engineering support. Professional engineering staff should be available to basic research groups for assistance in construction and maintenance of large scale prototype systems, including software and hardware. This can be accomplished through industrial collaborations or through placement of professional staff in university laboratories.

Responsibilities

Federal agencies historically have supported activities which advance basic research by developing and improving infrastructure for the nation's knowledge and human resource base in computing. The HPC Program will exploit existing mechanisms to meet needs in these areas.

The **DOE** has established advanced computational science research facilities at several national laboratories and universities. Although the DOE labs already maintain a strong university cooperation program, more needs to be done to provide closer ties with the academic computational science community below the top echelon. For example, an expansion of the summer program for high school students using national facilities would be beneficial in providing interested and trained students to the universities.

The national laboratories are ideal training centers for graduate students in the sciences because of the wealth of experience in solving real world problems. This environment makes a valuable addition to the training of new scientists and should be made available to many more senior graduate students, post-doctoral fellows and young faculty than is currently possible.

The **NSF**'s primary mission is broad support of basic research and human resources in science and engineering. NSF recently reorganized to support a new research directorate, Computer and Information Science and Engineering (CISE), to focus resources on computing as a strategic research area. CISE supports research grants for academic institutional improvement as well as research. The research community supported by CISE will be primary participants in this Program.

Several NSF Centers (Science and Technology Centers, Engineering Research Centers, and Supercomputer Centers) focus on topics central to the HPC Program. These Centers illustrate the type of university-industry and interagency programs which can be employed directly as testbeds and sources of high performance computing technology.

The five NSF National Supercomputer Centers, for example, have provided advanced hardware and software to advance the utility of computational science across an entire spectrum of researchers. More than 11,000 scientists at some 300 institutions have used these facilities during the past few years. The research facilities and advanced experimental systems developed under the Program can be made available broadly to the entire U.S. research community through the National Research and Education Network.

NASA supports leading-edge applications of high performance computing technology. It also supports development of computational science programs in universities.

3. Program Plan:
Basic Research and Human Resources

NASA Institutes (ICASE, RIACS, ICOMP, CESDIS) and Centers of Excellence (CASIS, ICLASS) provide settings at NASA Centers or at Universities where computer scientists and computational scientists can work together using state of the art equipment on a permanent or temporary basis (summers, sabbaticals, etc.) These programs would be for undergraduates, graduate students, postdoctorals, university faculty, and researchers from industry and government.

NASA has supercomputer facilities at several of its field centers (Ames, Goddard, Langley, Lewis, and Marshall). NASA has also established the Numerical Aerodynamics Simulation (NAS) Facility, which is a national facility for aerospace applications which operates not only state-of-the-art supercomputers, but advanced parallel computers like the Connection Machine. NASA has also established a significant Artificial Intelligence Laboratory in the Information Sciences Division at ARC. These facilities are used for a wide range of mathematical, algorithm, systems software, and computer architectural research. These facilities are available to NASA centers, institutes, and grantees, and to the aerospace community. Under this program NASA facilities will be expanded to include scalable testbeds to support interdisciplinary research which combines mathematics, algorithms, systems software, and computer architecture.

NOAA has supercomputer facilities, and has also created generic, broad spectrum workstation design facilities to support the Program for Regional Observing and Forecasting Systems (PROFS). Under this Component, NOAA will expand the opportunities for collaborative research at its facilities for development of algorithms and techniques for large scientific data bases, use of artificial intelligence in data management, and development of climate prediction models.

DARPA provides high performance computing systems for research community use on two scales: small-scale for experimentation, software and algorithm development by computer and computational science research groups, and medium-scale for shared-use facilities intended for access by dozens of groups via the National Research and Education Network. DARPA funding also supports key university and industrial labs for research and advanced development in computer and network architecture, network protocols and management, microsystems design and prototyping, advanced components and packaging, software tools and parallel algorithms.

4. Organization

Leadership of the HPC Program is the responsibility of the Office of Science and Technology Policy. It will be coordinated through the FCCSET Committee on Computer Research and Applications, whose members include representatives of the key agencies. The Committee will work closely with the President's Science Advisor and the various government funding agencies to ensure the continuing success of the Program. The components of the program that implement the Program will be executed by the cognizant agencies. Duties and responsibilities of the Committee include:

- Interagency planning and coordination;

- Policy development and technology assessment;

- Liaison with the industrial and university sectors; and

- Annual reporting of progress to the Office of Scientific and Technology Policy.

A High Performance Computing Advisory Panel will be formed, consisting of eminent individuals from government, industry, and academia. Members of the Advisory Panel will be selected by and will report to the Director of OSTP. The Panel will provide the Director and the Committee with an independent assessment of:

- Progress of the Program in accomplishing its objectives;

- Continued relevance of the Program goals over time;

- Overall balance among the Program components; and

- Success in strengthening U.S. leadership in high performance computing, and integration of these technologies into the mainstream of U.S. science and industry.

A broadly representative industry body will assist in making long-range demand and robustness projections for: high capacity research networks; the spectrum of computer architectures; the adequacy of software development; and the level of the manpower pool. This body will help assure a smooth transition between successive generations of high performance computing systems.

The FCCSET Committee on Computer Research and Applications has established subcommittees that will be responsible for planning, organizing, monitoring and coordinating the components of this Program. This includes liaison with the industrial and academic sectors, and published annual reports.

5. Budget

Budgets for the Program are presented in Table 1. Each budget element corresponds to a key activity in one of the four components of the HPC Program. The activities are described for each component in Section 3 of this plan. The yearly additional funding requested for this Program corresponds to the estimate given in the *HPC Strategy*, with some adjustment to yearly funding levels as a result of more detailed planning and inflation. Significant portions of the Program's funding will be allocated in each of the three participating sectors: universities, industry, and government laboratories.

Currently, the four principal funding agencies are spending about $500 Million per year on research and development for high performance computing. It is important that this funding continue with coordination by the FCCSET Committee as discussed in this plan, because the ability of the Program to achieve its goals depends upon maintenance of the broad base of computational and computer science and engineering research presently funded by the Federal government.

Preliminary planning estimates suggest that the first year of the program would require an augmentation of $150 million, which would then grow to an incremental annual level of $600 million by the fifth year.

Special attention has been devoted to the subcomponents "Early Systems for Evaluation" and "High Performance Computing Research Centers". There is an explicit strategy for investment in emerging high performance computing systems (including associated software) in these activities, to ensure that adequate funding is available. It is intended that the Early Systems for Evaluation budget sustain acquisition of the smallest scale systems which will allow characterization of their potential performance. For systems which prove to have good performance potential, the High Performance Computing Research Centers budget will support scaling these systems up, to demonstrate that potential in the Grand Challenges or other advanced applications. This will reduce risk to both producers of the systems and researchers using them, to provide the necessary incentive for early deployment in the most advanced applications.

The Basic Research and Human Resources component also requires special discussion, because it is funded in two ways. First, ten percent of the Program funding is set aside for this component. Second, it is intended that an additional fifteen percent of the total Program funding in the other three components will consist of basic research, carried out largely in Universities, which will also support the Program goals in Basic Research and Human Resources. Integrating this research with the rest of the Program allows a smooth flow of research from basic ideas through to applications.

Summary of Additional Funds
(Millions of Dollars)

Reference Page	Component	Year 1	Year 2	Year 3	Year 4	Year 5
17	**High Performance Computing Systems**	**55**	**91**	**141**	**179**	**216**
19	Research for Future Generations	11	17	24	32	37
19	System Design Tools	10	18	21	25	25
19	Advanced Prototype Development	22	36	65	86	116
20	Evaluation of Early Systems	12	20	31	36	38
23	**Advanced Software Technology and Algorithms**	**51**	**90**	**137**	**172**	**212**
24	Support for Grand Challenges	9	19	34	43	48
25	Software Components and Tools	15	30	41	60	78
26	Computational Techniques	6	10	18	19	31
26	High Performance Computing Research Centers	21	31	44	50	55
31	**National Research and Education Network**	**30**	**50**	**95**	**105**	**110**
33	Interagency Interim NREN	14	23	55	50	50
34	Gigabits Research and Development	16	27	40	55	60
34	Deployment of Gigabits NREN	(Funding begins after Year 5)				
34	Structured Transition to Commercial Service	(Funding begins after Year 5)				
37	**Basic Research and Human Resources**	**15**	**25**	**38**	**46**	**59**
	NOTE:	15% of the other three Components is also commited to this general area				
	TOTAL High Performance Computing Program	**151**	**256**	**411**	**502**	**597**

Table 1 – Budget Summary by Program Component

ACKNOWLEDGMENTS

Office of Science and Technology Policy guidance was provided by William R. Graham, Tom Rona, Robert Post, and Paul Huray. The Plan Drafting Committee was chaired by David B. Nelson from the Department of Energy; and included J. Mark Pullen, William L. Scherlis, and Stephen L. Squires from the Defense Advanced Research Projects Agency; Donald Austin, Daniel Hitchcock, Thomas Kitchens, and Norman H. Kreisman from the Department of Energy; Paul H. Smith from National Aeronautics and Space Administration; and Melvyn Ciment, Peter Freeman, and Stephen Wolff from the National Science Foundation. Special thanks are due to Sandy Merola and Dennis Hall from the Lawrence Berkeley Laboratory, for editing and production assistance.

APPENDIX A: SUMMARY OF GRAND CHALLENGES
FOR WHICH SOLUTION IS LIKELY TO BE POSSIBLE USING
SYSTEMS DEVELOPED UNDER THIS INITIATIVE

PREDICTION OF WEATHER, CLIMATE, AND GLOBAL CHANGE. The aim is to understand the coupled atmosphere, ocean, biosphere system in enough detail to be able to make long range predictions about its behavior. Applications include understanding CO_2 dynamics in the atmosphere, ozone depletion, climatological perturbations due to man made releases of chemicals or energy into one of the component systems, and detailed predictions of conditions in support of military missions.
Agencies: DOE, DOD, NASA, NSF, NOAA

CHALLENGES IN MATERIALS SCIENCES. High performance computing has provided invaluable assistance in improving our understanding of the atomic nature of materials. These have an enormous impact on our national economy. A selected list of such materials includes: semiconductors, such as silicon and gallium arsenide and superconductors such as the high Tc copper oxide ceramics that have been shown recently to conduct electricity at about 100 degrees Kelvin.
Agencies: DOD, DOE, NSF, NASA

SEMICONDUCTOR DESIGN. As intrinsically faster materials, such as gallium arsenide are used, a fundamental understanding is required of how they operate and how to change their characteristics. Essential understanding of overlay formation, trapped structural defects, and the effect of lattice mismatch on properties are needed. Currently, it is possible to simulate electronic properties for simple regular systems, however, materials with defects and mixed atomic constituents are beyond present capabilities.
Agencies: DOD, DOE, NSF

SUPERCONDUCTIVITY. The discovery of high temperature superconductivity in 1986 has provided the potential of spectacular energy-efficient power transmission technologies, ultra sensitive instrumentation, and devices using phenomena unique to superconductivity. The materials supporting high temperature superconductivity are difficult to form, stabilize, and use, and the basic properties of the superconductor must be elucidated through a vigorous fundamental research program.
Agencies: DOE, NSF, DOD

STRUCTURAL BIOLOGY. The function of biologically important molecules can be simulated by computationally intensive Monte Carlo methods in combination with NMR of crystallographic data. Molecular dynamics methods are required for the time dependent behavior of such macromolecules. The determination, visualization, and analysis of these 3D structures is essential to the understanding of the mechanisms of enzymic catalysis, recognition of nucleic acids by proteins, antibody/antigen binding, and many other dynamic events central to cell biology.
Agencies: DOE, HHS, NSF

DESIGN OF DRUGS. Predictions of the folded conformation of proteins and of RNA molecules, by computer simulation is rapidly becoming accepted as a useful, and sometimes primary tool in understanding the properties required in drug design.
Agencies: DOE, HHS, NSF

HUMAN GENOME. Comparison of normal and pathological molecular sequences is our current most revealing computational method for understanding genomes, and the molecular basis for disease. To benefit from the entire sequence of a single human will require capabilities for more than three billion subgenomic units, as contrasted with the ten to two hundred thousand units of typical viruses.
Agencies: DOE, HHS, NSF

QUANTUM CHROMODYNAMICS. In high energy theoretical physics, computer simulations of QCD are yielding first principle calculations of the properties of strongly interacting elementary particles. New phenomena have been predicted including; the existence of a new phase of matter, and the quark-gluon plasma. Properties under the conditions of the first microsecond of the big bang, and in the cores of the largest stars have been calculated by simulation methods. Beyond the range of present experimental capabilities, computer simulations of grand unified "theories of everything" have been devised using QCD (Lattice Gauge Theory).
Agencies: DOE, NSF

ASTRONOMY. Data volumes generated by Very Large Array (VLA) or Very Long Baseline Array (VLBA) radio telescopes currently overwhelms the available computational resources. Greater computational power will significantly enhance their usefulness in

SUMMARY OF GRAND CHALLENGES

exploring important problems in radio astronomy, resulting in better return on a major national investment.
Agencies: NASA, NSF

CHALLENGES IN TRANSPORTATION. In the nearer term, substantial contributions to vehicle performance can be made using more approximate physical modeling and reducing the amount of interdisciplinary coupling. Examples include, modeling of fluid dynamical behavior for three dimensional flow-fields about complete aircraft geometries, flow inside of engine turbomachinery, duct flow, and flow about ship hulls.
Agencies: NASA, DOD, DOE, NSF, DOT

VEHICLE SIGNATURE. Reduction of vehicle signature (acoustic and electromagnetic, and thermal characteristics) is critical for low detection military vehicles.
Agencies: NASA, DOD

TURBULENCE. Turbulence in fluid flows impacts the stability and control, thermal characteristics, and fuel performance of virtually all aerospace vehicles. Understanding the fundamental physics of turbulence is requisite to reliably modeling flow turbulence for the analysis of realistic vehicle configuration.
Agencies: NASA, DOD, DOE, NSF, NOAA

VEHICLE DYNAMICS. Analysis of the aeroelastic behavior of vehicles, as well as the stability and ride analysis of vehicles are critical assessments of land and air vehicle performance and life-cycle.
Agencies: NASA, DOD, DOT

NUCLEAR FUSION. Development of controlled nuclear fusion requires understanding the behavior of fully ionized gasses at very high temperatures under the influence of strong magnetic fields in complex three dimensional geometries.
Agencies: DOE, NASA, DOD

EFFICIENCY OF COMBUSTION SYSTEMS. To attain significant improvements in combustion efficiencies requires understanding the interplay between the flows of the various substances involved and the quantum chemistry which causes those substances to react. In some complicated cases the quantum chemistry required to understand the reactions is beyond the reach of current supercomputers.
Agencies: DOE NASA, DOD

ENHANCED OIL AND GAS RECOVERY. This challenge has two parts: to locate as much of the estimated 300 billion barrels of oil reserves in the US and then to devise economic ways of extracting as much of this as possible. Thus improved seismic analysis techniques as well as improved understanding of fluid flow through geological structures is required.
Agencies: DOE

COMPUTATIONAL OCEAN SCIENCES. The objective is to develop a global ocean prediction model incorporating temperature, chemical composition, circulation, and coupling to the atmosphere and other oceanographic features. This will couple to models of the atmosphere in the effort on global weather as well as having specific implications for physical oceanography.
Agencies: DOD, NASA, NSF, NOAA

SPEECH. Speech research is aimed at providing a communications interface with computers based on spoken language. Automatic speech understanding by computer is a large modeling and search problem in which billions of computations are required to evaluate the many possibilities of what a person might have said within a particular context.
Agencies: NASA, DOD, NSF

VISION. The challenge is to develop human-level visual capabilities for computers and robots. Machine vision requires image signal processing, texture and color modeling, geometric processing and reasoning, as well as object modeling. A competent vision system will likely involve the integration of all of these processes with close coupling
Agencies: NSF, DARPA, NASA

UNDERSEA SURVEILLANCE FOR ASW. The Navy faces a severe problem in maintaining a viable anti-submarine warfare (ASW) capability in the face of quantum improvements in Soviet submarine technology, which are projected to be so substantial that evolutionary improvements in detection systems will not restore sufficient capability to counter their advantages. An attractive solution to this problem involves revolutionary improvements in long-range undersea surveillance which are possible using very high gain acoustic arrays and active acoustic sources for ASW surveillance. These methods will be computationally intensive; even taking advantage of inherent parallelism and judicious design of algorithms, computational demands for the projected post-2000 era submarine threat mandate achieving signal processing computation rates of in excess of a trillion operations per second.
Agencies: DOD

APPENDIX B: GLOSSARY

bits– binary digits (the smallest units of digital information); also an abbreviation for "bits per second"

broadband ISDN (BISDN)– broadband integrated services data network, an evolving standard commercial communications offering which will provide data rates of hundreds of megabits per second

byte– one character of computer storage

common carrier– a regulated commercial company which offers communication services in an open market

flops– abbreviation for floating-point operations per second, a unit which characterizes the performance of a computer for certain scientific and engineering calculations

giga– prefix meaning billion, e.g. "gigaops" means "billion operations per second" and "gigabits" means "billion bits per second"

links– long-distance communications circuits, also known as "trunks"

mega– prefix meaning million, e.g. "megaops" means "millions operations per second" and "megabytes" means "million characters of storage"

mid-level network– a computer network with scope which falls between a nationwide network and a local network, such as one of the state or regional networks

ops– abbreviation for "operations per second", a general measurement of computer performance

policy-based routing– a computer network function which treats data packets in different ways depending on some policy, for example certain packets may be given high priority, certain others may be rejected as not authorized to use some portion of the network

telescience– science practiced at a distance, using telecommunications

tera– prefix meaning trillion, e.g. "teraops" means "trillion operations per second"

testbed– an configuration intended to allow experimentation with systems in an application environment

trunks– long-distance communications circuits, also known as "links"

value-added services– services provided in addition to basic communication links (and at extra cost); for example, computer networking using communications provided by a common carrier

A RESEARCH AND DEVELOPMENT STRATEGY FOR HIGH PERFORMANCE COMPUTING

Executive Office of the President

Office of Science and Technology Policy

November 20, 1987

EXECUTIVE OFFICE OF THE PRESIDENT
OFFICE OF SCIENCE AND TECHNOLOGY POLICY
WASHINGTON, D.C. 20506

This year the Federal Coordinating Council for Science, Engineering, and Technology (FCCSET) Committee on Computer Research and Applications began a systematic review of the status and directions of high performance computing and its relationship to federal research and development. The Committee held a series of workshops involving hundreds of computer scientists and technologists from academia, industry, and government. A result of this effort is the report that follows, containing findings and recommendations concerning this critical issue. It has been sent to the appropriate committees of Congress for their review.

A consistent theme in this report is the need for industry, academia, and government to collaborate and exchange information on future R&D efforts. Partners need to give one another signals as to their intent for future activities, and this report is a necessary first step in that process. The vision it represents must continue to grow. For that reason, I have asked the Committee to initiate the appropriate forums for discussing it further with the computing community.

Another theme has come out of this report: within four decades, the field of computer science has moved from a service discipline to a pervasive technology with a rigorous scientific basis. Computer science has become important to our national security and to our industrial productivity, and as such it provides the United States with many opportunities and challenges. Three of those opportunities are addressed in the report's findings and recommendations: High Performance Computers, Software Technology and Algorithms, and Networking. The fourth recommendation involves the Basic Research and Human Resources that will be required to conduct the other initiatives.

One thing is clear: the competition in an increasingly competitive global market cannot be ignored. The portion of our balance of trade supported by our high performance computing capability is becoming more important to the nation. In short, the United States must continue to have a strong, competitive supercomputing capability if it is to remain at the forefront of advanced technology. For that reason the Office of Science and Technology Policy is encouraging activities among the federal agencies together with the academic community and the private sector.

William R. Graham

William R. Graham
Science Adviser to the President and
Director, Office of Science and Technology Policy

CONTENTS

SUMMARY OF FINDINGS ON COMPUTER RESEARCH AND APPLICATIONS

1. <u>**HIGH PERFORMANCE COMPUTERS:**</u> **A strong domestic high performance computer industry is essential for maintaining U.S. leadership in critical national security areas and in broad sectors of the civilian economy.**

   o U.S. high performance computer industry leadership is challenged by government supported research and development in Japan and Europe.

   o U.S. leadership in developing new component technology and applying large scale parallel architectures are key ingredients for maintaining high performance computing leadership. The first generation of scalable parallel systems is now commercially available from U.S. vendors. Application-specific integrated circuits have become less expensive and more readily available and are beginning to be integrated into high performance computers.

2. <u>**SOFTWARE TECHNOLOGY AND ALGORITHMS:**</u> **Research progress and technology transfer in software and applications must keep pace with advances in computing architecture and microelectronics.**

   o Progress in software and algorithms is required to more fully exploit the opportunity offered by parallel systems.

   o Computational methods have emerged as indispensable and enabling tools for a diverse spectrum of science, engineering, design, and research applications.

   o Interdisciplinary research is required to develop and maintain a base of applications software that exploits advances in high performance computing and algorithm design in order to address the "grand challenges" of science and engineering.

3. <u>**NETWORKING:**</u> **The U.S. faces serious challenges in networking technology which could become a barrier to the advance and use of computing technology in science and engineering.**

   o Current network technology does not adequately support scientific collaboration or access to unique scientific resources. At this time, U.S. commercial and government sponsored networks are not coordinated, do not have sufficient capacity, do not interoperate effectively, and do not ensure privacy.

   o Europe and Japan are aggressively moving ahead of the U.S. in a variety of networking areas with the support of concentrated government and industry research and implementation programs.

4. <u>**BASIC RESEARCH AND HUMAN RESOURCES:**</u> **Federal research and development funding has established laboratories in universities, industry, and government which have become the major sources of innovation in the development and use of computing technology.**

[1]

SUMMARY OF RECOMMENDATIONS
FOR A NATIONAL
HIGH PERFORMANCE COMPUTING STRATEGY

1. <u>HIGH PERFORMANCE COMPUTERS:</u>   The U.S. Government should establish a long range strategy for Federal support for basic research on high performance computer technology and the appropriate transfer of research and technology to U.S. industry.

2. <u>SOFTWARE TECHNOLOGY AND ALGORITHMS:</u>   The U.S. should take the lead in encouraging joint research with government, industry, and university participation to improve basic tools, languages, algorithms, and associated theory for the scientific "grand challenges" with widespread applicability.

3. <u>NETWORKING:</u>   U.S. government, industry, and universities should coordinate research and development for a research network to provide a distributed computing capability that links the government, industry, and higher education communities.

4. <u>BASIC RESEARCH AND HUMAN RESOURCES:</u>   Long term support for basic research in computer science should be increased within available resources. Industry, universities, and government should work together to improve the training and utilization of personnel to expand the base of research and development in computational science and technology.

[2]

A RESEARCH AND DEVELOPMENT STRATEGY FOR HIGH PERFORMANCE COMPUTING

High performance computing refers to the full range of supercomputing activities including existing supercomputer systems, special purpose and experimental systems, and the new generation of large scale parallel architectures.

THE CHALLENGE

In the span of four decades, computing has become one of the most pervasive and powerful technologies for information management, communications, design, manufacturing, and scientific progress.

The U.S. currently leads the world in the development and use of high performance computing for national security, industrial productivity, and science and engineering, but that lead is being challenged. Through an increased foreign industrial capability, the U.S. technology lead in computing has diminished considerably in recent years, but the U.S. continues to maintain strength in basic science and technology. The technology is changing rapidly and the downstream rewards for leadership are great. Progress in computing can be accelerated through the continued pioneering of new hardware, software, algorithms, and network technology and the effective transition of that technology to the marketplace. A shared computing research and development vision is needed to provide to government, industry, and academia a basis for cooperative action. The successful implementation of a strategy to attain this vision and a balanced plan for transition from one generation of technology to the next can result in continued strength and leadership in the forthcoming decades.

High performance computing technology has also become essential to progress in science and engineering. A **grand challenge** is a fundamental problem in science or engineering, with broad applications, whose solution would be enabled by the application of the high performance computing resources that could become available in the near future. Examples of grand challenges are: (1) Computational fluid dynamics for the design of hypersonic aircraft, efficient automobile bodies, and

[3]

extremely quiet submarines, for weather forecasting for short and long term effects, efficient recovery of oil, and for many other applications; (2) Electronic structure calculations for the design of new materials such as chemical catalysts, immunological agents, and superconductors; (3) Plasma dynamics for fusion energy technology and for safe and efficient military technology; (4) Calculations to understand the fundamental nature of matter, including quantum chromodynamics and condensed matter theory; (5) Symbolic computations including speech recognition, computer vision, natural language understanding, automated reasoning, and tools for design, manufacturing, and simulation of complex systems. Many of these could be considerably advanced by the use of computer systems capable of trillions of operations per second.

THE STRATEGY

A **High Performance Computing Strategy**, involving close coordination of existing programs and augmented effort, is required to address this national challenge. This strategy involves the coordinated pursuit of computing technology goals through joint efforts of government, industry, and academia. The strategy will have impact in clarifying and focusing the direction of Federally-funded computing research, which continues to be the major source of innovation for computing technology and a primary catalyst for industrial development. Government support should be highly leveraged with resources provided by industry participants. To be effective, the strategy should also be defined and continually updated in cooperation with industry and academia by making them participants in developing and implementing a shared vision of the future to ensure continued U.S. leadership.

The high performance computing strategy is designed to sustain and focus basic Federally-funded research and promote the transfer of basic science from the laboratory to U.S. industrial development and finally to the marketplace. Technology development will be encouraged as appropriate to meet immediate needs as well as to create a foundation for long term leadership. Strong emphasis will be placed on continued transfer of the results of government funded R&D to industry and on cooperation with industry to insure the continued strength of American high technology trade in the international marketplace.

The basic elements of the strategy are research and development programs in high performance computer architecture, in custom hardware, in software and algorithms, and in networking technology, all supported by a basic research foundation. In each of these areas, major opportunities exist that require coordinated support and management, building on existing government programs. Access to high performance computing is essential for providing scientists and engineers at research institutions throughout the country with the ability to use the most advanced computers for their work. The strategy needs to concurrently address the appropriate Federal role in each

[4]

of the basic elements of the R&D process—basic research, applied research, and industrial development—in order to meet long term, intermediate, and short term technology development goals. Explicit attention must be directed to the flow of technology from basic to applied areas and to the marketplace, as well as back into the research community to create the next generation of computing infrastructure, achieving a cumulative effect. Technology developments within individual element areas will contribute extensively to other activities. Simultaneous and coordinated pursuit of the areas is therefore an important element of the strategy.

CURRENT STATUS AND TRENDS

● **High performance computing systems.** Improvements in materials and component technology are rapidly advancing computer capability. Memory and logic circuits are continuing to improve in speed and density, but as fundamental physical limits are approached, advances are being sought through improved computer architectures, custom hardware, and software. Computer architecture has begun to evolve into large scale multiple processor systems, and in the past four years a first generation of scalable parallel systems has progressed from the research laboratory to the marketplace. Scalable architectures provide a uniform approach that enables a wide range of capacity, from workstations to very high performance computers. Application–specific integrated circuits, such as for real–time signal processing, are being incorporated into special purpose computers.

At current performance levels our ability to model many important science, engineering, and economic problems is still limited. Formulations of computational models presently exist that for realistic solutions would require speeds of teraflops (trillions of floating point operations per second) and equivalent improvement in memory size, mass storage, and input/output systems. In addition, symbolic processing is complementing and enhancing numeric approaches. Achievement of this performance level in the next 5 years appears to be a feasible goal, based on credible extrapolations of processor capability, number of processors, and software sophistication. In developing the new architectural approaches, however, careful collaboration will be required with the applications community to assess the various approaches and to achieve transition to the new approaches where appropriate. As transitions are made, the high performance computing industry should strive to maintain its continued leadership and competitveness.

● **Software technology and algorithms.** As high performance computing systems evolve and become more critical in science, engineering, and other applications domains, software technology becomes an increasingly central concern. As experienced in many U.S. space and defense programs, for example, software can become the dominant computational cost element in large systems because of the need to support evolution throughout the system life cycle from design and

[5]

development to long term maintenance and transition to the next generation. Future software environments and tools should support the development of trustworthy systems capable of evolution, while increasing productivity of developers and users of the systems. Effective exploitation of the performance potential of the emerging parallel systems poses a special challenge both to software and to algorithm design.

High performance computing offers scientists and engineers the opportunity to use computer models to simulate conditions difficult or impossible to create and measure in the laboratory. This new paradigm of computational science and engineering offers an important complement to traditional theoretical and experimental approaches, and it is already having major impact in many areas. New approaches combining numeric and symbolic methods are emerging. The development of new instruments and data generation methods in fields as diverse as genetics, seismology, and materials accelerates demand for computational power. In addition, the opportunity is created to coordinate and focus effort on important grand challenges, such as computational fluid dynamics, weather forecasting, plasma dynamics, and other areas.

● **Computer network technology.** A modern high speed research network is one of the elements needed to provide high performance distributed computation and communication support for research and technology development in government, academia, and industry. A coordinated research network based on very high bandwidth links would enable the creation of large–scale geographically distributed heterogeneous systems that link multiple high performance workstations, databases, data generation sources, and extremely high performance servers as required, in order to provide rapid and responsive service to scientists and engineers distributed across the country. The existing national network is a collection of loosely coupled networks, called an internet, based on concepts pioneered in the U.S.

Technical issues being addressed include utilization of fiber optics to improve performance for the entire research and higher education enterprise of the nation. An additional issue of pressing concern, particularly within the governmental and industrial sectors, is that of computer and network security to ensure privacy and trustworthiness in a heterogeneous network environment. At present, responsibility for privacy and the assurance of trust are vested principally in the computers and switching nodes on the network. Further research, already actively underway, is urgently needed to develop models, methodology, algorithms and software appropriate to the scale of a coordinated research network.

[6]

● **Basic research and human resources in Computer and Computational Science.** Federal funding has historically been, and will likely remain, a major source of support for important new ideas in computing technology. Carefully managed and stable funding is required to maintain vigorous research in computer and computational science and sufficient growth in computer science manpower. It is important to maintain the strength of the existing major research centers and to develop new research activity to support the growth in computer and computational science. Interactions should be fostered among academia, industry, and national laboratories to address large problems and to promote transfer of technology. In the longer term, enhancement of the computing technology base will have significant impact in productivity, efficiency, and effectiveness of government, industry, and the research community.

IMPACT

Computing technology is vital to national security. Advanced computer systems and software are now integral components in most major defense, intelligence, and aerospace systems. Computing technology has a central role in energy research, oil exploration, weapons research, aircraft design, and other national security technology areas.

Major advances in science and engineering have also accrued from recent improvements in supercomputing capability. The existence of machines with hundred megaflop (hundreds of millions of floating point operations per second) speed and multimillion word memories has allowed, for the first time, accurate treatment of important problems in weather prediction, hydrodynamics, plasma physics, stress analysis, atomic and molecular structure, and other areas. The emerging machines with 1 to 10 gigaflop (billions of flops) speed and 100 to 300 million word memories are expected to produce comparable advances in solving numeric and symbolic problems.

Many of these advances in science and engineering are the result of the application of high performance computing to execute computational simulations based on mathematical models. This approach to science and engineering is becoming an important addition to traditional experimental and theoretical approaches. In applications such as the National Aerospace Plane, supercomputing provides the best means to analyze and develop strategies to overcome technical obstacles that determine whether the hypersonic vehicle can fly beyond speeds of Mach seven, where wind tunnels reach their maximum capability. The list of applications for which supercomputing plays this kind of role is extensive, and includes nearly all high–technology industries. The extent of its usage makes supercomputing an important element in maintaining national competitiveness in many high technology industries.

[7]

The high performance computing strategy will have impact in many sectors of the economy. Nearly all sectors of advanced industry are dependent on computing infrastructure. Any improvement in computing capability will have substantial leveraged impact in broad sectors, particularly as applications software increases in power and sophistication.

The computer hardware industry alone amounted to $65 billion in 1986, and U.S. technical market dominance, long taken for granted, is now challenged in this and other critical areas, including networking, microsystems and custom high-performance integrated circuit technology. Foreign investment in computing research and technology has grown considerably in the last decade.

As stated in the report of the White House Science Council, *Research in Very High Performance Computing*, November 1985, "The bottom line is that any country which seeks to control its future must effectively exploit high performance computing. A country which aspires to military leadership must dominate, if not control, high performance computing. A country seeking economic strength in the information age must lead in the development and application of high performance computing in industry and research."

BACKGROUND

The Federal Coordinating Council on Science, Engineering and Technology (FCCSET) was established by Congress under the Office of Science and Technology Policy (OSTP) to catalyze interagency consideration of broad national issues and to coordinate various programs of the Federal government. The FCCSET in turn, established a series of committees, with interagency participation to assess and recommend action for national science and technology issues. The committees have become recognized as focal points for interagency coordination activity, addressing issues that have been identified by direct requests through the OSTP and indirect requests by member agencies (such as the NSF requirement to provide an update to the Lax Report on Large Scale Computing in Science and Engineering). These studies have enabled the FCCSET Committee on Computer Research and Applications to develop a national view of computing technology needs, opportunities, and trends.

From its inception, the FCCSET Committee on Supercomputing (the original name of this committee) was chartered to examine the status of high performance computing in the U.S. and to recommend what role the Federal Government should play regarding this technology. The committee issued two reports in 1983 that provided an integrated assessment of the status of the supercomputer industry and recommended governme... actions. The FCCSET Committee on Computer Research and Applications concluded that it would be proper to include an update of the earlier reports to address the changes that have occurred in the intervening period as a complement to the technical

[8]

reports. The review was based upon periodic meetings with and site visits to supercomputer manufacturers and consultation with experts in high performance scientific computing. White papers were contributed to this report by industry leaders and supercomputer experts. The report was completed in September 1987 and its findings and recommendations are incorporated in the body of this report.

In developing the recommendations presented in this report, the FCCSET Committee reviewed findings and recommendations from a variety of sources, including those mentioned above. A related activity has been the preparation by the White House Science Council (WHSC) Committee on Research in Very High Performance Computing of the report *Research in Very High Performance Computing*, November 1985. The WHSC Committee, composed of respected individuals from academia, industry, and government, made recommendations related to the issues more recently addressed by the FCCSET Committee. In the areas addressed by both committees, there is a significant consistency of recommendations, and, indeed, progress in recent months further strengthens the case for the recommendations. The convergence of views expressed in the many reports, the strong interest in many sectors of government in developing a policy, the dramatic increase in foreign investment and competitiveness in computing and network technology, and the considerable progress in computing technology development worldwide are all indicators of the urgency of developing and implementing a strategy for nationwide coordination of high performance computing under the auspices of the government.

One of the of the direct requests that this report responds to is in Public Law 99–383, August 21, 1986, in which Congress charged the Office of Science and Technology Policy to conduct a study of critical problems and of current and future options regarding communications networks for research computers, including supercomputers, at universities and federal research facilities in the United States. The legislation asked that requirements for supercomputers be addressed within one year and requirements for all research computers be addressed within two years. Dr. William R. Graham, Director of the Office of Science and Technology Policy, subsequently charged the Federal Coordinating Council on Science Engineering and Technology (FCCSET) Committee on Computer Research and Applications to carry out the technical aspects of the study for OSTP.

It was recognized by the FCCSET Committee on Computer Research and Applications that networking technology needs to be addressed in the context of the applications of computing and the sources of computing power that are interconnected using the network technology. This report, therefore, presents an integrated set of findings and recommendations related to Federal support for computer and related research.

[9]

Three subcommittees carried out the work. Each of these committees contributed to the Findings and Recommendations contained in this report. The result is an integrated set of recommendations that addresses the technical areas.

- The **Subcommittee on Computer Networking, Infrastructure, and Digital Communications** invited experts in government, industry and academia to write white papers on networking trends, requirements, concepts applications, and plans. A workshop involving nearly 100 researchers, network users, network suppliers, and policy officials was held in San Diego, California in February 1987 to discuss the white papers and to develop the foundation for the report. Workshop leaders and other experts later met in Washington to summarize the workshop discussions and focused on six topics: access requirements and future alternatives, special requirements for supercomputer networks, internet concepts, future standards and services requirements, security issues, and the government role in networking. As a result of this work, the participants recommended that no distinction should be made between networks for supercomputers and other research computers and that the final report to the Congress should address networks generally. The requirements for both supercomputers and for other research computers are, therefore, addressed in this report.

- The **Subcommittee on Science and Engineering Computing** assessed computing needs related to computational science and engineering. The committee focused its deliberations on requirements for high performance computing, on networking and access issues, and on software technology and algorithms. Under the auspices of the Society for Industrial and Applied Mathematics (SIAM), and with the support of NSF and DOE, a workshop involving 38 recognized leaders from industry, academia, and national laboratories was held at Leesburg, Virginia in February 1987 on research issues in large–scale computational science and engineering. This workshop focused on advanced systems, parallel computing and applications. As a result of the workshop report, recommendations were made related to the role of computing technology in science and engineering applications.

- The **Subcommittee on Computer Research and Development** assessed the role of basic research, the development of high performance computing technology, and issues related to software technology. Contributing to this activity were two workshops. The National Science Foundation (NSF) Advisory Committee for Computer Research reviewed the field and produced an Initiatives Report in May 1987. This report recommended investment in three areas, including parallel systems and software technology. In September 1987, the Defense Advanced Research Projects Agency (DARPA) held a workshop on advanced computing technology in Gaithersburg, Maryland involving 200 researchers from academia, industry, and government. The workshop focused on large–scale parallel systems and software approaches to achieving high performance computing.

[10]

An important result of the activity of the FCCSET Committee on Computer Research and Applications and its subcommittees is that increased coordination among the Government elements is necessary to implement a strategy for high performance computing. The findings and recommendations presented here represent a consensus reached among the subcommittees and convey the powerful and compelling vision that emerged. As a result of this process, the next step would be for the members of the Committee on Computer Research and Applications to develop a plan to help ensure that the vision is shared between government, academia, and American industry. Subsequently, the Committee should develop an implementation plan for Federal government activities, including a detailed discussion of overall priorities.

[11]

1. HIGH PERFORMANCE COMPUTERS

- **<u>FINDING:</u>** **A strong domestic high performance computer industry is essential for maintaining U.S. leadership in critical national security areas and in broad sectors of the civilian economy.**

U.S. prominence in technology critical to national defense and industrial competitiveness has been based on leadership in developing and exploiting high performance computers. This preeminence could be challenged by dependency upon other countries for state of the art computers. Supercomputer capability has contributed for many years to military superiority. In addition, industrial applications now constitute more than half of the supercomputer market and are an important factor in U.S. industrial competitiveness. However, continued progress in computational science and engineering will depend in large part on the development of computers with 100 to 1000 times current capability for important defense, scientific, and industrial applications. These applications are represented by the grand challenges.

■ **U.S. high performance computer industry leadership is challenged by government supported research and development in Japan and Europe.**

The U.S. currently leads the world in research, development, and use of supercomputers. However, this leadership faces a formidable challenge from abroad, primarily from the Japanese. The 1983 FCCSET report stated that "The Japanese have begun a major effort to become the world leader in supercomputer technology, marketing, and applications." Most of the analyses and projections advanced in support of that statement have proven to be accurate.

Japanese supercomputers have entered the marketplace with better performance than expected. Japanese supercomputer manufacturers have attained a high level of excellence in high speed, high density logic and memory microcircuits required for advanced supercomputers. As a result, some U.S. computer manufacturers are dependent on their Japanese competitors for sole supply of critical microcircuits. Japanese manufacturers, universities, and government have demonstrated the ability to cooperate in developing and marketing supercomputers as well as in advancing high performance computing. Recent successes in dominating related high-technology markets underscore their financial, technical, and marketing capability.

[12]

475

■ **U.S. leadership in developing new component technology and applying large scale parallel architectures are key ingredients for maintaining high performance computing leadership. The first generation of scalable parallel systems is now commercially available from U.S. vendors. Application–specific integrated circuits have become less expensive and more readily available and are beginning to be integrated into high performance computers.**

The current generation of supercomputers achieve their performance through the use of the fastest possible individual components, but with relatively conservative computer architectures. While these computers currently employ up to eight parallel processors, their specific architectures cannot be scaled up significantly. Large scale parallel processing, in which the computational workload is shared among many processors, is considered to be the most promising approach to producing significantly faster supercomputers. The U.S. is currently the leader in developing new technology as well as components. However, exploiting these techniques effectively presents significant challenges. Major effort will be required to develop parallel processing hardware, algorithms, and software to the point where it can be applied successfully to a broad spectrum of scientific and engineering problems.

Government funded R&D in universities and industry has focused on an approach to large–scale parallelism that is based on aggressive computer architecture designs and on high levels of circuit integration, albeit with somewhat slower individual components. Unlike current supercomputers, the resulting systems employ 100s to 10,000s of processors. Equally important, these architectures are scalable to higher levels of parallelism with corresponding increase in potential performance.

The first generation of scalable parallel systems is now commercially available from U.S. vendors. These systems have demonstrated high performance for both numeric and non–numeric, including symbolic processing. Comparable systems do not yet exist outside the U.S. The second generation, with higher speed individual components and more parallelism, is already in development here. Experience with these systems has shown that, even with existing software, they are effective for certain classes of problems. New approaches to software for these large–scale parallel systems are in the process of emerging. These approaches suggest that parallel architecture may be effective for wide classes of scientific and engineering problems. An important benefit of the scalable architectures is that a single design, with its attendant components and software, may prove to be useful and efficient over a performance range of 10 to 100 or more. This allows one design to be used for a family of workstations, mini–supercomputers, and supercomputers.

[13]

● **RECOMMENDATION:** The U.S. Government should establish a long range strategy for Federal support for basic research on high performance computer technology and the appropriate transfer of research and technology to U.S. industry.

The program should build upon existing government supported efforts. However, government funding should not be viewed as a substitute for private capital in the high performance computer marketplace. A primary objective is to ensure continued availability of domestic sources for high performance computers that are required for Federal programs, both civilian and defense. These actions should include:

● Government should support, when appropriate for mission requirements, the acquisition of prototype or early production models of new high performance computers that offer potential for improving research productivity in mission areas. These computers could be placed in centers of expertise in order to allow sophisticated users to share initial experiences with manufacturers and other users, and to develop software to complement the vendor's initial offerings. These initial acquisitions should not require the vendor to supply mature operating systems and applications software typical of production computers. However, a criterion for acquisition should be that the hardware designs reflect a sensitivity to software issues, and that the computer has the potential for sustained performance in practical applications that approaches the peak hardware performance.

● Government agencies should seek opportunities to cooperate with industry in jointly funded R&D projects, concentrating especially on those technologies that appear scalable to performance levels of trillions of operations per second (teraops) for complex science, engineering, and other problems of national importance. Systems are needed for both numeric and symbolic computations.

However, since government mission requirements typically exceed those of industrial applications, cooperating with industry in R&D for computers to meet these missions will help to assure that the necessary computers are available. It will also drive supercomputer development at a faster pace than would be sustained by commercial forces alone, an important factor retaining and increasing U.S. leadership in this area.

● Government agencies should fund basic research to lay the foundation for future generations of high performance computers. Steps should be taken to ensure that development of state-of-the-art computers continues to be monitored for appropriate export controls.

[14]

2. Software Technology and Algorithms

- **FINDING:** Research progress and technology transfer in software and applications must keep pace with advances in computing architecture and microelectronics.

   - Progress in software and algorithms is required to more fully exploit the opportunity offered by parallel systems.

   - Computational methods have emerged as indispensable and enabling tools for a diverse spectrum of science, engineering, and design research and applications.

   - Interdisciplinary research is required to develop and maintain a base of applications software that exploits advances in high performance computing and algorithm design in order to address the "grand challenges" of science and engineering.

   A **grand challenge** is a fundamental problem in science and engineering, with broad application, whose solution will be enabled by the application of the high performance computing resources that could become available in the near future.

   As high performance computing systems evolve and are applied to more challenging problems, it is becoming increasingly clear that advances in software technology and applications are essential to realize the full performance potential of these systems. Software development, analysis, and adaptation remain difficult and costly for traditional sequential systems. Large scale complex systems including parallel systems pose even greater challenges. Market pressures for the early release of new computing system products have created a tradition of weak systems software and inadequate programming tools for new computers.

   Current approaches to software development provide only limited capabilities for flexible, adaptable, and reusable systems that are capable of sustained and graceful growth. Most existing software is developed to satisfy nearer term needs for performance at the expense of these longer term needs. This is particularly the case for applications in which specific architectural features of computers have been used to obtain maximum performance through low level programming techniques. The lack of portability of these programs significantly raises the cost of transition to newer architectural approaches in many applications areas. Approaches are beginning to emerge in the research community that have a potential to address the reuse and portability problems.

   Experiments with parallel computers have demonstrated that computation speeds can increase almost in direct proportion to the number of processors in certain applications. Although it is not yet possible to determine in general the most

[15]

efficient distribution of tasks among processors, important progress has nonetheless been made in the development of computational models and parallel algorithms for many key problem areas.

Access to advanced computing systems is an important element in addressing this problem. Experience has shown that the quality of systems and applications software increases rapidly as computing systems are made more available. Initial generic operating systems and extensions to existing programming languages can provide access through coupling high performance computers with existing workstations using either direct or network connections. However, in order to achieve the full potential impact of large scale parallel computing on applications, major new conceptual developments in algorithms and software are required.

The U.S. leads in many areas of software development. The Japanese, however, also recognize the need for high quality software capability and support in order to develop and market advanced machines. They have demonstrated the ability to effectively compete, for example in the area of sophisticated vectorizing compilers.

The U.S. will need to encourage the collaboration of computer scientists, mathematicians, and the scientists in critical areas of computing applications in order to bring to bear the proper mix of expertise on the software systems problem. Such collaboration will be enhanced by network technology, which will enable geographically dispersed groups of researchers to effectively collaborate on "grand challenges." Critical computer applications include problems in fluid dynamics, plasma physics, elucidation of atomic and molecular structure, weather prediction, engineering design and manufacturing, computer vision, speech understanding, automated reasoning, and a variety of national security problems.

[16]

- **RECOMMENDATION:** The U.S. should take the lead in encouraging joint research with government, industry, and university participation to improve basic tools, languages, algorithms, and associated theory for the scientific "grand challenges" with widespread applicability.

Software research should be initiated with specific focus on key scientific areas and on technology issues with widespread applicability. This research is intended to accelerate software and algorithm development for advanced architectures by increased early user access to prototype machines. It would also provide settings for developing advanced applications for production machines. Software technology needs to be developed in real problem contexts to facilitate the development of large complex and distributed systems and to enable transition of emerging parallel systems technology into the computing research community and into the scientific and engineering applications communities.

As part of a mixed strategy, longer term and more basic software problems of reliability and trust, adaptability, and programmer productivity must continue to be addressed. Languages and standards must be promoted that permit development of systems that are portable without sacrificing performance.

In applications areas including computational science and engineering, technology should be developed to support a smooth transition from the current software practice to new approaches based on more powerful languages, optimizing compilers, and tools supported by algorithm libraries. The potential of combining symbolic and numeric approaches should be explored. Progress in these areas will have significant impact on addressing the "grand challenges" in computational science and engineering. Although there are many pressing near term needs in software technology, direct investment in approaches with longer term impact must be sustained if there is to be significant progress on the major challenges for software technology while achieving adequate system performance.

Applications include (1) distributed access to very large databases of scientific, engineering, and other data, (2) high bandwidth access to and linking among shared computational resources, (3) high bandwidth access to shared data generation resources, (4) high bandwidth access to shared data analysis resources, such as workstations supporting advanced visualization techniques.

[17]

3. NETWORKING

- ## FINDING: The U.S. faces serious challenges in networking technology which could become a barrier to the advance and use of computing technology in science and engineering.

- Current network technology does not adequately support scientific collaboration or access to unique scientific resources. U.S. commercial and government sponsored networks presently are not coordinated, do not have sufficient capacity, do not interoperate effectively, and do not ensure privacy.

- Europe and Japan are aggressively moving ahead of the U.S. in a variety of networking areas with the support of concentrated government and industry research and implementation programs.

Computer network technology provides the means to develop large scale distributed approaches to the collaborative solution of computational problems in science, engineering, and other applications areas. Today, researchers sharing a local area network are able to exploit nearly instantaneous communication and sharing of data, creating an effect of linking their workstations and high performance servers into a single large scale heterogeneous computing facility. This kind of capability is now appearing in larger scale campus—wide computer networks, enabling new forms of collaboration. National networks, on the other hand, have low capacity, are overloaded, and fail to interoperate successfully. These have been expanded to increase the number of users and connections but the performance of the underlying network technology has not kept pace with the increased demands. Therefore, the networks which in the 1970s had significant impact in enabling collaboration, are now barriers. Only the simplest capabilities, such as electronic mail and small file transfers, are now usable. Capacity, for example, is orders of magnitude less than the rates required, even if the network is used only for graphics.

Other countries have recognized the value of national computing networks, and, following the early U.S. lead, have developed and installed national networks using current technology. As a result, these countries are now much better prepared to exploit the new opportunities provided by distributed collaborative computing than the U.S. is at the present time. The basic technologies for later generations are also being developed in the U.S., but there have been no major efforts to apply them to address the needs.

[18]

A longer term goal is the creation of large scale geographically distributed heterogeneous systems that link multiple superworkstations and high performance supercomputers to provide service to scientists and engineers distributed across the country. A well-coordinated national network could link these resources together when required on an *ad hoc* basis to provide rapid response to computational needs as they arise. This could reduce the number of sites needed for the physical presence of supercomputers. Present access to computer networks by researchers is dependent upon individual funding or location. There is unnecessary duplication in the links from various agencies to each campus. The development of improved networking facilities could greatly stimulate U.S. research and provide equitable access to resources.

Many scientific research facilities in the U.S. consist of a single, large, and costly installation such as a synchrotron light source, a supercomputer, a wind tunnel, a particle accelerator, or a unique database. These facilities provide the experimental apparatus for groups of scientific collaborators located throughout the country. Wide area networks are the logical mechanism for making data from such facilities more easily accessible nationwide. An important issue is that of computer and network security to ensure privacy and trustworthiness in a heterogeneous network environment. At present, responsibility for privacy and the assurance of trust are vested principally in the computers and switching nodes on the network.

Existing government-supported wide-area networks include ARPANET, HEPNET, MFENET, NSFNET, NASNET, MILNET, and SPAN, as well as private and commercial facilities such as TYMNET, TELENET, BITNET, and lines leased from the communication carriers. Longer-range estimates vary, but it is expected that by the year 1995 the nation's research community will be able to make effective use of a high capacity national network with capacity measured in billions of bits per second. Without improved networks, speed of data transmission will be a limiting factor in the ability of researchers to carry out complex analyses. The digital circuits most widely available today with transmission speeds of 56 kilobits per second (kb/s) are impediments to leading edge research and to optimal remote high performance computer use.

Point-to-point connections require interconnects through multiple vendors with cumulative costs. Greater network speed can reduce the time required to perform a given experiment and increase both the volume of data and the amount of detail that can be seen by researchers. Scientists accessing supercomputers would benefit because access speed is often critical in their work. Improved functionality frees scientists to concentrate directly on their experimental results rather than on operational details of the network. Increased network size extends these opportunities to thousands of individuals at smaller academic institutions throughout the nation. These modernization measures would significantly enhance the nation's position in scientific research. A national network would help maintain the U.S. leadership position in computer architectures,

[19]

microprocessors, data management, software engineering, and innovative networking facilities, and promote the development of international networking standards based on U.S. technology.

Integrated Systems Digital Networks (ISDN–voice and data) have been installed abroad on a national or regional scale. Research abroad is being conducted on service up to 1 Gb/s. Within the next five years, Integrated Services Digital Network (ISDN) circuits ranging from 64 kb/s to 1.5 Mb/s will be available in the larger metropolitan areas of the U.S. However, these services will fall short of the requirements for computer networks. By 1988 more than fifty Campus Area Networks will be operational at speeds approaching 100 Mb/s. Wide area networks operating at 1.5 Mb/s or less will not be able to handle the data volume expected.

Japan and Europe have extensive efforts with experimental nets in intermediate (40Mb) and high (gigabit) range. Japan is studying operational aspects of fiber nets using their national research network as a testbed, which includes exploring the feasibility of fiber optic services to residences.

To estimate the network bandwidth needed to support research at a major installation, the kinds and volume of traffic that would be used have been estimated at a representative campus, extrapolated ten years into the future. Three models were used to compute three independent estimates of the requirements for bandwidth needed by type of work, information needs by type of user, and information flowing at the installation boundary. In each model, the peak bandwidth was estimated for each type of service. For example, in the Task model, the need is dominated by that of at least one researcher to receive full color and full–motion high resolution images. A high–resolution color image contains about 30 megabits of information, so that a display rate of 30 frames per second requires a bandwidth of nearly one gigabit per second (Gb/s). In the User model, a research university with 35,000 students and 3,000 faculty and research staff using a mix of bandwidths again requires an aggregate bandwidth of approximately one Gb/s. In the Edge of the Installation model, bandwidth is estimated by the types of remote facilities being accessed and the expected number of simultaneous users; typical facilities include particle accelerators, supercomputers, and centers for imaging and/or animation. The aggregate bandwidth needed is one Gb/s. Thus three independent means of estimating bandwidth arrive at nearly the same requirement for a large research installation and one Gb/s can confidently be used as a lower bound on the bandwidth of a national research network.

[20]

● **<u>RECOMMENDATION</u>:** U.S. government, industry, and universities should coordinate research and development for a research network to provide a distributed computing capability that links the government, industry, and higher education communities.

A research network should be established in a staged approach that supports the upgrade of current facilities and development of needed new capabilities. Achievement of this goal would foster and enhance the U.S. position of world leadership in computer networking as well as provide infrastructure for collaborative research. The FCCSET Committee on Computer Research and Applications should provide a forum for interagency cooperations. Elements of the plan should include:

– *Stage 1.* Upgrade existing facilities in support of a transition plan to the new network through a cooperative effort among major government users. The current interagency collaboration in expanding the Internet system originated by DARPA should be accelerated so that the networks supported by the agencies are interconnected over the next two years.

– *Stage 2.* The nation's existing networks that support scientific research should be upgraded and expanded to achieve data communications at 1.5 Mb/sec for 200 to 300 U.S. research institutions.

– *Stage 3.* Develop a system architecture for a national research network to support distributed collaborative computation through a strong program of research and development. A long–term program is needed to advance the technology of computer networking in order to achieve data communication and switching capabilities to support transmission of three billion bits per second (3 Gb/s) with deployment within fifteen years.

– Develop policy for long term support and upgrading of current high performance facilities, including timetables for backbone and connection development, industry participation, access, agency funding, tariff schedules, network management and administration. Support should be given to the development of standards and their harmonization in the international arena.

Until the national research network can replace the current system, existing networks should be maintained and modified as they join the national network. Remedial action should be initiated as soon as possible. Upgrading the backbone to at least 1.5 Mb/s should be accomplished by 1990. This will ensure that the new generation of high performance computing can be effectively interconnected.

Industry should be encouraged to participate in research, development, and deployment of the national research network. Telecommunication tariff schedules

[21]

which have been set for voice transmission should be reviewed in light of the requirements for transmission of data through computer networking.

Prompt effective coordination is needed to increase user participation in the standards development process, to get requirements for standards expressed early in the development process, and to speed the implementation of standards in commercial off–the–shelf products. It is essential that standards development be carried out within the framework of overall systems requirements to achieve interoperability, common user interfaces to systems, and enhanced security.

[22]

4. BASIC RESEARCH AND HUMAN RESOURCES

- **FINDING:** Federal research and development funding has established laboratories in universities, industry, and government which have become the major sources of innovation in the development and use of computing technology.

  Many of the advances in computer science and technology in the U.S. were made possible by Federal programs of research support to universities and industry. For example, the advances that have occurred since 1983 in the area of parallel computing are the direct result of Federal research investment through agencies including DARPA and NSF. In the area of application of supercomputers to science and engineering, the majority of this investment came from the NSF Advanced Scientific Computing centers. In the area of parallel architectures, the major investment came from the DARPA Strategic Computing Program. Programs sponsored by DOE, NASA, and Defense to support critical mission needs have been a major source of investment in computational applications research. In industry, support for basic research is only a small fraction of industry research most of which is focused on nearer term product development. This can be attributed in part to the long term and high risk nature of basic research, but a more significant inhibitor of investment is the difficulty in the computer industry of maintaining proprietary protection for certain kinds of key fundamental advances.

- **RECOMMENDATION:** Long term support for basic research in computer science should be increased within available resources. Industry, universities, and government should work together to improve the training and utilization of personnel to expand the base of research and development in computational science and technology.

  Maintain vigorous research in Computer Science and sufficient growth of computer science manpower to support the scientific/technological basis of the computer field. Foster interactions among academia, industry, and national laboratories by creating interdisciplinary teams to address large scale problems. Extend the technology base to attain significant impact on competitiveness and industrial productivity.

  Innovative very high performance computing systems should be made available to universities and basic research laboratories in order to assist in the evaluation and exploitation of new technology and new industrial innovations.

[23]

Continue the following successful approaches to basic research and development: (1) The practice of loosely coordinated and flexible basic research supported through various federal sectors and applied to a diversity of institutions, (2) The mixed strategy of peer review to support a broad range of exploratory basic research throughout the academic community and the complementary technical program management approach of larger scale experimental systems programs which exploit new opportunities as they emerge, (3) Support for individuals and small groups in theoretical areas, (4) The practice of supporting the relevant basic research as part of larger experimental systems projects.

[24]

IMPLEMENTATION

Success of the National High Performance Computing Strategy will require an attitude of cooperation in which academia, industry and government work effectively together in developing and assessing new technology and in achieving the transition of promising new ideas into the marketplace. The rapid pace of developments in computing technology creates a number of implementation challenges that must be addressed explicitly if the Strategy is to have maximum impact.

The FCCSET Committee on Computer Research and Applications provides an appropriate forum for coordination of Federal agency programs. Specifically:

- The subcommittee on Computer Networking, Infrastructure, and Digital Communications will develop a coordinated implementation plan for the national research network.

- The subcommittee on Science and Engineering Computing will review the *grand challenges* through the use of high performance computing systems, including the research that will be involved.

- The subcommittee on Computer Research and Development will review the need for advanced software, algorithms, and hardware for future high performance computing systems.

All of the subcommittees will consider appropriate action to secure a foundation of basic research and human resources. In all three subcommittees we expect some overlap of responsibility and interchange of ideas to be compatible with success.

As has been firmly stated, the full cooperation through a shared vision between government, industry and the research community will be a necessary ingredient for the successful implementation of this strategy. The FCCSET Committee on Computer Research and Applications therefore calls for timely consideration of the vision and strategy by representative bodies of the research community and industry.

It is essential, however, that implementation of the strategy be undertaken in a timely manner. There is a need to follow through on the breakthroughs that occurred partially as a result of federal investment in the early 1980s. The fast pace of development dictates that appropriate Federal efforts are needed to help ensure continued excellence in high speed networking technology and leadership in high performance computing. Foreign investment in technology development in these key areas has increased dramatically. The prudent strategy is to maintain a consistent strong lead in research and to transfer the results as quickly as possible to American industry.

[25]

COST ESTIMATES

Many of the basic elements of the high performance computing strategy are already being implemented as part of ongoing agency programs at DOE, DARPA, NSF, NASA, and other Federal agencies, and important progress is being made. The FCCSET Committee activity has contributed to achieving a shared vision, and early coordination is already occurring in anticipation of implementation of the strategy. Implementation of the strategy involves three principal funding components, including the national research network, joint research to address the "grand challenges," and basic research in high performance computing architecture, custom hardware design, software, algorithms, and supporting technologies. Multiple agencies are involved in the implementation and funding of each of these components.

The funds that would be associated with each of these components are described below. Obviously, any incremental funding must be evaluated and approved within the context of current activities and research needs in other high priority fields. Currently, the Federal government is spending about $500M per year on all aspects of high

Summary of Additional Funds
(Millions of Dollars)

Current Funds			Yr 1	Yr 2	Yr 3	Yr 4	Yr 5
50 a	National Research Network	Stage 1	5	5	5	0	0
		Stage 2	5	5	55	55	55
		Stage 3	40	40	40	40	40
150 b	Joint Research in Computational Science and Engineering		30	60	90	120	150
300	Basic Research in Computer Science and High Performance Computing		60	120	180	240	300
500	TOTAL (above current funds)		140	230	370	455	545
	Funding Increase by Year (noncumulative)		140	90	140	85	90

a Estimated network research and support in grants and contracts.
b Estimated operating costs for existing computational science facilities.

[26]

performance computing. Funding for the activities recommended in this report would increase this base by $140M in additional resources for the first year, growing to an additional $545M per year in 5 years.

National Research Network. Current operating costs for the present collection of research–support networks operated by DARPA, NSF, DOE, and NASA is approximately $50M per year; the figure is uncertain because many subnetworks are funded by increments on research grants and contracts, rather than being centrally supported. Currently the interconnection of existing agencies' networks is planned within existing budgets. A significant increase in investment is needed to achieve the required capability. This investment could occur in three concurrent stages.

The *first stage* activity would involve an immediate upgrade to 1.5 Mbit/sec of the existing research–support networks. This would cost $15M over three years.

The *second stage* would expand upgraded network services (45Mbit/sec) to 200 to 300 research installations, using primarily fiber–optic trunk facilities. Development costs for this stage would be $5M per year of additional funding. Operation of the upgraded network would commence in three to five years, with operating costs of approximately $50M per year. Since the transition from the first stage to the second stage network could not be instantaneous, initially the full operating cost of the second stage network would necessitate additional funding; that requirement will diminish to the extent that the first stage network is phased out.

The goal of the *third stage* would be to deliver one to three Gbit/sec to selected research facilities, and 45 Mbit/sec to approximately 1000 research sites. Research and development costs for this project are estimated at $400M of new funds, spent over ten years; after ten years, operating costs would be about $200M per year unless some tariff relief is achieved.

Joint Research in Computational Science and Engineering. Current operating costs for existing computational science laboratory facilities is approximately $150M per year. Additional investment would be required to upgrade the existing facilities and/or to establish additional joint research activities, with government, industry, and university participation, to address approximately specific problem areas, including selected *grand challenges*. Many of these joint research efforts will involve multiple physical sites connected by the research network. The investment in these research activities supports pursuit of the grand challenges. This includes personnel to develop computational approaches in terms of theory, algorithms, and software, and the acquisition of modern computing equipment. Estimated Federal costs average $15M per year to establish and sustain each grand challenge. The joint research activities would be introduced at the rate of two per year. Overall investment will be approximately $30M per year initially, increasing to $150M per year in five years as new grand challenges are added.

[27]

Basic Research in Computer Science and High Performance Computing. Current Federal investment in advanced computer research is estimated at $300M in FY88. Over the past four years, investment in these areas has grown at 15% per year. The rate of increase appears to be declining, however, at a time when increased investment appears to be needed. Sufficient resources should continue to be allocated to take full advantage of the high performance computing opportunities that now exist including design and prototype development of systems capable of trillions of operations per second. A second important element is stable funding, which is required to preserve the long-term strength of the research community.

Other countries are also devoting considerable resources in this area. For example, the Japanese government supports two projects which directly address supercomputer development: The Fifth Generation Project and the Superspeed Project. Support for each of these is estimated to be in excess of $100M per year. In addition to this government support, Japanese industry is investing considerably more to develop high performance computers. Japanese government and industry are also investing amounts comparable to those recommended here to develop high bandwidth research networks.

ACKNOWLEDGMENTS

Office of Science and Technology Policy guidance was provided by Michael Marks. Stephen L. Squires, Defense Advanced Research Projects Agency, acted as Executive Secretary for this report. Technical assistance was provided by William L. Scherlis, Defense Advanced Research Projects Agency; along with Kathleen Bernard, Office of Science and Technology Policy; Charles N. Brownstein, National Science Foundation; Leslie Chow, National Aeronautics and Space Administration; and Michael Crisp, Department of Energy.

[28]

FCCSET COMMITTEE ON COMPUTER RESEARCH AND APPLICATIONS

Paul G. Huray (Chair)
Office of Science and Technology Policy

SUBCOMMITTEES

Science and Engineering Computing	Computer Research and Development	Computer Networking, Infrastructure and Digital Communications
James F. Decker (Chair) Department of Energy	Saul Amarel (Chair) Defense Advanced Research Projects Agency	C. Gordon Bell (Chair) National Science Foundation
James Burrows National Bureau of Standards	Donald Austin Department of Energy	Ronald Bailey National Aeronautics and Space Administration
John S. Cavallini Health and Human Services	C. Gordon Bell National Science Foundation	Sandra Bates National Aeronautics and Space Administration
Melvyn Ciment National Science Foundation	James Burrows National Bureau of Standards	James Burrows National Bureau of Standards
John Connolly National Science Foundation	Bernard Chern National Science Foundation	John S. Cavallini Health and Human Services
Craig Fields Defense Advanced Research Projects Agency	Peter Freeman National Science Foundation	Thomas Kitchens Department of Energy
Harlow Freitag Supercomputer Research Center	Lee Holcomb National Aeronautics and Space Administration	James Oberthaler National Institutes of Health
Randolph Graves National Aeronautics and Space Administration	Charles Holland Office of Naval Research	Dennis G. Perry Defense Advanced Research Projectes Agency
Norman H. Kreisman Department of Energy	Robert E. Kahn Computer Science Technology Board	Arnold Pratt National Institutes of Health
Lewis Lipkin National Institutes of Health	Daniel R. Masys National Institutes of Health	Shirley Radack National Bureau of Standards
Allan T. Mense Strategic Defense Initiative Office	Robert Polvado Central Intelligence Agency	Rudi F. Saenger Naval Research Laboratory
David B. Nelson Department of Energy	David Sadoff Department of State	Daniel VanBelleghem National Science Foundation
C. E. Oliver Air Force Weapons Lab	William L. Scherlis Defense Advanced Research Projects Agency	Stephen Wolff National Science Foundation
John P. Riganati Supercomputer Research Center	K. Speierman National Security Agency	
Paul B. Schneck Supercomputer Research Center	Stephen L. Squires Defense Advanced Research Projects Agency	
K. Speierman National Security Agency	Charles F. Stebbins Air Force Systems Command	
	Daniel F. Weiner, II Joint Tactical Fusion Program	

[29]

J

"Executive Summary," in *Information Technology and the Conduct of Research: The User's View,* Washington, DC: National Academy Press, 1989, pp. 1–5.

Executive Summary

Information technology—the set of computer and telecommunications technologies that makes possible computation, communication, and the storage and retrieval of information—has changed the conduct of scientific, engineering, and clinical research. This report examines present trends, future potential, and impediments to the use of information technology in support of research. Written from the viewpoint of the researcher using information technology and including many examples, the report offers a number of recommendations directed to two principal audiences: policymakers and leaders of institutions responsible for the support and management of research, and researchers themselves.

The first programmable, electronic, digital computer was created nearly five decades ago. At first, computers simply substituted for other means of carrying out arithmetic calculations; they were large, expensive, often unreliable, and accessible only to a minority of scientists and engineers. With the advent of the integrated circuit (the semiconductor "chip"), computational speed and power increased dramatically, and computer use became widespread. Recently, computer technology has been joined with telecommunications technology to create a new entity: information technology, which has done much to remove the constraints of speed, cost, and distance from the researcher.

On the whole, information technology has led to improvements in research. New avenues for scientific exploration have opened. Researchers can collaborate more widely and efficiently. Much more data are available for analysis. Analytic capabilities have improved significantly, along with the capability to present results as visual images. New information technologies offer further opportunities to improve research. But widespread use of computers in research has not come about without problems. Some of these difficulties are technological, some financial. Underlying many of them are complex institutional and behavioral constraints.

**INFORMATION
TECHNOLOGY AND
THE CONDUCT
OF RESEARCH**

The report examines three aspects of the research process: data collection and analysis, communication and collaboration among researchers, and information storage and retrieval.

In data collection and analysis, a number of trends are discussed, including

- Growth in the amount of information researchers can store and analyze;
- Creation of new families of computer-controlled instruments;
- Proliferation of computer networks dedicated to research; and
- Increasing availability of software "packages" supporting research activities.

Among the difficulties associated with data collection and analysis are uneven access to computing resources, problems in obtaining support for software development and maintenance, and unnecessary complexities of transmitting data over computer networks.

Communication and collaboration among researchers are changing. Not only can information be shared more and more quickly, but researchers are also developing new collaborative arrangements. Three technologies are involved: word processing, electronic mail, and computer communications networks. Word processing and electronic mail are arguably the most pervasive of all the routine uses of computers in research communication. Electronic mail—sending text from one computer user to another over the networks—is partially replacing written and telephone communication among many communities of scientists. Scientists increasingly use networks for conversation and for repeated exchanges of text and data files. Among the most important of the potential applications of information technology is the emergence of a truly national research network.

The principal difficulties with communicating via electronic mail and file transfer technologies involve incompatibility between different text and data processing systems and between network protocols. Also significant are network limitations: addressing conventions are cumbersome and unhelpful, locator services are nearly nonexistent, and overall network availability and reliability need improvement.

Electronic storage and retrieval of information hold enormous advantages: information can be stored economically, found quickly without going to another location, and moved easily. For all disciplines, both scientific data and reference databases promise to be significant sources of knowledge for basic research. However, a number of problems need to be resolved. Researchers have difficulty getting access to data stored by other researchers. Even when researchers get access to colleagues' data, they have difficulty reading them. Finally, when researchers get access to and read each others' databases, they often lack information on the quality of the data.

The primary difficulty encountered with reference databases is in conducting searches. Most information searches at present are incomplete, cumbersome, inefficient, expensive, and executable only by specialists.

There is a pressing need for new, more compact, and more permanent forms of data storage. Stored data gradually become useless, either because the storage media decay or the storage technology itself becomes obsolete. Underlying difficulties in information storage and retrieval are significant problems in the institutional management of resources.

New computer-based technologies offer the prospect of new ways of finding, understanding, storing, and communicating information, and should increase both the capabilities and the productivity of researchers. Among these new technologies are simulations, new methods of presenting observational and computational results as visual images, the use of knowledge-based systems as "intelligent assistants," and more flexible and intuitive ways for people to interact with, and control, computers.

The Panel has identified a number of problem areas in which institutional and behavioral impediments underlie many difficulties in the use of information technology in research. These areas include

- Issues of costs and cost sharing: financial impediments are chronic. Although institutions will continue to do their best, information technology for research will continue to need more funds. The Panel believes that increased support of information technology in research deserves high priority.

- The problem of standards: simplified, consistent standards for operation of, and interconnection among, computer systems could have major impacts on research communications and productivity; however, such standards are largely absent, and their development is a slow and controversial process.

- Legal and ethical constraints: the need to safeguard and maintain confidentiality of data on human subjects is a major issue; also likely to become increasingly significant is the question of responsibility in computer-supported decision making in engineering, clinical practice, or research.

- Gaps in training and education: learning to use information technology presently requires significant initial investments of time and effort, and researchers who make these investments often receive insufficient help. Although the problem is likely to diminish with time, it affects current attitudes of many researchers toward the use of information technology.

- The perceived risks of organizational change: organizations and administrators can understandably be reluctant to make the substantial changes required to make use of information technology.

- Of fundamental importance, the lack of an infrastructure for the use of information technology in research: access to expertise, and support mechanisms to encourage such experts; tools for developing and managing software; systems for storing and retrieving information; and support services for communication and collaboration among researchers.

The report concludes with three major recommendations.

RECOMMENDATION I

The institutions supporting the nation's researchers must recognize and meet their responsibilities to develop and support policies, services, and standards that help researchers use information technology more widely and productively. Specifically

- *Universities* should provide accessible, expert help in learning and using information technology.
- *University departments*, and *scientific and professional groups*, should establish career ladders for scientific programming positions.
- *Funding agencies* should provide support for scientific programming and for help services in learning and using information technology systems for research.
- *Scientific associations* should establish disciplinary standards for the storage and indexing of scientific data.
- *University departments*, and *scientific and professional groups*, should implement mechanisms for the evaluation, merit (peer) review, and dissemination of software useful in the conduct of research.
- *Vendors*, in collaboration with *scientific groups*, should establish standards for simplified and consistent user-machine interfaces.
- *Network administrators* should provide simple user interfaces and addressing schemes, add gateways to other networks, improve system reliability and capacity, and provide online help, such as guides to services and mail addresses of individuals who can answer questions.
- *Information service providers* should create simplified common standards for accessing and querying information sources and eventually provide unified access to information.
- *Software vendors*, and *scientific and professional groups*, should create program libraries and make them accessible through the networks.

RECOMMENDATION II

The institutions supporting the nation's researchers, led by the federal government, should develop an interconnected national information technology network for use by all qualified researchers. Specifically

- The Office of Science and Technology Policy (OSTP) in the Executive Office of the President, and the federal agencies responsible for supporting and performing research and development, should plan and fund a nationwide infrastructure for computer-based research communication.
- Planning and development of this nationwide infrastructure should be guided by users of information technology in research, rather than by technical experts in information technology or hardware or software vendors. The Panel believes strongly that such a national network is too important to the future of research to be left only to the technical experts.
- The national research network should be founded on the fundamental premise of open access to all qualified researchers/scholars that has nurtured the world's scientific community for centuries.

• The national research network should be developed in an evolutionary manner, making full use of the existing successful networks for research.

RECOMMENDATION III

To facilitate implementation of Recommendations I and II, and to focus attention on the opportunities and impediments associated with research uses of information technology, the Panel recommends the establishment at a national level of a user's group to oversee and advise on the evolution and use of information technology in support of scientific, engineering, and clinical research.

Specifically, the National Research Council (NRC) should charge a standing committee or board (whether existing or newly created) with the mandate to oversee and advise on research use of information technology. The membership of this board should include a majority of users from a variety of research disciplines.

K

High-Performance Computing & Networking for Science: Background Paper, U.S. Congress, Office of Technology Assessment, 1989.

BACKGROUND PAPER

CONGRESS OF THE UNITED STATES   OFFICE OF TECHNOLOGY ASSESSMENT

500

HIGH PERFORMANCE COMPUTING & NETWORKING FOR SCIENCE

BACKGROUND PAPER

CONGRESS OF THE UNITED STATES   OFFICE OF TECHNOLOGY ASSESSMENT

Recommended Citation:

U.S. Congress, Office of Technology Assessment, *High Performance Computing and Networking for Science—Background Paper*, OTA-BP-CIT-59 (Washington, DC: U.S. Government Printing Office, September 1989).

Library of Congress Catalog Card Number 89-600758

For sale by the Superintendent of Documents
U.S. Government Printing Office, Washington, DC 20402-9325
(Order form can be found in the back of this report.)

Foreword

Information technology is fundamental to today's research and development: high performance computers for solving complex problems; high-speed data communication networks for exchanging scientific and engineering information; very large electronic archives for storing scientific and technical data; and new display technologies for visualizing the results of analyses.

This background paper explores key issues concerning the Federal role in supporting national high performance computing facilities and in developing a national research and education network. It is the first publication from our assessment, *Information Technology and Research*, which was requested by the House Committee on Science and Technology and the Senate Committee on Commerce, Science, and Transportation.

OTA gratefully acknowledges the contributions of the many experts, within and outside the government, who served as panelists, workshop participants, contractors, reviewers, detailees, and advisers for this document. As with all OTA reports, however, the content is solely the responsibility of OTA and does not necessarily constitute the consensus or endorsement of the advisory panel, workshop participants, or the Technology Assessment Board.

JOHN H. GIBBONS
Director

High Performance Computing and Networking for Science Advisory Panel

John P. (Pat) Crecine, *Chairman*
President, Georgia Institute of Technology

Charles Bender
Director
Ohio Supercomputer Center

Charles DeLisi
Chairman
Department of Biomathematical
   Science
Mount Sinai School of Medicine

Deborah L. Estrin
Assistant Professor
Computer Science Department
University of Southern California

Robert Ewald
Vice President, Software
Cray Research, Inc.

Kenneth Flamm
Senior Fellow
The Brookings Institution

Malcolm Getz
Associate Provost
Information Services & Technology
Vanderbilt University

Ira Goldstein
Vice President, Research
Open Software Foundation

Robert E. Kraut
Manager
Interpersonal Communications Group
Bell Communications Research

Lawrence Landweber
Chairman
Computer Science Department
University of Wisconsin-Madison

Carl Ledbetter
President/CEO
ETA Systems

Donald Marsh
Vice President, Technology
Contel Corp.

Michael J. McGill
Vice President
Technical Assessment & Development
OCLC, Computer Library Center, Inc.

Kenneth W. Neves
Manager
Research & Development Program
Boeing Computer Services

Bernard O'Lear
Manager of Systems
National Center for Atmospheric
   Research

William Poduska
Chairman of the Board
Stellar Computer, Inc.

Elaine Rich
Director
Artificial Intelligence Lab
Microelectronics and Computer
   Technology Corp.

Sharon J. Rogers
University Librarian
Gelman Library
The George Washington University

William Schrader
President
NYSERNET

Kenneth Toy
Post-Graduate Research
   Geophysicist
Scripps Institution of Oceanography

Keith Uncapher
Vice President
Corporation for the National
   Research Initiatives

Al Weis
Vice President
Engineering & Scientific Computer
Data Systems Division
IBM Corp.

NOTE: OTA is grateful for the valuable assistance and thoughtful critiques provided by the advisory panel. The views expressed in this OTA background paper, however, are the sole responsibility of the Office of Technology Assessment.

iv

OTA Project Staff—High Performance Computing

John Andelin, *Assistant Director, OTA*
Science, Information, and Natural Resources Division

James W. Curlin, *Program Manager*
Communication and Information Technologies Program

Fred W. Weingarten, *Project Director*

Charles N. Brownstein, *Senior Analyst[1]*

Lisa Heinz, *Analyst*

Elizabeth I. Miller, *Research Assistant*

Administrative Staff

Elizabeth Emanuel, *Administrative Assistant*

Karolyn Swauger, *Secretary*

Jo Anne Price, *Secretary*

Other Contributors

Bill Bartelone
Legislative/Federal Program
  Manager
Cray Research, Inc.

Mervin Jones
Program Analyst
Defense Automation Resources
  Information Center

Timothy Lynagh
Supervisory Data and
  Program Analyst
Government Services Administration

[1]Detailee from NSF

v

List of Reviewers

Janice Abraham
Executive Director
Cornell Theory Center
Cornell University

Lee R. Alley
Assistant Vice President for
  Information Resources Management
Arizona State University

James Almond
Director
Center for High Performance
  Computing
Balcones Research Center

Julius Archibald
Department Chairman
Department of Computer Science
State University of New York
College of Plattsburgh

J. Gary Augustson
Executive Director
Computer and Information
  Systems
Pennsylvania State University

Philip Austin
President
Colorado State University

Steven C. Beering
President
Purdue University

Jerry Berkman
Fortran Specialist
Central Computing Services
University of California at Berkeley

Kathleen Bernard
Director for Science Policy
  and Technology Programs
Cray Research, Inc.

Justin L. Bloom
President
Technology International, Inc.

Charles N. Brownstein
Executive Officer
Computing & Information Science &
  Engineering
National Science Foundation

Eloise E. Clark
Vice President, Academic
  Affairs
Bowling Green University

Paul Coleman
Professor
Institute of Geophysics and
  Space Physics
University of California

Michael R. Dingerson
Associate Vice Chancellor for
  Research and Dean of the
  Graduate School
University of Mississippi

Christopher Eoyang
Director
Institute for Supercomputing
  Research

David Farber
Professor
Computer & Information
  Science Department
University of Pennsylvania

Sidney Fernbach
Independent Consultant

Susan Fratkin
Director, Special Programs
NASULGC

Doug Gale
Director of Computer
  Research Center
Office of the Chancellor
University of Nebraska-Lincoln

Robert Gillespie
President
Gillespie, Folkner
  & Associates, Inc.

Eiichi Goto
Director, Computer Center
University of Tokyo

C.K. Gunsalus
Assistant Vice Chancellor
  for Research
University of Illinois
  at Urbana-Champaign

Judson M. Harper
Vice President of Research
Colorado State University

Gene Hemp
Senior Associate V.P. for
  Academic Affairs
University of Florida

Nobuaki Ieda
Senior Vice President
NTT America, Inc.

Hiroshi Inose
Director General
National Center for Science
  Information System

Heidi James
Executive Secretary
United States Activities
  Board
IEEE

Russell C. Jones
University Research Professor
University of Delaware

Brian Kahin, Esq.
Research Affiliate on
  Communications Policy
Massachusetts Institute of Technology

Robert Kahn
President
Corporation of National
  Research Initiatives

Hisao Kanai
Executive Vice President
NEC Corporation

Hiroshi Kashiwagi
Deputy Director-General
Electrotechnical Laboratory

Lauren Kelly
Department of Commerce

Thomas Keyes
Professor of Chemistry
Boston University

Continued on next page

Doyle Knight
President
John von Neumann National
  Supercomputer Center
Consortium for Scientific
  Computing

Mike Levine
Co-director of the Pittsburgh
  Supercomputing Center
Carnegie Mellon University

George E. Lindamood
Program Director
Industry Service
Gartner Group, Inc.

M. Stuart Lynn
Vice President for
  Information Technologies
Cornell University

Ikuo Makino
Director
Electrical Machinery & Consumer
  Electronics Division
Ministry of International
  Trade and Industry

Richard Mandelbaum
Vice Provost for Computing
University of Rochester

Martin Massengale
Chancellor
University of Nebraska-Lincoln

Gerald W. May
President
University of New Mexico

Yoshiro Miki
Director, Policy Research Division
Science and Technology Policy Bureau
Science and Technology Agency

Takeo Miura
Senior Executive Managing Director
Hitachi, Ltd.

J. Gerald Morgan
Dean of Engineering
New Mexico State University

V. Rama Murthy
Vice Provost for Academic
  Affairs
University of Minnesota

Shoichi Ninomoiya
Executive Director
Fujitsu Limited

Bernard O'Lear
Manager of Systems
National Center for Atmospheric
  Research

Ronald Orcutt
Executive Director
Project Athena
MIT

Tad Pinkerton
Director
Office of Information
  Technology
University of Wisconsin-Madison

Harold J. Raveche
President
Stevens Institute of Technology

Ann Redelf
Manager of Information
  Services
Cornell Theory Center
Cornell University

Glenn Ricart
Director
Computer Science Center
University of Maryland in
  College Park

Ira Richer
Program Manager
DARPA/ISTO

John Riganati
Director of Systems Research
Supercomputer Research Center
Institute for Defense Analyses

Mike Roberts
Vice President
EDUCOM

David Roselle
President
University of Kentucky

Nora Sabelli
National Center for Supercomputing
  Applications
University of Illinois at
  Urbana-Champaign

Steven Sample
President
SUNY, Buffalo

John Sell
President
Minnesota Supercomputer Center

Hiroshi Shima
Deputy Director-General for
  Technology Affairs
Agency of Industrial Science and
  Technology , MITI

Yoshio Shimamoto
Senior Scientist (Retired)
Applied Mathematics Department
Brookhaven National Laboratory

Charles Sorber
Dean, School of Engineering
University of Pittsburgh

Harvey Stone
Special Assistant to the
  President
University of Delaware

Dan Sulzbach
Manager, User Services
San Diego Supercomputer Center

Tatsuo Tanaka
Executive Director
Interoperability Technology
Association for Information Processing,
  Japan

Ray Toland
President
Alabama Supercomputing Network
  Authority

Kenneth Tolo
Vice Provost
University of Texas
  at Austin

Kenneth Toy
Post-Graduate Research
  Geophysicist
Scripps Institution of
  Oceanography

August B. Turnbull, III
Provost & Vice President,
  Academic Affairs
Florida State University

Continued on next page

Gerald Turner
Chancellor
University of Mississippi

Douglas Van Houweling
Vice Provost for Information
  & Technology
University of Michigan

Anthony Villasenor
Program Manager
Science Networks
Office of Space Science and
  Applications
National Aeronautics and
  Space Administration

Hugh Walsh
Data Systems Division
IBM

Richard West
Assistant Vice President,
  IS&AS
University of California

Steve Wolff
Program Director for Networking
Computing & Information Science &
  Engineering
National Science Foundation

James Woodward
Chancellor
University of North Carolina
  at Charlotte

Akihiro Yoshikawa
Research Director
University of California, Berkeley
BRIE/IIS

NOTE: OTA is grateful for the valuable assistance and thoughtful critiques provided by the advisory panel. The views expressed in this OTA background paper, however, are the sole responsibility of the Office of Technology Assessment.

Contents

Chapter 1
Introduction and Overview Observations

The Office of Technology Assessment is conducting an assessment of the effects of new information technologies—including high performance computing, data networking, and mass data archiving—on research and development. This background paper offers a midcourse view of the issues and discusses their implications for current discussions about Federal supercomputer initiatives and legislative initiatives concerning a national data communication network.

Our observations to date emphasize the critical importance of advanced information technology to research and development in the United States, the interconnection of these technologies into a national system (and, as a result, the tighter coupling of policy choices regarding them), and the need for immediate and coordinated Federal action to bring into being an advanced information technology infrastructure to support U.S. research, engineering, and education.

RESEARCH AND INFORMATION TECHNOLOGY—A FUTURE SCENARIO

Within the next decade, the desks and laboratory benches of most scientists and engineers will be entry points to a complex electronic web of information technologies, resources and information services, connected together by high-speed data communication networks (see figure 1-1). These technologies will be critical to pursuing research in most fields. Through powerful workstation computers on their desks, researchers will access a wide variety of resources, such as:

- an interconnected assortment of local campus, State and regional, national, and even international data communication networks that link users worldwide;
- specialized and general-purpose computers including supercomputers, minisupercomputers, mainframes, and a wide variety of special architectures tailored to specific applications;
- collections of application programs and software tools to help users find, modify, or develop programs to support their research;

- archival storage systems that contain specialized research databases;
- experimental apparatus—such as telescopes, environmental monitoring devices, seismographs, and so on—designed to be set-up and operated remotely;
- services that support scientific communication, including electronic mail, computer conferencing systems, bulletin boards, and electronic journals;
- a "digital library" containing reference material, books, journals, pictures, sound recordings, films, software, and other types of information in electronic form; and
- specialized output facilities for displaying the results of experiments or calculations in more readily understandable and visualizable ways.

Many of these resources are already used in some form by some scientists. Thus, the scenario that is drawn is a straightforward extension of current usage. Its importance for the scientific community and for government policy stems from three trends: 1) the rapidly and continually increasing capability of the technologies; 2) the integration of these technologies into what we will refer to as an "information infrastructure"; and 3) the diffusion of information technology into the work of most scientific disciplines.

Few scientists would use all the resources and facilities listed, at least on a daily basis; and the particular choice of resources eventually made available on the network will depend on how the tastes and needs of research users evolve. However, the basic form, high-speed data networks connecting user workstations with a worldwide assortment of information technologies and services, is becoming a crucial foundation for scientific research in most disciplines.

MAJOR ISSUES AND PROBLEMS

Developing this system to its full potential will require considerable thought and effort on the part of government at all levels, industry, research institutions, and the scientific community, itself. It will present policymakers with some difficult questions and decisions.

Figure 1-1—An Information Infrastructure for Research

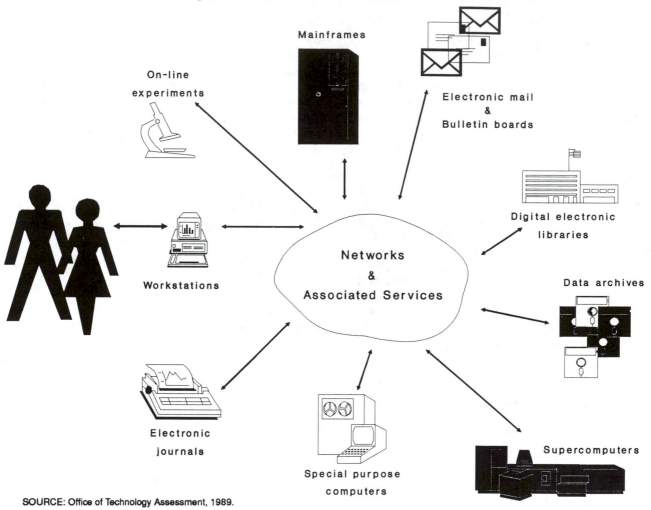

SOURCE: Office of Technology Assessment, 1989.

Scientific applications are very demanding on technological capability. **A substantial R&D component will need to accompany programs intended to advance R&D use of information technology.** To realize the potential benefits of this new infrastructure, research users need advances in such areas as:

- more powerful computer designs;

- more powerful and efficient computational techniques and software; overly high-speed switched data communications;

- improved technologies for visualizing data results and interacting with computers; and

- new methods for storing and accessing information from very large data archives.

An important characteristic of this system is that different parts of it will be funded and operated by different entities and made available to users in different ways. For example, databases could be operated by government agencies, professional societies, non-profit journals, or commercial firms. Computer facilities could similarly be operated by government, industry, or universities. The network, itself, already is an assemblage of pieces funded or operated by various agencies in the Federal Government; by States and regional authorities; and by local agencies, firms and educational institutions. **Keep-**

ing these components interconnected technologically and allowing users to move smoothly among the resources they need will present difficult management and policy problems.

Furthermore, the system will require significant capital investment to build and maintain, as well as specialized technical expertise to manage. **How the various components are to be funded, how costs are to be allocated, and how the key components such as the network will be managed over the long term will be important questions.**

Since this system as envisioned would be so widespread and fundamental to the process of research, access to it would be crucial to participation in science. **Questions of access and participation are crucial to planning, management, and policymaking for the network and for many of the services attached to it.**

Changes in information law brought about by the electronic revolution will create problems and conflicts for the scientific community and may influence how and by whom these technologies are used. **The resolution of broader information issues such as security and privacy, intellectual property protection, access controls on sensitive information, and government dissemination practices could affect whether and how information technologies will be used by researchers and who may use them.**

Finally, to the extent that, over the long run, modern information technology becomes so fundamental to the research process, it will transform the very nature of that process and the institutions—libraries, laboratories, universities, and so on—that serve it. **These basic changes in science would affect government both in the operation of its own laboratories and in its broader relationship as a supporter and consumer of research. Conflicts may also arise to the extent that government becomes centrally involved, both through funding and through management, with the traditionally independent and uncontrolled communication channels of science.**

NATIONAL IMPORTANCE— THE NEED FOR ACTION

Over the last 5 years, Congress has become increasingly concerned about information technology and research. The National Science Foundation (NSF) has been authorized to establish supercomputer centers and a science network. Bills (S 1067 HR 3131) are being considered in the Congress to authorize a major effort to plan and develop a national research and education network and to stimulate information technology use in science and education. Interest in the role information technology could play in research and education has stemmed, first, from the government's major role as a funder, user, and participant in research and, secondly, from concern for ensuring the strength and competitiveness of the U.S. economy.

Observation 1: The Federal Government needs to establish its commitment to the advanced information technology infrastructure necessary for furthering U.S. science and education. This need stems directly from the importance of science and technology to economic growth, the importance of information technology to research and development, and the critical timing for certain policy decisions.

Economic Importance

A strong national effort in science and technology is critical to the long-term economic competitiveness, national security, and social well-being of the United States. That, in the modern international economy, technological innovation is concomitant with social and economic growth is a basic assumption held in most political and economic systems in the world these days; and we will take it here as a basic premise. It has been a basic finding in many OTA studies.[1] (This observation is not to suggest that technology is a panacea for all social problems, nor that serious policy problems are not often raised by its use.) Benefits from of this infrastructure are expected to flow into the economy in three ways:

First, the information technology industry can benefit directly. Scientific use has always been a

---

[1]For example, U.S. Congress, Office of Technology Assessment, *Technology and the American Economic Transition*, OTA-TET-283 (Washington, DC: U.S. Government Printing Office, May 1988) and *Information Technology R&D: Critical Trends and Issues*, OTA-CIT-268 (Washington, DC: U.S. Government Printing Office, February 1985).

major source of innovation in computers and communications technology. Packet-switched data communication, now a widely used commercial offering, was first developed by the Defense Advanced Research Projects Agency (DARPA) to support its research community. Department of Energy (DOE) national laboratories have, for many years, made contributions to supercomputer hardware and software. New initiatives to develop higher speed computers and a national science network could similarly feed new concepts back to the computer and communications industry as well as to providers of information services.

Secondly, by improving the tools and methodologies for R&D, the infrastructure will impact the research process in many critical high technology industries, such as pharmaceuticals, airframes, chemicals, consumer electronics, and many others. Innovation and, hence, international competitiveness in these key R&D-intensive sectors can be improved.

The economy as a whole stands to benefit from increased technological capabilities of information systems and improved understanding of how to use them. A National Research and Education Network could be the precursor to a much broader high capacity network serving the United States, and many research applications developed for high performance computers result in techniques much more broadly applicable to commercial firms.

Scientific Importance

Research and development is, inherently, an information activity. Researchers generate, organize, and interpret information, build models, communicate, and archive results. Not surprisingly, then, they are now dependent on information technology to assist them in these tasks. Many major studies by many scientific and policy organizations over the years—as far back as the President's Science Advisory Committee (PSAC) in the middle 1960s, and as recently as a report by COSEPUP of the National Research Council published in 1988[2]— have noted these trends and analyzed the implications for science support. The key points are as follows:

- Scientific and technical information is increasingly being generated, stored and distributed in electronic form;
- Computer-based communications and data handling are becoming essential for accessing, manipulating, analyzing, and communicating data and research results; and,
- In many computationally intensive R&D areas, from climate research to groundwater modeling to airframe design, major advances will depend upon pushing the state of the art in high performance computing, very large databases, visualization, and other related information technologies. Some of these applications have been labeled "Grand Challenges." These projects hold promise of great social benefit, such as designing new vaccines and drugs, understanding global warming, or modeling the world economy. However, for that promise to be realized in those fields, researchers require major advances in available computational power.
- Many proposed and ongoing "big science" projects, from particle accelerators and large array radio telescopes to the NASA EOS satellite project, will create vast streams of new data that must be captured, analyzed, archived, and made available to the research community. These new demands could well overtax the capability of currently available resources.

Timing

Government decisions being made now and in the near future will shape the long-term utility and effectiveness of the information technology infrastructure for science. For example:

- NSF is renewing its multi-year commitments to all or most of the existing National Supercomputing Centers.
- Executive agencies, under the informal auspices of the Federal Research Internet Coordinating Committee (FRICC), are developing a national "backbone" network for science. Decisions made now will have long term influence on the nature of the network, its technical characteristics, its cost, its management, serv-

---

[2]Panel on Information Technology and the Conduct of Research, Committee on Science, Engineering, and Public Policy, *Information Technology and the Conduct of Research: The User's View* (Washington, DC: National Academy Press, 1989).

ices available on it, access, and the information policies that will govern its use.

- The basic communications industry is in flux, as are the policies and rules by which government regulates it.
- Congress and the Executive Branch are currently considering, and in some cases have started, several new major scientific projects, including a space station, the Earth Orbiting System, the Hubble space telescope, the superconducting supercollider, human genome mapping, and so on. Technologies and policies are needed to deal with these "firehoses of data." In addition, upgrading the information infrastructure could open these projects and data streams to broad access by the research community.

Observation 2: Federal policy in this area needs to be more broadly based than has been traditional with Federal science efforts. Planning, building, and managing the information technology infrastructure requires cutting across agency programs and the discipline and mission-oriented approach of science support. In addition, many parties outside the research establishment will have important roles to play and stakes in the outcome of the effort.

The key information technologies—high performance computing centers, data communication networks, large data archives, along with a wide range of supporting software—are used in all research disciplines and support several different agency missions. In many cases, economies of scale and scope dictate that some of these technologies (e.g., supercomputers) be treated as common resources. Some, such as communication networks, are most efficiently used if shared or interconnected in some way.

There are additional scientific reasons to treat information resources as a broadly used infrastructure: fostering communication among scientists between disciplines, sharing resources and techniques, and expanding access to databases and software, for instance. However, there are very few models from the history of Federal science support for creating and maintaining infrastructure-like resources for science and technology across agency and disciplinary boundaries. Furthermore, since the networks, computer systems, databases, and so on

interconnect and users must move smoothly among them, the system requires a high degree of coordination rather than being treated as simply a conglomeration of independent facilities.

However, if information technology resources for science are treated as infrastructure, a major policy issue is one of boundaries. Who is it to serve; who are its beneficiaries? Who should participate in designing it, building and operating it, providing services over it, and using it? The answers to these questions will also indicate to Congress who should be part of the policymaking and planning process; they will govern the long term scale, scope, and the technological characteristics of the infrastructure itself; and they will affect the patterns of support for the facilities. Potentially interested parties include the following:

Users

Potential users might include academic and industrial researchers, teachers, graduate, undergraduate, and high school students, as well as others such as the press or public interest groups who need access to and make use of scientific information. Institutions, such as universities and colleges, libraries, and schools also have user interests. Furthermore, foreign scientists working as part of international research teams or in firms that operate internationally will wish access to the U.S. system, which, in turn, will need to be connected with other nation's research infrastructures.

Collaborators

Another group of interested parties include State and local governments and parts of the information industry. We have identified them with the term "collaborators" because they will be participating in funding, building, and operating the infrastructure. States are establishing State supercomputer centers and supporting local and regional networking, some computer companies participate in the NSF National Supercomputer Centers, and some telecommunication firms are involved in parts of the science network.

Service Providers

Finally, to the extent that the infrastructure serves as a basic tool for most of the research and development community, information service providers will require access to make their products available to scientific users. The service providers may include government agencies (which provide access to government scientific databases, for example), libraries and library utilities, journal and text-book publishers, professional societies, and private software and database providers.

Observation 3: Several information policy issues will be raised in managing and using the network. Depending on how they are resolved, they could sharply restrict the utility and scope of network use in the scientific community.

Security and privacy have already become of major concern and will pose a problem. In general, users will want the network and the services on it to be as open as possible; however, they will also want the networks and services to be as robust and dependable as possible—free from deliberate or accidental disruption. Furthermore, different resources will require different levels of security. Some bulletin boards and electronic mail services may want to be as open and public as possible; others may require a high level of privacy. Some databases may be unique and vital resources that will need a very high level of protection, others may not be so critical. Maintaining an open, easily accessible network while protecting privacy and valuable resources will require careful balancing of legal and technological controls.

Intellectual property protection in an electronic environment may pose difficult problems. Providers will be concerned that electronic databases, software, and even electronic formats of printed journals and other writings will not be adequately protected. In some cases, the product, itself, may not be well protected under existing law. In other cases electronic formats coupled with a communications network erode the ability to control restrictions on copying and disseminating.

Access controls may be called for on material that is deemed to be sensitive (although unclassified) for reasons of national security or economic competitiveness. Yet, the networks will be accessible worldwide and the ability to identify and control users may be limited.

The above observations have been broad, looking at the overall collection of information technology resources for science as an integrated system and at the questions raised by it. The remaining portion of this paper will deal specifically with high performance computers and networking.

Chapter 2

High Performance Computers

An important set of issues has been raised during the last 5 years around the topic of high performance computing (HPC). These issues stem from a growing concern in both the executive branch and in Congress that U.S. science is impeded significantly by lack of access to HPC[1] and by concerns over the competitiveness implications of new foreign technology initiatives, such as the Japanese "Fifth Generation Project." In response to these concerns, policies have been developed and promoted with three goals in mind.

1. To advance vital research applications currently hampered by lack of access to very high speed computers.
2. To accelerate the development of new HPC technology, providing enhanced tools for research and stimulating the competitiveness of the U.S. computer industry.
3. To improve software tools and techniques for using HPC, thereby enhancing their contribution to general U.S. economic competitiveness.

In 1984, the National Science Foundation (NSF) initiated a group of programs intended to improve the availability and use of high performance computers in scientific research. As the centerpiece of its initiative, after an initial phase of buying and distributing time at existing supercomputer centers, NSF established five National Supercomputer Centers.

Over the course of this and the next year, the initial multiyear contracts with the National Centers are coming to an end, which has provoked a debate about whether and, if so, in what form they should be renewed. NSF undertook an elaborate review and renewal process and announced that, depending on agency funding, it is prepared to proceed with renewing at least four of the centers[2]. In thinking about the next steps in the evolution of the advanced computing program, the science agencies and Congress have asked some basic questions. Have our perceptions of the needs of research for HPC changed since the centers were started? If so, how?

Have we learned anything about the effectiveness of the National Centers approach? Should the goals of the Advanced Scientific Computing (ASC) and other related Federal programs be refined or redefined? Should alternative approaches be considered, either to replace or to supplement the contributions of the centers?

OTA is presently engaged in a broad assessment of the impacts of information technology on research, and as part of that inquiry, is examining the question of scientific computational resources. It has been asked by the requesting committees for an interim paper that might help shed some light on the above questions. The full assessment will not be completed for several months, however; so this paper must confine itself to some tentative observations.

WHAT IS A HIGH PERFORMANCE COMPUTER?

The term, "supercomputer," is commonly used in the press, but it is not necessarily useful for policy. In the first place, the definition of power in a computer is highly inexact and depends on many factors including processor speed, memory size, and so on. Secondly, there is not a clear lower boundary of supercomputer power. IBM 3090 computers come in a wide range of configurations, some of the largest of which are the basis of supercomputer centers at institutions such as Cornell, the Universities of Utah, and Kentucky. Finally, technology is changing rapidly and with it our conceptions of power and capability of various types of machines. We use the more general term, "high performance computers," a term that includes a variety of machine types.

One class of HPC consists of very large, powerful machines, principally designed for very large numerical applications such as those encountered in science. These computers are the ones often referred to as "supercomputers." They are expensive, costing up to several million dollars each.

---

[1]Peter D. Lax, *Report of the Panel on Large-Scale Computing in Science and Engineering* (Washington, DC: National Science Foundation, 1982).

[2]One of the five centers, the John von Neumann National Supercomputer Center, has been based on ETA-10 technology. The Center has been asked to resubmit a proposal showing revised plans in reaction to the withdrawal of that machine from the market.

A large-scale computer's power comes from a combination of very high-speed electronic components and specialized architecture (a term used by computer designers to describe the overall logical arrangement of the computer). Most designs use a combination of "vector processing" and "parallelism" in their design. A vector processor is an arithmetic unit of the computer that produces a series of similar calculations in an overlapping, assembly line fashion. (Many scientific calculations can be set up in this way.)

Parallelism uses several processors, assuming that a problem can be broken into large independent pieces that can be computed on separate processors. Currently, large, mainframe HPC's such as those offered by Cray, IBM, are only modestly parallel, having as few as two up to as many as eight processors.[3] The trend is toward more parallel processors on these large systems. Some experts anticipate as many as 512 processor machines appearing in the near future. The key problem to date has been to understand how problems can be set up to take advantage of the potential speed advantage of larger scale parallelism.

Several machines are now on the market that are based on the structure and logic of a large supercomputer, but use cheaper, slower electronic components. These systems make some sacrifice in speed, but cost much less to manufacture. Thus, an application that is demanding, but that does not necessarily require the resources of a full-size supercomputer, may be much more cost effective to run on such a "minisuper."

Other types of specialized systems have also appeared on the market and in the research laboratory. These machines represent attempts to obtain major gains in computation speed by means of fundamentally different architectures. They are known by colorful names such as "Hypercubes," "Connection Machines," "Dataflow Processors," "Butterfly Machines," "Neural Nets," or "Fuzzy Logic Computers." Although they differ in detail, many of these systems are based on large-scale parallelism. That is, their designers attempt to get increases in processing speed by hooking together in some way a large number—hundreds or even thousands—of simpler,

slower and, hence, cheaper processors. The problem is that computational mathematicians have not yet developed a good theoretical or experiential framework for understanding in general how to arrange applications to take full advantage of these massively parallel systems. Hence, they are still, by and large, experimental, even though some are now on the market and users have already developed applications software for them. Experimental as these systems may seem now, many experts think that any significantly large increase in computational power eventually must grow out of experimental systems such as these or from some other form of massively parallel architecture.

Finally, "workstations," the descendants of personal desktop computers, are increasing in power; new chips now in development will offer the computing power nearly equivalent to a Cray 1 supercomputer of the late 1970s. Thus, although top-end HPCs will be correspondingly more powerful, scientists who wish to do serious computing will have a much wider selection of options in the near future.

A few policy-related conclusions flow from this discussion:

- The term "Supercomputer" is a fluid one, potentially covering a wide variety of machine types, and the "supercomputer industry" is similarly increasingly difficult to identify clearly.
- Scientists need access to a wide range of high performance computers, ranging from desktop workstations to full-scale supercomputers, and they need to move smoothly among these machines as their research needs dictate.
- Hence, government policy needs to be flexible and broadly based, not overly focused on narrowly defined classes of machines.

HOW FAST IS FAST?

Popular comparisons of supercomputer speeds are usually based on processing speed, the measure being "FLOPS," or "Floating Point Operation Per Second." The term "floating point" refers to a particular format for numbers within the computer that is used for scientific calculation; and a floating

---

[3]To distinguish between this modest level and the larger scale parallelism found on some more experimental machines, some experts refer to this limited parallelism as "multiprocessing."

point "operation" refers to a single arithmetic step, such as adding two numbers, using the floating point format. Thus, FLOPS measure the speed of the arithmetic processor. Currently, the largest super-computers have processing speeds ranging up to several billion FLOPS.

However, pure processing speed is not by itself a useful measure of the relative power of computers. To see why, let's look at an analogy.

In a supermarket checkout counter, the calculation speed of the register does not, by itself, determine how fast customers can purchase their groceries and get out of the store. Rather, the speed of checkout is also affected by the rate at which each purchase can be entered into the register and the overall time it takes to complete a transaction with a customer and start a new one. Of course, ultimately, the length of time the customer must wait in line to get to the clerk may be the biggest determinant of all.

Similarly, in a computer, how fast calculations can be set up and presented to the processor and how fast new jobs and their associated data can be moved in, and completed work moved out of the computer, determines how much of the processor's speed can actually be harnessed. (Some users refer to this as "solution speed.") In a computer, those speeds are determined by a wide variety of hardware and software characteristics. And, similar to the store checkout, as a fast machine becomes busy, users may have to wait a significant time to get their turn. From a user's perspective, then, a theoretically fast computer can look very slow.

In order to fully test a machine's speed, experts use what are called "benchmark programs," sample programs that reproduce the actual work load. Since workloads vary, there are several different bench-mark programs, and they are constantly being refined and revised. Measuring a supercomputer's speed is, itself, a complex and important area of research. It lends insight not only into what type of computer currently on the market is best to use for particular applications; but carefully structured measurements can also show where bottlenecks occur and, hence, where hardware and software improvements need to be made.

One can draw a few policy implications from these observations on speed:

- Since overall speed improvement is closely linked with how their machines are actually programmed and used, computer designers are critically dependent on feedback from that part of the user community which is pushing their machines to the limit.
- There is no "fastest" machine. The speed of a high performance computer is too dependent on the skill with which it is used and programmed, and the particular type of job it is being asked to perform.
- Until machines are available in the market and have been tested for overall performance, policymakers should be skeptical of announcements based purely on processor speeds that some company or country is producing "faster machines."
- Federal R&D programs for improving high performance computing need to stress software and computational mathematics as well as research on machine architecture.

THE NATIONAL SUPERCOMPUTER CENTERS

In February of 1985, NSF selected four sites to establish national supercomputing centers: The University of California at San Diego, The University of Illinois at Urbana-Champaign, Cornell University and the John von Neumann Center in Princeton. A fifth site, Pittsburgh, was added in early 1986. The five NSF centers are described briefly below.

The Cornell Theory Center

The Cornell Theory Center is located on the campus of Cornell University. Over 1,900 users from 125 institutions access the center. Although Cornell does not have a center-oriented network, 55 academic institutions are able to utilize the resources at Cornell through special nodes. A 14-member Corporate Research Institute works within the center in a variety of university-industry cost sharing projects.

In November of 1985 Cornell received a 3084 computer from IBM, which was upgraded to a four-processor 3090/400VF a year later. The 3090/400VF was replaced by a six-processor 3090/600E in May, 1987. In October, 1988 a second 3090/600E was added. The Cornell center also operates several other smaller parallel systems, including an Intel iPCS/2, a Transtech NT 1000, and a Topologix T1000. Some 50 percent of the resources of Northeast Parallel Architecture Center, which include two Connection machines, an Encore, and an Alliant FX/80, are accessed by the Cornell facility.

Until October of 1988, all IBM computers were "on loan" to Cornell for as long as Cornell retained its NSF funding. The second IBM 3090/600, procured in October, will be paid for by an NSF grant. Over the past 4 years, corporate support for the Cornell facility accounted for 48 percent of the operating costs. During those same years, NSF and New York State accounted for 37 percent and 5 percent respectively of the facility's budget. This funding has allowed the center to maintain a staff of about 100.

The National Center for Supercomputing Applications

The National Center for Supercomputing Applications (NCSA) is operated by the University of Illinois at Urbana-Champaign. The Center has over 2,500 academic users from about 82 academic affiliates. Each affiliate receives a block grant of time on the Cray X-MP/48, training for the Cray, and help using the network to access the Cray.

The NCSA received its Cray X-MP/24 in October 1985. That machine was upgraded to a Cray X-MP/48 in 1987. In October 1988 a Cray-2s/4-128 was installed, giving the center two Cray machines. This computer is the only Cray-2 now at an NSF national center. The center also houses a Connection Machine 2, an Alliant FX/80 and FX/8, and over 30 graphics workstations.

In addition to NSF funding, NCSA has solicited industrial support. Amoco, Eastman Kodak, Eli Lilly, FMC Corp., Dow Chemical, and Motorola have each contributed around $3 million over a 3-year period to the NCSA. In fiscal year 1989 corporate support has amounted to 11 percent of NCSA's funding. About 32 percent of NCSA's budget came from NSF while the State of Illinois and the University of Illinois accounted for the remaining 27 percent of the center's $21.5 million budget. The center has a full-time staff of 198.

Pittsburgh Supercomputing Center

The Pittsburgh Supercomputing Center (PSC) is run jointly by the University of Pittsburgh, Carnegie-Mellon University, and Westinghouse Electric Corp. More than 1,400 users from 44 States utilize the center. Twenty-seven universities are affiliated with PSC.

The center received a Cray X-MP/48 in March of 1986. In December of 1988 PSC became the first non-Federal laboratory to possess a Cray Y-MP. Both machines were being used simultaneously for a short time, however the center has phased out the Cray X-MP. The center's graphics hardware includes a Pixar image computer, an Ardent Titan, and a Silicon Graphics IRIS workstation.

The operating projection at PSC for fiscal year 1990, a "typical year," has NSF supporting 58 percent of the center's budget while industry and vendors account for 22 percent of the costs. The Commonwealth of Pennsylvania and the National Institutes of Health both support PSC, accounting for 8 percent and 4 percent of budget respectively. Excluding working students, the center has a staff of around 65.

San Diego Supercomputer Center

The San Diego Supercomputer Center (SDSC) is located on the campus of the University of California at San Diego and is operated by General Atomics. SDSC is linked to 25 consortium members but has a user base in 44 States. At the end of 1988, over 2,700 users were accessing the center. SDSC has 48 industrial partners who use the facility's hardware, software, and support staff.

A Cray X-MP/48 was installed in December, 1985. SDSC's first upgrade, a Y-MP8/864, is planned for December, 1989. In addition to the Cray, SDSC has 5 Sun workstations, two IRIS workstations, an Evans and Sutherland terminal, 5 Apollo workstations, a Pixar, an Ardent Titan, an SCS-40 minisupercomputer, a Supertek S-1 minisupercomputer, and two Symbolics Machines.

The University of California at San Diego spends more than $250,000 a year on utilities and services for SDSC. For fiscal year 1990 the SDSC believes NSF will account for 47 percent of the center's operating budget. The State of California currently provides $1.25 million per year to the center and in 1988, approved funding of $6 million over 3 years to SDSC for research in scientific visualization. For fiscal year 1990 the State is projected to support 10 percent of the center's costs. Industrial support, which has given the center $12.6 million in donations and in-kind services, is projected to provide 15 percent of the total costs of SDSC in fiscal year 1990.

John von Neumann National Supercomputer Center

The John von Neumann National Supercomputer Center (JvNC), located in Princeton New Jersey, is managed by the Consortium for Scientific Computing Inc., an organization of 13 institutions from New Jersey, Pennsylvania, Massachusetts, New York, Rhode Island, Colorado, and Arizona. Currently there are over 1,400 researchers from 100 institutes accessing the center. Eight industrial corporations utilize the JvNC facilities.

At present there are two Cyber 205 and two ETA-10s, in use at the JvNC. The first ETA-10 was installed, after a 1-year delay, in March of 1988. In addition to these machines there is a Pixar II, two Silicon Graphics IRIS and video animation capabilities.

When the center was established in 1985 by NSF, the New Jersey Commission on Science and Technology committed $12.1 million to the center over a 5-year period. An addition $13.1 million has been set-aside for the center by the New Jersey Commission for fiscal year 1991-1995. Direct funding from the State of New Jersey and university sources constitutes 15 percent of the center's budget for fiscal year 1991-1995. NSF will account for 60 percent of the budget. Projected industry revenue and cost sharing account for 25 percent of costs. Since the announcement by CDC to close its ETA subsidiary, the future of JvNC is uncertain. Plans have been proposed to NSF by JvNC to purchase a Cray Research Y-MP, eventually upgrading to a C-90. NSF is reviewing the plan and a decision on renewal is expected in October of 1989.

OTHER HPC FACILITIES

Before 1984 only three universities operated supercomputers: Purdue University, the University of Minnesota, and Colorado State University. The NSF supercomputing initiative established five new supercomputer centers that were nationally accessible. States and universities began funding their own supercomputer centers, both in response to growing needs on campus and to increased feeling on the part of State leaders that supercomputer facilities could be important stimuli to local R&D and, therefore, to economic development. Now, many State and university centers offer access to high performance computers;[4] and the NSF centers are only part of a much larger HPC environment including nearly 70 Federal installations (see table 2-1).

Supercomputer center operators perceive their roles in different ways. Some want to be a proactive force in the research community, leading the way by helping develop new applications, training users, and so on. Others are content to follow in the path that the NSF National Centers create. These differences in goals/missions lead to varied services and computer systems. Some centers are "cycle shops," offering computing time but minimal support staff. Other centers maintain a large support staff and offer consulting, training sessions, and even assistance with software development. Four representative centers are described below:

Minnesota Supercomputer Center

The Minnesota Supercomputer Center, originally part of the University of Minnesota, is a for-profit computer center owned by the University of Minnesota. Currently, several thousand researchers use the center, over 700 of which are from the University of Minnesota. The Minnesota Supercomputing Institute, an academic unit of the University, channels university usage by providing grants to the students through a peer review process.

The Minnesota Supercomputer Center received its first machine, a Cray 1A, in September, 1981. In mid 1985, it installed a Cyber 205; and in the latter part of that year, two Cray 2 computers were installed within 3 months of each other. Minnesota

---

[4]The number cannot be estimated exactly. First, it depends on the definition of supercomputer one uses. Secondly, the number keeps changing as States announce new plans for centers and as large research universities purchase their own HPCs.

Table 2-1—Federal Unclassified Supercomputer Installations

Laboratory	Number of machines
Department of Energy	
Los Alamos National Lab	6
Livermore National Lab, NMFECC	4
Livermore National Lab	7
Sandia National Lab, Livermore	3
Sandia National Lab, Albuquerque	2
Oak Ridge National Lab	1
Idaho Falls National Engineering	1
Argonne National Lab	1
Knolls Atomic Power Lab	1
Bettis Atomic Power Lab	1
Savannah/DOE	1
Richland/DOE	1
Schenectady Naval Reactors/DOE	2
Pittsburgh Naval Reactors/DOE	2
Department of Defense	
Naval Research Lab	1
Naval Ship R&D Center	1
Fleet Numerical Oceanography	1
Naval Underwater System Command	1
Naval Weapons Center	1
Martin Marietta/NTB	1
Air Force Weapons Lab	2
Air Force Global Weather	1
Arnold Engineering and Development	1
Wright Patterson AFB	1
Aerospace Corp.	1
Army Ballistic Research Lab	2
Army/Tacom	1
Army/Huntsville	1
Army/Kwajalein	1
Army/WES (on order)	1
Army/Warren	1
Defense Nuclear Agency	1
NASA	
Ames	5
Goddard	2
Lewis	1
Langley	1
Marshal	1
Department of Commerce	
National Inst. of Standards and Technology	1
National Oceanic & Atmospheric Administration	4
Environmental Protection Agency	
Raleigh, North Carolina	1
Department of Health and Human Services	
National Institutes of Health	1
National Cancer Institute	1

SOURCE: Office of Technology Assessment estimate.

bought its third Cray 2, the only one in use now, at the end of 1988, just after it installed its ETA-10. The ETA-10 has recently been decommissioned due to the closure of ETA. A Cray X-MP has been added, giving them a total of two supercomputers. The Minnesota Supercomputer Center has acquired more supercomputers than anyone outside the Federal Government.

The Minnesota State Legislature provides funds to the University for the purchasing of supercomputer time. Although the University buys a substantial portion of supercomputing time, the center has many industrial clients whose identities are proprietary, but they include representatives of the auto, aerospace, petroleum, and electronic industries. They are charged a fee for the use of the facility.

The Ohio Supercomputer Center

The Ohio Supercomputer Center (OSC) originated from a coalition of scientists in the State. The center, located on Ohio State University's campus, is connected to 20 other Ohio universities via the Ohio Academic Research Network (OARNET). As of January 1989, three private firms were using the Center's resources.

In August, 1987, OSC installed a Cray X-MP/24, which was upgraded to an Cray X-MP/28 a year later. The center replaced the X-MP in August 1989 with a Cray Research Y-MP. In addition to Cray hardware, there are 40 Sun Graphic workstations, a Pixar II, a Stallar Graphics machine, a Silicon Graphic workstation and a Abekas Still Store machine. The Center maintains a staff of about 35 people.

The Ohio General Assembly began funding the center in the summer of 1987, appropriating $7.5 million. In March of 1988, the Assembly allocated $22 million for the acquisition of a Cray Y-MP. Ohio State University has pledged $8.2 million to augment the center's budget. As of February 1989 the State has spent $37.7 million in funding.[5] OSC's annual budget is around $6 million (not including the purchase/leasing of their Cray).

Center for High Performance Computing, Texas (CHPC)

The Center for High Performance Computing is located at The University of Texas at Austin. CHPC serves all 14 institutions, 8 academic institutions, and 6 health-related organizations, in the University of Texas System.

[5]Jane Ware, "Ohioans: Blazing Computer," *Ohio*, February 1989, p. 12.

The University of Texas installed a Cray X-MP/24 in March 1986, and a Cray 14se in November of 1988. The X-MP is used primarily for research. For the time being, the Cray 14se is being used as a vehicle for the conversion of users to the Unix system. About 40 people staff the center.

Original funding for the center and the Cray X-MP came from bonds and endowments from both The University of Texas system and The University of Texas at Austin. The annual budget of CHPC is about $3 million. About 95 percent of the center's operating budget comes from State funding and endowments. Five percent of the costs are recovered from selling CPU time.

Alabama Supercomputer Network

The George C. Wallace Supercomputer Center, located in Huntsville Alabama, serves the needs of researchers throughout Alabama. Through the Alabama Supercomputer Network, 13 Alabama institutions, university and government sites, are connected to the center. Under contract to the State, Boeing Computer Services provides the support staff and technical skills to operate the center. Support staff are located at each of the nodes to help facilitate the use of the supercomputer from remote sites.

A Cray X-MP/24 arrived in 1987 and became operational in early 1988. In 1987 the State of Alabama agreed to finance the center. The State allocated $2.2 million for the center and $38 million to Boeing Services for the initial 5 years. The average yearly budget is $7 million. The center has a support staff of about 25.

Alabama universities are guaranteed 60 percent of the available time at no cost while commercial researchers are charged a user fee. The impetus for the State to create a supercomputer center has been stated as the technical superiority a supercomputer would bring, which would draw high-tech industry to the State, enhance interaction between industry and the universities, and promote research and the associated educational programs within the university.

Commercial Labs

A few corporations, such as the Boeing Computer Corp., have been selling high performance computer time for a while. Boeing operates a Cray X-MP/24. Other commercial sellers of high performance computing time include the Houston Area Research Center (HARC). HARC operates the only Japanese Supercomputer in America, the NEC SX2. The center offers remote services.

Computer Sciences Corp. (CSC), located in Falls Church, Virginia, has a 16-processor FLEX/32 from Flexible Computer Corp., a Convex 120 from Convex Computer Corp, and a DAP210 from Active Memory Technology. Federal agencies comprise two-thirds of CSC's customers.[6] Power Computing Co., located in Dallas, Texas, offers time on a Cray X-MP/24. Situated in Houston, Texas, Supercomputing Technology sells time on its Cray X-MP/28. Opticom Corp., of San Jose, California, offers time on a Cray X-MP/24, Cray 1-M, Convex C220, and C1 XP.

Federal Centers

In an informal poll of Federal agencies, OTA identified 70 unclassified installations that operate supercomputers, confirming the commonly expressed view that the Federal Government still represents a major part of the market for HPC in the United States (see figure 2-1). Many of these centers serve the research needs of government scientists and engineers and are, thus, part of the total research computing environment. Some are available to non-Federal scientists, others are closed.

CHANGING ENVIRONMENT

The scientific computing environment has changed in important ways during the few years that NSF's Advanced Scientific Computing Programs have existed. Some of these changes are as follows:

The ASC programs, themselves, have not evolved as originally planned. The original NSF planning document for the ASC program originally proposed to establish 10 supercomputer centers over a 3-year period; only 5 were funded. Center managers have also expressed the strong opinion that NSF has not met many of its original commitments for

---

[6]Norris Parker Smith, "More Than Just Buying Cycles," *Supercomputer Review*, April 1989.

Figure 2-1—Distribution of Federal Supercomputers

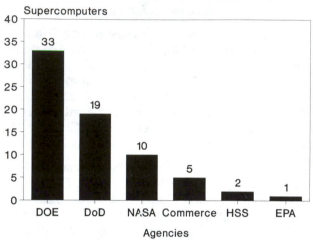

SOURCE: Office of Technology Assessment, 1989.

development of the Cray 3, a machine based on gallium arsenide electronics.

At the middle and lower end, the HPC industry has introduced several new so-called "mini-supercomputers"—many of them based on radically different system concepts, such as massive parallelism, and many designed for specific applications, such as high-speed graphics. New chips promise very high-speed desktop workstations in the near future.

Finally, three Japanese manufacturers, NEC, Fujitsu, and Hitachi have been successfully building and marketing supercomputers that are reportedly competitive in performance with U.S. machines.[7] While these machines have, as yet, not penetrated the U.S. computer market, they indicate the potential competitiveness of the Japanese computer industry in the international HPC markets, and raise questions for U.S. policy.

Many universities and State systems have established "supercomputer centers" to serve the needs of their researchers.[8] Many of these centers have only recently been formed, some have not yet installed their systems, so their operational experience is, at best, limited to date. Furthermore, some other centers operate systems that, while very powerful scientific machines, are not considered by all experts to be supercomputers. Nevertheless, these centers provide high performance scientific computing to the research community, and create new demands for Federal support for computer time.

Individual scientist and research teams are also getting Federal and private support from their sponsors to buy their own "minisupercomputers." In some cases, these systems are used to develop and check out software eventually destined to run on larger machines; in other cases, researchers seem to find these machines adequate for their needs. In either mode of use, these departmental or laboratory systems expand the range of possible sources researchers can turn to for high performance computing. Soon, desktop workstations will have performance equivalent to that of supercomputers of a decade ago at a significantly lower cost.

funding in successive years of the contracts, forcing the centers to change their operational priorities and search for support in other directions.

Technology has changed. There has been a burst of innovation in the HPC industry. At the top of the line, Cray Research developed two lines of machines, the Cray 2 and the Cray X-MP (and its successor, the Y-MP) that are much more powerful than the Cray 1, which was considered the leading edge of supercomputing for several years by the mid-1980s. IBM has delivered several 3090s equipped with multiple vector processors and has also become a partner in a project to develop a new supercomputer in a joint venture with SSI, a firm started by Steve Chen, a noted supercomputer architect previously with Cray Research.

More recently, major changes have occurred in the industry. Control Data has closed down ETA, its supercomputer operation. Cray Research has been broken into two parts—Cray Computer Corp. and Cray Research. Each will develop and market a different line of supercomputers. Cray Research will, initially, at least, concentrate on the Y-MP models, the upcoming C-90 machines, and their longer term successors. Cray Computer Corp., under the leadership of Seymour Cray, will concentrate on

---

[7]Since, as shown above, comparing the power and performance of supercomputers is a complex and arcane field, OTA will refrain from comparing or ranking systems in any absolute sense.

[8]See National Association of State Universities and Land-Grant Colleges, *Supercomputing for the 1990's: A Shared Responsibility* (Washington, DC: January 1989).

Finally, some important changes have occurred in national objectives or perceptions of issues. For example, the development of a very high capacity national science network (or "internet") has taken on a much greater significance. Originally conceived of in the narrow context of tying together supercomputer centers and providing regional access to them, the science network has now come to be thought of by its proponents as a basic infrastructure, potentially extending throughout (and, perhaps, even beyond) the entire scientific, technical, and educational community.

Science policy is also changing, as new important and costly projects have been started or are being seriously considered. Projects such as the supercollider, the space station, NASA's Earth Observing System (EOS) program, and the human genome mapping may seem at first glance to compete for funding with science networks and supercomputers. However, they will create formidable new demands for computation, data communications, and data storage facilities; and, hence, constitute additional arguments for investments in an information technology infrastructure.

Finally, some of the research areas in the so-called "Grand Challenges"[9] have attained even greater social importance—such as fluid flow modeling which will help the design of faster and more fuel efficient planes and ships, climate modeling to help understand long term weather patterns, and the structural analysis of proteins to help understand diseases and design vaccines and drugs to fight them.

REVIEW AND RENEWAL OF THE NSF CENTERS

Based on the recent review, NSF has concluded that the centers, by and large, have been successful and are operating smoothly. That is, their systems are being fully used, they have trained many new users, and they are producing good science. In light of that conclusion, NSF has tentatively agreed to renewal for the three Cray-based centers and the IBM-based Cornell Center. The John von Neumann Center in Princeton has been based on ETA-10 computers. Since ETA was closed down, NSF put the review of the JvNC on hold pending review of a revised plan that has now been submitted. A decision is expected soon.

Due to the environmental changes noted above, if the centers are to continue in their present status as special NSF-sponsored facilities, the National Supercomputer Centers will need to sharply define their roles in terms of: 1) the users they intend to serve, 2) the types of applications they serve, and 3) the appropriate balance between service, education, and research.

The NSF centers are only a few of a growing number of facilities that provide access to HPC resources. Assuming that NSF's basic objective is to assure researchers access to the most appropriate computing for their work, it will be under increasing pressure to justify dedicating funds to one limited group of facilities. Five years ago, few U.S. academic supercomputer centers existed. When scientific demand was less, managerial attention was focused on the immediate problem of getting equipment installed and of developing an experienced user community. Under those circumstances, some ambiguity of purpose may have been acceptable and understandable. However, in light of the proliferation of alternative technologies and centers, as well as growing demand by researchers, unless the purposes of the National Centers are more clearly delineated, the facilities are at risk of being asked to serve too many roles and, as a result, serving none well.

Some examples of possible choices are as follows:

1. Provide Access to HPC
- Provide access to the most powerful, leading edge, supercomputers available.
- Serve the HPC requirements for research projects of critical importance to the Federal Government, for example, the "Grand Challenge" topics.
- Serve the needs of all NSF-funded researchers for HPC.
- Serve the needs of the (academic, educational, and/or industrial) scientific community for HPC.

---

[9]"Grand Challenge" research topics are questions of major social importance that require for progress substantially greater computing resources than are currently available. The term was first coined by Nobel Laureate physicist, Kenneth Wilson.

2. Educate and Train

- Provide facilities and programs to teach scientists and students how to use high performance computing in their research.

3. Advance the State of HPC Use in Research

- Develop applications and system software.
- Serve as centers for research in computational science.
- Work with vendors as test sites for advanced HPC systems.

As the use of HPC expands into more fields and among more researchers, what are the policies for providing access to the necessary computing resources? **The Federal Government needs to develop a comprehensive analysis of the requirements of the scientific researchers for high performance computing, Federal policies of support for scientific computing, and the variety of Federal and State/private computing facilities available for research.**

We expect that OTA's final report will contribute to this analysis from a congressional perspective. However, the executive branch, including both lead agencies and OSTP also need to participate actively in this policy and planning process.

THE INTERNATIONAL ENVIRONMENT

Since some of the policy debate over HPCs has involved comparison with foreign programs, this section will conclude a brief description of the status of HPC in some other nations.

Japan

The Ministry of International Trade and Industry (MITI), in October of 1981, announced the undertaking of two computing projects, one on artificial intelligence, the Fifth Generation Computer Project, and one on supercomputing, the National Superspeed Computer Project. The publicity surrounding MITI's announcement focused on fifth generation computers, but brought the more general subject of supercomputing to the public attention. (The term "Fifth Generation" refers to computers specially designed for artificial intelligence applications, especially those that involve logical inference or "reasoning.")

Although in the eyes of many scientists the Fifth Generation project has fallen short of its original goals, eight years later it has produced some accomplishments in hardware architecture and artificial intelligence software. MITI's second project, dealing with supercomputers, has been more successful. Since 1981, when no supercomputers were manufactured by the Japanese, three companies have designed and produced supercomputers.

The Japanese manufacturers followed the Americans into the supercomputer market, yet in the short time since their entrance, late 1983 for Hitachi and Fujitsu, they have rapidly gained ground in HPC hardware. One company, NEC, has recently announced a supercomputer with processor speeds up to eight times faster than the present fastest American machine.[10] Outside of the United States, Japan is the single biggest market for and supplier of supercomputers, although American supercomputer companies account for less than one-fifth of all supercomputers sold in Japan.[11]

In the present generation of supercomputers, U.S. supercomputers have some advantages. One of American manufacturer's major advantages is the availability of scientific applications software. The Japanese lag behind the Americans in software development, although resources are being devoted to research in software by the Japanese manufacturers and government and there is no reason to think they will not be successful.

Another area in which American firms differ from the Japanese has been in their use of multiprocessor architecture (although this picture is now changing). For several years, American supercomputer companies have been designing machines with multiprocessors to obtain speed. The only Japanese supercomputer that utilizes multiprocessors is the NEC system, which will not be available until the fall of 1990.

---

[10]The NEC machine is not scheduled for delivery until 1990, at which time faster Cray computers may well be on the market also. See also the comments above about computer speed.

[11]Marjorie Sun, "A Global Supercomputer Race for High Stakes," *Science*, February 1989, vol. 243, pp. 1004-1006.

American firms have been active in the Japanese market, with mixed success.

Since 1979 Cray has sold 16 machines in Japan. Of the 16 machines, 6 went to automobile manufacturers, 2 to NTT, 2 to Recruit, 1 to MITI, 1 to Toshiba, 1 to Aichi Institute of Technology, and 1 to Mitsubishi Electric. None have gone to public universities or to government agencies.

IBM offers their 3090 with attached vector facilities. IBM does not make public its customers, but report that they have sold around 70 vector processor computers to Japanese clients. Some owners, or soon to be owners, include Nissan, NTT, Mazda, Waseda University, Nippon Steel and Mistubishi Electric.

ETA sold two supercomputers in Japan. The first was to the Tokyo Institute of Technology (TIT). The sale was important because it was the first sale of a CDC/ETA supercomputer to the Japanese as well as the first purchase of an American supercomputer by a Japanese national university. This machine was delivered late (it arrived in May of 1988) and had many operating problems, partially due to its being the first installment of an eight-processor ETA 10-E. The second machine was purchased (not delivered) on February 9, 1989 by the University of Meiji. How CDC will deal with the ETA 10 at TIT in light of the closure of ETA is unknown at this time.

Hitachi, Fujitsu, and NEC, the three Japanese manufacturers of supercomputers, are among the largest computer/electronic companies in Japan; and they produce their own semiconductors. Their size allows them to absorb the high initial costs of designing a new supercomputer, as well as provide large discounts to customers. Japan's technological lead is in its very fast single-vector processors. Little is known, as of yet, what is happening with parallel processing in Japan, although NEC's recent product announcement for the SX-X states that the machine will have multiprocessors.

Hitachi's supercomputer architecture is loosely based on its IBM compatible mainframe. Hitachi entered the market in November of 1983. Unlike their domestic rivals, Hitachi has not entered the international market. All 29 of its ordered/installed supercomputers are located in Japan.

NEC's current supercomputer architecture is not based on its mainframe computer and it is not IBM compatible. They entered the supercomputer market later than Hitachi and Fujitsu. Three NEC supercomputers have been sold/installed in foreign markets: one in the United States, an SX-2 machine at the Houston Area Research Consortium, one at the Laboratory of Aerospace Research in Netherlands, and an SX-1 has recently been sold in Singapore. Their domestic users include five universities.

On April 10, 1989, in a joint venture with Honeywell Inc., NEC announced a new line of supercomputers, the SX-X. The most powerful machine is reported to be up to eight times faster than the Cray X-MP machine. The SX-X reportedly will run Unix-based software and will have multiprocessors. This machine is due to be shipped in the fall of 1990.

Fujitsu's supercomputer, like Hitachi's, is based on their IBM compatible mainframes. Their first machine was delivered in late 1983. Fujitsu had sold 80 supercomputers in Japan by mid-1989. An estimated 17 machines have been sold to foreign customers. An Amdahl VP-200 is used at the Western Geophysical Institute in London. In the United States, the Norwegian company GECO, located in Houston, has a VP-200 and two VP-100s. The most recent sale was to the Australian National University, a VP-100.

Europe

European countries that have (or have ordered) supercomputers include: West Germany, France, England, Denmark, Spain, Norway, the Netherlands, Italy, Finland, Switzerland, and Belgium. Europe is catching up quickly with America and Japan in understanding the importance of high performance computing for science and industry. The computer industry is helping to stimulate European interest. For example, IBM has pledged $40 million towards a supercomputer initiative in Europe over the 2-year period between 1987-89. It is creating a large base of followers in the European academic community by participating in such programs as the European Academic Supercomputing Initiative (EASI), and the Numerically Intensive Computing Enterprise (NICE). Cray Research also has a solid base in academic Europe, supplying over 14 supercomputers to European universities.

The United Kingdom began implementing a high performance computing plan in 1985. The Joint Working Party on Advanced Research Computing's report in June of 1985, "Future Facilities for Advanced Research Computing," recommended a national facility for advanced research computing. This center would have the most powerful supercomputer available; upgrade the United Kingdom's networking systems, JANET, to ensure communications to remote users; and house a national organization of advanced research computing to promote collaboration with foreign countries and within industry, ensuring the effective use of these resources.[12] Following this report, a Cray X-MP/48 was installed at the Atlas Computer Center in Rutherford. A Cray 1s was installed at the University of London. Between 1986 and 1989, some $11.5 million was spent on upgrading and enhancing JANET.[13]

Alvey was the United Kingdom's key information technology R&D program. The program promoted projects in information technology undertaken jointly by industry and academics. The United Kingdom began funding the Alvey program in 1983. During the first 5 years, 350 million pounds were allocated to the Alvey program. The program was eliminated at the end of 1988. Some research was picked up by other agencies, and many of the projects that were sponsored by Alvey are now submitting proposals to Esprit (see below).

The European Community began funding the European Strategic Programme for Research in Information Technology (Esprit) program in 1984 partly as a reaction to the poor performance of the European Economic Community in the market of information technology and partly as a response to MITI's 1981 computer programs. The program, funded by the European Community (EC), intends to "provide the European IT industry with the key components of technology it needs to be competitive on the world markets within a decade."[14] The EC has designed a program that forces collaboration between nations, develops recognizable standards in the information technology industry, and promotes pre-competitive R&D. The R&D focuses on five main areas: microelectronics, software development, office systems, computer integrated manufacturing, and advanced information.

Phase I of Esprit, the first 5 years, received $3.88 billion in funding.[15] The funding was split 50-50 by the EC and its participants. This was considered the catch-up phase. Emphasis was placed on basic research, realizing that marketable goods will follow. Many of the companies that participated in Phase I were small experimental companies.

Phase II, which begins in late 1989, is called commercialization. Marketable goods will be the major emphasis of Phase II. This implies that the larger firms will be the main industrial participants since they have the capital needed to put a product on the market. The amount of funds for Phase II will be determined by the world environment in information technology and the results of Phase I, but has been estimated at around $4.14 billion.[16]

Almost all of the high performance computer technologies emerging from Europe have been based on massively parallel architectures. Some of Europe's parallel machines incorporate the transputer. Transputer technology (basically a computer on a chip) is based on high density VLSI (very large-scale integration) chips. The T800, Inmos's transputer, has the same power as Intel's 80386/80387 chip, the difference being in size and price. The transputer is about one-third the size and price of Intel's chip.[17] The transputer, created by the Inmos company, had its initial R&D funded by the British government. Eventually Thorn EMI bought Inmos and the rights to the transputer. Thorn EMI recently sold Inmos to a French-Italian joint venture company, SGS-Thomson, just as it was beginning to be profitable.

---

[12]"Future Facilities for Advanced Research Computing," the report of a Joint Working Party on Advanced Research Computing, United Kingdom, July 1985.

[13]Discussion paper on "Supercomputers in Australia," Department of Industry, Technoloy and Commerce, April 1988, pp. 14-15.

[14]"Esprit," Commission of the European Communities, p. 5.

[15]"Esprit," Commission of the European Communities, p. 21.

[16]Simon Perry, "European Team Effort Breaks Ground in Software Standards," *Electronic Business*, Aug. 15, 1988, pp. 90-91.

[17]Graham K. Ellis, "Transputers Advance Parallel Processing," *Research and Development*, March 1989, p. 50.

Some of the more notable high performance computer products and R&D in Europe include:

- **T.Node**, formerly called Supernode P1085, is one of the more successful endeavors of the Esprit program. T.Node is a massively parallel machine that exploits the Inmos T800 transputer. A single node is composed of 16 transputers connected by two NEC VLSI chips and two additional transputers. The participants in the project are The University of Southampton, Royal Signals, Radar Establishment, Thorn-EMI (all British) and the French firm Telemat. The prototype of the French T.Node, Marie, a massively parallel MIMD (multiple instruction, multiple data) computer, was delivered in April of 1988. The product is now being marketed in America.

- **Project 415** is also funded by Esprit. Its project leader is Philips, the Dutch electronics group. This project, which consists of six groups, focuses on symbolic computation, artificial intelligence (AI), rather than "number crunching" (mathematical operations by conventional supercomputers). Using parallel architecture, the project is developing operating systems and languages that they hope will be available in 5 years for the office environment.[18]

- **The Flagship** project, originally sponsored by the Alvey program, has created a prototype parallel machine using 15 processors. Its original participants were ICL, Imperial College, and the University of Manchester. Other Alvey projects worked with the Flagship project in designing operating systems and languages for the computer. By 1992 the project hopes to have a marketable product. Since cancellation of the Alvey program, Flagship has gained sponsorship from the Esprit Program.

- **The Supernum Project** of West Germany, with the help of the French Isis program, currently is creating machinery with massively parallel architecture. The parallelism, based on Intel's 80386 microprocessors, is one of Esprit's more controversial and ambitious projects. Originally the project was sponsored by

the West German government in their supercomputing program. A computer prototype was recently shown at the industry fair in Hanover. It will be marketed in Germany by the end of the year for around $14 million.

- **The Supercluster**, produced and manufactured by Parsytec GmbH, a small private company, exemplifies Silicon Valley initiative occurring in West Germany. Parsytec has received some financial backing from the West German government for their venture. This start-up firm sells a massively parallel machine that rivals superminicomputers or low-end supercomputers. The Supercluster architecture exploits the 32-bit transputer from Inmos, the T800. Sixteen transputer-based processors in clusters of four are linked together. This architecture is less costly than conventional machines, costing between $230,000 and $320,000.[19] Parsytec has just begun to market its product in America.

Other Nations

The Australia National University recently purchased a Fujitsu VP-100. A private service bureau in Australia, Leading Edge, possesses a Cray Research computer. At least two sites in India have supercomputers, one at the Indian Meteorological Centre and one at ISC University. Two Middle Eastern petroleum companies house supercomputers, and Korea and Singapore both have research institutes with supercomputers.

Over half a dozen Canadian universities have high performance computers from CDC, Cray Research, or IBM. Canada's private sector has also invested in supercomputers. Around 10 firms possess high performance computers. The Alberta government, aside from purchasing a supercomputer and supporting associated services, has helped finance Myrias Computer Corp. A wholly owned U.S. subsidiary, Myrias Research Corp. manufactures the SP-2, a minisupercomputer.

One newly industrialized country is reported to be developing a minisupercomputer of its own. The

---

[18]Julia Vowler, *Supercomputing Review*, "European Transputer-based Projects Issue Challenge to U.S. Supercomputing Supermacy," November/December 1988, pp. 8-9.

[19]John Gosh, "A New Transputer Design From West German Startup," *Electronics*, Mar. 3, 1988, pp. 71-72.

first Brazilian minisupercomputer, claimed to be capable of 150 mips, is planned to be available by the end of 1989. The prototype is a parallel machine with 64 processors, each with 32-bit capacity. The machine will sell for $2.5 million. The Funding Authority of Studies and Projects (FINEP) financed the project, with annual investment around $1 million.

Networks

Information is the lifeblood of science; communication of that information is crucial to the advance of research and its applications. Data communication networks enable scientists to talk with each other, access unique experimental data, share results and publications, and run models on remote supercomputers, all with a speed, capacity, and ease that makes possible the posing of new questions and the prospect for new answers. Networks ease research collaboration by removing geographic barriers. They have become an invaluable research tool, opening up new channels of communication and increasing access to research equipment and facilities. Most important, networking is becoming the indispensable foundation for all other use of information technology in research.

Research networking is also pushing the frontiers of data communications and network technologies. Like electric power, highways, and the telephone, data communications is an infrastructure that will be crucial to all sectors of the economy. Businesses demand on-line transaction processing, and financial markets run on globally networked electronic trading. The evolution of telephony to digital technology allows merging of voice, data, and information services networking, although voice circuits still dominate the deployment of the technology. Promoting scientific research networking—dealing with data-intense outputs like satellite imaging and supercomputer modeling—should push networking technology that will find application far outside of science.

Policy action is needed, if Congress wishes to see the evolution of a full-scale national research and education network. The existing "internet" of scientific networks is a fledgling. As this conglomeration of networks evolves from an R&D enterprise to an operational network, users will demand round-the-clock, high-quality service. Academics, policymakers, and researchers around the world agree on the pressing need to transform it into a permanent infrastructure. This will entail grappling with difficult issues of public and private roles in funding, management, pricing/cost recovery, access, security, and international coordination as well as assuring adequate funding to carry out initiatives that are set by Congress.

Research networking faces two particular policy complications. First, since the network in its broadest form serves most disciplines, agencies, and many different groups of users, it has no obvious lead champion. As a common resource, its potential sponsors may each be pleased to use it but unlikely to give it the priority and funding required to bring it to its full potential. There is a need for clear central leadership, as well as coordination of governments, the private sector, and universities. A second complication is a mismatch between the concept of a national research network and the traditionally decentralized, subsidized, mixed public-private nature of higher education and science. The processes and priorities of mission agency-based Federal support may need some redesigning, as they are oriented towards supporting ongoing mission-oriented and basic research, and may work less well at fostering large-scale scientific facilities and infrastructure that cut across disciplines and agency missions.

In the near term, the most important step is getting a widely connected, operational network in place. But the "bare bones" networks are a small part of the picture. Information that flows over the network, and the scientific resources and data available through the network, are the important payoffs. Key long-term issues for the research community will be those that affect the sort of information available over the network, who has access to it, and how much it costs. The main issue areas for scientific data networking are outlined below:

- research—to develop the technology required to transmit and switch data at very high rates;
- private sector participation—role of the common carriers and telecommunication companies in developing and managing the network and of private information firms in offering services;
- scope—who the network is designed to serve will drive its structure and management;
- access—balancing open use against security and information control and determining who

will be able to gain access to the network for what purpose;

- standards—the role of government, industry, users, and international organizations in setting and maintaining technical standards;
- management—public and private roles; degree of decentralization;
- funding—an operational network will require significant, stable, continuing investment; the financial responsibilities demarcated must reflect the interests of various players, from individual colleges through States and the Federal Government, in their stake in network operations and policies;
- economics—pricing and cost recovery for network use, central to the evolution and management of any infrastructure. Economics will drive the use of the network;
- information services—who will decide what types of services are to be allowed over the network, who is allowed to offer them; and who will resolve information issues such as privacy, intellectual property, fair competition, and security;
- long-term science policy issues—the networks' impacts on the process of science, and on access to and dissemination of valuable scientific and technical information.

THE NATIONAL RESEARCH AND EDUCATION NETWORK (NREN)

"A universal communications network connected to national and international networks enables electronic communication among scholars anywhere in the world, as well as access to worldwide information sources, special experimental instruments, and computing resources. The network has sufficient bandwidth for scholarly resources to appear to be attached to a world local area network."

EDUCOM, 1988.

". . . a national research network to provide a distributed computing capability that links the government, industry, and higher education communities."

OSTP, 1987.

"The goal of the National Research and Education Network is to enhance national competitiveness and productivity through a high-speed, high-quality network infrastructure which supports a broad set of applications and network services for the research

and instructional community."

EDUCOM/NTTF, March 1989.

"The NREN will provide high-speed communication access to over 1300 institutions across the United States within five years. It will offer sufficient capacity, performance, and functionality so that the physical distance between institutions is no longer a barrier to effective collaboration. It will support access to high-performance computing facilities and services . . . and advanced information sharing and exchange, including national file systems and online libraries . . . .the NREN will evolve toward fully supported commercial facilities that support a broad range of applications and services."

FRICC, Program Plan
for the NREN, May 23, 1989.

This chapter of the background paper reviews the status of and issues surrounding data networking for science, in particular the proposed NREN. It describes current Federal activities and plans, and identifies issues to be examined in the full report, to be completed in summer 1990.

The existing array of scientific networks consists of a hierarchy of local, regional and national networks, linked into a whole. In this paper, "NREN" will be used to describe the next generation of the national "backbone" that ties them together. The term "Internet" is used to describe a more specific set of interconnected major networks, all of which use the same data transmission protocols. The most important are NSFNET and its major regional subnetworks, ARPANET, and several other federally initiated networks such as ESNET and NASNET. The term internet is used fairly loosely. At its broadest, the more generic term internet can be used to describe the international conglomeration of networks, with a variety of protocols and capabilities, which have a gateway into Internet; which could include such things as BITNET and MCI Mail.

The Origins of Research Networking

Research users were among the first to link computers into networks, to share information and broaden remote access to computing resources. DARPA created ARPANET in the 1960s for two purposes: to advance networking and data communications R&D, and to develop a robust communications network that would support the data-rich conversations of computer scientists. Building on the resulting packet-switched network technology, other agencies developed specialized networks for their research communities (e.g., ESNET, CSNET, NSFNET). Telecommunications and electronic industries provided technology and capacity for these networks, but they were not policy leaders or innovators of new systems. Meanwhile, other research-oriented networks, such as BITNET and Usenet, were developed in parallel by academic and industry users who, not being grantees or contractors of Federal agencies, were not served by the agency-sponsored networks. These university and lab-based networks serve a relatively small number of specialized scientific users, a market that has been ignored by the traditional telecommunications industry. The networks sprang from the efforts of users—academic and other research scientists—and the Federal managers who were supporting them.[1]

The Growing Demand for Capability and Connectivity

Today there are thousands of computer networks in the United States. These networks range from tempoary linkages between modem-equipped[2] desktop computers linked via common carriers, to institution-wide area networks, to regional and national networks. Network traffic moves through different media, including copper wire and optical cables, signal processors and switches, satellites, and the vast common carrier system developed for voice communication. Much of this hodgepodge of networks has been linked (at least in terms of ability to interconnect) into the internet. The ability of any two systems to interconnect depends on their ability to recognize and deal with the form information flows take in each. These "protocols" are sets of technical standards that, in a sense, are the "languages" of communication systems. Networks with different protocols can often be linked together by computer-based "gateways" that translate the protocols between the networks.

National networks have partially coalesced, where technology allows cost savings without losing connectivity. Over the past years, several agencies have pooled funds and plans to support a shared national backbone. The primary driver for this interconnecting and coalescing of networks has been the need for connectivity among users. The power of the whole is vastly greater than the sum of the pieces. Substantial costs are saved by extending connectivity while reducing duplication of network coverage. The real payoff is in connecting people, information, and resources. Linking brings users in reach of each other. Just as telephones would be of little use if only a few people had them, a research and education network's connectivity is central to its usefulness, and this connectivity comes both from ability of each network to reach the desks, labs, and homes of its users and the extent to which various networks are, themselves, interconnected.

The Present NREN

The national research and education network can be viewed as four levels of increasingly complex and flexible capability:

- physical wire/fiber optic common carrier "highways";
- user-defined, packet-switched networks;
- basic network operations and services; and
- research, education, database, and information services accessible to network users

In a fully developed NREN, all of these levels of service must be integrated. Each level involves different technologies, services, policy issues, research opportunities, engineering requirements, clientele, providers, regulators, and policy issues. A more detailed look at the policy problems can be drawn by separating the NREN into its major components.

Level 1: Physical wire/fiber optic common carrier highways

The foundation of the network is the physical conduits that carry digital signals. These telephone wires, optical fibers, microwave links, and satellites are the physical highways and byways of data transit. They are invisible to the network user. To provide the physical skeleton for the internet, government, industry, and university network man-

---

[1] John S. Quarterman and Josiah C. Hoskins, "Notable Computer Networks," *Communications of the ACM*, vol 29, No. 10, October 1986, pp. 932-971; John S. Quarterman, *The Matrix: Networks Around the World*, Digital Press, August 1989.

[2] A "Modem" converts information in a computer to a form that a communication system can carry, and vice versa. It also automates some simple functions, such as dialing and answering the phone, detecting and correcting transmission errors.

agers lease circuits from public switched common carriers, such as AT&T, MCI, GTE, and NTN. In doing so they take advantage of the large system of circuits already laid in place by the telecommunications common carriers for other telephony and data markets. A key issue at this level is to what extent broader Federal agency and national telecommunications policies will promote, discourage, or divert the evolution of a research-oriented data network.

Level 2: User-defined subnetworks

The internet is a conglomeration of smaller foreign, regional, State, local, topical, private, government, and agency networks. Generally, these separately managed networks, such as SURANET, BARRNET, BITNET, and EARN, evolved along naturally occurring geographic, topical, or user lines, or mission agency needs. Most of these logical networks emerged from Federal research agency (including the Department of Defense) initiatives. In addition, there are more and more commercial, State and private, regional, and university networks (such as Accunet, Telenet, and Usenet) at the same time specialized and interlinked. Many have since linked through the Internet, while keeping to some extent their own technical and socioeconomic identity. This division into small, focused networks offers the advantage of keeping network management close to its users; but demands standardization and some central coordination to realize the benefits of interconnection.

Networks at this level of operations are distinguished by independent management and technical boundaries. Networks often have different standards and protocols, hardware, and software. They carry information of different sensitivity and value. The diversity of these logical subnetworks matters to institutional subscribers (who must choose among network offerings), to regional and national network managers (who must manage and coordinate these networks into an internet), and to users (who can find the variety of alternatives confusing and difficult to deal with). A key issue is the management relationship among these diverse networks; to what extent is standardization and centralization desirable?

Level 3: Basic network operations and services

A small number of basic maintenance tools keeps the network running and accessible by diverse, distributed users. These basic services are software-based, provided for the users by network operators and computer manufacturers in operating systems. They include software for password recognition, electronic-mail, and file transfer. These are core services necessary to the operation of any network. These basic services are not consistent across the current range of computers used by research. A key issue is to what extent these services should be standardized, and as important, who should make those decisions.

Level 4: Value-added superstructure: links to research, education, and information services

The utility of the network lies in the information, services, and people that the user can access through the network. These value-added services provide specialized tools, information, and data for research and education. Today they include specialized computers and software, library catalogs and publication databases, archives of research data, conferencing systems, and electronic bulletin boards and publishing services that provide access to colleagues in the United States and abroad. These information resources are provided by volunteer scientists and by non-profit, for-profit, international, and government organizations. Some are amateur, poorly maintained bulletin boards; others are mature information organizations with well-developed services. Some are "free"; others recover costs through user charges.

Core policy issues are the appropriate roles for various information providers on the network. If the network is viewed as public infrastructure, what is "fair" use of this infrastructure? If the network eases access to sensitive scientific data (whether raw research data or government regulatory databases), how will this stress the policies that govern the relationships of industry, regulators, lobbyists, and experts? Should profit-seeking companies be allowed to market their services? How can we ensure that technologies needed for network maintenance, cost accounting, and monitoring will not be used inappropriately or intrusively? Who should set prices for various users and services? How will intellectual property rights be structured for electronically available information? Who is responsible for the quality and integrity of the data provided and used by researchers on the network?

Research Networking as a Strategic High Technology Infrastructure

Research networking has dual roles. First, networking is a strategic, high technology infrastructure for science. More broadly applied, data networking **enables** research, education, business, and manufacturing, and improves the Nation's knowledge competitiveness. Second, networking technologies and applications are themselves a substantial growth area, meriting focused R&D.

Knowledge is the commerce of education and research. Today networks are the highways for information and ideas. They expand access to computing, data, instruments, the research community, and the knowledge they create. Data are expensive (relative to computing hardware) and are increasingly created in many widely distributed locations, by specialized instruments and enterprises, and then shared among many separate users. The more effectively that research information is disseminated to other researchers and to industry, the more effective is scientific progress and social application of technological knowledge. An internet of networks has become a strategic infrastructure for research.

The research networks are also a testbed for data communications technology. Technologies developed through the research networks are likely to enhance productivity of all economic sectors, not just university research. The federally supported Internet has not only sponsored frontier-breaking network research, but has pulled data-networking technology with it. ARPANET catalyzed the development of packet-switching technology, which has expanded rapidly from R&D networking to multibillion-dollar data handling for business and financial transactions. The generic technologies developed for the Internet—hardware (such as high-speed switches) and software for network management, routing, and user interface—will transfer readily into general data-networking applications. Govern-ment support for applied research can catalyze and integrate R&D, decrease risk, create markets for network technologies and services, transcend economic and regulatory barriers, and accelerate early technology development and deployment. This would not only bolster U.S. science and education, but would fuel industry R&D and help support the market and competitiveness of the U.S. network and information services industry.

Governments and private industries the world over are developing research networks, to enhance R&D productivity and to create testbeds for highly advanced communications services and technologies. Federal involvement in infrastructure is motivated by the need for coordination and nationally oriented investment, to spread financial burdens, and promote social policy goals (such as furthering basic research).[3] Nations that develop markets in network-based technologies and services will create information industry-based productivity growth.

Federal Coordination of the Evolving Internet

NREN plans have evolved rapidly. Congressional interest has grown; in 1986, Congress requested the Office of Science and Technology Policy (OSTP) to report on options for networking for research and supercomputing.[4] The resulting report, completed in 1987 by the interagency Federal Coordinating Council for Science, Engineering, and Technology (FCCSET), called for a new Federal program to create an advanced national research network by the year 2000.[5] This vision incorporated two objectives: 1) providing vital computer-communications network services for the Nation's academic research community, and 2) stimulating networking and communications R&D which would fuel U.S. industrial technology and commerce in the growing global data communications market.

The 1987 FCCSET report, building on ongoing Federal activities, addressed near-term questions over the national network's scope, purposes, agency authority, performance targets, and budget. It did not resolve issues surrounding the long-term operation of a network, the role of commercial services in

---

[3]Congressional Budget Office, *New Directions for the Nation's Public Works*, September 1988, p. xiii; CBO, *Federal Policies for Infrastructure Management*, June 1986.

[4]P.L. 99-383, Aug. 21, 1986.

[5]OSTP, *A Research and Development Strategy for High Performance Computing*, Nov. 20, 1987.

providing network operations and services, or interface with broader telecommunications policies.

A 1988 National Research Council report praised ongoing activities, emphasized the need for coordination, stable funding, broadened goals and design criteria, integrated management, and increased private sector involvement.[6]

FCCSET's Subcommittee on Networking has since issued a plan to upgrade and expand the network.[7] In developing this plan, agencies have worked together to improve and interconnect several existing networks. Most regional networks were joint creations of NSF and regional consortia, and have been part of the NSFNET world since their inception. Other quasi-private, State, and regional networks (such as CICNET, Inc., and CERFNET) have been started.

Recently, legislation has been reintroduced to authorize and coordinate a national research network.[8] As now proposed, a National Research and Education Network would link universities, national laboratories, non-profit institutions and government research organizations, private companies doing government-supported research and education, and facilities such as supercomputers, experimental instruments, databases, and research libraries. Network research, as a joint endeavor with industry, would create and transfer technology for eventual commercial exploitation, and serve the data-networking needs of research and higher education into the next century.

Players in the NREN

The current Internet has been created by Federal leadership and funding, pulling together a wide base of university commitment, national lab and academic expertise, and industry interest and technology. The NREN involves many public and private actors. Their roles must be better delineated for effective policy. Each of these actors has vested interests and spheres of capabilities. Key players are:

- universities, which house most end users;

- networking industry, the telecommunications, data communications, computer, and information service companies that provide networking technologies and services;
- State enterprises devoted to economic development, research, and education;
- industrial R&D labs (network users); and
- the Federal Government, primarily the national labs and research-funding agencies

Federal funding and policy have stimulated the development of the Internet. Federal initiatives have been well complemented by States (through funding State networking and State universities' institutional and regional networking), universities (by funding campus networking), and industry (by contributing networking technology and physical circuits at sharply reduced rates). End users have experienced a highly subsidized service during this "experimental" stage. As the network moves to a bigger, more expensive, more established operation, how might these relative roles change?

Universities

Academic institutions house teachers, researchers, and students in all fields. Over the past few decades universities have invested heavily in libraries, local computing, campus networks, and regional network consortia. The money invested in campus networking far outweighs the investment in the NSFNET backbone. In general, academics view the NREN as fulfillment of a longstanding ambition to build a national system for the transport of information for research and education. EDUCOM has long labored from the "bottom" up, bringing together researchers and educators who used networks (or believed they could use them) for both research and teaching.

Networking Industry

There is no simple unified view of the NREN in the fragmented telecommunications "industry." The long-distance telecommunications common carriers generally see the academic market as too specialized and risky to offer much of a profit opportunity.

[6]National Research Council, *Toward a National Research Network* (Washington, DC, National Academy Press, 1988), especially pp. 25-37.

[7]FCCSET or Federal Coordinating Council for Science, Engineering, and Technology, *The Federal High Performance Computing Program*, Washington, DC, OSTP, Sept. 8, 1989.

[8]S. 1067, "The National High-Performance Computer Technology Act of 1989," May 1989, introduced by Mr. Gore. Hearings were held on June 21, 1989. H.R. 3131, "The National High-Performance Computer Technology Act of 1989," introduced by Mr. Walgren.

However, companies have gained early experience with new technologies and applications by participating in university R&D; it is for this reason that industry has jointly funded the creation and development of NSFNET.

Various specialized value-added common carriers offer packet-switched services. They could in principle provide some of the same services that the NREN would provide, such as electronic mail. They are not, however, designed to meet the capacity requirements of researchers, such as transferring vast files of supercomputer-generated visualizations of weather systems, simulated airplane test flights, or econometric models. Nor can common carriers provide the "reach" to all carriers.

States

The interests of States in research, education, and economic development parallel Federal concerns. Some States have also invested in information infrastructure development. Many States have invested heavily in education and research networking, usually based in the State university system and encompassing, to varying degrees, private universities, State government, and industry. The State is a "natural" political boundary for network financing. In some States, such as Alabama, New York, North Carolina, and Texas, special initiatives have helped create statewide networks.

Industry Users

There are relatively few industry users of the internet; most are very large R&D-intensive companies such as IBM and DEC, or small high-technology companies. Many large companies have internal business and research networks which link their offices and laboratories within the United States and overseas; many also subscribe to commercial services such as MCI Mail. However, these proprietary and commercial networks do not provide the internet's connectivity to scientists or the high bandwidth and services so useful for research communications. Like universities and national labs, companies are a part of the Nation's R&D endeavor; and being part of the research community today includes being "on" the internet. Appropriate industry use of the NREN should encourage interaction of industry, university, and government researchers, and foster technology transfer. Industry

internet users bring with them their own set of concerns such as cost accounting, proper network use, and information security. Other non-R&D companies, such as business analysts, also are likely to seek direct network connectivity to universities, government laboratories, and R&D-intensive companies.

Federal

Three strong rationales—support of mission and basic science, coordinating a strategic national infrastructure, and promotion of data-networking technology and industrial productivity—drive a substantial, albeit changing, Federal involvement. Another more modest goal is to rationalize duplication of effort by integrating, extending, and modernizing existing research networks. That is in itself quite important in the present Federal budgetary environment. The international nature of the network also demands a coherent national voice in international telecommunications standardization. The Internet's integration with foreign networks also justifies Federal concern over the international flow of militarily or economically sensitive technical information. The same university-government-industry linkages on a domestic scale drive Federal interests in the flow of information.

Federal R&D agencies' interest in research networking is to enhance their external research support missions. (Research networking is a small, specialized part of agency telecommunications. It is designed to meet the needs of the research community, rather than agency operations and administrative telecommunications that are addressed in FTS 2000.) The hardware and software communications technologies involved should be of broad commercial importance. The NREN plans reflect national interest in bolstering a serious R&D base and a competitive industry in advanced computer communications.

The dominance of the Federal Government in network development means that Federal agency interests have strongly influenced its form and shape. Policies can reflect Federal biases; for instance, the limitation of access to the early ARPANET to ARPA contractors left out many academics, who consequently created their own grass-roots, lower-capability BITNET.

International actors are also important. As with the telephone system, the internet is inherently international. These links require coordination, for example for connectivity standards, higher level network management, and security. This requirement implies the need for Federal level management and policy.

The NREN in the International Telecommunications Environment

The nature and economics of an NREN will depend on the international telecommunications context in which it develops. Research networks are a leading edge of digital network technologies, but are only a tiny part of the communications and information services markets.

The 1990s will be a predominantly digital world; historically different computing, telephony, and business communications technologies are evolving into new information-intensive systems. Digital technologies are promoting systems and market integration. Telecommunications in the 1990s will revolve around flexible, powerful, "intelligent" networks. However, regulatory change and uncertainty, market turbulence, international competition, the explosion in information services, and significant changes in foreign telecommunications policies, all are making telecommunications services more turbulent. This will cloud the research network's long-term planning.

High-bandwidth, packet-switched networking is at persent a young market in comparison to commercial telecommunications. Voice overwhelmingly dominates other services (e.g. fax, e-mail, on-line data retrieval). While flexible, hybrid voice-data services are being introduced in response to business demand for data services, the technology base is optimized for voice telephony.

Voice communications brings to the world of computer telecommunications complex regulatory and economic baggage. Divestiture of the AT&T regulated monopoly opened the telecommunications market to new entrants, who have slowly gained long-haul market share and offered new technologies and information services. In general, however, the post-divestiture telecommunications industry remains dominated by the descendants of old AT&T, and most of the impetus for service innovations comes from the voice market. One reason is uncertainty about the legal limits, for providing information services, imposed on the newly divested companies. (In comparison, the computer industry has been unregulated. With the infancy of the technology, and open markets, computer R&D has been exceptionally productive.) **A crucial concern for long-range NREN planning is that scientific and educational needs might be ignored among the regulations, technology priorities, and economics of a telecommunications market geared toward the vast telephone customer base.**

POLICY ISSUES

The goal is clear; but the environment is complex, and the details will be debated as the network evolves

There is substantial agreement in the scientific and higher education community about the pressing national need for a broad-reaching, broad-bandwidth, state-of-the-art research network. The existing Internet provides vital communication, research, and information services, in addition to its concomitant role in pushing networking and data handling technology. Increasing demand on network capacity has quickly saturated each network upgrade. In addition, the fast-growing demand is overburdening the current informal administrative arrangements for running the Internet. Expanded capability and connectivity will require substantial budget increases. The current network is adequate for broad e-mail service and for more restricted file transfer, remote logon, and other sophisticated uses. Moving to gigabit bandwidth, with appropriate network services, will demand substantial technological innovation as well as investment.

There are areas of disagreement and even broader areas of uncertainty in planning the future national research network. There are several reasons for this: the **immaturity** of data network technology, services, and markets; the Internet's nature as strategic **infrastructure** for diverse users and institutions; and the uncertainties and complexities of overriding **telecommunications** policy and economics.

First, the current Internet is, to an extent, an experiment in progress, similar to the early days of the telephone system. Technologies, uses, and potential markets for network services are still nascent.

Patterns of use are still evolving; and a reliable network has reached barely half of the research community. Future uses of the network are difficult to identify; each upgrade over the past 15 years has brought increased value and use as improved network capacity and access have made new applications feasible.

The Internet is a conglomeration of networks that grew up ad hoc. Some, such as ARPANET, CSNET, and MFENET, were high-quality national networks supported by substantial Federal funding. Other smaller networks were built and maintained by the late-night labors of graduate students and computer centers operators. One of these, BITNET, has become a far-reaching and widely used university network, through the coordination of EDUCOM and support of IBM. The Internet has since become a more coherent whole, under Federal coordination led by NSF and DARPA and advised by the Internet Activities Board. Improvements in service and connectivity have been astounding. Yet the patchwork nature of the Internet still dominates; some campus and regional networks are high quality and well maintained; others are lower speed, less reliable, and reach only a few institutions in their region. Some small networks are gatewayed into the Internet; others are not. This patchwork nature limits the effectiveness of the Internet, and argues for better planning and stronger coordination.

Second, the network is a strategic infrastructure, with all the difficulties in capitalizing, planning, financing, and maintaining that seem to attend any infrastructure.[9] Infrastructures tend to suffer from a "commons" problem, leading to continuing underinvestment and conflict over centralized policy. By its nature the internet has many diverse users, with diverse interests in and demands on the network. The network's value is in linking and balancing the needs of these many users, whether they want advanced supercomputer services or merely e-mail. Some users are network-sophisticated, while many users want simple, user-friendly communications. This diversity of users complicates network planning and management. The scope and offerings of the network must be at least sketched out before a management structure appropriate to the desired mission is established.

Third, the network is part of the telecommunications world, rampant with policy and economic confusion. The research community is small, with specialized data needs that are subsidiary to larger markets. It is not clear that science's particular networking needs will be met.

Planning Amidst Uncertainty

Given these three large uncertainties, there is no straightforward or well-accepted model for the "best" way to design, manage, and upgrade the future national research network. Future network use will depend on cost recovery and charging practices, about which very little is understood. These uncertainties should be accommodated in the design of network management as well as the network itself.

One way to clarify NREN options might be to look at experiences with other infrastructures (e.g., waterways, telephones, highways) for lessons about how different financing and charging policies affect who develops and deploys technology, how fast technology develops, and who has access to the infrastructure. Additionally, some universities are beginning trials in charging for network services; these should provide experience in how various charging practices affect usage, technology deployment and upgrading, and the impacts of network use policies on research and education at the level of the institution.

Table 3-1 lists the major areas of agreement and disagreement in various "models" of the proper form of network evolution.

Network Scope and Access

Scope

Where should an NREN reach: beyond research-intensive government laboratories and universities to all institutions of higher education? high schools? nonprofit and corporate labs? Many believe that eventually— perhaps in 20 years—de facto data networking will provide universal linkage, akin to a sophisticated phone system.

[9]Congressional Budget Office, *New Directions for the Nation's Public Works*, September 1988; National Council on Public Works Improvement, *Fragile Foundations: A Report on America's Public Works*, Washington, DC, February 1988.

Table 3-1—Principal Policy Issues in Network Development

Major areas of agreement	Major areas of disagreement and uncertainty
Scope and access	
1. The national need for a broad state-of-the-art research network that links basic research, government, and higher education.	1a. The exact scope of the NREN; whether and how to control domestic and foreign access.
	1b. Hierarchy of network capability. Cost and effort limit the reach of state-of-the-art networking; an "appropriate networking" scenario would have the most intensive users on a leading edge network and less demanding users on a lower-cost network that suffices for their needs. Where should those lines be drawn, and who should draw them? How can the Federal Government ensure that the gap between leading edge and casual is not too large, and that access is appropriate and equitable?
Policy and management structure	
2. The need for a more formal mechanism for planning and operating the NREN, to supersede and better coordinate informal interagency cooperation and ad hoc university and State participation, and for international coordination.	2a. The form and function of an NREN policy and management authority; the extent of centralization, particularly the role of Federal Government; the extent of participation of industry users, networking industry, common carriers, and universities in policy and operations; mechanisms for standard setting.
Financing and cost recovery	
3. The desirability of moving from the current "market-establishing" environment of Federal and State grants and subsidies, with services "free" to users, to more formal cost recovery, shifting more of the cost burden and financial incentives to end users.	3a. How the transition to commercial operations and charging can and should be made; more generally, Federal-private sector roles in network policy and pricing; how pricing practices will shape access, use, and demand.
Network use	
4. The desirability of realizing the potential of a network; the need for standards and policies to link to information services, databases, and nonresearch networks.	4a. Who should be able to use the network for what purposes, and at what entry cost; the process of guiding economic structure of services, subsidies, price of for multi-product services; intellectual property policies.

SOURCE: Office of Technology Assessment, 1989.

The appropriate breadth of the network is unlikely to be fully resolved until more user communities gain more experience with networking, and a better understanding is gained of the risks and benefits of various degrees of network coverage. A balance must be struck in network scope, which provides a small network optimized for special users (such as scientists doing full-time, computationally intensive research) and also a broader network serving more diverse users. The scope of the internet, and capabilities of the networks encompassed in the internet, will need to balance the needs of specialized users without diluting the value for top-end and low-end users. NREN plans, standards, and technology should take into account the possibility of later expansion and integration with other networks and other communities currently not linked up. After-the-fact technical patches are usually inefficient and expensive. This may require more government participation in standard-setting to make it feasible for currently separated communities, such as high schools and universities, to interconnect later on.

Industry-academic boundaries are of particular concern. Interconnection generally promotes research and innovation. Companies are dealing with risk of proprietary information release by maintaining independent corporate networks and by restricting access to open networks. How can funding and pricing be structured to ensure that for-profit companies bear an appropriate burden of network costs?

Access

Is it desirable to restrict access to the internet? Who should control access? Open access is desired by many, but there are privacy, security, and commercial arguments for restricting access. Restricting access is difficult, and is determined more by access controls (e.g., passwords and monitoring) on the computers that attach users to the network, than by the network itself. Study is needed on whether and how access can be controlled by technical fixes within the network, by computer centers attached to the network, informal codes of behavior, or laws.

Another approach is not to limit access, but minimize the vulnerability of the network—and its information resources and users—to accidents or malice. In comparison, essentially anyone who has a modest amount of money can install a phone, or use a public phone, or use a friend's phone, and access the national phone system. However, criminal, fraudulent, and harassing uses of the phone system are illegal. Access is unrestricted, but use is governed.

Controlling International Linkages

Science, business, and industry are international; their networks are inherently international. It is difficult to block private telecommunications links with foreign entities, and public telecommunications is already international. However, there is a fundamental conflict between the desire to capture information for national or corporate economic gain, and the inherent openness of a network. Scientists generally argue that open network access fosters scientifically valuable knowledge exchange, which in turn leads to commercially valuable innovation.

Hierarchy of Network Capability

Investment in expanded network access must be balanced continually with the upgrading of network performance. As the network is a significant competitive advantage in research and higher education, access to the "best" network possible is important. There are also technological considerations in linking networks of various performance levels and various architectures. There is already a consensus that there should be a separate testbed or research network for developing and testing new network technologies and services, which will truly be at the cutting edge (and therefore also have the weaknesses of cutting edge technology, particularly unreliability and difficulty of use).

Policy and Management Structure

Possible management models include: federally chartered nonprofit corporations, single lead agencies, interagency consortium, government-owned contractor operations, commercial operations; and Tennessee Valley Authority, Atomic Energy Commission, the NSF Antarctic Program, and Fannie Mae. What are the implications of various scenarios for the nature of traffic and users?

Degree of Centralization

What is the value of centralized, federally accountable management for network access control, traffic management and monitoring, and security, compared to the value of decentralized operations, open access and traffic? There are two key technical questions here: to what extent does **network** technology limit the amount of control that can be exerted over access and traffic content? To what extent does technology affect the strengths and weaknesses of centralized and decentralized management?

Mechanisms for Interagency Coordination

Interagency coordination has worked well so far, but with the scaling up of the network, more formal mechanisms are needed to deal with larger budgets and to more tightly coordinate further development.

Coordination With Other Networks

National-level resources allocation and planning must coordinate with interdependent institutional and mid-level networking (the other two legs of networking).

Mechanisms for Standard Setting

Who should set standards, when should they be set, and how overarching should they be? Standards at some common denominator level are absolutely necessary to make networks work. But excessive standardization may deter innovation in network technology, applications and services, and other standards.

Any one set of standards usually is optimal for some applications or users, but not for others. There are well-established international mechanisms for formal standards-setting, as well as strong international involvement in more informal standards development. These mechanisms have worked well, albeit slowly. Early standard-setting by agencies and their advisers accelerated the development of U.S. networks. In many cases the early established standards have become, with some modification, de facto national and even international standards. This is proving the case with ARPANET's protocol suite, TCP/IP. However, many have complained that agencies' relatively precipitous and closed standards determination has resulted in less-than-satisfactory standards. NREN policy should embrace standards-setting. Should it, however, encourage wider participation, especially by industry, than has been the case? U.S. policy must balance the need for international compatibility with the furthering of national interests.

Financing and Cost Recovery

How can the capital and operating costs of the NREN be met? Issues include subsidies, user or access charges, cost recovery policies, and cost accounting. As an infrastructure that spans disciplines and sectors, the NREN is outside the traditional grant mechanisms of science policy. How might NREN economics be structured to meet costs and achieve various policy goals, such as encouraging widespread yet efficient use, ensuring equity of access, pushing technological development while maintaining needed standards, protecting intellectual property and sensitive information while encouraging open communication, and attracting U.S. commercial involvement and third-party information services?

Creating a Market

One of the key issues centers around the extent to which deliberate creation of a market should be built into network policy, and into the surrounding science policy system. There are those who believe that it is important that the delivery of network access and services to academics eventually become a commercial operation, and that the current Federal subsidy and apparently "free" services will get academics so used to free services that there will never be a market. How do you gradually create an information market, for networks, or for network-accessible value-added services?

Funding and Charge Structures

Financing issues are akin to ones in more traditional infrastructures, such as highways and waterways. These issues, which continue to dominate infrastructure debates, are Federal private sector roles and the structure of Federal subsidies and incentives (usually to restructure payments and access to infrastructure services). Is there a continuing role for Federal subsidies? How can university accounting, OMB circular A-21, and cost recovery practices be accommodated?

User fees for network access are currently charged as membership/access fees to institutions. End users generally are not charged. In the future, user fees may combine access/connectivity fees, and use-related fees. They may be secured via a trust fund (as is the case with national highways, inland waterways, and airports), or be returned directly to operating authorities. A few regional networks (e.g., CICNET, Inc.) have set membership/connectivity fees to recover full costs. Many fear that user fees are not adequate for full funding/cost recovery.

Industry Participation

Industry has had a substantial financial role in network development. Industry participation has been motivated by a desire to stay abreast of data-networking technology as well as a desire to develop a niche in potential markets for research networking. It is thus desirable to have significant industry participation in the development of the NREN. Industry participation does several things: industry cost sharing makes the projects financially feasible; industry has the installed long-haul telecommunications base to build on; and industry involvement in R&D should foster technology transfer and, generally, the competitiveness of U.S. telecommunications industry. Industry in-kind contributions to NSFNET, primarily from MCI and IBM, are estimated at $40 million to $50 million compared to NSF's 5 year, $14 million budget.[10] It is anticipated that the value of industry cost sharing (e.g., donated switches, lines, or software) for NREN would be on the order of hundreds of millions of dollars.

---

[10]Eliot Marshal, "NSF Opens High-Speed Computer Network," *Science*, p. 22.

Network Use

Network service offerings (e.g., databases and database searching services, news, publication, and software) will need some policy treatment. There need to be incentives to encourage development of and access to network services, yet not unduly subsidize such services, or compete with private business, while maintaining quality control. Many network services used by scientists have been "free" to the end user.

Economic and legal policies will need to be clarified for reference services, commercial information industry, Federal data banks, university data resources, libraries, publishers, and generally all potential services offered over the network.[11] These policies should be designed to encourage use of services, while allowing developers to capture the potential benefits of network services and ensure legal and economic incentives to develop and market network services.

Longer Term Science Policy Issues

The near-term technical implementation of the NREN is well laid out. However, longer-term policy issues will arise as the national network affects more deeply the conduct of science, such as:

- patterns of collaboration, communication and information transfer, education, and apprenticeship;
- intellectual property, the value and ownership of information;
- export control of scientific information
- publishing of research results
- the "productivity" of research and attempts to measure it
- communication among scientists, particularly across disciplines and between university, government, and industry scientists.
- potential economic and national security risks of international scientific networking, collaboration, and scientific communication;
- equity of access to scientific resources, such as facilities, equipment, databases, research grants, conferences, and other scientists. (Will a fully implemented NREN change the concentration of academic science and Federal funding in a limited number of departments and research universities, and of corporate science in a few large, rich corporations; what might be the impacts of networks on traditional routes to scientific priority and prestige?)
- controlling scientific information flow. What technologies and authority to control network-resident scientific information? How might these controls affect misconduct, quality control, economic and corporate proprietary protection, national security, and preliminary release of tentative or confidential research information that is scientifically or medically sensitive?
- cost and capitalization of doing research; to what extent might networking reduce the need for facilities or equipment?
- oversight and regulation of science, such as quality control, investigations of misconduct, research monitoring, awarding and auditing of government grants and contracts, data collection, accountability, and regulation of research procedures.[12] Might national networking enable or encourage new oversight roles for governments?
- the access of various publics to scientists and research information;
- the dissemination of scientific information, from raw data, research results, drafts of papers through finished research reports and reviews; might some scientific journals be replaced by electronic reports?
- legal issues, data privacy, ownership of data, copyright. How might national networking interact with trends already underway in the scientific enterprise, such as changes in the nature of collaboration, sharing of data, and impacts of commercial potential on scientific research? Academic science traditionally has emphasized open and early communication, but some argue that pressures from competition for research grants and increasing potential for commercial value from basic research have

---

[11]OMB, Circular A-130, 50 Federal Register 52730 (Dec. 24, 1985); A-130. H.R. 2381, The Information Policy Act of 1989, which restates the role of OMB and policies on government information dissemination.

[12]U.S. Congress, Office of Technology Assessment, *The Regulatory Environment for Science*, OTA-TM-SET-34 (Washington, DC: U.S. Government Printing Office, February 1986).

dampened free communication. Might networks counter, or strengthen, this trend?

Technical Questions

Several unresolved technical challenges are important to policy because they will help determine who has access to the network for what purposes. Such technical challenges include:

- standards for networks and network-accessible information services;
- requirements for interface to common carriers (local through international);
- requirements for interoperability across many different computers;
- improving user interfaces;
- reliability and bandwidth requirements;
- methods for measuring access and usage, to charge users that will determine who is most likely to pay for network operating costs; and
- methods to promote security, which will affect the balance between network and information vulnerability, privacy, and open access.

Federal Agency Plans: FCCSET/FRICC

A recently released plan by the Federal Research Internet Coordinating Committee (FRICC) outlines a technical and management plan for NREN.[13] This plan has been incorporated into the broader FCCSET implementation plan. The technical plan is well thought through and represents further refinement of the NREN concept. The key stages are:

Stage 1: upgrade and interconnect existing agency networks into a jointly funded and managed T1 (1.5 Mb/s) National Networking Testbed.[14]

Stage 2: integrate national networks into a T3 (45 Mb/s) backbone by 1993.

Stage 3: push a technological leap to a multigigabit NREN starting in the mid-1990s.

The proposal identifies two parts of an NREN, an operational network and networking R&D. A service network would connect about 1,500 labs and universities by 1995, providing reliable service and rapid transfer of very large data streams, such as are found in interactive computer graphics, in apparent real time. The currently operating agency networks would be integrated under this proposal, to create a shared 45Mb/s service net by 1992. The second part of the NREN would be R&D on a gigabit network, to be deployed in the latter 1990s. The first part is primarily an organizational and financial initiative, requiring little new technology. The second involves major new research activity in government and industry.

The "service" initiative extends present activities of Federal agencies, adding a governance structure which includes the non-Federal participants (regional and local networking institutions and industry), in a national networking council. It formalizes what are now ad-hoc arrangements of the FRICC, and expands its scale and scope. Under this effort, virtually all of the Nation's research and higher education communities will be interconnected. Traffic and traffic congestion will be managed via priority routing, with service for participating agencies guaranteed via "policy" routing techniques. The benefits will be in improving productivity for researchers and educators, and in creating and demonstrating the demand for networks and network services to the computing, telecommunications, and information industries.

The research initiative (called stage 3 in the FCCSET reports) is more ambitious, seeking support for new research on communications technologies capable of supporting a network that is at least a thousand times faster than the 45Mb/s net. Such a net could use the currently unused capabilities of optical fibers to vastly increase effective capability and capacity, which are congested by today's technology for switching and routing, and support the next generation of computers and communications applications. This effort would require a substantial Federal investment, but could invigorate the national communication technology base, and boost the long-term economic competitiveness of

---

[13]FRICC, *Program Plan for the National Research and Education Network*, May 23, 1989. FRICC has members from DHHS, DOE, DARPA, USGS, NASA, NSF, NOAA, and observers from the Internet Activities Board. FRICC is an informal committee that grew out of agencies' shared interest in coordinating related network activities and avoiding duplication of resources. As the de facto interagency coordination forum, FRICC was asked by NSF to prepare the NREN program plan.

[14]See also *NYSERNET NOTE*, vol. 1, No. 1, Feb. 6, 1989. NYSERNET has been awarded a multimillion-dollar contract from DARPA to develop the National Networking Testbed.

the telecommunications and computing industries. The gigabit network demonstration can be considered similar to the Apollo project for communications technologies, albeit on a smaller and less spectacular scale. Technical research needed would involve media, switches, network design and control software, operating systems in connected computers, and applications.

There are several areas where the FRICC management plan—and other plans—is unclear. It calls for, but does not detail any transition to commercial operations. It does not outline potential structures for long-term financing or cost recovery. And the national network council's formal area of responsibility is limited to Federal agency operations. While this scope is appropriate for a Federal entity, and the private sector has participated influentially in past Federal FRICC plans, the proposed council does not encompass all the policy actors that need to participate in a coordinated national network. The growth of non-Federal networks demonstrates that some interests—such as smaller universities on the fringes of Federal-supported R&D—have not been served. The FRICC/FCCSET implementation plan for networking research focuses on the more near-term management problems of coordinated planning and management of the NREN. It does not deal with two extremely important and complex interfaces. At the most fundamental level, the common carriers, the network is part of the larger telecommunications labyrinth with all its attendant regulations, vested interests, and powerful policy combatants. At the top level, the network is a gateway into a global information supermarket. This marketplace of information services is immensely complex as well as potentially immensely profitable, and policy and regulation has not kept up with the many new opportunities created by technology.

The importance of institutional and mid-level networking to the performance of a national network, and the continuing fragmentation and regulatory and economic uncertainty of lower-level networking, signals a need for significant policy attention to coordinating and advancing lower-level networking. While there is a formal advisory role for universities, industry, and other users in the FRICC plan, it is difficult to say how and how well their interests would be represented in practice. It is not clear what form this may take, or whether it will necessitate some formal policy authority, but there is need to accommodate the interests of universities (or some set of universities), industry research labs, and States in parallel to a Federal effort. The concerns of universities and the private sector about their role in the national network are reflected in EDUCOM's proposal for an overarching Federal-private nonprofit corporation, and to a lesser extent in NRI's vision. The FRICC plan does not exclude such a broader policy-setting body, but the current plan stops with Federal agency coordination.

Funding for the FRICC NREN, based on the analysis that went into the FCCSET report, is proposed at $400 million over 5 years, as shown below. This includes all national backbone Federal spending on hardware, software, and research, which would be funneled through DARPA and NSF and overseen by an interagency council. It includes some continued support for mid-level or institutional networking, but not the value of any cost sharing by industry, or specialized network R&D by various agencies. This budget is generally regarded as reasonable and, if anything, modest considering the potential benefits (see table 3-2).[15]

NREN Management Desiderata

All proposed initiatives share the policy goal of increasing the nation's research productivity and creating new opportunities for scientific collaboration. As a technological catalyst, an explicit national NREN initiative would reduce unacceptably high levels of risk for industry and help create new markets for advanced computer-communications services and technologies. What is needed now is a sustained Federal commitment to consolidate and fortify agency plans, and to catalyze broader national involvement. The relationship between science-oriented data networking and the broader telecommunications world will need to be better sorted out before the NREN can be made into a partly or fully commercial operation. As the engineering challenge of building a fully national data network is surmounted, management and user issues of economics, access, and control of scientific information will rise in importance.

---

[15]For example, National Research Council, *Toward a National Research Network* (Washington, DC: National Academy Press, 1988), pp. 28-31.

Table 3-2—Proposed NREN Budget ($ millions)

	FY90	FY91	FY92	FY93	FY94
FCCSET Stage 1 & 2 (upgrade; NSF)	14	23	55	50	50
FCCSET Stage 3 (gigabit+; DARPA)	16	27	40	55	60
Total	30	50	95	95	110
S. 1067 authorization	50	50	100	100	100
HR. 3131 authorization	50	50	100	100	100

SOURCE: Office of Technology Assessment, 1989.

The NREN is a strategic, complex infrastructure which requires long-term planning. Consequently, network management should be stable (insulated from too much politics and budget vagaries), yet allow for accountability, feedback, and course correction. It should be able to leverage funding, maximize cost efficiency, and create incentives for commercial networks. Currently, there is no single entity that is big enough, risk-protected enough, and regulatory-free enough to make a proper national network happen. While there is a need to formalize current policy and management, there is concern that setting a strong federally focused structure in place might prevent a move to a more desirable, effective, appropriate management system in the long run.

There is need for greater stability in NREN policy. The primary vehicle has been a voluntary coordinating group, the FRICC, consisting of program officers from research-oriented agencies, working within agency missions with loose policy guidance from the FCCSET. The remarkable cooperation and progress made so far depends on a complex set of agency priorities and budget fortunes, and continued progress must be considered uncertain.

The pace of the resolution of these issues will be controlled initially by the Federal budget of each participating agency. While the bulk of the overall investment rests with midlevel and campus networks, it cannot be integrated without strong central coordination, given present national telecommunications policies and market conditions for the required network technology. The relatively modest investment proposed by the initiative can have major impact by providing a forum for public-private cooperation for the creation of new knowledge, and a robust and willing experimental market to test new ideas and technologies.

For the short term there is a clear need to maintain the Federal initiative, to sustain the present momentum, to improve the technology, and coordinate the expanding networks. The initiative should accelerate the aggregation of a sustainable domestic market for new information technologies and services. These goals are consistent with a primary purpose of improving the data communications infrastructure for U.S. science and engineering.

L

High-Performance Computing: An Overview,
**U.S. Congress, Congressional Research Service,
December 18, 1990.**

High-Performance Computing: An Overview

Updated December 18, 1990

by
Stephen Gould
Science Policy Research Division

CONTENTS

High-Performance Computing:
An Overview

SUMMARY

Interest in high-performance computing grew rapidly during the 1980s within the international research and development community. High-performance computing is now widely considered to be a "keystone" technology -- one which supports advances in many areas of science and technology that, in turn, will likely have a large impact on future national competitiveness. The use of supercomputers, mini-supercomputers and graphics supercomputers is becoming common in major academic, Government, and industrial laboratories. While the United States currently leads the world in development and use of high-performance computer technology, foreign competitors are working diligently to catch up.

The Federal Government continues to play a leading role in the development of high-performance computing. Los Alamos National Laboratory, Lawrence Livermore National Laboratory, and other Federal laboratories are avid users of each new generation of supercomputers and major contributors to the software libraries serving supercomputer users. Research and development (R&D) programs funded by the National Science Foundation, the National Aeronautics and Space Administration, the National Institute of Standards and Technology, and the Departments of Defense and Energy are steadily advancing state-of-the-art software development, computer architectures, and high-speed networks. Federal spending related to development of high-performance computing science and technology is estimated to total $490 million in FY1991, an increase of 10% over FY1990 spending.

On Sept. 8, 1989, the White House Office of Science and Technology Policy (OSTP) submitted to Congress its 5-year program plan for support of high-performance computing and networking. The plan calls for a federally coordinated Government, industry, and university effort to accelerate the rate at which high-performance computing hardware and software and high-speed computer networks are developed and deployed. The plan also calls for additional Federal spending of $1.9 billion over a 5-year period for related education, facilities, networks and R&D. The timeframe and commitment for carrying out the plan are uncertain, subject to overarching budget constraints and securing necessary high-level approvals. Separate legislation considered by the 101st Congress (S. 1067 and H.R. 3131) called for a comparable effort to enhance and expand high-performance computing activities in the United States.

Questions to be addressed in evaluating Federal policies in this area include: What are the strengths and weaknesses of the U.S. supercomputer industry? How are U.S. companies doing vis-a-vis their foreign competitors? What priority is given to increased expenditures on high-performance computing and networks by industry, the research community, and pertinent Federal agencies in relation to other needs and programs? What mechanisms can be employed to ensure that computing and network resources are allocated to academic users efficiently and fairly?

ISSUE DEFINITION

Since 1983 the Federal Government has been actively promoting the widespread use of high-performance computers within the academic research community. Federal support for R&D on high-performance computers and for computer networks serving academic researchers began in the 1960s. A program plan drawn up in 1989 by the White House Office of Science and Technology Policy (OSTP) and legislation now being considered by Congress both propose to add substantial new resources to programs designed to bolster the development and use of high-performance computer technology and networks in order to maintain U.S. leadership in these areas. Issues related to these current proposals include the challenge posed by foreign high-performance computing capabilities, the priority that research networks and high-performance computing should be given relative to other research, education, and competitiveness needs, and what policy mechanisms can most effectively channel Federal support to academic computing and networks.

BACKGROUND AND ANALYSIS

"High-performance computing" is an activity made possible by a collection of technologies and resources, including computer hardware, software, communication networks, data bases, data collection instruments, and human-and computer-based expertise. The activity itself, however, employs whatever combination of such resources is necessary to solve highly complex, numerically intensive problems in the shortest possible period of time. An example is the calculation of wind resistance dynamics for a new automobile body design. Speed of computation depends on selecting an appropriate computer architecture for the problem to be solved, and using software optimized for both the problem and the architecture.

Interest in high-performance computing grew rapidly during the 1980s within the international research and development community. Supercomputers have proved to be powerful scientific and engineering tools that permit the solution of otherwise intractable problems and provide the means for making new discoveries and innovations. The use of supercomputers, mini-supercomputers and graphics supercomputers is becoming common in major academic, Government, and industrial laboratories. As a result, scientists and engineers are saving thousands of hours of computing time by using supercomputers to run their programs as much as 80 times faster than on conventional mainframes. High-performance computing has also opened up whole new territories of analytical exploration in such diverse areas as animal breeding, astrophysics, biomedicine, climate change studies, economics, materials and device engineering, and product design and testing.

High-performance computing is now widely considered to be a "keystone" or "enabling" technology that supports advances in many areas of science and technology that, in turn, may have a large impact on future national economic competitiveness. Accordingly, State governments and individual universities have begun to purchase their own high-performance computers in order to stay at the leading edge of science and technology and attract top researchers and innovation-oriented industry. In addition to the four supercomputer centers that continue to receive partial support from the National Science Foundation (NSF), at least 30 State and local centers are in operation. These include the Universities of Alabama, California, Colorado State, Florida, Georgia, Kentucky, Minnesota, Mississippi, Ohio State, Purdue, Texas, Utah and MIT, which have supercomputers connected with local or statewide networks. Most of these supercomputer facilities offer at least some access to industry, including small and medium-size businesses. NSF estimates that more than 11,000 professors, graduate students, and other researchers in academia are now using the supercomputer centers it supports. Using telephone lines or computer networks, it is now possible for academic scientists and engineers to gain remote access to at least 40 general purpose supercomputers, including some of the machines located within Department of Energy (DOE) and National Aeronautics and Space Administration (NASA) laboratories.

Primarily because the high-performance computers provide an alternative to expensive physical experimentation and prototyping, use of supercomputers has also been steadily growing among industrial researchers in a variety of commercial sectors. Virtually all major automobile companies now use supercomputers to help in the design of new models, most major oil companies employ them for geological exploration, and chemical and pharmaceutical companies have begun to put them to work modeling molecules or delving into problems in biotechnology.

High-Performance Computing Hardware

The overall driving force for creation of high-performance hardware options is the diversity of specific scientific and engineering application requirements. These requirements, in turn, create demands for computer designers and manufacturers to maximize speed, optimize utility, and optimize cost-effectiveness for different types of applications. No one computer is yet capable of simultaneously meeting these objectives for all applications. As a result, a diverse and expanding array of computing machines (described below) are being used to support high-performance computing needs. It is important to keep in mind that the "peak performance" of any particular supercomputer is the maximum speed of computation that can be obtained. The actual performance of a supercomputer can vary considerably and depends on a variety of factors, including the type of computing problem, and the sophistication of the algorithms (computational rules), software structure, and individual user.

General Purpose Supercomputers

Manufactured by Cray Research, Convex Computer, IBM, Fujitsu, Hitachi, and NEC, these machines offer a combination of high speed and flexibility. They are designed to perform well on a large variety of applications. Peak performance for general purpose machines ranges from several hundred million floating point operations per second (megaflops) to several billion floating point operations per second (gigaflops). General purpose supercomputers have become faster over the past few years mainly through use of parallel processing, which divides computing problems into parts that are handled simultaneously by a number of processors within each machine. For example, the Cray Y-MP has eight processors, and a machine being developed by Supercomputer Systems (with financial and technical backing from IBM) is expected to use 64 processors. General purpose supercomputers are generally the most expensive, ranging in price from about $1 million to over $25 million.

Massively Parallel Supercomputers

Manufactured by Thinking Machines, Ncube, Intel Scientific Computers, Myrias Computer, Active Memory Technology, and iP Systems KG, these supercomputers contain between 100 and 65,000 small processors in either single-instruction, multiple-data (SIMD) or multiple-instruction, multiple-data (MIMD) architectures. They divide a problem into pieces handled by each processor, and are particularly suited to applications that require relatively simple analysis of millions or billions of pieces of data, such as image processing, database searching, and analysis of fluid dynamics. They range in price from $250,000 to $20 million, and can operate at speeds equal to or greater than general purpose supercomputers. Intel's Touchstone Delta system, for example, performs at a rate of up to 32 gigaflops.

Mini-Supercomputers

Manufactured by a growing number of companies, these machines offer a fraction of full-scale supercomputing performance at an even smaller fraction of the cost. Peak performance is generally between 20 megaflops and 200 megaflops, and prices are mostly between $100,000 and $1,000,000. Their attractive price- performance ratio and relatively low price range have attracted many new users to supercomputing, including small and mid-sized companies. Given that faster machines are often only available to researchers in a shared-use mode with many other users, some scientists and engineers prefer to have dedicated use of a minisupercomputer even if their applications take 10 or 20 times longer to run.

Graphics Supercomputers

These machines increasingly have performance comparable to mini-supercomputers, or even low-end general purpose supercomputers, but are specially designed to run visualization software. Visualization techniques allow researchers to convert the numerical output of computer models into pictures that make it easier to analyze and understand the phenomena that the numbers describe. Graphics supercomputers are often used to process the numerical output of programs run on other types of supercomputers.

Special Purpose Supercomputers

For some applications, high performance can be attained at the lowest cost by building computing machines whose architecture and components are optimized to run just one type of application. For example, a machine designed to solve a particular category of differential equations in mathematical physics can be built in about the same time, and at the same expense, as it takes to prepare the software required for this application to run well on a general purpose supercomputer. Some customized machines can run through certain kinds of calculations faster than on any general purpose supercomputer. Scientists traditionally have been intimately involved in the design of their data collection instruments. While not common, the design of special purpose computers is becoming part of scientific instrument building for some scientists.

Software

Software is the set of program instructions used to direct computer operations. Software design is an important determinant of the efficiency and speed of high-performance computers. It is often stated that a shortage of software is hindering the full exploitation of currently available supercomputers. While this software "bottleneck" or "lag time" may be especially pronounced in the area of high-performance computing, it is a longstanding problem afflicting virtually the entire spectrum of computing machines -- from the latest personal computers to new engineering workstations to virtually every supercomputer now in use. This situation persists despite significant progress in software development technologies.

Factors that limit software availability for high-performance computing include:

-- **Diversity of machine architectures being employed** -- What works well on one supercomputer does not necessarily work well or at all on another model. While software "portability" between machines within some categories of high-performance machines has improved, there is nothing resembling the portability associated with the universe of IBM-compatible personal computers or mainframes.

-- **Increasing use of parallel architectures** -- A parallel program differs from a sequential one as radically as a parallel computer differs from its sequential counterpart. A sequential program does one thing at a time, whereas a parallel program must create, manage, coordinate and ultimately pull together many simultaneous threads of activity. Parallel programming, which often requires brand-new approaches to creating data structures and algorithms, is still in its infancy.

-- **Demands of scientific and engineering computation** -- Much scientific and engineering software is application specific, unique, and not portable between machines. This means that to exploit high-performance computing in their research, many users must devote substantial time and effort to learning how to create their own software, and developing, validating, and maintaining it.

While software availability continues to be a problem, there are signs of improvement. Standardized versions of FORTRAN (the dominant programming language), improved FORTRAN optimized compilers, and the adoption of UNIX as a common operating system by many supercomputer manufacturers are making it easier to both develop high-performance computing software and to move applications from the machine of one manufacturer to that of another. Expanding broad-spectrum libraries of algorithms optimized for each manufacturer's systems are also aiding the application development process.

Applications

The primary benefit of increasingly powerful high-performance computers is more realistic simulations of complex phenomena -- with applications throughout the realm of science and technology. Technologists who design composite materials, chemicals, biologically derived substances, complex structures and machines, or electronic devices are increasingly adopting high-performance computing as a primary tool. Scientists seeking fundamental new knowledge in a variety of disciplines are also turning to computational experiments performed on supercomputers to tackle once intractable problems. Prominent applications include: investigation of superconducting materials; semiconductor design; design of drugs; understanding the human genome and the molecular basis for disease; automotive design; aerospace design; enhancement of oil and gas recovery; and prediction of weather, climate, and global change.

Several proposed large-scale science projects, from the superconducting supercollider and large array radio telescopes to the Earth Observation System satellite project, would create torrential new data flows that would demand more powerful information management and processing systems. Research areas in the so-called "grand challenges" of science and engineering, such as fluid flow modelling, modelling of long term weather patterns, and the structural analysis of proteins, require substantially more powerful technologies for data processing, communication, and storage than are currently available.

Networks

Since state-of-the-art supercomputers are expensive, high-performance computing often involves gaining remote access to centralized facilities via computer networks. In 1985, NSF launched NSFNET to facilitate remote access to NSF-funded supercomputer centers by the academic research community. NSFNET has subsequently become the core of a rapidly developing "internet" which links a number of governmental, private and international research networks. Twelve regional networks in the United States now connect to the high-speed interstate transmission lines maintained by NSF. Local-area networks within more than 1,000 colleges, universities, and other institutions, in turn, connect researchers with the regional networks. The internet has become the primary pathway used by academic researchers to connect to supercomputers not located on their campus.

The Federal Research Internet Coordinating Committee (FRICC), a collaboration of the Defense Advanced Research Projects Agency (DARPA), DOE, Department of Health and Human Services (DHHS), NASA, and NSF has begun transforming the present internet into a National Research and Education Network (NREN) in order to provide a distributed computing capability that links the Government, industry, and higher education communities. The carrying capacity of the network, currently 1.5 million bits per second (megabits), can be used in two ways: to handle the aggregate volume of transmissions that individually do not require high speed, or to provide ultrafast communications for such applications as interactive supercomputer use, image file transfer, and transfer of very large data files. While both types of traffic make use of NSFNET's capacity, support of high-performance computing is not currently its dominant use.

Current Federal Initiatives

On Sept. 8, 1989, OSTP submitted to Congress its 5-year program plan for support of high-performance computing and networks. The plan calls for a federally coordinated Government, industry, and university collaboration to accelerate the rate at which high-performance computing hardware and software and high speed computer networks are developed and deployed. Total Federal spending for related education, facilities, networks and R&D would be doubled over the 5-year period -- from approximately $490 million per year to about $1 billion per year. The timeframe and commitment for carrying out the plan are uncertain, subject to overarching budget constraints and securing necessary high-level approvals.

Key elements of current Federal support for high-performance computing research include four national supercomputing centers supported by NSF, broad support of basic research and human resource development by NSF's Computer and Information Science and Engineering directorate, DARPA's Strategic Computing program, and various advanced computational science research facilities sponsored by DOE and NASA. The current research internet is tied together by Federal transcontinental computer networks, including the NSF's NSFNET, DOD's ARPANET and MILNET, DOE's ESNET, and NASA's Science Network, that are interconnected to each other and to many other commercial and regional networks. Progress toward national goals is coordinated among Federal agencies through the Committee on Computer Research and Applications of the Federal Coordinating Council on Science, Engineering and Technology.

OSTP's program plan contains four interdependent, complementary program components, categorized as high performance computing systems, advanced software technology and algorithms, national research and education network, and basic research and human resources. The plan seeks to:

-- Support computational advances through R&D oriented towards addressing major scientific and technological challenges;

-- Increase the use of high-performance computing by reducing the risks to industry for R&D and encouraging cooperation among Government, industry, and academia;

-- Continue use of Government-funded facilities as a market for new, leading-edge commercial high-performance computing products;

-- Support the necessary research, network and computational infrastructures on which U.S. high-performance computing capabilities are based; and

-- Support the necessary human resource base.

High-Performance Computing Systems

The current goal of research programs is to support the development of computing systems capable of sustaining trillions of floating-point operations per second on significant problems. This will require developing a new technology base through a program of research in computer architectures, microelectronics and packaging, and associated systems software. The DARPA Strategic Computing program, DOE, and NASA plan to increase funding for the industry/university partnerships that have established U.S. leadership in highly parallel, high-performance computing systems. One result of previous funding is the advanced parallel computer commercialized by Thinking Machines Corporation. NSF, NASA, DOE, and DOD (including DARPA, the Army Research Office, the Office of Naval Research, and the Air Force Office of Scientific Research) will share responsibility for long-range research on the foundations of high-performance systems. For example, NSF is providing funding to a Science and Technology Center jointly operated by Rice University, California Institute of Technology, Argonne National Laboratory, and Los Alamos National Laboratory that is exploring more effective applications of parallel architectures.

Advanced Software Technology and Algorithms

The OSTP plan emphasizes that the ability to exploit high-performance computing technology to address problems of competitive and national importance is determined primarily by software capability. A current focus of Federal support for software research related to high-performance computing is the development of basic tools, languages, algorithms, and associated computational theory to enable solution of "Grand Challenge" application problems in science and engineering. As defined by OSTP, a Grand Challenge is "a fundamental problem in science or engineering, with potentially broad economic, political, and/or scientific impact, that could be advanced by applying high-performance computing resources." DOE, NASA, NSF, NOAA, and DARPA share responsibility for clearly defining the computational requirements of the Grand Challenges, and selecting applications areas in which collaborative groups are to be formed. Software research expected to have broad impact on software productivity and on systems capability and reliability will also be supported.

The National Research and Education Network

This national computer network will seek to broadly support communication among individuals and organizations involved in open research and scholarly pursuits in the United States. NREN's first stage, now complete, involved upgrading the existing research internet to 1.5 megabits per second for all primary telecommunication links. The second stage would provide upgraded network services to 200 to 300 research facilities, using a shared backbone network with 45 megabit per second capacity. Research and development for a third stage would be carried out during the period of the 5-year plan, but actual deployment would be anticipated at a later date. This stage would provide one to three gigabit per second networking service to selected research facilities, and 45 megabit per second networking to approximately 1,000 sites nationwide. Deployment of this third stage might coincide with a transition from Government sponsorship of the NREN to commercial network service paid for by users. NSF has assumed responsibility for overseeing the operation of NREN, upgrading and extending the network, providing advanced network services, and promoting the development of collaboration technology. DARPA is the lead agency for supporting advanced networking technology research and development.

Basic Research and Human Resources

A significant constraint hindering broad progress in high-performance computing is a shortage of personnel in computing technology and in computational science and engineering. OSTP's plan therefore calls for: upgrading 10 university computer science departments toward the standards of the current ten best departments; upgrading an additional 25 computer science departments to nationally competitive quality; sponsoring the creation of at least ten interdisciplinary computational science and engineering programs in universities; and attaining a level of 1,000 new computer science Ph.D.s per year by 1995. Related goals include expanding support for basic research in computing technology, improving the facilities available to support basic research and advanced education, and improving linkages between computing technology and other science and engineering disciplines.

Congressional Initiatives

Congress has shown substantial interest in the health and progress of high-performance computing since the early 1980s. Recognizing the pivotal role played by supercomputers and networks within the U.S. infrastructure for science and technology, Congress has been quite supportive of related Federal programs and activities given that budgetary pressures have been increasing steadily throughout the decade. Support for high-performance computing has been closely linked in congressional thinking with fostering U.S. competitiveness in high-technology industries and responding to powerful economic/technological challenges from abroad.

Legislation considered by the 101st Congress (S. 1067 and H.R. 3131) would have provided explicit authority for expanding Federal support for research, development, and application of high-performance computer technology and research networks in the United States. The National High-Performance Computer Technology Act -- initially introduced in the 100th Congress -- would have authorized the Federal Government to establish a high-capacity research and education computer network; develop an information infrastructure of data bases, services, and knowledge banks to be available for access over the network; promote increased development and distribution of computer software; accelerate the development of high-performance computer systems; and expand relevant basic research and education programs. The Act would have authorized additional appropriations of $1.75 billion over a 5-year period for these activities, and required an annual report from the Federal Coordinating Council for Science, Engineering, and Technology summarizing the achievements and progress of related Federal efforts during the preceding year. S. 1067 was passed by the Senate, but not by the House. Nevertheless, Congress approved an increase of almost 10% for spending on high-performance computing initiatives for FY1991. Legislation based on S. 1067 is likely to be introduced in the 102nd Congress.

Issues

It is difficult to independently ascertain the health of high-performance computer and network technology development in the United States, or assemble a knowledge base upon which sound budgetary decisions can be made. Much has been written about the importance of these technologies, and this reflects broad support in principle within industry, Government, and academia for Federal investments in high-performance computing and networking. However, there is a dearth of in-depth, objective analyses of current Federal (and private sector) programs and expenditure levels, what they are accomplishing, and what can be expected in the future under alternative spending options.

There is also inadequate definition of the linkages and dependencies between science and technology that can be expected to lead to advances in high-performance computing and networking and a much broader set of research and development activities related to electronics, computers, and telecommunications. While they demonstrate specialized architectures and some specialized features, high-performance systems to a large extent are the sum of a diverse array of generic component technologies. For example, massively parallel computers use many of the same components found in mass-production personal computers. It is thus difficult to separate out the technology base or prospects for high-performance systems from progress in the electronics industry as a whole.

Questions to be addressed in evaluating Federal policies in this area are multifaceted. What are the strengths and weaknesses of the U.S. supercomputer industry? How are U.S. companies doing vis-a-vis their foreign competitors? What priority is to be given to increased expenditures on high-performance computing and networks by industry, the research community and pertinent Federal agencies in relation to other needs and programs? What current Federal programs contribute to progress in high-performance computing and networks? What policy mechanisms can be employed to ensure that computing and network resources are allocated to academic users efficiently and fairly? What benefits have compensated network sponsors to date for their investments? To what extent has Federal sponsorship of research networks helped or hindered the development of commercial network services? The remainder of this section seeks to highlight the context for some of these questions.

Foreign Competition

In the view of some observers -- including a subcommittee of the Institute of Electrical and Electronics Engineers -- the United States runs a serious risk of losing its supercomputer industry to Japan. Over the past decade, Japan has devoted considerable effort to developing state-of-the-art, high-performance computers. The competitive position of the three leading Japanese manufacturers of supercomputers is bolstered by the fact that they are also among the world's leading manufacturers of semiconductors. As vertically integrated electronics manufacturing giants, Fujitsu, Hitachi, and NEC, each dwarf their non-IBM supercomputer competitors in size and resources. The three Japanese firms primarily produce single-processor machines based on individual processors more powerful than any U.S. manufacturer is expected to deliver in the foreseeable future. Multi-processor versions of Japanese machines expected to become available in 1991 may far outstrip the performance of the best U.S. general purpose supercomputers. The vulnerability of U.S. manufacturers is seen to be intensified by a substantial reliance on Japanese semiconductors.

Despite the apparent strength of the Japanese challenge, U.S. manufacturers continue to dominate the high-performance computing market. IBM's vector facility, while notably slower (800 megaflops) than some competing machines, has sold more units worldwide than other U.S. and Japanese manufacturers combined. Among the faster machines, Cray Research has more installations than the Japanese manufacturers combined. U.S. mini-supercomputer manufacturers, led by Convex Computer and Alliant Computer Systems, are preeminent in meeting the high-performance computing demand among customers unable or unwilling to buy high-end supercomputers costing millions of dollars. U.S. manufacturers are also preeminent in producing massively parallel supercomputers, which are expected to indefinitely retain leadership in achieving the highest speeds if software technology can keep up. For both practical and political reasons, Japanese supercomputers have been virtually shut out of the U.S. market to date -- two of the three Japanese supercomputers now located in the United States are owned by a Norwegian company. By contrast, more than 50 IBM-3090 series mainframe computers with vector facilities are in use in Japan, along with 17 Cray, 2 Control Data/ETA, and about 110 Japanese supercomputers.

Academic High-Performance Computing and Networking

Use of the NSFNET and the research internet by individual researchers is currently not constrained by any individual budget because network costs are directly paid by network sponsors. At least partly because there is no way to charge individual users or meter individual usage, demand for network capacity has been steadily growing by as much as 40% per month. Users have little incentive to use network resources efficiently, nor is there incentive to use alternate communication services even if alternatives ultimately cost research sponsors less per unit of service. Both to control overall network costs and to facilitate a transition from Government and private subsidies to commercial service, a major challenge is to implement a system to allocate costs to users in proportion to the amount of network services they use.

Allocation of high-performance computer resources has given rise to a similar problem. It has long been a rule-of-thumb for academic researchers to "use whatever machine you can get your hands on." However, there is widespread resistance to using shared systems if individually controlled high-performance computers are available. Accordingly, demand for access to supercomputer centers is generally the greatest among those who have no alternative either because their research demands the most powerful machines or because the power of other computers they have access to is grossly inadequate. In some cases, researchers can now obtain time on expensive general purpose supercomputers more easily than access to less expensive scientific workstations or mini-supercomputers, and use such time for problems not requiring the full power of the supercomputer. Conversely, some researchers make do with less powerful machines even though they could benefit substantially from using more powerful systems.

Robert Kahn, president of the Corporation for National Research Initiatives, has argued that researchers need to be provided with the freedom to choose among various computing and network alternatives, and the ability to pay the full costs of the alternative chosen. Essentially, this would entail allowing users to operate within a free market with funds secured through the normal mechanisms available for obtaining research support. A major obstacle is that this approach would require fairly uniform cooperation from a diverse array of research support agencies in giving academic computer and network users the additional funds they need to pay for whatever resources best meet their needs.

Funding Priority Within the Research Community

A plethora of important new or ongoing research initiatives are currently competing for "new money" that is in chronically short supply. The task of upgrading the high-performance computing infrastructure could claim a high relative priority as a recognized prerequisite for the success of other major science and technology initiatives now being considered. However, it is not clear what degree of priority is given to high-performance computing by agencies such as DARPA, DOE, NASA, and NSF relative to their other programs and initiatives. It is also uncertain what priority various segments of the research community place on high-performance computing relative to their other interests. In a zero-sum fiscal environment, the broad support being voiced for expanded funding for computing and networks could quickly dissipate.

It is difficult to judge the merit of allocating additional resources to high-performance computing without an adequate understanding of the impact of current programs and expenditure levels, and of what a substantially increased allocation of resources will accomplish. Little documentation is available on how budgets for high-performance computing are spent each year by DARPA, DOE, NASA, and NSF and what results are being obtained. No projections have been made of what progress can be made if future funding does not increase.

Impact of National Research and Education Network

Networking advocates assert that continuing development of NREN will provide a means of increasing the effectiveness of the U.S. research community through remote access to powerful resources and new capabilities for collaboration. However, there is little empirical evidence on the nature and extent of a network's ability to enhance the research process and increase research productivity. Many claims about existing and proposed research networks are characterized by enthusiasm and idealism either not documented by empirical studies, or documented with narrow anecdotes about very successful high-profile users.

The computer networks used by the research community have been developed within the public sector, or on an ad hoc basis by their users. There has been little opportunity for private sector vendors of network services to compete with these research networks since the subsidies enjoyed by users are not available for purchasing services from commercial vendors. For example, a primary use of the research networks is for electronic mail. Electronic mail services supplied by commercial vendors are used extensively by private industry, but are only rarely used by academia. There has been no opportunity for commercial network vendors to bid for the business of academia in a manner similar to the way vendors of long-distance telephone services compete for university customers. Continuing development of subsidized computer networks by Government and ad hoc organizations might serve to constrain the availability of flexible, broadband data communications services on the public switched telecommunications network useful to a broader segment of potential customers (e.g., small and medium-sized businesses and nonprofit organizations).

Exercising Federal Leadership

Because it is an enabling technology with broad economic impact, there is widespread interest in doubling Federal spending on high-performance computing in order to further boost U.S. competitiveness. Since Federal programs related to high-performance computing are scattered among various departments, agencies, and components, responsibility for oversight and funding of research and development activities is distributed among a number of committees and subcommittees within the U.S. Congress. As is the case with other crosscutting R&D topics relevant to national competitiveness, efforts to specifically adjust the level of resources directed toward achieving national goals will depend on a high degree of consensus among Federal agencies and congressional committees.

OSTP emphasizes that its program plan is for planning purposes only and does not necessarily imply agreement on funding priorities at either the agency level or Presidential level. If one or more agencies choose not to seek increased funding for high-performance computing, or if other budget priorities preclude approval of agency budget increases by the Executive Office of the President, the additional resources called for in OSTP's 5-year plan may not materialize.

To the extent that congressional committees are interested in allocating additional resources to high-performance computing and networking in the absence of Federal agency requests, getting such resources to the diverse relevant programs is problematic. Jurisdiction for authorizing legislation for DOD, DOE, NASA, and NSF is splintered. Choosing one lead agency empowered to allocate new resources among the various Federal programs may simplify congressional action, but could trigger counterproductive "turf battles" within the executive branch. The National Institute of Standards and Technology within the Department of Commerce was given a charter by Congress in 1988 to act as a catalyst for technology development, but is considered by many to be ill-equipped to perform that role.

LEGISLATION

H.R. 3131 (Walgren)
National High-Performance Computer Technology Act of 1989. Provides for a coordinated Federal research program to ensure continued United States leadership in high-performance computing. Introduced Aug. 3, 1989; referred to Committee on Science, Space, and Technology (Subcommittee on Science, Research, and Technology). Hearings held Oct. 3, 1989, and Mar. 15, 1990.

H.R. 4329 (Roe)
American Technology Preeminence Act. Provides for enhancing the position of U.S. industry through application of the results of Federal research and development, including a national high performance computer technology program. Introduced Mar. 21, 1990; referred to Committees on Science, Space, and Technology and on the Judiciary. Reported, with amendment, June 14, 1990 (H.Rept. 101-481). Passed House, amended, July 11, 1990. S. 1191 Passed in lieu, July 11, 1990.

S. 1067 (Gore)
National High-Performance Computer Technology Act of 1989. Provides for a coordinated Federal research program to ensure continued United States leadership in high-performance computing. Introduced May 18, 1989; referred to Committee on Commerce, Science, and Transportation (Subcommittee on Science, Technology, and

Space).   Hearings held June 21, July 26, and Sept. 15, 1989.   Reported, with amendment, July 23, 1990 (S.Rept. 101-387). Passed Senate, Oct. 15, 1990.

S. 1191 (Hollings)
Technology Administration Authorization Act of 1989. Authorizes appropriations for Department of Commerce's Technology Administration. Introduced June 15, 1989; referred to Committee on Commerce, Science, and Transportation. House incorporated H.R. 4329 as an amendment. Passed House July 11, 1990.

S. 1976 (Johnston)
DOE National High-Performance Computer Technology Act of 1989. Provides for continued United States leadership in high-performance computing. Introduced Nov. 21, 1989; referred to Committee on Energy and Natural Resources. Hearings held, Mar. 6, 1990. Reported July 19, 1990 (S.Rept. 101-377).

CONGRESSIONAL HEARINGS, REPORTS, AND DOCUMENTS

U.S.   Congress.   House.   Committee on Science and Technology.   American Technology Preeminence Act. Report, 101st Congress, 2d session. May 10, 1990. Washington, U.S. Govt. Print. Off., 1990. 88 p.

U.S. Congress. House. Committee on Science and Technology. Subcommittee on Science, Research, and Technology. High performance computing. Hearing, 101st Congress, 1st session. Oct. 3, 1989. Washington, U.S. Govt. Print. Off., 1989. 173 p.

----- U.S. supercomputer industry. Hearing, 101st Congress, 1st session. June 20, 1989. 140 p.

U.S.   Congress.   Senate.   Committee on Commerce, Science, and Transportation. Subcommittee on Science, Technology, and Space.   Computer networks and high-performance computing.   Hearings, 100th Congress, 2d session. Aug. 11, 1988. Washington, U.S. Govt. Print. Off., 1988. 146 p.

----- National High-Performance Computer Technology Act of 1989, S. 1067. Hearings, 101st Congress, 1st session. June 21, July 26, and Sept. 15, 1989. Washington, U.S. Govt. Print. Off., 1990. 413 p.

U.S.   Congress.   Senate.   Committee on Commerce, Science, and Transportation. High-Performance Computing Act of 1990. Report, 101st Congress, 2d session. July 23, 1990. Washington, U.S. Govt. Print. Off., 1990. 33 p.

U.S. Congress. Senate. Committee on Energy and Natural Resources. Department of Energy. High-Performance Computing Act of 1990. Report, 101st Congress, 2d session. July 19, 1990. Washington, U.S. Govt. Print. Off., 1990. 27 p.

FOR ADDITIONAL READING

Executive Office of the President. Office of Science and Technology Policy. The Federal high performance computing program. Sept. 10, 1989. [Washington] 1989.

National Academy of Sciences. Committee on Science, Engineering, and Public Policy. Information technology and the conduct of research: the user's view. Washington, National academy press, 1989.

National net '88 double issue: public and private initiatives to create a national education and research network. Educom bulletin, v. 23, nos. 2 (summer) and 3 (fall), 1988: 2-72.

National Research Council. Computer Science and Technology Board. Toward a national research network. Washington, National academy press, 1988.

The next computer revolution (special issue). Scientific American, v. 57, no. 4, October 1987: 56-169.

The world in a grain of silicon. The economist, v. 311, no. 7606, June 10, 1989: 79-80, 82.

U.S. Congress. Office of Technology Assessment. High performance computing and networking for science (background paper). Washington, U.S. Govt. Print. Off., 1989.

U.S. Library of Congress. Congressional Research Service. Building the national research education network, by Stephen Gould. [Washington] 1990.
       CRS Issue Brief 90126

----- The Federal research internet and the national research and education network: prospects for the 1990s, by Stephen Gould. July 26, 1990.
       CRS Report 90-362

M

The Federal Research Internet and the National Research and Education Network: Prospects for the 1990s,
U.S. Congress, Congressional Research Service, July 26, 1990.

Stephen Gould
Analyst in Information Science and Technology
Science Policy Research Division

July 26, 1990

THE FEDERAL RESEARCH INTERNET AND THE NATIONAL RESEARCH AND EDUCATION NETWORK: PROSPECTS FOR THE 1990'S

SUMMARY

The Federal Research Internet is a loosely organized system of interconnected, unclassified computer networks that links over 100,000 computers nationwide and overseas. The Internet, which began in 1969 as an experimental prototype network called ARPANET, has come to play an integral role within the research community. It includes research networks funded by Federal agencies as well as scores of local and regional networks that use common data communication protocols. The Internet supports a vast, multi-disciplinary community of researchers within government, universities, and industry, including physicists, electrical engineers, mathematicians, medical researchers, chemists, astronomers, computer scientists, and social scientists. It allows users of any one of the thousands of computers it connects to reach any other user and have access to distant resources such as supercomputers and scientific databases.

Today's Internet is far from providing uniformity in the type and quality of service provided to users, and despite its size does not yet reach the entire research and education community. While compatibility among component networks has been steadily increasing, many of the networks currently being used are still fragmented into separate operational regimes. To remedy such weaknesses, continued evolution of the Internet until it becomes a user-friendly, unified high-speed research network with nationwide coverage is envisioned by Federal sponsors and academic participants.

Plans for transforming the Internet into a National Research and Education Network (NREN) are moving forward under the leadership of the National Science Foundation (NSF), the White House Office of Science and Technology Policy (OSTP), and the Federal Networking Council. The Council is a collaboration of the NSF, the Defense Advanced Research Projects Agency, the Department of Energy, the National Aeronautics and Space Administration, and the Department of Health and Human Services that oversees operation of the Internet. While not formally a part of OSTP's Federal Coordinating Council on Science, Engineering and Technology (FCCSET) structure, the Federal Networking Council works closely with the FCCSET Committee on Computer Research and Applications in conducting its activities.

Federal leadership and funding have played a significant role in the development of the research networks and computational resources to be linked within the NREN. Policy issues of continuing importance to Congress as this infrastructure takes shape are likely to include the setting of investment priorities for Federal funds; assuring equitable access among various classes of users; resolving intellectual property rights issues as they pertain to electronic information management and dissemination; weighing the extent of international linkages; balancing public sector and private sector roles in development, financing and management of the NREN; and evaluating its long-term impacts related to science, technology, education, and commerce. In the near term, the relationship of the NREN to the interests of the U.S. telecommunications and information industries is likely to demand Congressional attention.

CONTENTS

THE FEDERAL RESEARCH INTERNET AND THE NATIONAL RESEARCH AND EDUCATION NETWORK: PROSPECTS FOR THE 1990'S

INTRODUCTION

If information maintained in electronic or digital form is the lifeblood of the "information age," then interconnected computer networks are surely becoming primary circulatory systems that nourish the health of business, science, and technology. Electronic information holds substantial advantages over printed information in that it is more economical to manage and store, can be searched more effectively, can be retrieved quickly without going to another location, and can be moved around easily. Computer networks that are national or international in reach are fast becoming an essential means of exploiting these inherent advantages. While isolated computers offer their users powerful ways of processing information, extensive interconnection of computers is a prerequisite for obtaining the full benefits associated with managing information in electronic or digital formats.

This report will provide a brief overview of the continuing evolution of the primary computer network structures serving the U.S. academic research community. The development of a national electronic information infrastructure for science and technology--with common resources ranging from databases to telescopes and supercomputer facilities--is an ongoing process that is similar to, parallels, and is encouraged by the development of computer networks serving scientists, engineers, and other academic disciplines. Development of academic computer networks and the larger electronic infrastructure have been substantially aided by research and operational support provided by various Federal agencies.

Information technology is now often defined as the combination of computer technology and telecommunications technology that makes possible computation, communication, and the storage, retrieval and processing of information. In the academic research community, information technology now includes:

o computer hardware of all kinds, from microprocessors dedicated to specific operations to the most powerful supercomputers;
o communications networks that link, through their computers, scientists, engineers, and other professionals to each other and to resources of various kinds; and
o computer software that researchers use to design and run projects, collect and analyze data, and manage the information that the projects yield.

Extensive use of these tools is rapidly changing the conduct of science, engineering, and other disciplines. It has steadily reduced constraints of speed, cost, and distance associated with data collection and analysis, modeling of complex phenomena, communication and collaboration among researchers, and information storage and retrieval.[1] Computer networks play a central role in obtaining each of these benefits, and in facilitating Federally-supported research and development activities. In recognition of these contributions, legislation has been introduced in Congress that would authorize a significant expansion in Federal support for research, development, and application of high-performance computers, and expansion and enhancement of computer networks serving the research and education communities.

Anatomy of a Network

A computer network is a set of computers communicating by common conventions called protocols over communications media. Both local and long distance communication between computers generally takes place over telephone lines, while communication within a university or research center is often routed over a dedicated wiring system. One type of network, known as a circuit switch network, allows computer-to-computer linkages that are analogous to a telephone connection that carries one conversation. Another, known as a packet-switch network, can accommodate many conversations at once. The academic research community has tended to favor use of packet-switch networks.

Computers that are linked by a network are called network nodes, and those that people use directly are called hosts. There may also be special computers whose purpose is to serve as packet switches that transfer packets around the network. Two or more networks may be interconnected by a special host called a gateway, router, bridge, or repeater. Computer network protocols usually involve the exchange of discrete units of information called messages over some form of physical medium, such as coaxial cable, fiber optic cable, microwaves, or a twisted pair of copper wires. Routes between computers must be kept up-to-date, time must be synchronized, and reliability must be ensured. Any combination of communications media can be employed in the same network.

In packet switch networks, messages are broken into small chunks of equal size called packets, and then interleaved with data packets from other sources on the same telecommunications channel. Routed through switching centers as an independent entity, a packet is temporarily stored at each node until an output link becomes available to forward it to the next node along the way to its destination. Packets are reassembled for presentation only at their final destination. The software modules that make routing choices (based on address and other information contained within each packet) are kept abreast of traffic conditions on the network by their own electronic exchanges. Since this process utilizes the entire communications channel bandwidth of the packet switch network, the cost per message is generally

---

[1] National Academy of Sciences, Committee on Science, Engineering, and Public Policy. Information Technology and the Conduct of Research: The User's View. Washington, National Academy Press, 1989. p. 11-30.

less than that associated with circuit switch networks where, because computers tend to generate and exchange information in intermittent bursts, a dedicated circuit may be idle during much of the connection time.

Demand for Wide-area Network Services

Advancements in information technology fuel a number of trends related to data collection and analysis that in turn encourage increased use of wide-area computer networks among researchers. Growth in the amount of information that researchers can electronically or digitally store and analyze with their individual workstations has substantially increased the demand for direct electronic access to central, large-scale data repositories with holdings such as seismic studies, weather data, genetic information, and data from space exploration missions. Creation of new families of computer-controlled instruments and machines has opened up enticing opportunities to widely share such resources through remote control and interaction. Examples of computer-controlled facilities include the Berkeley-Illinois-Maryland Millimeter Array telescope in Hat Creek, California, and the Continuous Electron Beam Accelerator being built in Newport News, Virginia. The development of regional centers housing expensive high-performance computers requires the availability of high-quality wide-area networks to maximize the distribution of benefits of these expensive resources within the research community. The users of the four supercomputer centers funded by the National Science Foundation (NSF) as well as the supercomputers housed at more than 30 state and local facilities benefit substantially from network access.

Use of computer networks is contagious, and in itself fuels greater demand. The more researchers that are introduced to the opportunities associated with computer networks and obtain connections, the greater the value inherent in network access. Increased connectivity among researchers and computational resources breeds greater demand for network access which, when fulfilled, breeds further demand. The most popular network function to date, and thus a major factor fueling network growth, is electronic mail (e-mail). E-mail, the process of sending text from one computer user to another over the network, is partially replacing written and telephone communication within many research communities. Accordingly, networks have become a primary channel for conversation and for repeated exchanges of text, data, and software files.[2] In the future, e-mail system users are expected to be able to convey information with integrated text, sound, graphics and video.

Growth in demand for wide-area networks is also a reflection of new interdependencies within and among universities, government agencies, and private industry. A broad consensus favoring increased efforts to promote effective technology transfer among these sectors serves to promote greater communication and collaboration between them. To maintain national competitiveness, it has become increasingly important to share scientific and

---

[2] National Academy of Sciences, op. cit., p. 2.

technical developments as they happen in fields such as opto-electronics, biotechnology, and superconductivity. As a high-speed conduit for such information, wide-area networks are recognized as both facilitating the conduct of research and the transfer of research to those who develop and use technology.

Development of the Internet

The network of computer networks known as the Internet originated with the development of the ARPANET, an experimental network established in 1969 by the Defense Advanced Research Projects Agency (DARPA). With ARPANET, DARPA sought to demonstrate the potential of computer networking based on packet-switching technology that allows many users to economically share a single communication channel. In the 1970's, DARPA sponsored several additional networks and supported the development of a set of rules and procedures for addressing and routing messages across separate networks so that they could be linked together. Called the "Internet protocols," these rules and procedures provided a universal language allowing electronic messages to be sent across multiple interconnected networks.

In the 1980's the number of networks attached to ARPANET grew as technological advances facilitated network connections. ARPANET had become so heavily used by 1983 that the Department of Defense split off operational traffic associated with military research and development programs onto a separate network known as MILNET. In recognition of the exploding demand for network services, DARPA officials also sought to shift the burden of serving general academic research needs away from the Department of Defense.

Beginning in 1985, the National Science Foundation (NSF) assumed responsibility within the Federal government for coordinating the development of the Internet. Since then, NSF has actively worked to foster the creation of networks serving the academic research community, to interconnect the networks serving various segments of the research community, and to build expanded data communication capacity to better serve research needs. In 1986, NSF began funding a backbone network called NSFNET in order to provide remote access to its supercomputer centers. Regional and local area campus networks are linked to NSFNET's interstate backbone to connect researchers at more than 220 colleges and universities. Regional networks include partial-statewide networks like the Bay Area Regional Research Network in northern California, statewide networks like the New York State Educational Research Network, and multistate networks like the Southern Universities Research Association Network.

Other Federal agencies also operate networks on the Internet to support their missions, including the Department of Energy (HEPNET, MFENET, and ESNET), the Department of Health and Human Services, and the National Aeronautics and Space Administration (NASNET and SPAN). This loosely organized confederation of Federal, regional, and local networks, which use the Internet protocols, make up the current Internet. The Internet now supports a vast, multidisciplinary community of researchers within government, universities, and industry, including physicists, electrical engineers, mathematicians, medical researchers, chemists, astronomers, economists, computer scientists, and social scientists.

The Internet's evolution from a prototype network to a large-scale multinetwork has accelerated rapidly in the 1980's. In late 1983, the Internet was comprised of about 50 networks. By January 1990, the number had grown to over 1000. The number of host computers connected to the Internet has grown from about 200 in 1982 to over 20,000 in early 1987 and over 100,000 by the end of 1989. NSF estimates that about one million researchers are active users of the academic networks that are connected to the Internet. Funding for Internet operations comes from the five Federal agencies involved in operating research networks and from universities, States, and private companies involved in operating and participating in local and regional networks and the NSFNET backbone.[3] While Federal funding plays a key role, a substantially greater share of financial support for Internet operations comes from the non-Federal sources of funding. A Federal Networking Council, operating under the auspices of the White House Office of Science and Technology Policy, coordinates the functioning and integration of agency networks at the Federal level. However, management of the Internet is decentralized, residing primarily at the host site and individual network levels.[4]

Researchers and educators currently use the Internet and other networks for a variety of functions:

o   Electronic mail (e-mail) and electronic publishing.
o   Software and data file transfer/exchange.
o   Graphics and image file transfer.
o   Remote computer access (interactive and batch) to supercomputers and other specialized research instruments.
o   Remote access to computerized databases.[5]

---

[3] NSFNET is operated with contributions of funds and/or services from NSF, the State of Michigan, IBM, and MCI. Regional networks are operated with the support of various types of public and private sector partnership arrangements.

[4] U.S. General Accounting Office. Report to the Chairman, Subcommittee on Telecommunications and Finance, Committee on Energy and Commerce, House of Representatives. Computer Security: Virus Highlights Need for Improved Internet Management. June 1989.

[5] For an expanded discussion of network applications, see National Research Council. Computer Science and Technology Board. Toward a National Research Network. Washington: National Academy Press, 1988.

Not all individual academic networks are currently equally suited for or even capable of each of these applications. Actual network uses, therefore, depend on which network an individual user is connected to.

The National Research and Education Network

Today's Internet is far from providing uniformity in the type and quality of service provided to users, and despite its size does not yet reach the entire research and education community. While compatibility among networks has been steadily increasing, many of the networks currently being used are still fragmented into separate operational regimes. Communication options are often limited in terms of the kinds of computer equipment, systems, and applications that can use the networks effectively. Interconnection points between some networks are weak if available, thus limiting the extent to which geographically dispersed colleagues can reliably use the networks to communicate and collaborate with each other. Since instruction, documentation, and troubleshooting support for network users are in many cases scarce, the researchers able to most effectively use existing networks are those who have developed a degree of expertise in computer networking technology.

To remedy these weaknesses, continued evolution of the Internet until it becomes a user-friendly, unified high-speed research network with nationwide coverage is envisioned by Federal sponsors and academic participants. Supporters see a truly national research network as one of the elements required to obtain a high performance distributed computation and communication infrastructure that will accelerate the pace of research and technology development in government, academia, and industry. A coordinated research network based on very high capacity links would enable the creation of large-scale geographically distributed research support systems that could link academic researchers with numerous high performance workstations, databases, data generation sources, and the most powerful high-performance computers.

The Federal Networking Council, which includes representatives of DARPA, DOE, HHS, NASA, and NSF, is transforming the Internet into a full-fledged National Research and Education Network (NREN). This is being done through the sharing of communications circuits, network access points, and even entire networks, leading to streamlined operations and reduced costs. The plan developed by the Council calls for the NREN to be developed in three stages. For NREN 1, now nearly complete, the agencies have completed an upgrade of their networks to 1.5 megabit per second (T1) trunks. Under the supervision of DARPA, "policy-based routing" mechanisms are being devised that will allow better interconnection of these trunks. For NREN 2 the agencies will acquire a common set of 45 megabit per second (T3) transcontinental trunks, to be known as the Research Interagency Backbone.

Chapter 3.

When this is fully operational, it will be interconnected with the NSFNET backbone, resulting in an interim NREN that provides upgraded network services to 200 to 300 research institutions. Deployment of NREN 2 is now getting underway and, subject to the availability of funding, is expected to be completed within 5 years. Progress on the development of NREN is being monitored by the Federal Coordinating Council on Science, Engineering and Technology's Committee on Computer Research and Applications.

The NREN concept is based on a fundamental premise of open access to all qualified researchers and scholars. By the time NREN 2 is complete, it is expected that every university and major laboratory will be connected to the NREN through one of the regional networks. It is anticipated that the regional networks will continue to be operated with the financial sponsorship of State and local governments and industry as private and autonomous business entities. NREN 2 technologies are expected to form a base from which commercial providers can offer compatible networking services nationally. Deployment of NREN 3, an operational national network with gigabit-capacity trunks, will include a structured process resulting in transition of the network from a government operation to a commercial service.[6] It is anticipated that deployment of NREN 3 will get underway during the mid-1990's if the necessary technology and funding are available.

Dimensions of the Intellectual Utility

An extensive array of information resources will likely become stitched together by the NREN to form a more cohesive electronic information infrastructure within the United States. Reference databases, which store in electronic formats information that primarily helps researchers find out about printed literature of interest, comprise what may be the most extensive category of resources. These computer-searchable services have expanded enormously over the past twenty-five years. The National Library of Medicine's MEDLINE, the Library of Congress' MARC, the National Agriculture Library's AGRICOLA, and NASA's RECON databases are examples of the reference services that could be integrated into NREN. Increasingly, reference databases are being expanded to include full-text retrieval capabilities. Other reference resources include the U.S. National Technical Information Service which electronically maintains abstracts of unclassified, publicly available reports, software packages and data files from over 300 government agencies related to hundreds of subject areas.

Scientific and engineering data sets found in source databases preserve information and measurements relating to topics of broad common interest to various segments of the research community. For example, GenBank is an

---

[6] For a more complete description of NREN plans and agency responsibilities, see Executive Office of the President, Office of Science and Technology Policy. The Federal High Performance Computing Program. Sept. 10, 1989, [Washington]. p. 31-36.

electronic library of known genetic sequences. Descriptions of the molecular structures of all chemical substances reported in the scientific literature since 1961 are maintained by the Chemical Abstracts Service. The National Oceanic and Atmospheric Administration (NOAA) and NASA have thousands of computer tapes holding data drawn from observations of the earth, the atmosphere, and space. Ongoing and anticipated large-scale data-generation and observational efforts will produce ever larger files that could be made widely available to researchers for analysis through the NREN.

Knowledge banks take a variety of forms, including electronic bulletin boards, ongoing computer conferences, multi-function databases, and expert systems. BIONET, which serves the molecular biology community, offers a research news bulletin board that has become a forum where scientists can post interesting developments and highlight the expertise and research interests of their laboratories for the rest of the electronic community. A service initiated by the Welch Medical Library of the Johns Hopkins University makes available an online gene map along with over 4,300 descriptions of specific disorders and substances related to genetic diseases that are updated every week. Prototype expert systems being developed will assist researchers in interpreting mass spectra of organic molecules, in troubleshooting particle beam lines for high energy physics, in chemical synthesis planning, in planning experiments in molecular genetics, and in automated theory formulation in chemistry, physics, and astronomy.

Software libraries will be a major component of the future U.S. information infrastructure. Such repositories are maintained by various research organizations to support the needs of their community of computer users. In many disciplines, it is common to use standard software packages for certain classes of problems. A key function of the NSF-funded supercomputer centers is to make available large collections of software relating to diverse scientific and engineering supercomputing applications, since few research groups or universities can afford to maintain their own comprehensive libraries. Another type of software library, NASA's AdaNET seeks to promote the principles of software engineering and software reuse by being an authoritative source of information and software "parts" that keep users abreast of new innovations.[7]

Prototyping services such as the Metal Oxide Semiconductor Implementation System (MOSIS) represent yet another type of resource that could be connected to the NREN. MOSIS serves the research community as a broker for commercial silicon foundry services by contracting for the manufacture of custom very large-scale integrated chips. Orders for circuit design that are submitted electronically are batched by MOSIS and sent on to one of several foundries for cost-effective, rapid prototype fabrication.

---

[7] National Aeronautics and Space Administration. Scientific and Technical Information Division. Software Reuse Issues. Washington: NASA Conference Publication 3057, 1989. p. 149, 155.

Sharing of expensive instrumentation is important to many research disciplines and is likely to become more so. A wide variety of facilities provide the experimental apparatus required by groups of scientific collaborators located throughout the country. Many research facilities consist of a single, large, and expensive installation such as a radio telescope, synchrotron light source, wind tunnel, particle accelerator, or supercomputer. Other unique facilities are comprised of computers that host specialized analytic software or unique databases. A primary function of the NREN will be to facilitate access to these unique scientific resources.

Future information infrastructure development efforts may include standardizing, cross-linking, and developing a master index for diverse databases in order to form a universally-accessible digital library system. This could greatly simplify access to information sources from printable documentation to complex data structures from any workstation on the national network. As one step in this direction, a prototype digital data library designed to organize data from large, interdisciplinary science projects is being developed at the National Center for Supercomputer Applications at the University of Illinois.[8] There are also likely to be expanded efforts to incorporate textbook type knowledge in computer-based formats into sophisticated expert systems and comprehensive knowledge banks related to science and technology. Proposals for a network-accessible "electronic transaction framework" would provide a testbed for exploring new ideas in computer-based interactions related to custom design of electronic and optical devices, flexible manufacturing systems, and rapid procurement/bidding systems.[9]

National Collaboratories

The Internet and NREN are providing the technical means to facilitate the operation of a new generation of cohesive "centers without walls"--centers, institutes and laboratories that exist outside of normal organizational structures and without a single geographical location or common administrative structure. In March 1989, a workshop sponsored by NSF's Directorate for Computer and Information Science was convened at Rockefeller University to develop recommendations for a research agenda that would focus on advancing mechanisms to more effectively support remote interaction by researchers with colleagues, instruments and data. Workshop participants envisioned use of high-speed computer networks to support functional "collaboratories" that allow scientists, engineers, and other

---

[8] Waldrop, M. Mitchell. Learning to Drink from a Fire Hose. Science, May 11, 1990. p. 674-5.

[9] U.S. Congress. Senate. Committee on Commerce, Science, and Transportation. Subcommittee on Science, Technology, and Space. Computer Networks and High Performance Computing. Hrgs. 100th Cong., 2nd Sess. Washington, U.S. Govt. Print. Off., 1988. p. 39-41, 44.

professionals to work with remote facilities and each other as if they were co-located. More than just use of network services, a collaboratory would be enabled by a combination of technology, tools and infrastructure that permit the maintenance of an effective, ongoing interface among physically remote colleagues and facilities.[10]

Functions envisioned for collaboratories include fostering interdisciplinary research, managing unique instrumentation, and assembling a critical mass of the factors that contribute to research productivity. To be successful, a collaboratory must allow a geographically dispersed community of researchers to interactively share ideas, data, and instruments with much the same ease as individuals who are collocated now enjoy. Without the constraints of distance, opportunity and choice would determine the composition, size and duration of disciplinary or interdisciplinary research teams. Collaboratories could offer new alternatives for managing and using inherently remote instruments like space telescopes and unmanned deep ocean vehicles. Some of the largest scientific challenges, such as comprehensively documenting and understanding global change, require research efforts that are necessarily distributed among a geographically-dispersed array of researchers, instruments, and databases. To meet such challenges, effective remote interaction will be essential to problem solving.

Research required for the development of collaboratories will focus on integration of existing computer-based/controllable research tools into a unified system architecture, creating smoothly functioning interfaces between such tools, making the enhancements and modifications required to make the tools fully accessible and usable by the research community, and evaluating and improving the degree to which the tools work together to support scientific and engineering research. The component parts of a collaboratory will include software that helps team members to facilitate project organization and management, and coordination of action, joint design, and resource scheduling. General collaborative tools include e-mail systems that perform with increased interoperability, graphics capability, privacy, security, and user support services; electronic file transfer protocols that enable team members to share their results in the form of computer files and engage in cooperative development and analysis activities; and software for the operation of remote facilities and instruments (with access control and authentication for safety and security). Other tools that could enhance research productivity and strengthen interfaces within a collaboratory are listed in Table 1. In addition to specialized instrumentation, hardware components for the collaboratory are envisioned to include high performance workstations equipped with high definition color displays, computer network links capable of conveying information at speeds in excess of 1 billion bits per second, and

---

[10] Towards a National Collaboratory: Report of an Invitational Workshop. Washington: NSF/CISE, 1989. p. 1.

supercomputers with processor power capable of between several billion to several trillion calculations per second.[11]

Getting There from Here

Development of the NREN is taking place amid a much larger set of activities in the United States that seek to integrate computers and telecommunications. In the computer industry, linking and combining diverse hardware and software components into a seamless web of functionality is known as "systems integration." Systems integration is one of the industry's fastest growing services, with $17 billion in total revenue projected for 1990- up from approximately $1 million in 1975.[12] It is estimated that by 1993, 60 percent of all personal computers in the United States will be connected together. Linking computers and communications through digital technology, and integrating voice, data, and video, is rapidly expanding the options available for factory and office automation and consumer electronics.

A fully developed NREN and National Collaboratory each will require monumental systems integration accomplishments. The ultimate goal of the NREN--and many commercial systems integration and telecommunications activities--is to make computer networking "as pervasively available as telephone service is today," with the corresponding ease of inter-computer communication providing benefits to the entire Nation by improving the productivity of all information-handling activities.[13] The vision guiding the National Collaboratory concept is one of achieving seamless access by all scientists, engineers, and other professionals to colleagues, instruments, data, information, and knowledge.[14] While much is being done within government, universities and industry that will contribute to the eventual completion of these electronic infrastructures, much coordinated work remains to be done.

While scientific data and reference databases promise to be significant repositories of knowledge to be accessible through the NREN, there are many practical problems hindering their integration into networks. One obstacle is the current state of information/data storage, management and preservation. In many cases, stored machine-readable data is gradually becoming useless, either because of storage media decay or the storage technology itself is obsolete. Access to data is often problematic. For various reasons, researchers have difficulty getting access to data stored directly by other

---

[11] Towards a National Collaboratory: Report of an Invitational Workshop. op. cit., p. 7.

[12] Wall Street Journal, Dec. 14, 1989, p. B-1.

[13] Executive Office of the President, op. cit., p. 35.

[14] Towards a National Collaboratory: Report of an Invitational Workshop. op. cit., p. 6.

researchers. Even when they get access, they may have trouble reading them in the absence of standardized formats or adequate documentation, and often lack information on the quality of the data. Because of inconsistent formats and retrieval procedures between databases, many searches of even the best commercially maintained databases are incomplete, cumbersome, inefficient, expensive, and executable only by specialists.[15]

Poor interoperability of existing software tools and demand for new software that outstrips production capabilities together create a major obstacle to network based integration of research support systems and tools. Improvements in software and algorithms have become the primary determiners of the power, flexibility, and reliability of computing systems. There is a generalized need for the vast array of existing and emerging knowledge pertaining to software to be codified, unified, distributed, and extended more systematically. Providing better access to information with national online libraries, intelligent user support technologies, intelligent scientific instruments, and increased levels of user friendliness throughout the electronic infosphere will require a steady stream of software innovations.

Relative to the telephone system, today's computer networks are not very easy to use. Principal difficulties with communicating via electronic mail and file transfer technologies involve incompatibility between different text and data processing systems and between network protocols. Network addressing conventions are cumbersome and unhelpful, address locator services are not well established, and overall network availability and reliability is in many cases well below the standards associated with voice networks.

To date, the speed of networks has not nearly kept pace with the increase in the power of computers. Use of supercomputers has introduced capabilities for computational analysis, simulation, and modeling that generate very large data, graphic or video files. Such files cannot be communicated across current research networks in reasonable timeframes. Without higher capacity networks, the speed of data transmission remains a limiting factor in the ability of researchers to carry out complex analyses using remote resources. Greater network speed would reduce the time required to perform a given experiment and increase both the volume of data and the amount of detail that can be seen by researchers.

Congressional Issues

Federal leadership and funding have played a significant role in the development of the research networks and computational resources to be linked within the NREN. To successfully establish universal interoperability among the diverse, expansive array of Federally-sponsored networks, databases, software libraries, research instruments and facilities, supercomputers, and large-scale scientific projects would require a sustained

---

[15] National Academy of Sciences, op. cit., p. 2.

commitment by the Congress and key Federal agencies throughout this decade. To ensure steady progress toward a unified electronic infrastructure in the United States, Congress will need to provide coordinated oversight over not only numerous related initiatives serving the research community, but the process of integrating the resulting research-oriented information collection and management systems into a larger national infrastructure that can serve multiple national needs related to economic development and industrial and service sector productivity.

Several policy issues are likely to be of continuing importance to Congress as the NREN infrastructure takes shape. Periodically reviewing and setting investment priorities for Federal funds may be necessary to ensure that steady progress on diverse infrastructure components is sustained. Priority is currently being given to expansion of telecommunications links for various backbone networks and research on high-speed networking. However, as high-speed network service becomes more widely available to the research and education communities, priority might shift towards making more data collection instruments, databases and knowledge banks maintained or supported by the Federal government accessible through the NREN. Developing a comprehensive digital library system, for example, by itself would be an enormous enterprise requiring substantial Federal participation.

Congress might be called upon to provide guidance on balancing public sector and private sector roles in the development, financing and management of the NREN. While industry has had a substantial role in network development, operation of the Internet has been primarily a public sector enterprise. Representatives of the telecommunications and information industries have urged that creation of a commercial market for delivery of network access and services to academics should be a central focus of NREN policy, and that private industry be given a greater role in developing and managing the network. While the OSTP plan and pending legislation call for a transition of NREN from being a government operation to being a commercial service, some academic network advocates believe it should be kept a public enterprise.

Congress is likely to play a major role in determining the exact scope of the NREN and in assuring equitable access among various classes of users. It has yet to be decided whether the NREN will reach beyond major research universities and government laboratories to all institutions of higher education, high schools, nonprofit and corporate laboratories, or new high-technology entrepreneurs. A balance might have to be struck between providing a network optimized for users doing computationally intensive research and those with more diverse needs. Access and equity questions will be associated with cost recovery policies for various user categories. While open access is desired by many network users, privacy and security concerns (i.e., sabotage) might dictate some type of access controls. A desire to capture information for national economic gain may call into question the extent of international linkages.

Congress might **also** get involved in resolving intellectual property rights issues as they **pertain** to electronic information management and dissemination--which **present** major challenges to those seeking to preserve the economic value of information or assert rights associated with ownership. Copyright issues loom large in considering how to create and manage a comprehensive digital library system. Management of Federal scientific and technical information resources (and other Federal information resources) might deserve timely evaluation in the context of NREN development. Providing extensive electronic access to such resources has the potential to be a valuable NREN asset.

Four legislative proposals are now before Congress that would provide explicit authority for Federal support of the NREN along with support for research, development, and application of high-performance computers. The National High-Performance Computer Technology Act (S. 1067 and H.R. 3131) would authorize the Federal government to take the lead in establishing the NREN and in promoting the development of the information infrastructure of databases, services, and knowledge banks to be available for access over the network. The Act would assign primary responsibility for coordinating the development of the NREN and the associated information infrastructure to the National Science Foundation. The DOE National High-Performance Computer Technology Act (S. 1976) contains similar provisions relating to Department of Energy programs, but would assign responsibility for development of the NREN to the Department. Title VII of the American Technology Preeminence Act (H.R. 4329) emphasizes the role of OSTP's Federal Coordinating Council for Science, Engineering, and Technology in planning the NREN and defining the organizational arrangements to be used for managing its operation.

Involvement by a wide range of Federal agencies and programs will be necessary to fully develop the NREN and the array of scientific and technical resources to be connected to it. A wide variety of authorization and appropriations legislation might include infrastructure components or have policy impacts on network development and use.

CONCLUSIONS

Perhaps the most important prospects for an extensive electronic infosphere involve not the amount of information and knowledge that will become more rapidly accessible, but the availability of tools that help users effectively find and understand the information they seek. With an information overload afflicting many sectors of activity, improved retrieval tools are crucial to the overall success of networking for most users. Among the tools beginning to be developed are knowledge-based systems known as "intelligent assistants" to help users sort through and organize available information, and new methods of presenting observational and computational results as visual images. Devising automated "knowbots" that periodically search multiple databases and digital libraries for needed information and bring it back to their users through the network may be possible within a decade. Success of the NREN will also depend in general on more flexible and intuitive ways for people to interact with, and control, the computers connected to the network.

There are obviously many component parts required to complete the NREN. Many of the technological building blocks are already available and in place. Other necessary tools, technologies and linkages will be developed during the 1990's. The full capabilities now envisioned are not likely to be available until after the year 2000.

NREN and a completed National Collaboratory mechanism ultimately offer the prospect of new ways of finding, understanding, storing, and communicating information, and should increase both the capabilities and the productivity of scientists, engineers, and other professionals. However, these electronic infrastructures represent more than a distributed computational paradise for scientists and engineers. They can be both a testbed for and prototype of an electronic information infrastructure that could be available to every home, office and factory in the United States. The same combination of technology, tools and infrastructure that will allow scientists, engineers, and other professionals to work smarter and more effectively interface with remote colleagues and facilities can also promote greater productivity, flexibility, and innovation in other sectors of the economy and society.

TABLE 1: Collaboratory Infrastructure Tools

o smart agents for the design of experiments, including expert systems for planning, scheduling, coordination, and operation design of experiments;

o smart data gathering tools for intelligent screening and identification of significant data;

o interoperable data description protocols to facilitate multidisciplinary use and analysis of data from multiple sensors and computer models;

o information fusion techniques for overall integration and understanding of data from heterogeneous sources;

o standard file representations for higher level functionality in shared files;

o standardization and adoption of user-friendly formats to facilitate database use;

o multimedia e-mail (graphics, sound, spread sheets, scanned images, full-motion video);

o computer conferencing software to support structured discussions in an open architecture environment;

o real-time computer supported multi-media teleconferencing;

o publication mechanisms for digital technical reports and journals;

o digital libraries with search mechanisms for finding information contained in documents of all types, including software, video, and other "unusual forms" (i.e., linearly-encoded scientific data), within in a distributed database;

o hypertext capabilities that work across local- and wide-area networks;

o protocols that facilitate integration of services over distributed libraries;

o artificial intelligence tools for scanning and recognizing the contents of documents;

o intelligent agents or "knowbots" that conduct searches of distributed digital libraries to find desired information;

o hypermedia databases that track research team interactions and provide ongoing record of design decisions, operational problems and corrections, and research approaches;

o online, interactive mechanisms for an user education and training support;

o remote experiment schedulers;

o automated scheduling negotiation processes;

o access control and authentication procedures to provide secure means for sharing control of resources; and

o software for simulation of scientific instruments in order to replace construction of expensive physical prototypes and enable collaborative development and evolution of shared instruments.

SOURCE: These concepts are drawn from "Towards a National Collaboratory: Report of an Invitational Workshop," 1989.

N

Building the National Research and Education Network, U.S. Congress, Congressional Research Service, January 7, 1991.

Updated January 7, 1991

by
Stephen Gould
Science Policy Research Division

CONTENTS

Building the National Research
and Education Network

SUMMARY

The National Research and Education Network (NREN) is a computer network being built to support broadly communication and resource sharing among institutions and individuals engaged in unclassified research and scholarly pursuits in the United States. NSFNET, a computer network launched by the National Science Foundation in 1985, currently serves as the primary cross-continental backbone for the NREN, which now links over one thousand university and college campuses, industrial research laboratories, and governmental research centers across the nation. Using the NREN, hundreds of thousands of students, researchers, and educators can directly access supercomputers and other state-of-the-art scientific and technical resources.

The overall goal of the NREN is to enhance national competitiveness and productivity through a high-capacity, high-quality computer network infrastructure that supports a broad set of applications and network services for the research and education communities. Transforming the NREN into a nationwide system of "information superhighways" that transport digitized information at several billion bits per second between high-performance computational resources and individual workstations is but one part of achieving this goal. Development of extensive digital libraries that make vast quantities of information quickly and easily available to researchers over the network is also an integral part of the infrastructure to be ultimately embodied in the NREN. Both in terms of capacity and resources connected to it, the NREN today is only a rough prototype of what supporters have in mind for the turn of the century.

The NREN is emerging from a larger national computer network, the Federal Research Internet. Like the Internet, the NREN currently is a loosely organized system of interconnected, unclassified computer networks. While Federal funding plays a key role in the ongoing development of NREN, a substantially greater share of financial support for its operations comes from the non-Federal participants, including industry. The Federal Networking Council, operating under the auspices of the White House Office of Science and Technology Policy (OSTP), seeks to coordinate the functioning and integration of NREN components at the Federal level. However, development and management of the NREN is decentralized, residing primarily at the local host site and individual network levels. A central question is whether NREN goals can be met by continued development on a decentralized basis, or whether one organization should assume a dominant role in NREN development, management, and funding. IBM and MCI Communications recently launched a new nonprofit organization that will seek to extend the capabilities of the NREN to additional education and research institutions.

Plans for substantially accelerating the evolution of the NREN during the next five years have been formulated by OSTP and are reflected in authorizing legislation now being considered by Congress. While these plans recognize that the ongoing development will require extensive coordination and involvement by government, universities and industry, just how NREN goals will be achieved is still an open question.

ISSUE DEFINITION

The informal collaboration among network researchers, users and sponsors that has guided the growth of both the Federal Research Internet and the emerging National Research and Education Network (NREN) is viewed by many participants as inadequate to meet future needs or fulfill the promise they believe computer networking holds. To ensure network reliability, broad coverage, user support, and the timely introduction of improved services, technology and capacity, some participants believe that a new public corporation is required to plan and oversee the development and effective operation of the NREN. Other supporters favor designating one Federal agency to take overall responsibility for NREN development. Some industry representatives argue that commercial vendors of telecommunications services should play a primary role in NREN development in order to more directly stimulate the universal availability of integrated broadband networks and services in the United States. In short, the primary issues are how the NREN will be developed and what the role of the Federal Government will be.

BACKGROUND AND ANALYSIS

Computer networks devoted to research and education have been in a period of rapid growth since the early 1980s. Until recent years, the design of these networks was often derived from and tailored to the special requirements of individual groups or research sponsors. As the use of microcomputers spread on college and university campuses and in Government, university, and industrial research laboratories, demand arose for wide access to common networks. This demand helped fuel the evolution of the Federal Research Internet, which is not a true network but an interconnection of autonomous computer networks that use common rules and procedures for addressing and routing messages. Called the "Internet protocols," these rules and procedures provide a universal language that allows electronic messages to be sent across multiple interconnected networks. The Internet includes networks funded by Federal agencies as well as scores of public and private local and regional networks.

Development of a general purpose national infrastructure to supply computer networking and other related services to the research and education communities began in earnest in 1985. At that time, the National Science Foundation (NSF) initiated support for the creation of computer networks explicitly designed to be used by any person or organization involved in open research and scholarly pursuits. Instead of catering to the needs of a particular scientific or engineering discipline or the interests of a particular mission orientation (i.e., research and development activities related to space exploration, health care, energy or defense), the transcontinental backbone networks, the mid-level State and regional networks, and the campus-wide networks within colleges and universities that collectively form the emerging NREN are shared by a diverse, multidisciplinary community of educators, students and researchers. While the interconnected networks that comprise the emerging NREN are also considered parts of the Internet, they are distinguished from many other Internet networks by their open membership policies.

A striking feature of both the current NREN and the larger Internet is that no one organization is responsible for the development and operation of either system. Neither system is a membership organization or has a governing board or council, although various committees set up by participating organizations and sponsors do have a role in consensus-based policymaking and coordination. Because of this, characterizing any particular autonomous network as being part of NREN or the Internet can be subjective. Nevertheless, the following section will briefly describe the emerging NREN's component parts.

Today's National Research and Education Network

NREN is a 3-level structure or hierarchy comprised of the following:

-- an interstate backbone network known as NSFNET, sponsored by NSF, the State of Michigan, IBM Corporation, and MCI Communications Corporation;

-- a mid-level tier of regional networks, including partial-statewide networks like the Bay Area Regional Research Network (BARRNET), statewide networks like the New York State Educational Research Network (NYSERNET), and multistate networks like the Southeastern Universities Research Association Network (SURANET); and

-- a third level composed of institutional and campus-wide networks within college and university campuses and Government and industrial laboratories that have the responsibility for directly serving most NREN users.

NSFNET is managed by Merit, Inc., a nonprofit organization affiliated with the University of Michigan at Ann Arbor that also manages the Merit Computer Network, a statewide network that links universities and other institutions in Michigan; CICNET, a regional network in the upper midwest; and the University of Michigan's campus network. The four supercomputer centers sponsored by NSF are directly connected to NSFNET along with the NSF-supported National Center for Atmospheric Research and more than a dozen regional networks.

The regional networks within NREN are operated with the financial support of various types of public and private sector partnership arrangements. Some regional networks are managed by a specially created nonprofit organization or a preexisting academic association. Others have no organizational or legal status, existing only as projects or accounts within a member institution. Participating institutions generally pay fixed annual fees to connect to the regional networks, typically $10,000-50,000 per year depending on the size of the institution and the carrying capacity of the telecommunications channel connecting it to the network. Some of the regional networks received partial start-up funding from NSF. The third-level institutional and campus-wide networks are financed primarily by the institutions they serve. Some universities have received one-time grant funding from NSF to connect their campus-wide networks to a mid-level network.

Each of the networks within the NREN are operated independently, although the participating institutional networks must often abide by guidelines set by the regional network(s) they connect to and by the NSFNET. Most academic computer networks provide some type of user guidelines, and generally do not permit commercial use unrelated to research or instruction carried out at nonprofit institutions. Connectivity to the NREN has been expanded unevenly by the mid-level networks. While some have been aggressively pursuing corporate research centers and other new users, others have been content to provide a service to their university-based membership.

The NREN has grown dramatically over the past three years. By 1990, there were more than 1500 identifiable networks connected together through the mid-level networks and NSFNET, including well over 100,000 computers. Data traffic on the NSFNET backbone has increased nearly 20% per month since mid-1988, and is now over 2.5 billion packets per month. The number of active NREN users is expected to grow from about 1 million today to 4-6 million within ten years, while computer connections to the network increase to 500,000. NREN also connects with other Federal agency networks as well as to international research and industrial networks in Canada, Europe, Central and South America, and the Pacific Rim. An upgrade of NSFNET to a carrying capacity of 45 megabits per second (from 1.5 megabits) is now underway to accommodate continued growth in NREN connections as well as provide improved performance.

In September 1990, IBM, MCI Communications, and Merit, Inc. announced the formation of a nonprofit company to extend the capabilities of NSFNET and the NREN to additional education and research institutions and to commercial companies that provide services to education and research. IBM and MCI have each pledged $5 million in start-up financing to the new organization, which will be known as Advanced Network and Services, Inc. (ANS). Merit, which holds a contract with NSF to operate NSFNET, will run network operations for ANS. Prices to be charged by ANS to new institutional network subscribers are approximately $300,000 per year for 45 megabit capacity service and $55,000 for 1.5 megabit capacity service. According to officials of the new company, ANS is planning to offer an expanded network capacity that will permit transmission speeds of one billion bits per second within two years.

Network Applications

The NREN and the Internet together support a vast, multi-disciplinary community of researchers and educators within universities, government, and industry. Professionals with disciplines ranging from astrophysics to medical science to economics use the networks for their own purposes. While the resources they use via the networks are equally diverse, most network applications currently fall within the following categories:

-- national and international electronic mail (including destinations reached via gateways to commercial networks);

-- file transfer, including complex documents, graphical or image data, and databases relating to individual research projects;

-- access to software libraries;

-- remote connection to supercomputers and other high-performance computers with specialized architectures;

-- remote connection to computers dedicated to complex, large-scale scientific and technical modelling (i.e., modelling the atmosphere or the economy);

-- remote connection to computer-controlled scientific instruments such as particle accelerators and telescopes;

-- interactive searching of bibliographic, abstract, and full-text literature databases;

-- access to specialized databases such as satellite, medical, economic and legal data; and

-- use of specialized knowledge banks -- computers hosting various expert systems, online scientific and technical journals, informal topical bulletin boards, and ongoing computer-based conferences.

By connecting educators and researchers to these resources, NREN facilitates global sharing of expensive scientific tools and widely dispersed sources of information. As a multifaceted communications system, the NREN also promotes the sharing of ideas and collaborations among distant colleagues. Most of the resources available via NREN are also accessible to users by other means (i.e., travel or use of other communications systems). However, use of NREN for access often saves time and can minimize costs by greatly expanding the power and reach of a personal computer workstation.

National Research and Education Network of the Future

Today's NREN is far from providing uniformity in the type and quality of service provided to users, and despite its already substantial reach does not connect with the entire research and education community. Use of the network for many applications is not easy, and instruction, documentation, and troubleshooting support for users are in many cases scarce. The individuals able to most effectively use NREN to access the full range of current resources are those who have developed a degree of expertise in computer networking technology. Many other users have learned the operational requirements of only the resources they need the most. Continued evolution of the NREN until it becomes a user-friendly, unified high capacity telecommunications utility with nationwide coverage is envisioned by Federal sponsors and academic participants.

One characteristic being sought for the future NREN is the capacity to convey digitized information at the rate of several billion bits (gigabits) per second. While unnecessary for many network applications, such capacity would greatly enhance the ability of researchers to carry out complex analyses using remote resources. Use of supercomputers has introduced capabilities for computational analysis, simulation, and modeling that generate very large data, graphic or video files that cannot be transferred across the current NREN in a timely manner. Major scientific projects that are ongoing or proposed, from particle accelerators and large array radio telescopes to the NASA Earth Observation System satellite project, will create vast streams of new data that will also make high-capacity networks desirable for distribution within the research community. Various potential network applications, including fully interactive remote use of supercomputers, will not be possible until high-capacity network links are in place.

Applications that are expected to be developed as NREN capacity increases include the following:

-- transfer of electronic mail and data files in multimedia formats, including high resolution graphics, full motion video, and sound;

-- multimedia, computer-based conferencing facilities;

-- development and use of network utilities that rely on resources that are distributed across the network, like a unified digital library that can automatically draw upon geographically dispersed collections.

-- facilities enabling scholars to dynamically and collaboratively build and maintain databases that contain all that is known on a particular subject; and

-- knowledge management systems that provide standard, consistent and intuitive interfaces to network resources and services.

Another attribute associated with plans for the future NREN is network access to a much more extensive array of information and data collection resources. Some types of existing resources will be more readily integrated into NREN than others. Computer-searchable services, such as the National Aeronautics and Space Administration's RECON, the National Agriculture Library's AGRICOLA, the Library of Congress' MARC, and the National Library of Medicine's MEDLINE databases are examples of resources that can be made accessible over the NREN in the near term.

Some NREN proponents envision making the vast collections housed in the Library of Congress and other major libraries available to students, educators and researchers via the network. Since most library collections are not in machine-readable formats, substantial efforts would be required to accomplish this type of accessibility. Existing data archives like those maintained by NASA and the National Oceanic and Atmospheric Administration, which house thousands of computer tapes holding data drawn from observations of the earth, the atmosphere, and space, are also candidates for NREN access. While these collections are in machine-readable formats, many data archives are also not yet equipped to make their data readily available via NREN. A wide variety of facilities that house large and expensive scientific instruments that are shared by the research community are not currently equipped to provide remote access or operational control via computer networks. For example, while the Continuous Electron Beam Accelerator being built in Newport News, Virginia is designed to be computer-controlled from remote locations, most existing large high-energy physics installations are not.

A third characteristic of the future NREN is more extensive coverage of the research and education communities. A primary goal associated with NREN development is the broadest possible participation by individuals and organizations in education, industry, and Government that are involved in research and education. The larger the relevant community served by NREN, the greater the value inherent in network access will be since communication is a key network function. As indicated earlier the current NREN is distinguished from other networks by its non-exclusivity, but creating open access to all qualified researchers and scholars will be accomplished only with substantial additional NREN growth.

Current Federal Initiatives

In September 1989, the White House Office of Science and Technology Policy (OSTP) submitted to Congress its 5-year program plan for support of high-performance computing and networks. The plan calls for a federally coordinated Government, industry, and university collaboration to accelerate the rate at which high-performance computing hardware and software and high-capacity computer networks are developed and deployed. Total Federal spending for related education, facilities, networks and R&D would be doubled over the 5-year period, from approximately $500 million per year to about $1.1 billion per year. Expenditures related to NREN development would also increase substantially, with an additional $390 million spent over the five-year period. This funding would include research and development projects required to obtain gigabit-capacity network technology, but does not cover the cost of deploying the technology in the NREN.

OSTP's plan divides NREN development into three stages. The first stage, begun in 1988, involved upgrading the existing research internet to carry 1.5 million bits (megabits) per second on all telecommunication links within the NSFNET backbone. The second stage, which is now underway, will provide upgraded network services to 200 to 300 research facilities, using a shared backbone network with a carrying capacity of 45 megabits per second. By the end of the second stage, OSTP expects that every university and major laboratory will be connected to a mid-level network that is part of the NREN. Recognizing that present mid-level network services vary widely in reliability and scope, the plan calls for increased interaction of the Federal Government with the mid-level networks to develop homogeneous and universal networking services.

Before NREN can attain the gigabit transmission capacity envisioned for the third stage, a significant array of technical problems related primarily to message switching and software capability will have to be solved. Research and development on these problems will be carried out during the period of OSTP's five-year plan, but actual deployment of the third-stage NREN is anticipated at a later date. This stage is intended to provide 1-3 gigabit per second networking service to selected research facilities, and 45 megabit per second networking to approximately 1000 sites nationwide.

The OSTP plan designates NSF as the lead agency for deploying the operating NREN, and the Defense Advanced Research Projects Agency (DARPA) as the lead agency for research and development on advanced networking technology. The Federal Networking Council, a collaboration of the NSF, DARPA, the Department of Energy, NASA, and the Department of Health and Human Services that operates under the auspices of OSTP, seeks to maintain overall coordination of the activities of Federal agencies related to the NREN and Internet.

It is the goal of the OSTP plan that the NREN infrastructure eventually becomes a commercial offering nationwide. Thus, deployment of the third-stage NREN may coincide with a transition from Government sponsorship of the NREN to a commercial network service paid for directly by users. The plan notes that since some of the mid-level networks are private and autonomous organizational entities, elements of the emerging NREN can already be considered part of the private sector. The plans of IBM, MCI, and Merit for their new joint venture may also accelerate this transition.

Congressional Initiatives

Legislation considered by the 101st Congress would have provided explicit authority for expanding Federal support for building the NREN. S. 1067, the High-Performance Computing Act of 1990, would have provided for a coordinated Federal research program in high-performance computing, including development of a multi-gigabit-per-second NREN by 1996 to link government, industry and the education community. The Act would have assigned NSF the primary responsibility for deploying the high capacity NREN and developing an information infrastructure of network services and resources, and would have authorize additional appropriations for NSF of $195 million over a 5-year period for the NREN. S. 1067 was passed by the Senate, but not by the House. Similar legislation is likely to be introduced in the 102nd Congress.

Issues

Federal leadership and funding have played a significant role in the development of both the computer networks and computational resources being linked within the NREN. Yet, taken as a whole, the NREN is being developed and expanded in an ad hoc manner with no one organization or identifiable group setting overall priorities or goals. The NREN instead reflects the individual priorities and goals of the wide assortment of participants, from particular Federal agencies to various interest groups, university-based consortia, and corporate backers. This may well continue to be the case even if NREN-related legislation is passed by Congress.

Substantial progress has been made with this decentralized approach in cooperatively establishing extensive interoperability among systems of diverse organizational origin and geographical location. However, not all interested constituencies within the research and education communities are being well served, and some network applications have been better accommodated than others. On one hand, it is easy to understand the viewpoint of participants who feel that the informal collaboration that has guided NREN development to date is inadequate to meet future needs or fulfill the promise they believe computer networking holds. But given the well-established momentum that the decentralized approach to network development has, it is also somewhat difficult to envision a successful transition of the NREN to being a centrally directed enterprise since some key participants are not interested in foregoing the autonomy they have over the networks that directly serve their needs. For example, various Federal agencies, while generally agreeable to participating in a cooperative NREN effort, appear reluctant to give up operating control over their research-oriented networks to another agency or non-Federal organization.

Both the OSTP plan for NREN development and the NREN-related provisions of S. 1067 designate NSF as the organization responsible for NREN development, a role it has played for more than five years. NSF's approach to NREN development has fostered the network's decentralized nature. In seeking to use its available funding for academic networking as "leverage" to encourage investment from other sources, NSF has provided partial support to groups organized to primarily serve the needs of their particular constituencies. Universities and research groups that have been unsuccessful in obtaining a special NSF grant or network participation funding from other sources currently have little or no access to the NREN. This has in part led to interest among some NREN supporters in formation of a new public corporation with a broad mandate to plan and oversee the operation and expansion of the NREN.

No matter which organization oversees future NREN development, the task of establishing universal interoperability among the diverse, expansive array of federally sponsored networks, databases, software libraries, research instruments and facilities, supercomputers, and large-scale scientific projects would likely require a sustained commitment by the Congress and key Federal agencies throughout this decade. To ensure steady progress toward a unified electronic infrastructure in the United States, Congress may wish to provide coordinated oversight over not only numerous related initiatives serving the research community, but the process of integrating the resulting research-oriented information collection and management systems into a larger national infrastructure that can serve multiple national needs related to economic development and industrial and service sector productivity.

Several other policy issues are likely to be of continuing importance to Congress as the NREN infrastructure takes shape. Periodically reviewing and setting investment priorities for Federal funds may be necessary to ensure that steady progress on diverse infrastructure components is sustained. Priority is currently being given to expansion of telecommunications links for various backbone networks and research on high-speed networking. However, as high-speed network service becomes more widely available to the research and education communities, priority might shift towards making more data collection instruments, databases and knowledge banks maintained or supported by the Federal Government accessible through the NREN. Developing a comprehensive digital library system, for example, by itself would be an enormous enterprise requiring substantial Federal participation.

Congress may wish to provide guidance on balancing public sector and private sector roles in the development, financing and management of the NREN. While industry has had a substantial role in network development, operation of the Internet has been primarily a public sector enterprise. Representatives of the telecommunications and information industries have urged that creation of a commercial market for delivery of network access and services to academics should be a central focus of NREN policy, and that private industry be given a greater role in developing and managing the network. While the OSTP plan and pending legislation call for a transition of NREN from being a Government operation to being a commercial service, some academic network advocates believe it should be kept a public enterprise.

Congress is likely to play a major role in determining the scope of the NREN and in assuring equitable access among various classes of users. It has yet to be decided whether the NREN will reach beyond major research universities and Government laboratories to all institutions of higher education, high schools, nonprofit and corporate laboratories, or new high-technology entrepreneurs. A balance might have to be struck between providing a network optimized for users doing computation-intensive research and those with more diverse needs. Access and equity questions will be associated with cost recovery policies for various user categories. While open access is desired by many network users, privacy and security concerns (i.e., sabotage) might dictate some type of access controls.

Congress might also wish to be involved in resolving intellectual property rights issues as they pertain to electronic information management and dissemination -- which present major challenges to those seeking to preserve the economic value of information or assert rights associated with ownership. Copyright issues loom large in considering how to create and manage a comprehensive digital library system. Management of Federal scientific and technical information resources (and other Federal information resources) might deserve timely evaluation in the context of NREN development. Providing extensive electronic access to such resources has the potential to be a valuable NREN asset.

Continued involvement by a wide range of Federal agencies and programs will be necessary to fully develop the NREN and the array of scientific and technical resources to be connected to it. Accordingly, a wide variety of authorization and appropriations legislation coming before Congress might include infrastructure components or have policy impacts on network development and use.

LEGISLATION

H.R. 3131 (Walgren)

National High-Performance Computer Technology Act of 1989. Provides for a coordinated Federal research program to ensure continued U.S. leadership in high-performance computing. Introduced Aug. 3, 1989; referred to Committee on Science, Space, and Technology (Subcommittee on Science, Research, and Technology). Hearings held Oct. 3, 1989, and Mar. 15, 1990.

H.R. 4329 (Roe)

American Technology Preeminence Act. Provides for enhancing the position of U.S. industry through application of the results of Federal research and development, including a national high performance computer technology program. Introduced Mar. 21, 1990; referred to Committees on Science, Space, and Technology and on the Judiciary. Reported, with amendment, June 14, 1990 (H.Rept. 101-481). Passed House, amended, July 11, 1990. S. 1191 Passed in lieu, July 11, 1990.

S. 1067 (Gore)

High-Performance Computing Act of 1990. Provides for a coordinated Federal research program to ensure continued U.S. leadership in high-performance computing. Introduced May 18, 1989; referred to Committee on Commerce, Science, and Transportation (Subcommittee on Science, Technology, and Space). Hearings held June 21, July 26, and Sept. 15, 1989. Reported, with amendment, July 23, 1990 (S.Rept. 101-387). Passed Senate, amended, Oct. 25, 1990.

S. 1976 (Johnston)

Department of Energy High-Performance Computing Act of 1990. Provides for continued U.S. leadership in high-performance computing. Introduced Nov. 21, 1989; referred to Committee on Energy and Natural Resources. Reported, with amendment, July 19, 1990 (S.Rept. 101-377).

CONGRESSIONAL HEARINGS, REPORTS, AND DOCUMENTS

U.S. Congress. House. Committee on Science and Technology. American Technology Preeminence Act. Report, 101st Congress, 2nd session. May 10, 1990. Washington, U.S. Govt. Print. Off., 1990. 88 p.

U.S. Congress. House. Committee on Science and Technology. Subcommittee on Science, Research, and Technology. High performance computing. Hearing, 101st Congress, 1st session. Oct. 3, 1989. Washington, U.S. Govt. Print. Off., 1989. 173 p.

U.S. Congress. Senate. Committee on Commerce, Science, and Transportation. High-Performance Computing Act of 1990. Report, 101st Congress, 2nd session. July 23, 1990. Washington, U.S. Govt. Print. Off., 1990. 33 p.

U.S. Congress. Senate. Committee on Commerce, Science, and Transportation. Subcommittee on Science, Technology, and Space. Computer networks and high-performance computing. Hearings, 100th Congress, 2nd session. Aug. 11, 1988. Washington, U.S. Govt. Print. Off., 1988. 146 p.

----- National High-Performance Computer Technology Act of 1989. Hearings, 101st Congress, 1st session. Jun. 21, July 26, and Sept. 15, 1989. Washington, U.S. Govt. Print. Off., 1989. 413 p.

U.S. Congress. Senate. Committee on Energy and Natural Resources. Department of Energy High-Performance Computing Act of 1990. Report, 101st Congress, 2nd session. July 19, 1990. Washington, U.S. Govt. Print. Off., 1990. 27 p.

FOR ADDITIONAL READING

Executive Office of the President. Office of Science and Technology Policy. The Federal high performance computing program. Sept. 10, 1989. [Washington] 1989.

Kahn, Robert E. Networks for advanced computing. Scientific American, v. 257, no. 4, October 1987: 136-143.

National Academy of Sciences. Committee on Science, Engineering, and Public Policy. Information technology and the conduct of research: the user's view. Washington, National academy press, 1989.

National net '88 double issue: public and private initiatives to create a national education and research network. Educom bulletin, v. 23, nos. 2 (summer) and 3 (fall), 1988: 2-72

National Research Council. Computer Science and Technology Board. Toward a national research network. Washington, National academy press, 1988

U.S. Congress. Office of Technology Assessment. High performance computing and networking for science (background paper). Washington, U.S. Govt. Print. Off., 1989.

U.S. Library of Congress. Congressional Research Service. The Federal research internet and the national research and education network: prospects for the 1990s, by Stephen Gould. July 26, 1990.
    CRS Report 90-362 SPR

----- High-performance computing: an overview, by Stephen Gould. CRS Issue Brief. Updated regularly.
    CRS Issue Brief 90015

Wintsch, Susan. Toward a national research and education network. Mosaic, v. 20, no. 4, winter 1989: 32-42.

O

S. 343,
Department of Energy High-Performance Computing Act of 1991,
U.S. Congress, Senate, Committee on Energy and Natural Resources, February 5, 1991.

To provide for continued United States leadership in high-performance computing.

IN THE SENATE OF THE UNITED STATES

FEBRUARY 5 (legislative day, JANUARY 3), 1991

Mr. JOHNSTON (for himself, Mr. WALLOP, Mr. FORD, Mr. DOMENICI, Mr. BINGAMAN, and Mr. CRAIG) introduced the following bill; which was read twice and referred to the Committee on Energy and Natural Resources

---

A BILL

To provide for continued United States leadership in high-performance computing.

1   *Be it enacted by the Senate and House of Representa-*

2   *tives of the United States of America in Congress assembled,*

3   **SECTION 1. SHORT TITLE.**

4   This Act may be referred to as the "Department of

5   Energy High-Performance Computing Act of 1991".

6   **SEC. 2. FINDINGS.**

7   The Congress finds that:

8   (a) advances in high-performance computer science and

9   technology are vital to the Nation's defense, scientific ad-

1 vancement, international competitiveness and long-term
2 prosperity;

3 (b) the Department of Energy and other Federal agen-
4 cies have a critical need for a nationwide high-capacity com-
5 puter network;

6 (c) the Department of Energy is the Federal agency
7 having the greatest degree of expertise and knowledge in the
8 research, development and use of high-performance comput-
9 ers, associated software and networks;

10 (d) the Department of Energy's expertise and knowl-
11 edge is due in part to its ownership and use of the greatest
12 number of high-performance computers of any Federal
13 agency;

14 (e) the Department of Energy's expertise and knowl-
15 edge is also due in part to its numerous national laboratories
16 that have personnel with particular expertise in the research,
17 design, development and use of high-performance computers,
18 associated software and networks; and

19 (f) the Department of Energy is the Federal agency that
20 is particularly well equipped to undertake additional research
21 and development of high-performance computing hardware
22 and associated software, and to design, implement and
23 manage a multi-gigabit per-second nationwide computer net-
24 work connecting Federal departments and agencies.

1 **SEC. 3. PURPOSES.**

2   The purposes of this Act are:

3   (a) to promote the research and development of high-

4 performance computers and associated software; and

5   (b) to create a multi-gigabit per-second nationwide com-

6 puter network for use by the Department of Energy and

7 other Federal departments and agencies.

8 **SEC. 4. DEFINITIONS.**

9   For the purposes of this Act, the term—

10   (a) "Secretary" means the Secretary of Energy;

11   (b) "Department" means the Department of Energy;

12   (c) "Federal laboratory" means any laboratory, or any

13 federally-funded research and development center, that is

14 owned or leased or otherwise used by a Federal agency or

15 department and funded by the Federal Government, whether

16 operated by the Government or by a contractor;

17   (d) "national laboratory" means any Federal laboratory

18 that is owned by the Department of Energy;

19   (e) "educational institution" means a degree granting

20 institution of at least a Baccalaureate level; and

21   (f) "software creation" means any innovation or prepa-

22 ration of new computer software of whatever kind or descrip-

23 tion whether patentable or unpatentable, and whether copy-

24 rightable or noncopyrightable.

25   (g) "Director" means the Director of the Office of Sci-

26 ence and Technology Policy.

SEC. 5. DEPARTMENT OF ENERGY HIGH-PERFORMANCE COM-PUTING PROGRAM.

(a) The Secretary, acting in accordance with the authority provided by the Federal Nonnuclear Energy Research and Development Act of 1974 (42 U.S.C. 5901 et seq.) shall establish a High-Performance Computing Program (hereinafter referred to as the "HPC Program").

(b) Within one year after the date of the enactment of this Act, the Secretary shall establish a management plan to carry out HPC Program activities. The plan shall—

(1) be developed in conjunction with the Director's overall efforts to promote high-performance computing;

(2) summarize all ongoing high-performance computing activities and resources at the Department that are not classified or otherwise restricted;

(3) describe the levels of funding for each aspect of high-performance computing that are not classified or otherwise restricted;

(4) establish long range goals and priorities for research, development, and application of high-performance computing at the Department, and devise a strategy for achieving them; and

(5) ensure that technology developed pursuant to the HPC Program is transferred to the private sector in accordance with applicable law.

1 **SEC. 6. DEPARTMENT OF ENERGY HIGH-PERFORMANCE COM-**

2 **PUTING PROGRAM ACTIVITIES.**

3 (a)(1) The Secretary shall establish a national multigiga-

4 bit-per-second computer network to be known as the "Feder-

5 al High-Performance Computer Network".

6 (2) The Secretary shall provide for the linkage of the

7 Federal agencies and departments, and other persons as the

8 Secretary may deem appropriate.

9 (3) The Network shall be designed, implemented and

10 managed by the Secretary of Energy, in consultation with

11 other Federal departments and agencies.

12 (4) The Secretary may make use of existing Federal fa-

13 cilities and networks as may be appropriate to carry out the

14 requirements of this section, *Provided,* That the Federal de-

15 partment or agency concurs in such use.

16 (b) The Secretary shall promote education and research

17 in high-performance computational science and related fields

18 that require the application of high-performance computing

19 resources by making the Department's high-performance

20 computing resources more available to undergraduate and

21 graduate students, post-doctoral fellows, and faculty from the

22 Nation's educational institutions.

23 (c) The Secretary shall establish at least two Collabora-

24 tive Consortia, and as many more as the Secretary deter-

25 mines are needed to carry out the purposes of this Act, by

26 soliciting and selecting proposals:

1   (1) Each collaborative consortium shall—

2   (A) undertake basic research and develop-

3   ment of high-performance computing hardware

4   and associated software technology;

5   (B) undertake research and development of

6   advanced prototype networks;

7   (C) conduct research directed at scientific

8   and technical problems whose solutions require

9   the application of high-performance computing re-

10   sources;

11   (D) promote the testing and uses of new

12   types of high-performance computing and related

13   software and equipment;

14   (E) serve as a vehicle for computing vendors

15   to test new ideas and technology in a sophisticat-

16   ed computing environment; and

17   (F) disseminate information to Federal de-

18   partments and agencies, the private sector, educa-

19   tional institutions, and other potential users on the

20   availability of high-performance computing facili-

21   ties.

22   (2) Each Collaborative Consortium shall be com-

23   prised of a lead institution, which has responsibility for

24   the direction and performance of the consortium, and

25   participants from industry, Federal laboratories or

1 agencies, educational institutions, and others, as may

2 be appropriate.

3   (3) Each lead institution shall be a national labo-

4 ratory which has the experience in research on prob-

5 lems that require the application of high-performance

6 computing resources.

7   (4) The consortium may fund research and devel-

8 opment associated with prototype computing technolo-

9 gy provided that industrial participants in each consor-

10 tium shall not be reimbursed for costs associated with

11 their own involvement.

12   (d) The provisions of the National Cooperative Research

13 Act of 1984 (15 U.S.C. 4301–4305) shall apply to research

14 activities taken pursuant to this section..

15   (e) Each Collaborative Consortium may be established

16 by a Cooperative Research and Development Agreement as

17 provided in section 12 of the Stevenson-Wydler Technology

18 Innovation Act of 1980 (15 U.S.C. 3710a).

19   (f) The Secretary shall report annually to the Committee

20 on Energy and Natural Resources of the Senate and the

21 Committee on Science, Space, and Technology of the House

22 of Representatives regarding the HPC Program.

23 **SEC. 7. GOVERNMENT AND PRIVATE SECTOR COOPERATION.**

24   In accordance with applicable law, the Secretary may

25 cooperate with, solicit help from, provide funds to, or enter

1 into contracts with private contractors, industry, government,

2 universities, or any other person or entity the Secretary

3 deems necessary in carrying out the provisions of this Act.

4 **SEC. 8. OWNERSHIP OF INVENTIONS AND CREATIONS.**

5   (a) Except as otherwise provided by the National Com-

6 petitiveness Technology Transfer Act of 1989 (103 Stat.

7 1674) and any other applicable law, title to any invention or

8 software creation developed under this Act shall vest in the

9 United States and shall be governed by the provisions of sec-

10 tion 9 of the Federal Nonnuclear Energy Research and De-

11 velopment Act of 1974 (42 U.S.C. 5908).

12   (b) Trade secrets and commercial or financial informa-

13 tion that is privileged and confidential and which is obtained

14 from a non-Federal party participating in research or other

15 activities under this Act may be withheld in accordance with

16 section 552(b)(4) of title 5, United States Code.

17   (c) The Secretary, for a period of up to five years after

18 the development of information that results from research

19 and development activities conducted under this title and that

20 would be a trade secret or commercial or financial informa-

21 tion that is privileged or confidential, under the meaning of

22 section 552(b)(4) of title 5, United States Code, if the infor-

23 mation had been obtained from a non-Federal party, may

24 provide appropriate protection against the dissemination of

1 such information, including exemption from subchapter II of

2 chapter 5 of title 5, United States Code.

3 **SEC. 9. AUTHORIZATION.**

4   There is authorized to be appropriated such sums as are

5 necessary to carry out the purpose of this Act.

○

P

Grand Challenges:
High Performance Computing and Communications,
the FY 1992 U.S. Research and Development Program,
Committee on Physical, Mathematical, and Engineering
Sciences, Federal Coordinating Council
for Science, Engineering, and Technology,
and Office of Science and Technology Policy, 1991.

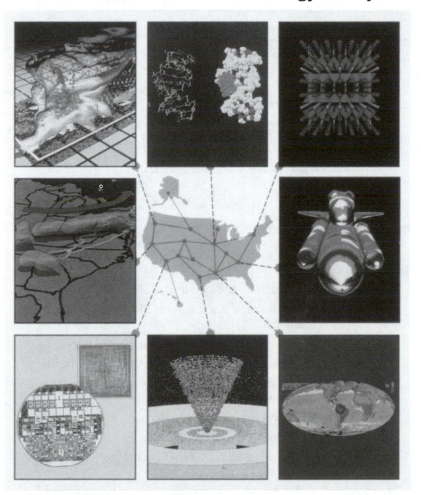

A Report by the Committee on
Physical, Mathematical, and Engineering Sciences

To Supplement the President's Fiscal Year 1992 Budget

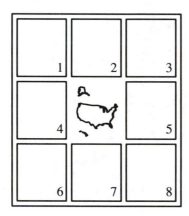

On the Cover:

1. Numerically modelled thunderstorm.

2. Computational model of chemical carcinogen binding with DNA molecule.

3. Visualization of structure of superconducting material.

4. Simulation of acid rain pollutants over Ohio River basin.

5. Aerodynamic characteristics of space vehicle: computer simulated versus wind tunnel data.

6. Photo of wafer and multi–chip prototypes.

7. Numerical simulation of fuel jet.

8. Computer image of earth's biosphere components generated from satellite data.

The images used in this report were produced by ongoing scientific projects in areas of the planned HPCC program. They were selected to illustrate the breadth of subject matter of the HPCC program, and are elaborated upon in Chapter 4. The U.S. map suggests how the National Research and Education Network supports geographically distributed collaborative research activities.

Grand Challenges:
High Performance Computing
and Communications

The FY 1992 U.S. Research and Development Program

A Report by the Committee on
Physical, Mathematical, and Engineering Sciences

Federal Coordinating Council for Science,
Engineering, and Technology

Office of Science and Technology Policy

To Supplement the President's Fiscal Year 1992 Budget

Office of Science and Technology Policy
Federal Coordinating Council for Science, Engineering, and Technology
Committee on Physical, Mathematical, and Engineering Sciences

Acting Chairman

Charles Herzfeld, Department of Defense

Members

Barry Williamson, Department of the Interior
Charles E. Hess, Department of Agriculture
Robert White, Department of Commerce
William Raub, Department of Health and Human Services
James Decker, Department of Energy
John B. Childers, Department of Education
Norine Noonan, Office of Management and Budget
Eugene Wong, Office of Science and Technology Policy
Arnold Aldrich, National Aeronautics and Space Administration
Erich Bretthauer, Environmental Protection Agency
Fredrick M. Bernthal, National Science Foundation

Executive Secretary

Jane Stutsman, National Science Foundation

FCCSET Directorate

Maryanne C. Bach, Executive Director
Charles H. Dickens, Senior Staff Associate
Jean Grace, Executive Assistant

High Performance Computing and Communications Working Group

David Nelson, Department of Energy, Chairman
Barry Boehm, Defense Advanced Research Projects Agency, Co–Chairman
Charles N. Brownstein, National Science Foundation, Co–Chairman
Lee Holcomb, National Aeronautics and Space Administration, Co–Chairman
Lawrence E. Brandt, National Science Foundation
John S. Cavallini, Department of Energy
Melvyn Ciment, National Science Foundation
Jack D. Fellows, Office of Management and Budget
Stephen M. Griffin, National Science Foundation
Paul E. Hunter, National Aeronautics and Space Administration
Gary M. Johnson, Department of Energy
Thomas A. Kitchens, Department of Energy
Norman H. Kreisman, Department of Energy
Albert T. Landberg, Jr., National Institute of Standards and Technology
Fred Scoresby Long, National Oceanic and Atmospheric Administration
Daniel R. Masys, National Library of Medicine
Joan H. Novak, Environmental Protection Agency
William L. Scherlis, Defense Advanced Research Projects Agency
Paul H. Smith, National Aeronautics and Space Administration
K. Speierman, National Security Agency
Stephen L. Squires, Defense Advanced Research Projects Agency
Stephen Wolff, National Science Foundation

EXECUTIVE OFFICE OF THE PRESIDENT
OFFICE OF SCIENCE AND TECHNOLOGY POLICY
WASHINGTON, D.C. 20506

MEMBERS OF CONGRESS:

I am pleased to forward with this letter "Grand Challenges: High Performance Computing and Communications, The FY 1992 U. S. Research and Development Program," a report by the Committee on Physical, Mathematical, and Engineering Sciences of the Federal Coordinating Council for Science, Engineering, and Technology, a supplement to the President's Fiscal Year 1992 Budget.

The report presents an ambitious and well-coordinated research and development program designed to sustain and extend U.S. leadership in all advanced areas of computing and networking. The program not only provides a far-sighted vision for the underlying technologies but also gives recognition to the importance of both human resources and those applications that serve major national needs. This is a program of national investment that will bring both economic and social dividends.

The program is strategically related to other key components of the President's overall approach to challenges in science, technology, and education. It provides for the use of improved computational and communications technologies to contribute to more effective solutions of grand challenge problems.

The goal of the Federal High Performance Computing and Communications (HPCC) Program is to accelerate significantly the commercial availability and utilization of the next generation of high performance computers and networks. Recent advances offer the potential for a thousand-fold improvement in useful computing capability and a hundred-fold improvement in available computer communications capability by 1996. These advances will come through improvements in hardware and software. This increased capability will greatly expand the availability of these resources for research and education. It is my personal view, moreover, that the successful implementation of this program will lay the foundation for changes in education at all levels.

Several years of effort on the part of senior government, industry, and academic scientists and managers are reflected in this program. Acting Chairman Charles Herzfeld and his interagency committee members, associates, and staff are to be commended on the excellent work that is manifest in both the program and the report.

D. Allan Bromley
Director

613

Table of Contents

List of Figures

Grand Challenges: High Performance Computing and Communications

The FY 1992 U.S. Research and Development Program

Executive Summary

EXECUTIVE SUMMARY

- High performance computing and computer communications networks are becoming increasingly important to scientific advancement, economic competition, and national security. The technology is reaching the point of having a transforming effect on our society, industries, and educational institutions. The goal of the Federal High Performance Computing and Communications (HPCC) Program is to accelerate significantly the commercial availability and utilization of the next generation of high performance computers and networks in a manner consistent with the Strategic and Integrating Priorities shown in Figure 1.

- The HPCC Program is the result of several years of effort on the part of senior government, industry, and academic scientists and managers to design a research agenda to extend U.S. leadership in high performance computing and networking technologies.

- For FY 1992 the HPCC Program proposes to invest $638 million in the four complementary and coordinated components shown in Figure 1. This investment represents a $149 million, or 30%, increase over the FY 1991 enacted level.

- The HPCC Program is driven by the recognition that unprecedented computational power and capability is needed to investigate and understand a wide range of scientific and engineering "grand challenge" problems. These are fundamental problems whose solution is critical to national needs. Progress toward solution of these problems is essential to fulfilling many of the missions of the participating agencies. Examples of grand challenges addressed include: prediction of weather, climate, and global change; determination of molecular, atomic, and nuclear structure; understanding turbulence, pollution dispersion, and combustion systems; mapping the human genome and understanding the structure of biological macromolecules; improving research and education communications; understanding the nature of new materials; and problems applicable to national security needs.

- The HPCC Program nurtures the educational process at all levels by improving academic research and teaching capabilities. Advanced computing and computer communications technologies will accelerate the research process in all disciplines and enable educators to integrate new knowledge and methodologies directly into course curricula. Students at all levels will be drawn into learning and participating in a wide variety of research experiences in all components of this program.

- The FY 1992 Program and this document were developed by the HPCC Working Group under the direction of the Committee on Physical, Mathematical, and Engineering Sciences of the Federal Coordinating Council for Science, Engineering, and Technology.

Figure 1   **The High Performance Computing
and Communications Program**

Goals: Strategic Priorities

Extend U.S. technological leadership in high performance computing and computer communications.

Provide wide dissemination and application of the technologies both to speed the pace of innovation and to serve the national economy, national security, education, and the global environment.

Spur gains in U.S. productivity and industrial competitiveness by making high performance computing and networking technologies an integral part of the design and production process.

Strategy: Integrating Priorities

Support solutions to important scientific and technical challenges through a vigorous R&D effort.

Reduce the uncertainties to industry for R&D and use of this technology through increased cooperation between government, industry, and universities and by the continued use of government and government–funded facilities as a prototype user for early commercial HPCC products.

Support the underlying research, network, and computational infrastructures on which U.S. high performance computing technology is based.

Support the U.S. human resource base to meet the needs of industry, universities, and government.

Program Components

High Performance Computing Systems
  Research for Future Generations of Computing Systems
  System Design Tools
  Advanced Prototype Systems
  Evaluation of Early Systems

Advanced Software Technology and Algorithms
  Software Support for Grand Challenges
  Software Components and Tools
  Computational Techniques
  High Performance Computing Research Centers

National Research and Education Network
  Interagency Interim NREN
  Gigabits Research and Development

Basic Research and Human Resources
  Basic Research
  Research Participation and Training
  Infrastructure
  Education, Training, and Curriculum

1. PROGRAM GOALS AND OVERVIEW

Introduction

High performance computing (HPC) is emerging as a powerful technology for industrial design and manufacturing, scientific research, communications, and information management. A robust U.S. high performance computing and computer communications capability contributes to leadership in critical technology and national security areas. Improved computational and communications technologies contribute to more effective approaches to problem solving, new products and services, and enhanced national competitiveness across broad sectors of the economy.

Recent advances offer the potential for a thousand–fold improvement in useful computing capability and a hundred–fold improvement in available computer communications capability by 1996. Based on several years of planning, under the auspices of the Federal Coordinating Council for Science, Engineering, and Technology (FCCSET), Federal agencies and the technical community have developed the Federal High Performance Computing and Communications (HPCC) Program to realize this potential and to meet the challenges of advancing computing and associated communications technology and practices. Agencies have realigned and enhanced their high performance computing research and development programs, coordinated their activities with other agencies, and shared common resources to develop the program presented in this document.

Needs and Benefits

High performance computing has become a vital enabling force in the conduct of science and engineering research over the past three decades. Computational science and engineering has joined, and in some areas displaced, the traditional methods of theory and experiment. For example, in the design of commercial aircraft, many engineering issues are resolved through computer simulation rather than through costly wind tunnel experiments. This trend has been powered by computing hardware and software, computational methodologies and algorithms, availability and access to high performance computing systems and infrastructure, and the growth of a trained pool of scientists and engineers. This process has been nurtured by Federal investment in advanced research, agency supercomputer centers, and national networks through DARPA, DOE, NASA, NSA, and NSF. These facilities have contributed to national mission areas such as energy, space, health, defense, environment, weather, and basic science and

619

technology that could not be effectively addressed without the use of such advanced facilities.

High performance computing technology is knowledge and innovation intensive. Its development and use engages the entire scientific and engineering community. Building upon fundamental research of the early 1980's, a new computing technology of scalable parallel processing computers emerged. By the mid–1990's, this innovative approach to high performance computing systems promises to achieve sustained performance improvements of a thousand–fold compared to current systems.

In a growing number of science and technology fields, progress and productivity in modern research are increasingly dependent on the close interaction of people located in distant places, sharing and accessing computational resources across networks. Although the U.S. is the world leader in most of the critical aspects of computing technology, this lead is being challenged.

The Federal HPCC Program is a strategic Federal investment in the frontiers of computing and computer communications technologies and is formulated to satisfy national needs from a variety of perspectives including: technology, science applications, human resources, and technology transition. Needs are derived from the agency missions and based on the underlying science, engineering, and technology base required to carry out these missions. Many of these mission needs are related to solving very intensive large scale computing problems. These fundamental problems often cut across various agencies and missions and are called grand challenge problems (Figure 2).

The industrial and academic sectors provide major sources of innovation, cost effective development, and support of information technologies and their application to grand challenge problems. As these technologies are developed, the results support the Federal agency missions and become available nationally. The program provides for development of these revolutionary technologies within a framework of a partnership among government, industry, and academe and allows for rapid transition of laboratory results into new products that will then be applied within the program.

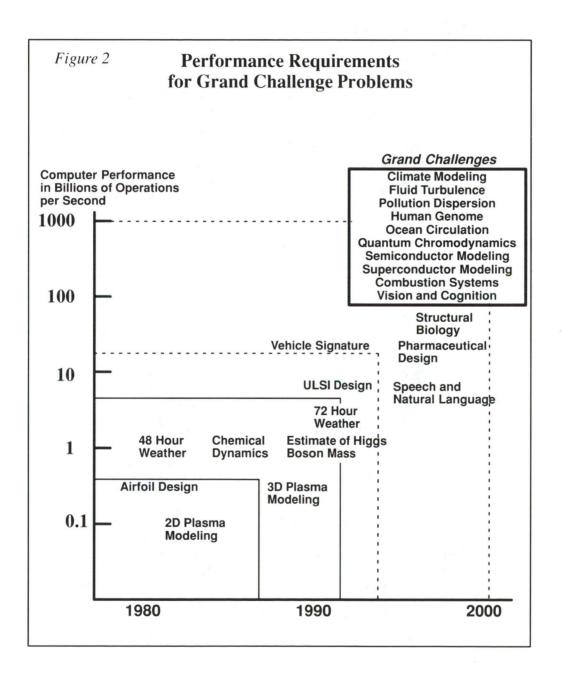

Figure 2

Performance Requirements
for Grand Challenge Problems

Program Description

The Program consists of four integrated components representing the key areas of high performance computing and communications:

High Performance Computing Systems (HPCS)— the development of the underlying technology required for scalable parallel computing systems capable of sustaining trillions of operations per second on large problems.

Advanced Software Technology and Algorithms (ASTA)— the development of generic software technology and algorithms for grand challenge research applications to realize the performance potential of high performance computing systems in a networked environment.

National Research and Education Network (NREN)— the development of a national high speed network to provide distributed computing capability to research and educational institutions and to further advanced research on very high speed networks and applications.

Basic Research and Human Resources (BRHR)— support for individual investigator and multidisciplinary long term research drawn from diverse disciplines, including computer science, computer engineering, and computational science and engineering; initiation of activities to significantly increase the pool of trained personnel; and support for efforts leading to accelerated technology transition.

Advances in high performance computing enable advances in almost every other science and engineering discipline. There is a complex web of research interdependencies among the four components, and each area contributes to progress in other areas. Because of these dependencies, achieving and maintaining balance between the research components is a primary goal and the most important priority in the current context and environment. The HPCC Program is designed to provide balanced support both for technology areas including components, systems, software, and algorithms, and for applications, infrastructure, and human resources to achieve rapid overall research progress and productivity.

The component activities are planned to produce a succession of intermediate benefits on the way to meeting the long range programmatic goals. The HPCC Program builds on Federal programs already in place, providing additional resources in selected areas. Computational science and engineering grand challenges as illustrated in Figure 2 are the focal points for these efforts.

Goals

The goals of the High Performance Computing and Communications Program are to:

Extend U.S. technological leadership in high performance computing and computer communications.

Provide wide dissemination and application of the technologies both to speed the pace of innovation and to serve the national economy, national security, education, and the global environment.

Spur gains in U.S. productivity and industrial competitiveness by making high performance computing and networking technologies an integral part of the design and production process.

These goals will be realized by achieving: computational performance of one trillion operations per second (10^{12} ops, or teraops) on a wide range of important applications; development of associated system software, tools, and improved algorithms for a wide range of problems; a national research network capable of one billion bits per second (10^9 bits, or gigabits); sufficient production of Ph.D.'s and other trained professionals per year in computational science and engineering to enable effective use and application of these new technologies.

Strategy

The goals will be met through coordinated government, industry, and university collaboration to:

Support solutions to important scientific and technical challenges through a vigorous R&D effort.

Reduce the uncertainties to industry for R&D and use of this technology through increased cooperation between government, industry, and universities and by the continued use of government and government–funded facilities as a prototype user for early commercial HPCC products.

Support the underlying research, network, and computational infrastructures on which U.S. high performance computing technology is based.

Support the U.S. human resource base to meet the needs of industry, universities, and government.

At the program component level the strategy will: exploit and extend scalable parallelism and engage in intensive software development in HPCS; use common requirements of the grand challenges to foster HPC software progress in ASTA to strengthen HPC software development and coordination; evolve from the current Internet network to the NREN using a series of testbed systems; and strengthen academic activities in computer science and computational science and engineering as part of BRHR.

Program Execution Strategy

The strategy is based on the strengths of partnerships among the Federal agencies and other organizations. Major portions of the program will be cost–shared and leveraged by the participation of industry and universities. This general approach operates well today and provides strong evidence that the HPCC Program can be successful in the future. The specific elements of the approach are to:

Create a balanced, critical–mass program. The program must achieve sufficient scope and balance among the components. A technology program that created extremely fast processors without comparable memory, input–output, and mass storage systems would not succeed. Neither would a program that created powerful computers without adequate software, network access, and capable people. Similarly, a program that created only high performance networks would not satisfy the increased performance requirements needed for grand challenges. The HPCC Program must operate at a sufficient scale and coverage of technology areas that the new technologies can be effectively applied to grand challenge problems with acceptable levels of risk. The HPCC Program achieves balance by the extensive participation of experienced users, applications developers, and researchers in the HPCC disciplines throughout the design, development, and implementation process.

Build on agency strengths. The strategy builds on agency strengths by giving appropriate agencies the responsibility to coordinate activities for areas of demonstrated capability. It also ensures that the strengths of the other agencies are included by integrating their participation in various task areas. DOE, NASA, NSF, DOC (NOAA, NIST), and DOD (DARPA, NSA) have decades of experience in applying the world's most powerful computers, and thus provide a valuable perspective on high performance computing requirements and applications. NSF has the demonstrated technical and operational expertise needed for deploying high performance national networks in the research community, and is uniquely positioned to support basic research in computer science, computational science, and other scientific areas that can benefit from high performance computing in interdisciplinary programs. DARPA, having pioneered technologies for high performance computing systems and microelectronic components, has a strong existing research program in teraops computing and gigabit networking, and offers rapid technology transition into commercial products in support of DOD science, technology, and applications base. EPA, NIH, and NOAA provide complementary HPCC requirements perspectives and application bases. NIST has extensive experience in HPC systems and networks instrumentation and evaluation, and provides a means for standards development.

Accelerate Technology Transfer. The transfer of technology from research to development and to application can be a very slow process due to a number of barriers to the use of new technology: high initial cost, inadequate and user–unfriendly software and systems, and lack of standards. The HPCC Program relies upon substantial industry participation to overcome these barriers and yield the benefits derived from moving new technologies to industry. The strategy accelerates technology transition by using a participative development process for each of the task areas, and by stimulating the growth of shared knowledge and capabilities. An example of this is the creation of network–accessible repositories of scalable HPC software and associated user groups to provide usage feedback and improvement of the HPC software base.

Overcome Barriers. To overcome high costs of creating successive generations of high performance computers, the program will emphasize scalable computer designs. Scalable computing and networking technologies enable exploratory use with small, lower cost prototype systems needed to eventually support the acquisition of larger systems. The development of user–friendly software and systems as part of the investment in the HPC software base is a major, integral part of the program. The central role of mission agencies, and the broad academic scientific research community involvement, ensures that the hardware, software, and networking technology developed will be responsive to user needs. A strategy of cooperative government, industry, and university activities is used to manage and coordinate the coupling of these sectors to achieve maximum synergy.

2. HIGH PERFORMANCE COMPUTING AND COMMUNICATIONS PROGRAM COMPONENTS

The HPCC Program is composed of four integrated and coordinated components that are designed to enhance scientific productivity and support long term agency needs. The emerging scientific computing environment is that of advanced workstations with high resolution color displays connected to a high speed computer communications network and high performance computing resources. The regional and national networks provide a means to gain access to additional high performance computing systems and research resources. Realizing the full potential of these teraops computing and gigabits networking systems will require advanced software technology and algorithms and people educated and trained to use these tools and resources in this dynamic field.

High Performance Computing Systems (HPCS)

The HPCS component produces scalable parallel computing systems through the development of prototype systems. The program is designed to attack computational science problems by developing innovative systems that will provide a one–hundred to one–thousand–fold increase of sustained computing capability over machines that follow the more conventional design evolution path (See Figure 3). DARPA will coordinate the research and development effort that will produce teraops systems.

The program is structured to focus on technological challenges in the earliest stages of the product development cycle. Critical underlying technologies are developed in prototype form along with associated design tools. This allows empirical evaluation of alternative solutions as the prototype systems mature. Evaluation is performed throughout the development cycle, with experimental results being fed back into the design process to refine successive generations of systems. There is risk inherent in creating new technologies, and each project will be managed according to its proximity to commercial introduction. Larger projects which are close to yielding commercial products are performed on a cost shared basis with industry.

HPCS is composed of the four subcomponents shown below.

Research for Future Generations of Computing Systems. This activity produces the underlying component, packaging, and scaling concepts. These projects ensure that the required advanced technologies will be available for the new systems while providing a foundation for the more powerful systems that need to follow.

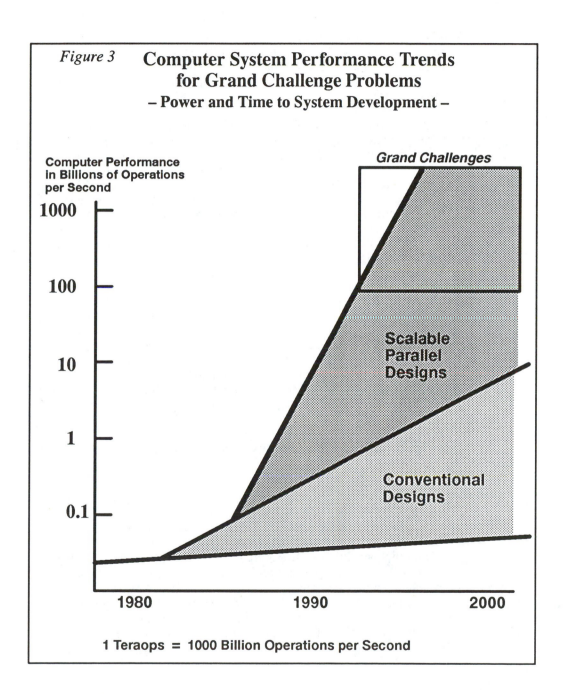

Figure 3 — **Computer System Performance Trends for Grand Challenge Problems** – Power and Time to System Development –

System Design Tools. This activity develops computer aided design
tools and frameworks for enabling multiple tools to work together to
enable design, analysis, simulation, and testing of systems
components. The tools will enable rapid prototyping of new system
concepts.

Advanced Prototype Systems. This activity consists of focused
development of experimental systems that are designed and
developed on a cost shared basis with industry. The 100 gigaops
systems provide a basis for the teraops systems. New models of
computation will be introduced and successive generations of
computer systems, along with systems software, will encompass
broader grand challenge domains. Modular technologies will enable
a wide variety of system configurations using common components.
Systems with 100 gigaops sustained performance will be developed
by the early 1990's. The teraops level will be reached by the mid
1990's.

Evaluation of Early Systems. Experimental systems will be placed at
sites with high levels of expertise to provide feedback to systems
architects and software designers. Performance evaluation criteria for
systems and results of evaluation will be made widely available.
Because of scalability, early systems can be acquired at smaller
scales to evaluate their potential performance. As noted below, the
ASTA component will support, on a cost shared basis, the acquisition
of large scale systems for experimental use in grand challenge
applications.

Advanced Software Technology and Algorithms (ASTA)

Dramatic improvements in algorithm design and software technology
are essential to achieving sustained teraflops computing system
performance. Improvements in hardware, especially for scalable
parallel systems, must be matched with new and innovative algorithms
and software to enable researchers to expand the boundaries of
computational capabilities. In Figure 4, this point is illustrated for broad
classes of scientific computing problems by showing that comparable
improvements in throughput have resulted from advances in
computational methods as from improved hardware technology. In this
case, hardware improvements yielded a speed–up of 1000 over 20 years,
while software and algorithms improvements yielded a speed–up of
3000 over the same period, for an aggregate speed–up of more than a
million.

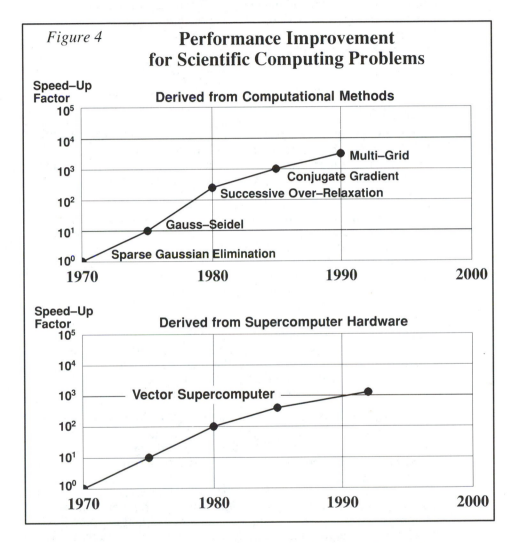

Figure 4

Performance Improvement for Scientific Computing Problems

The ASTA component of the Federal High Performance Computing and Communications Program has three goals:

Enable solution of grand challenge application problems in science and engineering.

Improve system user–friendliness, reliability, and software productivity.

Use experience gained on leading edge applications to help guide future software efforts.

The emphasis is on the development of advanced algorithms and software technology required to address applications problems on the scale of grand challenges. The ASTA component is comprised of four subcomponents, as shown below.

Software Support for Grand Challenges. The HPCC Program is designed to demonstrate new computing technology capabilities by confronting an expanding number of grand challenge application problems. The goal is to reduce the risks to researchers inherent in adopting innovative high performance computing technologies. Grand challenge application problems will be selected based upon their scientific importance, the potential for cost sharing with sources directly concerned with the specific scientific and engineering applications, and the potential for leveraging across sectors.

Software Components and Tools. The multidisciplinary research teams will have common needs in software technology and programming environments, advanced compiler technology, optimization and parallelization tools, interoperability and data management, visualization, debugging and analysis, and performance measurement. Advances in these generic software areas will minimize the need for specialized researchers to master advanced, complex computing science skills. Coordination of the development of advanced software technology and algorithms among the participating agencies will be important to ensure effective and efficient use of resources. A particular focus of this element will be to develop advanced software applications that exploit the NREN using distributed file systems and national software libraries.

Computational Techniques. The focus of the HPCC Program on scalable parallel computing systems dictates that significant advances in computational techniques will be needed. The design and theory of algorithms are as important as hardware or networking improvements in reaching teraflops computational performance. Research in computational techniques will include parallel algorithms, numerical and mathematical analyses, parallel languages, computational models, and program refinement techniques. Higher level languages will be developed to enable computational scientists to work directly at the level of the abstract computational problem being addressed and to more easily explore specific implementation approaches.

High Performance Computing Research Centers. High performance computing research centers and testbed facilities will provide a large number of researchers access via the NREN to both conventional and innovative supercomputing architectures. Many of these centers will introduce innovative architectures and will be the focus of technology transfer activities and form the base for training new generations of computer and computational scientists.

National Research and Education Network (NREN)`

The NREN component of the HPCC Program dramatically expands and enhances the U.S. portion of an existing worldwide infrastructure of interconnected computer networks called the Internet. A substantial fraction of the domestic Internet is supported and loosely coordinated by Federal agencies, principally DARPA, DOE, NASA, and NSF.

Collaboration among scientists is an important and integral facet of the U.S. research environment. It can be greatly improved by increasing the level of network connectivity and by introducing new capabilities into the existing infrastructure. The NREN design will not only address broad network connectivity, but will also provide the basis for necessary higher level capabilities and services.

Many educational institutions, government laboratories, and industrial research facilities are currently connected to the Internet. Yet, it still falls short of a widespread, uniform, and high performance national infrastructure. In order to satisfy the HPCC Program goals, the NREN must not merely provide network access to research and educational institutions at all levels and locations, it must also deliver new capabilities. Some of these, such as distance learning, may initially be extensions of current technology. All capabilities will benefit from, and many will be enabled by, a program of research into very high speed technology. This technology is needed to support access to digital libraries, large scale distributed computing resources, as well as to perform computationally intensive applications that require real time visualization of modeling and simulation results, rapid interrogation and retrieval of scientific data from specialized data bases, remote control of experiments and simulations, and teleconferencing.

In addition to serving the needs of the scientific and research communities, the NREN will provide valuable experience necessary for the successful development of a broader, privately–operated national information infrastructure. Such an infrastructure would allow consumers, businesses, and schools and government at all levels to share quality information and entertainment when and where they want it at a reasonable cost.

Applications conducted over a computer network vary in their flow of information from steady, as in a bulk file transfer, to "bursty," as in human–computer interaction via keyboard. Similarly, some applications can be carried out at relatively low communication rates, while others by their nature require high speeds. A number of scientific networking applications are characterized on the graph of speed versus burstiness in Figure 5. Traffic seen in the early days of networks appears near the bottom of the chart. More advanced applications are furthest from the origin and require more sophisticated protocols and network capabilities. This chart illustrates that a gigabit network is needed not only to carry the aggregation of low speed traffic, but also to accommodate high speed uses.

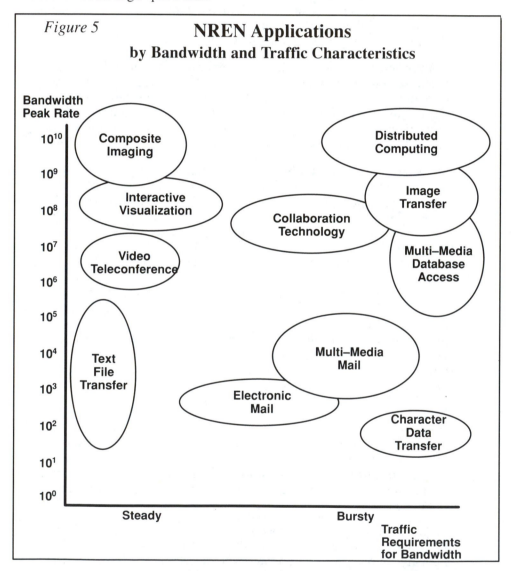

Figure 5

NREN Applications
by Bandwidth and Traffic Characteristics

The vision of the NREN is of an interconnection of the nation's educational infrastructure to its knowledge and information centers. In this system, elementary schools, high schools, two and four year colleges, and universities will be linked with research centers and laboratories so that all may share access to: libraries, databases, and diverse scientific instruments such as supercomputers, telescopes, and particle accelerators. The NREN enables communication and fosters collaboration among and within these communities. By reducing the traditional impediments of geographical isolation, the NREN improves the quality and raises the level of education nationwide. The NREN contributes to the success of the Basic Research and Human Resources component of the High Performance Computing and Communications Program. By making unique scientific and informational resources accessible beyond their physical locations, it permits widespread participation in the HPCC Program by scientists, university researchers, and students, and it enables the development of large scale distributed computing resources.

Interagency Interim NREN. The NSF will coordinate the Interim NREN activities by upgrading its backbone network, by assisting regional networks to upgrade facilities, capacity, and bandwidth, and by interconnecting the backbone networks of other agencies. A significant effort in its implementation will be the development and deployment of safeguards to enhance security and control over access to the connected computer systems, and that of the network components themselves in order to minimize vulnerability to careless or malicious attack. Coordination among participating agencies and the non Federal networking community will be expanded through the creation of a National Networking Council.

Gigabit Research and Development. DARPA will coordinate the research and development effort that will culminate in initial deployment of gigabits per second capability. Coordination of research efforts on very high speed switches, protocols, and computer interfaces will be necessary.

Basic Research and Human Resources (BRHR)

This component addresses long term national needs for more skilled personnel, enhancement of education and training, and materials and curriculum development in the high performance computing science and engineering areas. The NREN and ASTA components include support for research in the large scale project environment. The BRHR component is designed to encourage investigator initiated, long term research on experimental projects that will maintain the flow of innovative ideas and talented people into high performance computing areas.

Drawing the best and brightest of our Nation's youth into scientific and technological careers is a formidable challenge that will have profound effects on overall U.S. scientific and technological competitiveness. This component of the program will establish industry, university, and government partnerships to improve the training and utilization of personnel and to expand the base of research and development personnel in high performance computing science, technology, and applications.

The BRHR component of the HPCC Program has five goals:

> Improve the flow of human resources into high performance computing.

> Improve the university infrastructure to stay at the leading edge.

> Expand collaboration and resource sharing among the Federal, academic, and industrial sectors.

> Facilitate multidisciplinary research on high performance computing and communications.

> Create a critical mass of users by building a base with common systems, tools, and interfaces.

The BRHR component is organized across the four sub–components shown below.

Basic Research. These activities support increased participation of individual investigators in the conduct of innovative multidisciplinary research in computer science, computer engineering, and computational science and engineering related to high performance computing. The strategy is to increase the number of multi–disciplinary awards across all disciplines where computational methods are critical to achieving advances or scientific breakthroughs. Program activities include: research on scientific algorithm development for highly parallel computers;

generic computational algorithm development; scaling techniques; prediction techniques for concurrent systems; resource management strategies for highly parallel distributed systems; fault tolerant strategies for parallel and distributed systems; and research on heterogeneous software environments.

Research Participation and Training. These activities address the human resources pipeline in the computer and computational sciences, at post–doctoral (training and re–training), graduate, and undergraduate levels. Program activities include: workshops and seminars; post–doctoral fellowships in computational science and engineering; career training in medical informatics through grants to young investigators; institutional training and post–doctoral programs; knowledge transfer exchange programs at national laboratories, centers, universities, and industry; and software dissemination through national databases and libraries.

Infrastructure. These activities will improve university and government facilities for computer science, computer engineering, and computational science and engineering research related to high performance computing. Program activities include: improvement of equipment in computer science, computer engineering, and computational science and engineering academic departments, centers and institutions; development of scientific databases; and distribution of integrated system building kits and toolsets.

Education, Training and Curriculum. These activities will expand and initiate activities to improve undergraduate and pre–college education and training opportunities in high performance computing and computational science and engineering for both students and educators. The introduction of associated curriculum and training materials at all levels is an integral part of this effort. Program activities include: bringing people to national centers for training, technology transfer, and educational experiences; using professional scientists and engineers to provide curriculum development materials and instruction for high school students in the context of high school supercomputer programs, supercomputer user workshops, summer institutes, and career development informatics for health sciences.

3. PROGRAM DEVELOPMENT AND AGENCY BUDGETS

Program Planning

Leadership for the HPCC Program is provided by the Office of Science and Technology Policy (OSTP), through the Federal Coordinating Council for Science, Engineering, and Technology (FCCSET) Committee on Physical, Mathematical, and Engineering Sciences (PMES). The membership of the PMES includes senior executives of many Federal agencies.

The planning process for the HPCC Program was coordinated by a PMES working group through information exchange, the common development of interagency initiatives, and the review of individual agency HPCC proposals and budgets.

Evaluation Criteria

Each participating agency HPCC contribution was reviewed against formal evaluation criteria during the planning and budget process. A review of participating agencies was performed using these evaluation criteria to develop the FY 1992 agency requests for the Program. The evaluation criteria are shown in Figure 6.

Agency Budgets

Over the last three years of the planning process of this initiative, the participating agencies have mutually adjusted their activities within the base to achieve greater efficiency in addressing the goals of the HPCC Program. For FY 1992, $638 million is being proposed, a $149 million or 30 percent increase over the FY 1991 enacted level. The budget is shown in Figure 7.

The funds proposed from Federal sources are not intended to carry out the entire HPCC Program. Portions of this program will be cost shared by organizations from the participating sectors. The funding estimates are based on analyses of the practical experience of prior computing and computer networking programs. These estimates were then reviewed as outlined above. Cost sharing will occur with various U.S. industrial and university partners to a large extent in the HPCS and the NREN components. Cost sharing will occur in the ASTA component with agency programs and other computational applications programs, for example, in specific grand challenge areas, via multidisciplinary collaborations. This component also includes deployment of high performance systems to HPCC research centers. The close coupling of support in the Program will result in significant leverage, accelerate technology transfer, stimulate U.S. industry and markets, and enable the solution of computationally intensive applications. In addition, although HPCC is not intended to include classified programs, the technology produced will have an important impact in these national security areas. Figure 7 illustrates the relative levels of investment in the four program components.

Figure 6

Evaluation Criteria
for the
Federal High Performance Computing
and Communications Program

Relevance/Contribution. The research must significantly contribute to the overall goals and strategy of the Federal High Performance Computing and Communications (HPCC) Program, including computing, software, networking, and basic research, to enable solution of the grand challenges.

Technical/Scientific Merit. The proposed agency program must be technically/scientifically sound and of high quality, and must be the product of a documented technical/scientific planning and review process.

Readiness. A clear agency planning process must be evident, and the organization must have demonstrated capability to carry out the program.

Timeliness. The proposed work must be technically/scientifically timely for one or more of the HPCC program components.

Linkages. The responsible organization must have established policies, programs, and activities promoting effective technical and scientific connections among government, industry, and academic sectors.

Costs. The identified resources must be adequate, represent an appropriate share of the total available HPCC resources (e.g., a balance among program components), promote prospects for joint funding, and address long–term resource implications.

Enhancements to Existing Program Research. Existing agency HPCC programs will receive adequate support before new initiatives are funded.

Agency Approval. The proposed program or activity must have policy–level approval by the submitting agency.

Figure 7

High Performance Computing and Communications
Budgets by Agency and Program Component
(Dollars in Millions)

Agency	Base FY 1991	HPCC FY 1992	FY 1992 HPCC Component			
			HPCS	ASTA	NREN	BRHR
DARPA	**183.0**	**232.2**	103.3	38.5	32.9	57.5
DOE	**65.0**	**93.0**	15.0	58.0	12.0	8.0
NASA	**54.0**	**72.4**	14.2	49.8	7.4	1.0
NSF	**169.0**	**213.0**	24.0	103.0	32.7	53.3
DOC/NIST	**2.1**	**2.9**	0.3	0.6	2.0	0.0
DOC/NOAA	**1.4**	**2.5**	0.0	1.8	0.7	0.0
EPA	**1.4**	**5.2**	0.0	4.5	0.0	0.7
NIH/NLM	**13.5**	**17.1**	0.0	8.9	4.2	4.0
Total	**489.4**	**638.3**	**156.8**	**265.1**	**91.9**	**124.5**

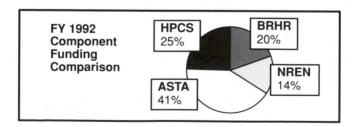

FY 1992 Component Funding Comparison

HPCS 25%
BRHR 20%
NREN 14%
ASTA 41%

HPCC — High Performance Computing and Communications

Components of HPCC:
HPCS — High Performance Computing Systems
ASTA — Advanced Software Technology and Algorithms
NREN — National Research and Education Network
BRHR — Basic Research and Human Resources

Agency Program Descriptions

The agency responsibilities under the Federal HPCC Program are outlined in Figure 8. Several agencies have been assigned a coordinating responsibility in specific technical areas:

- DOE and NASA will coordinate activities in HPC system evaluation, testbed development, and applications software capabilities.

- NASA will coordinate the accumulation of and access to the HPC software base. This will be facilitated by a wide area file system technology that is currently being deployed for early experimental use by DARPA which will be extended to include the NREN as it matures and is deployed by NSF.

- DARPA will coordinate activities in the development of scalable parallel HPC systems, including their basic units of replication, system modules, and the necessary associated systems software. DARPA will also coordinate activities in gigabit network technology research.

- NSF will coordinate activities for the broad deployment of the National Research and Education Network working with all agencies with mission specific requirements.

- NSF will coordinate activities in basic research and human resource development, while each agency retains its role as required to accomplish their own missions.

- NIST will coordinate activities in HPC system instrumentation, evaluation, and in standards issues.

Each agency participates in all of the identified activities to ensure that the resulting capabilities are a good match to user needs. DOC/NOAA, HHS/NIH/NLM, and EPA bring distinctive applications areas of broad interest and network user bases.

Figure 8

HPCC Program: Agency Responsibilities: HPCS, ASTA		
Activity / Agency	High Performance Computing Systems	Advanced Software Technology & Algorithms
DARPA	· Technology development and coordination for Teraops systems	· Technology development for parallel algorithms and systems software
DOE	· Technology development · Systems evaluation	· Energy applications centers · Energy computation research · Software tools
NASA	· Aeronautics and space application testbeds · Systems development for space flight	· Software coordination · Research in: · Aerospace computations · Information management
NSF	· Basic architecture research	· Basic research in: · Software tools, databases · Grand challenges · Computer access
DOC/ NIST		
DOC/ NOAA		· Ocean and atmospheric computation research · Software tools
EPA		· Research in environmental computations, databases, and application testbeds
NIH/ NLM		· Medical application testbeds · Software tools · Medical computation research

National Research and Education Network	Basic Research and Human Resources	Activity / Agency
· Technology development and coordination for gigabits networks	· University programs	**DARPA**
· Energy deployment mission facilities · Gigabits applications research	· Basic research and education programs	**DOE**
· Aerospace deployment mission facilities	· Research initiation and university block grants	**NASA**

· Facilities coordination and deployment
· Gigabits research
	· Programs in:
	  · Basic research
	  · Education
	  · Training / curricula
		NSF

· High speed network research and standards		**DOC/ NIST**
· Ocean and atmospheric mission facilities		**DOC/ NOAA**
· States environmental mission assimilation	· Technology transfer to States · University programs	**EPA**
· Medical mission facilities	· University programs	**NIH/ NLM**

Table title: **HPCC Program: Agency Responsibilities: NREN, BRHR**

Defense Advanced Research Projects Agency (DARPA)

DARPA, as the DOD lead agency for advanced technology research, will focus on developing the high performance computing and networking technologies needed for the Defense and overall HPCC Programs. DARPA programs have produced both the computing and networking foundation for the HPCC Program, including the first generation of scalable parallel computing systems and large scale computer networks, and the associated system software and supporting technologies. DARPA has worked with industry to pioneer the application of these new technologies within Defense and on a cooperative basis with other Federal agencies.

The DARPA HPCC Program builds upon the DARPA Strategic Computing Program. As the HPCC Program builds up, the Strategic Computing Program integrates its results with Defense specific needs such as embedded systems, accelerators of specific problem domains, and grand challenges problems related to defense. DARPA will continue this mode of executing the HPCC Program, cooperating with various defense organizations, and working closely with AFOSR, ARO, ONR, Defense Service Laboratories, NSA, other Defense organizations, and other Federal agencies as appropriate.

High Performance Computing Systems will be produced in the four main subareas: Research for Future Generations of Computing Systems, System Design Tools, Advanced Prototype Systems, and Evaluation of Early Systems. Systems capable of sustaining 100 gigaops for large problems will available for deployment by late 1993 and the teraops systems will be available by 1996.

In *Advanced Software Technology and Algorithms*, DARPA projects will produce scalable libraries for Defense problem domains and programming and analysis tools for scalable parallel and distributed heterogeneous systems in a workstation/server configuration that will be open to the integration of embedded systems and accelerators.

For the *National Research and Education Network* component, high performance networking technologies will be produced to satisfy the gigabit technology needs of the NREN and to provide a dual use technology base for Defense. This networking technology includes development of new protocols and switch and transmission technologies, and it will be capable of supporting a wide range of advanced network services.

The *Basic Research and Human Resources* component will focus on fundamental scientific issues in these three technology development areas in cooperation with other basic research programs and provide for smaller individual investigator projects to complement the larger projects. In addition, the relevant and related basic research will also be integrated into the larger projects as it matures.

Department of Energy (DOE)

The Department of Energy will participate in all components of the High Performance Computing and Communications Program. In the area of *High Performance Computing Systems,* the DOE will be an early customer of small versions of systems with advanced architectures and will evaluate these systems on energy related applications. The DOE will consider cooperative development of advanced systems between its national laboratories and vendors, especially integration of very high speed computer and networking hardware with software systems. The DOE will support research and development on algorithms and systems software for parallel computing systems.

The *Advanced Software Technology and Algorithms* effort will include research and development of: parallel algorithms for grand challenge applications, software and tools for early prototypes of 100 gigaflops and teraflops systems, prototype computational science programming environments that meet standards and are transportable, and support for high performance computing research centers to facilitate the transition from research on parallel machines into the applications and the programming environments. The DOE will fund several grand challenge collaborations, initiate a software component and tools program with strong industrial participation, and initiate an applications driven computational research program. The DOE will evaluate proposals and make research awards related to grand challenges in global climate change, molecular biology, human genome research, materials and chemical sciences, combustion research, waste remediation, fusion energy, and other areas within its mission.

The DOE will participate in the cooperative interagency *National Research and Education Network.* The Energy Sciences Net (ESNet) will be incorporated into the NREN and will provide quality network access to the energy research facilities. ESNet will maintain compatibility and will be upgraded in concert with NREN. Gigabit network support technology will be developed for DOE applications distributed across multiple energy research centers at the national laboratories and universities.

The DOE's *Basic Research and Human Resources* activities will include: stimulating research in computational science, expanding training programs at the national laboratories for high school teachers and college students in computing techniques, initiation of a high school supercomputer access program, and provision of fellowships in computational science with internship at national laboratories.

National Aeronautics and Space Administration (NASA)

NASA's HPCC Program participates in all four components of the Federal Program, through a vertically integrated program focused on NASA's grand challenges in: Computational Aerosciences, Earth and Space Sciences, and Remote Exploration and Experimentation.

The goal of NASA's program is to accelerate the development and application of high performance computing technologies to meet NASA's science and engineering requirements. In cooperation with the other Federal agencies, NASA's program will deploy teraflops computer capabilities essential for computational design of integrated aerospace vehicle systems and for predicting long term global change, and will enable the development of massively parallel techniques for spaceborne applications.

NASA's program is focused on bringing together interdisciplinary teams of computer scientists and computational physicists to develop these technologies within three vertically integrated projects that are unique to NASA's missions. These technologies include applications algorithms and programs, systems software, peripherals, networking, and the actual high performance computing hardware. NASA will develop a suite of software tools to enhance productivity. These include: load balancing tools, run time optimizers, monitors, parallelization tools, as well as data management and visualization tools.

NASA's role includes coordinating the *Advanced Software Technology and Algorithm* component for the Federal program; acquiring experimental hardware for testbeds in computational aerosciences, earth and space systems sciences, and remote exploration and experimentation; and supporting the development of the National Research and Education Network. To encourage vigorous research into the underlying theory and concepts of high performance computing, NASA will foster interactions among academia, industry, and national laboratories and will strengthen the basic research in high performance computing at the NASA centers and research institutes and in universities.

NASA's considerable expertise in experimental parallel computer testbeds and small, scalable testbed systems will be used to demonstrate high performance computing technologies as a step toward full–scale computational capabilities. A key to successful exploitation of massively parallel computing power will be the blending of application–driven and architecture–driven computer systems to most effectively meet NASA's needs.

National Science Foundation (NSF)

The NSF HPCC Program impacts the activities of all science and engineering disciplines by providing computing and networking infrastructure support and by developing enabling technologies for advanced computing and communications platforms and paradigms.

In the area of *High Performance Computing Systems*, research will be initiated on new architectures and systems optimized for specific research applications. New tools for systems level automated design and component packaging will be supported to permit the design of application–specific devices and systems.

In *Advanced Software Technology and Algorithms*, research will be initiated on scientific database technology and implementation of prototype networked databases and associated software. Advanced applications tools for research computing environments will be supported to enable nationwide access to the full complement of parallel machines for research on grand challenge problems. Areas of research focus will include numeric and symbolic computing, algorithm development, optimization of applications software for new parallel computers, scientific visualization, automated programming tools, and new methods of scientific and technical information exchanges.

NSF coordination of the *National Research and Education Network* activities will accelerate the harmonizing of multiple agency networks and protocols into a single NREN. The number of nodes will be increased to expand distributed information resources, and to increase redundancy, capacity, control, and security. Mid–level nets will be assisted to upgrade facilities and service very high bandwidth requirements. Support will be provided for research on new protocols for gigabit networks, switch and transmission technology, routing, congestion, and flow control. The exploration of pricing mechanisms for network services and network applications and structured transition to commercial service will be initiated.

In *Basic Research and Human Resources,* support will include multidisciplinary research and university infrastructure for computer science, computer engineering, and computational science and engineering. To increase the human resource pool in computing hardware and software systems areas, support will be expanded for graduate and post–doctoral positions. Curriculum improvement, teacher training, and support for centers to provide education and training in the use of experimental and parallel supercomputers are integral parts of this component.

National Institute for Standards and Technology (DOC/NIST)

The NIST research program is directed toward developing performance monitoring tools and promoting "open systems" software. NIST has proposed to augment its current HPC research program by promoting the commercialization of protocol and security mechanisms for medium speed networks.

The goal of NIST's activities in high performance computing is to develop hardware performance monitoring tools, promote "open system" software, and support a classification system for indexing and distributing scientific software so that industry and the research community can effectively exploit the power of future generations of high performance computers. In support of *The National Research and Education Network*, NIST will develop and speed commercialization of network protocols and security mechanisms that can achieve the desired gigabit speeds on future versions of the network. NIST will participate in the HPCC Program by:

Developing hardware monitoring methods leading to load characterization and performance measurement techniques for ultra–high–speed systems which will be made available on a publicly accessible database.

Conducting research on new protocols and related security primitives necessary to sustain gigabit network speeds and standards to provide interoperability, common user interfaces to systems, and enhanced security for the network.

Establishing a network testbed at NIST instrumented to collect performance data and test new network protocols, management routines, and security mechanisms for gigabit networks.

National Oceanic and Atmospheric Administration (DOC/NOAA)

The National Oceanic and Atmospheric Administration operational and research programs are directed toward weather prediction, ocean sciences, the Climate and Global Change Program, and the Coastal Oceans Program, together with data management activities for all agency programs. The HPCC Program will allow extensive development of new forecast models, studies in computational fluid dynamics, and the incorporation of evolving computer architectures and networks into the systems that carry out agency missions.

The NOAA High Performance Computing Program is focused in two components:

Advanced Software Technology and Algorithms. This component provides support for: grand challenges in atmospheric and oceanic sciences; development of advanced numerical models to simulate the general circulation of the oceans and atmosphere in support of NOAA missions and the activities of collaborating research groups; development of new computational methods for solving atmospheric, oceanic, and related problems on new computer architectures; data management R&D; support for basic research in strategies, techniques, and tools required for the management and analysis of large–scale distributed scientific databases and distributed data handling, including quality control; and development of algorithms for massively parallel processors, together with their standardized software component libraries and tools for the solution of oceanic and atmospheric analysis and forecasting problems.

NOAA will acquire, install, and operate advanced computational facilities for the evaluation of near operational prototype computers having massively parallel architectures and will develop algorithms appropriate for these architectures.

The National Research and Education Network component provides networking in support for NOAA's climate and global change research community and a wide range of agency missions in oceanography, weather prediction, and environmental sciences research. NOAA will evaluate advanced network protocols and hardware technologies related to its missions.

Environmental Protection Agency (EPA)

The EPA research program is directed toward the advancement and dissemination of computational techniques and software tools which form the core of ecosystem, atmospheric chemistry and dynamics models. The models extend the computational capability of environmental assessment tools to handle multi–pollutant interactions and optimization of control strategies.

The *Advanced Software Technology and Algorithms* component will develop new approaches for coupling numerical equation solvers to the high performance features of emerging computer architectures including specific techniques for solution of partial differential equations on massively parallel architectures. These solvers will be designed to operate on a flexible, generic grid system decoupled from specific applications to provide a testbed for evaluation and optimization. The resulting solution framework can serve as the computational engine for a variety of interdisciplinary applications.

Advancement of scientific visualization techniques can provide exceptional benefits in increasing the pace at which environmental problems are solved. EPA's program includes basic research to improve user interfaces and computational algorithms related to image rendering and manipulation of geometric images. The main focus is on simultaneous representations of multiple data sets and real–time visualization in a heterogeneous distributed processing environment. Related research on storage and access techniques for massive environmental data bases across multiple architectures will be conducted.

The *Basic Research and Human Resources* component includes the establishment of technology transfer centers to propagate the use of HPCC technology to State and local environmental groups, and Federal managers for optimization of pollution control and prevention strategies. A main goal of a Technology Transfer Center is to provide non–sophisticated users with training and guidance in the application of a variety high performance computing tools to solve important environmental challenges. The program also supports cross–discipline career training through universities and other institutions to ensure a continuing base of technical professionals knowledgeable in the use of high performance computing technology for environmental problem solving.

National Institutes of Health / National Library of Medicine (HHS/NIH/NLM)

The HHS/NIH program includes molecular biology computing, creation, and transmission of digital electronic images, the linking of academic health centers via computer networks, the creation of advanced methods to retrieve information from life sciences databases, and training in biomedical computer sciences. The HPCC program will complement the Human Genome Project by providing new methods for computer based analysis of normal and disease genes.

The *Advanced Software Technology and Algorithms* component will develop advanced software technology and algorithms in two areas of importance in biomedical research and education: biotechnology computing and digital images. In the area of biotechnology computing, the program will support development of molecular sequence comparison algorithms, new database methods, and algorithms to predict biological structure and function from genetic code. The biomedical images area will support new methods for representing, linking, and rendering images of biological structure

The *National Research and Education Network* component has two sub–components: connections among academic medical centers and their growing array of computerized information sources; and development of intelligent gateways that link conceptually related databanks in the life sciences. The academic medical centers of the country are confronted with a growing array of disconnected computer–based information sources, ranging from patient records, x–rays and laboratory systems, to basic research tools such as protein and DNA sequence databanks. Development of advanced software systems capable of representing and linking these dissimilar data types, and communicating them among centers for research and health care, is the goal of this part of the program. The focus of the Gateways HPCC program is the building of systems that are capable of translating a user's request into multiple computer–based vocabularies, selecting appropriate databases from a wide range of widely–available resources, and retrieving information in a manner that does not require users to understand the structure and syntax of the systems being queried.

The *Basic Research and Human Resources* component addresses the need to train biomedical researchers and health care providers in the use of advanced computing and network communications to aid in their work. The successful predoctoral and postdoctoral grants program for career training in medical informatics administered by the National Institutes of Health will be expanded.

4. GRAND CHALLENGE AND SUPPORTING TECHNOLOGY CASE STUDIES

This section incorporates examples of high performance computing and computer communications technologies and several illustrative grand challenge applications in computational science and engineering, that are presented on the cover of this report. The examples were chosen to illustrate the diversity and significance of application areas that have been addressed to date. The list of grand challenges is too long to allow an example from each area, thus lack of representation of certain areas does not imply lack of importance. A more complete description of the grand challenges can be found in the Federal High Performance Computing Program report issued in September 1989.

Forecasting Severe Weather Events

Making accurate predictions about the behavior of the atmosphere is of critical importance to reducing losses due to storms, hurricanes, floods, and other weather related phenomena. Current operational small scale weather prediction models have been constrained by two broad deficiencies: inadequate size of the data sets necessary to define the detailed atmospheric structures and insufficient computer resources to support high resolution. During the next five years, major progress will be made on the first deficiency by using a combination of new ground–based and remote–observing systems. This leaves inadequate computer power as the primary stumbling block preventing high resolution models from playing operational roles in our national weather prediction efforts.

The high–resolution, operational weather prediction models of the future will represent a new generation of numerical formulations. The primary differences will be in the treatment of vertical motions and small scale processes which in the past have been considered to be "sub–grid scale." This means that physically significant events, such as convection, must be treated as parameterized processes and fine scale details in, for example, thunderstorm evolution that can affect the surroundings cannot be directly addressed by the model. Likewise, fine scale observations of local importance, such as moisture gradients around wet areas, which can provide local forcing, currently cannot be incorporated adequately.

To meet this scientific and national need, new technologies need to be developed and incorporated into existing facilities so that a less than 5 km resolution model can be operational before the end of the century. This would allow updated forecasts on a 6–hourly or shorter basis. Such models have already shown significant advances in the accuracy of predicting a wide variety of weather events, from severe thunderstorms to lake effect snowfalls in research applications. Each reduction of the model resolution by one–half requires an increase of computer power of almost an order of magnitude, as well as comparable increases in supporting memory, mass storage and networks. For example, a 5 km model could require up to a 20 teraflops computer system to meet operational schedules using this model.

Researchers have used supercomputers to model thunderstorms numerically. Wind, temperature, pressure, and other variables are calculated every few seconds at several hundred thousand locations in the area of the developing storm. Mathematical equations are then used to simulate the storm's evolution. In this graphic, particles which are released near the ground at regular intervals are colored orange when rising and blue when sinking. Yellow signifies paths of individual particles.

Cancer Genes

DNA is the blueprint of life, the molecular thread in the nucleus of each of our cells which guides the assembly of molecules and complete living organisms. When the DNA code is altered by mutation, serious diseases can result, such as cancer; this phenomenon was known to scientists studying animal tumors in the 1970's. They isolated cancer–causing genes, called "oncogenes" from animal tumors, and later found that similar genes existed in normal human DNA. This was a profound mystery. Why would we be carrying the seeds of our own destruction in our genetic blueprint?

In 1984, two separate research groups used a computerized searching algorithm to compare a newly discovered oncogene to all known genes. To their astonishment, the cancer causing gene matched a normal gene involved in growth and development. Suddenly, it became clear that cancer might be caused by a normal growth gene being switched on at the wrong time. This fundamental and unexpected insight was an early example of a field that is now known as Computational Biology, the science of using computers to store and analyze data from complex molecules in living cells.

The databases used in 1984 for these comparisons contained information about several thousand molecular units; now they contain over 30 million. Moreover, the current multi–agency genome research programs of NIH, NSF, and DOE will acquire data on tens of billions of molecular units, ranging from simple organisms to human beings. The best computer algorithms for determining the similarity of molecules require time proportional to the length of the molecules being compared; if the methods used to analyze oncogenes in 1984 were applied to the three billion base pairs of the human genome, they would require hundreds of years of computer time on today's fastest supercomputers. New computer designs and software methods will be essential to cope with the explosive growth of molecular data. Functioning as intellectual amplifiers to detect similarities and differences in molecules whose size and complexity are too vast for the unaided human mind, the computer systems to be developed by the HPCC program will be a critical tool for the life sciences in the 1990's, and the health care systems of the 21st Century.

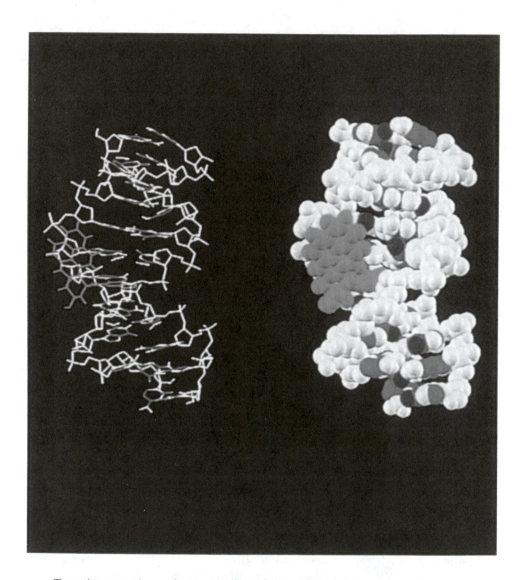

Two views are shown for the binding of a chemical carcinogen to a short stretch of DNA. The stick model on the left shows the overall structure of the DNA–carcinogen complex. The space filling model on the right shows the actual intimate binding of the carcinogen, hiding deep within the DNA. This chemical contact leads to mutations in the DNA code, and ultimately to a tumor.

Predicting New Superconductors

In 1988, the world was excited by the discovery that a particular yttrium–barium–copper–oxide compound superconducts at a temperature of 93° Kelvin, still very cold, but much warmer than any previous superconductor. This discovery sparked a worldwide effort to expand research to discover new superconducting materials. The economic benefit of a high–temperature superconductor is beyond calculation, portending the development of, for example, much more efficient power transmission and lightweight, powerful magnets to revolutionize the transportation business. Advanced computing is a central part of the arsenal of research tools which will be necessary to reach that payoff.

Despite these early successes, many questions remain before it is understood how some materials superconduct when very similar compounds do not. This understanding will be critical to predicting new superconductors, which might work at even higher temperatures, be less expensive, carry more current, or be more amenable to manufacturing processes. Increasing progress in all these areas is required before the impact of these new materials will be felt.

The solution of physical models requires intensive calculations to understand the material structure. High performance computing can shorten the discovery process by allowing the development of accurate simulations to point experimenters in the most promising directions. For example, most of the groups looking for new superconductors are trying various copper–oxide combinations. Researchers are using high performance computers to explore the possibility of various combinations of elements that may lead to new superconducting materials.

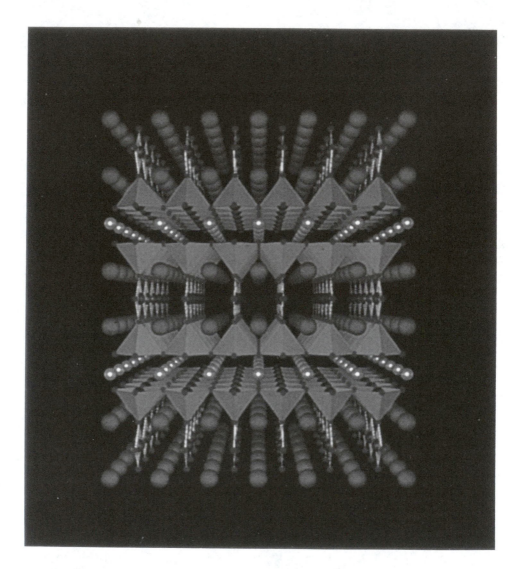

Researchers have used visualization techniques to investigate the structure of materials which are thought to be involved in the superconducting mechanism. In this graphic, barium cations (green) and yttrium cations (silver) are shown with their associated oxygen defects. The copper atoms (blue) and oxygen atoms (red) are found in two types of CuO_4 environments, one of which is depicted in yellow, the other in light blue.

Air Pollution

The ability of the atmosphere to absorb and to cleanse itself of pollutant contaminants was taken for granted until the 1950's when "killer fogs" in London, England and Donora, Pennsylvania caused the deaths of hundreds of people. Since then, technological advances in controlling source emissions have reversed the trend of steadily increasing pollution, even in the face of continued industrial growth. However, reduction strategies of individual pollutant types do not always produce the desired results. In fact, these simple solutions can even make air quality worse due to complex chemical interactions of the remaining airborne contaminants. Pollutants may travel long distances from industrial centers to sensitive areas where they are deposited in transformed products such as ozone and acid rain. These complexities of pollutant transport and transformation are costly and difficult to study experimentally, therefore, numerical models of the atmosphere have been developed to assess the effects of man–made emissions on air quality.

The new Clean Air Act mandates the use of numerical models to demonstrate the effectiveness of proposed regulatory control strategies. The potential cost to society to implement these proposed controls is estimated to reach tens of billions of dollars. Current models have been useful in evaluating alternative control strategies, but do not yet have the capability to produce optimum solutions. Present computing limitations on existing supercomputers force simplifications in the scientific descriptions of chemical and physical processes, and slow examination of alternatives. Control strategies for each pollutant are often determined independently with little evaluation of multiple pollutant interactions. Remedial solutions determined for a particular scale of space and time are not readily extendable to other scales of pollutant dispersal.

High performance computing will enable multi–scale numerical explorations with cross–pollutant interactions to be performed in a timely manner so as to be useful to legislated control and prevention requirements. Advanced computer designs and software methods will also enable cost optimization of pollutant control tradeoffs. Improved visualization techniques will enhance the interpretation and evaluation of massive amounts of environmental measurement and computer simulation data. High performance computing models will lead to a better understanding of the actions needed to minimize pollutant damage to materials and environmental damage to crops while making our air safer to breathe for future generations.

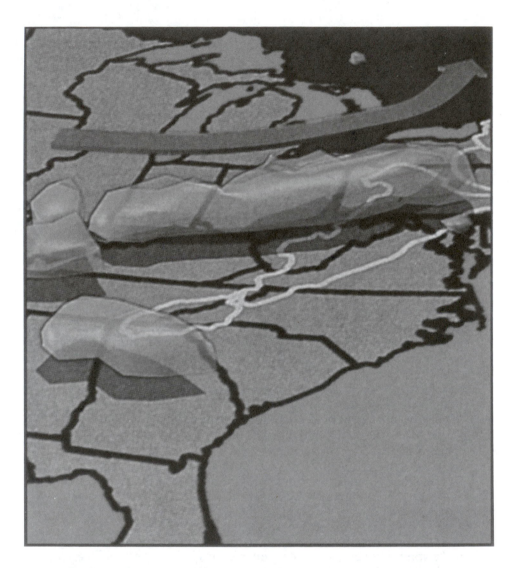

Using a supercomputer, atmospheric researchers have simulated the transport, chemical transformation, and surface deposition of sulfur compounds responsible for acid rain. Visualization specialists have depicted the movement of sulfur compounds from major sources in the Ohio river valley to sensitive lakes in the Adirondacks. The yellow cloud represents high concentrations of sulfur compounds. Several sensitive aquatic regions are outlined in green and a typical wind flow pattern is presented in red.

Aerospace Vehicle Design

Being able to predict the aerodynamic characteristics of in–flight vehicles is important for designers. Reproducing such flight regimes in wind tunnels is time consuming, costly, and in some cases impossible. Computational aerodynamics simulations are less costly and much faster than complex wind tunnel tests and are able to simulate many inaccessible flight regimes. These capabilities will be particularly important in the design of supersonic and hypersonic aircraft to serve international markets.

Computational aerosciences directly contributes to maintaining U.S. preeminence in aerospace science and engineering disciplines. The computational technology developed in such computational aerodynamics problems will directly transfer to the U.S. aerospace industry and aircraft manufacturers. Other potential beneficiaries are in diverse fields where fluid dynamics is an important design aspect such as automobile manufacture, ship design, and medicine (e.g., heart/cardiovascular flow simulation).

Massively parallel computing systems and advanced parallel software technology and algorithms will enable the development and validation of multidisciplinary, coupled models. These models will allow the numerical simulation and design optimization of complete aerospace vehicle systems throughout the flight envelope.

Shown here is a comparison between supercomputer simulation data and actual wind tunnel model data for the pressure distribution along the integrated space shuttle, solid rocket boosters and external tank flying at Mach 1.55. Note the excellent agreement between the two.

Energy Conservation and Turbulent Combustion

For the foreseeable future, 90% of the energy needs of the United States will be met by the combustion of fossil fuels. Two of the largest uses are for electrical power generation and in automobiles. Computational models offer a means of improving the design and efficiency of internal combustion engines.

Automobile engines are most efficient when run at high temperatures, but increased temperatures also lead to increased nitrogen oxide emissions. The burning of alternative fuels such as methanol is complicated by the emission of carcinogens. The effects of the emissions are influenced by local climatic conditions, making it necessary to consider the total system of fuel, engine, and atmosphere when seeking better designs. Our environment is too delicate and cannot be used as a testbed, so the atmospheric effects must be simulated.

A full three dimensional engine design code has been developed and implemented on a supercomputer. The code is designed to handle the most complex engines, such as the stratified charge and the two–stroke engines. The code represents an approximation to reality, because not all of the physical phenomena are well understood. Moreover, even if they were, the limited capabilities of existing computers would not allow this detailed information to be included.

For example, over 400 chemical processes of hydrocarbon and nitrogen chemistry are known to occur in internal combustion engines, yet only ten or less of the most significant reactions are used in simulations, in order to allow the calculation to run in a few hours on today's large supercomputers. Since the 400 hydrocarbon–nitrogen reactions are known, the real problem could be addressed with better algorithms running on a machine 10,000 times more powerful, a teraflops machine. This computational technology is needed by many private industrial engine firms as well as universities and government laboratories.

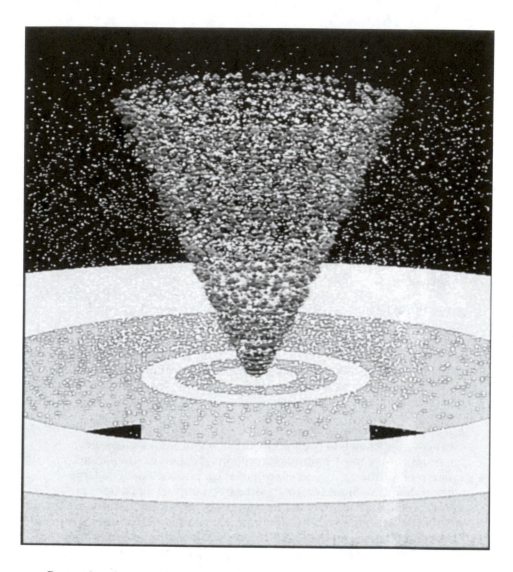

Researchers have used high performance computers to accomplish the
numerical simulation of the properties of a conical fuel jet. The colors of the
particles within the jet indicate the droplet size. The smallest particles are blue,
intermediate size particles are shown in yellow, while the particles with the
largest diameters are depicted in red. The smaller light blue particles around the
jet represent the swirling air surrounding the spray.

Microsystems Design and Packaging

Since the invention of the integrated circuit in 1958, the number of transistors fabricated on a microchip has doubled every two years, providing a medium to incorporate ever–increasing complex electronic design into chips, components, and packages. By analogy, the complexity of detail incorporated in a single integrated circuit 1 cm square is equivalent to representing the map features, at a city block level, of the entire Eastern United States. A similar analogy for a 5 cm square module densely packed with a collection of chips would be the equivalent of a map of North and South America. Determining the interconnecting paths, selecting the right modules, testing the interfaces, and choosing the mix of technologies are part of the design process to build the scalable components for workstations to supercomputers.

In the computing world, scalable architectures based on the 1–2 million transistor custom structures of today will evolve in the mid 1990's to system approaches exploiting 10–million–transistor chips, standard component parts, and special interface electronics, all combined in optimally designed modules adhering to standard interfaces. System clock speeds will continue to improve, and the diversity of microchip technologies combined in a single module will allow unprecedented flexibility for designers.

Managing this complexity explosion would be overwhelming without the use of computationally based approaches that enable teams of designers to systematically reduce the time to develop such systems. Today, computational tools enable complex microcircuits to be developed on first pass, at the same time that packaging technologies such as multichip modules can be demonstrated. High performance computing applied to the technology design process will enable the exploration of design alternatives and rapid exploitation of new technologies.

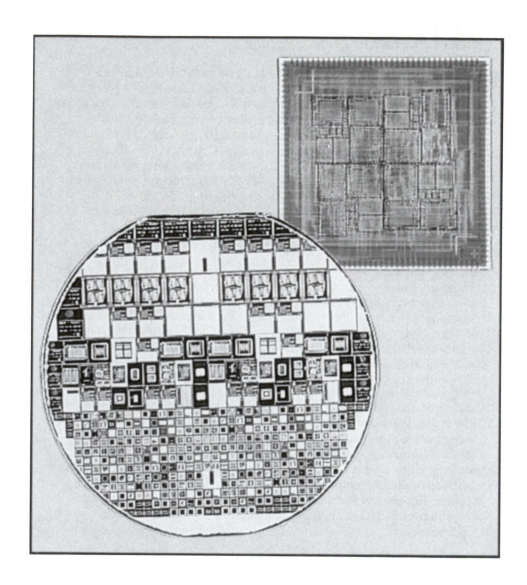

The figure shows both current and future components of the innovation design cycle. In the lower left of the photograph is a multiproject wafer using an industry/academia/government supported prototyping capability. The multiproject wafer shown is 4 inches in diameter, shares resources with 82 projects, and represents approximately 200 million transistors distributed over the wafer. Proven experimental prototypes are used as components of larger modules, interconnected with advanced technology. In the upper right hand corner is an example of an advanced interconnect module of 36 diverse microchips, packed together 1.5 inches on a side. Advanced computationally intensive design tools are essential to realize these high performance components.

Earth's Biosphere

The Earth's biosphere is a complex physical system. There are a multitude of phenomena which can change the state of the biosphere on a local, regional, and global scale. In order to predict the directions and consequences of changes in the state and condition of the biosphere, detailed scientific models are required, which in turn are constructed from massive amounts of experimental and computational data.

Experimental information is derived from satellite and ground based sensors. By the late 1990's, the sensors will have the resolution required to provide data in support of much more accurate and informed decision making on issues such as pollution and global warming. Because the sensors will generate terabytes of data each day, which will be combined with local data sets on the ecosystem, major improvements in the capability for collecting, analyzing, distributing, and archiving data are necessary.

The effort of constructing valid scientific models which describe the dynamics and underlying processes of the biosphere will involve interdisciplinary teams of experts from the geophysical, life, physical, computer, and computational sciences. They will work together to construct computational models which will validate our empirical understanding of the biosphere, and help predict how worldwide activities affect the global ecosystem. Computer and computational scientists will develop the advanced software technology and algorithms for handling massive amounts of data and working with high resolution, coupled models of the Earth's atmospheric–biospheric–oceanic interactions. Efforts in software development and experimentation will predict how local current conditions may impact future global conditions allowing the linking of ecosystem models to global climate models. The result of this collaborative effort will be a much deeper understanding of our environment and the impact of human activities upon it.

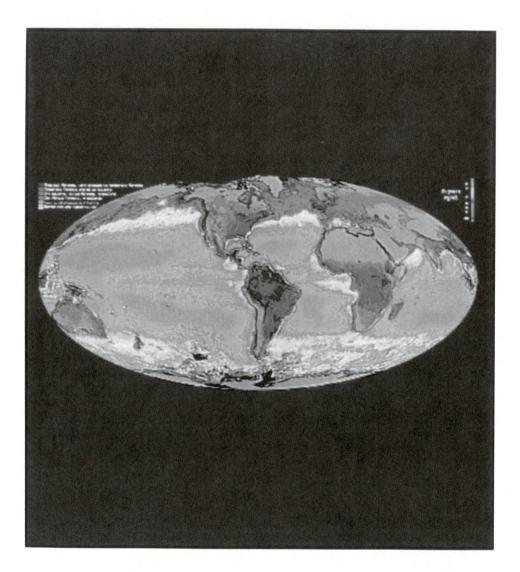

A global view of the Earth's ocean chlorophyll and land vegetation is depicted here. The image was derived from accumulated satellite data. Generating this image required over 2 terabytes (10^{12} bytes) of raw data. Data such as these are the baseline "snapshot" of our current biosphere and are vital to understanding short and long term component interactions of the Earth's biosphere for such purposes as crop productivity improvement, fishing and weather prediction.

High Speed Networks

The development of more powerful computers feeds both the demand for, as well as the growth of, more powerful data communications capability. As computing technology progresses, greater demands are placed on network performance as researchers conceive of new tasks and modalities of use that require even higher performance.

Current developments in large scale scientific computing are leading to truly distributed computing, allowing a given job to be executed on several different machines communicating partial results among themselves, sharing in different facets of calculations, and jointly assembling a final result for output. Such intermachine communication is inherently capable of taking place at speeds that stress local area network technology and are a hundred or more times faster than are possible on today's long haul networks. As an example, some of the nation's leading radiology departments have committed to digital transfer of radiology images on broadband local networks operating at speeds of 100 to 1000 million bits per second.

In order for the NREN to support these and other demanding applications, not yet contemplated, a substantial directed research and development effort is needed in the areas of protocols (the formal structure of inter–computer communications), high speed computer interfaces for computers, and network equipment, such as switches. Multi–gigabit networks represent a change in kind, not just in degree, from today's networks. For example, consider that in a coast–to–coast communication at three gigabits per second there are at any instant "in flight" nearly nine megabytes of data, which is more than the memory of most personal computers and workstations.

Some gigabit research has already begun, and several experimental facilities have been established in a productive collaboration of academic, industrial, and governmental organizations, but HPCC support will be needed to carry the research program to the stage that commercial providers can use the technology to install and operate a multi–gigabit NREN.

Education Using the NREN

Computers increasingly fill important niches in all phases of the learning process, providing flexible instruments for interactive instruction and student based learning experiences. Their use in education both provides the skills needed to function in our increasingly technology–intensive world, and aids teaching and learning of all science and engineering topics. The development of the National Research and Education Network will accelerate and transfer the technology of computer communications to the needs of educators and students. The result will be to empower them to share resources and ideas on a national scale.

In a recent project, classes in many locations chose a day to measure the length of the sun's shadow from a vertical measuring stick on the school grounds at 12 noon. Each class consulted maps and geography books to find its school's latitude, and sent the results to a shared database located in the U.S. and Canada. All schools then received the database of measurements from around the world, and each class used the complete database to calculate the curvature of the earth, and from that, the earth's diameter. A normally dry recitation of facts became an engaging problem solving exercise because the students themselves derived the answer from their shared measurements. Along the way they learned geography, geometry, statistics, and how to collect and share data over computer networks.

This project, implemented by the use of the network, is a learning laboratory without walls, similar to the way research scientists take advantage of high speed digital networks to conduct shared research that is "distance independent." The HPCC Program will face the challenge of "scaling–up" today's Internet, making it "user–friendly" and improving its services so that it is readily accessible to all U.S. educational institutions.

Glossary

ASTA
    Advanced Software Technology and Algorithms

Bit
    Acronym for binary digit

BRHR
    Basic Research and Human Resources

Byte
    A group of adjacent binary digits operated upon as a unit (usually connotes a group of eight bits)

CAD
    Acronym for "computer aided design".

Computer Engineering
    The creative application of engineering principles and methods to the design and development of hardware and software systems.

Computer Science
    The systematic study of computing systems and computation. The body of knowledge resulting from this discipline contains theories for understanding computing systems and methods; design methodology, algorithms, and tools; methods for the testing of concepts; methods of analysis and verification; and knowledge representation and implementation.

Computational Science and Engineering
    The systematic application of computing systems and computational solution techniques to mathematical models formulated to describe and simulate phenomena of scientific and engineering interest.

flops
    Acronym for "floating point operations per second". The term "floating point" refers to that format of numbers which is most commonly used for scientific calculation. Flops is used as a measure of a computing system's speed of performing basic arithmetic operations such as adding, subtracting, multiplying, or dividing two numbers.

Giga–
    10^9 or billions of ... (e.g.: gigabits)

Grand Challenge
    A Grand Challenge is a fundamental problem in science and engineering, with broad economic and scientific impact, whose solution could be advanced by applying high performance computing techniques and resources.

HPCC
   High Performance Computing and Communications

HPCS
   High Performance Computing Systems

High Performance Computing
   High performance computing encompasses advanced computing,
   communications, and information technologies, including scientific
   workstations, supercomputer systems, high speed networks, special
   purpose and experimental systems, the new generation of large scale
   parallel systems, and applications and systems software with all
   components well integrated and linked over a high speed national network.

Mega–
   10^6 or millions of ... (e.g.: megaflops)

Network
   Computer communications technologies that link multiple computers to
   share information and resources across geographically dispersed locations.

NREN
   National Research and Education Network

ops
   Acronym for "operations per second". Ops is used as a rating of the speed
   of computer systems and components. In this report ops is generally taken
   to mean the usual integer or floating point operations depending on what
   functional units are included in a particular system configuration.

Parallel Processing
   Simultaneous processing by more than one processing unit on a single
   application.

Peta–
   10^{15} or thousands of trillions of ... (e.g.: petabytes)

Supercomputer
   At any given time, that class of general–purpose computers that are both
   faster than their commercial competitors and have sufficient central
   memory to store the problem sets for which they are designed. Computer
   memory, throughput, computational rates, and other related computer
   capabilities contribute to performance. Consequently, a quantitative
   measure of computer power in large–scale scientific processing does not
   exist and a precise definition of supercomputers is difficult to formulate.

Tera–
   10^{12} or trillions of ... (e.g.: teraops)

Q

Seeking Solutions: High-Performance Computing for Science,
U.S. Congress, Office of Technology Assessment, 1991.

BACKGROUND PAPER

CONGRESS OF THE UNITED STATES   OFFICE OF TECHNOLOGY ASSESSMENT

Recommended Citation:

U.S. Congress, Office of Technology Assessment, *Seeking Solutions: High-Performance Computing for Science—Background Paper*, OTA-BP-TCT-77 (Washington, DC: U.S. Government Printing Office, April 1991).

Foreword

High-performance "supercomputers" are fast becoming tools of international competition and they play an important role in such areas as scientific research, weather forecasting, and popular entertainment. They may prove to be the key to maintaining America's preeminence in science and engineering. The automotive, aerospace, electronic, and pharmaceutical industries are becoming more reliant on the use of high-performance computers in the analysis, engineering, design, and manufacture of high-technology products.

Many of the national and international problems we face, such as global environmental change, weather forecasting, development of new energy sources, development of advanced materials, understanding molecular structure, investigating the origin of the universe, and mapping the human genome involve complex computations that only high-performance computers can solve.

This is the second publication from our assessment on information technology and research, which was requested by the House Committee on Science and Technology and the Senate Committee on Commerce, Science, and Transportation. The first background paper, *High Performance Computing & Networking for Science*, published in 1989, framed the outstanding issues; this background paper focuses on the Federal role in supporting a national high-performance computing initiative.

OTA gratefully acknowledges the contributions of the many experts, within and outside the government, who served as panelists, workshop participants, contractors, reviewers, and advisors for this document. As with all OTA reports, however, the content is solely the responsibility of OTA and does not necessarily constitute the consensus or endorsement of the advisory panel, workshop participants, or the Technology Assessment Board.

JOHN H. GIBBONS
Director

High-Performance Computing and Networking
for Science Advisory Panel

NOTE: OTA appreciates and is grateful for the valuable assistance and thoughtful critiques provided by the advisory panel members. The panel does not, however, necessarily approve, disapprove, or endorse this background paper. OTA assumes full responsibility for the background paper and the accuracy of its contents.

iv

OTA Project Staff—High-Performance Computing

John Andelin, *Assistant Director, OTA*
Science, Information, and Natural Resources Division

James W. Curlin, *Telecommunication and Computing Technologies Program Manager*

Fred W. Weingarten,[1] *Project Director*

Elizabeth I. Miller, *Research Assistant*

Administrative Staff

Elizabeth Emanuel, *Office Administrator*

Karolyn St. Clair, *Secretary*

Jo Anne Price, *Secretary*

---

[1]Through June 30, 1990.

Contents

Chapter 1
High-Performance Computing and Information Infrastructure for Science and Engineering

Introduction

Information technology is a critical element for science and engineering. The United States is building a nationwide computer-communication infrastructure to provide high-speed data services to the R&D community, but the mere installation of hardware is not enough. Whether very fast data communication networks and high-performance computers deliver their promised benefits will depend on the institutions, processes, and policies that are established to design and manage the new system.

OTA was asked by the House Committee on Science, Space, and Technology and the Senate Committee on Commerce and Transportation to examine the role that high-performance computing, networking, and information technologies are playing in science and engineering, and to analyze the need for Federal action. An OTA background paper, released in September 1989, explored and described some key issues.[1] This background paper examines high-performance computing as part of the infrastructure proposed in the Office of Science and Technology Policy (OSTP) initiative. A detailed OTA report on the National Research and Education Network (NREN) is scheduled for release later in 1991.

Six years ago, Congress directed the National Science Foundation (NSF) to establish an Advanced Scientific Computing Program designed to increase access by researchers to high-performance computing. That program resulted in the establishment of five national centers for scientific supercomputing. Since then, one of the centers has been left unfunded; but the other four are still operating.

During the last 5 years, legislation has been introduced in Congress calling for the establishment of a high-capacity, broadband, advanced national data communications network for research. Over the years, congressional interest has grown as this concept has evolved into a plan for an integrated national research and education network (NREN)

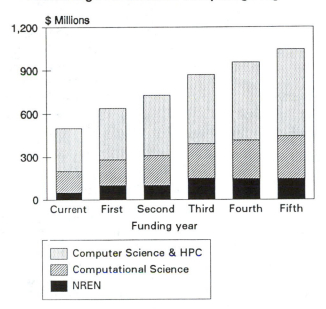

Figure 1—Estimated Proposed Funding Levels for Federal High-Performance Computing Program

SOURCE: Office of Science and Technology Policy, *The Federal High-Performance Computing Program* (Washington, DC: Office of Science and Technology Policy, 1989), app. C, p. 26.

consisting of an advanced communication network linked to a variety of computational and information facilities and services.

In September 1989, at the request of Congress, OSTP submitted a draft plan developed by the Federal Coordinating Council for Science, Engineering, and Technology (FCCSET). The plan called for a "National High-Performance Computing Initiative" that includes both a national network and initiatives to advance high-performance computing (see figure 1). In testimony to the 101st Congress, the director of OSTP stated that this Initiative was among the top priorities on the science agenda. On June 8, 1990, the National Science Foundation announced a $15.8 million, 3-year research effort aimed at funding 5 gigabit-speed testbed experimental networks. These test networks are the first step in developing a high-speed nation-

---

[1]U.S. Congress, Office of Technology Assessment, *High Performance Computing & Networking for Science*, OTA-BP-CIT-59 (Washington, DC: U.S. Government Printing Office, September 1989).

wide broadband advanced communication network in collaboration with the Defense Advanced Research Project Agency (DARPA).

OSTP set forth its plans for a Federal High-Performance Computing and Communications Program (HPCC) in a document released on February 4, 1991, supporting the President's Fiscal Year 1992 budget.[2] The Program proposes to invest $638 million in fiscal year 1992, an increase of about 30 percent over the 1991 level. These funds will support activities in four program areas: 1) high-performance computing systems; 2) advanced software technology and algorithms; 3) National Research and Education Network; and 4) basic research and human resources.

High-Performance Computing: A Federal Concern

Concern about information technology by high-level policymakers is a recent phenomenon. Researchers who see the importance of data exchange have managed to secure funding for computers and communications out of the limited Federal agency research budgets. Agencies such as DARPA and NSF have quietly developed computer and network-related programs without major administration initiatives or congressional actions. But the atmosphere is now different for several reasons.

First, researchers cannot consistently obtain needed information resources because of the cost. High-end scientific computers cost several million dollars to purchase and millions more per year to operate. Universities grew reluctant in the late 1970s and early 1980s to purchase these systems with their own funds, and government investment in computers slowed. In the meantime, researchers learned more about the use of high-performance computing. The machines became more powerful, doubling in speed about every 2 years. The scientific community slowly became aware of the lost opportunities caused by lack of access to high-performance computers and other powerful information technologies.

Second, information resources—computers, databases, and software—are being shared among disciplines, institutions, and facilities. These are being linked as common resources through networks to users at desktop workstations. A need has grown for better coordination in the design and operation of these systems; this will be particularly important for a national data communications network.

Third, although the U.S. computer industry is relatively strong, there is concern about increasing competition from foreign firms, particularly Japanese. Over the last decade, the Japanese Government has supported programs, such as the Fifth Generation Project (it is now planning a Sixth Generation initiative) and National Superspeed Computer Project, designed to strengthen the Japanese position in high-performance computing. During the last 2 years there have been difficult trade negotiations between the United States and Japan over supercomputer markets in the respective countries. This has raised concern about the economic and strategic importance of a healthy U.S. high-performance computing industry.[3]

Fourth, concern for the Japanese challenge in high-performance computing goes beyond the competitiveness of the U.S. supercomputer industry. Computational simulation in engineering design and manufacturing is becoming a major factor in maintaining a competitive posture in high-technology industries such as automotives, aerospace, petroleum, electronics, and pharmaceuticals. It is in the availability and application of high-performance computing to increase productivity and improve product quality where the greatest future economic benefits may lie.

Finally, the infrastructure of this interlinked set of technologies is considered by some to be a strong basis for the development of a universal broadband information system. A very high-capacity digital communication network and information services, as visualized, would carry entertainment, educational, and social services to the home and support a broad range of business and education services. A

---

[2]OSTP, *Grand Challenges: High-Performance Computing and Communications*, (Washington, DC: OSTP, 1991), p. 57.

[3]High-performance computers are considered to be strategically important to the United States because of the central role computers play in the economy, security, manufacturing, and research and development. *See* Office of Science and Technology Policy, *The Federal High Performance Computing Program* (Washington, DC: Office of Science and Technology Policy, 1989), pp. 12-13. *See* U.S. Congress, Office of Technology Assessment, *Making Things Better: Competing in Manufacturing*, OTA-ITE-443 (Washington, DC: U.S. Government Printing Office, February 1990), p. 241, for a comprehensive view of the U.S. competitive position in manufacturing, including computer-related industries. An assessment of the status of the U.S. supercomputing industry will be included in a forthcoming OTA report on Japan and International Trade.

Photo credit: Cray Research, Inc.

The CRAY Y-MP/832 computer system is the top-of-the-line supercomputer of Cray Research, Inc. It contains 8 central processors and 32 million 64-bit words of memory.

nationwide network for research and education could be a starting point, and could gradually broaden to this vision.

Multiple Goals for an Initiative

The supporting arguments for a Federal High-Performance computing/networking initiative center on three objectives:

1. *To advance U.S. research and development* critical to U.S. industry, security, and educa-

tion by providing researchers with the most powerful computers and communication systems available. This objective is based on a vision of computers and data communication technologies forming a basic infrastructure for supporting research. This goal has been proposed in several reports and policy papers.[4]

2. *To strengthen the U.S. computer industry* (particularly the high-performance computers and high-speed telecommunications) by testing new system concepts and developing new techniques for applications. Federal Coordinating Council for Science, Engineering, and Technology (FCCSET) and the Institute of Electrical and Electronics Engineers, among others, strongly endorse this view.[5]

3. *To enhance U.S. economic and social strength* by stimulating the development of a universal information infrastructure through development of new technologies that could serve as a system prototype.[6]

Strong sentiment exists among some Members of Congress for each of these three objectives. Furthermore, the goals are closely related and nearly inseparable—most discussion and proposals for computing and networking programs reflect elements of all three.

Not everyone in Congress or the executive branch agrees that all goals are equally important or even appropriate for the Federal Government. Some consider the current level of government spending to advance scientific knowledge to be adequate, and they believe that other needs have higher priority. Others point out that since information technology is now central to all R&D, it is important to create a modern information infrastructure in order to realize the benefits from government investment in science and engineering.

[4]Peter D. Lax, ''Report of the Panel on Large-Scale Computing in Science and Engineering'' (Washington, DC: National Science Foundation, 1982), p. 10. EDUCOM, Networking and Telecommunications Task Force, *The National Research and Education Network: A Policy Paper* (Washington, DC: EDUCOM, 1990) p. 3.
    ''The goal of the National Research and Education Network is to enhance national competitiveness and productivity through a high speed . . . network infrastructure which supports a broad set of applications and network services for the research and instructional community.''

[5]Executive Office of the President, Office of Science and Technology Policy, *The Federal High Performance Computing Program* (Washington, DC: September 1989), p. 1.
    ''[A goal of the High Performance Computing Program is to] maintain and extend U.S. leadership in high performance computing, and encourage U.S. sources of production.''

[6]*Congressional Record* comments on introduction of bill. For example, Senator Gore stated the following, when introducing his bill, S1067:
    ''The nation which most completely assimilates high performance computing into its economy will very likely emerge as the dominant intellectual, economic, and technological force in the next century.
    U.S. industry must produce advanced yet economical systems which will meet the needs of users found in each of the major sectors. . . . If this is not done by U.S. Government leadership, it will be done by foreign leadership to the detriment of U.S. national interests.''

Some disagree with an initiative that resembles "industrial policy"—i.e., policy aimed at supporting specific private sector enterprises. They argue that the government should not intervene to support either the supercomputer or the telecommunications industry. Proponents of government intervention argue that the dominant position of the U.S. supercomputer industry has historically resulted from heavy Federal investments in computing for research and that the future health of the industry will require continued Federal attention.

Some ask why science should get early preferred access to what ultimately may become a universal communication service, and suggest that selectively providing such resources to science might delay broader adoption by the public that promises even greater payoffs. They are also wary of the government providing or subsidizing telecommunication services that should, in their view, be provided by the private sector. They argue that a universal network is best achieved through the expertise and resources of the commercial communication and information industries. Proponents of Federal action maintain that the science network will be an important prototype to develop and test new standards and technologies for extremely high-speed packet-switched data communication. Furthermore, in their view, a network oriented to research and education would be a valuable testbed for developing applications and better understanding how a universal network would be used.

These debates reflect in part different philosophies, values, and expectations about future events that must be resolved in a political process. The assumptions underlying each of these three goals—advance U.S. R&D, strengthen the U.S. computer and telecommunications industry, and enhance U.S. economic and social strength—are generally soundly based because:

1. **Scientific users need access to advanced computers, communication systems, databases, and software services**—Scientific and engineering research in the United States cannot retain its world-class position without the best available information and communication technologies. These include advanced computer systems, very large databases, and high-speed data communications, local workstations, electronic mail service, and bulletin boards. Such technology does not simply enhance or marginally improve the productivity of the research process; it enables research that could not be performed otherwise. Simulating the complex behavior of the Earth's climate, analyzing streams of data from an Earth satellite or visualizing the interactions of complex organic molecules are impossible without these new technologies. Furthermore, many more important applications await the as-yet-unrealized capabilities of future generations of information technology.

2. **Major Federal research applications have stimulated the computer industry and will likely continue to do so**—Scientific and engineering applications have stretched the capacities of information technologies and tested them in ways that other applications cannot. Eventually, the techniques and capabilities developed to serve these demands make their way into the broader community of computer users. Although the computer industry structure and markets are changing, this form of technology transfer will likely continue.

3. **U.S. economic growth and societal strength can be assisted by the development of a national information infrastructure that couples a universal high-speed data communication network with a wide range of powerful computational and information resources**—In a recent report, *Critical Connections: Communication for the Future*, OTA stated:

> Given the increased dependence of American businesses on information and its exchange, the competitive status among businesses and in the global economy will increasingly depend on the technical capabilities, quality, and cost of [their] communication facilities ... Failure to exploit these opportunities is almost certain to leave many businesses and nations behind.[7]

In that report, OTA listed "modernization and technological development of the communication infrastructure" as one of the five key areas of future policy concern. The high-performance computing

---

[7]U.S. Congress, Office of Technology Assessment, *Critical Connections: Communication for the Future,* OTA-CIT-407 (Washington, DC: U.S. Government Printing Office, January 1990), p. 6.

and networking initiative reflects a mixture of three basic goals: 1) enhancing R&D, 2) accelerating innovation in U.S. information technology, and 3) stimulating the development of a universal broadband digital network in the United States. Achieving the last goal will ultimately bring information and educational opportunities to the doorstep of most American homes.

An Infrastructure for Science

Science and Information Technology Are Closely Linked

Whether computers are made of silicon chips, optical glass fibers, gallium arsenide compounds, or superconducting ceramics, and regardless of the architecture, the basic elements of computers are the same—data, logic, and language.

- *Data* is the substance that is processed or manipulated by the technology; often, but not always, numerical.
- *Logic* is the nature of the process, from basic arithmetic to extremely complex reasoning and analysis.
- *Language* is the means of communicating from the user to the machine what is to be done, and from the machine to the user the result of that action.

These three elements are also basic to science. They characterize the nature of research and the work of scientists.

- Researchers collect data from measurements of natural phenomena, experiments, pure mathematics, and, increasingly, from computer calculations and simulations. Data can take many forms, e.g., numbers, symbols, images, sounds, and words.
- Researchers build logical structures—theories, mathematical and computer models, and so on—to describe and understand the phenomena they are studying.
- Researchers communicate their work among themselves in common scientific languages. This communication is a continuing process— both formal and informal—that lies at the heart of the scientific method. It is based on exposing ideas to the critical review of peers, allowing the reproduction of experiments and analyses, and encouraging the evolution of understanding based on prior knowledge.

Scientists invented the computer to serve research needs during World War II. In the late 1960s, research needs led to the development of ARPANET —the first nationwide communication system designed specifically to carry data between computers. NSF operated a Computer Facilities Program in the late 1960s and early 1970s that assisted universities in upgrading their scientific computing capabilities for research and education. Today, computers are used throughout society, but researchers, joined by industry, are still driving the evolution of information technology and finding new applications for the most powerful computer and communication technologies.

The invention of the printing press in the 15th century created the conditions for the development and flourishing of modern science and scholarship. Not only did the press allow authors to communicate their ideas accurately, but the qualities of the medium stimulated entirely new methods and institutions of learning. Similarly, electronic information technology is again changing the nature of basic research. The character of the research—the way data are collected, analyzed, studied, and communicated—has changed because of technology.

Computational research has joined experimentation and theory as a major mode of investigation. Scientists now use computer models to analyze very complex processes such as the flow of gases around a black hole or the wind patterns around the eye of a hurricane or typhoon (see boxes A and B). These and other areas of research, such as global climate change, can be accomplished only with high-performance computing. They cannot use conventional mathematical and experimental approaches because of the complexity of the phenomena.

Research is generating data at unprecedented rates. The human genome database is projected to eventually contain over 3 billion units of information. Earth observation experiments in space will collect and send to Earth trillions of units of data daily. A single image of the United States, with resolution to a square yard, contains nearly a trillion data points. Current data storage technologies are unable to store, organize, and transmit the amounts of data that will be generated from these projects. Long-term storage capabilities must be researched and developed. "Big science" projects, such as those mentioned above, should devote a portion of their budgets for R&D in high-capacity data storage

Box A—Black Holes: The Mysteries of the Universe

A black hole is an object in space, whose mass is so dense that nothing is able to escape its gravitational pull, not even light. Astronomers think the universe is populated with black holes that are the remains of collapsed stars. Much of the research conducted on the universe has implications for other areas of study, such as physics. Below is a visualization of the three dimensional flow of gases past a black hole. The computer codes used to create this image can also be used to determine the accuracy of computer generated models of three dimension fluid flows.

Collaborative efforts between two NSF-funded supercomputer centers, the National Center for Supercomputing Application (NCSA) in Illinois and The Cornell Theory Center, resulted in a video of the phenomenon pictured. The computer code used to derive the data was written by researchers at Cornell and was run on Cornell's IBM 3090 computer. NCSA remotely accessed the data via NSFNET from Cornell. At the Illinois center researchers worked with a scientific animator who, using Waverfront Technologies Graphic Software tools and a graphics packaged designed at NCSA, processed the data on a Alliant computer. The research team created a rough contoured image of the cell with the Alliant. The researchers returned to Cornell and modified the contouring graphics programs, creating a videotape on Silicon Graphics workstation at Cornell. The project was the first joint effort between NSF supercomputer centers. Utilizing the expertise of two centers was instrumental in graphically depicting three-dimensional fluid flow.

PHOTOGRAPH
NOT AVAILABLE

systems if such large projects are to be successful. New forms of institutions and procedures to manage massive data banks are also needed.

Journal articles have been the major form of communication among scientists. Publishers are beginning to develop electronic journals, accessed directly over communication networks or distributed in computer readable form. The different nature of electronic storage means that these new "publications" will likely look, behave, and be used differently than printed journals. They may contain information in a variety of forms: high-definition video, moving images, sound, large experimental data sets, or software. Using so-called "hypermedia" and multimedia techniques, these electronic journals can be linked to other related articles, films, and so on. They can evolve and change over time, containing later annotations by the original author or others, or references to later articles that advanced or stemmed from the original work.

Scientists communicate with each other continually by letter, telephone, conferences, and seminars, and by meeting personally around the departmental coffee pot. These modes of communication are often as important to research as formal publications. All of these modes will likely continue in some form, but digital communication systems provide many new powerful ways to communicate—electronic mail, computer conferences, and bulletin boards. Proximity, time, and travel are less important in using these new communication paths. With bulletin boards and electronic mail, information can be exchanged much faster than by mail and with accuracy and detail that is impossible to achieve with telephone. Since the participants need not travel, computer conferences can accommodate large numbers of participants. Sessions can take place over weeks or months, and people can participate in the electronic meeting wherever they are at whatever time is convenient.

A National Infrastructure for Research and Education

These information technologies and applications are merging into an interconnected network of resources referred to in telecommunication's parlance as an "Information Infrastructure." This infrastructure is a conceptual collection of linked resources made up of:

Box B—Supertyphoon Hope

A typhoon is a tropical storm confined to the western Pacific Ocean, referred to as hurricanes in the Western Hemisphere. The cyclonic storms are usually accompanied by extremely low atmospheric pressure, high winds of over 100 knots, and vast amounts of rainfall. These storms can wreak havoc when they reach land, at which time they dissipate. A series of computer-generated images that trace the 6-day evolution of supertyphoon Hope are shown here. The supertyphoon's course was simulated using a computer model. Researchers were able to measure the precision of their model by comparing its results to the data gathered during the storm in 1979. Developing accurate weather models continues to be difficult despite advances in technology. Weather models must incorporate many variables such a winds, temperatures, the oceans, and atmospheric pressures.

Researchers processed their weather model at the National Center for Atmospheric Research (NCAR) remotely from their home institute, Florida State University (FSU). Using a NASA computer network, the group accessed an IBM 4381 computer, which served as the front end machine for a Cray X-MP. After the data were processed at NCAR, it was transferred to magnetic tapes and mailed to FSU for further analysis. (An increase in bandwidth now allows the researchers to separate large data sets into sections and send them over high bandwidth computer networks.) At FSU the data were translated into images using a Silicon Graphics Workstation. Data collected from the storm in 1979 are stored on computers at NCAR. The data were used to measure the accuracy of FSU's weather model. The computer-generated storm was accurate within hours of the actual events of Supertypoon Hope.

The facilities at NCAR were especially suited for the needs of the FSU researchers since both the staff and resources were geared towards atmospheric and ocean modeling. Researchers frequently visit NCAR for user conferences and have become familiar with many of the technical support staff.

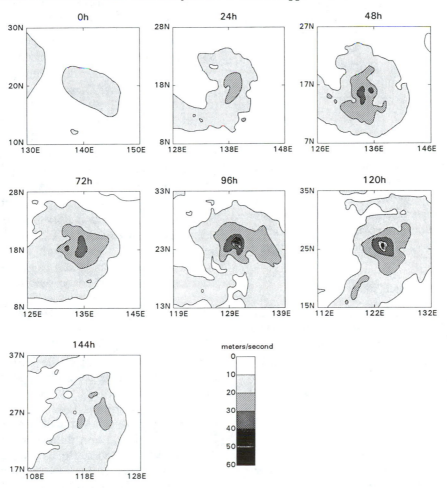

A Nationwide High-Speed Broadband Advanced Information Communication Network

This computer-to-computer network is composed of many parts—local networks on campuses and in research facilities, State and regional networks, and one or more national "backbone" networks interconnecting them all. This domestic backbone would link to networks in other countries. Some of the domestic networks will be private commercial networks; others may be operated by private nonprofit organizations, and still others may be government-funded and/or managed.

Specialized and General Purpose Computers

Users will be able to access the newest, most powerful supercomputers. There will be a variety of specialized machines tailored to specific uses and applications because of the developing nature of current computer architectures. They will be used for database searches, graphical output, and artificial intelligence applications such as pattern recognition and expert systems. Researchers will have access to a heterogeneous computing environment where several specialized machines, each with their own strengths, are linked through a software network that will allow users to simultaneously exploit the power of each computer to solve portions of a single application.

Collections of Specialized Applications Programs

Some application programs are extremely large and represent years of development effort. They may be maintained and updated centrally and made available over the network. Groups can also make available libraries of commercial or public domain software that could be distributed to local computers.

Remote Access to Research Instruments

Some research facilities house one-of-a-kind instruments, unique because of their cost or their site location, such as telescopes, environmental monitoring devices, oceanographic probes, seismographs, space satellite-based instruments, and so on. Remote use and control of these instruments is possible through the network infrastructure.

Services To Support and Enhance Scientific Communication

These services include electronic mail and conferencing systems, bulletin boards, and electronic journals through which researchers can communicate with each other. They also will include scholarly bibliographic reference and abstracting services, and online card catalogs linked to key research libraries.

"Digital Libraries" and Archives

These resources would contain collections of reference materials—books, journals, sound recordings, photographs and films, software, and other types of information—archived in digital electronic form. These also include major scientific and technical databases such as the human genome database, time-series environmental data from satellites, and astronomical images. Some visionaries see the network eventually providing access to a connection with a "Global Digital Library," a distributed collection of facilities that would store electronically most of the world's most important information.

Facilities for Analyzing and Displaying the Results of Computations

Researchers who simulate large, complex systems must develop ways to interpret these simulations to replace examining enormous quantities of computer-generated numbers. These researchers need to interact with the model; directly controlling the computer is the next step. Researchers are developing new ways to "see" their models by visualizing them directly or by use of methods such as holograms that provide three-dimensional views. Other researchers are developing tactile systems that, through special gloves and visors, allow a person to "feel" simulated objects or act as if they were moving about in a simulated environment ("virtual reality"). Researchers on the network will draw on specialized centers of technology and expertise to help them develop interfaces with computations and databases.

The Current Federal Picture

Recent Studies

Over the last 8 years, the key Federal science agencies and private groups have assessed the role of information technology in science and engineering research. These studies have concluded that computers and communication technology are critically important to R&D and the competitive position of the United States in the global economy. The studies pointed out shortcomings in the current system and recommended Federal actions.

The Lax Report

In 1982, the Panel on Large Scale Computing in Science and Engineering issued a report that became known as the "Lax Report" after its chairman, Peter Lax. It was jointly funded by the NSF and the Department of Defense. The panel noted that the U.S. research establishment seriously lacks access to high-performance computing. It found that this deficiency harms U.S. preeminence in R&D and threatens the current strong position of the U.S. computer industry. To remedy this, the panel recommended a national supercomputer program consisting of four basic components:

1. establish national supercomputing centers and develop "a nation-wide interdisciplinary network through which users will have access to facilities";
2. support research in software and algorithms—particularly work on parallelism and other new computer architectures for high-performance computing in the future;
3. support education and training programs for new users in order to assist the research community in using supercomputer applications; and
4. support research aimed at developing new, faster, supercomputers.

Variation of these four elements are repeated in the subsequent proposals and initiatives.

The Bardon/Curtis Report

At the request of Congress, NSF undertook an internal review of the Lax Report designed to form a program plan. The 1983 report, which became known as the Bardon/Curtis Report, offered an ambitious program plan with several recommendations for NSF:

1. "greatly increase its [NSF's] support for local computing facilities, including individual workstations, systems for research groups, specialized computer facilities, and local area networks";
2. establish 10 supercomputer centers;
3. support the establishment of networks to link users with the supercomputer centers; and
4. "support a program of academic research in the areas of advanced computer systems design."

National Academy of Sciences/COSEPUP

In 1989, the Committee on Science, Engineering, and Public Policy of the National Academy of Sciences (NAS) published a report, *Information Technology and the Conduct of Research,*[8] which examined the needs of science for new technological initiatives. This report, prepared by a panel chaired by Donald Langenberg, emphasized the changing form of research and its increased dependence on new information technologies. The report advised against leaving the design and operation of these programs only to the technical experts. Systems designers must learn what the users need, then design the system. The panel made two recommendations to do this:

- "The institutions that support U.S. research, including universities, industry, and Government should develop and support policies, services, and standards that help researchers use information technology more widely and productively, and
- "The institutions supporting the nation's researchers, led by the Federal government, should develop an interconnected national information technology network for use by all qualified researchers."

The panel recognized that industry, the universities, libraries, professional societies, and the Federal Government share responsibilities for this. The Federal role, according to the committee, should include leadership and coordination in the development of technologies and services to support the research and education needs in addition to funding.

National Association of State Universities and Land Grant Colleges (NASULGC)

In 1989, NASULGC issued a report, *Supercomputing for the 1990's: A Shared Responsibility*, on the need to make high-performance computing available for academic research, that contained recommendations for the Federal Government and universities. It points out that a computing infrastructure would have to include facilities operated by a variety of institutions beyond the Federal Government. Federal policy, it suggests, should be tailored to encouraging and leveraging private, regional, and local efforts. Recommendations for Federal action include:

---

[8]NAS report.

- supporting the national supercomputer centers and maintaining them at the technological leading edge;
- "fostering and encouraging university, state, and regional supercomputing facilities" (of which the report identified 27);
- supporting the development of a national network; and
- assuring the "constancy" of support.

These recommendations reflect concern that the support of NSF national centers would draw funds away from computing at non-NSF centers. The report notes that the non-NSF centers will also play an important role in the future of scientific computing. NASULGC further observes that changing policies and unpredictable funding disrupts operations and discourages the development of facilities.

EDUCOM

EDUCOM is an association of higher education institutions. It functions as a clearing house for information and expertise about computers and communication technologies. EDUCOM's university consortium created and manages BITNET, a private, shared network that serves the networking needs of academics at a low cost. Its Networking and Telecommunications Task Force examined the Federal networking and computing initiatives and has produced several policy statements and reports.

A statement, released in March 1990, focuses on the network. It makes a series of specific recommendations on implementing the NREN, but its statement of the basic goal for a network is broad:

> [NREN]. . . is to enhance national competitiveness and productivity through a high-speed, high-quality network infrastructure which supports a broad set of applications and network services for the research and education community.[9]

Common Themes

The series of reports strikes some common themes. Three points, in particular, are important to the current policy debate.

First, the network has become the key element. Seen first as simply a means to access expensive or highly specialized computing resources (similar to the initial intentions for ARPANET), the network has become the basic foundation for the information infrastructure, connecting researchers and students not only to computers, but providing access to a wide range of services.

The network is actually an internet, a family of networks (networks within networks), the design and operation of which needs coordination and leadership from the Federal science agencies. OTA's forthcoming report on the NREN will explore these issues in depth.

Second, educational needs are now part of the NREN plan although it is undecided how wide the range of users and institutions will be. In any event, this will affect network architecture and operating policies. Once referred to as a National Research Network (NRN), it is now known as a National Research and Education Network (NREN). This evolution was natural. It is impossible to separate education from research at the graduate level. There are also strong arguments for including undergraduates, secondary schools, and even primary schools in the system. To better coordinate the educational community's views on how the NREN may assist education, the Department of Education and State and local educators must be actively involved in the policy process.

The question of scope of the network extends to research in non-science scholarly disciplines, some of which are not well-funded by Federal programs. The wide range of services offered, including access to libraries, bibliographic services, electronic mail, bulletin boards, computer conferencing, and so on, extends the network's potential scholarly beneficiaries beyond just scientists and engineers.

A third commonly raised issue in the reports is the need to look beyond mere hardware. Computers need software that make them accessible and usable by researchers. A network needs software tools and data-bases that allow scientists to communicate effectively with one another. Databases need inquiry systems (search engines), indices, tables of contents, directories, hypertext, and other tools to enable users to search, identify, and retrieve the information they need for their work. To properly develop an infrastructure that is useful to all science, attention must be paid to software as well as hardware.

Other groups also rely on access to scientific information. Public interest groups with concerns of

---

[9]EDUCOM, The National Research and Education Network, op. cit., footnote 4, p. 3.

public safety and health, the environment, energy, defense policy, and so on, rely on access to scientific publications and databases and attendance at conferences and seminars. The press, particularly the specialized scientific and technical press, must access conferences, journals, and other forms of electronic communication.

In most cases, these applications, which enable effective access and use of information, are neither simple nor obvious. Developing them will require significant research and software development as well as better understanding of how information technology can best assist scholars in their work. The answers to these questions will also depend on the nature and breadth of the constituency for the network. Different users will have different skills, analytical strategies, and research styles depending, in part, on the traditions of their particular disciplines and their level of training.

The Government's Role Is Changing

The Federal Government has major responsibilities for the health of basic and academic research in the United States, both as a user of the products and from its role in supporting science and engineering to advance the economy and improve the quality of life. The government is already participating heavily in the development and management of the existing R&D information infrastructure—in using it, funding it, and in setting policies. The government must deal with additional responsibilities resulting from the new infrastructure. The challenge will be to organize and assemble a government entity to: 1) identify and determine promising technological directions for the high-performance computing infrastructure; 2) evaluate progress over the course of the High-Performance Computing (HPC) initiative; and 3) make course corrections at the appropriate times.

First, facilities need to be highly interconnected. They must connect physically and logically with the network. Digital signals must conform to standards and protocols in the same way that electrical appliances must plug into standard 110 volt, 60 Hz AC power outlets. Users must be able to transmit and receive communications, programs, and data seamlessly and transparently to and from each nook and cranny in the system. Government policies and programs must be coordinated if interconnectability is to be achieved.

Second, many of the shared resources cut across agencies, institutions, disciplines, and programs. This feature of sharing is most obvious in the physical network; but it is also true for many of the computing facilities, data archives, and network services such as directories, bulletin boards, and electronic mail. Thus, many policy decisions regarding the use and access to these resources and services must be made at an interagency level. Furthermore, new private networks and service corporations now provide networking services to public and private customers. The policies of these private entities will become more important as the network moves towards full commercialization.

Third, the facilities will be expensive and require large capital investments. The Federal Government will be asked to share these costs with States, local governments, other countries, research and educational institutions, industrial users, service providers, and individual users. Private entities may be expected to contribute substantially as well. But while technological risks may be acceptable to private companies. The commercial risks may be unacceptable without government support.

Fourth, many of the resources on the network will be unique and of great national—even international—importance, e.g., a supercomputer dedicated to global climate modeling or the human genome database. Access to these scarce resources must reflect a cooperative set of goals, to determine access, decide who can use it, and to set national priorities. Federal policies are needed to balance and ensure equitable access and security. The Executive Office of the President (OSTP) and congressional committees may be called on to referee conflicts among competing interests from time to time. A well-organized Federal management system responsible for policy oversight and operation of the HPC and network infrastructure can anticipate or avoid many problems, and thus reduce the need for political resolutions.

Finally, the government must assist in advancing the state of computer and communication technologies to hasten the development of more powerful high-performance computers, faster data communications, and more effective software. Several studies by NAS, OSTP, and others have identified ''Grand Challenges in Research'' of critical national importance, but which are currently unachievable because of inadequate computing power.[10] What is needed are computers that are hundreds—even thousands—of times faster than the best now available. Similarly, the "data explosion" demands better and faster storage technology to archive large data sets. The rapidly growing communication needs of science require switched wide-area digital communication networks capable of moving billions of units of information per second to and from researchers.

The Structure of Federal Policy

Researchers foresee computers that will soon perform a trillion arithmetic steps ("teraflops") per second, data communication systems that can transmit billions of units of data ("gigabits") per second, and electronic storage systems that can store correspondingly large amounts of information and absorb and disgorge it at rates matched to the speed of the computers and communication lines. New hardware will require new streamlined software to operate the high-speed computers and communications networks efficiently.

Developing, Managing, and Funding Major Resources

A striking trend in information technology is the development of inexpensive input and output devices—computers, telephones, facsimile machines, and so on—that are affordable and easy to use. But the opposite is happening in the development of advanced computers and communications technology. High-performance computers, data networks, and archiving facilities are extremely expensive to build and operate. They are complicated technologies that require experts to develop and operate. Such expensive and complicated systems must be located in a few central facilities and made available to network users through such installations as the National Supercomputer Centers, NSFNET, the planned Human Genome Data Archive, and so on.

Allocating Resources and Assuring Equitable Access

The network raises a number of allocation and access issues that must be resolved. The number of high-performance computers and elaborate research instruments, such as telescopes or particle accelerators, are limited because of their high capital and operating costs. Universal access is not feasible, yet these facilities are critical to certain types of research. An equitable, fair process for allocating time on these facilities is crucial.

Network utility features, such as electronic mail, bulletin boards, journals, and so on, are basic to research in any field. Without them, one is locked out of the profession of science. Every researcher must have access to these services.

Updating Information Policies

Policies that currently govern the existing networks were developed to resolve conflicts over access and control of the information, e.g., protecting the privacy and confidentiality of communications and data on the network, or enforcing intellectual property rights. There are many more information policy questions concerning the rights and responsibilities to various electronic forms of communication that must still be addressed. Should "electronic mail" be protected like first class mail? Should bulletin board operators be legally responsible for messages placed on their boards? Does the First Amendment of the U.S. Constitution protect the sender? Should intellectual property protections be granted to electronic databases? If so, what form? Answers to these and other information policy questions will determine how the network is used and what services will be offered.

Adapting Science Policy

Just as an information infrastructure may change the way science is *done*, it may also lead to the need to change Federal science policy to accommodate these changes. High-performance computers may

---

[10]OSTP defines Grand Challenges as "...a fundamental problem in science or engineering, with potentially broad economic, political, and/or scientific impact, that could be advanced by applying high performance computing resources." Examples include: 1) Computational fluid dynamics for the design of hypersonic aircraft or efficient automobile bodies and recovery of oil; 2) Computer based weather and climate forecasts, and understanding of global environmental changes; 3) Electronic structure calculations for the design of new materials such as chemical catalysts, immunological agents and superconductors; 4) Plasma dynamics for fusion energy technology and for safe and efficient military technology; 5) Calculations to improve the understanding of the fundamental nature of matter, including quantum chromodynamics and condensed matter theory; and 6) Machine vision to enable real-time analysis of complex images for control of mechanical systems. *See* Office of Science and Technology Policy, *The Federal High Performance Computing Program* (Washington, DC: 1989), p. 8.

change research priorities and create new ways for research groups to organize and work together.

Determining the Type of Technology

The purpose of the technology will drive future policies. Management questions arising from the design and operation of a nationwide, ultra-high speed communication network may differ in nature from the problems of supporting and operating National Supercomputer Centers. But decisions related to both will collectively determine how effectively a national information infrastructure will be used in research and education.

On the other hand, information policy issues—that relate to the information that flows through the network-connected facilities—are seamlessly linked. Although the technical means for protecting and controlling information moving over the system may differ from computer to computer, or application to application, information policies are less dependent on the nature of the technology than on the generic issues. Privacy protection, access control, data security, and intellectual property protection are problems that need to be addressed across the board. Similarly, changes in the framework of Federal Government support and oversight of science policy will affect all technologies, disciplines, and agencies.

Determining Access

Depending on how one views the NREN, it is seen serving widely different user groups, ranging from a few federally funded high-end researchers engaged in ''Big Science,'' to the scholarly community, to education from kindergarten through secondary schools. Both technical design decisions and policy will affect these various users in different ways. Who the intended user will be is a critically important consideration in making NREN policy. It is a subject dealt with in detail in a forthcoming OTA Report that focuses on the network as a broadband advanced communication infrastructure to simultaneously deliver data, video, and voice service.

Major Strategic Concerns

The mutual dependence and interconnectedness of a national information infrastructure will force the Federal Government to develop long-term strategies to guide the overall development of the NREN: this must be done in concert with a coordinated program to provide high-performance computer-based tools for science, research and education.

Breadth of Scope

Long-Range Planning Needs

Creating the infrastructure, the network, and its related resources, is not a one-time job. There are misconceptions that information infrastructure is a static concept only needing to be plugged in. This is not so; new applications will appear and the capabilities of technology will continue to grow and change. The system will, therefore, be a continually evolving assembly of technologies and services. Therefore planning and operating the NREN must be considered a dynamic process. An institutional framework must be developed to ensure its success.

Studies on information technology and science (including OTA's) rely on anecdotal examples, ''gee-whiz'' speculation about future applications, and the subjective views of the research and education community. These arguments are persuasive and sufficient to justify the support for the NREN, but they do not contribute sufficiently to long-term management and planning for the operation of the infrastructure. The Federal investment in computer, communication, and data resources for science and engineering should be based on a periodic assessment of needs and changing technologies. This assessment should include:

- surveys of existing resources—public, private nonprofit, and commercial, such as:
  —specialized and general purpose high-performance computing facilities;
  —Federal, State, and local data communication networks;
  —scientific and technical databases; and
  —software packages for research uses.
- utilization levels of existing facilities by categories such as:
  —field of research;
  —government, academic, or industrial use; and
  —research, graduate education, undergraduate education, or pre-college education.
- Barriers to efficient use of facilities, such as:
  —policy or legal barriers;
  —lack of standards for interconnection of systems; and
  —user difficulties such as lack of training, inadequate user interfaces, or lack of software and services.

- Projections of future computing needs (particularly, assessments of the need for new, large-scale research initiatives.)

Although NSF attempts to keep tabs on the computational and information needs of the science community, the pace of technological development and massive new science projects make such information more important during periods of tight budgets. These data are difficult to compile, and special efforts are needed to provide such planning data to those decisionmakers responsible for anticipating future national computing needs.

Chapter 2

Policy Considerations for High-Performance Computing

Currently the National Science Foundation (NSF) sponsors five leading edge computational centers, the four national supercomputer centers and the National Center for Atmospheric Researcher (NCAR) (see app. A). When the centers were established, one goal of the NSF initiative was to nationally provide researchers with access to leading edge technology. Prior to the NSF program, U.S. researchers and scientists had little opportunity—outside of Federal laboratories—to access supercomputers. Since their creation, the centers have been extremely successful in providing access to supercomputing resources to academic and industrial researchers.

The success of the NSF centers has made them the target of a debate over funding strategies for their support. It is noteworthy that they are not the only such facilities funded by the Federal Government or even by NSF. Computers, especially large-scale computers, always have required relatively large institutional structures to operate. The Department of Energy (DOE) and the Department of Defense (DoD) fund many more computational centers at a considerably higher cost than the NSF. Government establishment and support of scientific computing facilities date back to the earliest days of computing. Furthermore, high-performance computing is becoming increasingly important to all of science and engineering. The issue is not whether science, education, and engineering in the United States need high-performance computing centers, but rather how these centers should be supported, and how the costs of that support should be allocated over the long term.

It is imperative that the United States: 1) continue to steadily advance the capabilities of leading edge computer technology; 2) provide the R&D community with adequate computing resources; and 3) expand and improve the use of high-performance computing in science and engineering.

Advancing Computer Technology

Computers lie on the nearly seamless lines between basic research, applied research, and the development of new technologies. A program intended to advance the state-of-the-art of high-performance computing must include:

- physics research on fundamental devices, superconductors, quantum semiconductors, optical switches, and other advanced components;
- basic research in computer science and computer engineering, including theoretical and experimental work in computer architecture and a variety of other fields such as distributed systems, software engineering, computational complexity, data structures, programming languages, and intelligent systems;
- applied research and assembly of experimental laboratory testbed machines for exploring new concepts;
- experimentation, evaluation, and development of software for new prototype computers, e.g., the Connection Machine, Hypercube or neural nets;
- development of human resources and facilities for computing research needed to support a high-performance computing initiative, which requires additional trained researchers and research facilities;
- research and development of new technologies for data storage and retrieval (this may be the biggest technological bottleneck in the future); and
- creation of new algorithms tailored for advanced architectures to meet the needs of scientists and engineers for greater computational capabilities.

Difficulties and Barriers

Funding

The term "computational science" is used to define research devoted to applying computers to computationally intensive research problems in science and engineering. It is focused on developing techniques for using high-performance computing to solve scientific problems in fields such as chemistry, physics, biology, and engineering. Though growing, the base funding level for computer and computational science and engineering is currently low.

Defense Advanced Research Projects Agency (DARPA), NSF, DOE (particularly national laboratories such as Los Alamos and Lawrence Livermore Laboratory), the National Institute of Science and Technology (NIST), National Aeronautics and Space

Administration (NASA), and the National Institutes of Health have all contributed to improving the state-of-the-art of computer technology and its application to science and technology. There is, however, no clear lead agency to focus a national high-performance computing program.

A significant or substantial increase in the support of computational science as part of a high-performance computing initiative would require a relatively large additional investment. There is disagreement among researchers in the various disciplines about increasing funding for computational science. Some fear that investments in this area would reduce funds available for other research activities.

Procurement Regulations

In addition to the expense involved, obtaining prototype machines for experimental use has become more difficult because of some agency interpretations of Federal procurement law. In the past, research agencies have stimulated the development of advanced computer systems by purchasing early models for research use. Contracts for these machines were sometimes written before the machine was manufactured. The agency would then participate in the design and contribute expertise for software development. This cooperative approach was one key to advancing high-performance computing in the 1960s and 1970s. Unfortunately, the process has become more difficult as Federal procurement regulations for computing systems have become tighter and more complex.

Policy Issues

Federal support of computing R&D is intertwined with the political debates over technology policy, industrial policy, and the appropriate balance of responsibility between the Federal Government and the private sector in developing computer technology. Computing researchers study basic, and often abstract, concepts including the nature of complex processes and algorithms. But, the results of their work can have important practical implications for the design of computer hardware and software.

Computing research is often based on the study of prototypes and artifacts rather than natural phenomena. Consequently, Federal support is sometimes viewed as technological—rather than scientific—in nature. Moreover, Federal defense procurement directly supports the U.S. computer and software

industry. Because of this relationship with industry, the High Performance Computing Initiative invariably blends the role of traditional Federal science policy with Federal efforts to support precompetitive activities of a strategically important industry. This has led to confusion and debate over the goals and appropriateness of the proposed High Performance Computing Initiative.

Providing Access to Resources

Federal support for educational and research computer resources must broker their use among many different users with different needs at many different institutions. Policies that serve some users well may shortchange others. There are three general objectives that serve all: 1) provide funds for acquiring computer hardware and software; 2) assist in meeting operational expenses to maintain and manage facilities; and 3) ensure that scarce computational resources are distributed fairly to the widest range of users.

No single Federal program for supporting scientific computing is likely to serve the needs and policy objectives for all facilities and user groups. Support must come from a variety of coordinated programs. For example, since the inception of NSF's Advanced Scientific Computing programs, debates over support of the national supercomputer centers have reflected many different, and often contradictory, views of the roles the centers should play and the constituencies they serve.

Difficulties and Barriers

Diversity of Sources

Computers are expensive to buy and to operate. For larger machines, usage crosses many disciplines and users are associated with many different academic institutions and industrial organizations. Supplying computer time can be a significant burden on research budgets, and support is often found by pooling funds from several sources.

No Natural Limits

Researchers seem to have an insatiable appetite for computer time. This perplexes policymakers who are used to dealing with expenditures for fixed cost items. One can estimate the number and kind of laboratory apparatus a chemist might need or microscopes a biology laboratory can use, based on the physical requirements of the researchers. However, the modeling of a complex organic chemical molecule for the design of a new pharmaceutical could saturate significant supercomputer resources. The potential use for supercomputer capacity appears to be limitless.

Administrators at research laboratories and government funding agencies have difficulties assessing computing needs and justifying new expenditures, either for purchase of additional computer time or for investments in upgrading equipment. It is even harder to predict future needs as researchers conceive new applications and become more sophisticated in developing innovative computer uses. These conflicting demands on the Federal science budget require careful balancing.

Disincentives to Investment

Support for computing resources may come from individual institutions themselves by underwriting the capital investment. The capital investment and operation costs are partially recaptured through fees charged back to the users. However, this model has not worked successfully, for a couple of reasons.

First, a multimillion dollar high-performance computer is a risky investment for an individual research institution. The risk is even greater for experimental machines whose potential use is difficult to anticipate. The institution must gamble that: 1) there is sufficient potential demand among research staff for the facilities; 2) federally supported researchers will have adequate funds to cover the costs; and 3) researchers with funds will choose to use the new computer rather than an outside facility.

Networks expand the possible user community of the facility, but they also provide access to competing systems at other institutions. In the past, researchers were, by and large, captive users of their own institutional facilities. Networks free them from this bondage. Now, researchers can use "distributed" computer resources elsewhere on the network. Faced with a wider "market" for computer time, research institutions may have less incentive to invest in more advanced systems, and instead upgrade local area networks to link with the NSFNET high-capacity backbone. On the other hand, networks can improve the efficiency and cost-effectiveness of computing by distributing computing capabilities.

Pricing policies for computer time must be carefully scaled to recover the costs of capital investments in hardware. High-computing costs can result in loss of revenue as researchers seek better rates at other institutions. The government requires that federally supported researchers pay no more than nonsupported researchers for computer time. But to ensure that operations break even, computer centers are forced to charge a rate equal to the costs divided by usage. This policy seems reasonable and equitable on the surface, but it results in higher rates for computer time when machine usage is light and lower rates as it grows. This pattern produces an upside-down market similar to that of the electric utilities before capital costs forced them to shave peak loads by charging a premium for power during periods of high usage. This is the reverse of airline rates where fares are lower when seats are empty and higher when planes are full.

Support Strategies

These disincentives and barriers have tended to limit investments in high-performance computers for research at a time when an increasing amount of important research requires access to more computational capacity. The Office of Science and Technology Policy's (OSTP) High Performance Computing Initiative, funding agencies' program plans, and pending legislation are aimed at balancing the Nation's R&D needs with high-performance computing capacity.

Four basic funding strategies to achieve this goal are described below:

Fully Support Federally Owned and Operated Centers

The most expedient strategy is to establish government-owned and operated facilities. The government could directly fund investments for hardware and software, and the centers' operational costs. There currently are several government funded and operated computational centers administered by the mission agencies. (See app. A, table A-1.) Government-financed computational centers provide a testbed for prototype machines and novel architectures that can help bolster the U.S. computer industry against foreign competition. Software development, critically needed for high-performance computing, is commonly a major activity at these centers.

A Federal high-performance computing initiative could select specific computational centers for full funding and operation by the Federal Government. A Federal agency might be needed to supervise the creation and management of the centers. Hardware would be owned or leased by the government. The center might be operated by a government contractor. The personnel, support staff and services, could either work directly for the government or a government contractor. These centers would be in addition to the existing mission agency computing centers.

Federally owned and operated computational centers currently exist under the management of several Federal mission agencies. The national laboratories—Los Alamos, Sandia, and Livermore—are operated by the DOE. Much of their work relates to national security programs, such as weapons research. NASA, DoD, and the Department of Commerce operate high-performance computing centers. NASA's centers primarily conduct aerospace and aerodynamic research. DoD operates over 15 supercomputers, whose research ranges from usage by the Army Corps of Engineers to Navy ship R&D to Air Force global weather prediction to intelligence activities of the National Security Agency (NSA). However, they do not fill the general needs of the science and education community. Access to these mission agency centers is limited, and only a small portion of the science community can use their facilities. The Federal Government could similarly own and operate computational centers for academic missions as well.

While federally owned and operated computing centers might risk experimentation with novel, untested computer concepts that academic or industrial organizations cannot afford, there is a possibility that this strategy could blossom into an additional layer of bureaucracy. The advantages of having direct government control over allocating computer time based on national priorities and acquiring leading edge technologies is offset by the risk of having government managers making decisions that should best be made by practicing scientists and engineers as is currently done at the NSF centers. Such shortcoming in systems management may be overcome by using nongovernment advisors or boards of governors, but centers could find it difficult to ensure stable year-to-year funding as national budgets tighten and competition for research dollars increases.

Fully or Partially Support Consortia or Institutionally Operated Centers

Federal science agencies can provide partial or full support to institutions for purchasing new computers. This is currently done by NSF and DOE. NSF provides major funding for four national supercomputer centers and the National Center for Atmospheric Research (NCAR) facility. DOE partially funds a supercomputer facility at Florida State University. The agencies provide funds for the purchase or leasing of computers and also contribute to the maintenance of the centers and their support staff. This has enabled the centers to maintain an experienced staff, develop applications software, acquire leading edge hardware, and attract computational scientists.

The government, through the NSF, provided seed funds and support to establish the centers and operate them. The NSF centers are complete computational laboratories providing researchers with leading edge technology, support services, software development, and computer R&D. The States and institutions in which the NSF centers are located have contributed about 35 percent of the expenses of the centers, and in addition the private sector has also contributed to the centers through direct funding and with in-kind contributions. Private firms are able to become partners with and use the centers' resources in return for their contribution. The national centers have attracted a user base exceeding that of the mission agency computational centers and including nearly every aspect of research, science, and education in U.S. universities.

The allocation of resources at these centers differs from that of the mission agency centers. The process of obtaining computing time at these centers is more open and competitive than at government-operated centers. The competitive process is aimed at fair allocation of the computing resources through a peer review process. Government subsidization of the operation of the computing centers has increased the use of computational resources, and increased the user base. For example, before the NSF national centers, there were only three or four places in the United States where high-performance computers were available if the research was not funded by mission agencies. Now, a growing number of States and universities operate computational centers to support research.

Some individuals have proposed that certain high-performance computing centers be assigned specialized missions. For instance, one center might emphasize biomedical research, or fluid dynamics; another, the responsibility for one of the other ''grand challenges,'' such as global warming. NCAR is often used as an example of a successful discipline-oriented computational center to be used as a model for further specialization.

NCAR's computational center is partially funded by the NSF, but its research is specific to its mission in atmospheric science. In this way, it differs from the other four national NSF centers. NCAR's research includes climate, atmospheric chemistry, solar and solar-terrestrial physics, and mesoscale and microscale meteorology. The center houses a ccre staff of researchers and support personnel, yet its computational tools and human resources are available to the international atmospheric research community. Computer networks enable researchers around the Nation to access NCAR's facilities. NCAR, through its staff, research, hardware, and networks, has become a focal point for atmospheric research.

The advantage of a subject or discipline-specific computational center is that it focuses expertise and concentrates efforts on selected, important national problems. The staff is familiar with the type of work done within the disciplines and often knows the best ways to solve specific problems using computational science. Computers can be matched to fill the specific needs of the center rather than attempt to use a general purpose machine to serve (sometimes inadequately) the needs of diverse users. Experts in the field would have a central focus for meeting, comparing and debating research findings, and planning future research strategies much as atmospheric scientists now do at NCAR.

There are also disadvantages to discipline-specific centers. The ''general'' high-performance computing centers are a focal point for bringing together diverse users and disciplines. Researchers, scientists, computer scientists and engineers, and software engineers and designers work collaboratively at these centers. This interdisciplinary atmosphere makes the centers a natural incubator for the advancement of computational science, which is an essential component of research, by fostering communication among experts in various fields. It is noteworthy that NCAR, a mission-specific center, has a general purpose supercomputer identical to that at the general high-performance computing centers (i.e., a Cray Y-MP). Moreover, many atmospheric scientists also compute at the other NSF supercomputing centers.

The NSF centers were established to foster research and educational activities so that academic research could keep up with the needs and progress of the Federal research laboratories, the U.S. industrial research and engineering community, and foreign competitors, but subsidizing a select group of centers may create an impression of ''elitism'' within the science and technology community. The current funding of NSF centers authorizes only four federally funded centers. There has been no open competition for other computational centers in the NSF process since the selection in 1983-84, so equity within the community is often questioned. But the centers' plans are reviewed annually, and a comprehensive review was undertaken in 1989-90 that culminated in the closure of the Princeton University center. Some nonfederally funded State and university centers question why these installations are perpetually entitled to government funds while others are closed out of the competition.[1]

NSF's subsidization of its centers tends to establish a hierarchy within the computational community. However, objective competition among the centers would be hard to referee since the measures for determining eminence in computation are imprecise and subjective at best. The government must be leery of creating proclaimed ''leaders'' in computational science, because it risks setting limits instead of pushing the frontiers of computing.

Provide Supercomputing Funds to Individual Research Projects and Investigators

The Federal Government could choose to support computational resources from the grass-roots user level instead of institutional grants. Federal science agencies could provide funds to researchers as part of their research grants to buy and pay for computer services. In this way, the government would indirectly support the operational costs of the centers. Capital improvement would likely still need support

---

[1]Gillespie, Folkner & Associates, Inc., ''Access to High-Performance Computer Resources for Research,'' contractor report prepared for the Office of Technology Assessment, Apr. 12, 1990, p. 36.

from the Federal Government because of the unpredictability of funding through user control and the need for long-term planning for maintaining and upgrading computer technology.

Some believe that funding the researcher directly for purchasing computer services would create competition among computational centers that could lead to improvements in the efficiency of the operation of computer centers and make them more responsive to the needs of the users. If scientists could choose where to ''purchase'' supercomputing services, they would likely choose the center that provides the best value and customer service. Scientists could match the services they seek with the specialties of each center to meet their individual needs. Proponents of funding computer services through individual research grants believe that creating efficient, market-oriented computational centers should be a goal of the high-performance computing program.

Centers vying for users might be captured by the largest users since they would have the most computing funds to spend. Well-funded users could force centers to cater to their needs at the expense of smaller users by the sheer purchasing power they represent. The needs of small users and new users could be slighted as centers compete for the support from big users. Competition among centers for users could have a downside if it should lead to isolation and lack of cooperation, and interfere with communication among the centers.

Upgrades and new machines involve large financial investments that user-derived funds may not be able to provide. The uncertainty of future funding in a competitive environment would make long-range planning difficult. High-performance computers generally must be upgraded about every 5 years because the technology becomes outdated and maintenance too costly. National centers aimed at maintaining leading edge technology must upgrade whenever state-of-the-art technology emerges. Therefore, supplemental funding would be required for capital outlays even if user funds were used to offset operational expenses.

Critics of direct funding of researchers for supercomputer time claim that the money set aside for supercomputing should be dedicated solely for that use. They believe that if researchers were given nonearmarked funds for computer services, they might use them instead to buy minisupercomputers or graphic workstations for themselves, or to fund graduate students. They believe that much of the money would never reach the supercomputing centers, leading to unstable and unpredictable budgets. Direct funding of researchers for computing time was tried in the 1970s, and led to many of the problems identified in the Lax report.

Proponents of user-controlled funding believe that researchers can best decide whether supercomputing is necessary or not for their projects, and if minisupercomputers would suffice, then perhaps that is the best option.

Provide Incentives for State/Private Institutions To Supply Computational Services

Universities are heavily investing in information technologies and computational resources for the sciences. These non-Federal efforts should be encouraged. The government could provide matching funds to State and private institutions to contribute to the capital costs for computers and startup. Even a small amount of government seed money can help institutions leverage funds needed to establish a computing center. Supplemental assistance may be needed periodically for upgrading and maintaining up-to-date technology.

Some believe that temporary financial seeding of new centers is the best way for the Federal Government to subsidize supercomputing. Providing matching funds for several years to allow time for a center to become self-sufficient may be the best strategy for the Federal Government to assist in achieving supercomputing excellence.

After the seed period expires, centers must eventually upgrade their machines. Without additional funds to purchase upgrades they might fall behind new centers that more recently purchased state-of-the-art technology. Should this happen, a number of computational centers might be created, but none of them may end up world-class centers.

Expanding and Improving Usage

High-performance computers are general analytical tools that must be programmed to solve specific computational problems. Learning how to use the potential power of high-performance computers to solve specific problems is a major research effort itself. Research on how to apply high-performance computers to problems goes hand-in-hand with research on how to design the computers themselves. A Federal program to advance high-performance computing must strike a careful balance by supporting programs that advance the design of high-performance computers while at the same time advancing the science and engineering of computing for the R&D community.

It is important to distinguish *computational science* from *computer science and engineering*. Computer science is the science in which the object of intellectual curiosity is the computer itself. Computational science is the science in which the computer is used to explore other objects of intellectual curiosity. The latter discipline includes fields of basic research aimed at problems raised in the study of the computer and computing. They are not driven by specific applications. Although distinct, the two fields are closely related; researchers in each area depend on results and questions raised in the other.

Broader applications of computers often flow from advances made in research computing. Research in visualization, driven by the need to better understand the output of scientific calculations, has led to computer graphics technology that has revolutionized the movie and television industry and has provided new tools for doctors, engineers, architects, and others that work with images.

To advance the science of using high-performance computing, Federal programs must support five basic objectives:

1. **Expand the capabilities of human resources**—Individuals educated, trained, or skilled in applying the power of high-performance computers to new problems in science and technology are in high demand. They are sought by businesses, industries, and an assortment of institutions for the skills they bring to solving complex problems. There is a shortage of scientists, engineers and technicians with such skills. A Federal high-performance computing initiative must ensure that the pipeline for delivering trained personnel remains full.

2. **Develop software and hardware resources and technologies**—The research and development of technologies that can be applied to major research problems—"grand challenges"—must continue. Special efforts are needed to ensure progress in the development of software in order to harness the power of high-performance computing for the solution of R&D problems.

3. **Strengthen the scientific underpinnings of computation**—This can be accomplished through the support of computer science and engineering as well as computational science.

4. **Construct a broadly accessible, high-speed advanced broadband network**—Such a network will provide the scientific and educational community with access to the facilities, the data, and the software needed to explore new applications.

5. **Develop new algorithms for computational science**—Algorithms are mathematical formulas used to instruct computers (part of computer programs and hardware). They are the basis for solving computational problems. New and better algorithms are needed to improve the performance of hardware and software in the computing environment.

Difficulties and Barriers

Computer and computational sciences compete with many other disciplines, for science funding. They are relatively young fields and are growing from a small funding base. Funding levels for computing research is relatively small compared with the more mature disciplines. Stimulating growth in computer and computational science encounters a "chicken and egg" problem.

The size and level of activity of a research field is partially related to funds available. A Federal initiative designed to increase the research activity in computer and computational sciences must anticipate additional demands for Federal research funds. Furthermore, to maintain a healthy level of research activity, adequate funds to ensure future growth must be provided or talent will abandon the field to seek research money elsewhere. The small number of researchers working in computer and computational science may be cited as justification for *not* increasing levels of support, yet low levels of support limit the number of researchers and research positions.

Computational science is, in all but a few disciplines, a relatively new field. New researchers looking to establish their careers need assurance that their work will be recognized and accepted by their peers. Peer acceptance affects both their ability to obtain research funds and to publish articles in scientific journals. If computational methods are new to the field, the researcher may face a battle to gain acceptance within the traditional, conservative disciplines.

In many cases, researchers are in the early stages of understanding how to program radically new types of computers, such as massively parallel computers and neural nets. Researchers wishing to use such a computer need the assistance of those who can program and operate these computers for the duration of a project. There is currently a scarcity of such talent.

A NSF program dedicated to computational science and engineering may be needed. The program could fund computational scientists from a cross section of traditional disciplines such as biology, chemistry, and physics. Funds for programs aimed at developing human resources, such as fellowships, young investigator grants, and so on, may also need to be earmarked for computational science. Direct funding for computational sciences would overcome the tendency of the disciplines to favor the funding of conventional research and their reluctance to try new methodologies.

Computational Centers

The most difficult issues, which programs in NSF's Advanced Scientific Computing Division are addressing, stem from the problems in putting leading edge technology in the hands of knowledgeable users who can explore and develop its potential.

In the mid-1980s, NSF formed five national supercomputer centers. Three of them—the University of California at San Diego, Pittsburgh, and University of Illinois at Champaign-Urbana—were based on Cray supercomputers. One, at Cornell University, installed modified IBM computers, and the Princeton Center was based on a machine to be built by ETA, a subsidiary of Control Data that has since gone out of business. Subsequently, NSF did not renew the Princeton Center for a second 5-year period.

There have been many changes in the high-performance computing environment since the establishment of those centers. These changes include: 1) the evolution of the mini-supercomputer, 2) the establishment of other State and institutional supercomputing centers, 3) the increase in use and interest in applications of high-performance computing to research, 4) the emergence of the Japanese as a force in the design, manufacturing, and use of high-performance computers, and 5) the emergence of a national network. Because of these changes—particularly in light of budget pressures and the high cost of the program—questions are being asked about the future directions of NSF support for these centers.

The basic conflict arises from several concerns:

1. the need for the NSF programs that support computational centers to determine what their ultimate goals should be in an environment where technological changes and user needs are constantly changing;
2. the need of computer centers and their researchers for stable, predictable, and long-term support in contrast to the reluctance of the government to establish permanent institutions that may make indefinite claims on Federal funding; and
3. the view that any distribution of NSF high-performance computing funds should be openly competitive and based on periodic peer review.

Purposes for Federal High-Performance Computing Programs

Leading Edge Facilities

Leading edge facilities provide supercomputing to academe and industry and provide facilities for testing and experimenting with new computers. Academics are provided an opportunity to train with leading edge technology; researchers and engineers learn about new computer technology.

A leading edge facility's responsibilities go beyond merely providing researchers access to CPUs (central processing units). Manufacturers of high-performance computers rely on these centers to test the limits of their equipment and contribute to the improvement of their machines. Leading edge technology, by its nature, is imperfect. Prototype machines and experimental architectures are provided a testbed at these centers. Scientists' experiences with the technology assist the manufacturers in perfecting new computing equipment. Bottlenecks, defects, and deficiencies are discovered through use at the centers. Moreover, user needs have led to the creation of new applications software, computer codes, and software tools for the computers. These needs have forced the centers to take the lead in software development.

Several computational centers have industrial programs with large corporate sponsors. These corporations benefit from leading edge computational centers in two ways. First, industry gains access to the basic research conducted at universities on supercomputers. Second, industry learns how to use leading edge computer technology. The support services of these facilities are available to corporate sponsors and are a major attraction for these corporations. Corporate researchers are trained and tutored by the centers' support staff, and work with experienced academic users. They gain a knowledge of supercomputing, and this experience is taken back to their corporations. Participating corporations often leave the programs when they gain sufficient knowledge to operate their own supercomputer centers.

A high-performance computing plan that establishes and maintains leading edge facilities benefits a broad range of national interests. Academics learn how to use the technology, manufacturers use their experiences to improve the technology, and industry gains an understanding of the value of supercomputing in the work place.

Increasing the Supply of Human Resources

An important aspect of any high-performance computing program is the development of human resources. National supercomputer centers can cultivate human resources in two ways. First, researchers and scientists are taught how to use high-performance computers, and new users and young scientists learn how to use modern scientific tools. Second, national centers provide an atmosphere for educating and cultivating future computer support personnel. Users, teachers, and technicians are critical to the future viability of supercomputing.

Producing proficient supercomputer users is an important goal of a high-performance computing program. Researchers with little or no experience must be trained in the use of the technologies. Education must begin at the graduate level, and work its way into undergraduate training. Bringing supercomputer usage into curricula will help familiarize students with these tools. The next generation of scientists, engineers, and researchers must become proficient with these machines to advance their careers. The need for competent users will increase as supercomputers proliferate into the industrial

sector. Already there are reports of a shortage of supercomputer trained scientists and engineers.[2]

Support staff is an essential element of computational centers. The support services, which include seminars and consultation and support, educate the next generation of users. Support personnel are the trouble-shooters, locating and correcting problems, and optimizing computer codes. The NSF national centers have excellent staff, some of whom have moved to responsible positions at State and university-operated centers. The experience they gained at the NSF national centers contributes to the viability of new high-performance computing operations in industry and elsewhere in academe. The importance of the services that support personnel provide is often overlooked by policymakers, yet their contributions to supercomputing are invaluable. The greatest asset of a proficient high-performance computing center is the staff, not the computer. A high-performance computing program must emphasize the importance of developing human resources by producing educated users and users who will educate.

Advancing Computational Science

High-performance computer centers are a focal point for bringing together diverse users and disciplines. Researchers, scientists, computer scientists and engineers, and software engineers and designers work collaboratively at these centers. This interdisciplinary atmosphere makes the centers a natural incubator for the advancement of the computational sciences, which is an essential component of supercomputing. A national high-performance computing program could promote the computational sciences by fostering communication among experts in various fields.

Researchers and scientists know what questions to ask, but not necessarily how to instruct computers to answer them. Computational scientists know how to instruct computers. They create the computer instructions sets, computer codes, and algorithms for computers so that researchers can most efficiently utilize the technology. The development of computer codes and software is often a collaborative effort, supported by previous codes, software tools, and support staff, many of whom are computational scientists. Providing the methodology for utilizing

---

[2]Michael Schroeder, ''How Supercomputers Can Be Super Savers,'' *Business Week*, Oct. 8, 1990, p. 140.

these tools is as important as providing the tools themselves.

Developing New Software Applications

New algorithms and codes must be developed to allow optimum use of supercomputer time. One of the more frequent criticisms of many high-performance computing operations has been the use of suboptimal codes. Supercomputer time is wasted when outdated or less than optimal codes are used. Creating codes is a specialty in itself. The development of codes is so labor intensive and time consuming that using an outdated code, as opposed to creating a new one, is sometimes more time efficient, although it may waste costly supercomputer time. A high-performance computing program could advance the usage of new and efficient codes by promoting computational science.

Providing Access to More Supercomputing CPUs

Supercomputing CPUs offer researchers computing power and speed unattainable from conventional mainframes. High-performance computer centers provide, at a minimum, access to supercomputing cycles. Supercomputing CPUs currently are a scarce resource in high demand. Any Federal high-performance computing program will increase the amount of supercomputing cycles available to researchers. It is uncertain, however, how much increase in CPUs the government should provide. Supercomputers are used in the advancement of all scientific disciplines, for both ''big'' and ''little'' science projects. All areas of research benefit from high-performance computing. Notwithstanding any reasonable level of effort, the government will be unable to provide enough supercomputing resources to meet all researchers' needs. They will always seek more and faster supercomputing power.

Computer facilities whose main goal is to provide supercomputing CPUs are often called ''cycle shops.'' The NSF centers *are not* cycle shops. At cycle shops, support services are minimal: A skeletal support staff, enough personnel to keep the machines up and running, is all that is required. This limits cycle shops' usefulness to primarily experienced users. Only proven technology can be used. Training, education, and software development are not major activities at such facilities. User applications have to be ''canned'' and ready for use. These centers are the antithesis of leading edge facilities. Cycle shops are more economical for experienced users in need of large amounts of CPU time. This is not the majority of users, however.

Improving Data Storage Capabilities

Increasing importance is being placed on data storage capabilities. Researchers now realize the limits of current data storage technologies. A high-performance computing program can stimulate research in high-capacity storage and retrieval technologies.

Data storage technologies do not have the public appeal and visibility that supercomputers do. For this reason, they have been overlooked in supercomputing R&D, yet data storage is an integral part of high-performance computing. Supercomputers often use and produce large data sets. Computational centers are increasingly running into data memory and storage problems. New technologies for gathering data, e.g. satellites and automated sensors, are placing even greater demands on storage facilities. These data are often used in computing, and are converted into new data sets that require additional storage.

The Federal Government could take the initiative in R&D on new storage technologies, emphasizing its importance to high-performance computing. The amount of data handled at supercomputing centers will increase as the user base multiplies, and as data sharing increases through the use of high-capacity communications networks through the National Research and Education Network (NREN). Storage technologies are currently pushing their limits, and breakthroughs are needed if they are not to become the limiting factor in high-performance computing.

Chapter 3

High-Performance Computers: Technology and Challenges

Computers and the R&D Process

Scientists use the theories and techniques of mathematics for building and describing models in logical ways and for calculating the results they yield. As early as the third century B.C., the Alexandrian scholar Eratosthenes estimated the circumference of the earth to an accuracy within 5 percent of what we now consider to be the correct figure. He did so by making assumptions about the nature of the physical universe, making measurements, and calculating the results.[1] In essence, he did what modern scientists do. He constructed a hypothetical model that allowed him to apply mathematical tools—in this case, trigonometry and arithmetic—to data he collected.

Scientific models are used both to test new ideas about the physical universe and to explore results and conclusions based on those models. Eratosthenes discovered a new ''fact''—the size of the earth. Had his calculations, instead, confirmed a result already discovered by some other means, he would have accomplished a different research purpose; he would have provided evidence that the model of the universe was correct. Had they differed with known fact, he would have had evidence that the model was incorrect. Science advances, step by step, through a process of building models, calculating results, comparing those results with what can be observed and, when observations differ, revising the models.

Modes of Research Computing

Just as mathematics is central to science, computers have become basic instruments of research to modern science and play a wide variety of roles. Each of the roles is based on mathematical modeling, using the interactive solution of thousands of equations.

To Perform Complex Calculations

Sometimes the basic mathematics and structure of a physical process are well known—the equations that describe the flow of air around a solid object, for example. Researchers may wish to calculate the results of this process in experimental designs such as a new aircraft wing or the shape of an automobile. Calculating results from flow equations are enormously time-consuming even on the most powerful computers of today. Scientists must simplify these problems to fit the capabilities of the computers that are available. They sacrifice accuracy and detail in their model to achieve computability.

To Build New Theories and Models

At other times, researchers seek to understand the dynamics of a process, like the aging of a star or formation of a galaxy. They create computer models based on theories and observe how the behavior of those models do or do not correspond to their observations.

To Control Experimental Instruments and Analyze Data

Most modern scientific instruments have some computational power built in to control their performance and to process the measurements they make. For many of these, from the largest particle accelerators or space platforms to more modest instruments, the computer has become an integral and indispensable part.

Such research instruments generate enormous flows of information—some at rates up to several trillion units (terabits) a day. Unpackaging the data flow, identifying the elements, and organizing those data for use by scientists is, itself, a sizable computational task. After the initial steps, still more computer power is needed to search this mountain of data for significant patterns and analyze their meanings.

To Better Understand and Interact With Computer Results

At the most basic level, computers produce numbers; but numbers usually represent a physical object or phenomenon—the position of an atom in a protein molecule, the moisture content in a cloud, the stress in an automobile frame, or the behavior of an explosive. To make sense to researchers, the streams of numbers from a computer must be

---

[1]Thomas S. Kuhn, *The Copernican Revolution* (Cambridge, MA: Harvard University Press, 1985), p. 274.

converted to visual displays that are easier to understand when seen by the eye. Researchers are now concentrating on visualization—pictorial displays that incorporate images, motion, color, and surface texture to depict characteristics of an analysis on a computer screen.

Some researchers are exploring more advanced techniques that use other senses such as sound and touch to convey results to the human mind. By incorporating all of these technologies, they may eventually be able to create what is called "virtual reality," in which a scientist equipped with the proper gear could interact directly with a model as though he or she were standing in the midst of the phenomenon that was modeled. A biochemist could "walk" around and about a protein molecule, for example, and move atoms here and there, or a geologist could explore the inside of an active volcano.

To Provide "Intelligent" Assistance

Computer operations are not restricted to only computational operations on numbers. The popularity of word processors shows that computers can manipulate and perform logical operations on symbols, whether they represent numbers or not. Experts in the "artificial intelligence" community have been exploring how computers can assist researchers in ways other than direct computation of results. They have worked on systems that can prove mathematical theorems or perform tedious manipulations of algebraic expressions, systems that help chemists find new forms of molecules, and natural language inquiry systems for databases.

A national research and educational network (NREN) would create a critical need for such help in the future so that scientists are not overwhelmed by the complexity and amount of information available to them. New tools such as "knowbots"—small autonomous programs that would search databases throughout the network for information needed by the researcher—have been proposed.

Implications for Federal Programs

The traditional view of the "scientific computer" as one specifically intended for high-speed arithmetic computation is changing as researchers use computers for an increasingly rich variety of tasks. Any Federal initiative supporting computational science must create an environment that supports a wide variety of machines with improved capabilities, many of which serve specialized user communities.

Numerical computation is still critically important, but so are applications such as database manipulation, artificial intelligence, image production, and on-line control of experimental instruments. Even the design of computers meant to do numerical calculations is becoming more specialized to address specific types of problems.

The NREN is a crucial element of efforts to make high-performance computing widely available to the U.S. research community. Members of research groups who need these specialized computers are widely scattered throughout the country, and so are the computers they need.

The Evolution of Computer Technology

Government and Computer R&D

Like much of the new electronics technology of the day, computers in large measure grew out of work done during World War II for defense research programs. After the war, many engineers and scientists who staffed those programs took their knowledge into the private sector to begin the commercial U.S. computer industry.

The Federal Government remains a major purchaser, user, and force in shaping computer technology. Its influence is particularly strong in scientific computing; many computational researchers either work for the government in national laboratories or are substantially funded by government agencies. The computing needs of the defense agencies, and the weapons programs of the Department of Energy (earlier the Atomic Energy Commission (AEC)), demanded continual advancement of the speed and power of scientific computing.

Computers that meet the specifications of scientific users were not, until recently, commercially successful or widely available. As a result, Federal agencies needing these large scientific machines had to fund their development. Control Data's 6600 computer in the mid-1960s was among the first large scientific machines designed for national defense needs to be marketed successfully in the private sector.

Even though scientific computers were not originally successful in the nongovernment market, their technology was. The ''Stretch'' computer, designed and built by IBM for the AEC, provided many innovations that were later used in the design of the IBM 360 series that was the basic IBM product line for over a decade. Federal science agencies such as the National Science Foundation (NSF), Defense Advanced Research Projects Agency (DARPA), and the Office of Naval Research (ONR) have also contributed over the years to the development of computer architecture through their computer science and engineering research programs.

The government role in support of basic and applied research in computing and in testing prototype machines and making them available to researchers is critical to the well-being of small specialized firms in high-performance computing.

Government support for research in computer architecture has gone through cycles. In the early days, it was in research laboratories that computer scientists first developed many of the architectural concepts that formed the basis for general purpose computers. As computers became more complex and their manufacture a more refined art, academic research on computer design waned. Perhaps the decreased interest in architecture research resulted from the notion at that time that the major computer design issues had been settled and the development of new generations of machines should be left to the industry. The academic research that continued was mostly paper-and-pencil design simulated on conventional computers.

During the last decade, advances in microelectronics created opportunities to explore radical new designs with relatively inexpensive off-the-shelf chips from manufacturers, or custom designs. Experts were predicting the end of performance improvements that could be wrung from traditional design concepts, while the costs for coaxing performance improvements were increasing dramatically. As a result, computer scientists and engineers are again exploring alternate approaches, and academic research has now returned to the development and testing of prototypes, this time in cooperation with industry. Now, as then, the basic question is whether these experimental designs are more efficient and effective for performing specific types of calculations.

Computer scientists and engineers basically look in three directions to improve the efficiency and increase the speed of computers:

1. the fundamental technology of the computer components;
2. the architecture of the computer; and
3. the software programs and algorithms to instruct and control the computers.

These three areas of investigation are distinct fields of research, but they have an important influence on each other. New devices allow computer designers to consider different approaches to building computers, which, in turn, can lead to new ways of programming them. Influences can just as easily go the other way: new software techniques can suggest new machine architectures. One of the problems with introducing radically new types of computers into common use is that entirely new theories of programming must be developed for them, whereas software techniques for traditional machines have taken place over 40 or 50 years of development and refinement.

Fundamental Technologies

Basically, computers are complex assemblies of large numbers of essentially similar building blocks. These building blocks—all of which are generally different types of logical switches that can be set in one of two states (on-off)—are combined to form the memory, registers, arithmetic units, and control elements of modern digital computers (*see* box C). The advance of computer technology at this level can be seen as the clustering of more and more of these basic switches into increasingly smaller, faster, cheaper, and more reliable packages.

Integrated Circuits—Electrical engineers predict that, by 2000, chip manufacturers will be able to put over one billion logic gates (switches) on a single chip. Some silicon chips already contain more than a million gates. This level of complexity begins to allow producers to put huge computational power on one processor chip. By the end of the decade, it is expected that a single chip will have the complexity and the power of a modern supercomputer, along with a significant amount of memory.

This trend is influencing research in computer design. Computer scientists and engineers use the term ''architecture'' to describe the art of arranging the flows of data and the detailed logical processes within the computers they design. Given the com-

Box C—The Building Blocks of Modern Computer Hardware

From electro-mechanical relays to vacuum tubes to silicon-based very-large-scale integrated circuits, the electronic technologies that form the basic components of computers have steadily and rapidly advanced year by year since the 1940s. One measure of improvement is the number of transistors (the basic building block of logic and memory) that can be placed on a chip. Increase in transistor density is expected to continue throughout the coming decade, although "traditional" silicon technology, the basis of microelectronics for the last few decades may begin reaching its maximum cost/performance benefit. It may become too costly to derive future performance advancements out of silicon.

In the past, as each type of technology—mechanical switches, vacuum tubes, and transistors—reached its limits, a new technology has come along that allowed information technology to continue improving; this phenomenon is likely to continue. Researchers are exploring several basic technologies that, if successful, could continue these rates of growth, not only through this decade, but well into the next century.[1]

Gallium Arsenide Compounds

Gallium Arsenide (GaAs) is a compound with semiconductor properties similar to, but in some ways superior to, silicon. Spurred in part by interest from the Department of Defense, researchers have developed GaAs to the point where such devices are being produced for commercial application. But will it ever be cost-effective to manufacture devices complex enough and in quantities sufficient to build full-scale computers in a cost-effective way? Some manufacturers are trying.

Cray Computer Corp. (CCC), a separate company spun off from its parent Cray Research, and Convex Computers—a manufacturer of entry-level supercomputers—are attempting to use GaAs-based components for their new machines. Although offering much greater speeds for the machine, these components have proved to be difficult to manufacture and to assemble into a large-scale mainframe. Their efforts are being watched closely. Some experts think that some of these manufacturing difficulties are inherent and that GaAs will remain a valuable but expensive "niche" technology, possibly useful for high-speed and costly applications, but not serving as the "workhorse" all-purpose replacement for silicon in everyday applications.[2]

Superconductivity

For years it has been known that some materials attain a state known as "superconductivity" when cooled sufficiently. A superconductive material essentially transmits electricity without (or with low) resistance. Using superconductivity, a switch known as a "Josephson Junction" (JJ) can be built that could, in theory, serve as the basis of computer logic and memory.

The problem has been that "sufficiently cooled" has meant very cold indeed, nearly the temperature of liquid helium, only 4 degrees Kelvin.[3] Although it is possible to attain these temperatures, it requires extensive and complex apparatus either for refrigerating or for using liquid helium, a very temperamental substance to deal with. Problems with reliably manufacturing JJs have also been difficult to solve. Because JJs could move computer capabilities beyond silicon limits if these problems were solved, some manufacturers, particularly the Japanese, have continued to explore low-temperature superconductivity.

Within the last few years, however, the discovery of materials that exhibit superconductivity at higher temperatures has led to a renewed interest in the JJ.[4] "High temperature" is still very cold by normal standards, around 50 to 100 degrees Kelvin, but it is a temperature that is much more economical to maintain. Significant materials problems still confound attempts to manufacture JJs reliably and in the bulk necessary to manufacture computers. However, investigators have just begun exploring this technology, and many of them expect that these

---

[1]U.S. Congress, Office of Technology Assessment, *Microelectronics Research and Development—Background Paper*, OTA-BP-CIT-40 (Washington, DC: U.S. Government Printing Office, March 1986).

[2]Marc H. Brodsky, "Progress in Gallium Arsenide Semiconductors," *Scientific American*, February 1990, pp. 68-75.

[3]Kelvin is a unit of measurement that uses as its reference, "absolute zero," the coldest temperature that matter can theoretically attain. In comparison, zero degrees Centigrade, the temperature at which water freezes, is a warm 273 degrees Kelvin.

[4]U.S. Congress, Office of Technology Assessment, *Commercializing High-Temperature Superconductivity*, OTA-ITE-388 (Washington, DC: U.S. Government Printing Office, August 1988).

problems will be solved, in part because of the potential importance of the technology if it can be tamed. It has been suggested that Japanese manufacturers continue to work on low-temperature prototypes in order to gain experience in designing and building JJ-based computers that could be useful if and when high-temperature technology becomes available.

Other Advanced Technologies

Researchers are also investigating other promising technologies, such as "optical switching" devices. Fiber optics already offers significant advantages as a communication medium, but signals must be converted back to electrical form before they can be manipulated. It might be attractive in terms of speed and economy if one could handle them directly in the form of light.

Other researchers are working on so-called **"quantum effect"** devices. These devices use silicon—and in some cases GaAs—materials, but take advantage of the quantum, or wave-like, behavior of electrons when they are confined in very small areas (say, on the order of 100 atoms in diameter.)[5] Again, problems of manufacturing, particularly devices as small as this, present major difficulties to be overcome.

---

[5]Henry I. Smith and Dimitra A. Antoniadis, "Seeking a Radically New Electronics," *Technology Review*, April 1990, pp. 27-39.

---

plexity that modern chips can embody, a chip designer can use them to build bigger, more elaborate constructs. Such a designer might be thought of more as a "city planner"—someone who arranges the relationships between much larger structures and plans the traffic flow among them.

Computer design is helped considerably by modern technology. First, through use of automated design and "chip foundries" for producing customized chips (some of which can be accessed via a network), designers can move from paper-and-pencil concepts to prototype hardware more easily. Many of the new high-performance computers on the market use processor chips custom-designed for that specific machine; automated chip design and manufacture shorten the time and improve the flexibility in producing custom chips.

Second, the market offers a variety of inexpensive, off-the-shelf chips that can be assembled to create new and interesting experimental designs. One of the best known successful examples of this type of research is a project initiated at the California Institute of Technology. There, researchers designed and built a customized computer to help them with certain specialized physics calculations. They developed the first "hypercube" machine using a standard line of processor chips from Intel. Intel supported the project in the early days, principally through the donation of chips. Later, as the design concept proved itself and attracted the attention of government agencies, full-scale research support was provided to the group.

The impact of that low-budget project has been enormous. Several companies (including Intel) are in, or are planning to enter, the high-performance computer market with computers based on the hypercube design or one of its variations. Universities are beginning to realize the potential of specialized, low-budget machines, among them Caltech, Rice, and Syracuse. Three NSF centers (National Center for Supercomputing Applications, Pittsburgh Supercomputing Center, and the San Diego Supercomputer Center) also have installed these architectures for access by the nationwide academic community.

Based on the history and trends in computer architecture research, it appears that: 1) it is feasible to design and build computers with architectures customized for particular tasks; 2) the availability of powerful, inexpensive chips, has prompted academic laboratories to return to research in computer architecture; 3) new ideas in computer architecture can likely be commercialized quickly; and 4) universities that have access to fabrication facilities are more likely to develop new, specialized machines.

In the past, such customized machines would have been considered curiosities, with no chance of competing with traditional designs. The computer industry at that time was conservative, and users were unwilling to take chances on new ideas. Now, some entrepreneurs will gamble that if the system has distinct advantages in power and cost, new markets will open, even for systems based on radical new design theories.

But bringing a new high-performance machine to market is neither cheap nor simple. Millions of dollars—sometimes hundreds of millions—must be spent refining the design, developing software, and solving manufacturing problems, before a design concept moves from the laboratory into general use. The speed and ease of this transfer depends heavily on whether the technology is evolutionary or revolutionary.

It is difficult to say which computer technologies will become the foundation for building computers over the next decade. Despite the fact that all of the alternative technologies have difficulties to be overcome, it is likely that one or more new component technologies will be developed to fuel the rapid growth of computer capability into the next decade and beyond. But advances in fundamental technology alone will not be sufficient to achieve the increases in computer power that are needed by research users.

Computer Architecture

The term "computer architecture" denotes the structural design of a computer system. It includes the logical behavior of major components of the computer, the instructions it executes, and how the information flows through and among those components. A principal goal of computer architecture is to design machines that are faster and more efficient for specific tasks.

"Supercomputer" is commonly used by the popular media to describe certain types of computer architectures that are, in some sense, the most powerful available. It is not, however, a useful term for policy purposes. First, the definition of computer "power" is inexact and depends on many factors, including processor speed and memory size. Second, there is no clear lower boundary of "supercomputer power." IBM 3090 computers come in a wide range of configurations, but are they "supercomputers"? Finally, technology is changing rapidly, and with it the conceptions of the power and capability of various computers. Here, the term "high-performance computers" (HPC) (distinguished from the Federal program to advance high-performance computing referred to as the "high-performance computing initiative") includes a variety of machine types.

One class of high-performance computing consists of large, advanced, expensive, powerful machines, designed principally to address massive computational science problems. These computers are the ones often referred to as "supercomputers." Their performance is based on central processing unit (CPU) power and memory size. They use the largest, fastest, most costly memories. A leading edge "supercomputer" can cost up to $20 million or more.

A large-scale computer's power comes from a combination of very high-speed electronic components and specialized architecture. Most machines use a combination of "vector processing" and "parallel processing" (parallelism) in their design. A vector processor is an arithmetic unit of the computer that produces a series of similar calculations in an overlapping, assembly-line fashion (many scientific calculations can be set up in this way).

Parallel processing is the use of several processors that simultaneously solve portions of a problem that can be broken into independent pieces for computing on separate processors. Currently, large, mainframe high-performance computers such as those of Cray and IBM are moderately parallel, having from two to eight processors.[2] The trend is toward more parallel processors on these large systems. The main problem to date has been to figure out how problems can be set up to take advantage of the potential speed advantage of larger-scale parallelism.

The availability of software for supercomputer application is a major challenge for high-performance computing in general, but it is particularly troublesome in the case of large parallel processing systems. Parallel processing requires that the complexity of the problem be segregated into pieces that can run separately and independently on individual processors. This requires that programmers approach solutions in a very different manner from the way they program information flow and computations on vector processors. Until the art of parallel programming catches up with the speed and sophistication of hardware design, the considerable power of parallel computing will be underutilized. Software development for supercomputing must be given high priority in any high-performance computing initiative.

---

[2]To distinguish between this modest level and the larger scale parallelism found on some more experimental machines, some experts refer to this limited parallelism as "multiprocessing."

Some machines now on the market (called "mini-supers" or "minisupercomputers") are based on the structure and logic of a large supercomputer, but use cheaper, slower electronic components and lower performance technology. They are relatively less expensive than high-end supercomputers. These systems sacrifice some speed, but cost much less to manufacture. An application that is demanding but does not require a full-size supercomputer may be more efficiently run on a minisuper.

Other types of specialized systems also have appeared on the market. These machines gain computation speed by using fundamentally different architectures. They are known by colorful names such as "Hypercubes," "Connection Machines," "Data Flow Processors," "Butterfly Machines," "Neural Nets," or "Fuzzy Logic Computers." Although they differ in design concept, many of these systems are based on large-scale parallelism. Their designers get increased processing speed by linking large numbers—hundreds or even thousands—of simpler, slower, and cheaper processors. But computational mathematicians and scientists have not yet developed a good theoretical or experimental framework for understanding how to arrange applications to take full advantage of these massively parallel systems. Therefore, these systems are still, by and large, experimental, even though some are on the market and some users have developed applications software for them. Experimental as these systems are however, many experts believe that any significantly large increase in computational power must grow out of experimental systems such as these or from other forms of massively parallel architecture or hybrid architectures.

"Workstations," the descendants of personal desktop computers, are increasing in power; new chips being developed will soon offer computing power nearly equivalent to a Cray 1 supercomputer of the late 1970s. Thus, although high-end high-performance computers will be correspondingly more powerful, scientists who wish to do heavy-duty computing will have a wide selection of options in the future. Policymakers must recognize that:

- The term "supercomputer" is a fluid one, potentially covering a wide variety of machine types; similarly, the "supercomputer industry" is increasingly difficult to identify as a distinct entity.

- Scientists need access to a wide range of high-performance computers from desktop workstations to full-scale supercomputers, and they need to move smoothly and seamlessly among these machines as their research needs require.
- Government policies should be flexible and broadly based to avoid focusing on a narrowly defined class of machines.

Mere computational power is not always the sole objective of designers. For example, in the case of desktop computers like the Apple MacIntosh or NEXT Computers, or the more powerful engineering workstations, much effort has gone into improving the communication between the machine and the operator (user interface). Computers are being designed to be more easily linked through data communication networks. Machines are being designed to do specialized tasks within computer networks, such as file management and internetwork communication. As computer designers develop a wider variety of machines specialized for particular tasks, the term "high performance" covers a wider range of applications and architectures, including machines that are oriented to numerical scientific calculation.

Computer Performance

Computers are often compared on the basis of computer power—usually equated to processing speed. The convention used for measuring computer power is "FLOPS" (floating point operations per second). The term "floating point" refers to a particular format for numbers (scientific notation) within the computer that is used for scientific calculation. A floating point "operation" refers to a single arithmetic step, such as multiplying or dividing two numbers, using the floating point format. Thus, FLOPS measure the speed of the arithmetic processor. Currently, the largest supercomputers have processing speeds ranging up to several billion FLOPS. DARPA has announced a goal of developing in this decade a "teraflop" machine, a computer that executes one trillion FLOPS.

Peak computer speed and computer systems performance are two different things. Peak computer speed is the raw theoretical performance that is the maximum possible for the computer architecture. Computer system performance, the actual speed under use, is always lower—sometimes much lower. Theoretical peak speed alone is not a useful measure of the relative power of computers. To understand why, consider the following analogy.

At a supermarket checkout counter, the calculation speed of the cash register does not, by itself, determine how fast customers can checkout. Checkout speed is also affected by the speed that the clerk can enter each purchase into the cash register and the time it takes to complete a transaction with each customer—bag the groceries, collect money, make change—and move on to the next. The length of time the customer must wait in line to reach the clerk may be the most important factor of all, and that depends on how many clerks and cash registers are provided.

Similarly, in a computer, how quickly calculations can be set up and input to the processor and how quickly new jobs and their data can be moved in, completed, and the results moved out of the computer determines how much of the processor's speed can actually be harnessed (some users refer to this as ''solution speed''). Solution speed is determined by a variety of architectural factors located throughout the computer system as well as the interplay between hardware and software. Similar to the store checkout, as a fast machine becomes busy, users may have to wait in line. From a user's perspective, then, a theoretically fast computer can still deliver solutions slowly.

To test a machine's speed, experts use ''benchmark programs,'' i.e., sample programs that reproduce a ''standard'' workload. Since workloads vary, there are several different benchmark programs, and they are continually being refined and revised. Measuring a supercomputer's speed is a complex and important area of research. Performance measurement provides information on what type of computer is best for particular applications; such measurements can also show where bottlenecks occur and, hence, where hardware and software improvements should be made.

One can draw some important implications from these observations on computing speed:

- Computer designers depend on feedback from users who are pushing their machines to the limit, because improvements in overall speed are closely linked to how the machines are programmed and used.

- There is no ''fastest'' machine. The speed of a high-performance computer depends on the skill of those that use and program it, and the type of jobs it performs.

- One should be skeptical of claims of peak speeds until machines have been tested by users for overall systems performance.

- Federal R&D programs for improving high-performance computing must stress software, algorithms, and computational mathematics as well as research on machine architecture.

Supercomputer Centers

The National Supercomputer Centers

In February 1985, National Science Foundation (NSF) selected four sites to establish national supercomputing centers: Cornell University, the University of Illinois at Urbana-Champaign, the University of California at San Diego, and the John von Neumann Center in Princeton. A fifth site, Pittsburgh, was added in early 1986. Funding for Princeton's Von Neumann Center was later dropped. The four remaining NSF centers are described briefly below.

The Cornell Theory Center

The Cornell Theory Center is located on the campus of Cornell University. Over 1,900 users from 125 institutions access the center. Although Cornell does not have a center-oriented network, 55 academic institutions are able to utilize the resources at Cornell through special nodes. A 14-member Corporate Research Institute works within the center in a variety of university-industry cost-sharing projects.

In November 1985 Cornell received a 3084 computer from IBM, which was upgraded to a four-processor 3090/400VF a year later. The 3090/400VF was replaced by a six-processor 3090/600E in May 1987. In October 1988 a second 3090/600E was added. The Cornell Center also operates several other smaller parallel systems, including an Intel iPCS/2, a Transtech NT 1000, and a Topologix T1000. Some 50 percent of the resources of Northeast Parallel Architecture Center, which include two Connection machines, an Encore, and an Alliant FX/80, are accessed by the Cornell facility.

Until October 1988, all IBM computers were "on loan" to Cornell for as long as Cornell retained its NSF funding. The second IBM 3090/600, procured in October, will be paid for by a NSF grant. Over the past 4 years, corporate support for the Cornell facility accounted for 48 percent of the operating costs. During those same years, NSF and New York State accounted for 37 percent and 5 percent, respectively, of the facility's budget. This funding has allowed the center to maintain a staff of about 100.

The National Center for Supercomputing Applications

The National Center for Supercomputing Applications (NCSA) is operated by the University of Illinois at Urbana-Champaign. The center has over 2,500 academic users from about 82 academic affiliates. Each affiliate receives a block grant of time on the Cray X-MP/48, training for the Cray, and help using the network to access the Cray.

The NCSA received a Cray X-MP/24 in October 1985. That machine was upgraded to a Cray X-MP/48 in 1987. In October 1988 a Cray-2s/4-128 was installed, giving the center two Cray machines. This computer is the only Cray-2 now at a NSF national center. The center also houses a Connection Machine 2, an Alliant FX/80 and FX/8, and over 30 graphics workstations.

In addition to NSF funding, NCSA has solicited industrial support. Amoco, Eastman Kodak, Eli Lilly, FMC Corp., Dow Chemicals, and Motorola have each contributed around $3 million over a 3-year period to the NCSA. In fiscal year 1989 corporate support amounted to 11 percent of NCSA's funding. About 32 percent of NCSA's budget came from NSF, while the State of Illinois and the University of Illinois accounted for the remaining 27 of the center's $21.5-million budget. The center has a full-time staff of 198.

Pittsburgh Supercomputing Center

The Pittsburgh Supercomputing Center (PSC) is run jointly by the University of Pittsburgh, Carnegie-Mellon University, and Westinghouse Electric Corp. More than 1,400 users from 44 States utilize the center. Twenty-seven universities are affiliated with PSC.

The center received a Cray X-MP/48 in March 1986. In December 1988 PSC became the first non-Federal laboratory to possess a Cray Y-MP. For a short time, both machines were being used simultaneously; however the center has now phased out the Cray X-MP. The center's graphics hardware includes a Pixar image computer, an Ardent Titan, and a Silicon Graphics IRIS workstation.

The operating projection at PSC for fiscal year 1990, a "typical year," has NSF supporting 58 percent of the center's budget while industry and vendors account for 22 percent of the costs. The Commonwealth of Pennsylvania and the National Institutes of Health both support PSC, accounting for 8 percent and 4 percent of budget respectively. Excluding working students, the center has a staff of around 65.

San Diego Supercomputer Center

The San Diego Supercomputer Center (SDSC) is located on the campus of the University of California at San Diego and is operated by General Atomics. SDSC is linked to 25 consortium members but has a user base in 44 States. At the end of 1988, over 2,700 users were accessing the center. SDSC has 48 industrial partners who use the facility's hardware, software, and support staff.

A Cray X-MP/48 was installed in December 1985. SDSC's first upgrade, a Y-MP8/864, was planned for

December 1989. In addition to the Cray, SDSC has five Sun workstations, two IRIS workstations, an Evans and Sutherland terminal, five Apollo workstations, a Pixar, an Ardent Titan, an SCS-40 minisupercomputer, a Supertek S-1 minisupercomputer, and two Symbolics machines.

The University of California at San Diego spends more than $250,000 a year on utilities and services for SDSC. For fiscal year 1990 the SDSC believes NSF will account for 47 percent of the center's operating budget. The State of California currently provides $1.25 million per year to the center and in 1988 approved funding of $6 million over 3 years to SDSC for research in scientific visualization. For fiscal year 1990 the State is projected to support 10 percent of the center's costs. Industrial support, which has given the center $12.6 million in donations and in-kind services, is projected to provide 15 percent of the total costs of SDSC in fiscal year 1990.

Other High-Performance Computer Facilities

Before 1984 only three universities operated super-computers: Purdue University, the University of Minnesota, and Colorado State University. The NSF supercomputing initiative established five new supercomputer centers that were nationally accessible. States and universities began funding their own supercomputer centers, both in response to growing needs on campus and to increased feeling on the part of State leaders that supercomputer facilities could be important stimuli to local R&D and, therefore, to economic development. Now, many State and university centers offer access to high-performance computers (HPC);[1] and the NSF centers are only part of a much larger HPC environment including nearly 70 Federal installations (see table A-1).

Supercomputer center operators perceive their roles in different ways. Some want to be a proactive force in the research community, leading the way by helping develop new applications, training users, and so on. Others are content to follow in the path that the NSF National Centers create. These differences in goals/missions lead to varied services and computer systems. Some centers are "cycle shops," offering computing time but minimal support staff. Other centers maintain a large support staff and offer consulting, training sessions, and even assistance with software development. Four representative centers are described below.

Minnesota Supercomputer Center

The Minnesota Supercomputer Center, originally part of the University of Minnesota, is a for-profit computer center owned by the University of Minnesota. Currently, several thousand researchers use the center, over 700 of which are from the University of Minnesota. The Minne-

Table A-1—Federal Unclassified Supercomputer Installations

Laboratory	Number of machines
Department of Energy:	
Los Alamos National Lab	6
Livermore National Lab, NMFECC	4
Livermore National Lab	7
Sandia National Lab, Livermore	3
Sandia National Lab, Albuquerque	2
Oak Ridge National Lab	1
Idaho Falls National Engineering	1
Argonne National Lab	1
Knolls Atomic Power Lab	1
Bettis Atomic Power Lab	1
Savannah/DOE	1
Richland/DOE	1
Schenectedy Naval Reactors/DOE	2
Pittsburgh Naval Reactors/DOE	2
Department of Defense:	
Naval Research Lab	1
Naval Ship R&D Center	1
Fleet Numerical Oceanography	1
Naval Underwater System Command	1
Naval Weapons Center	1
Martin Marietta/NTB	1
Air Force Weapons Lab	2
Air Force Global Weather	1
Arnold Engineering and Development	1
Wright Patterson AFB	1
Aerospace Corp	1
Army Ballistic Research Lab	2
Army/Tacom	1
Army/Huntsville	1
Army/Kwajalein	1
Army/WES (on order)	1
Army/Warren	1
Defense Nuclear Agency	1
National Aeronautics and Space Administration:	
Ames	5
Goddard	2
Lewis	1
Langley	1
Marshal	1
Department of Commerce:	
National Institute of Standards and Technology	1
National Oceanic and Atmospheric Administration	4
Environmental Protection Agency:	
Raleigh, North Carolina	1
Department of Health and Human Services:	
National Institutes of Health	1
National Cancer Institute	1

SOURCE: Office of Technology Assessment estimate, September 1989.

sota Supercomputing Institute, an academic unit of the university, channels university usage by providing grants to the students through a peer review process.

---

[1]The number cannot be estimated exactly. First, it depends on the definition of supercomputer one uses. Secondly, the number keeps changing as States announce new plans for centers and as large research universities purchase their own HPCs.

The Minnesota Supercomputer Center received its first machine, a Cray 1A, in September 1981. In mid-1985, it installed a Cyber 205; and in the latter part of that year, two Cray 2 computers were installed within 3 months of each other. Minnesota bought its third Cray 2, the only one in use now, at the end of 1988, just after it installed a ETA-10. The ETA-10 has recently been decommissioned due to the closure of ETA. A Cray X-MP has been added, giving the center a total of two supercomputers. The Minnesota Supercomputer Center has acquired more supercomputers than anyone outside the Federal Government.

The Minnesota State Legislature provides funds to the university for the purchasing of supercomputer time. Although the university buys a substantial portion of supercomputing time, the center has many industrial clients whose identities are proprietary, but they include representatives of the auto, aerospace, petroleum, and electronic industries. They are charged a fee for the use of the facility.

The Ohio Supercomputer Center

The Ohio Supercomputer Center (OSC) originated from a coalition of scientists in the State. The center, located on Ohio State University's campus, is connected to 20 other Ohio universities via the Ohio Academic Research Network (OARNET). As of January 1989, three private firms were using the center's resources.

In August 1987, OSC installed a Cray X-MP/24, which was upgraded to a Cray X-MP/28 a year later. In August 1989 the center replaced the X-MP with a Cray Research Y-MP. In addition to Cray hardware, there are 40 Sun Graphic workstations, a Pixar II, a Stallar Graphics machine, a Silicon Graphic workstation, and an Abekas Still Store machine. The center maintains a staff of about 35..

The Ohio General Assembly began funding the center in the summer of 1987, appropriating $7.5 million. In March 1988, the Assembly allocated $22 million for the acquisition of a Cray Y-MP. Ohio State University has pledged $8.2 million to augment the center's budget. As of February 1989 the State has spent $37.7 million in funding.[2] OSC's annual budget is around $6 million (not including the purchase/leasing of their Cray).

Center for High Performance Computing (CHPC)

The Center for High Performance Computing is located at the University of Texas at Austin. CHPC serves all 14 institutions, 8 academic institutions, and 6 health related organizations, in the University of Texas system.

The University of Texas installed a Cray X-MP/24 in March 1986, and a Cray 14se in November 1988. The X-MP is used primarily for research. For now, the Cray 14se is being used as a vehicle for the conversion of users to the Unix system. About 40 people staff the center.

Original funding for the center and the Cray X-MP came from bonds and endowments from both the University of Texas system and the University of Texas at Austin. The annual budget of CHPC is about $3 million. About 95 percent of the center's operating budget comes from State funding and endowments. Five percent of the costs are recovered from selling CPU time.

Alabama Supercomputer Network

The George C. Wallace Supercomputer Center, located in Huntsville, Alabama, serves the needs of researchers throughout Alabama. Through the Alabama Supercomputer Network, 13 Alabama institutions, university, and government sites are connected to the center. Under contract to the State, Boeing Computer Services provides the support staff and technical skills to operate the center. Support staff are located at each of the nodes to help facilitate the use of the supercomputer from remote sites.

A Cray X-MP/24 arrived in 1987 and became operational in early 1988. In 1987 the State of Alabama agreed to finance the center. The State allocated $2.2 million for the center and $38 million to Boeing Services for the initial 5 years. The average yearly budget is $7 million. The center has a support staff of about 25.

Alabama universities are guaranteed 60 percent of the available time at no cost, while commercial researchers are charged a user fee. The impetus for the State to create a supercomputer center has been stated as the technical superiority a supercomputer would bring, which would draw high-tech industry to the State, enhance interaction between industry and the universities, and promote research and the associated educational programs within the university.

Commercial Labs

A few corporations, such as the Boeing Computer Corp., have been selling high performance computer time for a while. Boeing operates a Cray X-MP/24. Other commercial sellers of high performance computing time include the Houston Area Research Center (HARC). HARC operates the only Japanese supercomputer in america, the NEC SX2. The center offers remote services.

Computer Sciences Corp. (CSC), located in Falls Church, Virginia, has a 16-processor FLEX/32 from Flexible Computer Corp., a Convex 120 from Convex Computer Corp., and a DAP210 from Active Memory Technology. Federal agencies constitute two-thirds of

---

[2]Jane Ware, ''Ohioans: Blazing Computer,'' *Ohio*, February 1989, p.12.

CSC's customers.[3] Power Computing Co., located in Dallas, Texas, offers time on a Cray X-MP/24. Situated in Houston, Texas, Supercomputing Technology sells time on its Cray X-MP/28. Opticom Corp., of San Jose California, offers time on a Cray X-MP/24, Cray 1-M, Convex C220, and C1 XP.

---

[3]Norris Parker Smith, ''More Than Just Buying Cycles,'' *Supercomputer Review*, April 1989.

Index

National Academy of Sciences (NAS): 9, 11
National Aeronautics and Space Administration (NASA),
   7, 16, 18
National Association of State Universities and Land
   Grant Colleges (NASULGC): 9-10
National Center for Atmospheric Research (NCAR): 7, 15, 18,
   19
National Center for Supercomputing Applications (NCSA): 6
National Institute of Science and Technology (NIST): 16
National Laboratories
   Livermore: 16, 18
   Los Alamos: 16, 18
National Science Foundation (NSF): 14, 15, 27
   Advanced Scientific Computing Division: 22
   Computer Facilities Program: 5, 16
   supercomputing centers: 8, 12, 13, 15, 18, 19, 20, 22, 23, 24
National Security Agency: 18
National Superspeed Computer Project: 2
Network
   architecture: 10
   BITNET: 10
   high-speed broadband: 21
   Internet: 10
   national: 10, 22
   National Research and Educational Network (NREN): 1, 7, 8,
      10, 13, 24, 26
   National Science Foundation (NSF): 1, 5, 6, 8
   NSFNET: 6, 12, 17
   State and local: 13
   switched wide-area digital: 12
   universal: 4, 5, 12

Office of Science and Technology Policy (OSTP): 1, 11, 17

Parallel computers (parallelism), 8
Pittsburg Supercomputer Center: 29
Policy
   industrial: 3
   information: 12, 13
   science: 12
Princeton University: 19, 22
Privacy: 12

Research
   applied: 15
   atmospheric chemistry: 19
   basic: 15
   biomedical: 19
   fluid dynamics: 19

global climate change: 5
"Grand Challenges," 11
instruments: 8
physics: 15
Rice University: 29

Science, computational: 15, 16, 23
Scientific and engineering applications: 4
Scientific instruments
   method: 5, 24
   oceanographic probes: 8
   satellites: 8
   seismographs: 8
Search engines: 10
Senate Committee on Commerce and Transportation: 1
Silicon chips: 5
Silicon Graphics workstation: 6
Software: 2, 4, 6, 7, 8, 10, 15, 17, 21, 23, 24, 30, 32
   public domain, 8
Standards and protocols: 9, 11
State supercomputing centers: 20
Supercomputer
   definition: 30
   leading edge: 22
Superconductivity: 28-29
Syracuse University: 29

Technologies
   automated chip design: 29
   chip foundaries: 29
   computer: 15
   data storage: 5, 24
   gallium arsenide: 5, 28
   integrated circuits (IC): 27
   microelectronics: 27
   visual: 26
Technology, leading edge: 15
Typhoon Hope: 7

U.S. Constitution, First Amendment: 12
University of California, San Diego: 22, 29
University of Illinois, Champaign-Urbana: 22, 29

Virtual reality: 8, 26

Wavefront Technologies Graphic Software: 6
World War II: 5, 26

U. S. GOVERNMENT PRINTING OFFICE ; 1991 - 33-982 QL 3

APPENDIX R

GLOSSARY

anonymous FTP: Anonymous File Transfer Protocol; allows Internet users to login to a remote host computer and retrieve files without having an account on the remote host; see TCP/IP.

ANS: Advanced Network Services, Inc.; a not-for-profit company organized and supported by Merit, Inc., IBM Corporation, and MCI Communications Corporation.

ANSI: American National Standards Institute.

ARL: Association of Research Libraries; one of the principals of the Coalition for Networked Information.

ARPA: Advanced Research Projects Agency in the Department of Defense; responsible for computing and communication research and development (R&D); precursor of DARPA; see ARPANET and DARPA.

ARPANET: Advanced Research Projects Agency Network; the first packet-switching network; founded in 1968; served as early backbone of the Internet.

asynchronous: Not occurring at the same time or not occurring regularly.

backbone: A high-capacity electronic trunk connecting lower capacity branches which are networks themselves, e.g., NSFNET.

bandwidth: The capacity (however measured) of a communication channel; often expressed by a baud rate, e.g., gigabits per second.

BARRNet: Bay Area Regional Research Network; a regional mid-level network in NSFNET; located in the San Francisco Bay area.

baud rate: The rate at which information is transmitted; ordinarily expressed in bits per second.

BITNET: Because It's Time Network; the primary, cooperative academic electronic network in the United States; supports electronic mail, file transfer, and mailing lists or bulletin boards; managed by CREN; see EARN.

broadband: Used to describe a communication channel with a bandwidth greater than the 300-3000 Hertz required for a voice-only audio channel; or a kind of local area network that can transmit voice, video, and other forms of information at high speed and through numerous channels.

broadcast: Transmission of simultaneous signals from one source to multiple receivers.

bulletin board: A computerized message system, often available only on request, that allows users to read and post, i.e., broadcast, messages; often dedicated to a particular topic, e.g., "18th century English literature;" sometimes referred to as a newsgroup, mailing list, or discussion group.

CAUSE: An organization of computing and other information technology professionals in higher education; one of the principals in CNI.

CERFNET: California Education & Research Federation Network; a regional mid-level network in NSFNET.

channels: Divisions of a single transmission medium into discrete communication paths by transmitting information at different frequencies.

CICNET: Committee on Institutional Cooperation Network; computer network whose major members are the Big Ten universities and the University of Chicago; a regional NSFNET mid-level network.

circuit-switched network: A network which connects users, machines, or channels by connecting terminals on different circuits; as distinguished from a packet-switching network.

CMC: Computer-Mediated Communication; includes such functions as computer conferencing, bulletin boards, and electronic mail.

CNI: Coalition for Networked Information; organization formed by EDUCOM, CAUSE, and the Association of Research Libraries; to promote the use and provision of network information resources.

CNRI: Corporation for National Research Initiatives; a private corporation performing and supporting research on networking.

coaxial cable: A central wire surrounded by insulation and a braided series of wires that carry information at very high rates and with high transmission quality; as distinguished from a twisted pair.

Coalition for Networked Information: See CNI.

command: An input or output instruction to a computer.

common carrier: An organization, subject to certain legal and other restrictions, which provides a transportation service for a fee with little regard for the identity or content of what is transported; the description has been extended to some communication organizations, e.g., telephone companies; see MFJ and value-added network.

communication channel: Connection between terminals and computers; may include hardwire connection, telephone lines, satellites, and microwaves.

compression: A technique for compacting data by decreasing the amount of redundant or unnecessary data stored.

computer conferencing: Use of computerized facilities to allow geographically remote meeting participants to interact as if they were in physical proximity.

computer network: The connection of at least two computers so that they can share software, functions, hardware, and other capabilities; each computer is then a node of the network.

CREN: Corporation for Research and Educational Networking; governing body of BITNET and CSNET.

CSNET: Computer + Science Network; intended to facilitate research and to encourage collaboration among computer scientists; allows electronic mail, file transfer, and interactive login; now managed by CREN.

DARPA: Defense Advanced Research Projects Agency; see ARPA.

datagram: A packet which is individually routed.

dial-up: Access to a computer or computer system through a public telephone system.

DIALOG: A major commercial supplier and vendor of online databases.

duplex: To transmit messages in two directions concurrently on the same communication channel.

EARN: The European counterpart of BITNET.

echoing: Monitoring information sent by displaying the data on a screen as it is transmitted.

EDUCOM: A cooperative of universities and colleges to support the use of information technologies in higher education; one of the principals in the Coalition for Networked Information.

EFF: The Electronic Frontier Foundation; concerned with the protection of civil rights in the electronic environment.

emulation: A microcomputer's imitation of a mainframe terminal.

FARNET: Federation of American Research Networks.

FCCSET: Federal Coordinating Council for Science, Engineering, and Technology; in the Office of Science and Technology Policy in the Executive Office of the President.

FNC: Federal Networking Council; oversees U.S. networking policy and initiatives.

Free-Net: Cleveland Free-Net, a free, publicly available network.

FRICC: Federal Research Internet Coordinating Committee; a cooperative group of five Federal agencies which coordinates national network planning among Federal agencies.

FTP: File Transfer Protocol; one of three high-level protocols available on the Internet; see TCP/IP.

gateway: A means of accessing an online resource; in a networked environment, a computer connecting two or more networks.

gigabit: Approximately one billion bits (1024 x 1024 x 1024 bits).

HCI: Human-Computer Interaction; used to describe a user's communication with a machine rather than with another person.

HPC: High Performance Computing.

Hz: Hertz; a measure of frequency of transmission; one hertz equals one cycle per second.

host: A computer which offers access to remote users; more generally, the central or controlling processor in a network.

IEEE: Institute for Electrical and Electronics Engineers.

IIA: Information Industry Association; a leading trade asssociation of database generators and vendors, publishers, and other information businesses.

interactive: A mode of communication in which the computer responds to commands given by the user in real time.

internet: Internetwork; any connection of two or more networks.

Internet: The global collection of interoperating networks using the TCP/IP protocol suite; shares resources and serves as a research testbed.

IP: Internet Protocol; provides addresses, packet management, and other technical functions; see Protocol and TCP/IP.

ISBN: Integrated Services Digital Network; digital telephone network currently being installed globally to replace the existing analog network; voice, data, and video can be transmitted digitally from a source.

ISO: International Standards Organization for networks; composed of the national standards groups of the individual member countries; see NISO.

JVNCNET: John von Neumann [Supercomputer] Center Network; a consortium network connecting several supercomputers at the John von Neumann Supercomputer Center at Princeton Unviersity, which was one of the five NSF supercomputer centers funded in 1985, to several Northeastern states; a supercomputer consortium NSFNET mid-level network.

knowbot: KNOWledge roBOT; a proposed piece of active software which would "mine" the networked information landscape according to specific user profiles and instructions; faces many technical, ergonomic, legal, and other obstacles.

LAN: Local Area Network; a high-speed, short haul network; usually digital as opposed to analog.

LOS NETTOS: Greater Los Angeles Network; a regional NSFNET mid-level network.

LSP: Linked Systems Protocol; convention, or standard, for digital bibliographic information retrieval; see Z39.50.

MARC: MAchine Readable Cataloguing; developed by the U.S. Library of Congress and the British Library.

megabit: Approximately one million bits (1024 x 1024 bits).

Merit: Connects state-supported universities in Michigan; a regional NSFNET mid-level network; the Merit organization manages NSFNET.

MIDNET: Midwestern States Network; a regional mid-level NSFNET network.

MFJ: The Modified Final Judgment; Judge Greene's decision, and that decision's amendments, on the divestiture of AT&T; forbids telephone companies from providing enhanced or value-added information services, i.e., those which are based on computer processing; see common carrier and value-added network.

mid-level network: A network connecting NSFNET to campus, local area, and other institutional networks; regional, discipline-based, or based on a supercomputer consortium; see NSFNET.

MILNET: Military Network; a network connecting Department of Defense contractors for the purpose of sharing unclassified military research; part of the Internet.

MRNET: Minnesota Regional Network; a regional mid-level NSFNET network.

multiplex: To transmit more than two simultaneous messages through the same communication channel.

NBS: U.S. National Bureau of Standards; now the National Institute of Standards and Technology (NIST).

NCSANET: National Center for Supercomputing Applications Network; a regional NSFNET mid-level network; connects supercomputers at the National Center for Supercomputing Applications at the University of Illinois at Urbana-Champaign, one of the five NSF supercomputer centers funded in 1985, and the NSFNET to sites in Illinois, Indiana, and Wisconsin.

NEARNET: New England Academic and Research Network; a regional NSFNET mid-level network.

network: A series of connected points or nodes.

network architecture: A network's design.

NIC: Any network information center; supports users by providing information about services available on that network.

NISO: National Information Standards Organization; the U.S. representative to ISO.

NIST: U.S. National Institute of Standards and Technology; formerly the National Bureau of Standards (NBS).

NLM: National Library of Medicine; one of the first providers of a distributed online information system.

node: Where communication channels in a network converge; used to refer to particular geographic places, institutions, and computers.

NORTHWESTNET: Northwestern States Network; a regional mid-level NSFNET network connecting Alaska, Idaho, Montana, North Dakota, Oregon, and Washington.

NREN: The proposed National Research and Education Network.

NRI: Same as CNRI.

NSF: National Science Foundation.

NSF supercomputer centers: Funded in 1985, they included the San Diego Supercomputer Center (University of California at San Diego), the National Center for Supercomputer Applications (University of Illinois at Urbana-Champaign), the Theory Center and Cornell National Supercomputing Facility (Cornell University, Ithaca, NY), the John von Neuman Supercomputer Center (Princeton University, Princeton, NJ), and the Pittsburgh Supercomputing Center (Carnegie-Mellon University, Westinghouse Electric Corporation, and the University of Pittsburgh, Pittsburgh, PA); five of the first nodes of NSFNET; in 1990, four of the centers were given funding for another five years to 1995 (Phase II of the NSF effort), but the Princeton center was not.

NSFNET: National Science Foundation Network; high-speed national internetwork or network of networks which interoperate but which remain technically and administratively autonomous (see TCP/IP); current backbone of the U.S. Internet; offered as the backbone for the proposed NREN. The mid-level wide area networks which make up NSFNET are BARRNET, CERFNET, CICNET, CREN/CSNET, JVNCNET, LOS NETTOS, MERIT, MIDNET, MRNET, NCSANET, NEARNET, NORTHWESTNET, NYSERNET, OARNET, PREPNET, PSCNET, SDSCNET, SESQUINET, SURANET, THENET, USAN, VERNET, and WESTNET.

NTIA: National Telecommunication and Information Administration; in the U.S. Department of Commerce.

NYSERNET: New York State Educational and Research Network; the mid-level NSFNET regional network for New York State.

OARNET: Ohio Academic Resources Network; a regional NSFNET mid-level network.

OCLC: The Online Computer Library Center; located in Ohio; one of the primary bibliographic utilities and information research organizations in the United States.

OIRA: Office of Information and Regulatory Affairs at OMB; a lead Federal agency for information policy development.

OMB: Office of Management and Budget; in the Executive Office of the President; see OIRA.

OPAC: Online Public Access Catalogue; a publicly accessible computer file which contains cataloguing information about a library or information center's collection; many such OPACs are available on the Internet.

OSI: Open Systems Interconnect[ion]; a developing set of international protocols to connect unlike computer systems.

OSI Reference Model: The seven-layered model used to describe the functions supported by OSI.

OSTP: Office of Science and Technology Policy; in the Executive Office of the President.

OTA: Office of Technology Assessment; a research agency of the U.S. Congress; producer of technical and analytic reports at the request of Congress.

packet: A uniformly sized unit of data sent through a packet-switching network; the unit contains the information to be sent, control information, and a destination; fundamental unit of the TCP/IP protocol suite; see datagram.

packet-switching network: Computer network in which self-contained packets are sent and reassembled and which can send data from more than one user at the same time; as distinguished from a circuit-switched network.

PC: the IBM Personal computer; used generically to describe microcomputers.

PDN: Public data network, e.g., SprintNet and Tymnet.

PRA: Paperwork Reduction Act passed in 1980; PL 96-511; established the Office of Information and Regulatory Affairs (OIRA) in the Office of Management and Budget (OMB).

PREPNET: Pennsylvania Research and Economic Partnership Network; a regional mid-level NSFNET network.

protocol: Formal description or convention of allowable message formats and actions that computers must follow in order to exchange messages, e.g., TCP/IP, a layered protocol suite.

PSCNET: Pittsburgh Supercomputing Center Network; a supercomputer consortium, regional NSFNET mid-level network connecting the Pittsburgh Supercomputing Center, one of the five NSF supercomputer centers funded in 1985, to sites in Maryland, Michigan, Oklahoma, and Pennsylvania.

PSI: Performance Systems International, Inc.; for-profit corporation located in Reston, Virginia, and founded by former principals of NYSERNET; provides a number of network services; the history of and relationship between NYSERNET and PSI has been offered as a model for future netwrok development.

PTT: Post, Telephone, and Telegraph; in many countries other than the United States, a government organization exists with a monopoly to provide these information services.

random access: Direct retrieval of stored information without sequential sorting.

RBOCS: Regional Bell Operating Companies, e.g., NYNEX

real time: Used to describe a computer system which operates at sufficient speed to appear interactive to a user.

redundant: Used to describe data not considered essential to a message's meaning, e.g., unused fields in a file.

refresh rate: The number of times per second that a computer monitor screen display is redrawn.

regional network: A computer network with nodes in a particular, defined geographic area, e.g., NYSERNet is one of the regional mid-level networks of NSFNET.

remote: Geographically distant from a computer, without a direct, hardwired connection.

RFC: Request for Comments on the Internet; ordinarily generated by system administrators for comments, then accepted as a network standard.

RLG: Research Libraries Group; consortium of large, prestigious research libraries in the United States.

RLIN: Research Libraries Information Network; links libraries in the United States; operated by RLG.

rlogin: Remote login; an Internet service similar to Telnet.

ROM: Read Only Memory; a format which allows an electronic storage device to be read but not written to.

routing: The assignment of a message to a particular communication channel or series of channels.

SDSCNET: San Diego Supercomputer Center Network; a supercomputer consortium, regional mid-level network of NSFNET connecting the Center, one of the five NSF supercomputer centers funded in 1985, to sites in California and Hawaii.

sequential: Retrieval of stored information only after preceding information has been read in order; distinguished from random access.

server: A computer which shares its resources, such as data files, with other computers on a network.

SESQUINET: Texas Sesquicentennial Network; a regional mid-level NSFNET network connecting sites in Texas.

simplex: Data transmission in only one direction; as distinguished from duplex or multiplex.

SMTP: Simple Mail Transfer Protocol; the Internet electronic mail protocol; layered on IP; see TCP/IP.

SprintNet: A public packet-switching (telecommunications) network or PDN operated by US Sprint; formerly Telenet.

STI: Scientific and Technical Information.

SURANET: Southeastern Universities Research Association Network; a regional mid-level network in NSFNET connecting sites throughout the Southeastern United States.

synchronous: Occurring at the same time or at regular intervals.

T1: A line that can carry 1.544 megabits per second (Mbps).

T3: A line that can carry 44.746 megabits per second; the stated minimal target for the proposed NREN.

TCP: Transmission Control Protocol; a transport layer protocol, or convention, for the Internet; see TCP/IP.

TCP/IP: Transmission Control Protocol/Internet Protocol; the suite of application and transport protocols (FTP, Telnet, SMTP, and UDP) which are run over IP.

Telnet: Internet standard protocol for remote terminal connection (remote login); see rlogin.

THENET: The Texas Higher Education Network; a state-based, regional NSFNET mid-level network.

twisted pair: Two copper wires twisted together; the ordinary analog telephone wire.

traffic: The messages on a communications channel.

Tymnet: A public packet-switching network or PDN operated by McDonnell Douglas Network Systems Company.

UDP: User Datagram Protocol; a transport protocol for IP.

UNIX: Operating system developed by Bell Laboratories to support simultaneous multiple tasks and multiple users.

USAN: The University Satellite Network connecting several major universities to the National Center for Atmospheric Research in Colorado using satellite links.

USENET: Sometimes identified as the User's Network; a highly decentralized, cooperative, international bulletin board system, with thousands of discussion groups.

user group: An organization of the users of a particular computer system; often acts as a lobby to represent users' concerns to system managers and others.

USENIX: UNIX users' group.

UUCP: UNIX to UNIX Copy Program; both a computer network and a communication protocol.

UUNET: UNIX to UNIX Network; a publicly available general network with electronic mail capabilities, but not bulletin boards or computer conferencing.

value-added network: A computer network that provides services, functions, or facilities, e.g., retransmission of messages, beyond those provided by common carriers like telephone companies; see common carrier and MFJ.

VERNET: Virginia Education and Research Network; a regional mid-level NSFNET network.

virtual machine: A logical construct that simulates personal control of one or more multi-user computer systems; appears to the user to be one machine.

voice-grade: Used to describe a telephone line expressly designed for the transmission of human voice signals; these signals are in the range of 300-3000 Hertz (or cycles per second).

WAN: Wide Area Network; may use microwaves and satellites as well as computer networks.

WESTNET: Southwestern States Network; a regional mid-level NSFNET network connecting Arizona, Colorado, New Mexico, Utah, and Wyoming.

Z39.50: The Linked Systems Protocol for online bibliographic retrieval; promulgated by NISO.

Author Index

Subject Index